ISABELLA OF SPAIN

THE LAST CRUSADER

The Betrothal of Isabel and Fernando
*(From a Contemporary Tapestry in the Collection
of John N. Willys, Ambassador to Poland)*

ISABELLA
OF SPAIN

The Last Crusader

By

WILLIAM THOMAS WALSH

Illustrated

"Thou art the glory of Jerusalem, thou art
the joy of Israel, thou art the honour of our
people: For thou hast done manfully, and thy
heart has been strengthened, because thou hast
loved chastity, and after thy husband hast not
known any other: therefore also the hand of
the Lord hath strengthened thee, and therefore thou shalt be blessed for ever. And all
the people said: So be it, so be it."
—Judith 15:10-12

TAN BOOKS AND PUBLISHERS, INC.
Rockford, Illinois 61105

Copyright © 1930 by William Thomas Walsh.

First published November, 1930 by Robert M. McBride and Company, New York.

Library of Congress Catalog Card No.: 87-71866

ISBN: 0-89555-320-1

Printed and bound in the United States of America.

TAN BOOKS AND PUBLISHERS, INC.
P.O. Box 424
Rockford, Illinois 61105

1987

To My Father
In Grateful Memory

WORKS BY WILLIAM THOMAS WALSH

The Mirage of the Many (1910)
Isabella of Spain (1930)
Out of the Whirlwind (novel, 1935)
Philip II (1937)
Shekels (blank-verse play, 1937)
Lyric Poems (1939)
Characters of the Inquisition (1940)
"Gold" (short story)
Babies, not Bullets! (booklet, 1940)
Thirty Pieces of Silver (a play in verse)
Saint Teresa of Ávila (1943)
La actual situatión de España (booklet, 1944)
El caso crucial de España (booklet, 1946)
Our Lady of Fátima (1947)
The Carmelites of Compiègne (a play in verse)
Saint Peter, the Apostle (1948)

CONTENTS

ILLUSTRATIONS

FOREWORD

THIS book attempts to tell the amazing story of Queen Isabel of Castile as it appeared to her contemporaries, against the blood-spattered background of her own times. It is a tale so dramatic, so fascinating, that it needs no embellishing or piecing out with the wisdom—or folly—of another age. To probe the inner cosmos of men and women long dead by the light of a pseudo-science, to strip away with pitiless irony all noble or generous appearances, to pry open with an air of personal infallibility the very secret hinges of the door to that ultimate sanctuary of the human conscience which is inviolable even to father confessors—that is an office for which I have neither the taste nor the talent; and if I have fallen unawares into any such pitfalls of the devils of megalomania, I beg forgiveness in advance. Under the naive rhetoric of the fifteenth century chroniclers there is ample material for what Joseph Conrad called rendering the vibration of life and Michelet called the resurrection of the flesh without resorting to subjective interpretation. And it has seemed all the more imperative to follow the sources objectively and let them speak for themselves as far as possible, because, strange as it may appear, the life of Columbus's patron and America's godmother has never been told completely and coherently in our language.

For nearly a century the "official" biography has been Prescott's "History of the Reign of Ferdinand and Isabella." He was a careful and patient scholar to whom we owe a debt of no small size. Yet he was incapable of understanding the spirit of fifteenth century Spain, because with all his erudition he could never wholly forget the prejudices of an early nineteenth century Bostonian. And modern research has opened up treasures of source material unknown to him. Llorente, whom he followed with blind confidence on the Inquisition, has been proved not only wildly inaccurate but deliberately dishonest, and is distrusted by all reliable historians; many of the original documents unearthed by Lea[1] and the extremely valuable

ones published by Padre Fidel Fita in the Bulletin of the Royal
Academy of History at Madrid were not available until half
a century or more after Prescott wrote. The Columbian investigations of Harrisse, Thacher and others have almost completed
the portrait of a Discoverer who is human rather than legendary. The studies of Señor Amador de los Rios, Dr. Meyer
Kayserling and M. Isidore Loeb have shed new light upon
the history of the Spanish Jews. Bergenroth's decoding of the
Spanish state papers, many of them still in cipher when Prescott wrote, has provided a new approach to Isabel's relations
with France, England, and the Holy Roman Empire.

Nearly all the biographies of Isabel in the English language,
and some in French, have followed the conclusions of Prescott
and have adopted his attitude, even when they have made use
of later material. When not openly hostile they have generally
approached the fifteenth century with an air of condescension
—the worst possible attitude for an historian, for condescension is not a window, but a wall. Even to begin to understand a
person (the representative of an age), you must have enough
sympathy to imagine yourself standing in his place, holding
the same beliefs, having the same information, feeling the same
emotions. You can never achieve more than a caricature of
him if you keep reminding yourself that he is a medieval igno-
ramus with faults and passions that you imagine you do not
share. You will understand him better if you say at the outset,
"Let us see what he believed about himself and the world, and
assume as a working hypothesis that it is true: would I, in
his place, have done differently?" Humility is the mother of
all virtues, even in the writing of history.

Again, to understand a woman crusader who changed the
course of civilization and the aspect of the entire world, as
Isabel did, it is essential to begin by visualizing the European
stage on which she appeared. When she was born there was no
such nation as Spain. She was European, Christian in con-
sciousness, rather than Spanish. All the chroniclers of the time
—Bernaldez, Pulgar, Zurita—repeatedly keep the reader informed of what is going on in all parts of Europe, not merely
in Spain, just as an American newspaper reports events of
interest to all the United States, not alone the state where it is
published. But some of the modern biographies of Isabel manage to convey the impression that she thought of Italy or

England as we think of Siam. Christendom—the whole European culture—was an entity more real to the average European than the limits of the country he lived in. Only by recapturing Isabel's concept of a unified Christian civilization can we begin to comprehend the world she was born in.

It was a dying world. The west was like some old ship eaten by intestine fires and ready to founder under the waves of a triumphant Mohammedanism. For Christendom had hardly subdued the barbarism that snuffed out the light of Rome when it was forced to begin a titanic struggle for its very existence—not merely the First Crusade or the Fourth Crusade that our histories mention, but a super-crusade that kept Europe on the defensive for a thousand years, from the early eighth to the late seventeenth century. Even the fanaticism and the militarism of our medieval ancestors were imposed upon them by the continual necessity of warding off attacks by fanatical and militaristic foes. After the barbarian migrations came the ravages of Magyars and Vikings; and finally the ruthless millions of Islam.

When Isabel was born, the Turks had been steadily carrying fire and scimitar through eastern Europe, slaying men, women and children; they had reached the Danube, overrun Asia Minor, taken lower Hungary, gobbled up a great part of the Balkans. In Isabel's third year, 1453, they blasted their way into Constantinople and made themselves masters of Greece. Successive Popes exhorted the European rulers to forget their quarrels and jealousies and unite to save Christendom from being overwhelmed. But Christian princes were too busy fighting Christian princes from one end of Europe to the other. France and England, at the end of the Hundred Years' War— it was only twenty years before Isabel's birth that Saint Joan was burned—were exhausted; yet Louis XI was preparing to crush feudalism in France, and England was on the eve of the Wars of the Roses that rent her for a generation. Poland had been desperately defending herself from predatory German barons on the west and Lithuanian heathen on the east. The survivors in Hungary, Albania and the Balkans were rallying to make an almost hopeless resistance to the Mohammedans. Italy was divided into rival states, chief of which were Rome, Naples, Milan, Florence, Genoa, and Venice—all involved in dynastic and commercial feuds, and corrupted by too much

wealth and by the paganism that had returned in the shadow
of the Renaissance. No one but the people on the first line of
defense would listen to the Popes. The Emperor Frederick III,
ruler of all central Europe, was too busy planting a garden
and catching birds. The King of Denmark stole the money
donated for a crusade from the sacristy of the cathedral at
Roskilde. And all this while Mohammed II, the Grand Turk,
was fighting his way to the east shore of the Adriatic, and
seemed certain to carry out the threat of a predecessor, Bajazet
the Lightning, to feed his horses on the altar of Saint Peter's
in Rome.

Meanwhile the Mohammedans had long since driven a wedge
into western Europe, by way of Spain. Of the three great
peninsulas that Christendom had planted, like colossal feet, in
the Mediterranean, they now possessed Greece, and were preparing to assail Italy. But Spain had been their battleground
for nearly eight hundred years.

Hardly had the Mohammedan Arabs subdued and organized
the Berbers of north Africa when they were invited by the
Spanish Jews to cross the nine-mile strip of water at Gibraltar
and possess themselves of the Christian kingdom. The plot
was discovered, and the Jews sternly punished. A second attempt, however, was successful at a moment when the Visigoth
monarchy was perishing of its own follies. "It remains a fact,"
says the *Jewish Encyclopedia*, "that the Jews, either directly
or through their correligionists in Africa, encouraged the
Mohammedans to conquer Spain."[2] In 709 the Arab general
Tarik led an army of Berbers, in which there were many
African Jews, across the straits. Defeating and slaying King
Roderigo, with the aid of Christian traitors, at the great battle
of Jerez de la Frontera, they carried death in all directions
through the peninsula. Wherever they went, the Jews threw
open to them the gates of the principal cities, so that in an
incredibly short time the Africans were masters of all Spain
save the little kingdom of the Asturias in the northern mountains, where the Christian survivors who were unwilling to
accept Islam reassembled and prepared to win back their heritage. Meanwhile the Berbers entered France along the Mediterranean coast.[3] The whole western culture of Rome was in
jeopardy a second time, from the same enemy; for by a striking coincidence it was the same Berber race that had followed

Hannibal across the Alps into Italy nearly a thousand years before. The fate of all Christendom hung on the issue of a battle.

The glorious victory of Charles Martel in 732 saved our culture; but Spain remained lost to Christendom for centuries. Christian churches were turned into mosques, old Roman cities were gradually transformed into the oriental pleasure grounds of the caliphs. Córdoba under the Ommiad, Abd er Rahman III, in the tenth century was more beautiful than Bagdad, and next to Constantinople the most magnificent city in Europe. Medicine, mathematics and philosophy were taught in its schools. At a time when the Christians to the north were fighting for the mere right to exist, the caliphs enjoyed an income greater than those of all the kings of Europe combined.

Slowly and painfully, but with hope born of their faith, the Christian knights fought their way south into the lands of their ancestors. With much expense of blood they gradually carved out five small Christian states: Castile and Leon on the great central plateau, Navarre in the shadow of the Pyrenees; Aragon, originally a Frankish colony, in the northeast, and Catalonia—remnant of the old Spanish March—on the eastern coast. Alfonso VI of Castile took Toledo in 1085—though the Saracens, reinforced by hordes of Almoravides from Africa, later defeated him. Alfonso Sanchez recovered Saragossa and the sacred site where Saint James the Apostle (Santiago) had built the first Christian church in Spain. Aragon and Catalonia united. Portugal became independent in 1143. And then, in 1160, the military failure of Alfonso VIII placed in peril all that had been gained.

At a critical moment the great voice of Pope Innocent III, summoning all Europe to join in the Spanish Crusade, prevented a second catastrophe. Ten thousand knights and 100,000 infantry came from France and Germany in time to reinforce the armies of Castile and Aragon. They vanquished the mighty Saracen host in the battle of Las Navas de Tolosa in 1212, crushed them utterly, left 200,000 of them dead on the field.

It was the turning point of the age-long Crusade. In the following generation Fernando III, the Saint, recaptured Córdoba, Seville, Jerez and Cádiz. Luxuriant Andalusia, south of Castile, was regained. When the fifteenth century began, nothing was left to the Moors but the Kingdom of Granada in the extreme south. It was, however, the richest, most fertile, most delightful part of Spain, populous and warlike, sustained by abundant farm lands and pasturage, and protected from military attack by the enormous natural fortifications formed by the snowy peaks of the Sierra Nevada. The city of Granada and the score of almost impregnable towns that encircled it could put into the field a well-equipped army of 50,000. But even more menacing to the security of the Christian kingdoms was the fact that the Moors could obtain almost unlimited reinforcements and supplies from the Mohammedan millions of Africa, and at short notice. So long as Islam retained any foothold in Spain, there was perpetual danger that the seven hundred years of heroic effort might yet be lost.

To prevent such a debacle, to complete the reconquest, Christian Spain had need of political unity under a strong leader. But the problem of unity was far more intricate than the one with which Louis XI was beginning to grapple in France. He, too, had an arrogant feudal nobility to suppress, anarchy to reduce to order, a bankrupt country to make productive. But he had an enormous advantage in the fact that his people were so nearly one in race and were one in religion. There was no such fundamental unity to build upon in Spain, where the Jews constituted a powerful minority resisting all efforts at assimilation. Of the openly professing Jews of the synagogue there were only some 200,000 in 1450, and they were allowed complete freedom of worship. But far more numerous were those Jews—there must have been at least 3,000,000 of them—who observed the rites and customs of the Old Law in secret, while outwardly they pretended to be Christians. They were called *Conversos* or "New Christians." The Jews of the synagogue sometimes called them *Marranos*, from the Hebrew *Maranatha*, "the Lord is coming," in derision of their belief, or feigned belief, in the divinity of Jesus Christ. The *Conversos* were assimilated in a superficial sense, for many of them married into the noblest families in Spain, enjoyed all the privileges of Christians, and had gradually gathered into their hands most of the wealth, the political power, and even the control of taxation; but it was generally felt that in a crisis they would prove to be Jews at heart, enemies of the Christian faith, and the allies, as in the past, of the half-oriental and circumcized Moors. How to fuse elements almost as immiscible as oil and water into a unity capable of resolving chaos into order and pushing back to the Mediterranean the western salient of the mighty battle line of Islam—that was the challenge that the times had hurled. at Isabel's immediate ancestors, and found them wanting. It was a task which, if at all possible, demanded constructive genius of the highest order. By some mysterious ordering of circumstance, by a falling out of events more romantic than fiction, it was committed to the hands of a woman.

ISABELLA OF SPAIN

I

ISABEL OPENS HER EYES UPON A MUD-
DLED WORLD, AND MEETS A KING AND
THE KING'S MASTER

ISABEL was born to the purple in no ordinary sense. She was more than the daughter of King Juan II of Castile and his second wife, Doña Isabel, of Portugal. Under the pink and white of her skin pulsed the blood of crusaders and conquerors, the blood of Alfred the Great, of William the Conqueror, of the iron Plantagenet Henry II and the fiery Eleanor of Aquitaine, of Edward I and Edward III of England, of Philip the Bold of France, of Alfonso the Wise of Castile. She was descended on both sides from Louis IX of France and his cousin Fernando III of Castile, both kings, both crusaders and both canonized saints. She derived Lancastrian blood through both parents from John of Gaunt, brother of the Black Prince. Yet her arrival in a chaotic world on the twenty-second of April, 1451, caused hardly a stir even in the little town of Madrigal. Her father, who was at Segovia, announced the event by proclamation: "I, the King . . . make known to you that by the grace of Our Lord this Thursday just past, the Queen, Doña Isabel, my dear and well-beloved wife, was delivered of a daughter; the which I tell you that you may give thanks to God." The infanta was baptized a few days later in the Church of Saint Nicholas, with no especial pomp or display. When the voices of her sponsors rumbled among the arches and arabesques of the old church, renouncing Satan and all his works on her behalf, there was no prophet on hand to cry out that one of the most remarkable women in all history had been born.

During the long and painful confinement of Isabel's mother,

there were certain symptoms of poisoning which, although they yielded to antidotes, left her a victim of a chronic nervous depression. In an epoch when the illnesses of the great were often ascribed to the malice of their foes, it was inevitable that people should whisper the name of Don Álvaro de Luna, Constable of Castile and Grand Master of the Order of Santiago, especially as that gifted and charming gentleman had long been suspected of having murdered the King's first wife, Doña María of Aragon, and her sister, the Dowager Queen Leonor of Portugal.

Lean, dark and sinister, exquisite in silk and jewels, handsome even in his late middle age, this nephew of the anti-Pope Benedict had been absolute master, for a long generation, of King Juan and of all Castile. He looted the Crown to make himself fabulously rich, he corrupted the Church by naming unworthy friends for benefices, he alienated the nobles by his insolence and arrogance, he infuriated the populace by giving high offices and privileges to Jews and Moors, he sowed discord in Aragon, Navarre, France and Italy for his own ends, and he led a life so dissolute that many blamed him for all the moral decay that made the court notorious. It was in his time, said the chronicler Palencia, that Castile saw the beginning of certain *infames tratos obscenos*, "infamous obscene customs which have since increased so shamefully." Intimate friend as well as prime minister, he dominated the King completely. He told him what to wear, what to eat, and even when to enter the bedroom of Queen María. Various interpretations were attached to the royal complacency. Many suspected the Constable of sorcery. Some said that he was protecting the weak-willed King from his own immoderation; others questioned the legitimacy of Don Enrique, the heir to the throne. But the gossip troubled the King not at all, so long as he was spared the boredom of administration, and left free to indulge his passion for poetry and music, for with all his weaknesses he was a loyal patron of the fine arts.

When Queen Leonor was driven out of Portugal by her brother-in-law, the regent, Don Pedro, she visited her sister, the Queen of Castile; and De Luna, who was friendly to Don Pedro, resented her presence as a threat to his own supremacy. Queen María died, after an illness of only three days. There were strange spots on her body, says the chronicler, "like those caused by herbs." Her sister died of the same mysterious ailment. The enemies of Don Álvaro had their opinion.

The King, who was disappointed in his son Enrique, thought of marrying again. His choice fell upon Fredagonde, daughter of Charles VII of France. But Don Álvaro had other plans for him. He had already, in fact, arranged for his master's marriage to the young Princess Isabel, first cousin of King Alfonso V of Portugal and niece of the Regent Don Pedro. The Constable feared the effect of a French alliance on his own position. On the other hand, his friend Don Pedro would know how to influence his young and inexperienced niece in the right direction, and Don Álvaro flattered himself that she would become a pliant instrument in his hands for the domination of the King. Women had always found him irresistible.

In the year 1447, consequently, there came to Burgos a slender princess from the west, whose face was rather melancholy in repose, though it became singularly beautiful, like the glass of some Gothic window, when the light of any emotion shone through it. She was the daughter of the Infante Don Juan, a younger son of Juan the Great of Portugal; her grandmother was Philippa, one of the daughters of John of Gaunt. Her welcoming was magnificent even for a country with a weakness for royal brides. There were dances, banquets, speeches, bull-fights, tourneys, glittering processions. Don Álvaro had arranged everything.

But Isabel had grown up in the court of a strong monarch, and had very definite notions of what a King should be. Her husband the slave of a haughty subject? Intolerable! That any one should attempt to regulate her domestic routine was not even to be thought of. And when Don Álvaro bowed over her hand with his most disarming smile, she read his heart; and, feeling that this man with the soft voice and the touch that made one think of a dark snake, would destroy her, body and soul, unless she destroyed him, she decided without hesitation that he must be destroyed.

To the further annoyance of the Constable, King Juan fell in love with his young wife. Assured by a fortune teller that he would live to be ninety, and finding himself still handsome and charming in his forties, he gave himself up to love and to gluttony, without consulting Don Álvaro as to his comings and goings. The Queen began to feel for him the affection that weak and likable men often inspire in strong-minded women. Pious, energetic, and incapable of compromise where any principle was involved, she threw her influence on the side of the nobles who were constantly plotting for the downfall of the favorite even after he crushed them at the first battle of Olmedo. The suspicion that de Luna had attempted to poison her at the time of the Infanta Isabel's birth urged her on to hasten his fall. Three years after the birth of the Princess Isabel, she brought forth her son, Alfonso; and while he was still in the womb, she accomplished her desire.

The murder of Don Alfonso Perez de Vivero gave her the opportunity she sought. He was the King's messenger, but Don Álvaro, angered because he had forsaken his party for the Queen's, had him thrown out of a window on Good Friday afternoon, in 1453. This conduct agreed so well with the popular impression that the Constable was a Catholic in name only, and a dabbler in black magic, that the indignation against him was extreme. The Queen made use of it to complete her ascendancy over the King. She induced him to have Don Álvaro seized and taken to Valladolid, where a council of his enemies was waiting to pass judgment upon him. At the crucial moment, some of the *Conversos* whom he had raised to power joined the party of the Queen. Their ingratitude was decisive.[1]

De Luna was as unruffled and confident in misfortune as he had been in power. He knew that, if he could talk with the King for five minutes, his personal charm would gain a pardon. It had on other occasions. No one knew better than he how difficult it was for Don Juan to punish any one; in fact, de Luna had once advised him never to speak with any man whom he had condemned. The Queen reminded her husband of that excellent counsel when he thought of receiving the Constable in audience. Seconded by those who feared the vengeance of Don Álvaro if he returned to power, she adjured him, in the name of Castile, of their love, of their children, of the God so long defied by de Luna, to prove himself a true King by administering strict justice. Twice during the trial, Juan is said to have signed an order for the release of his friend, and to have been shamed out of sending it by the Queen, who remained at his side night and day. When he ratified the sentence of the Court, his tears fell upon the paper.

Meanwhile in Valladolid, that drab city, preparations for

the execution had been completed with almost indecent haste, and at 8 o'clock on the morning of June 2, a crowd was gathering in the Plaza Major before a huge scaffold covered with black velvet, surmounted by a crucifix and a block. Against this sable background, thumbing the edge of the great sword of the Kings of Castile, stood the tall figure of an executioner, masked, silent, wrapped in robes of scarlet. The Plaza was almost filled with peasants, cattle herders, gayly dressed hidalgos who had ridden from far places to see their master's undoing. A trumpet sounded, and down the principal street came a little procession to the sound of muffled kettle-drums: first, a particolored herald with gaudy cap and tabard, proclaiming in a loud voice the high crimes of Don Álvaro de Luna; next, two ranks of men-at-arms in leather jerkins and cuirasses, and finally, mounted on a mule, the imperturbable Grand Master, wearing high-heeled shoes with diamond buckles, and muffled to the chin in a long Castilian cloak, while his confessor rode beside him.

The condemned dismounted, gazed serenely about at the brilliant assembly of his foes and the idly curious, smiled as if to say that one could expect no more from human nature, and with a firm step went up to meet the man in scarlet. Never had he looked more noble and gracious than when he raised his fine head and gazed thoughtfully out of his dark eyes over the heads of the people. A murmur of admiration and pity rippled through the crowd; whereat Don Álvaro placed his hand over his heart and bowed to them with grave gallantry. After another word with his confessor, he loosened the tasseled cord at his neck and handed his cloak to his page Morales, revealing on his breast the sword and cockleshell of Santiago, emblems of the great Crusade that he had sacrificed to avarice and ambition. He handed the page his hat; a ring, as a keepsake. If he glanced down the narrow street to see whether the King's messenger was coming, if he began to doubt the promises of his astrologers, he betrayed no uneasiness when he turned again to the spectators and in a resonant voice wished happiness and prosperity to the King and people of Castile. The sunlight sparkled on his coal black hair, on the jewels at his feet and his waist, on the newly ground steel of the sword of justice. Don Álvaro casually examined the block and the sword, took from his bosom a black ribbon, handed it to the

executioner for the binding of his hands. This done, he knelt
before the crucifix and prayed with fervor. A silence like the
dying of the wind in a field of wheat fell over the murmuring
crowd. The Grand Master was placing his head on the block.
The man in red made a pantherlike movement. There was a
flash of steel. Cries and shrieks burst from the Plaza. The
head rolled in the dust. *Castile! Castile for the King Don
Juan and his wife Lady Isabel!*

It was the young Queen's hour of victory, but the chalice of
her triumph was bitter. For the King suffered the remorse of
the imaginative, and all the rest of his miserable days passed
in self-reproaches for the doom of his friend. Eyen the birth
of his son Alfonso, November 15, 1454, left him unconsoled.
He died the following July, after a reign of forty-eight indolent years, moaning, "Would to God I had been born the son
of a mechanic instead of the son of a King!" He had encouraged art and literature, he had given power and privileges to
the Jews, he was father to a princess in whom his intellect
and her mother's will compounded to form greatness. History
has remembered little more of him. His magnificent tomb is in
the Cartuja de Miraflores, two miles from Burgos.

After his funeral and the coronation of the new King
Enrique IV, the Queen withdrew from the court with her two
children, and made her residence in the small castle of Arévalo,
in Old Castile. Alfonso was an infant in the cradle. The
Infanta Isabel was a self-possessed little blonde girl of three
years, with wide shoulders and sturdy legs, who regarded the
world frankly and analytically through large blue eyes in which
there were tiny streaks and specks of gold and green.

The melancholy that had fallen upon the Queen when Isabel
was born became habitual. After the King's death she was
seldom free from illness, never from anxiety. Her allowance
from her stepson Enrique, who had never liked her much,
came so irregularly that the little family was sometimes reduced
to the bare necessities, almost to actual want. But as all other
resources failed her, the pious Queen turned more than ever to
the solace of religion, and spent what remained of her superb
will in the service of her children. Isabel remembered her lying
in bed, ill; in white mourning garments, weeping for the King;
in the chapel, kneeling in reverence before the uplifted Host.

The child remembered something vague but terrifying about

the execution of Álvaro de Luna, for it was much talked about, and sung about in popular ballads. She recalled being told at the age of six that King Enrique was arranging for her marriage to Prince Fernando, the five year old second son of the King of Aragon. Fernando! The name was like a bell chiming in a far country of romance. It was odd to be the betrothed of a Prince that one had never seen.

At Arévalo Isabel formed her first friendship, one that lasted until the day of her death. Beatriz de Bobadilla was a child of her own age, daughter of the governor of the castle. Beatriz was dark and emotional, while Isabel was fair, reserved and strangely mature. They became inseparable. They played games together in the inclosed garden of the Alcázar, they learned to read by the bedside of the Queen, they approached the altar in the chapel together to receive their first Holy Communion. Sometimes they rode with the governor and his troops through the little walled town into the flat checkered country, where fields of wheat and saffron extended one after another as far as one could see—the wheat almost the color of Isabel's hair, and the saffron very fragrant on the wind. Cows and horses grazed in the pastures along the meandering Araja. Beyond the green places lay a flat desert, stark and treeless and full of unknown things to be feared. The lights and shadows alternated on this level plateau in broad undulating bars, like the waves of a great dark sea.

Sometimes they rode as far as Medina del Campo, where the greatest fair in Spain was held three times a year, and merchants came from all over southern Europe to buy choice Castilian wools and grains, and blooded steers and horses and mules from Andalusia. There were cavaliers from Aragon, sailors from Catalonia on the east coast, mountaineers from Guipúzcoa on the north, turbaned Moors from Granada in the south, blue-eyed Castilian farmers, bearded Jews in gaberdines, peasants from Provence and Languedoc, sometimes even an Englishman or a German. The people interested her, but not so much as the horses. Before Isabel was ten she scorned the mule that etiquette ordained for women and children, and kept her seat on a spirited horse. Days in the saddle made her hard, straight, resourceful, fearless, indifferent to fatigue, contemptuous of pain; a vigorous girl with delicate pink complexion, a firm prudent mouth, a lower jaw a trifle heavy, indicating unusual energy and will. She became a skilled huntress, commencing with hares and deer, but later following the black wild boar, and on one occasion slaying a good-sized bear with her javelin. Her brother Alfonso learned also to handle a sword and to tilt with lances.

Isabel grew up without a knowledge of Latin, but her education in other respects was sound and well balanced. She learned to speak Castilian musically and with elegance, and to write it with a touch of distinction. She studied grammar and rhetoric, painting, poetry, history and philosophy. She embroidered intricate Moorish designs on velour and cloth of gold, and illuminated prayers in Gothic characters on leaves of parchment. A missal that she painted, and some banners and ornaments for the altar in her chapel, are in the Cathedral at Granada. She had inherited a love for music and poetry. She read her father's favorite poet, Juan de Mena, and probably a Spanish translation of Dante. Her tutors, having studied at Salamanca University, must have given her at second hand the philosophy of Aristotle on which Saint Thomas Aquinas had built the great synthesis that was the foundation of medieval teaching.

Some notion of how science was taught at the period may be had from a philosophical and allegorical novel called the *Vision deleytable*, written by the Bachelor de la Torre about 1461 for the instruction of Prince Charles of Viana, Isabel's second fiancé. "I perceive that motion is the cause of heat," says the young hero; and goes on to discuss why there are perpendicular lines on the sun, what makes the wind blow, why climates differ, why materials are different, what causes the sensations of smell, taste, hearing, why some plants are large and others small, the properties of medicines—and all this sugar-coated in the form of a novel! The tragedies of Seneca were known in Spain. One of the first books published after the introduction of printing in Isabel's reign was a translation of *Plutarch's Lives* by Alonso de Palencia[2]; another by the same author was *Josephus's History*. Spanish versions of the *Odyssey* and the *Aeneid* were popular in the court of Isabel's brother. Books of medicine and surgery and anatomical charts were fairly common in a country where the Jews had long excelled in the healing art. From singing the *Cancioneros* that had been so dear to her father, Isabel evoked from the past the heroic story of her crusading ancestors; and from the chronicles of her own time, there unrolled before her keen intelligence and strong imagination a picture of the fascinating and terrifying world into which she had been born.

She was a King's daughter and the half-sister of a King, and there were certain inevitable questions that she must have asked her mother. What manner of man was Don Enrique IV, and what was he doing to bring back the glories of Saint Fernando and Alfonso the Wise, and heal the scars that the gemmed boots of Don Álvaro had left upon the face of a Castile weary of wars and feuds?

His Majesty occasionally rode to Arévalo to visit his relatives. Isabel remembered his coming there one day with two cavaliers, the Marqués of Villena and his brother Don Pedro Giron. These gentlemen, she learned afterwards from her mother, were the King's closest companions, his *criados*, who advised him in everything and who therefore were the two most powerful persons in the realm. Perhaps that was why they cut a more magnificent figure than King Enrique himself. They wore fine silks, bordered with cloth of gold, large and brilliant jewels, heavy gold chains cunningly wrought by smiths in Córdoba. The King looked shabby beside them. Loose-jointed, tall and awkward, he wore his long woolen cloak in a slovenly way, and instead of the boots that Castilian cavaliers wore, had his small delicate feet shod in buskins, like those of the Moors, with mud on them, so that they looked all the more peculiar on the ends of his long legs. But his face puzzled the little princess even more than his queer clothes and his familiar way of speaking to the servants. His skin was very white and rather puffy. His eyes were blue, somewhat too large, and somehow different from the eyes of other people. His nose was wide, flat and decidedly crooked, the result, it was said, of a fall he had as a boy. At the top of that prominent organ were two vertical furrows into which the bushy royal eyebrows curled up in a most peculiar manner. His beard was shaggy, with auburn streaks in it, and stuck out so oddly and abruptly that it made his face in profile look concave. But it was the eyes that one kept looking at and wondering about. There was a strange look of grievance and bewilderment in them, an inquietude that vaguely disturbed one. What did they remind her of? His chaplain, who wrote a eulogy of him after his death, recorded that Enrique's "aspect was fierce, like that of a lion that by its very look strikes terror to all beholders."[3] But it did not remind the chronicler Palencia of a lion at all. It reminded him of one of those monkeys that Isabel had seen in a wooden cage at the fair at Medina del Campo. His eyes glittered and roved about and looked ashamed, just like a monkey's.[4]

His Majesty talked of one thing and another, sometimes turning for confirmation of what he said to the Marqués of Villena, who nodded or put in a suave word in his slow drawl. This gentleman, had he had the good or evil fortune to be born later, would have been called a self-made man; for in the time of King Juan he was one Juan Pacheco, a page introduced at court by Don Álvaro de Luna. Though a professing Christian, he was one of many with Jewish blood in their veins who owed their prosperity to the great Constable; on both sides he was descended from the Jew Ruy Capon.[5] But, with other *Conversos* of the court, he had requited his benefactor by helping to overthrow him. Prince Enrique, whose elevation was thus hastened, rewarded Pacheco by making him Marqués of Villena and his intimate companion and adviser.

Of the three men, the Marqués was the most likable, because there was a twinkle in his shrewd eyes, and his beard and mustache were positively fascinating, so ingeniously had they been curled. Besides, he smelled delightfully of ambergris. He had a long aquiline nose, quite hooked in the middle and pointed at the tip; and somewhat too near the base of it, a narrow mouth with full lips, giving a curiously cherubic expression to the whole face. On either side of the mouth a carefully waxed and twisted mustache drooped somewhat dejectedly for a short distance, and then of a sudden turned out and up into two jaunty and devil-may-care points. The Marqués could be charming when he wanted to be, and on this particular occasion he made himself most agreeable.

His brother, Don Pedro Giron, was also of that numerous class of Castilians known as *Conversos*, or New Christians. He must have made at least some pretence of being a Catholic, else he could hardly have attained to the Grand Mastership of the illustrious military Order of Calatrava, founded by two Cistercian monks and consecrated to the rule of St. Benedict. He was a sleek, well-fed man, probably a sensual and passionate man. He hardly glanced at the Queen, but his eyes returned from time to time to gloat upon the fresh blonde beauty of the young princess, and his look was one of those under which a woman has almost the sensation of being forcibly disrobed.

After the King and the two cavaliers had gone, Isabel found her mother weeping in her apartment. She may have divined that the royal visit in some way concerned her, but she was too young to be told of the indecent proposal that Don Pedro had made on another occasion to the Queen, and at the instigation—so he said—of King Enrique himself.[6]

II

ENRIQUE THE LIBERAL he was called on his accession in 1454, and liberal he was in more than one sense
of the word. There was a certain grandeur in his contempt for all practical and mercenary considerations. A favorite
had only to ask him for money or land belonging to the
crown, and he complied graciously. He ordered castles, monuments and monasteries built wherever and whenever the fancy
seized him. He signed schedules and important state papers
without even reading them. He gave his friends orders on the
exchequer, leaving the sum blank for the beneficiaries to fill
in to suit themselves; and when a conscientious treasurer objected, Enrique silenced him with one of his royal aphorisms:
"Instead of accumulating treasures like private persons, a king
ought to spend them for the welfare of his subjects. I give to
my enemies to make them my friends, and give to my friends
to keep them from becoming my enemies." It was simple, very
simple. And it must be said for him that he was as generous
with the property of others as he was with his own. Having
acquired the vast Castilian estates of King Juan of Aragon
as security for a loan, he gave most of them to his friend
Pacheco. The Marqués smiled more cherubically than ever,
but there were several other needy deservers who thought the
King's generosity had been misplaced. However, a king with
such a philosophy was sure to have friends as long as his
funds held out.

Enrique the Liberal was far from orthodox in his opinions
and conduct. His chosen companions were Moors, Jews and
Christian renegades; indeed, any man who ridiculed the Christian religion was sure of at least a smile from his Majesty, if
not a pension. One of the favorite daily pastimes at the King's
table was the invention of new and original blasphemies; ob-

scene jokes were made about the Blessed Virgin and the Saints. The King attended Mass, but never confessed or received Communion. If his laxity pleased the enemies of the Church, it offended the mass of the people, who were predominantly Catholic. A petition addressed to Enrique a few years later by the chief Christian nobles and prelates said: "It is especially notorious that there are in your court and in your palace and about your person individuals who are infidels, enemies of our holy Catholic faith, and others, Christians in name only, but of very questionable faith, particularly those who believe and say and affirm that there is no other world but to be born and to die like beasts; and there are continually blasphemous people and renegades . . . whom your Lordship has exalted to high honors and dignities in your realms."

The Moorish guard which Enrique had constantly with him, and which he paid more generously than his Christian troops, did not tend to increase his popularity in a country where Christians had been slowly winning back their lands from the Moors during seven centuries of almost continuous warfare, and where a new Moorish conquest was always a possibility to be feared—indeed, Mohammed the Little had ravaged the *vega*, fruitful plain, of Christian Andalusia in 1455, the second year of Enrique's reign. Small wonder that in a crusading country muffled curses followed the King when he rode by at the head of his Saracen retainers.

Not that Enrique was at all warlike; on the contrary, he was decidedly a pacifist. He never wearied of protesting that bloodshed was abhorrent to him. Out of this, perhaps, grew another trait in which he was considerably ahead of, or behind, his time: a sympathy, amounting almost to affection, for criminals. It gave him such acute pain to order the execution of a thief or a murderer that he generally avoided it. In fact, his tolerance for the enemies of society was so well known that a drunken highwayman named Barrasa went boldly to tell him how he and another footpad, known as Alonzo the Horrible, had assassinated a wayfarer, and to prevent his identification, had peeled the skin off his face. The King, delighted with their ingenuity, made Barrasa his equerry. Similarly, when the renegade Bartolomé del Marmol, after joining other apostate Christians in a series of atrocities, including the murder and mutilation of forty Christians, attempted to return to the town where he was born, the people armed themselves and chased him into the wilderness; but King Enrique welcomed him, and gave him a post in the Moorish Guard.

Unfortunately, the King appeared to have but little affection left for the non-criminal classes. He had three respectable artisans hanged in Seville merely because in a peevish moment he had given his word he would do so. He appointed officials who used their offices to tyrannize over the people and make themselves rich. He "farmed out" the privilege of collecting taxes to the wealthy Rabbi Jusef of Segovia, whose great influence in the King's counsels was unpopular with the exploited masses, and to Diego Árias de Ávila, a converted Jew, to whom he gave almost plenary powers, including the right to exile citizens, or put them to death *without a hearing* for non-payment of taxes; and with these powers, unprecedented in Castile, Enrique annulled the rights of appeal and of asylum. To his excessive laxity on one hand and excessive severity on the other there could be only one ending: a state of anarchy. The nobles, both those who were sure of the King's protection and those who were learning to despise his authority, began to consider themselves petty kings in their own jurisdictions, and when they had disputes with neighbors, they went to war. Others, as the value of Enrique's inflated currency depreciated, began to coin their own money. The robber barons and highwaymen preyed on the farmers, laborers and merchants, until many of the victims, unable to make an honest living, became criminals themselves. In Seville the King gave Xamardal, Rodrigo de Marchena and other bandits the privilege of taxing fish, beasts of burden, leather, and tasters of wine. There was hardly a corner in Castile where a man was safe from robbery and murder, hardly a road where a girl or a woman was safe from rape and mutilation. Public and private morality had never been so low since Christianity came into the land.

The stench of the court began to pervade the air of all Spain. Enrique alone seemed to be impervious to the strong odor; indeed, it was a curious fact that his sense of smell, like some of his other instincts, differed—literally, not figuratively—from those of other men. The odor of decay pleased him; he found horses' skulls and burning leather delightful. He disliked sunlight, and broad and clean horizons, preferring the gloom and obscurity of the forests around Madrid, where he loved to chase wild animals with Moors, rustics and criminals. Such were some of the reports that sifted through the gossips of the court to every hamlet on the peninsula, and ultimately to every capital in Europe. And among the most scandalous were those concerning the King's two marriages.

Precociously familiar with all vices and described by his tutor, Fray Lupe de Barrientos as a youth "born for the ruin of the throne and the reproach of nations," Enrique at the age of fourteen wedded Blanche, the gentle daughter of King Juan of Aragon. After several childless years, he had the marriage annulled in 1446 by the Bishop of Segovia, on the ground of impotence. From that time on, the King was known as *Enrique El Impotente*.

When he succeeded his father in 1454, he needed an heir, and the Marqués of Villena, virtual ruler of the kingdom, volunteered to select a suitable mate for him.

Villena, who "could disguise all vices but his avarice, which he could neither hide nor moderate"[1] lived in constant fear of losing rich Castilian possessions of Juan of Aragon. To forestall another match with the House of Aragon, or any alliance that might indirectly touch his interests, he chose for Enrique's second wife the lovely Princess Juana, sister of King Alfonso V of Portugal, a witty vivacious girl of fifteen. Enrique offered a rich dowry and asked none. Alfonso, not at all sorry to extend his influence in Castile, persuaded his sister to accept, though she must have known her suitor's reputation, for by this time ballads about him were being sung in the streets in Spain and Portugal. Perhaps her vanity made her imagine that being a queen was worth any price. At any rate, she accepted. Thus for the second time a woman came from Portugal to change the history of Castile.

Juana arrived at Badajoz in 1455 with twelve pretty maids of honor and a long retinue of cavaliers. At the border they were met by the young blades of the Castilian court, who conducted them in triumph to Córdoba, where the Archbishop of Tours performed the marriage. Never were so many brilliant banquets, receptions, processions, bull-fights, feasts and jousts held in honor of any Princess in Castile, never had the Court been so captivated as it was by the brunette beauty, the fresh charm and the tireless gaiety of this young Queen. She danced so divinely that the French ambassador made a vow never to dance with any other woman. At one of the banquets the servants of the Archbishop of Seville passed around salvers full of choice rings and precious stones, that Doña Juana and her ladies might choose such as agreed with their complexions.

Whatever may have been the motive of Juana in consenting to marry the mere wreckage of a man, she could hardly have been prepared for the pain and humiliation of the next few months. Her husband desired an heir, and according to Palencia, he demanded that the Queen have a child by one of his intimates.[2] Juana's instincts being sound, she refused.

Enrique attempted to punish her. He neglected her, he gave her no money, he made her virtually a prisoner, he snubbed her in public. Juana still resisted. The King then sought, and in this he may have been advised by that smiling Marrano with the perfumed beard, the Marqués, to arouse her jealousy by paying court to one of her ladies-in-waiting, Doña Guiomar de Castro. With principles more elastic than those of her royal mistress, Guiomar made the most of her elevation, even to the extent of patronizing the Queen in the presence of the court. That was more than Portuguese pride could endure. Juana's fan, smartly slapped across Guiomar's face, left white marks that on the next day were red. Immediately two factions were formed, the party of Her Majesty, and the party of the Lady Guiomar. The Queen in great anguish wrote her royal brother all that she had suffered, but it does not appear that Alfonso V allowed any solicitude for her honor to come between him and his Castilian policy. However, the Marqués of Villena let it be known that he was a partisan of the Queen. At his insistence, Enrique packed Lady Guiomar off to the country, with the gift of a beautiful estate and an income so large that she was later able to marry the Count de Trevino.

Enrique was becoming the jest of the peninsula. Having got out of him all they could, Doña Guiomar and several others amused their friends with anecdotes of which he was the hero. The gossips next began to look with more care into Enrique's relations with various men and boys, and their conclusions were reflected in a scurrilous passage of the *Coplas de Mingo Revulgo*.

Enrique in self-defense posed as the lover of the corrupt Catalina de Sandoval. He even pretended to be jealous of her lover and had him beheaded. But the scandal was already well known; and a storm was rising. The chief opposition came from the Catholic nobles and those of the clergy who were not Enrique's creatures. At Toledo Cathedral the Dean, Don Francisco de Toledo, denounced him from the pulpit. Don Alfonso Carrillo, Archbishop of Toledo and primate of Spain, reproved the King first in private and then in public for his evil life and the scandals of his court and government. Enrique's reply to the Archbishop was to attack the ecclesiastical immunities, to ridicule church documents and ceremonies and to curtail Carrillo's jurisdiction. In the past this method had been known to silence the criticisms of a certain type of churchman. But in Carrillo Enrique had a different kind of man to deal with; one whom his worst enemies, and he had many, had never accused of lack of courage; and the Archbishop now returned to the attack with all the thunderous gravity and majesty for which he was noted.

It was Enrique's move. It amused him to find that he could kill two birds with one stone. He had grown tired of his affair with the Countess de Sandoval, and was looking for some pretext to get rid of her. The happy thought occurred to him that he might at the same time annoy the Archbishop of Toledo. With a stroke of his pen he removed from office the pious and efficient abbess of the convent of San Pedro de las Dueñas in Toledo, and bestowed the office on the Countess. The convent, he explained, needed to be reformed! Catalina proceeded to reform the community by destroying its discipline and teaching the young nuns the vices she had made notorious in the palace.

The cynics of the King's table found it all very diverting. The court wag, Don Gonzalo de Guzman, said in a company of nobles, "There are three things that I will not *lower* myself to take up: the pompous drawl of the Marqués of Villena, the gravity of the Archbishop of Toledo, and the virility of Don Enrique." Others, who had the interests of the Church and the State at heart, saw no humor in the situation. One of these was the Archbishop himself. Another was Don Fadrique Enriquez, the Admiral of Castile.

Don Fadrique, a diminutive[3] but very forceful and important gentleman, one of the great land-owners of Castile, had lately increased his prestige by marrying his daughter Juana to King Juan of Aragon. He now began conspiring with other powerful nobles against the hated Marqués and the despised King. With this revolutionary Junta the Archbishop of Toledo allied himself.

Enrique saw that he had gone too far. His natural impulse would have been to make his peace with the conspirators; but the Marqués of Villena, fearing the influence of the Admiral and the Archbishop, suggested another alternative more profitable to him and more flattering to the King. Why not divert the public gaze from these petty domestic difficulties by a glorious Crusade against the Moors? Nothing was more likely to arouse the national, the racial and the religious emotions of the Castilians. Their ancestors had won back the soil foot by foot from the Infidel; even now from the south came daily stories of Moorish raids into Christian territory, of cattle driven off, of men killed and women ravished. Enrique had long been detested for his partiality for these enemies of the commonwealth, and particularly for his rebuke to the Duke of Medina Sidonia for taking Gibraltar from the Arabs. Here was his·opportunity to regain the public esteem and at the same time to divide or win over the conspirators. The Archbishop of Toledo could hardly refuse to support a popular war that he himself had long advocated. Enrique may have found the idea amusing. He appointed as regents in his absence the Archbishops of Toledo and Count Haro, a Christian gentleman of character and ability. A bull of crusade was obtained from Pope Pius II, indulgences were offered under the usual conditions, a fund of 4,000,000 maravedis was raised for expenses, and 30,000 troops assembled at Córdoba in 1557.

History does not record a more pusillanimous crusade than this. Enrique led his eager host through Andalusia, crossed the Sierra Nevada, and invaded the wide blossoming *vega* surrounding Granada. But it soon became plain that his purpose was not war, but a holiday. He marched up to fortified towns and marched away again without a blow. Some of his cavaliers having been killed in skirmishes with straggling Moors, he forbade skirmishes in future. When some young soldiers set fire to wheat fields and cut down fruit trees, as was customary in these wars, he whipped them with his own hand, and had their ears cut off. It was a sin, said he, to destroy food. The Moors seemed to attach no great importance to the crusade, for they never came out in force from their walled towns to

offer battle; and the suspicion grew in the Christian army that
Enrique had assured them they had nothing to fear. From
time to time he met groups of them secretly, sat on the ground
with them, and to the great scandal of the chronicler who
reports it, ate their honey, raisins, figs and butter without the
slightest dread of being poisoned. A king who was a true
crusader could hardly have taken that risk. It was his daily
custom, too, to retire to an orchard and solace himself with
Moorish music. Like the Moors, he rode *a la jineta*, as no
other Castilian king had ever done. There is even some evidence that the Moors believed Enrique to be in sympathy with
their sect.

Betrayed, as they thought, by their king, the cavaliers of
Castile left the orange groves and nightingales of the south
without fighting a battle. The chief damage was done to the
farms of the Christians of Andalusia. Almost the only shots
of the Crusade were fired by Queen Juana, who, riding into
camp with nine other dizzily attired damsels, sped two arrows
against the Moorish walls of Cambril.

The Archbishop of Toledo, dourly administering the public
business from Valladolid, learned of the issue of the "war"
with a disgust intensified by the realization that he had been
tricked. To make matters worse, he discovered that the King
had given 80,000 florins of the money the Pope had authorized
him to collect for a crusade to Don Beltran de la Cueva, one
of his intimates. After a public protest in which he was joined
by Don Pedro Gonzalez de Mendoza, Carrillo made open cause
with Don Fadrique the Admiral and other lords returning
in anger and shame from Granada. The King came back, therefore, to find the conspiracy he had hoped to destroy merely
postponed. In fact the Marqués, who was always well informed by his brother Don Pedro Giron and various spies,
was not long in perceiving that the country was in a pretty
muddle indeed; for Don Fadrique was in communication with
his son-in-law the King of Aragon, the last person in the
world that Villena wished to see drawn into the affairs of
Castile.

After a little reflection the Marqués had one of those happy
inspirations that occur to statesmen. Casting about for help
against Juan of Aragon, he naturally bethought him of that
monarch's enemies. As luck would have it, the King of Aragon

had fallen out, since his second marriage, with his son Carlos of Viana, in whom the stepmotherly jealousy of Juana Enriquez saw only an obstacle. With Carlos, then, Pacheco arranged an alliance, sealed by the promise of the hand of the Princess Isabel.

The Queen of Aragon had no intention of enduring such a slight. She was a woman to whom power was necessary and inevitable, and the birth of a son, Fernando, in 1452, had given her an additional motive for dispossessing Carlos. It was she who arranged the betrothal of Fernando and Isabel in 1457, but her husband's understanding with the Castilian rebels put a damper on that for the time being, and now Villena's arrangement with Carlos threatened definitely to end her hopes. Her ascendancy over the aging King of Aragon was such, however, that she induced him to have Carlos seized and cast into prison.

Carlos, a scholar of forty, thin, sad, kindly and tubercular, was much loved in Catalonia, and when the Catalans learned of his arrest they rebelled and forced King Juan to release him. Father and son had an affectionate meeting and signed a treaty. Carlos entered Barcelona in triumph. But presently he died after a short illness. The Catalans openly declared that agents of his father and stepmother had poisoned him. The suspicion was probably unjust.

Carlos had two sisters. One of them was Blanche, the former wife of Enrique IV of Castile, and to her he left his title to the Kingdom of Navarre. The other was Eleanor, Countess of Foix, a jealous and unscrupulous woman. Having betrothed her son Gaston to a sister of Louis XI, she now obtained the aid of the Spider King in removing poor Blanche from the scene of action. This was done by shutting her up in a convent at Orthez with the connivance of her father, Juan of Aragon. There Blanche died, poisoned by her sister. The murderess lived only three weeks to enjoy the fruits of her crime.

As all three of the children of the King of Aragon by his first marriage were dead, little Fernando now had a clear field, and his mother renewed her efforts to ally him to the royal house of Castile. But at this moment the Catalans, who hated her furiously, again revolted, and pursuing her to Gerona, fifty miles from Barcelona, besieged her and the ten year old Prince Fernando in a tower. She coolly directed the defense

Enrique IV, "El Impotente"
(*From the "Boletín de la Real Academia de la Historia"*)

for several days. But the rebellion had grown so alarmingly that the old King was unable to go to her rescue. He obtained 700 French lances, with archers and artillery, however, from Louis XI, together with a loan of 200,000 crowns, for which he pledged, as security, the two valuable provinces of Roussillon and Cerdagne. Louis hoped that the loan would never be paid. To that worthy end he did his best to keep Juan in trouble.

Meanwhile Enrique IV had ignored the dying appeal of Blanche, or rather, answered it by coming to terms with her father and her other enemies. The situation in Castile had changed somewhat. The conspirators, discouraged by the unexpected entanglements in which their ally, Juan of Aragon, had become involved, had given up their schemes for the time being. Enrique, therefore, had no further need of help from Navarre. Besides, his personal affairs had unexpectedly taken a favorable turn.

Juana his wife had given up the struggle for her soul.

Precisely at what point, or why, or how she struck her colors —whether Enrique's cruelties and importunities wore down her patience, or whether the temptations of the lewd court were too strong for her rather voluptuous nature, or whether in her loneliness and despair at being forsaken by her brother she threw herself into the arms of some attractive and sympathetic male—the details have not come down to us; only the fact of her fall and its effect on the destiny of nations.

About this time a new character appears in the royal drama. The peerless knight-at-arms, Sir Beltran de la Cueva, began to display himself in the company of both their Majesties, and the three appeared everywhere together. Don Beltran was tall, robust, and florid of countenance; expert with sword and lance, and always ready to quarrel for a delicate point of honor. The King, it was observed, had seldom been more pleased with any of his favorites; he seemed fairly infatuated with him, so that he bore it meekly when Beltran flew into paroxysms of rage against him, permitting him to act as if he were lord of the palace, and to knock down the porters and kick them if doors were not opened quickly enough. The nobles fervently detested Beltran for his arrogance and insolence; and it goes without saying that the Marqués of Villena saw no virtue in him at all. Others of the King's cronies praised him, and com-

monly greeted one another with "Have you heard Don Beltran's newest blasphemy?"

One day as their Majesties were approaching Madrid after
entertaining the Count of Armagnac with three days' hunting
in the country, they found their road barred by a knight in
silvered armor, with trappings of gold on his horse, who sat
immovable and stately by an open field at a turn of the way,
his lance couched as if for combat. The royal cavalcade halted
by the road side while two officers spurred ahead to inquire
who the mysterious cavalier might be, and why he impeded
the King's highway. Meanwhile their Majesties noticed some
tiers of scaffolding that had been erected on the field and were
filling with spectators. The officers returned to report that
the knight errant was Don Beltran de la Cueva, who had been
there since early morning challenging each knight that came
by that road to tilt six rounds with him, or else to leave his
left glove on the ground in token of his cowardice. Don Beltran
did this to vindicate the superlative beauty of his mistress over
all the other women in the world. Any knight who managed
to break three lances with him had his permission to go to
yonder archway, which glittered with all the letters of the
alphabet painted with gold, and take thence the initial of the
lady of his choice. But so far none of the letters had been
removed.

The Queen was enchanted at coming upon this adventure.
The King, who had been in one of his cloudy moods, cried,
"A passage of arms! Magnificent!" And all the rest of that
day the royal party watched the encounters, which came frequent and furious as knight after knight went down before
the invincible lance; and when the dusk came slowly over the
brown *vega*, it was agreed by all, from His Majesty to the
village yokels, that Don Beltran had nobly maintained the
cause of his lady. Her name, for reasons of his own, he re-
frained from publishing. But he did not deny that she was of
high degree.

The King was so diverted by that day's sport that he commanded a monastery to be built on the spot where Beltran had
withstood all comers; and the monastery of *San Jerónimo del
Paso*, St. Jerome of the Passage of Arms, remains there still
as a witness to the truth that good is sometimes brought about
by strange instrumentalities.

Not long after the passage of arms it was bruited about the Court that Queen Juana, after seven childless years, had conceived at last. In the following March (1462) she gave birth at Madrid to a girl. The King's joy was exuberant. He showered favors right and left. Don Beltran de la Cueva, as if in honor of the event, and as a reward for his many distinguished services, was made Count of Ledesma. The child was named after her mother, Juana; but every one called her *La Beltraneja*, that is to say, the daughter of Beltran. She was baptized with great pomp and magnificence by the Archbishop of Toledo. The new Count of Ledesma and all the court were present. The godfathers were the Marqués of Villena and the French ambassador. It was observed that the Marqués had lost something of his cherubic expression of late.

The godmother was the Infanta Isabel, a grave, determined, very beautiful child of eleven, who had been brought from Arévalo on a mule, surrounded by troopers. She made her responses in a cool musical voice that vibrated through the church, a voice that seemed intended to command and to be obeyed. The Marqués looked at her. He had almost forgotten her. Perhaps some use could be made of her one of these days.

Enrique next summoned the Cortes and requested the delegates of the seventeen cities to take the oath of allegiance to the Infanta Juana, as heir to the throne of Castile. The delegates, after some murmuring, complied. The first person to kiss the little Infanta's hand was the Princess Isabel.

After this ceremony she returned to Arévalo. Her mother was not well. Isabel's visit to the court had disturbed her. Some friends had lately brought her the latest gossip about Enrique and Juana and their intimates. It made the Dowager ill even to think of such things. Youths in feasts and tourneys were displaying devices boasting of their desire for the Queen and Lady Guiomar. When the Marqués of Villena was ill, Enrique had gone to his house at dawn to divert him by singing and playing an accompaniment on the lute. There was a story about the youth, Francisco de Valdes, who fled to Aragon to escape his attentions. As for the Moors of the royal guard, the scandals about them were too numerous and too vile to remember. One of them made the Dowager Isabel tremble with loathing and anger. To say nothing of their *torpe liviandad*

contra leyes de naturaleza, some of the dusky ruffians had violated several young women and girls; and when the outraged
fathers went to King Enrique demanding vengeance, he informed them that they had evil minds, they were insane. He
increased the wages of the Moors, and had the fathers whipped
on the streets.

About the time that these horrors found echoes in sleepy
Arévalo, there was a clatter of horsemen's hoofs at the gate
of the Alcázar; and one of Enrique's officers brought the
Dowager Queen a brief note from her stepson.

She was commanded to send the Infanta Isabel and the
Infante Alfonso to the Court without delay, to take up their
permanent residence there. Enrique added by way of explanation that they would be more virtuously brought up under
his personal care.

Something broke in the Queen Dowager's heart. The melancholy that she was subject to now became habitual, a mild
but incurable form of insanity. Isabel and her brother sadly
made their preparations, and sadly they took leave of their
mother. Neither felt like talking as they rode, followed by
squires and men-at-arms, along the King's highway to Madrid.

III

THE massive gate of the old Moorish Alcázar at Madrid swung slowly open with a groan and a crunch. From within came the sound of female voices, young and shrill and shrieking with laughter, and the beating of many hoofs on a stone pavement. A dozen small mules in gold and crimson trappings came galloping through the gate, each bearing a damsel in a low-cut sleeveless gown, with skirts so short that when the wind flapped them back, the bare thighs of the riders were revealed; and the hucksters and beggars who had fled from the middle of the narrow street with hoarse cries and curses saw that the legs of all were painted with cosmetics, brilliantly white in the afternoon sunshine. The girls wore costumes of the most varied character. One had a saucy bonnet, another went bare-headed and let her bobbed reddish hair stream in the wind; there was still another in a man's hat cocked on one side, another with a Moorish turban of silken gauze woven with threads of gold, and yet another whose black hair was covered with a little kerchief in the Viscayan manner. One was girded about the breasts with leathern thongs taken from a cross-bow, one had a dagger in her girdle, one carried a sword, several had knives of Vittoria hung around their necks.[1]

These were the young women with whom Isabel was to live, sleep, eat and talk during the next two years, and it was in the apartment of one of them that Alfonso, at the age of nine, was to peer through the crack of a door a few months later and behold the peerless knight-at-arms, Don Beltran de la Cueva, tiptoeing by candlelight into the boudoir of her Serene Majesty. The life to which the two children from the austere castle of Arévalo were introduced so suddenly was a devil-may-care succession of balls, tourneys, pageants and comedies, bull-fights, intrigues and scandals. Each day there was a new blasphemy by Don Beltran, each day a new story of the Queen's indiscretion, each day a new joke about the King's virility. "The young women of the court are very expert for their age in the art of seduction," wrote Palencia. "The lasciviousness of their costumes arouses the young people, and their words are extremely audacious." When they are not engaged in lovemaking, he adds, "they are indulging in sleep, or covering their bodies with cosmetics and perfumes. The desire which devours them night and day would astonish even the foolish virgins."

In Castile, as in Italy, a cycle of civilization was ended, and the late Middle Ages were dying in a miasma of levity, cynicism, depravity. It was in this very year that a new King in Paris plucked one Master Francois Villon from the shadow of the gibbet. It was then that young Girolamo Savanarola began to thunder predictions of the destruction of Italy by an outraged God. Spain, too, had found evil as well as good in the cup of the Renaissance. Her condition was worse, in many respects, than that of Italy. The demoralization that usually follows war had been magnified and made chronic by eight centuries of almost continuous conflict, struggles between Christians and Mohammedans, between Castile and Portugal, between Castile and Aragon. Human life was very cheap. Contact with Moslems profoundly modified the influence of the Christian Church among the people; polygamy, for example, was not uncommon, though it usually took the form of open concubinage. And the Jews, although possessors of a far nobler moral code than the Mohammedans, acted everywhere as a powerful dissolvent, as will later appear, of the Christian faith which was the foundation of the morality of the people among whom they lived. Many of the clergy were depraved. And the Court was unspeakably foul. Isabel was disgusted by what she saw and heard there. But for the present her youth protected her.

Enrique kept his promise to provide instruction for both children. Alfonso learned the accomplishments of a cavalier, studied with a tutor, and attempted to fulfil the obligation his mother had imposed of being Isabel's knight and protector.

He scowled at Juana's damsels, he scowled at the Moorish guards.

The Princess was instructed in music, painting, poetry, sewing, grammar. She spent a long while every day in prayer, beseeching God to keep her and Alfonso safe and without sin, and she especially invoked the aid of the Blessed Virgin, of Saint John the Evangelist, and of Saint James the Apostle, the patron saint of Castile.

It was not until the Princess was about sixteen that Juana attempted to induce her to join the debaucheries of the Court. Isabel, in tears, fled to her brother.

Alfonso buckled on his sword and strode to the Queen's apartment. The substance of his speech was that her Majesty had spoken more like a harlot than a queen, and that he, Alfonso, Prince of Castile, forbade her to mention any further evil to his sister, Doña Isabel. Juana listened, amused and contemptuous, to her fourteen-year-old mentor and said nothing. From that day on she made no further attempt to corrupt the Princess.

Alfonso next made a visit to the ladies in waiting. He forbade them under pain of death to address his sister. They listened in silence, holding their laughter until he had gone, for after all, one does not laugh at the brother of a King. However, they told the Queen, with much hilarity, what had passed.

Isabel and Alfonso did not escape so easily from the strong political currents of that Court. Although the birth of *La Beltraneja* had at first strengthened the King's hand against the conspirators, the conviction was growing that she was not his daughter, and men all over Castile were saying that Alfonso ought to be acknowledged as heir to the throne. Many who had merely grumbled at the greed and dishonesty of the Marqués were ready to take arms against the swaggering and blasphemous Don Beltran; and the Archbishop at a meeting of nobles denounced him for infamous crimes.

The conspirators detested the Queen's lover so whole-heartedly that they began to find some excellence even in the Marqués. The Archbishop, who was Pacheco's uncle, had never had any serious grievance against him. The Admiral and others, much as they hated him, were willing to make a truce with him until they had given the *coup de grâce* to the

Count of Ledesma. Villena wavered for some time between
the Junta and the party of the Queen. With all his vast possessions that he had wheedled from the King, he was never
content, and never would be without the Grand Mastership
of the Order of Saint James, an office of such power and
revenues that it was bestowed only in the royal family. By
voice of the Order, the exalted honor had been conferred upon
Prince Alfonso. But, it seemed to the Marqués, the Prince
was very young to hold so important a dignity. His intuition
led him to the Queen's ante-chamber not long after she had
suffered Alfonso's curtain lecture, and he managed, with many
smiles and compliments, to persuade her that the Prince ought
to resign the Mastership, at least until he was older. Alas,
there was another possibility, one too sad even to think about.
"Whom the gods love ——" But Pacheco's insinuations to
Her Majesty may have been invented by the malice of his
enemies. In 1462, however, the King announced that his
brother the Prince had "resigned" the Mastership. Pacheco
smiled to the very roots of his curly beard.

Now, although Juana had helped the Marqués to this extent,
she had views of her own on the appointment of Alfonso's
successor. She had not thought it necessary to trouble Villena
with the information that he had a rival for the Mastership.
The first intimation the Marqués had of this development was
one cold day when the King, on the moment of departing for
Madrid, announced the nomination of Don Beltran.

The atmosphere was violently charged when the Court went
to Almazan to spend Christmas. There, as luck would have
it, an embassy of Catalans came to renounce their allegiance
to Juan of Aragon, because he had brought French troops to
fight them at Gerona, and to offer it to Castile in return for
aid. Flattered and elated, Enrique sent them 2,500 lances—a
small force, but large enough to embarrass Aragon at that
particular moment. Juan, in desperation, appealed to Louis XI,
who promptly offered his services as mediator. Nothing pleased
the French king better than to promote a quarrel and then
arbitrate it with some advantage to himself.

The three monarchs and the queens of Castile and Aragon
met with much pomp and display by the banks of the River
Bidassoa in April, 1463. It must have been one of the first
great royal spectacles that Isabel and her brother witnessed.

After the usual tourneys, feasts and music, the French king
and Enrique went to the river bank for a formal meeting, of
which Philippe de Comines has left a vivid picture. The Castilians wore gaudy colors and much gold, and even the slovenly
Enrique was overdressed and loaded with jewelry for the
occasion, while the French appeared in raiment of severe simplicity, following the example of the sardonic Louis, who had
on a short home-spun coat, "as ill-made as possible, for sometimes he worse very coarse cloth, and particularly then. His
hat was old and differing from everybody's else, with a leaden
image of the Blessed Virgin Mary upon it. The Castilians
laughed heartily at his dress, supposing it his stinginess."
Enrique, a little uncomfortable in his grandeur, looked down
with amazement in his watery blue eyes at the bent figure of
an old King dressed like a merchant. "In short, the conversation broke up, and they parted, but with such scorn and
contempt on both sides, that the two kings never loved each
other very heartily afterwards." Of Enrique the French chronicler cannot resist adding, "He was a person of no great sense,
for he had given away all his patrimony, or suffered it to be
embezzled from him." But by all odds the most gorgeous personage at that meeting was the new Grand Master of Santiago,
Don Beltran, who, having arrived at Euenterabia with an
escort of 300 Moorish horsemen from Granada, was seen
crossing the swift river in a boat with a sail of cloth of gold,
and as he stepped ashore with a lordly air, it was observed
that he was shod with buskins thickly studded with precious
stones; and thus he went to wait upon the King of Castile.

The actual negotiations, managed by the Queen of Aragon
on one side and by the Marqués and the Archbishop on the
other, ended in a solemn treaty whereby peace was declared,
and Juan of Aragon ceded to Enrique, as the invader, the
fortified town of Estrella in Navarre. It was only later, when
Enrique sent a force to occupy the place and was denied
entry to it, that he saw how brazenly he had been duped.
Every one else had gained something from the adventure.
Juan of Aragon, thanks to his shrewd and charming wife,
was relieved of an invasion at an embarrassing time. Louis
XI, as arbiter between two nations, had increased his prestige
and gained an excuse for later interference in Spain. But
Enrique had been bought off by a purely imaginary gift. He

was furious. Unable to punish Louis or Juan, he denounced the Archbishop and the Marqués as scoundrels and traitors. His suspicions took on some color from the friendship between Carrillo and King Juan, and the fact that not long after this, the Queen of Aragon entertained Villena *en tête-à-tête* at dinner, while the noble ladies of her court waited on him as if he had been a prince of the blood.

Enrique hesitated to proceed openly against the Marqués. Like most cowards of his type, he preferred indirect methods. If his enemies were at all formidable, he liked to have them under his eyes, where he could watch them and punish them cautiously with petty slights and coolnesses. He was afraid of the Archbishop, and felt that he had gone far enough with him for the present. But the Marqués, that treacherous friend, that viper, his own creature, must be humiliated somehow and brought to heel, as in past times. By way of letting Villena know that he had fallen from favor, His Majesty left Madrid without notifying him. The Marqués learned unofficially that the King, the Queen and Don Beltran had gone to Estremadura on the Portuguese border, taking with them the Infanta Isabel.

This could only mean that Beltran, with the Queen's connivance, had finally gained Pacheco's place in the royal confidence. But why had they taken the Princess with them? The spies of Villena enlightened him; their Highnesses had gone to Gibraltar to meet the King of Portugal. Alfonso the African, as he had been called since his successful crusade across the straits, was now in his corpulent middle age, but Queen Juana, his sister, had decided to extend her sphere of influence and his by giving him the Princess Isabel in marriage. Don Beltran saw the point, and between them he and the Queen managed to win over Enrique, particularly as His Majesty was in high feather on being apprised that Juana again had hopes of a male heir. Nothing had been said of all this to Villena, for since his dinner with the Queen of Aragon he had been advocating her plan of marrying Isabel to her son Fernando.

Meanwhile the widowed Alfonso V, at Gibraltar, was so pleased with the pink and white beauty and placid wisdom of the twelve-year-old princess that he invited her to become Queen of Portugal. Isabel thanked him for the honor, which she protested was far beyond her deserts, but begged to inform him that according to the laws of Castile and the wishes of the King her father, now with God, she could not marry without the consent of the three estates of Castile assembled in a Cortes; and naturally, before she could venture on so serious a step, she would have to sound the opinions of many nobles and prelates and commons. Either the child thought of that astute reply herself, or the Archbishop of Toledo, to whom her brother Alfonso had lately appealed for protection, had been instructing her in the rudiments of diplomacy. With her precocious maturity of judgment she probably saw through the wiles of Juana and Beltran, and formed a correct estimate of the character of Alfonso V.

Events suddenly begin to gallop at a melodramatic tempo. Back in Madrid, Isabel hears some alarming news. During her absence her brother has been seized at the King's orders and locked up in a secret chamber of the Alcázar. He makes various attempts to communicate with her, but fails. Perhaps it is just as well for her peace of mind. Later she will hear that Queen Juana has visited him and has tried to induce him to take some "herbs" for his health; but Perucho Monjarán, a Viscayan, has secretly advised him not to touch them. The Prince's tutor, sent to teach him Latin, instructs him in certain Renaissance vices. The boy orders him away. In his desperation he manages to get a message of appeal to Carrillo. The Archbishop sends him a promise of help.

The Archbishop keeps his word. He is seen in gleaming mail, armed cap-à-pie, on a huge black war horse, and over his cuirass flutters a crimson cloak with a great white cross emblazoned on it. Couriers fly over the roads from one end of the kingdom to the other. The feudal retainers of the Admiral are on the march northward. The conspirators have decided upon war. The people, disturbed by many wild rumors, are restless, surly, afraid—whatever happens, it cannot be much worse for them. The great nobles take sides. Many who despise Enrique are drawn to him by loyalty to the ideal of legitimate succession. One of these, Don Pedro Gonzalez de Mendoza, Bishop of Calahorra, resists the urgent appeals of the conspirators, who value his character and the influence of his illustrious family. This man will play an important part in the destiny of Isabel and of Castile. Meanwhile all men are asking what Villena will do. With his usual caution he attempts to solve his difficulties by his own methods before resorting to arms; he tries several times to have Don Beltran assassinated, and on one occasion the peerless knight barely escapes. That decides the question for the Marqués. He takes the plunge, he joins the rebels. With him goes his disreputable brother, Don Pedro Giron, Grand Master of the Order of Calatrava.

Assembling their forces at Burgos in the north, the leaders of the Junta appeal to public opinion in a series of memorable *representaciones* openly addressed to the King. Certain writers of later ages will misrepresent this document, seeing in it nothing but the peevish expression of the greed of Villena, the vanity of Carrillo, and the jealousy of Don Beltran's other enemies, and failing to discern what gives it such grave importance: the fact that it voices the outraged faith and moral indignation of a whole people. The rebels, whether sincerely or for political purposes, are undoubtedly speaking for the democracy of Spain. The *representaciones* are like a mirror in which Enrique may be seen as he appeared to the first people in Europe to exercise the right of representative and elective government. The signatures of many of the greatest lords and prelates of Castile are affixed to the charges.

The King is censured in plain terms for his unchristian opinions and conduct, and his blasphemous and infidel associates, to whose influence are attributed "the abomination and corruption of sins so heinous that they are not fit to be named, for they corrupt the very atmosphere, and are a foul blot upon human nature"; sins "so notorious that their not being punished makes one fear the ruin of the realms; and many other sins and injustices and tyrannies have increased in your reign, that did not exist in the past."

The King's Moorish guard and the renegade Christians, whom he has made rulers of Castile, have "raped married women and corrupted and violated virgins, and men and boys against nature; and good Christians who dared to complain were publicly whipped."

The noblemen declare that that King has allowed in his court open "gibes and blasphemies about holy places and the sacraments . . . especially the Sacrament of the body of our good and very mighty Lord. . . . This is a heavy burden on your conscience, by whose example countless souls have gone and will go to perdition." He has destroyed the prosperity of the Christian laboring classes by allowing Moors and Jews to exploit them. His profligacy has so debased the currency that prices have soared beyond all reason, and merchants cannot dispose of their goods at the fairs. His officials practise extortion and bribery on a huge scale, while hideous crimes go unpunished, and robber barons capture citizens and hold them for ransom. He has made a mockery of justice and government by his vicious appointments. He has corrupted the Church by casting good bishops out of their sees and replacing them by hypocrites and politicians.

Then comes a paragraph in which it is not difficult to see a trace of the subtle hand of the Marqués of Villena:

"The thing that fairly makes our hearts bleed* is to see Your Highness in the power of the Count of Ledesma."

And perhaps it was the plain-speaking Archbishop of Toledo, he who had denounced Don Beltran as a monster, who is responsible for the next bombshell:

"Doña Juana, the one called the Princess, is not your daughter."

Finally, the grave charge is made that Don Beltran "has used the King's authority to gain possession of the illustrious *señores Infantes* Don Alfonso and Doña Isabel; to the great injury of your royal dignity and the shame of the inhabitants of these kingdoms, for *they fear lest certain persons under the influence of the will of the said Count procure the death of the said Infantes,* so that the succession of these kingdoms may devolve upon the said Doña Juana."

In conclusion, the barons "beg and require" that no marriage shall be forced upon the Princess Isabel without the consent of the three estates of the realm, assembled in a Cortes, in accordance with the will of her father King Juan, "and as reason dictates."

The Grand Mastership of Santiago must be restored to Prince Alfonso.

Prince Alfonso must be recognized as heir to the throne in place of *La Beltraneja.*

When Enrique received those *representaciones* at Valladolid, he ran immediately to the Queen and the Count, and

* Literally, "weep drops of blood," *lloran gotas de sangre.*

enacted a scene, while Don Beltran swore, and Juana listened
in contemptuous silence. The King was lost, he was betrayed,
he would be killed, he must surrender. The next moment he
was for cutting off the heads of all the rebels. He thought of
fleeing to Portugal. He thought of giving battle. Why could
no one advise him? Where was Villena? Why had he ever let
him go away?

His paroxysm over, he listened to reason and became confident again. The Queen was certain that her child would be
a boy. His birth would rob the conspirators of the issue they
had raised over La Beltraneja.

It was not to be. Juana's son was born prematurely, dead,
and La Beltraneja was again the center of the conflict. Enrique, in a new panic assembled his council and asked for
advice.

In the opinion of some, the King still had the whip hand,
if only he acted firmly and promptly. Belief in the sacredness
of royal authority was stronger in Castile than in Aragon.
And if Villena was jealous of Beltran, who was more envied
than Villena? His enemies would be the King's friends. . . .
At length the aged Bishop of Cuenca, who had been a counsellor of King Juan II, declared that there were no two sides
to the question they were wasting time upon; a king who
hoped to preserve his royal authority could have no dealings
with rebels who defied him, except to offer them battle.

Enrique's flabby mouth curled into a sneer. "Those who
need not fight nor lay hands on their swords," he said, "are
always free with the lives of others."

A moment of eloquent silence. The King, it appeared, would
purchase peace at any price. There was nothing more to be
said. The old Bishop arose, his eyes aflame, his voice trembling with bridled anger.

"Henceforth," he cried, "you will be called the most unworthy King Spain has ever known; and you will repent of
it, Señor, when it is too late!"

Enrique sent an hysterical appeal to the Marqués of Villena. That dexterous gentleman, after quickly weighing the
pros and cons, informed his fellow conspirators that it would
be unwise, dishonorable, disloyal, not to say impious, to take
the field against the lawful king until all peaceful means had
been employed, and he volunteered, if they would delegate

him, to obtain from Enrique the best possible terms for all of them. With some reluctance, they agreed, knowing that if any one could manage the King, it was Villena. A series of conversations followed between the King and the Marqués. The upshot was an agreement known as the Concord of Medina del Campo, perhaps the most humiliating document ever signed by a monarch. For Enrique agreed to these stipulations:

Don Alfonso is recognized as Prince of the Asturias and lawful heir to the throne—virtually a confession of La Beltraneja's illegitimacy.

Don Beltran, Count of Ledesma, will resign the Grand Mastership of Santiago in favor of Alfonso, and will retire from the Court with certain of his henchmen.

Enrique will not increase certain taxes without the consent of the Cortes.

Enrique will hereafter confess his sins and receive Holy Communion at least once a year.

Isabel's brother had suddenly become a personage of the first importance in Castile. The question arose, who should be his guardian. With amazing short-sightedness, Enrique delivered him into the custody of the Marqués. The royal humiliation was complete.

It gradually dawned upon both the King and the barons that the only ones to profit by the whole transaction had been the Prince and the Marqués. The diminutive but explosive Don Fadrique, Admiral of Castile, was furious. The Marqués, he informed his associates, had made fools of them all.

"He of Villena," complained the Admiral bitterly, "always manages to maintain two kings in a circle of noblemen, partisans of the one or of the other; and he, placing one foot on the man on either side of him, sprinkles all of us indiscriminately." The laughter was loud, but there were contrapuntal shouts of rage against the Marqués.

Don Fadrique was not the man to expend all his energies on aphorisms. While Villena was finding a safe place for the keeping of Prince Alfonso, the Admiral came to a mysterious agreement with the Archbishop of Toledo. Taking French leave of their fellow conspirators before the sun was up, the two galloped as fast as horses would carry them to Madrid, where they requested an immediate audience with the King. Admitted to Enrique's presence, they humbly professed that they had seen the errors of their ways, and were so mortified at the thought of the treachery into which they had been inveigled that they had come to repudiate it and offer His Majesty their loyalty anew. Villena they denounced as an unscrupulous traitor who had betrayed the King and the whole country. With Alfonso in the Marqués's custody, there would henceforth be two kings in Castile, whenever it pleased Villena to raise the flag of revolt. The Archbishop and the Admiral felt it their duty to come to the King's assistance. They advised him to revoke the Concord of Medina del Campo, and to demand the restoration of Don Alfonso by that archtraitor Villena.

Enrique, alternately frightened and flattered, placed himself in the hands of the two late conspirators. To show his gratitude, he gave them the deeds to valuable properties they had long desired. As soon as they left to take possession of their new estates, he repudiated the Concord of Medina, and sent a sharp request to Villena to return the Infante Alfonso to court without delay.

The Marqués and his friends enjoyed a hearty laugh at the King's naïveté. But it was not until Enrique sent an appeal to the Archbishop to return to Madrid that he realized how completely he had been tricked. His messenger reported having met Carrillo riding fully armed to rejoin the rebels, and on parting at the cross-roads, the Archbishop shouted in his booming voice: "Tell your king that I have had enough of him and of his affairs. He shall see who is the true sovereign of Castile."

Enrique soon learned what that meant. Carrillo and the Admiral, reunited to Villena, had Alfonso proclaimed king at Valladolid. They were planning a larger assembly of the insurgent lords near Ávila, and they sent a secret courier inviting the Infanta Isabel, who was living in great suspense with Queen Juana. She pondered, and sent her regrets. The King was almost in despair. The Queen was ill. Don Beltran reluctantly resigned the Mastership of Santiago on condition that he receive, among other compensations, the title of Duke of Albuquerque, and retired to Cuellar. There was a tenseness everywhere. Something was about to happen.

Early in July, 1465, there appeared in Ávila a long procession of cavaliers with the Archbishop and the Marqués

at their head, on either side of the Prince Don Alfonso, all
on caparisoned horses and sheathed in armor from head to
foot. The little Prince sat as straight as possible and looked
neither to the right nor to the left. His visor was up, showing
a glint of his yellow hair to the people who stood on both sides
of the rocky narrow street, shouting "Long live the King!
Long live the King Alfonso!" The cavalcade passed through
one of the gates in the huge granite wall, near one of the
machicolated towers, and filed out into the plain, followed
by the populace.

Ávila is perched near the summit of a wild mountain gorge
in the heart of a bleak and arid terrain where almost everything is gray—gray shadows, gray earth, gray rocks, even the
sunlight has a grayish tinge, wherever it manages to penetrate. In the old river bed by the town are scattered piles of
enormous boulders of granite, polished by the floods of centuries. One goes down past them into a wide treeless waste
stretching out to the dark white-capped mountains of the
Guadarama; and the shadows on this plain lie in great waves
of grayness, that seem to heave sometimes like the surge of
an infinite sea. Standing on the crest near the city walls, one
might hesitate to go down into that shadow, for it is like
going into some limbo and leaving the sunlight and fair
fortune and inviting a dreadful and mysterious doom. A hush
falls on the troops as they ride; there is hardly a sound but
the beating of hoofs and the creaking of saddle leather, on
this fifth day of July.

In the middle of the *vega* a theater has been rudely constructed about a high platform on which men are moving
about, and even from a distance one can see what appears to be
a royal personage on a throne near the edge, for the sun
sparkles on his crown and sceptre and a great sword of justice like that of the kings of Castile. A strange position, his,
for so exalted a personage. He slumps down in his chair like
a drunkard. One gets another glimpse of him: he is sitting
stiff and straight like a scarecrow. When Alfonso and his
friends reach the amphitheater, they see that it actually is a
scarecrow, or something very like one. It is an effigy of King
Enrique IV, royally clad in a mantle lined with miniver over
a black mourning robe. His jeweled collar, the gold chain on
his neck, the pearls, rubies and emeralds at his girdle, the

slovenly Moorish buskins—nothing has been left out of the picture. The royal banner of Castile floats over his head; and around the platform, as if guarding the mock king, stand knights, men-at-arms, cross-bowmen and lancers. A huge crowd is gathering in from all sides as Alfonso, the Archbishop and the Marqués dismount and ascend the platform. All the crafts, all the guilds, are represented there; one sees the brown cowls of Franciscans and the black and white of Dominicans; Moorish sheiks, in turbans; whiskered Jews in their gaberdines, students from Salamanca University, cavaliers wearing the insignia of the three military orders, peasants from Aragon with hempen sandles, Castilian lords in long woolen mantles. The Prince looks down on the crowd. Trumpets bray, kettledrums rumble.

An altar has been sent up on one side of the platform. The Archbishop of Toledo has taken off his armor and put on his vestments, red and white, with a glimmer of gold. A bell rings. The Archbishop makes the sign of the cross. He has begun to say Mass. The crowd kneels . . . the Host and the Chalice gleam as they are held up in the sunlight. . . . *"Domine, non sum dignus,"* says the Archbishop, striking his breast . . . the Last Gospel . . . the Mass is over. A great murmuring is liberated from the crowd. They press closer to the platform and the men-at-arms. They know there is to be something more. They are hardly prepared for what happens.

The Archbishop, his ruddy face very grave, advances to the effigy of Enrique, deliberately takes off the crown, and says,

"Thus lose the royal dignity which you have guarded so ill."

The Count of Benavente, seizing the sceptre:

"Thus you lose the government of the realms, as you deserve."

Diego Lopez de Zuniga now cries, "Lose also the throne and the reverence due to kings!" and he kicks the stuffed image off the seat into the dust of the *vega*.

Trumpets and kettledrums. A shout of triumph from the partisans of Alfonso. Shrieks and groans of horror from many parts of the crowd; even some loud sobbing; for in Castile a king, whatever he may be as a man, represents the sovereignty of the people, which comes from God. The rebels, however, proceed with their program. Alfonso is led to the empty throne, seated, the crown placed on the blond head . . . shouts . . . trumpets and kettledrums . . . pandemonium.

The news of the outrage offered him at Ávila plunged Enrique into a profound gloom. It seemed to him, and to others, like the beginning of his last chapter. "Naked came I out of my mother's womb," he quoted, "and naked shall I return thither." He shut himself up, strummed his lute, sang some sad songs. Why had he ever offended the Marqués of Villena?

But the rebels at Ávila had done their work too thoroughly. They had made something of a martyr of Enrique, they had certainly wounded the Castilian reverence for the idea of kingship, while the Moors and Jews and the large class of office-seekers who had obtained favors from him looked on with indignation. The reaction in his favor gained impetus from the support of Don Pedro Gonzalez de Mendoza, Bishop of Calahorra, a scholar and a statesman whose powerful house was allied by blood ties to most of the great families of the north. Little as Mendoza respected the character of the King, he was under no illusions as to the unselfishness of Villena or the cool judgment of Carrillo. Consequently, when those rebels urged him to join the faction of Prince Alfonso and good government, he replied, "It is well-known, gentlemen, that every kingdom is like a body, of which we have the King for a head. If the head is sick, it seems more sensible to endure the pains rather than cut it off. . . . Holy Scripture forbids rebellion and commands obedience. . . . We ought to preserve the welfare of the greatest number, even if some are unhappy, rather than plunge all into the evils of civil war and anarchy. . . . Prince Alfonso, being only eleven years old, cannot reign for some years yet. Admitting that Don Enrique is weak and vicious, Castile will be no better off under a boy"—and one imagines Mendoza adding under his breath, "controlled by men like Pacheco."

The Bishop's letter raised some disturbing questions in the mind of the Marqués. Suppose Enrique should win? What would become of the rebels and their estates, their lives? It was no part of Villena's philosophy to be on the losing side of anything. He hastened, therefore, to Enrique with a little pro-

gram which he flattered himself would be to the advantage of
both:

Villena to give Enrique money, urgently needed, and 3,000 lances
equivalent to some 10,000 men, who were ravaging the estates of the
King's friends in Andalusia. Villena to hand over Prince Alfonso
to the King. All the Pachecos, Villena's influential relatives, presumably to return to their allegiance, and leave Carrillo and the
Admiral isolated and at the King's mercy.

The King, on his part, to banish Don Beltran, Duke of Albuquerque,
and with him Mendoza, bishop of Calahorra. *The King to give the
Infanta Isabel in marriage to Villena's brother, Don Pedro Giron,
Master of Calatrava.*

Enrique listened without resentment to the proposal of a
Marrano, a descendant of the Jew Ruy Cápon, to ally himself
with Castilian royalty. Seeing in it only the solution of his
difficulties, he readily agreed to sacrifice his half-sister and
his friends. He communicated his intention to the Queen, and
the Queen informed Isabel.

The Infanta could hardly believe her senses. It was no new
thing for her to be pledged to some complete stranger—she
had been promised at various times to Fernando of Aragon,
to Carlos of Viana, to Alfonso V of Portugal; and there
was much talk at one time of her marrying a brother of
Edward IV of England, probably that Earl of Gloucester
who became notorious as Richard III. But all had royal blood,
all had qualities she could respect. Don Pedro Giron had
neither. He was reputed to be a scoundrel of many vices. And
if all that men said against him were false, the fact remained
that it was he who made certain insulting proposals to Isabel's
mother. Marry that man? Never!

She wept in the arms of her friend Beatriz de Bobadilla.
What was the matter? The King . . . the King's orders . . .
marriage. But marry whom? Don Pedro Giron . . . Mother
of God! . . . When Beatriz recovered her speech she ran out
of the room, and returned presently holding a small silver
dagger. "You will never marry that monster," she cried, "for
I swear before God that if he comes to take you, I will plunge
this in his heart."

Isabel mournfully shook her head. It was typical of her
to reject at once, on instinct, any suggestion of violence. God
alone had power over life and death, except when He delegated it to kings. To God, then, she must turn for succor. She

locked herself in her room. She fasted for three days; and during the next three days and nights she knelt almost continually before a Crucifix, passionately repeating over and over again, with tears,

"Dear God, compassionate Savior, do not let me be given to this man! Either let him die, or let me die!"

All this was duly reported to the King, who merely smiled. . . . Even the Queen, perhaps with some memory of her own unhappy struggle tugging at the mantle of cynicism that she had draped over her finer feelings, and a pang of sympathy for the hollow eyes and pale cheeks that told of the girl's anguish, predicted that Isabel would never consent. But Enrique replied that he would bring the little fool to her senses by persuasion if possible, otherwise, by force. Perhaps she needed to be taught who was king of Castile! He had already sent word to Don Pedro Giron to come at once to Madrid to be married, and that was all there was to that. The Alcázar, the whole city was in a bustle of preparation. Decorations were made. Gowns were ordered for the Queen and her ladies and Isabel. The Court buzzed with the new gossip and enjoyed it immensely.

A courier returned from Don Pedro Giron, who was at his castle at Almagro, with word that the King's instructions pleased him very well, and that he would go to Madrid with all possible haste. With his black mustache newly waxed and pointed, with kingly raiment on his back and a kingly retinue assembled under the banner of Calatrava, the rake of forty-three set forth to meet his bride of fifteen.

Isabel continued her prayers. Beatriz de Bobadilla, fingering her dagger, did nothing but repeat, over and over,

"God will never permit it, and neither will I."[2]

IV

O N THE first evening after his departure from Almagro
with a gaudy retinue and much music and flying pennons and the jests and laughter that ought to follow
a bridegroom, Don Pedro Giron came to Villarubia, a small
place near Villareal, and there, impatient though he was, the
darkness compelled him to stop.

"A few more days," he said, to console himself, "and I
will sleep with a Princess."

But no man knows with certainty where he will sleep in a
few days. During that very night the Master of Calatrava
became violently ill with quinsy. Doctors were summoned, the
best Jewish physicians that could be found. But they could do
nothing against the invisible hand that seemed to be slowly
choking Don Pedro. A frenzy seized him when he realized
the hopelessness of his condition. False *Converso* that he was,
he cast aside all pretence of being a Catholic, and refused to
receive the sacraments or say any Christian prayers.

On the third day after his departure he died, blaspheming
God for His cruelty in refusing to add only forty more days
to his forty-three years, that he might enjoy his royal bride.[1]
It was with silent worms that Don Pedro made his bed; and
all his treasures and titles passed into the hands of his three
bastard sons.[2]

Isabel received the news of his death with tears of joy and
gratitude, for she considered it a direct answer to her prayers,
and hastened to the chapel to fall on her knees and offer thanks.
That night she slept very soundly after her long vigil.

It was otherwise with King Enrique and the Marqués of
Villena. The death of Pedro, as Castillo recorded, was "very

grievous" to them, for with him fell all their beautiful house
of cards. And the rebels, impatient for action after a long
truce, were mobilizing again. Villena felt that he had his own
future to consider, and as usual, he considered it. The choice
between the King and the rebels was not difficult. The Marqués
mounted his horse and rejoined the Archbishop and the
Admiral.

There was nothing for Enrique to do but abdicate or prepare for battle. His plight, after all, was not hopeless. He
could count on Mendoza, the influential bishop of Calahorra;
and the royal forces numbered some 70,000 infantry and
14,000 cavalry. The King at last made up his mind to fight.

War could hardly be worse than the chaotic peace of the
last few months. Every man's hand seemed to be against his
neighbor's; every little baron preyed on the farms and nearby
towns as if he were in an enemy's country; murders, robberies, burnings and rapes were daily commonplaces; government itself appeared like a form of persecution of the weak
and protection for the avarice and brutality of the strong,
and while pestilence and famine struck down the poor on every
side, old feuds rekindled and brawls flamed into petty wars.
A typical example: the Marqués of Astorga sent troops to
pillage the lands of the Count of Benavente. The Count's people, 350 men, women and children, took refuge in a church
at Gordoncillo. The soldiers set fire to the church, and all
within it perished.

Far more serious in its immediate consequences and its
repercussions in later Spanish history was the war that began
that summer between the *Conversos* and the Old Christians
of Toledo. The canons of the Cathedral there—some of them
were *Conversos*—controlled the revenues of the neighboring
town of Maqueda, including a tax on bread.[3] This privilege, so
hateful to the poor, they sold at auction to certain Jews. A
Christian of influence named Alvar Gomez ordered an *alcalde*
to beat the Jews and drive them out of the city. This was done.
The canons had the *alcalde* arrested, but while they were
deliberating as to his punishment and the settlement of the
whole dispute, Fernando de la Torre, a wealthy leader of the
Conversos, decided to take the law into his own hands. A rash
and violent man, he announced that the *Conversos* had secretly
assembled 4000 well-armed fighting men, six times as many

as the Old Christians could muster; and on July 21 he led his forces to attack the Cathedral. The crypto-Jews burst through the great doors of the Church, crying, "Kill them! Kill them! This is no church, but only a congregation of evil and vile men!"[4] The Christians in the church drew swords and defended themselves. Others ran to their aid, and a bloody battle was fought before the high altar.

Meanwhile strong reinforcements of Christians came galloping from Alofria and launched a counter attack on the luxurious section where most of the *Conversos* lived. They burned down the houses on eight of the principal streets. They captured Fernando de la Torre and his brother and hanged them; then they massacred the *Conversos* indiscriminately.

A few days later Isabel's brother arrived at Toledo with Villena and the Archbishop. A delegation of Old Christians waited on the fourteen-year-old prince and offered him their support against Enrique if he would approve of the massacre and of further measures to be taken against the now terrified and disarmed *Conversos*.

"God forbid that I should countenance such injustice!" said the young Prince without hesitation.

When the Marqués of Villena reminded him that in that case the Old Christians of Toledo would probably declare for the King, Alfonso replied,

"Much as I love power, I am not willing to purchase it at such a price."[5]

On another occasion Alfonso declared that the nobles ought to be shorn of their power to defy kings and tyrannize over the people. "But I suppose I must endure this patiently until I am a little older," the boy added, significantly. The Marqués was beginning to find this obstinate Prince and his lofty but purely academic sentiments a little tiresome.

With such support as they could get in Toledo, the rebels gathered a force approximately as large as the King's. The rival armies now came face to face near Olmedo, on that very field where Enrique as a boy had appeared in arms among the enemies of his father. From Alfonso's camp the stalwart Archbishop of Toledo sent his message of defiance to the King; and he took pains to let Don Beltran know that his time had come, since forty cavaliers had sworn to accomplish his death on the morrow. Beltran's retort was to send back by

Carrillo's messenger a detailed description of the armor he intended to wear in the battle.

Early the next day, Thursday, August 20, 1467, the battle began with a charge of cavalry and the shattering of lances; then they dismounted and fought with swords all the rest of the day; the footmen, too, were engaged, and there was great carnage. On the King's side, a magnificent streak of silver and steel and gold bounding here and there over the piles of dead showed where Beltran was defending himself against his forty sworn executioners. Many fell before that invincible arm, for whatever else the King's favorite may have been, he was no coward. His great strength and skill preserved him that day for service in a nobler cause.

In the very thick of the *mêlée* appeared Alfonso, "the King of Ávila" sword in hand, in full armor, laying about him so sturdily that several men fell under his blows. By his side, on a great chestnut steed, rode the fiery Archbishop Carrillo, wearing over his gleaming Toledo cuirass, a scarlet cloak emblazoned with a white cross. Now he hewed a path for Alfonso through the enemy host, and now he rescued the Infante from the onslaught of too many cavaliers. Early in the day Carrillo's arm was wounded, and the blood trickled down his gauntlet; yet when the rebels finally gave way, he, with Alfonso, was the last to leave the field, and his hoarse voice, like an angered bull's, could be heard egging on his tired cavalry to one more attempt, until darkness covered all.

Enrique watched the struggle from a hillside. At the first sign of a retreat among his troops, he fled in panic, thinking the battle lost; and when the tide turned and the rebels finally yielded ground to Don Beltran and his companions, the King was nowhere to be found. Pulgar, the chronicler, discovered him next day hiding in a village several miles away.

Both sides claimed the victory. Enrique's army had remained in possession of the field. The rebels had taken the greater number of prisoners and of pennons, including the royal standard.

The two armies, tired of battle, drew apart. The conspirators were having disagreements, for Carrillo and the Admiral had no confidence in Villena. On the other side, Enrique remained with a small guard at the town of Olmedo, where the Queen and La Beltraneja joined him. He was a pathetic

figure, bewildered, penitent, and not without noble sentiments.
Mariana represents him as falling down before a crucifix and
crying, "Thine aid I implore, my Lord, Christ the son of
God, by whom Kings reign; to Thee I commend my person
and dignity. I beg that this punishment, which is less than I
deserve, may be for the good of my soul. Lord, give me
patience to endure it, and permit not the people to suffer for
my sins!"[6]

News of the King's misery was presently dispatched to
Carrillo, who had gone to Ávila to recuperate from his wound.
The old politician at once engaged some of the henchmen of
Pedro Árias to go to Olmedo and attempt to seize the King.
One evening they managed to get into the royal residence with-
out being detected. Enrique fled half naked through the fields.
Knocking at the door of a cottage, he borrowed some clothes
from a villager, and thus disguised, mounted a mule that an-
other countryman lent him, and did not stop to look behind
till he reached Madrid.

The Queen and Isabel, for greater safety, went with La
Beltraneja to Segovia. Within its thick battlements they seemed
safe enough for the present. The rebels, however, sent a large
force of cavalry to capture them. The Queen fled with her
baby and a few personal effects.

Isabel had to decide quickly whether she would accompany
the Queen or wait and surrender to the insurgents. She was
not unwilling to get out of Juana's hands. Besides, her brother
Alfonso was in the approaching army. She waited for him,
joyfully.

Brother and sister had much to say to each other, after
months of uncertainty and fears for each other's safety. On
Alfonso's birthday, they rode to see the fair at Medina del
Campo, where they had gone as children with Beatriz de
Bobadilla from Arévalo. They must have remembered that
other birthday of his when he was solemnly entertained by
one of the little moralistic dialogues of Juan de Encina, and
Isabel took the part of a Muse with a long chiffon robe and a
flower in her hair. They must have remembered their mother,
sitting in a melancholy stupor at Arévalo. The future seemed
like a wilderness of struggles and perils. Isabel, if she escaped
the poison of powerful foes, might find some happiness or
lifelong misery in a political marriage. Alfonso, if *he* escaped

the cup of treachery, might expect a soldier's death, or exile —or an unstable throne, set up in the midst of chaos.

When Alfonso rejoined the Archbishop at Ávila, Isabel remained at Segovia. There, in obedience to her mother, she made it her first concern to find a good confessor and to converse with priests and nuns known to be holy and intelligent. It may have been then that she first met Fray Tomás of Torquemada, prior of the Dominican convent at Segovia since 1452. He was the nephew of a cardinal; some said the descendant of converted Jews.[7] There is no evidence that he was her confessor at this period. The coincidence of their being in the city at the same time has been made the slender foundation of a later legend of fantastic proportions, in which Torquemada is made to solicit from the young Princess a promise that when she becomes Queen she will establish the Inquisition. Not only is proof lacking, but the whole story is highly improbable, since Isabel at that time had no expectation of being Queen.[8]

It is not improbable, however, that she talked with the prior of Santa Cruz, and may even have discussed the evils of the times with him, as she did with many other intelligent men. It would have been the usual thing, and consistent with her character, to ask him to pray for King Enrique. Most likely, too, she would have asked him to pray for her, and for her brother.

Alfonso, surely, had need of prayers.

Early in July, 1468, there galloped into Segovia a courier from the village of Cardeñosa, about six miles from Ávila. He said that the King of Ávila had ridden to Plasencia with the Marqués of Villena, the Conde de Benavente and others, to meet a group of nobles whose support the rebels were anxious to gain. The Archbishop of Toledo was not present, having gone elsewhere on a similar errand. Alfonso was, therefore, completely in Villena's hands. After the conferences they rode back by way of Cardeñosa, and stopped there for the night. Alfonso became suddenly ill. His condition was disturbing. He had expressed a wish to see his sister.

Isabel was on horseback in a trice, and with a small escort at her heels galloped over the winding dusty ways to Ávila, and thence to Cardeñosa. As she dismounted, the Archbishop of Toledo, who had lately arrived, came to meet her. She had

only to look at the stern set of his face to know the truth:
Alfonso was dead. The Archbishop had got there in time to
administer the sacraments; but the lad's illness had been acute,
and no medicine could save him. The girl went into the little
room where her brother lay, and fell on her knees beside the
corpse. When she came out she was pale and weeping; but it
was not her way to speak much when deeply moved. Carrillo
and Alfonso's attendants told her what had happened. On the
day before, July 4, the Prince had eaten trout, of which he
was particularly fond. Either the fish had been poisoned by
some one acting in the interest of Enrique and Juana and La
Beltraneja, or Alfonso had been seized with a peculiarly violent attack of the summer fever, which had carried off many
in Castile that summer; or it was acute ptomaine poisoning.
A mystery it has remained to this day.

After the funeral, Isabel rode back in stoical silence to
Ávila. What should she do, what must become of her now?
To return to the King and Queen was out of the question.
Villena she hoped never to see again—the very thought of
him made a great burning of dread and indignation pass over
her body from head to foot. For the present she decided to
remain at the Cistercian convent of Saint Ann at Ávila. The
nuns received her with kindness, and she spent several days
there alone with her sorrow, in meditation and prayer.

Early one morning there was a clatter of horses' hoofs in the
crooked streets, and the townspeople peeped out of their gray,
flat-roofed houses to see the red mantle and white cross of the
Archbishop of Toledo, passing pell-mell at the head of a troop
of cavaliers. At the Convent of Saint Ann, Carrillo leaped off
his horse, and knocked at the gate with the hilt of his sword.
The Archbishop of Toledo, begging audience of the Princess
Lady Isabel!

In silence and sad dignity the Infanta received him and
several other *grandes*. She wore a severely simple robe of
white wool, very long. One after another they knelt before her
and kissed her hand. She waited for them to speak. Carrillo
was the spokesman. All good men, he said, regretted the death
of her brother, Don Alfonso; his death was a national calamity.
The Princess Isabel was now the hope of Castile. They had
come to offer her their fealty with the ancient crown of the
Kings of Castile and Leon.

Isabel listened calmly to the sonorous voice. When the gray-haired Archbishop had finished, she replied quietly but very positively that her brother, King Enrique, was the lawful king of Castile, having received the sceptre from her father, King Juan II; and as kings reigned by the permission of God and were responsible to him for the authority they held, no lawful power in Castile could take it from him without his consent, so long as he lived. She did not condemn her brother Don Alfonso for what he had done, for no doubt he had acted according to his conscience; but as for her, she would never seek power by unconstitutional means, lest doing so she lose the grace and blessing of God, and all her efforts come to nothing. So long as her brother Don Enrique lived, he might be sure of her obedience and loyalty. "For if I should gain the throne by disobedience to him, how could I blame any one who might raise his hand in disobedience against me?"

Carrillo pleaded with her passionately, almost in tears. Her refusal would mean ruin to the friends of her brother, for without a leader their cause would fall to pieces, and their estates, their very lives, would be exposed to the vengeance of Enrique and his Queen. And could anyone doubt that the enemy would find a means of getting rid of Isabel herself, so formidable a rival to the child of Don Beltran? Let her reconsider her unwise decision, for the very fate of Castile hung upon her words, and all the murders and burnings and unmentionable crimes that would continue would be her responsibility. The Princess shook her head. No.

Carrillo bowed and withdrew, very red in the face. Isabel returned to her prayers and her needlework.

The rebels had no choice now but to make peace. Villena in particular, who had reason to fear Carrillo's influence with the Princess, at once declared that she had been quite right in refusing the crown. Carrillo, with bitter reluctance, had to join the others in suing for terms.

Enrique needed money so badly that he was willing to make almost any concessions. He met the barons near Ávila, at the Toros de Guisando, four great stone bulls sculptured more than a thousand years before, and bearing an inscription showing that Julius Caesar had won a victory there. Isabel insisted upon going to the meeting with Carrillo, in spite of his fears

for her safety and his prediction that the agreement would
be a farce.

The event appeared to justify her confidence. The universal
hunger for peace brought about a compromise distinctly favorable to her. Villena, seeing the impossibility of uniting the
country under any other heiress so long as Isabel lived, counseled the King to acknowledge her *for the present*. The King,
again in the hands of his old favorite, coolly sacrificed Queen
Juana and Don Beltran. How low their credit had fallen is
apparent in the stipulations to which Enrique signed his name:

(1) He granted a general amnesty to all the insurgents.

(2) He agreed to ask the Pope to annul his marriage to Queen
Juana and to send her back to Portugal within four months.

(3) He acknowledged Isabel as Princess of the Asturias and heiress
to the throne of Castile and Leon.

(4) He agreed to convoke a Cortes within forty days, to give
legal sanction to Isabel's title, and to discuss necessary reforms in
government.

(5) He promised never to compel Isabel to marry against her
wishes, on condition that she would not marry without his consent.

(6) He agreed to give Isabel the cities of Ávila, Búete, Molina,
Medina del Campo, Olmedo, Escalona and Ubeda, for her proper
maintenance as heiress.

Thus once more, on that Monday, September 19, 1468,
Enrique insulted his wife and virtually admitted the illegitimacy of La Beltraneja. Having signed the agreement, he
tenderly embraced Isabel, saluting her as heiress of the realms.
All the nobles present advanced to kiss her hand, and to swear
allegiance to her between the hands of the Papal Legate,
Antonio de Veneriz, Bishop of Leon, who absolved them
from their previous oath under coercion to La Beltraneja.

So far so good. The next step was to assemble the Cortes
at Ocaña, and this Enrique proceeded to do. Naturally there
were long and involved debates over the woes of the land and
the means that ought to be used to remedy them. Enrique,
having promised to take all the proposals under advisement,
dissolved the Cortes. The delegates had taken the oath of
allegiance to Isabel, but had not formally ratified the treaty
of Toros de Guisando.

The Archbishop of Toledo now had the satisfaction of saying "I told you so," to the Infanta. In that sly little smile of
the Marqués of Villena he imagined he saw something more

than pleasure at being restored to royal intimacy. He had no doubt that the Marqués had put the King up to signing the Treaty of Toros de Guisando with the deliberate intent of scrapping it afterward, and of calling together the Cortes at Ocaña to gain more time. But there was something else in the wind.

Carrillo was right in suspecting that the Marqués was determined to get Isabel out of the country as soon as possible.

In fact, Villena had already convinced the King that the simplest method, and one that would have the additional merit of preventing her union with Fernando of Aragon, would be to marry her at once to Alfonso V. He assured Enrique that the mere threat of compulsion would bring her to her senses.

If Enrique had any final scruples against forcing Isabel's consent, they were silenced by the arrival at Ocaña of a magnificent embassy from Portugal, under the Archbishop of Lisbon, who came with Alfonso's instructions not to return without the plighted troth of the Princess. Villena had egged on the chivalrous Alfonso to the final attempt; and he had well timed his conversations with the King. Fortune helped him further by sending to Ocaña at that time an Aragonese envoy with a new request for the hand of the Infanta for Prince Fernando.

But while the King and his favorite were disposing of her future, Isabel was giving some serious thought to the matter herself. She had three suitors: Alfonso V, Fernando of Aragon, and the Duke of Guyenne, brother and heir apparent of Louis XI. The first she had met and appraised. Of the others she had no accurate information. She had decided to find out what manner of men they were before she committed her happiness to any of them. Very secretly, therefore, she had sent her chaplain, Alonso de Coca, to Paris and Saragossa to observe the two suitors at close range. To be sure, a Princess must consider the good of all rather than her own preference; but if one could find a way to make one's private happiness coincide with the general weal, so much the better. For some while this had been the burden of her daily prayers; and now came Alonso de Coca back from his long journey at an opportune moment with the news she sought. The French Duke, said he, was a "feeble, effeminate prince, with limbs so emaciated as to be almost deformed, and eyes so weak and watery that he was unfit for all knightly pursuits." Ah! and what of Don Fernando? Oh, there was a proper man, "a very proper man, comely in face and symmetrical in figure, with a spirit that is equal to anything he might desire to do."[9]

Between two such princes, it was not very difficult for a vigorous attractive girl of sixteen to make her choice. And now by unique good fortune it became evident that the man more fit for knightly exercises was also the candidate to whom Castilian policy ought to point. Enrique and Villena had no principles; but Carrillo argued powerfully in favor of Fernando, and his argument showed that he had the vision of a statesman.

Think of the advantage, said he, of joining the two largest and most populous sections of the Spanish peninsula into one nation with common blood, speech, customs and traditions! Such a nation under able leadership could soon sweep the Moorish power into the Mediterranean and back to Africa. It would also be able to resist the encroachments of France from the North, and Portugal from the West. With Castile's army and Aragon's navy and merchant marine, it could easily become the greatest nation in Europe. On the other hand, if Isabel went to Portugal, she would become a foreigner and no doubt would be excluded from the Castilian succession by the astute Villena; while her children, if she had any, could hardly hope to inherit the crown of Portugal, since Alfonso V had a male heir, Dom João, by his first marriage. As for the Duke of Guyenne, he would probably never become king, for Louis at last had an infant son; and even if he did, Castile would be only an appendage of France. Thus the political wisdom of the Archbishop. From certain other nobles to whom she had written asking for advice, Isabel received similar counsel.

Nevertheless she obeyed Enrique's request that she receive the Archbishop of Lisbon and his embassy. Having listened with grave courtesy to their speeches, she replied that she thanked them for their good will, and would carefully consider all that they had said. This did not please the Archbishop, nor Enrique when he heard it. The King now notified Isabel that he desired her consent to the Portuguese marriage without further delay; otherwise she would be imprisoned at the

Prince Alfonso, Isabel's Brother
(*From the Effigy on his Tomb*)

Alcázar at Madrid, where he would find a means of teaching her the obedience due to kings.

Carrillo had left town, but the Infanta got word to him of the King's ultimatum through her *maestresala*, Gutierre de Cárdenas. The Archbishop advised her to temporize with the Portuguese, consent without delay to the Aragonese proposal, and fear nothing; for in any emergency he himself would bring an army to her rescue. Fernando, he said, was "a boy and man of good discretion," whom most of the great Castilian lords, his blood relations, would gladly see king of their country. Carrillo himself, said Cárdenas, was in hiding for the present, having been warned by some one at court, perhaps his kinsman Villena, that Enrique planned to have him seized and put to death for his open advocacy of the marriage with Fernando. Cárdenas and the Admiral, who was Fernando's maternal grandfather, discussed the whole problem with Isabel at great length. "Since the modesty customary to damsels prevented them from deciding concerning their own marriages," she had certain scruples. Cárdenas managed to overcome them by arguing that as her father was dead, and her mother incapacitated by illness, she must be guided by public opinion. The three estates, nobles, clergy and common people, wished her to marry Fernando, he said. After a moment of reflection the girl replied,

"God, the witness of hearts, knows that before my own affection I look first to the welfare of these kingdoms. And since the votes of the nobles appear to point in this direction, and it seems pleasing to God, I will conform to His will and submit to the opinion of all."[10]

It was decided in her little informal cabinet, that Gutierre de Cárdenas and Alonso de Palencia should go at once to Aragon with her consent. They left at night, muffled in long cloaks, a little troop armed to the teeth, and rode by cow paths and lonely trails, avoiding larger places, toward the border.

In the interim, Isabel followed the advice of the Admiral and the Archbishop in dealing with the embassy from Portugal. She agreed with their view that Enrique's threat to coerce her, in violation of the treaty of Toros de Guisando, absolved her from her promise not to marry without his consent, and considered herself justified under the circumstances in dissimulating. She told the Archbishop of Lisbon, therefore, that one very important obstacle to her marriage with Alfonso V, was their blood relationship within the degrees forbidden by Holy Mother Church. If the Pope saw fit to grant a dispensation, of course that would put a different complexion on the whole affair.

There was nothing for them to do but send to Rome for a dispensation, which was granted in due course by Pope Paul II. But Enrique did not wait for the return of his messenger to Rome, for Villena had got wind somehow of the departure of Cárdenas and Palencia, and had rightly conjectured their destination; whereat the King was furious, and ordered Isabel's arrest.

News of the royal decision spread rapidly from the palace to every quarter of the town. There was much gossiping and putting of heads together and running to and fro, all very mysterious, as when something extraordinary is bruited in an ant hill.

When Isabel arose next morning, rather surprised to find herself still at liberty, she saw through her window various groups of citizens in many kinds of costumes, patrolling the road in front of her apartment, and picketing the palace gates. Pikes, javelins, long spears, axes, swords, daggers, maces— they carried all manner of weapons. What were they doing there? She learned with joy that the people of Ocaña had seized arms and rebelled in defense of her person and her right to wed whom she pleased. Even the children joined in the popular demonstration. All that day she heard them singing in the street,

> *Flores de Aragon*
> *dentro in Castilla son!*
> *Pendon de Aragon!*
> *Pendon de Aragon!*

Boys and girls were waving the pennants of Aragon and of Castile. Scurrilous gibes at Enrique and the Queen and La Beltraneja had been nailed on the walls and on the palace doors. Men and boys went about singing ballads contrasting the gray hairs of that old rooster Alfonso V with the handsome head of Fernando, who seemed to have grown almost overnight into the hero of a popular legend. Ribald songs about the King and the Marqués were sung under the very windows of the royal family.

Watching the demonstrations, Isabel felt perhaps for the first time the power latent in the mob. Cárdenas, she saw, had been right in what he had said about the people; and she had no doubt at all that God had ratified her judgment through the mouths of the humble. Autocrat though she was by birth and instinct, it was her good fortune now and henceforth in all the great crises of her public life to find her own volition supported and enlarged by the popular voice. Like Caesar, like Napoleon, she had an egotism that was intuitively democratic.

Bernaldez, writing of this occasion in the ripeness of his age, considers the singing of the children a happy omen for better days in Castile. "*Domine, ex ore infantium et lactantium perfecisti laudem,*" he quotes, and adds that "in that time of pride, heresy, blasphemy, avarice, rapine, wars and feuds and factions, thieves and foot-pads, gamesters, pimps, murderers, public tables for rent where the names of Our Lord and Our Lady were blasphemed, renegades, slaughterings and all manner of wickedness, Our Lord put words of joy into the mouths of children: *Flores de Aragon . . . Beati oculi qui vident quod vos videtis.*" Bernaldez reflects the popular sentiment concerning the young princess. In the eyes of burghers and farmers, her chaste piety, well advertised both by praise and by ridicule, seemed almost angelic against the foul background of the Court, and Isabel herself like some white flower sturdily growing out of a mephitic heap of garbage. If anyone could restore peace, it was she.

Naturally the King and the Marqués did not share the enthusiasm of their humbler subjects. But there was nothing to do for the present but countermand the order for Isabel's arrest. Moreover, a new rebellion had flared up in the South and was making such headway that the Marqués considered it imperative for Enrique and him to go there at once with all the troops available. The affair of the Princess could wait until they returned.

They left Isabel safe, but hardly of tranquil mind. Where was Carrillo? Why had he not hastened to her assistance? In the midst of her anxieties came a laconic message from him urging her to flee from Ocaña without delay, and to hide for the present in her own town of Madrigal.

Isabel left Ocaña one night with a few friends, and rode to the town of her birth.

She had hardly got there when a disturbing message came from Cárdenas and Palencia. Having left Valladolid in the middle of the night, to thread their way through unfrequented country roads, they had reached Burgos de Osma. There a few cautious inquiries convinced them that the Bishop of Burgos, who happened to be a nephew of Villena, was hand-in-glove with the King's party; further, that sentiment along the Aragonese border was hostile to Isabel and her plan to marry Fernando. The Count of Medina Celi and most of the powerful Mendozas had sworn to seize or slay the prince if he attempted to pass through their fiefs on his way to meet his bride. All this Cárdenas sent to the Princess by a courier who trailed her from Ocaña to Madrigal; and he added a strong recommendation that she ask Carrillo to hurry 300 lances to Burgos de Osma, to open a way for the Prince if the latter decided to come.

Having sent back this message, Cárdenas and Palencia spurred on to Saragossa, arriving September 25, 1469. They could hardly have picked a less opportune moment. Fernando had been fighting desperately all summer. His Homeric father was at Urgel, encircled by his foes and threatened by a mutiny of his unpaid troops. The Catalans had rebelled again, this time in the interest of John of Lorraine. Louis XI had allowed that pretender to pass with troops through the very Roussillon that he had received as security from Aragon.

The situation could hardly have been worse when Juan of Aragon became blind from a double cataract. His Amazonian wife, though ill with cancer, placed herself at the head of one Aragonese army to besiege Rosas, while Prince Fernando raised another and hastened to a junction with her near Gerona. There the Prince narrowly escaped capture and death; but he compelled John of Lorraine to raise the siege of Gerona and withdraw for the present. Then the Queen died, exhausted by her strenuous labors, leaving her husband blind, helpless, penniless, with no one to depend upon but a fifteen-year-old son.

In September, when Cárdenas and Palencia arrived in Aragon, a Jewish physician and astrologer had just restored the sight of one of the King's eyes by couching. Juan urged the Jew to heal the other eye. The doctor pleaded that the planets

were unfavorable. Juan threatened him with death, but the
Jew refused to operate until October, when he couched the
other eye with complete success. Juan, restored to sight at 80,
put on his armor, took the field at the head of his troops,
besieged Barcelona, and entered it in triumph. Later in December, the sudden death of his enemy, John of Lorraine,
relieved him of much military pressure.

But when Isabel's envoys arrived in September, his affairs
looked desperate. The marriage of his son to Isabel was a
hope close to his heart, for the union of Aragon and Castile
seemed to him the only means of keeping his foe Louis XI
out of the Pyrenees. To send Fernando to Castile at present,
however, seemed nothing but folly. There was the situation at
home. . . . There was the watch kept by the Bishop of Burgos
and Medina Celi and the Mendozas on the border. . . . There
was the lack of money. Juan of Aragon, however, was not
the man to give up while there was breath in his lungs. Fernando signed the marriage agreement. He bade Cárdenas tell
Isabel he would join her at the first possible moment. Meanwhile, to prove his sincerity and his love, he sent her as a
dowry a necklace of pearls and balas rubies, valued at 40,000
gold florins, that had belonged to his mother, and 8,000 florins
in gold coin. The necklace had been pawned, but Fernando
borrowed money from some of the rich Jews of Aragon to
redeem it.

The two Castilian gentlemen found Isabel still at Madrigal,
safe but not incognita. The spies of Villena had been too alert
for that, and so, apparently, had those of Louis XI; for within a few days the Princess found herself waited upon by the
Cardinal of Albi and a glittering entourage, who came to
renew the suit of the Duke of Guyenne. Louis had been following all the maze of negotiations concerning Isabel with the
most ardent curiosity. Her marriage either in Portugal or in
Aragon would be injurious to French interests, since both
these countries were allies of Louis's enemy, England; and the
Aragonese match, in particular, would be a blow at Louis's
aspirations beyond the Pyrenees, for it would raise up a new
and powerful Spanish state to resist him. He sent the Cardinal
with instructions to spare no eloquence on behalf of his de-
crepit brother, Guyenne.

Nothing could have been more ceremoniously correct than

the meeting of the Princess and the Cardinal. What a beautiful thing it had been, that old and admirable friendship between her father and the monarchs of France! "Surely, if your Highness's father were alive he would *never* consent to your marrying either Don Alfonso or Don Fernando; and surely in the other world it would give great joy to the soul of the King your Father, if your marriage to the Duke were concluded."[11] These and more practical reasons the ambassador urged; and offered besides to win over King Enrique to the marriage with the Duke, and thus reconcile him with Isabel.

The Princess heard the embassy, gave much honor to the Cardinal, and replied, "Before all things I shall beg God in all my affairs, and especially this one which touches me so nearly, that He will show me His will, and raise me up for whatever may be for His service and for the welfare of these kingdoms."[12]

There was a second interview; and this time the Princess bade them reply to the King of France that "she had determined after mature consideration not to dispose of this matter of her marriage without following the advice of the *grandes* and cavaliers of these kingdoms, with whom she would consult on that which the Cardinal had proposed to her; and having their vote, would do whatever God might ordain and they might counsel." Isabel was learning from one diplomat after another the art of saying with great earnestness something that sounds important and means little or nothing.

"The Cardinal didn't like this answer," her secretary naïvely concludes, "but it was the one he had to go away with."[13]

It was at this crisis that Cárdenas and Palencia came back from Aragon with Fernando's signature and the balas rubies. After she had thanked and dismissed them, she fell on her knees in gratitude to Almighty God; for this, she felt, was the answer to all her prayers.

Her position, nevertheless, was far from secure. Villena and the King were expected almost any day from Estremadura. The Marqués already had emissaries in Madrigal, spying upon Isabel, and making daily reports to his nephew, the Bishop of Burgos, who by a curious coincidence happened to be there at the time. His instructions were to watch Isabel's every move and to notify the Marqués what she was doing, whom she talked with, what plans she might be hatching. Within a week the Bishop had a description of Fernando's necklace. He promptly relayed it to Villena.

The Marqués was furious. He went immediately to the King. Unless His Majesty was willing to have his royal authority flouted by the Aragonese and an obstinate girl, he must act firmly before his return to the North. A strong force should be sent at once to seize the Princess. Enrique ordered 400 lances, all the cavalry he could spare, to Madrigal.

Isabel's face was calm, but her mind was uneasy. She felt a thousand dangers hanging over her. She thought of flight. But to what place and with whom? She did not wish to go without the Archbishop. Where was the Archbishop? Why was there not even a message from him?

Somewhere in the town she heard shouts, the sound of feet running, and then the clatter of many horses' hoofs galloping over the cobble-stones. She imagined the worst. She could see before her nothing but imprisonment—a dungeon, the poisoned cup . . . darkness. There was no time to fly. She fell on her knees and prayed.

A servant opened the door at the end of the chamber and came timidly in, followed by an overshadowing form in gleaming Toledo armor, whose spurs rattled as he came. The girl arose and faced him.

It was Carrillo.

V

PRINCE FERNANDO COMES DISGUISED AS A TEAMSTER, AND LOVE COMES DISGUISED AS PRINCE FERNANDO

IF THE Bishop of Burgos had looked out of his window a few minutes later, he might have seen the Princess and the Archbishop cantering past to join the three hundred horsemen waiting outside the gates of Madrigal.

She followed him without question. As they rode along he explained with his slow pompous gravity why he had not come before, why he had carried her off so suddenly, why he had brought so small a force instead of the "army" he had promised. Difficulty with one of his towns . . . rents uncollectable . . . scarcity of money . . . greed of mercenary soldiers.

Much as she liked and trusted the Archbishop, she was beginning to see in him the weakness that existed, it would seem, in every man. In Carrillo, it was a form of pride—the excessive love of glory. If he always had his broad hand out, like the Marqués of Villena, for royal favors, there was this difference: Pacheco hoarded his gains to gloat over them in the secrecy of his perfumed beard, while the Archbishop wanted them only to give them away again to his friends and flatterers. His vanity made him generous, and his generosity made him improvident, so that with all his titles and possessions he was continually without funds. A strange mingling of the priest and the soldier he was. He had built the monastery of St. Francis at Alcalá de Henares, had founded a chair at the college there, had reformed certain abuses among the priests of the diocese, and otherwise had given evidence of a real desire to promote the health of the Church. Yet the priest in him was constantly being betrayed by the man of war. And he lacked a sense of humor. But on that day Doña Isabel was grateful to him for snatching her away only a few hours before the arrival of Enrique's troops in Madrigal.

At the end of their fifty-mile ride they saw many cavaliers coming from the city of Valladolid to welcome them; and the citizens waved flags and cheered them and cried, "Castile! Castile, for the Princess Lady Isabel!"

All very gratifying, but as the Archbishop shrewdly observed, the citizens of Valladolid would weigh little against Enrique's army. Isabel was still in great danger. No money, no troops; no troops, prison or exile. The only glint of hope Carrillo could see was the possibility that Fernando of Aragon might somehow be smuggled over the frontier. Isabel, as a wife, would have a stronger status, and could either find a refuge in Aragon, or rally what support she could in Castile and confront Enrique with the *fait accompli*. So argued Carrillo. Isabel agreed. They despatched a swift messenger to Aragon bidding Fernando come in disguise—otherwise the attempt would be futile. The Prince replied that come he would if possible.

The King and the Marqués were already on their way back from Estremadura. Isabel's capture was not the only business that drew them northward. They had had certain disquieting reports concerning Queen Juana. After betraying her and her child in the Treaty of Toros de Guisando, they had sent her under a guard to Alehejos, as the "guest" of the Archbishop of Seville. Still young and beautiful, she was a woman "to whom talk of love was pleasing, and other things which youth is accustomed to demand and modesty to deny. . . . Delighting more in the beauty of her face than in the glory of her reputation, she did not preserve the honor of her person as she ought, nor that of the King, her husband."* Forbidden to visit her daughter Juana, who was at Buytrago; strictly guarded by Don Inigo Lopez de Mendoza, Count of Tendilla, she found a way of winning over a boy named Don Pedro, a nephew of the Archbishop, who brought horses to a place under the castle wall one dark night, and lowered her from the battlements in a large basket. Unhappily the rope broke, and Juana tumbled in a heap. Her face and right leg were bruised, but there was nothing more serious; and she continued the adventure with Don Pedro. On the way to Buytrago they stopped to pass the time of day with the Duke of

* Pulgar, Crónica.

Albuquerque at his castle of Cuellar. All these events were reported to the King and the Marqués.

While they were on their way north, a small caravan of merchants was leaving Tarazona, in Aragon, to the east. Going as rapidly as their mules and asses, laden with goods, could proceed, they traveled long after sundown by out-of-the-way trails that went only through small villages. Some of them, for merchants, had uncommonly fine features and soft skins. And one of their servants, a young muleteer, had a certain distinction even in ragged garments, with a soiled cap pulled over his eyes.

When they stopped at an inn, the muleteer waited on the rest at table. He had frank alert eyes, a symmetrical, well-nourished body, and strong shapely hands. The candlelight on his brown hair gave it a somewhat reddish tinge. When he smiled, and he rarely did, one noticed his small, white, rather irregular teeth. At night, while the merchants were asleep, he tossed restlessly about, or got up to pace the courtyard of the inn and study the stars.

Working their way west along the river Douro to Soria, the merchants followed a rocky trail across the mountains, and late on the second night of their journey came to Burgos de Osma. The gates of the castle, the first on their way that did not belong to one of the enemies of the Princess Isabel, were already locked for the night. While the merchants stopped at a little distance to deliberate, the young muleteer, more impatient, ran ahead, and knocked loudly at the gate.

Overhead suddenly opened a window, from which the inmates, accustomed to visits from marauders or robber barons, let fly a shower of stones. A rock as big as a man's head grazed the ear of the young muleteer below.

"Do you want to kill me, you fools?" he cried, "It is Don Fernando! Let me in!"

There were footsteps ringing on stone pavements, the rattle of chains and the slow creaking of the mighty gates . . . the voice of the Alcaide, identifications and apologies.

Early next morning the Alcaide conducted the Prince to Dueñas in Leon, where friends of Isabel met him, and as soon as he had changed his clothing, escorted him to Valladolid. Isabel, with the Archbishop and Beatriz de Bobadilla and other friends, was waiting for him at the palace of Juan de Vivero.

As he entered the hall, an excited courtier cried, *"Ese es! Ese es!"*—in commemoration of which his descendants have always been permitted to have "SS" on their escutcheons—"This is he! This is he!"

As the Prince came across the hall with a slow, deliberate step, like that of a man who knows what he wants, Isabel watched him with a fascinated, half painful curiosity; this stranger was her husband! He was then seventeen years old, but responsibility had made him seem older, and a lofty brow, made higher by incipient baldness, gave a look of great intelligence to his face. He had bushy eyebrows, and quick daring eyes. It was easy to believe all that had been said of him—that he was simple in his dress, sober in his tastes, always master of himself in all circumstances, always the prince. Somewhere in his face—on one portrait at any rate—there was, oddly enough, a hint of something Semitic.[1] When he smiled, his face seemed handsome. When he spoke to Isabel, his voice, ordinarily rather hard and authoritative, became musical, persuasive, as it always did with those he liked or wished to please.

There were the usual formalities. Carrillo was present, and the Admiral of Castile, Fernando's grandfather, and other notables. Conventional compliments passed in prolix and musical Castilian. Isabel and Fernando were thinking their own thoughts.

Isabel was then eighteen, eleven months older than Fernando and perhaps an inch taller, "the handsomest lady I ever beheld," said one courtier, and if no way remains to judge whether or not he flattered—for the portraits of her are poor and do not resemble one another—those who saw her agreed at least on the fine proportions of her athletic body, her graciousness and poise, the classic purity of her features, the beauty and harmony of her gestures and all her movements, the music of her rather low and distinct voice, the copper and bronze lights in her hair and that delicate blonde coloring that no painter could have imitated. Like Fernando, her second cousin, she was descended on both sides from the English House of Lancaster, from the Plantagenets. To that kingly race perhaps she owed her fair skin and hair and her blue eyes with the green and gold flecks swimming about in their depths.

Fernando arrived on the eleventh of October. On the twelfth

Isabel wrote the King a long letter announcing her intention, justifying her course and begging his blessing.[2] If possible she would have waited for a reply; but the Archbishop, the Admiral and the Prince, with convincing arguments, urged an immediate marriage.

Yet Isabel still hesitated. She was related by blood to Fernando within the degrees forbidden by the Church. The necessary dispensation would have to come from Rome, and she anticipated a long delay by Pope Paul II, who had been prejudiced against her by Villena's agents for the past five years. The Prince replied with his most disarming smile that every difficulty had been foreseen. His father, King Juan of Aragon, had obtained the dispensation more than five years ago from the previous Pope, Pius II, during those early negotiations for Isabel's hand. Fernando's grandfather, the little Admiral, produced the bull, and handed it to the Archbishop with a great flourish. The document was in blank authorizing Fernando to marry *any* person related to him within the fourth degree of kinship. Evidently the wily Juan had not pinned all his hopes on Isabel! At any rate, the Archbishop, with more than his ordinary gravity, declared that there was no further obstacle to the marriage; and he performed it on Wednesday, October 18, at Juan de Vivero's palace, in the presence of some two thousand persons.

Fernando had already sworn at Cervera to the conditions dictated by Castilian fear of the Aragonese and by Isabel's conviction that only a strong Castilian sovereign with a united public opinion could bring harmony out of chaos; and before the conclusion of the marriage ceremony he solemnly repeated the oath. He agreed to respect all the laws and usages of Castile; to reside there and never leave the country without his wife's consent; to make no appointment, civil or military, without her consent; to leave all nominations to church benefices in her hands; to alienate no property belonging to the crown; to continue the holy war against the Moors of Granada; to provide always for the maintenance and comfort of Isabel's mother the Queen Dowager at Arévalo; to treat King Enrique with respect and filial devotion, as the lawful ruler of Castile. All public ordinances were to be signed jointly by Isabel and Fernando, unless one of them happened to be out of the kingdom. Isabel, if she succeeded Enrique, was to be the undisputed

sovereign of Castile, Fernando to have the title of King only
by courtesy—a necessary concession to the traditional Castilian
fear of Aragonese intrigue.

All this was hypothetical, depending on what Villena's malice
and the King's weakness might manage to effect. But for the
present Isabel was completely happy, probably for the first
time, possibly for the last time, in her restless life. She loved
her husband with all the ardor of a nature that despised half
measures, and Fernando loved her as much as it was possible
for his colder and more practical spirit to love any one. Of
the two she was the better educated and undoubtedly the more
lofty and magnanimous of soul. But perhaps their very incom-
patibilities contributed to the success of their marriage, for it
is difficult to imagine Isabel living amicably with a man as
intense and unbending as she was. Certain it is that both
exercised from the start a remarkable understanding and forbearance; and the same tact and common sense, carried over
into the intricate business of government, enabled them to work
together so successfully that it was said "they acted in all
things as one person."

Fernando accomplished whatever business he had to do
quietly and methodically. Though he was most scrupulous about
the cleanliness of his person, he wore the plainest sort of
clothes as a rule. On feast days of the Church or other grand
occasions, however, he would wear around his neck a gold
chain set with pearls. He loved games of various kinds. In
youth he played pelota, later he spent much of his leisure at
chess and backgammon, and to the end of his days he was
devoted to cards.

Isabel's relaxations were poetry and music, conversation on
literature, philosophy and theology, and of course, riding and
hunting. But her patience must have been tried severely at
times by her husband's devotion to cards. She disliked all games
of chance; and as for professional gamblers, we have the word
of Lucio Marineo for it that she classed them with blasphemers. "Hell," this Italian moralist and man of letters
assures us *en passant*, "is full of gamblers." And in summarizing the strong aversions of the Princess, whose guest he was,
he adds that while she paid great honor to grave, worthy and
modest persons, she fairly abhorred libertines, loquacious fel-
lows, the importunate and the fickle; "and she did not wish

to see nor to hear liars, coxcombs, rascals, clairvoyants, magicians, swindlers, fortune-tellers, palm readers, acrobats, climbers and other vulgar tricksters."[3]

Perhaps it was fortunate, then, that Fernando was a man who loved peace, and where no vital principle was involved, preferred to compromise rather than fight. No one but Isabel ever curbed his more earthy and selfish nature; no one else evoked from him so much that was fine and generous. There was between them, moreover, one strong bond that helped to smooth over their differences. Both were sincerely religious. Fernando never broke his fast until he had heard Mass, even when traveling. But Isabel not only heard Mass daily, but "was in the habit every day of saying all the canonical hours" like a priest or a nun,[4] besides long prayers in private and "extraordinary devotions." In many personal habits, too, they were in complete agreement. Fernando ate sparingly and drank moderately. Isabel never touched wine at all. "She was abstemious," wrote Marineo, "and as we vulgarly say, a waterdrinker."

The happy autumn of 1469 passed quickly. Christmas came, and still there was no word from King Enrique. Isabel began to watch the road for royal couriers. Not only her future security but her very bread and butter depended upon her halfbrother's forgiveness. Several times that winter she was not only without money, but had difficulty in obtaining the barest necessities. Fernando could expect no help from his father, and Isabel could collect none of her revenues without the King's permission. Three days after their marriage she sent a second missive by certain cavaliers, explaining to Enrique that since he himself had broken the treaty of Toros de Guisando by attempting to force her to marry Alfonso V against her will, she was free from all obligation. The King replied laconically that he would consult his ministers, meaning, doubtless, Pacheco. No further message came from the court.

To complicate the situation further, Isabel conceived early in 1470. They were still at Valladolid. Where they would be when the child was born was a profound mystery. And yet they were both overjoyed, and going together to Mass early in the morning, knelt before the high altar and returned thanks to God for the great favor He had shown them in their adversity. Isabel wore a dress of somewhat faded elegance, and

Fernando's doublet showed signs of wear. But what did youth and love care for such contemptible trifles?

At last came a reply from the King. Isabel, he said, had deliberately disobeyed him. She had broken the solemn treaty of Toros de Guisando. He must treat her as any other rebel and enemy of the public weal. And that, very likely, meant war.

Valladolid, full of the spies of the Marqués, was no longer safe. At the Archbishop's suggestion Isabel went to his brother's house at Dueñas with her husband, to await her delivery.

Villena meanwhile sent secretly to Louis XI, advising him that Isabel's was a lost cause, and suggesting that the Duke of Guyenne ask for the hand of La Beltraneja. Louis followed the advice.

In June Isabel wrote a third letter to the King, offering her "filial" obedience and Fernando's, and begging him, for the sake of peace and justice, to recognize her claim as his heir and to unite with her in abolishing anarchy and misery. Enrique made no reply.

Isabel's child was born at Dueñas on the first day of October, 1470. She accepted the universal pain of women with fortitude, but it was not so easy to face the ordeal in the presence of several officials appointed for the occasion in obedience to a rule that had been observed in Castile ever since the mother of Pedro the Cruel was accused of having palmed off the son of a Jew on her royal husband, who insisted upon a male heir. Isabel stipulated that her face be covered with a silk veil; not that she feared crying out, for she knew how to suffer in silence, but in case she could not control the muscles of her face, she did not choose to have the witnesses see a Princess of Castile so much as wince.

The child was a girl, fair-haired, and called by her mother's name.

A few days later, the Princess sat up and dictated a long letter to the King. She reminded him of her conciliatory letters, unanswered; renewed the offer of her obedience, and indirectly made a shrewd appeal to the public dislike for the French with whom Enrique was negotiating.

"And now from many sources we are informed that instead of your accepting our just supplication, you have permitted certain foreign people, extremely odious to our nation, to intrude themselves by various wiles and devices, and to take other steps against us and against the right and legitimate succession belonging to us; the which your Highness, of your own free will, swore to me the Princess publicly, while I was in your power within view of Toros de Guisando, in the presence of the legate of our most Holy Father, and with his authority; and you imposed the same oath on our very reverend fathers in Christ the Archbishops of Toledo and Seville and the Master of Santiago and the Count of Placencia and the Bishops of Burgos and Soria and other Dukes and Counts and *ricos-hombres* gathered there at that time; and later, in the town of Ocaña, by your Lordship's order, many other prelates and cavaliers swore to it, and the *procuradores* of the cities and towns of these realms, as your Worship well knows, and as everybody knows. And, very excellent Señor, since we still desire that you send to bid us serve and respect and obey you as a king and lord and a true father, for which we are willing to answer to God, Our Lord, in the heavens, the true knower of public and secret intentions, and to your inhabitants in this land, and even to strangers, we have decided to write this present letter to Your Grace; in which with the reverence of children and servants we beg that it may please you to accept our just supplication, and to receive our obedience and service, laying aside all grievances and displeasures in the service of Our Lord and for the pacification of these your realms and possessions, and showing mercy to us, whose intent never was, nor shall be to anger you, nor do you any despite. And if by chance, very excellent lord, it should not please your Highness to do this in as kindly a spirit as we beg it, then we ask what in justice you cannot deny us: that before the commencement of those rigors which would be difficult to stop after they begin and could cause such great offenses to God and irreparable damage to these your kingdoms (moreover we believe they might extend to a very large part of Christendom) your Grace should please to hear us and to maintain our just cause."[5]

After citing the approval of her cause by prelates, members of religious orders, and others, Isabel lays aside diplomatic amenities and thrusts home with what amounts to an ultimatum:

Fernando of Aragon

"Hence, very mighty Señor, since we so sincerely offer you peace, and submit ourselves to the judgment and sentence of your subjects: we supplicate your royal lordship and, if necessary, demand with that Almighty God who is accustomed to be and is a true and just judge between emperors and kings and great lords, that it may not please you to deny us that which you cannot and ought not deny to the least in your kingdoms. This we supplicate and demand of your Grace, once and for all, with as much insistence as we can and as much reverence as we ought. Likewise we intend to publish it in your kingdoms and beyond them: for if this is not received in the spirit in which we offer it, then in the defence of our just cause we will do what is permitted to all by divine and human sanction, and we shall be without blame before God and before the world; and to this we ask your Highness that we may have your definite reply."

Enrique bestirred himself to answer that Isabel had been ill-advised to marry without his consent, "on account of the evils which such things produce in the realms," and he attributed it entirely to her disobedience that "it is not yet pleasing to God that the mischiefs and wars which exist in the kingdom shall cease."

Knowing that some nobles would support him because he was the King, and others because they would wish to be on the stronger side, he had decided to fight. His next move was to summon Queen Juana and her eight-year-old daughter from Buytrago to Lozaya, where the Marqués of Villena and several other cavaliers took the oath of allegiance to La Beltraneja as heiress to Castile and Leon; after which the Cardinal of Albi, as proxy for the Duke of Guyenne, solemnly pronounced the words of betrothal with her. The Court proceeded to Segovia for feasting and processions. La Beltraneja remained under the protection of the Marqués of Villena.

In all this news, full of the threat of civil war, the only encouragement for Isabel was a report that Don Pedro Gonzalez de Mendoza, who as Bishop of Calahorra had once refused to join the rebels at Burgos, now declined to take the new oath, saying that when he took it previously all the nobles in the kingdom had done so. Knowing Mendoza's respect for legitimacy and all the other machinery of peace and order, Isabel hoped his refusal might mean that he was

beginning to doubt that the country could ever be united under
the standard of La Beltraneja, and she saw in him a possible
ally.

She found other unexpected friends in hunger and fear.
There was famine that winter in Castile. The roads were full
of foot-pads and cut-throats. Money had almost disappeared
and goods were exchanged by primitive barter. Corpses of
wayfarers were found every morning in city streets, strangled
or starved. There was pestilence everywhere, everywhere the
tolling of funeral bells and the digging of graves. White, bony
faces stared from the gray walls of houses as cavalcades of
nobles or troopers rode by; and curses followed them, curses
especially bitter against the Marqués and King Enrique, to
whose infamies the commoners attributed the wrath God was
visiting upon them and their children.

Spring brought Isabel other confederates: Biscay and Guipúzcoa had declared for her. She heard that Villena, having
begged and received from Enrique the town of Sepulveda, was
refused admittance, and the inhabitants sent their allegiance
to her and Fernando. The citizens of Aranda de Duero cast
out the officers of Queen Juana and raised the flag of Isabel,
who rode there with Carrillo to receive their homage. Agreda
ejected the Duke of Medina Celi, to whom Enrique had given
the place, and declared for the Princess.

Even death seemed to have joined the ranks of Isabel's partisans. The Duke of Guyenne suddenly expired after eating a
peach, which the enemies of his brother, Louis XI, were only
too eager to believe had been poisoned by the royal command.
At any rate, Isabel was rid of a troublesome suitor; while La
Beltraneja, thrown back on the matrimonial market, was offered by Enrique to her uncle the King of Portugal. Alfonso
declined the honor, alleging scruples.

Pope Paul II, who had generally leaned to the side of
Enrique IV as the legitimate sovereign, died in the summer of
1471. The election of the devout and learned Franciscan, Francesco della Rovere, as his successor, proved most favorable
to Isabel. As she was henceforth to have some very important
relations with this Pope, Sixtus IV, it is necessary to consider
for a moment the condition of the Church at that time, and
the part the Pope played in the life of Europe.

VI

IN THE Middle Ages the Pope, as spiritual father of
Christendom, had been the head of what was virtually a
League of Nations, or more accurately, of feudal divisions,
for there was little nationalism of the modern sort. The Church
was almost coextensive with society, made up, to be sure, of
the good, the bad and the indifferent, saints and sinners, wheat
and tares, but cemented by a common faith and a common
standard of ethics. Unlike the twentieth century League of
Nations, which is abortive chiefly because nations are unwilling to surrender their sovereignty even in part to the mere
abstraction of a super-state, the medieval Pope, as the visible
successor of Saint Peter and the Vicar of Christ on earth,
was almost universally respected by Christians, and imposed
upon all the conflicting masses that made up our western
world a common culture and a comparative harmony. Thus on
a foundation of faith and good will, the Church accomplished
what the Roman Empire had been able to effect only by sheer
force. The medieval harmony varied with circumstances and
the abilities of different Popes, but it will be found that the
balance was more often disturbed by the attempts of the State
to subvert the Church to the purpose of tyranny than from
the encroachments of the Church upon the province of the
State. Men attempted to solve the problem of balance by nice
definitions of the spiritual and temporal powers. It was the
accepted view that both Church and State were of divine origin, and must be sovereign in their respective spheres. The
Church had no power over civil legislation or administration
in merely secular matters, such as the election or appointment

of officers and the collection of taxes; but it was the Pope's right and duty to interfere with kings or lawgivers where there was question of sin or of the salvation of souls.[1] The Church prohibited slavery as immoral; encouraged the co-operation of employer and employee in guilds, insisted upon the sanctity of marriage, arbitrated wars, forbade wars of aggression, reduced the violence of conflict by the Truce of God. In extreme cases the Pope could and did release from their allegiance the subjects of evil or tyrannical kings; on the other hand he could excommunicate a notorious rebel, or a heretic, or a disturber of the peace. Such was the theory that Christendom accepted, and considering what human beings are, it was remarkably successful in practice. "The work done by the Curia was enormous, ranging from arbitration between kings to minute regulations about disputes in a parish. The Pope, needless to say, could not transact all this business unaided. His chancery became the most technical and also the most efficient administrative machine which ever existed. Every stage in the preparation of a bull or mandate was carefully scrutinized to secure authenticity, prevent forgery and guarantee that each formality, from the acquiescence of the pontiff to the consideration of technical objections by the parties, had been observed. . . . The medieval methods of cultivation and restraint are not in favor nowadays, but if we reflect upon the magnitude of the task, the condition of society and the amazing energy of its life in the early Middle Ages, it cannot justly be said that they were unduly repressive. And, by maintaining as a practical guide in life the conception of an ordered universe, in which there is a fundamental harmony between moral and physical law, the Church turned the faces of the European peoples in the only direction along which social and scientific advance was possible."[2] But during a century or more before the birth of Isabel, the harmony and balance of Christendom had been violently disturbed by forces beyond the power of any Pope to control.

In 1347 there had come out of the darkness of Asia a mysterious and irresistible disease, that slew a man in two or three days at the most, sometimes in a few hours. From the black spots that were its dreadful symptoms and from the grisly black of the corpses, it was called the Black Death. Within two years after its appearance at Constantinople it had spread to every corner of Europe, killing at the very least 25,000,000 people. Some cities perished utterly. In most, a third to half of the people died. Nor was there safety on remote farms or in mountain villages. People died of fear. Mothers forsook their sick children. Whole masses went insane. Some in despair plunged into orgies of vice, others rushed to the monasteries to throw over the walls pest-tainted gold from which the monks shrank in horror. Ghostly ships with flapping sails were washed on the shores of France and Spain, and the curious fishermen who boarded them found only black rotting corpses on the decks, and themselves went ashore to die. The scourge fell with special virulence upon the laborers, and even more so on the clergy, constantly exposed to contagion as they were by the necessity of administering the sacraments to the sick and the dying. In one Italian monastery only one monk survived to bury his thirty-six brethren.

The Church in Isabel's time had not yet recovered from the terrible blow. It had almost annihilated her priesthood; and even to fill partially the places of the dead, she had been compelled to lower her standard, accepting men ignorant of Latin. There was a weakening everywhere of ecclesiastical morale and discipline. Meanwhile, at the time when men had most need of it, the authority of the Papacy was long impaired by the enforced exile of the Popes at Avignon, as virtual prisoners of the French Kings for seventy years.

It was not until 1377 that Gregory XI returned to Rome. One of the deplorable results of the exile was the Great Schism. Europe was bewildered by the spectacle of two and even three claimants to the chair of Saint Peter. The crisis ended only when Nicholas V was recognized by the whole Church in 1447—only four years before the birth of Isabel. Moral corruption had become widespread, both in Church and State. The need of reform was a primary issue.

But while Christendom fairly writhed with internal pangs, its very existence was threatened by the almost continuous onslaughts of powerful and aggressive foes without. Of these the most dangerous were the Mohammedans, who from the very beginning had preached and practised conquest by the sword. The Pope was the only man to whom all Christians might look for leadership, and it was the Pope alone whose voice repeatedly thundered above the follies and passions of

Europe, calling upon princes to lay aside their selfish quarrels and unite in the defense of their common civilization. For a thousand years the energies of Europe were drained by what was virtually one gigantic defensive crusade. When Urban II preached "the first crusade," so-called, in 1095, Islam, now the arch-foe, had dominated Christian Spain for nearly four centuries, and had thrown a wedge into the very heart of Europe. From the eighth century the encroachments of Moslem power had constituted a standing major problem for nearly every Pope, and for some of them an almost overwhelming one.

In the lifetime of Isabel's father, Pope Eugene IV preached a crusade against the Ottoman Turks, who were overrunning Hungary, and Duke Hunyadi of Transylvania led crusaders from all parts of Europe into Servia and routed the Moslems at Nisch. But after the Hungarians made peace, against the advice of the Pope, the Turks crossed the Hellespont, crushed the Christians at Vanna, and in 1448 defeated Hunyadi. Nicholas V, the first Pope in Isabel's lifetime, sent twenty-nine galleys to defend Constantinople in 1453. His successor, the Spanish Pope Calixtus III, made the stopping of the Turkish advance the one great aim of his pontificate. He sold his art treasures and table service to obtain money for the Crusade to regain Constantinople: his fleet drove the enemy from Lemnos and other places, but in the end he failed because the European princes were too stupid or too selfish to perceive the danger. Under the scholarly Pius II, there appeared in Rome the battle-scarred face of Skanderbeg, who had been warring for a whole generation for the independence of Albania, while greedy Venetian traders plotted his ruin, and now he came, at sixty, begging for help. When he died in 1468, he had failed to save his country, but he had averted the conquest of Italy.

The next pope, Paul II, sent money to Albania repeatedly, and called upon all rulers to join the crusade. But in the spring of 1470 Mohammed II launched a fleet of 400 ships against Negroponte, a supposedly impregnable place on the island of Euboea, and in July, while the Pope was trying to reconcile Venice and Naples and appease the enmity of Ferrante II of Naples, the news came that the impossible had happened, that Venice had lost the pearl of her Grecian dominions. There was consternation in Rome, in all Italy, even in Spain. "All

Venice," wrote the Milanese ambassador, "is struck with dismay; the inhabitants, half dead with fear, say the loss of all their possessions on the mainland would have been a less disaster." Malipiero wrote, "The glory and credit of Venice are destroyed. Our pride is humbled." This disaster frightened warring Italian princes enough so that by the end of 1470, the Pope had succeeded in uniting them in a defensive alliance against the Turks. But Paul II died the following summer, leaving Christendom in a critical state.

He bequeathed to his successor two mighty problems—the two overshadowing issues of the whole fifteenth century: the corruption in the Church, and the Turkish invasions. By a peculiar sinister irony, each one of these evils contributed constantly to the perpetuation of the other. The weakening of ecclesiastical discipline and the scandalous lives of many political prelates made it more difficult for the Pope to organize Europe against the enemy. Yet the enormous demands of the Crusade left him neither time nor energy for the thorough house-cleaning that was needed. To break the vicious circle, the times called for a Pope of holy and irreproachable life, who was at the same time statesman of masterful genius, a Gregory VII, an Innocent III.

At this moment (1471) the tiara was placed on the gray hairs of a man in whom many saw the promise of greatness. Sixtus IV was a Franciscan monk, devout, earnest, even ascetic. As general of his order he had been a capable administrator, an energetic reformer, and an eloquent preacher. His powerful head suggested unusual energy and force, his face bore marks of thought, toil, self-discipline. His private life was blameless. He was generous to a fault, and valued money so little that if he saw some lying on his table, he commanded that it be given to the poor. He paved Rome and restored its walls and bridges. Although he was a poor friar of lowly birth, he became after his elevation a discerning patron of the arts and sciences. It was he who built the Sistine Chapel, re-established the Vatican Library and opened it for general use, and employed such painters as Ghirlandajo, Botticelli and Perugino. He assumed office with the lofty purposes of reforming the Church and prosecuting the Crusade with all vigor.

The one rock on which the good intentions of Sixtus might

possibly be wrecked was nepotism, the source of so many evils in the Church. And it so happened that Sixtus did love his relatives more than a Pope should. As soon as he was elevated they flocked to Rome from their native Liguria, with hands open for favors and benefices. Sixtus made two of his nephews cardinals: Giuliano della Rovere, aged twenty-eight, and Pietro Riario, aged twenty-five.

Giuliano, afterwards Pope Julius II, was grave and resolute, with great handsome dark eyes, a truly Renaissance character of Titanic energies, like Michael Angelo. Nature seemed to have intended him for a soldier and a statesman. His youth was that of a Renaissance noble, turbulent and ambitious. In later life he reformed himself, and commenced the reform of the Church several years before the excommunication of Luther.

Pietro was proud, sensual, ostentatious, absolutely unworthy of the rich benefices that his generous uncle showered upon him. He was not the son of Sixtus, as enemies of the Pope insinuated, but of Paolo Riario of Savona.[3] "He seemed to vie with the ancients in pomp and grandeur—and, it may be added, in vices. All morality was openly defied by this upstart. Instead of the habit of Saint Francis, he went about in garments laden with gold, and adorned his mistress from head to foot with costly pearls."[4] When the Princess Leonora of Naples visited Rome, Pietro had a splendid wooden house, a veritable palace, built for her and her attendants before the Church of the Apostles. The banquet hall of the palace was kept cool by three great bellows, hidden among precious tapestries. Even the meanest vessels in the house were of silver and gold. Riario's banquet to the Princess recalled the pagan luxury of imperial Rome. Servants in silk first gave the guests sweet-meats, oranges encrusted in silver, and malvoisie, with rose water for their hands. Three courses followed, forty-four dishes in all, including stags roasted whole and in their skins, goats, hares, calves, herons, peacocks with their feathers, and finally a bear with a staff in his jaws.[5]

Riario gained much influence over Sixtus, but fortunately perhaps for the Church, he died of his excesses after three years of glory. His banquet gives some hint of how the Renaissance, taken as a philter, had made all Italy drunk with the desire to imitate the pagan past in which it suddenly discovered an ancestor. The Renaissance as the recovery of classical art

and wisdom was one thing, the Renaissance as the return of
classical vices and futilities was quite another. It was the pagan
side of the glorious awakening that troubled sober churchmen
and philosophers, and it was that phase—for passion is always
a better publicity agent than saintliness—that chroniclers most
carefully set down and historians are tempted to exaggerate.
Against the meagre records that we find of many holy lives in
homes and cloisters, of men and women in difficult surroundings attempting to follow the example of Christ, of aristocratic
women toiling in scores of charity hospitals, of associations of
the rich to lend money to the poor without interest, of men
inspired by religion to risk their lives serving in the "burial
societies" in time of pestilence—against this humble background of daily felicity and charity, and against the most magnificent art that human hands ever created, fall the blacker and
more gigantic shadows of such smiling scoundrels as Cesare
Borgia and his brother the Duke of Gandia, such veritable
monsters as Sigismondo Malatesta, and a whole army of such
able and noisy scribblers as Machiavelli, ridiculing the humility
and self-abnegation of Christianity and glorifying all the passions—lust, avarice, pride, selfishness—that the Church had
labored so many centuries to restrain. If any of the pious
imagined that the unity of the Middle Ages had finally done
for all the false gods and demons of the dead world, they were
to have many harsh reminders of a conflict that would end only
with time. For they found themselves surrounded by men who
seemed consumed with a curious ambition to be their own remote ancestors, so to speak—for the pagans, as usual, were
the reactionaries, and the believing Christians the misunderstood minority looking forward to a better age. There was
something grotesque in the religious veneration that the
humanists of the Roman Academy, who had rejected the
dogmas of the Church, laid at the moldy shrines of poets and
philosophers who had not had a toothache in well over a thousand years; something almost too fantastically human in their
burning candles before the picture of Plato, as if he were a
saint; something positively bewildering in the mental processes of a priest—such as Marsilio Ficino, teacher of Pico della
Mirandola—who could gravely address his congregation as
"beloved in Plato" instead of "beloved in Christ." Bewildering is indeed the word for this epoch in which there flourished,

side by side, the sublimest art and the most abominable crimes
—sometimes united in a single person, as in Cellini; an ex-
traordinarily long list of the most splendid saints, and vain-
glorious autocrats addicted to the worst vices of Nero's time
and owning no principle but the vicious one of Machiavelli
that the end justifies the means. It was as though Pan, awakening from a long sleep in the Falernian hills, had come down
on stealthy hoofs to the Campo di Fiore early in the morning
to jeer at Cardinal Ascanio Sforza riding forth with his
hounds and his hawks for the hunting; as though Priapus had
crawled from the ruins of some forgotten garden on the
Palatine to leer through the oleanders by the palace of the
beautiful Vanozza near the bridge of San Angelo.

Yet the Church, as Pastor justly remarks, was not by any
means the author of the evils that corrupted her. She had
tried to restrain the tyranny of the state, but the state had
enslaved her. She had opposed militarism, but the elemental
necessity of self-defense had entangled her. She had preached
against the fatal excesses at the root of most human miseries,
and even now in her period of weakness, her friars, especially
Dominican and Franciscan, thundered in the vein of Savonarola, against the sins of princes and prelates. But the insidious forces that she had set her face against had made their
way into her own sacred places. And over the anxious and
ascetic form of Sixtus IV fell the ominous shadow of a Spanish Cardinal, his vice-chancellor, Roderigo Borja—in Italy
called Borgia.

When Borgia handed the tiara of Saint Gregory the Great
to Francesco della Rovere on the day of his coronation, August 25, 1471, it was generally believed that the new Pope
would immediately commence the needed reform of the
Church. But the Turkish victories in the east and the panic
of all Italy took precedence over all other issues. The overshadowing necessity was to unite Europe in a league of self-
defense. Measures for holding a great Congress of all Christendom were earnestly discussed at a Consistory on the thirtieth.
But after many discussions and much correspondence, nothing
came of it; for the rulers, as usual, were indifferent.

In December, Sixtus appointed five of the Cardinals Legates
de Latere, with the object of "calling upon the whole Christian world to defend the Catholic Faith against the Turk, the

enemy of the name of Jesus." He sent the venerable Bessarion to France, Burgundy and England, Angelo Capriano to the Italian states, Marco Barbo to Germany, Hungary and Poland, and Oliviero Carafa to command the fleet to be organized with the aid of the King of Naples. He sent Cardinal Borgia to his native country Spain.

At the same time the Pope issued a bull in which he described the Turkish preparations for the conquest of all Christendom, and called upon the princes to join in the common defense.

The result was discouraging. Bessarion was unable to make peace between the hostile Louis XI and Charles the Bold. England was harassed by her own troubles. Barbo found the Emperor indifferent. The Italian princes were at sixes and sevens. The Pope did what he could with the slender means at his command. He made an alliance with Usunhassan, the Mohammedan enemy of the Grand Turk. Having blessed the banners of the Christian fleet, he rode on horseback to bless the ships at anchor in the Tiber, and bid godspeed to the eighty-seven galleys about to sail for the east to attack Satalia. Satalia resisted. The Neapolitans quarreled with the Venetians, and went home in a huff. The fleet took Smyrna. But on the whole the Turks continued their victorious progress with little opposition. By 1475, they had conquered the Crimea, and began preparations for a grand final assault on Italy itself, while Lorenzo de' Medici, egged on by Louis XI, was stirring up a new agitation against the Pope among the Italian states.

Of all the papal peacemakers, Borgia probably accomplished most. When he sailed from Ostia for Spain in May, 1472, he was just forty years of age, tall and powerfully built, a commanding and majestic figure to behold. On nearer view one saw that he had coal black eyes, extremely penetrating, though they had a habit of blinking; but his nose was crooked, and there was a certain coarseness in the whole face that corresponded well to his reputation. The legend that makes him a morose, inhuman monster is false. He was a child of his age, however, and a notable example of the evils of nepotism, for his uncle, Pope Calixtus III, had made him a Cardinal and enriched him at the age of twenty-three; and power and luxury had been the ruin of him. But he was a gentleman of courtly manners, a charming conversationalist, a good judge of men,

an administrator of great capacity, a cavalier irresistibly attractive to women. Had it not been for the priestly office that
he dishonored, he might have passed as a man of average
morality in Renaissance Italy.

It was high time for peace in Castile if civilization was
not to vanish utterly from that chaotic country. A hundred
robber barons and some thousands of thieves and murderers
preyed upon the countryside. Seville was being reduced to a
shambles, its exquisite gardens torn up, its houses razed, its
citizens mowed down by a veritable warfare between the Duke
of Medina Sidonia and the fiery young Marqués of Cádiz. In
Toledo, since the riots of 1467, the wealthy Marranos had
lived almost in a state of siege. There were similar conditions
in other cities. And, as if anything were needed to complete
the general despair, the crops of 1472 were a failure everywhere in Andalusia, the granary of all Spain. Bernaldez gives
an illuminating glimpse of the famine prices that prevailed. A
fanega of wheat (about 1.6 bushels) or of corn sold for 700
to 800 maravedis; an ox for 3,000 maravedis; a cow 2,000;
wine, 75 maravedis per gallon. Now, if we estimate a maravedi
at about 2 American cents of 1929, and there are good reasons
for believing that ratio nearer the truth than the generally
accepted lower figures, this means that while a man could
purchase an ox for $60, and a cow for $40, and wine for $1.50
the gallon, he must pay $10 for a bushel of wheat—and $12
at the Puerto de Santa Maria. In that terrible year of starvation a man with a wife and children might have to give a cow
—if he had one—for four bushels of wheat or corn.

Cardinal Borgia rode in his usual magnificent state through
the desolate country as the guest of Archbishop Carrillo, con-
versing with men of importance and getting the lay of the land.
It took him a very little while to see that the recognition of
Princess Isabel must be the first step in any peace program
worth considering. And, as it was plain that the Marqués of
Villena held the key to the whole situation, he went to visit
him. Several conversations were held before Pacheco would
consent to meet Isabel and Fernando; and then a new obstacle
appeared. When Carrillo learned that the Prince and Princess
were going to Guadalajara for the conference, under the protection of the Marqués of Santillana, brother of Bishop Mendoza, he jealously withdrew, and had to be coaxed back by the

persuasive eloquence of Borgia. The papal legate, meanwhile, was making excellent progress with the Marqués of Villena, probably by appealing to his self-interest—the only logic that Pacheco understood.

And then, when all was going well, the peacemakers struck another snag. Isabel sent to the parleys as her representative, the converted Jew Andres de Cabrera, who had married her girlhood friend Beatriz de Bobadilla. She liked and trusted Cabrera. Moreover, he was governor of the Alcázar at Segovia, where part of the royal treasure was kept. He had formerly been one of Villena's intimate friends, but of late a coolness had arisen on his discovery that the Marqués was attempting to steal his governorship and certain other privileges. Therefore, when Pacheco heard that Cabrera was to take part in the deliberations at Guadalajara, he washed his hands of the whole business and left Enrique to patch up a peace as well as he could.

Meanwhile Beatriz de Bobadilla went to Segovia in disguise to win the King's consent to Borgia's program. As a result, Enrique agreed to recognize Isabel as his heiress, and invited her to Segovia to receive his blessing and kiss his brotherly hand.

She accepted, and went under the protection of Cabrera. There is a picture of her on a white horse, riding in triumph through a crowded street, with the King on foot holding her bridle. Enrique received her graciously, as one long lost. Nothing of royal magnificence was lacking in the entertainment he offered her.

After one great public banquet for the Princess and Fernando, the King had a sharp pain in his side, and took to his bed. Prayers were offered for his recovery. He did recover, but ever after suffered from what was believed to be a disease of the liver. The usual suspicion of poisoning was whispered about.

Meanwhile Cardinal Borgia was acclaimed everywhere as the man whose tact and intelligence had made possible at least the beginnings of peace. He had averted what promised to be an ugly civil war at the worst possible moment, even if the active participation of Castile and Aragon in the European crusade was out of the question; and though historians have written of his "failure" in Spain, it is difficult to see what more he could have done under the circumstances. He was feted and honored, at any rate, in Castile. From Segovia he went with the Prince and Princess to Alcalá de Henares, where Carrillo entertained them with all the princely generosity and splendor for which he was noted. The day before the Cardinal's party arrived, so many hens were requisitioned by the Archbishop on the farms near Alcalá, that on the morrow "hardly a cock remained that did not behold himself with consternation standing solitary on the deserted steps of the hen-roost."[6]

Isabel and her husband visited Carrillo while Borgia was his guest and then returned to Segovia. It was hardly a safe place; yet where was there a safer? And the turn of the tide of her fortunes had brought her new encouragement, new adherents. Several young knights, attracted by what they had heard of her beauty, her wisdom and her courage, went to her court to offer their swords for any service she might command. One of them was Gonsalvo de Córdoba, a youth of her own age, with the figure and presence of a Greek god. Handsome, witty, eloquent, a lover of poetry and music, he had almost superhuman strength and skill, and a nature so happy and so genial that the whole court loved him and called him "the Prince of Youth." With the sword he had no equal. On horseback with lances, he was second to none but Prince Fernando, the best horseman in Spain. Though he had no means and was dependent on the charity of his brother the lord of Montilla, he dressed like a duke and gave gifts like a king. He had the virtues of Don Beltran de la Cueva, without his vices; for Gonsalvo was sober and chaste in his life, and sincerely devout. Isabel wrote his name in a little book that she and Fernando kept for a memorandum of people of merit who might sometime be useful.

She still needed all her friends. For already, while she was dancing at Segovia, the Marqués was cantering to Cuellar to sow the seeds of new mischief. There his old enemy, Don Beltran, was chafing under the boredom of exile and hankering for any enterprise that had red blood in it. Between them the two royal favorites hatched a plot to assassinate Isabel's friends Cabrera and his wife, and then to seize the Prince, the Princess and the Archbishop of Toledo. Into this pretty conspiracy they drew the Count of Benavente by promising to have La

Beltraneja married to his cousin the Infante Don Enrique of Aragon. The three then broached the scheme to Enrique. Here was a chance, they argued, to settle the succession once and for all, and at the same time to get revenge on Carrillo, whose treachery, as any honest man could see, was at the bottom of all the evils of Castile.

The King liked the suggestion so well that he smuggled armed men into Segovia to wait concealed for the psychological moment to arrest Isabel, Fernando and Carrillo. His cowardice, however, made him first seek the moral support of men who could control public opinion. Fortunately, the first he approached was Bishop Mendoza. He received the following note in reply:

"May it never please God, Señor, that I should do despite to those Princes who came into your power with your consent. And since at the time when it pleased you they should come, you did not advise me of their coming, even less should you now advise me of their peril. But since it has already pleased you to acquaint me of it, I request you, in God's name, not to conceive such a deed in your soul; for I doubt not that you will have against you the whole realm, and especially the cities, who are convinced that the succession belongs by right to this princess, your sister; and there might follow as a consequence of your act, a great deal of inconvenience, and even an actual danger to your royal person."[7]

Seldom had Enrique received from a subject a communication so terse and so barren of all the conventional phrases of court flattery. He sighed, and deferred action.

Isabel had already got wind of the plot, however, through Beatriz de Bobadilla. Of her own peril she took little account, but it seemed to her that Fernando, a stranger in Castile, was in much graver danger, and she persuaded him to go to Turuegano, on the theory that they would be safer apart. When Carrillo begged her not to stay in Segovia, she replied that her friend the Alcaide would protect her person; whereupon Cabrera, at her request, increased her guard. Enrique then gave up his project and withdrew to Madrid, followed by the Marqués of Villena.

The Marqués bedevilled the tired king with complaints and reproaches until Enrique, to silence him, gave him the city of

Madrid, regardless of the fact that he had bestowed it on
Cabrera.

Cabrera was already inclined toward Isabel's cause, through
the influence of his wife. Henceforth he was heart and soul in
her service.

Whether or not Isabel spoke with Fray Tomás de Torquemada during her long stay at Segovia in 1473, history does not
say. But it is known that she conferred with several distinguished men, both priests and laymen, about the increasing
gravity of the situation between the Old Christians and the
Conversos. For another incident, destined to have sanguinary
consequences, had occurred while she was visiting Carrillo at
Alcalá.

On March 14, the second Sunday of Lent, the Christians
of Córdoba had arranged to have a solemn procession to the
Cathedral. From this function the authorities had excluded
the "New Christians," possibly in connection with the persecution following the Toledo incident of 1467, possibly because
the *Conversos* had become so secure in Córdoba that they
openly attended the synagogues, and mocked the Christian
religion. At any rate, they were excluded. The houses in the
old Moorish city were covered with gaudy spring flowers, the
streets carpeted and shaded with hundreds of tapestries. The
procession, brilliant with many colors, moved slowly through
the town to the sound of austere music. At its head was borne
a statue of the Blessed Virgin Mary.

As the statue passed the house of one of the wealthiest *Conversos*, a girl threw a bucketful of dirty water from one of the
upper windows. It splashed upon the statue.[8] There was a
horrified silence, then a roar of indignation, and cries of "Sac-
rilege!" and the old cry of "Death to the *Marranos*!" A black-
smith named Rodriguez set fire to the *Converso's* house with
the taper he was carrying. Men in the procession drew their
swords, broke ranks, and rushed into the houses of the secret
Jews. The massacre that followed was more bloody than the
one in Toledo.

In Córdoba, however, the *Conversos* found a powerful
champion in Don Alonzo de Aguilar, lord of Montilla. Their
gold is said to have been a convincing argument with him;
furthermore, he had married a woman of Jewish descent, a
daughter of the Marqués of Villena. He and his brother Gon-

salvo de Córdoba drew their swords in defense of the "New Christians." The Old Christians, led by the Count of Cabra, besieged Don Alonzo and his partisans in the Alcázar. The battle raged for several days. Don Alonzo and Gonsalvo cut their way out with difficulty.

A virtual state of war persisted for nearly four years between the two factions—Don Alonzo and the *Conversos* on one side, and the Count of Cabra and the Old Christians on the other. But even more deplorable was the reaction in other cities of Andalusia and Castile. The old frenzy against the secret Jews flamed up in a dozen places—Montoro, Adamur, La Rambla, Santaella, Ubeda, Jaen—and everywhere the *Marranos* were put to the sword. But perhaps the most thorough and brutal of the massacres occurred at Segovia on May 16, 1474. And its direct cause was a crime by which Don Juan Pacheco, Marqués of Villena, brought upon his memory the just scorn of Christians and Jews alike.

None knew better than he what deadly passions slumbered in that rocky city where the stern keep towered over the Jewish *alhama*, the houses of the rich *Conversos*, and the Dominican convent of Santa Cruz. None knew better than he, who had both Jewish and Christian relatives in the vicinity, how little provocation was needed to start a street battle in Segovia. The Jews there had always been numerous and assertive. And they were specially hated by the Christians, in consequence of certain crimes imputed to them. In 1405 Dr. Mayr Alguadés and other prominent Jews were executed for the theft of a consecrated Host from the Cathedral; and certain other Jews, who sought to have the Bishop poisoned in revenge—they bribed his cook—were drawn and quartered.[9] But in Isabel's recent memory—about the time of her brother's death in 1468—a most acute crisis resulted from the conviction of several Jews accused of a heinous crime in one of the small towns near Segovia. Colmenares records it in his *History of Segovia*:

"At this time in our town of Sepúlveda, the Jews, incited by Salomón Pichón, rabbi of their synagogue, stole a boy in Holy Week, and inflicting upon him the greatest infamies and cruelties (inflicted) upon the Redeemer of the world,[10] put an end to that innocent life: incredible obstinacy of a nation incorrigible to so many chastisements of Heaven and earth! This misdeed, then, like many others in the memorials of the

time, leaked out and came to the notice of our Bishop Don
Juan Árias de Ávila,[11] who, as higher judge at that time in
causes pertaining to the Faith, proceeded in this matter; and
investigating the crime, ordered brought to our city[12] sixteen
Jews of the principal offenders. Some finished in the fire;[13]
and the rest were drawn and hanged in that part of the meadow
occupied today by the monastery of San Antonio el Real.
Among them a boy, with signs of repentance and many supplications, begged for Baptism and for his life, that he might
do penance by entering and serving in a certain monastery of
the city. All his requests were granted—though it is known for
certain that as a double apostate he fled within a few days.
Better advised were the people of Sepúlveda, who, distrusting
those (Jews) who remained there, killed several and forced
the rest to go out of that territory, (thus) completely uproot-
ing so pestilent a seed."[14]

This passage, containing as it does the lurid spark of a much
greater subsequent conflagration, is highly important in the
light it sheds upon the state of public opinion in Segovia
during the spring of 1474, when Pacheco cast his acquisitive
eyes in that direction. Don Juan Árias de Ávila, son of Jewish parents, was still the bishop there; and the Alcaide, or
royal governor, was Cabrera, the friend whom Pacheco had
betrayed.

Cabrera was a man of capacity, but he was a *Converso*,
and therefore unpopular with the Old Christians. When the
gust of rage passed through the cities of Castile after the
Córdoba massacre of 1473, the Marqués saw a chance to pay
old scores, get rid of Cabrera, and then obtain the rule of
Segovia from the King. All this might be done under cover
of a popular uprising against the *Conversos*. Pacheco, regardless of the Jewish blood that flowed in his own veins, arranged the massacre, sent his troops secretly to Segovia, rode
thither himself.[15]

On Sunday, May 16, the *Conversos* awoke to find Segovia
full of armed men, crying for their blood. Hoofs rang on the
pavements, swords rattled, bullets pelted the walls, while Pacheco's men everywhere carried fire and slaughter into the houses
of the "converted" Jews. The flames greedily lapped over the
hillside, devouring house after house. The corpses lay in great
tangled piles on the streets.

Fortunately news of the plot had somehow reached Cardinal Borgia, the papal legate, at Guadalajara. He sent a warning to the King, who notified Cabrera at the eleventh hour. The Governor had barely time to snatch his sword, rally some of his troops, and dash to the rescue of the *Conversos*. He fought with reckless bravery and great skill. His men, inspired by his valor, swept the streets clear of Pacheco's men, they rode down the Old Christian mob. The Marqués and his hirelings fled from the city.

When Isabel and Fernando arrived at Segovia, there were still foul smelling splotches of blood on the pavements and the walls of houses—the whole place stunk of charred timbers, rotting flesh, carnage, pestilence. Isabel commended Cabrera in the warmest terms, affectionately welcomed his wife Beatriz, passionately denounced those who had been the fanatical tools of Pacheco. On a recent occasion she had already shown, with a spirit reminiscent of her brother Alfonso, that she had no intention of currying popularity by even a tacit approval of the massacres. She had found Valladolid fairly boiling with hatred, the populace ready to fall upon the detested Marranos at the slightest provocation. Some of her partisans, influential cavaliers of the city, began egging on the multitude. Isabel and Fernando fortunately learned of it in time. Putting principle above party advantage, both condemned the nefarious work in unequivocal language; in fact, they stopped a riot that had already begun.[16]

The plain speech of the young Prince and Princess cost them dear, for several of their most valuable adherents in Valladolid went over to the cause of Enrique. From then on the lives of Fernando and Isabel were actually in danger.[17] They fled from the city with Carrillo, stayed for another while at Dueñas, and later proceeded to Segovia.

During the days that followed Isabel and her husband discussed the state of Castile with several of the chief men of Segovia, with Cabrera, with the bishop Don Juan Árias de Ávila, possibly with the humble and abstemious Fray Tomás of Torquemada, prior of the Dominican convent of Santa Cruz. There were counsels of anger and counsels of despair. What could save the land from utter ruin, from an anarchy that might end in a second conquest of the peninsula by the

Mohammedans, applauded by Jews and *Conversos*? What could make the children of Israel stop exploiting the Christians and proselytizing, even as Christians, to destroy Christianity? and what could make the Christians stop massacring the Marranos on every provocation? The answer must have been obvious to the young princes. It was probably then that they formed the solid resolution that if ever they came to the throne of Castile they would subordinate all lesser considerations to the one great essential need of a government strong enough to be feared and respected by all classes. If the royal absolutism, the new cesarism of Spain was not conceived among the cinders and bloodstains of Segovia, it was probably quickened there.

Isabel and Fernando also discussed with their advisers certain projects for the reform of the Spanish Church. Carrillo was setting an example in his diocese. He had issued an edict that forbade dicing and the wearing of gaily colored clothes by clergymen; priests must say Mass at least four times a year, and bishops at least three; and both were adjured not to lead a riotous or military life—"except to take service with kings or princes of the blood." That such an ordinance was needed speaks volumes for the laxity in the Spanish Church, and the crying necessity of further reforms.

A pity it was that Carrillo did not confine his great energies to ecclesiastical matters. His vanity was always betraying him. It was a bitter day for him, in March, 1473, when Mendoza was made Cardinal of Spain, an office that Carrillo felt belonged in justice to him as primate. Pope Sixtus IV evidently thought otherwise, for he had sent the red hat to Mendoza, who received it at Segovia amid acclamations in the presence of the Princess Isabel. Carrillo's sensitive vanity was cut to the quick at the thought that she whom he had served so well could sponsor what he considered a public slight to him. He could think of no word for it but ingratitude. In a great huff of disappointment, he retired to his estates at Alcalá, where he began certain alchemistic researches with one Doctor Alarcon, an astrologer, in the hope of producing gold to pay his debts and restore his fortunes. Under the influence of superstition, the disintegration of his strong character was rapid.

The next year was a fortunate one for Isabel and for Castile. "In 1474, Our Lord sent rain and great fertility and abundance," wrote the curate of los Palacios. Ordinarily the flux of prosperity would have strengthened Villena's position, but death, so often the friend of Isabel, again took a hand in the game; he took the curl out of that perfumed beard and stiffened the long grasping fingers, and laid the owner of so many farms and cities in his elegant tomb at El Parral. An abscess on his cheek finally checkmated the old politician, October 4, at Santa Cruz, while he was besieging another town that Enrique had given him. His last words were: "Has the castle surrendered?"[18]

The King, in his fifty-first year, was left forlorn and in failing health. A new problem arose to vex his harassed soul; who ought to succeed Villena in the mighty office of Grand Master of the Order of Santiago? There were three claimants, Don Alonzo de Cárdenas, the Count of Parades, and Pacheco's son, the young Marqués of Villena. Now it happened that the young Marqués went to Vazalmadrid, three leagues from Madrid, to solicit the vote of the Count of Osorno. That gentleman seized his visitor and threw him into a dungeon. The news made the King ill, for since Pacheco's death he had discovered in himself a sentimental fondness for the younger Marqués. Disregarding the advice of his *fisicos*, who were becoming alarmed over his kidneys and his liver, he proceeded to Madrid, and with Cardinal Mendoza, Count Haro and Carrillo, went to demand of Osorno the release of the Marqués. The Count said that the elder Villena had promised him certain moneys and lands for his vote for the Grand Mastership some years before, but after his election had failed to keep the promise. When the money was paid he would release the Marqués, and not before. Enrique remained twenty days arguing with the Count. Successful at last, he returned to Madrid with his favorite; but the strain had been too much for him and his illness suddenly became acute. The physicians could do no more. Thereupon the Cardinal of Spain and others urged the King to make a will, since he might be at the point of death, to settle forever the question of the succession by stating categorically whether or no Juana, La Beltraneja, was his daughter. The King sighed, but made no answer. At eleven o'clock that night he ordered his secretary to write a short paper naming Cardinal Mendoza and the young Marqués of Villena his executors, and commanding that his daughter do whatever they and certain other great lords might agree upon. According to Castillo, his chaplain and apologist, he confessed his sins "for a long hour" to Fray Pedro Mazuelo, prior of St. Jerome of the Passage of Arms, the monastery that Enrique had built to commemorate Don Beltran's championship of the mysterious high-born lady some fifteen years before. Asked once more whether or no La Beltraneja was his daughter, he sighed, turned away his head, and expired. It was two o'clock in the morning of December 12, 1474.

In his last moments the King had expressed a wish to be buried by the side of his mother Queen María at Santa María de Guadalupe. Castillo adds that "he was so wasted in his flesh that there was no need to embalm him." For the time being his remains were taken to San Jerónimo del Paso. Poor Enrique! He lay in state on the spot where he had watched Don Beltran hurl so many champions to the ground.

Isabel heard the news that very day at Segovia. The people were quiet but uneasy. Fernando was absent, having gone to Roussillon to fight for his father, but Cabrera and Beatriz importuned the Princess to be crowned immediately before the partisans of La Beltraneja could act. Isabel first put on mourning garments and went to the Church of St. Michael, where she had the flags of Castile and of the city lowered and covered with black, heard Mass, and prayed for the repose of her brother's soul. As she returned to the Alcázar, she heard her name shouted in the windy streets. Children were running about screaming the tidings that the courier had brought from Madrid: *"Es muerto Don Enrique! Viva la Princesa! Castilla! Castilla por la Reina Doña Isabel!"*

On that cold twelfth of December it lay with the Christian Jew Cabrera whether she or Juana Beltraneja would be Queen of Castile. Perhaps the deciding factor was the word of his wife, Isabel's girlhood friend of Arévalo. Cabrera remained faithful. The chief men of Segovia were notified that Doña Isabel would be crowned in the public square on the morrow, Saint Lucy's Day.

From her mother's virtue and will power, from the degeneracy of Enrique, from the itching greed of Pacheco, from the stepmotherly hate of Juana of Castile and motherly love of Juana of Aragon, from the anger and loyalty of Carrillo, the integrity of Mendoza and the courage of Cabrera, from pestilence and famine and a thousand years of war, slow time had strangely distilled this moment. The Middle Ages were past. Modern Spain was about to be born.

VII

ISABEL IS CROWNED QUEEN OF CASTILE
—A LITTLE MARITAL DIFFERENCE—
PORTUGAL DECLARES WAR

ISABEL, looking down from the Alcázar on the keen frosty morning of December thirteenth, sees a town crammed full of people from the four gates and the stern walls to the scornful towers rising on perpendicular rocks above the Enseña. All is murmuring, a confused singing, joy, expectancy. The great keep above her is like the prow of a mighty gray ship eager to cut through the wide shadowy sea of grayness that the plain makes, to the harbors of new worlds. Merchants who got up before daylight are finding the best places to hawk their wares. From the four roads through the four gates come troops of men armed cap-a-pie, escorting this or that nobleman, with the flourish of pennons, the deep blatting of sackbuts, the braying of trumpets, the squeaking of flageolets, the rumble of kettledrums, the flare of many brilliant colors, the flash of gold and silver on man and beast; everywhere the stern glitter of burnished steel.

Isabel sits on her white palfrey in the courtyard of the Alcázar waiting for the gate to open. Gems sparkle on her bridle, at her throat, at the arch of her little foot against the cloth of gold with which her mount is caparisoned. She is twenty-three years old, a supple but robust figure clad from head to foot in white brocade and ermine. Her face is flushed a deeper pink than usual, her eyes very blue and very clear.

The massive gate is open at last. Two officers of Segovia in archaic splendor hold her jeweled bridle. Andres de Cabrera, the Alcaide, takes his place beside her. On the other side is the Archbishop Carrillo, with purple and gold vestments over his breastplate of Toledo steel. A few cavaliers in doublet and hose, with jaunty little velvet hats, follow.

Isabel rides slowly into the view of the people. "Viva la

Reina !" A shout like the roaring of waves on rocks comes from thousands of throats and is reëchoed down the crooked windings of the main street. Framed in endless colors, from the shade of filthy rags to the subtlest nuances of porphyry and saffron, are rows of eyes and teeth gleaming from swarthy faces, lean and yellow faces, white faces drawn taut over hungry cheek-bones, faces of cunning and lust and lawlessness, faces peace-loving and holy, faces sensual and fat, faces proud and stern, faces of men and women sick of wars and crimes, faces of children, wondering.

"*Viva la Reina!*" A blast of trumpets. The faces, with much screaming, praying, blessing, cursing, laughing, are pushed back against the cracked walls. A gorgeous procession moves slowly along the narrow, stony street: prelates and priests in chasubles worked in gold thread over purple silk, walking two by two and chanting "*Te Deum Laudamus!*"— nobles in rich velour, glistening with precious stones and gold chains, councilmen of Segovia in ancient heraldic costumes, spearmen, cross-bowmen, men at arms, flag-bearers, musicians, a great rabble following. Isabel, to whom looking like a queen comes natural, takes her place near the head of the procession. All move slowly ahead. "Viva la Reina! Castile for the Queen, Lady Isabel !"

In front of Isabel on a great horse rides a herald, holding point upward the Castilian sword of justice, naked, menacingly bright in the sunlight, symbol that this young woman in white on the white jennet has the power of life and death over all who behold her, and some ten millions besides. Then follow two pages, bearing on a pillow the gold crown of King Fernando the Saint.

Arriving at the plaza, where a high platform has been draped with stuffs of rich colors, Isabel dismounts, slowly ascends the steps, and seats herself on the throne with great deliberation and composure, as though she had been born for that very thing and nothing else. Trumpets . . . silence . . . speeches . . . the great crown of Saint Fernando is placed on the light auburn hair. Shouts of rapture and triumph from all sides. Andres de Cabrera kneels before her and hands her the keys of Segovia and of the Alcázar; the herald cries in a loud voice, "Castile! Castile! Castile for the King Don Fernando and his wife Lady Isabel, Queen Proprietress of this King-

dom!" More shouting. Royal flags and pennons of cities,
hidalgos and military orders snap in the wind. The bells of all
the churches and convents ring out jubilantly. Muskets and
arquebusses are fired from the keep of the Alcázar. Heavy
lombards thunder from the city walls.

Isabel is a queen at last.

Dignitaries, prelates and nobles, advanced to take the oath
of allegiance and kiss the new sovereign's hand. Carrillo knelt,
that great surly warrior-priest, and Gutierre de Cárdenas, and
the capable Alonso de Cárdenas, and the Prince of Youth,
Gonsalvo de Córdoba, and the wiry Admiral Fadrique, and
Count Haro. At the last, wonder of wonders, came the peerless knight-at-arms, Don Beltran de la Cueva, Duke of Albuquerque, to kiss the hand of Isabel. What could this mean,
except that he had reason to know that the Infanta Juana was
not the legitimate daughter of the late King?

But others who should have been there were missing. Where
was the Duke of Arévalo? Where was Don Diego Lopez
Pacheco, Master of the Order of Calatrava? The Count of
Urena? The Marqués of Villena, lord of so many manors and
cities?

When the obeisances were finished, Isabel went down from
the dais and walked to the Cathedral, where she humbly prostrated herself before the high altar, giving thanks to her
Maker for bringing her safely through so many perils to such
great honor, and asking the grace to rule according to His
will, and to use the authority He had given her with justice
and wisdom. This was a formula with some kings. Isabel was
passionately in earnest.

After God, she looked to Fernando for help in her almost
impossible task and after him, to the Cardinal of Spain.
Mendoza was not present, however. He had remained at
Madrid to sing the high mass of requiem over the poor remains of King Enrique. All was done magnificently, as befitted
royal obsequies in a country with a weakness for splendid
funerals; and, since the treasury at Madrid was empty, the
Cardinal paid all the expenses, including the cost of a splendid
tomb as Guadalupe, where the King's body was laid by that
of his mother. It was Mendoza, too, who wrote the epitaph
commencing "Al Muy Alto y Esclarecido Señor Don Enrique," remarkable for the purity and naturalness of its

Castilian in an age of bombastic rhetoric. His duty performed, he rejoined Isabel at Segovia.

Fernando was riding from the north as fast as horses could carry him. The news of Enrique's death and Isabel's coronation had reached him in Perpignan where he had gone early in the autumn to answer a desperate appeal from his father. The aged king, lacking supplies and money, had been on the point of being captured when Fernando arrived with what troops he could shark up on the way.

Fernando then went as governor-general of Aragon to Saragossa, to endeavor to bring some order out of a state of the wildest anarchy. The whole community was being cowed and exploited by Ximenes Gordo, a rich *Converso*, who had taken command of the city troops and imposed his turbulent will on the populace. He had long been in the bad graces of Fernando as a partisan of Charles of Viana. The young Prince, on his arrival, invited Gordo to a private conference, and received him in a small apartment as though he were an intimate friend. The flattered tyrant, imagining he had another Enrique to deal with, did not perceive that he was trapped until the Prince began to enumerate his offenses. It was too late to escape, for there were guards at the door, and in the next room a priest and a hangman, to whose respective ministrations Fernando calmly delivered his guest. The body was exposed in the marketplace that noon.[1]

While Fernando was carrying out the severe policy that he and Isabel had agreed was necessary—though such summary executions were contrary to the laws of Aragon—he learned of the coronation at Segovia through a letter from Carrillo, and it was a grievous blow to his masculine pride. Even more painful was a second letter from Gutierre de Cárdenas describing the revival of the ancient ceremony of carrying the nude sword of justice before the Queen. Fernando cried out:

"Tell me, you who have read so many histories, did you ever hear of carrying the symbol of life and death before queens? I have known it only of kings!"

An autocrat, a soldier, and a true Aragonese, Fernando had assumed that his wife would be glad to leave in his hands the chief burden and responsibility of kingship. It was a shock to discover that she intended to interpret their marriage agreement literally. He was encouraged in his resentment by his

father, the King of Aragon, and by his grandfather, the Admiral of Castile. Even Isabel's friend Carrillo—also the friend
of Fernando's father—wrote that it was not wise to leave too
much power in the hands of a woman.

In Aragon, where the law from time immemorial had excluded women from the succession, such an attitude seemed
perfectly natural and just. In Castile, where no Salic law
existed, it was bound to appear a selfish usurpation, especially
as Fernando had agreed in the marriage treaty, which he
perhaps had considered a mere formality, to respect Isabel's
title. By the time he reached Segovia the whole court was
agog with gossip, controversies, conjectures.

Isabel was deeply wounded when her husband's friends questioned her right to rule alone. It was not her first disappointment in Fernando. A bitter moment it was for her when she
first learned that the Papal dispensation under which she had
married her second cousin had been forged by his father,
with the connivance of Admiral Fadrique and probably with
the knowledge of Fernando. It was a double wound. Isabel's
piety would never have consented to the slightest infraction
of the law of the Church which she believed to be the one
instrument established by Jesus Christ for the salvation of
mankind; and it was her nature to despise any taint of fraud.
But she suffered most as a woman suffers who finds her husband capable of deceiving her at the very outset of their life
together. She knew no peace until an authentic bill of dispensation was obtained from Rome.

There was yet another disillusionment in store for her when
it came to her ears that Fernando had had an illegitimate
child by another woman with whom he had been intimate
just before his marriage. Henceforth she was to know the
cruel torment of a jealousy which her pride could not always
conceal. Yet even in her jealousy there was something individual and queenly. If she happened to notice that Fernando
looked with more than casual interest on some pretty maid of
honor in her court, she overwhelmed the girl with gifts, arranged a good marriage for her, or sent her off to a fine estate
with a handsome pension. Other ladies of the Renaissance
would have found less tactful and generous ways to rid themselves of their rivals. Perhaps there was more than piety in

the custom Pulgar ascribes to her of having about her "old women who were virtuous and of good family."

If the thought of taking revenge on Fernando in kind had ever occurred to her, she would have put it away immediately as a temptation from the devil. The theory that two wrongs could make a right never troubled her lucid mind. But though she was inflexible in her principles, she was learning, perforce, to be tolerant of mortal weakness. Fernando the hero, Fernando the Prince Charming of that happy year of poverty, was dead. She continued in spite of all to love Fernando the man. He was the child of his age. And men in camps had temptations that women were spared. So Isabel may have reasoned, to numb the aching of her heart. "She much loved the king her husband and fulfilled her duties to him immeasurably."[2]

When Fernando arrived at the gate of Saint Martin, all the great nobles and prelates who were in Segovia went forth to greet him as King of Castile—King not by any right of his own, but as the consort of the lawful Queen. Yet the Aragonese faction, if small, was so influential and clamorous that many feared a new division in the state. The danger was averted by the conciliatory efforts of Cardinal Mendoza, representing Isabel, and Carrillo, as attorney for Fernando. But it was the Queen herself whose tact and dignity maneuvered her husband into a position where he could only acquiesce as gracefully as possible. "She was a woman of great heart; she hid her anger, and dissimulated it, and as this was known, all the nobles and others feared to incur her indignation."—Pulgar, who wrote that, had preserved her words on this crucial occasion:

"This subject, Señor, need never have been discussed, because where there is such union as by the grace of God exists between us, there can be no difference. Already, as my husband, you are King of Castile, and your commands have to be obeyed here; and these realms, please God, will remain after our days for your sons and mine. But since it has pleased these cavaliers to open up this discussion, perhaps it is just as well that any doubt they have be clarified, as the law of these our kingdoms provides. This, Señor, I say, because, as you perceive, it has not pleased God thus far to give us any heir but the Princess Doña Isabel our daughter. And it could happen that after our days some one might come who, being descended from the royal house of Castile, might allege that these realms belonged to him even by the collateral line, and not to your daughter the Princess, on account of her being a woman. . . . Hence you see well, Señor, what great embarrassments would ensue for our descendants. And . . . we ought to consider that, God willing, the Princess our daughter has to marry a foreign prince, to whom will belong the government of these realms, and who may desire to place in command of the fortresses and royal patrimony other people of his nation, who will not be Castilians; whence it may follow that the kingdom may pass into the hands of a foreign race. And that would be a great burden on our consciences, and a disservice to God, and a great loss to our successors and subjects. And it is well that this declaration be made now to avoid any misunderstandings in the future."

Fernando evidently could think of no reply. "The King, knowing this to be true, was much pleased," says the chronicler, "and gave orders that nothing further be said on the subject." Thirty years later he was to see how far-sighted she was in her providence for her children and for the country. But never again, with one notable exception, would they have a serious difference of opinion. Henceforth in most public affairs they were to act as one person, both signatures on all documents, both faces on all coins. "Even if necessity parted them, love held their wills in unison. . . . Many persons tried to divide them, but they were resolved not to disagree." Pulgar sees something divine in this unanimity.

There was surely no time now for differences of any sort. To bring order out of anarchy, to restore the prestige of the crown, to reform the clergy and the secular officials, to recover from robber barons the crown lands illegally granted by Enrique, to deflate the currency and restore prosperity to the farms and industries, to cope with the Jewish problem, the Moorish problem, the *Converso* problem—this task seemed impossible for a young woman and a young man with no money and no troops. It would be difficult enough if they could count on peace. They had no such assurance. To the west they had a possible enemy in Alfonso V, the uncle of La Beltraneja, whose vanity still smarted under Isabel's rejections. To the north they had a probable enemy in Louis XI, the most profound and subtle diplomatist in the chaos that was Europe. Saint Jeanne d'Arc had made the French nation possible; he was making it a permanent reality. Could Isabel be the Jeanne d'Arc and Fernando the Louis XI of Spain, where the task was more complicated? Louis thought not. When they sent Pulgar to announce to him the death of Enrique and to request him to return Roussillon and Cerdagne to Aragon, the Spider King went into deep mourning for his royal "brother," but as for the two provinces, he felt obliged to keep them until he was properly reimbursed for his great expenses in aiding Juan of Aragon against the Catalans.

Isabel commenced her reign by sweeping out of sight the worst of the *criados* who had made her brother's court so infamous in ballad and execration. The Moorish guard went straggling south to Granada to seek service with their own. The highwaymen and cutthroats and extortioners found their way to prisons or to gallows or to join the desperate robber barons who sneered at the notion that the young queen's reforms would be more than a brief gesture. They soon had to admit that she was going about the task in a businesslike way. First she appointed able and trustworthy men to the principal offices in the kingdom: Mendoza, the Cardinal of Spain, as Chancellor; Count Haro as Constable of Castile; Fernando's uncle Fadrique as Admiral of Castile; Gutierre de Cárdenas as Treasurer and Bursar. Such leaders, confident of royal backing, immediately began to oust imposters and hang thieves and murderers right and left, until "with the justice that they executed, the men and citizens and laborers and all the people in general who longed for peace were joyful, and gave thanks to God, because they had lived to see a time in which it pleased Him to have mercy on these kingdoms. . . . And the King and Queen, with this justice which they administered, gained the hearts of all in such a manner that the good had love for them and the evil had fear."[3]

All this, however, was in the limited sphere where their authority was accepted. Estremadura, Galicia, Guipúzcoa and Andalusia were battle-grounds of pillage and anarchy. The young Marqués of Villena, from his town of Madrid, cast a cold unappreciative eye on the new administration functioning in Segovia. From his father Juan Pacheco he had inherited the view that royalty was a mere convenience for the enrich-

ment of noblemen. Knowing Isabel's need of money, soldiers
and friends, and confident in the possession of a valuable ace
in the custody of her rival La Beltraneja, now twelve years
old, he decided that the moment was ripe to make certain demands. For himself he asked the Grand Mastership of the
Order of Santiago, and confirmation of the doubtful titles to
the places his father had wheedled from Enrique El Impotente: Alcaráz, Trujillo, Requena, Escalona, Madrid, the Mar-
quisate of Villena and the incomes of all. For his brothers, Don
Pedro Puertocarrero and Don Alonzo Tellez Giron, he asked
similar favors. His two cousins, the Duke of Arévalo and
the Count of Urena made simultaneous demands. The young
Marqués informed the Queen that if she refused, he and his
friends would proclaim Juana sovereign of Castile.

To this political blackmail Isabel and Fernando replied that
there could be no division in the kingdom over Juana, for
it was notorious that she was not the daughter of King
Enrique. To settle the question forever, they would be glad
to have her properly married, and to ask the Pope to dispose
of the Mastership. Juana meanwhile should be placed with
some one agreeable to both parties. Villena, perhaps knowing
that Sixtus IV was friendly to Isabel, replied that he would
keep the Infanta until he received his title. Meanwhile he
began making overtures to Alfonso V, Juana's uncle, with a
view to drawing him into Castile with an army. Isabel, hearing of this development, was much troubled.

It may have been only a coincidence that about the time
Villena made his threat of a new civil war, his great-uncle the
Archbishop of Toledo approached the Queen at Segovia with
a request for certain lands and titles which she and Fernando
had promised him some while before their coronation. Fernando now found himself in a dilemma. The men who held
the offices Carrillo craved had since rendered loyal service to
Juan of Aragon and to Fernando himself in the war with
France. To keep Carrillo his friend, he must make them his
enemies—unless indeed the Archbishop would compromise.

Isabel was willing to go to any length to satisfy the friend
of her perilous childhood. She begged him to accept gifts and
offices at least equivalent to those he demanded. The Archbishop sternly replied that he would take what he had been
promised and nothing else. While Isabel and Fernando were

Juana—"La Beltraneja"
Claimant to the Throne of Castile

casting about for some other way to pay the obligation, he vanished secretly from Segovia, without telling them where he was going. They heard that he was at home in Alcalá de Henares, spending the remains of his fortune on the alchemistic experiments of his friend, Doctor Fernando de Alarcon, and of one Beato, who was gaining much influence over him. Alarcon had rendered services from time to time to the Marqués of Villena. Young Pacheco was suspected of paying him to whet the Archbishop's anger against the King and the Queen.

Isabel's opinion of Carrillo's real motive is probably reflected in the words of her secretary: "Some imputed his discontent to pride, and some to greed, but we believe that it was chiefly envy of the Cardinal of Spain, because of the honor paid him by the King and Queen."

Don Pedro Gonzalez de Mendoza, to give him his full name, was indeed becoming indispensable to Isabel and Fernando as their difficulties multiplied. Son of that distinguished soldier and poet, the Marqués of Santillana, who was the first to translate Dante into Castilian, he was learned, acute, charming, and capable. But it was his character, even more than his talents, that commended him to Isabel and Fernando. He was one of the few men whom they could trust absolutely in any emergency. He was not ascetic, like Fray Tomás of Torquemada; in his youth he had been a man of the world, as an illegitimate son bore witness. But he had none of the turbulent pride or vanity of men like Carrillo. His piety, if not radiant, was a sincere and steady glow; his patriotism rooted in the pride of an honorable old family; his sense of social solidarity and responsibility at once firm and sensitive. In this crisis he gave a new proof of his superiority to Carrillo by riding to Alcalá and pleading with the old Archbishop to lay all rancor aside and support the King and Queen in their policy of giving Castile the peace and stability that all decent men desired. There had been too many civil wars. They led to nothing but anarchy and ruin. It would be tragic, perhaps fatal, to have another. All must make some sacrifice for the public good. And to disarm the Archbishop's envy, the Cardinal offered to efface himself and let Carrillo play the chief rôle in a reform Cortes to be assembled at Segovia in the spring.[4]

Carrillo replied somewhat stiffly that he had always considered Isabel the legitimate heiress,[5] and would gladly see a Cortes assembled. But his tone was too ceremonious to reassure the Cardinal. He returned to Segovia to report to the Queen that he feared something was brewing between Carrillo and Villena and Alfonso V of Portugal.

If Alfonso, enriched by the discovery of gold at Saint George La Mina in 1471, should invade Castile with several thousand men, who could withstand him? Isabel had scarcely 500 troops. Fernando might muster as many more with what doubtful help his father could send him. Meanwhile the strength that ought to be available to repel an invasion was being squandered in a score of miniature wars, guerrillas in the original sense of the word. There was the *Marrano* or *Converso* war in Toledo, the war of nobles in Seville—the war between Christians and *Conversos* in Segovia—every town had one.

There was the three-cornered war for the Grand Mastership of Santiago, which Villena claimed against Alonso de Cárdenas and the Count of Paredes. The Duke of Medina Sidonia, conqueror of Gibraltar, now entered that struggle as a partisan of Villena. He was a strong champion, for during the past three years he had accumulated a considerable army in his constant warfare with the young Marqués of Cádiz in and about Seville.

On the ninth of January of this crucial year of 1475, the Duke rode out of Seville at the head of 2,000 cavalry and 2,000 infantry, to put the quietus on Alonso de Cárdenas, and to seize certain towns belonging to the Order of Santiago, in the jurisdiction of Cárdenas. They went forth gaily, many noble youths in armor singing to the delight of the debonair duke; and at the head of the column marched musicians playing lustily on various instruments—the Duke had even taken along the nine singers from the Cathedral of Seville.[6] Cárdenas was absent from his post, fighting against the Count of Feria, a friend of the Duke, who had seized the town of Jerez, belonging to Santiago, and had barricaded himself in the Church of Saint Bartholomew. There on the eleventh Cárdenas attacked him. They fought from early morning until dusk and the Count fled. The Duke, vowing vengeance on Cárdenas, swooped down, musicians and all, on the rich farms of Santiago, and collected a huge toll of cows, bulls, oxen, horses, which his troops drove before them toward Llerena. It was carnival time in Llerena when the Duke approached. He camped for the night at Guadalcanal, a few miles away, intending to overtake Cárdenas next morning.

Cárdenas was a man of some imagination. Isabel had already written his name in that little book of hers, and his action on this occasion justified her opinion. In the dead of night he made a forced march with his 350 horsemen, galloped into Guadalcanal, where the Duke had not even troubled to post a guard, and fell upon the sleepers with shouts of "Cárdenas!" and the blast of trumpets. As Cárdenas arrived at the Duke's headquarters, says Bernaldez, the Duke departed, scantily clad. The four thousand having fled in panic before the three hundred and fifty, the victors ransacked the camp, taking "all the musical instruments, cows, oxen, mules, horses, silver, garments, and the nine choir singers" of Seville, and in the morning rode back to Llerena with their booty.

All this was the mere rumbling of thunder on the left.

Isabel and Fernando were at Valladolid with Cardinal Mendoza when the storm overtook them in the shape of a letter from Alfonso V. Everyone knew, said he, that his niece Juana was the daughter of King Enrique and the legitimate queen of Castile, and since he was about to marry her, he was entitled to call himself King of Castile and Leon. He had been promised the aid of the Marqués of Villena, the Duke of Arévalo, the Master of Calatrava, the Count of Urena, *the Archbishop of Toledo* and others of the greatest houses in Castile, and he ventured to predict that the Count of Benavente, the Marqués of Cádiz, and Don Alonso de Aguilar, all his relatives, would join him too, and so would Don Beltran, Duke of Albuquerque, when they saw him enter Castile with a great army as King. Fourteen Castilian cities had already pledged their allegiance to him. What could Isabel and Fernando, who had neither money nor troops, attempt in his despite when he invaded Castile? And by the grace of God he would do it.[7]

Though bombastic in phraseology, as were most official communications of the period, the threat was not an empty one. Spies brought word that Alfonso was assembling a huge army. The most notorious criminals and robber barons in

Castile were flocking to his standard; and with them many others who "desired wars and tumults, thinking that new ventures bring new gains."[8] With Mendoza's help, Isabel and Fernando framed a reply to Alfonso. They were amazed at his unjust demands. It was wrong to destroy the peace of two kingdoms. The very Castilians who now supported the claim of Juana had forced Enrique to disown her. . . . They cared nothing for Alfonso or Juana, only their own interest. . . . When Enrique had offered Juana to Alfonso, he had refused, knowing her title was doubtful. But if he insisted upon fighting, they would be waging a just defensive war, and the blame for the necessary loss of life and property would be his.

Neither the sovereigns nor the Cardinal had any illusion that the letter would deter Alfonso. It was really addressed to public opinion; it was propaganda.

The Queen was still unwilling to believe that Carrillo had gone over to her enemies. Vain and quarrelsome he was, but not treacherous; she resolved not to give him up without a struggle. The appeal of her secretary to the Archbishop probably reflects the Queen's thoughts pretty faithfully under its florid rhetoric. There are phrases that recall the frank impetuosity of her own letters.

" 'Cry out and do not cease,' says Isaias, Very Reverend Lord; and we likewise shall not see the people of this realm stop weeping for their woes, and shall not cease to cry out to you, who are said to be their author. . . . Consider, Very Reverend Lord, your venerable days, and the years of your life, consider the thoughts of your soul, and consider that in the time of King Enrique your house was a refuge for angry and discontented cavaliers, who made leagues and plots against the royal sceptre, and encouraged the disobedient and scandalous people of the kingdom; and always have we seen you rejoicing in arms to destroy the tranquillity of the people, with allies very foreign to your profession, enemies of the public peace. . . . Leave off, Señor, being the cause of scandals and of blood. For if God did not permit David, because he was a man of blood, to build the house of prayer, how can your Lordship, having been in such bloody wars as have occurred, mingle with a clean conscience in the duties which your priestly office requires? . . . How can you, a priest, take arms without perverting your habit and religion? How can

you, the father of consolation, take arms without afflicting
and making to weep the poor and the wretched, and giving
joy to tyrants and robbers and men of scandals and of blood,
by the criminal division which you create and encourage? Tell
us, in God's name, Señor, if you in your days intend to make
an end to our miseries? . . . Do not be willing any longer
to tempt God with such inconstancies, do not desire to arouse
his judgments which are terrible and terrifying."

Carrillo took no formal notice of this appeal. A cavalier,
one of his friends, replied for him that he had no intention
of injuring the King and Queen in any way. To this gentleman Pulgar now wrote, evidently aiming over his head at
the Archbishop:

. . . "The Archbishop served the King and Queen so well
in the beginning that if he had persevered in their service,
every one would have said that the beginning, the middle and
the end of their reign belonged to the Archbishop, and all the
glory would be his. . . . But God said, *'Gloriam meam non
dabo'* to the Archbishop. I will permit those Alarcons to say
what is contrary to the King and the Queen, the King of
Portugal to help rid the kingdom of them, and then in spite
of all their will and their power, I will give my glory to this
Queen, who ought to have it by right, that the people may
see that all the archbishops in the world are not sufficient to
remove or place kings on the earth; for I have reserved that
prerogative for my own tribunal."

When the Archbishop's friend again defended him in general terms, the Jewish secretary wrote a scathing reply, now
descending to bitter sarcasm, now rising to the solemn indignation of a Hebrew prophet. He attempts to prove that Isabel
can accomplish even the impossible, with divine aid. To show
how great works can be carried on through peril and difficulty,
he refers to Aeneas, Jupiter, Hercules and Romulus, all of
whom God mysteriously aided, even through the agency of
wild beasts. . . . King Fernando similarly had been preserved
through many wars and plots. Isabel was in her mother's arms
when she fled from peril to peril, fatherless, "and, what is
most keenly felt by royalty, in extreme lack of necessary
things, enduring threats, dwelling in fear and danger." Did
Isabel herself, recalling her childhood in this moment of bitterness, insert the personal reminiscence? . . . Pulgar con-

tinues ironically: "If this lord, your friend, thinks to buy this
kingdom like a bonnet, I don't wish to believe it, even if
Alarcon and el Beato tell me so. I prefer to believe in these
divine mysteries rather than in these human thoughts. Was it
for this that Don Enrique died without heirs, and for this
that Prince Carlos and Don Alfonso died, and for this that
other great obstructors died, for this that God has made all
these causes and mysteries that we have seen—in order that
your friend the Archbishop may dispose of such great realms
in accordance with his peevishness? I don't believe it."

The words may be Pulgar's, but the energy, the passionate
sincerity, and the supreme confidence in God are all so characteristically Isabel's that if it were not for some of the
rhetorical embellishments one could imagine her dictating the
letters. No reply came from Carrillo. Alonso de Palencia, who
tried to persuade him to return to the Queen's service, thought
him a little bit insane. The Archbishop told him Doctor Alarcon had had revelations more marvelous than Saint Paul's.

To King Alfonso Pulgar directed one final appeal; "respectfully" reminding him that his cause was unjust, that he
was the tool of selfish men, "and as for the fine promises they
have made you of the possession of Castile with little work
and much glory, a saying of Saint Anselm occurs to me:
'Very beautiful is the door that invites to danger.'

"The people greatly love the Queen, for they know her to
be the certain daughter of King Juan . . . and no slight
account ought to be taken of this, for *the voice of the people
is the divine voice,* and to oppose the divine is to attempt with
feeble vision to conquer the invincible rays of the sun." The
secretario threatens Alfonso with the certain visitation of
God's justice, and goes so far as to make a prophecy that is
interesting in the light of subsequent events: "Thus, my Lord,
you will spend your life suffering and giving and asking, which
is the business of a subject, rather than reigning and issuing
orders, which is the end you desire, and the one these cavaliers
promise you."

Alfonso ignored both pleadings and threats. The Cardinal
of Spain made one final effort to avert the disaster, by asking
him for several days' truce in which to seek an understanding
"that will be for God's service and safeguard the honor of

both parties." Alfonso replied in courteous terms that the Cardinal's request came too late.

Isabel had either to fight with such effectives as she could muster, or to surrender, and it was not in her nature to admit defeat while she could lift a finger. The common people, she was confident, were on her side, and most of the clergy. If Alfonso only allowed her time enough, she could raise a democratic volunteer army of considerable size. On the task of whetting the popular patriotism through prelates and other friends she now focussed her tremendous energies of soul and will.

It was at this moment that she found herself again pregnant. To another woman it would have been the final straw. Isabel only prayed more fervently, and resolved to do what she could in the time that remained.

Mendoza and others assured her that her only hope was in conciliating the Archbishop of Toledo. It was being said everywhere, "Whoever gets the Archbishop will win." The Queen was advised to go to Alcalá and appeal to Carrillo in person. She called a meeting of her council at Lozaya to consider this unprecedented compromising of the royal dignity. Some said that if Carrillo saw her, his pride would succumb to his generosity and the old affection he bore her. Others said it would be fatal for a Queen to approach a subject as a petitioner; the reaction on public opinion would be deplorable.

Isabel, after a moment of reflection, said:

"Since I have great confidence in God, I have little hope in any service and little fear of any injury that the Archbishop can do the King my lord and me. And if the Archbishop were another and a greater person, I would attach more weight to my going to him. But since he is my subject, and has been familiarly in my service, I wish to go to him, because I think that the sight of me will change his will, and enable him to withdraw from that new enterprise which he thinks of embracing. And merely to satisfy the opinion of the people, who know that he has served the King my lord and me, I wish to make this attempt, that I may not let him do wrong if it is possible to prevent it. Moreover, I do not wish to keep with me the accusing thought that if I *had* gone to him in person, he might have withdrawn from this evil road which he wishes to take."[9]

Though experienced diplomats groaned inwardly, there was nothing more to be said, since the Queen had made up her mind. Without further ado she mounted a horse and took the high road for Toledo with the Duke of Infantado, Count Haro and the Duke of Alba. At Colmenar Viejo she made a halt while the noblemen went on to Alcalá to prepare the Archbishop for her visit.

Carrillo received Count Haro with gloomy courtesy. The Count, at great length, appealed to his pride, his vanity, his generosity, his loyalty. Obviously moved, the old prelate asked to be excused that he might confer with his friends. Haro waited. After an hour the Archbishop returned. His manner was stern, somewhat truculent. Evidently Alarcon, the alchemist, and el Beato, the star-gazer, had done their work in the interim. The Count now informed him that the Queen was near by, and would call upon him at any hour he desired.

Carrillo frowned, and flushed to the roots of his white hair.

"If she comes in one gate of Alcalá," he said, "I will go out the other. I took her from the distaff and gave her a sceptre, and I will send her back to the distaff!"

Haro went back to Colmenar. The Queen was in the church when he sent her word of his return. It was like Isabel, anxious though she was for news, to wait until Mass was over before she received him. He briefly made his report.

The Queen could hardly believe his words. Pale with anger and disappointment, she put her hands to her hair in a tortured gesture, as if to hold her wits together, and closed her eyes. She remained silent until she was mistress of herself. Then looking up, she said, "My Lord Jesus Christ, in your hands I place all my affairs, and I implore your protection and aid"; and, mounting her horse, rode on toward Toledo.[10]

Worse news awaited her there. Alfonso V, with 20,000 men, had crossed the border into Estremadura on the Feast of Corpus Christi, May 25, with a great fanfare of trumpets and kettledrums, and had marched to Plasencia, where his Castilian allies joined him. There the young Marqués of Villena presented to him the Infanta Juana. On a platform hurriedly erected in the public square, the plain, rather pop-eyed girl of thirteen was pronounced the wife of the fat mustachioed king of fifty, her uncle. All present kissed their hands and hailed them King and Queen of Castile and Leon.

Isabel proceeded methodically to interview leaders of public opinion and to raise such troops and supplies as she could. Fernando in the north was engaged in a similar task, riding desperately from place to place—Salamanca, Toro, Zamora— appealing to the people's patriotism against the invader. He found them sluggish, tired of wars, ready to purchase peace at almost any price, as the 40,000,000 well-fed Spaniards of the fifth century had bought it from 30,000 Vandals. The baseborn alcaide of Castro Nuño,[11] whom Bernaldez calls "a menial corrupt fat worm, the powerful scourge of the countryside," to whom seven great cities paid tribute, turned a cold and suspicious eye on the hard young King with the long nose. Moreover, Fernando had been unpopular with many in Castile since the attempt of his friends to rob Isabel of her rights. It was evident that the chief appeal to the country must come from Isabel herself. But there was no time for her to say or dó much. Alfonso had only to continue his march, cut her off, take her prisoner or put her to flight, and he was master of the kingdom.

Isabel, wearing a breastplate of steel over her plain brocade dress, pressed her lips silently together as she mounted her horse and took the road to the north.

VIII

INSTEAD of marching to seize Isabel, Alfonso V proceeded to Arévalo, in the heart of Castile, and camped
there. His reasons were excellent. From the center of the
kingdom he could negotiate with nobles in all parts of the
country; likewise, his presence there would leave Isabel and
Fernando no central place in which to assemble an army.
Thus counseled the wisdom of the wise, but it was a wisdom
that turned out to be folly, since it gave Isabel the one thing
she needed—time.

She pounced upon her advantage with all the energy of an
awaking genius. Tireless, seemingly ubiquitous, she was almost constantly on horseback, going from one end of the
kingdom to the other, making speeches, holding conferences,
sitting up all night dictating letters to her secretaries, holding
court all morning to sentence a few thieves and murderers to
be hanged, riding a hundred miles or two, over cold mountain
passes, to plead with some lukewarm nobleman for five hundred soldiers. She knew and understood the word NECES-
SITY. She did not yet know the meaning of the word
IMPOSSIBLE. All things were possible to God, and God
was on her side. If she suffered from certain physical miseries,
that was only to be expected; the work had to be done, it was
necessary. Wherever she went the common people cheered
her, and their ancient hatred for the Portuguese who had
humiliated their ancestors at Aljubarrota (1385) flamed anew
under the molten fire of her words. She would always conclude each harangue with a passionate prayer:

"Thou, O Lord, who knowest the secrets of the heart, of
me Thou knowest that not by an unjust way, not by cunning

or by tyranny, but believing truly that these realms of the King my father belong to me rightfully, have I endeavored to obtain them, that what the kings my forebears won with so much bloodshed may not fall into the hands of an alien race. Lord, in whose hands lies the sway of kingdoms, I humbly beseech Thee to hear the prayer of Thy servant, and show forth the truth, and manifest Thy will with Thy marvellous works: so that if my cause is not just, I may not be allowed to sin through ignorance, and if it is just, Thou give me wisdom and courage to sustain it with the aid of Thine arm, that through Thy grace we may have peace in these kingdoms, which till now have endured so many evils and destructions."[1]

Moved to tears by her exhortations, the people believed her words, because it was obvious that she herself believed them with the irresistible sincerity of a child. Thanks to her skill as a propagandist and Alfonso's inertia, the end of June saw a considerable mobilization of hidalgos and the proletariat at several points. Isabel herself took command of several thousand men at Toledo, rode among them in armor, like Jeanne d'Arc; gave commands, organized, exhorted.

It was little better than a rabble, some on horses, some on mules, more on foot; but it was a rabble animated by a religious confidence in the powers of the young Queen. At their head she marched to Valladolid, to make a junction with the troops Fernando was bringing from the mountains of the north, from Old Castile, Biscaya, Guipúzcoa and the Asturias by the sea. None came from Andalusia, because of the distance and the civil wars there. None came from Murcia, for Isabel thought it more practical to have her adherents there make war on the estates of the Marqués of Villena, to keep him from helping Alfonso. But a host of 42,000 men seemed to have sprung up by some miracle at Valladolid.

They were indifferently equipped and badly disciplined. Of the twelve thousand cavalry, only 4,000 were properly armored and caparisoned. The rest rode *a la jineta*, Moorish fashion. The 30,000 infantry included yokels from farms, runaway apprentices, even jailbirds released wholesale by Fernando on condition that they fight. There was no time to be meticulous. While Isabel struggled with the commissariat, Fernando quickly whipped the recruits into thirty-five battalions. Leaving Valladolid in July, he struck southwest to the River Douro.

Isabel, making her headquarters at Tordésillas, where she could watch developments and maintain Fernando's line of communications, suffered a painful reaction from her gigantic labors as soon as the tension relaxed. The result was a miscarriage.

Alfonso, having shilly-shallied for two months at Arévalo waiting for reinforcements, had finally marched to Toro and Zamora, both of which opened their gates to him. These two powerful places on the Douro commanded the gateway from Portugal into the most populous part of Castile. Their loss was a sore blow to Fernando, and to make matters worse, he learned that Louis XI, recognizing Alfonso as King of Castile, had sent an invading army into Guipúzcoa. His only hope of success against such great odds was to strike a sharp decisive blow at Alfonso and then march north against the French. Rapidly, therefore, he followed the Portuguese along the river to Toro. In his enthusiasm he rejected the opinion of veteran cavaliers that Toro, protected in the rear by the river and flanked by bristling forts, could be taken only after a long siege. Investing the town, he sent his cartel to Alfonso, daring him to bring out his army and fight, or better still, to settle the issue by personal combat and thus avoid the shedding of innocent blood. Alfonso replied that he would gladly fight Fernando if he were sure of the security of his person, and suggested that Queen Isabel and Queen Juana be exchanged as hostages. If cavaliers on both sides smiled at the thought of the fat Alfonso meeting the lean and able-bodied Fernando in the lists, the Portuguese may have found a subtle revenge in linking the name of Isabel with that of the poor child whom every one in Castile had been calling a bastard these thirteen years. Fernando retorted that it was futile to speak of exchanging the queens, "because of the inequality existing between them, an inequality notorious to all the world." He offered the Princess Isabel or any other hostage.

Alfonso replied that he would accept only Queen Isabel, for if he won the duel and she remained free, the war would continue—a singular tribute from an enemy to Isabel's genius. There the parleys ended.

Fernando had besieged Toro only three days when he discovered, to his consternation, that his communications had
been cut by the Alcaide of Castro Nuño, who had gone over
to the Portuguese. Within twenty-four hours bread jumped
in price from two to ten maravedis a loaf, and Fernando's
forty-two thousand men were threatened with starvation or
surrender. A hasty council of war was held in a church. So
noisy and irate was the discussion, for the younger cavaliers
declared for attacking Toro at once, that it was bruited through
the camp that they were trying to seize the King. The rabble
crowded about the church doors crying "Give us our King!
Give us our King!" until Fernando showed himself, saying,
"Here I am, brothers! You need not fear treason. These are
all my loyal vassals."

Fernando sided with his younger officers, for he counted on
the spoils of Toro and Zamora to pay his men. But with all his
impetuosity, there was in him a streak of caution that made
him see what was obvious to the older captains, that if he tried
to storm Toro without heavy artillery he would fail, and must
then withdraw under less favorable circumstances. He ordered
a retreat.

The soldiers grumbled at first and, as they went, broke
their ranks and fell to pillaging the countryside. If Alfonso
had pursued immediately, he could have cut them to pieces.
As it was, only a remnant of the great host straggled back to
Medina del Campo at the heels of a silent and crestfallen
Fernando. July was not yet past, and Isabel's labor had gone
for nothing. A final drop of wormwood in her cup was the
news that Carrillo had joined Alfonso with 500 lances, probably 2,000 men.

The convalescent Queen wasted no time in recriminations.
Fernando had had his lesson and would profit by it. Her duty
was to persuade the country to give her a second and a better
army. Nothing stimulated her like a task that others called
impossible. The word "fate" like the word "impossible" was
hardly in her vocabulary. Failure to her meant rather God's
chastisement of human stupidity and inefficiency. They were
justly punished for their impatience, their rash presumption,
their sins and the sins of their fathers. God had tried them,
to see how they would remain faithful in misfortune, but he
would never forsake them, for they trusted in His mercy;

He would surely give them the victory if they but persevered. Let them avoid their past mistakes and walk humbly before Him—God was reasonable; and was anything difficult for Him? Thus the Queen consoled Fernando.

At her summons, the three estates met in Cortes at Medina del Campo to shake their heads gloomily over various proposals to raise money for the payment of soldiers and the purchase of artillery. To Isabel's courage and will they paid almost the tribute of idolatry; but idolatry could not be turned into maravedis. It was the Cardinal of Spain who suggested a practical solution. The Church, like the State, said he, lacked funds; but all the churches possessed treasures of silver plate accumulated as gifts and heirlooms throughout many centuries. The clergy wanted peace. If any one could restore it to the land, the Queen could. Let them lend her half the silver treasures of the Church, to melt into money.

The clergy voted unanimously to make the loan for three years, with no security but the Queen's personal word. Into the receptacles placed in all the churches poured priceless relics, some of them a thousand years old. At the thought of melting them down in that great patriotic holocaust, the Queen suffered acutely, and might have drawn back if the Cardinal had not overcome her scruples. What were souvenirs and baubles compared to peace? A sum of 30,000,000 maravedis, possibly half a million dollars in our money, was realized. The debt lay heavy on Isabel's conscience until it was liquidated. She commanded the fathers of the monasteries of San Jerónimo to make sure that all churches were repaid at the end of three years.

The help of the Church marked the turning point in Isabel's fortunes. Troops were paid; new recruits enlisted, confiding in the Queen's promises; gunpowder and heavy lombards were brought from Italy and Germany; merchants eager to give the Queen credit brought in food and clothing, and the great camp near Valladolid sang with the clangor of smiths and armorers, the tramp of drill squads, the neighing of horses, the creaking and roaring of artillery, the putter of arquebus and *espingarda* practice. By December 1, less than five months after the retreat from Toro, the new army was ready for the field. Fernando had not over 15,000 men, but they were

disciplined and well armed. Once more he marched toward
Toro.

Alfonso had been delayed by troubles he had not anticipated. Villena had had to withdraw from the Portuguese army
all his forces to meet an attack by the Count of Paredes, one
of Isabel's captains. Even the town of Villena rebelled against
him, declaring for the Queen. From the border of Estremadura, Alonso de Cárdenas, he who had defeated the Duke of
Medina Sidonia, invaded Portugal with fire and sword, taking
with him as lieutenant the Prince of Youth, Gonsalvo de
Córdoba; and from Portugal came frantic appeals to Alfonso
to return and protect his own kingdom, even while he was
urging his son Dom João, to bring him reinforcements. On
the whole Alfonso was bitterly disappointed in his Castilian
allies. Many were like Don Beltran who, after waiting a long
while to see which way the die would fall, suddenly appeared, like a bird of brilliant plumage, in Fernando's camp.

Mendoza took advantage of Alfonso's disillusionment to
send him a secret message suggesting peace. The fat king
offered to retire on condition that he keep Toro and Zamora,
besides the kingdom of Galicia and a sum of money. Isabel
was willing to buy him off, but declared she would never
consent to giving away a single battlement of her father's
kingdom.

At this juncture, the people of Burgos appealed to Isabel
for help against the tyranny of their alcaide, who had gone
over to the enemy. It was an important place. Fernando sent
there his bastard brother the Duke of Villahermosa and Count
Haro with as many troops as he could spare, and later, when
the situation became critical, went himself, at the Queen's
instance, and besieged the enemy in the Church of Santa Maria
la Blanca. Isabel sent him some of her artillery for the purpose. Portuguese reinforcements compelled him to withdraw,
but he returned with more troops, and instituted a long siege.
Isabel, anticipating that Alfonso, then at Peñafiel, would attempt to relieve Burgos or to cut off Fernando, went from
Tordésillas in person to post careful guards on all the roads
to the north. She galloped to Toledo, 130 miles south, to bring
back new levies from that place. She made a wide and rapid
swing to Leon, more than 200 miles to the north, to rescue
the province from a treacherous governor, whom she faced

down with her usual aplomb. She kept in touch with Fernando, with half a dozen armies, with nobles and clergy in all parts of the kingdom, and through them with the public opinion to whose impulses she was so sensitive.

To keep Alfonso occupied while Fernando was at Burgos, she sent the Count of Benavente to make a raid on the Portuguese, with instructions not to hold Peñafiel if he took it, for the defenses were weak, but to withdraw at once and attack elsewhere. Flushed with a few small successes, the Count forgot his instructions and was defeated and captured one night by King Alfonso.

Leaving Toro in the hands of the robber baron, Juan de Ulloa, Alfonso then led his army twenty miles down the Douro to Zamora. Isabel from Tordésillas followed every move he made. It was clearly Zamora that she must strike, and she intended to strike as soon as Fernando could leave the siege of Burgos in other hands. Advices from him said that his sappers were mining the walls.

At this critical moment the Queen received startling information from Zamora, information that made her pore over her map all night, her greenish-blue eyes afire with the anticipated triumph of military genius when it detects a vital flaw in an enemy's defenses. There on the map in the light of the flickering candle lay the River Douro like a great eel making a winding trail across Old Castile, Leon and Portugal, to be swallowed at last in the Atlantic. Here was Toro, and here, westward, was Zamora, on a high place, inaccessible except by a powerfully fortified bridge, commanded by a skilled leader, Francisco de Valdez. And Valdez had just sent the Queen a secret messenger to say that he was willing to deliver the fort commanding the bridge if she would send troops by night to take it.

Fernando was the only man whose courage and resourcefulness she dared trust in so secret and important an operation. But realizing that his absence from Burgos might be fatal to the morale of his troops there, she wrote him in code that he must pretend illness and then slip away unnoticed. Besides the Queen, no one knew of the plot but the Cardinal, and a monk who acted as intermediary. The King trusted no one but his brother, the Admiral and Count Haro. These three, quietly taking charge of operations, let it be known next day that he was confined to his quarters by a slight illness. But during the night, Fernando, leaving his quarters alone, had gone to a place outside Burgos where his secretary had horses waiting, and by riding all night through a bleak country where more than one enemy would have been glad to capture him, he arrived just before dawn at Valladolid. Isabel, having galloped there to meet him, hid him during the day in her bedroom. She had a small picked force of cavalry assemble under tried leaders who had no idea where they were going. As soon as it was dark, Fernando placed himself at their head.

The King had ridden sixty miles the night before from Burgos to Valladolid; it was another hard ride of fifty to Zamora, and the road passed under the very walls of Toro, which the enemy held. At Tordésillas, a third of the distance, the Queen had fresh horses ready. They bolted past Toro without being challenged.

Zamora was twenty miles farther on. Just beyond Toro a courier from Valdez met them. He begged them in God's name to hurry, for Alfonso suspected something. On the evening before he had ordered Valdez to let certain troops pass the bridge, evidently with secret instructions to seize the fort and Valdez. The governor replied that it was too late; they must wait until morning. If Fernando failed him, he was lost.

Fernando arrived in time. Having taken possession of the fort commanding the bridge, he had only to hold it until Isabel brought up reinforcements and artillery. A few big guns on that bridge would command the Alcázar of Zamora, though not the town itself.

Isabel had the guns on the road before dawn. It would take two or three days to bring them up.

Alfonso almost had a stroke when he saw the Castilian flag over the bridge. He would have ordered an immediate attack with all his power if Carrillo had not dissuaded him, pointing out that the approach to the bridge from the town was too narrow for more than two men to pass by at a time. Besides, he said, Fernando would never have put himself in such a hazardous position without the expectation of heavy reinforcements during the day. Isabel's bluff had succeeded.

During the next night Alfonso abandoned his untenable position in the Alcázar, and withdrew a league into the open country, leaving a strong force in the town. Fernando occupied the castle.

Like a chess-player directing a dozen games simultaneously, Isabel sat in her armor at Tordésillas planning her next move. Her instinct told her that Fernando's moment was at hand. She feared that the memory of his previous debacle might make him err this time on the side of caution. To add to her anxiety, disquieting intelligence reached her from the north. Louis XI, as Alfonso's ally, had sent into Guipúzcoa 40,000 men, who were making straight for the strategic point of Fuenterrabía, that city where Isabel as a child of twelve had seen the meeting of three kings. The town is powerfully situated at the mouth of the Alduida. At high tide the sea nearly surrounds it, covering half the thick lofty walls. The people of the town appealed to Isabel for help against the invaders. She commanded two of her nobles in Guipúzcoa to hasten there with what troops they had and sent Juan de Gamboa, a cavalier she trusted, to assume command of the town and hold it. Gamboa arrived barely in time to organize a defense. For the next three months he held out desperately against enormous odds.

From Fernando came word that Alfonso had challenged him to leave the fortress of Zamora and fight. With the reinforcements Isabel had sent her husband, the Castilian army was somewhat larger than the Portuguese. Six months before, Fernando would have rushed forth to join battle. Now he was resolved to wait for the most favorable moment. At a counsel of war, the veteran Conde de Alva de Liste had said to him, "It is always a mistake to do what the enemy wants you to do. Alfonso wants you to fight. Refuse." Fernando had accepted his counsel; yet he wanted Isabel's opinion, for he considered her intuitions more valid than his own.

Her heart said that the moment to fight had come, but her reason told her it was impossible to make a sensible decision without being on the ground, and her place in the present crisis was at headquarters. She sent the Cardinal of Spain, in whose judgment she had unlimited confidence, to advise the King what to do. Mendoza saw the whole picture at a glance. The peasants were manifesting signs of war-weariness. Inaction was wearing down the morale of Fernando's army. The men were clamoring for money again, and desertions were becoming numerous. The Cardinal helped to meet the financial difficulty by giving the King all his family plate, even the renowned table-silver that had belonged to his father the Marqués of Santillana, to melt into money. And his opinion was that the Castilians should give battle at once.

Leaving a garrison on the bridge and in the Alcázar, Fernando took his army into the plain and drew up in battle array, to wait for Alfonso. Four hours passed. The Portuguese did not appear; the Castilians returned that night to Zamora.

The next day Alfonso was reinforced by his fiery son, Dom João, with 20,000 troops. The shoe was now on the other foot. Looking out one morning from his fort on the bridge, Fernando saw himself besieged by a greatly superior force. It was too late to fight. He remained cooped up for the next fortnight, chafing under the taunts of the Portuguese.

Isabel, at Tordésillas, slept less than ever, and prayed more. She forgot to eat and grew thin. She thought of everything but herself. In her officers and men her almost superhuman powers inspired a fanatical devotion. They considered her a saint.[2] Like Saint Jeanne d'Arc, she insisted upon clean living and clean speech; there were no blasphemies or obscenities in any camp where she was; and rough soldiers knelt daily at prayer in the field, while Mass was being said, and took it as a matter of course because the Queen requested it.

She saw plainly the A, B, C, of all military success: attack, attack, attack. If Alfonso's force outnumbered hers, it must be divided. She sent a force to attack Toro. She hurled others against Castro Nuño and Siete Iglesias, on the right flank of the invaders. Alfonso was obliged to send help to all these places. And then Isabel had an inspiration. Fuentesauco, almost at the enemy's rear, had poor defenses and a small garrison, and yet it directly commanded his line of communications. She gave the word, and the Count of Trevino, with 2,000 cavalry, swooped down on the place and seized it.

His communications broken and his forces divided, Alfonso found the tables turned on him again. His army was suffering from the bitterly cold nights. A scarcity of food threatened him. Unwilling to make an open bid for peace to an inferior force, he secretly offered to cross the Douro with only two companions if Fernando would meet him privately by the

river bank. Fernando was willing. While he waited on the
edge of the stream, he saw a boat put forth from the opposite
bank. Under the weight of the fat Alfonso, it sprang a leak,
half filled with water, and was rowed heavily back to land.
Another rendezvous was arranged for one hour after midnight. At one o'clock by the clock of Zamora, Fernando went
to the river. He waited an hour, decided that Alfonso had
changed his mind, and returned to his camp. Alfonso, crossing an hour later, found no one. The clock of Zamora struck
three. It was two hours fast. No third interview was arranged.
Pulgar saw in all this the hand of Providence, saving Isabel
from the payment of the indemnity that Fernando probably
would have promised Alfonso to rid the land of him.

His supplies running low, the Portuguese was now reduced
to sending an official embassy to Fernando, suggesting a fif-
teen-day truce. Fernando called a council of war. Most of his
officers advised accepting the truce; for if Alfonso was in
difficulty now, his plight would be even worse in two weeks.
The Cardinal of Spain arose. His words had great weight,
because all felt them to be in a sense the words of Queen
Isabel:

"My lord, for the reconciliation and peace of the human
race God our Redeemer suffered many injuries; and you, for
the peace of your realms, ought to suffer the injury which it
appears the King of Portugal has done you in establishing
his camp where he has. But that you suffer by a truce of
fifteen days does not appear to me to be to your advantage
nor to that of the Queen my lady, nor to the honor of your
royal crown. He wants a truce to take his camp away and
set it up again where he pleases, and all for his safety, without hindrance from anybody. . . . In this matter, Señor, I
will speak not as a son of religion and the cloth which I have
received, but as the son of the Marqués of Santillana, my
father, who by his own great practise in arms and that of his
ancestors was well versed in this military science. No cavalier
should tolerate, and especially a king so powerful as you, that
another king, a foreigner, should enter his realms and take
up a position where he wishes, and abandon it with impunity
when he finds it convenient to do so, unless necessity con-
strains. . . . The Queen by words and deeds, and by supply-
ing your host with troops and supplies, has shown her great

determination. . . . If this were permitted, all her efforts would be in vain. Here they are, in a foreign country, running short of supplies. Surely, God has given you this advantage. . . . If we delay further, we shall be subject to the vicissitudes of fortune. And thus in a little while you and the Queen will retain but slight power to give, and even less to utilize, the justice which is your office; whence it must follow that these realms will be reduced again into a dissolution of tyrannies, to the disservice of God."[3]

Fernando felt that this was substantially what Isabel would have said, had she been there. He sent Alfonso a refusal, appending a reproof from Cardinal Mendoza for the destruction of the beautiful monastery of Saint Francis.

The next day, March 1, 1476, was Friday, always a fortunate and conspicuous one in Spanish history. At the first streak of dawn Fernando's guards on the bridge brought him word that the enemy had broken camp and vanished. A reconnoitring party reported that the Portuguese, sending their baggage ahead during the night, and breaking camp just before dawn, were proceeding rapidly eastward along the southern bank of the Douro, undoubtedly making for Toro. Fernando joyfully gave the order for the pursuit. Trumpets blared, arms were seized, the ranks were formed. At last!

Crossing the river was slow work. The narrow bridge had been further restricted by bulwarks hastily thrown up by the Castilians. So eager were the *peones* to fight that many of them swarmed across in boats, or on the dam, or by swimming. Fernando detailed 200 knights to whip them into order on the opposite side. The cavalry crossed by the bridge, two by two. It took more time to form a battle array on the south bank. The morning was well spent when the army, in three sections, followed the tracks of the invaders along the river. The air was cold and damp. Light clouds obscured the sun from time to time, shadowing the gray landscape.

By the middle of the afternoon they came to a small hill, half-way between Zamora and Toro. Beyond that hill, lying between the river and a mountain ridge, was a flat place, known as the Field of Pelayo Gonzalez; and beyond the field was a narrow pass where the mountains jutted down against the Douro. If the Portuguese intended to give battle, that field would be the place they would choose. But if they had already

gone through the narrow defile, they would be safe in Toro
before the Castilians could pass through. Fernando hastily
called his captains together. Several nobles advised returning
to Zamora. It was too late to begin a battle, and the horizon
looked rainy. Cardinal Mendoza volunteered to go alone over
the hill and reconnoitre.

"If they are retreating in disorder we can pursue them," he
said. "If they are ready for battle, we may still retreat if we
wish, without their seeing us." The young King nodded. The
Cardinal, a linen rochet over his chain armor and a visor pro-
jecting over his black eyes, spurred ahead, followed by a single
orderly, and disappeared over and through the *portillo*. In
a moment he returned, his face set, his eyes agleam from what
he had beheld. Something bred in his blood during a thousand years of war had silenced in him the voice of the statesman and the voice of the priest.

"Señor," he said quietly, "the King of Portugal is not proceeding in flight, as they said, but has his regiments drawn up
in battle formation; and if you now order your troops to
retreat, and do not attack, he will wrest from you this day
all the honor which you think to take from him, since you
have not put him to flight. Hence it seems to me that you
ought to command all your people to advance and form a
battle front, if the King of Portugal waits for you, and trust
God, in whose hands are all victories, to give you today the
triumph you hope for."[4]

The captains were silent, waiting for the King to speak.

"Forward!" said Fernando. The captains galloped back to
their posts, and gave the word.

Slowly the Castilian host went over the rising ground and
defiled into the plain. The sun, far down the western sky,
was at their backs, shining murkily from under a heavy curtain of gray clouds. The dismal light smote the Portuguese full
in the eyes. It played over their bluish armor and their multicolored pennons and the cloth of. gold on their caparisoned
horses. It glittered in little points on the tips of lances held
aloft and ready to be couched, and on many it glimmered
dully from the tails of foxes, hoisted by the cavaliers for luck.
While the Spanish came over the hill and descended into the
shadowy flats, the Portuguese re-formed and closed their ranks
and waited.

A cloud swallowed the sluggish sun. Now both armies were in shadow, the Portuguese standing grim and silent, the Castilians swarming and seething from columns of four into long battle lines, a rhythmical confusion subsiding into order.

Fernando commanded the center, opposite Alfonso. On his left, by the river, Cardinal Mendoza and the Duke of Alba opposed Carrillo and the Count of Faro. On the Castilian right, six squadrons of horse under six captains faced the powerful wing of Prince Dom João, who had with him the Portuguese artillery and a squadron of cavaliers under the fighting Bishop of Évora. On each side the infantry were massed behind the wing of cavalry that impinged on the river bank. Gunpowder had only begun to do away with the warfare of chivalry. The *peones* were still considered largely an auxiliary arm, to dispatch or capture fallen knights, to run among horses and hamstring them and, increasingly, to fire crossbows, *espingardas* or Moorish muskets, and arquebusses.

While the Castilians were forming, Alfonso was making a speech to his army: they were at least as numerous as the enemy; let them fight bravely and victory was certain. The trumpets sounded. On both sides the cavalry spurred their horses, lowered their spears, galloped to the shock. A fine cold drizzly rain began to fall.

A long splintering crash as the hosts came together and were interlocked . . . the splitting of lances, the rattle of armor, the thumping of horses; riders catapulted to the ground to lie still or rise and draw swords, footmen running out among them with daggers and axes . . . the melée grimly settled down to a business-like hacking and thrusting with swords. "Fernando!" cried the Castilians. "Alfonso!" shouted the Portuguese. Where the standards of the rival kings fluttered back and forth on the waves of steel, there was the fiercest fighting and shouting and letting of blood and piling up of slain. On the left the Cardinal of Spain, his bishop's rochet torn and spattered with blood that looked almost black in that leaden dusk, fought with the fury of a tiger, laying men flat to right and left of him as he pressed forward through the ranks of Portuguese. On the right, Dom João's artillery thundered; the echoes rumbled from the river to the crags, followed by the brisk rattle of his musketry. At this the six squadrons of Fernando's Galician and Asturian cavalry broke and fled, pursued by the yelling Portuguese.

Entangled with their foes, neither Fernando nor the Cardinal could go to the help of their right wing; and, to make matters worse, Dom João doubled back after a brief pursuit of the scared mountaineers, and fell upon their flank. The fighting was desperate, to the death. Back and forth, up and down they swayed in the cold crepuscular rain, while the shouts became hoarser and the moanings of the wounded more frequent under foot, and the darkness came swiftly down from the slaty sky, and still neither side had the victory. Thus for three hours the fortune of the battle hung in the balance. They fought silently now, panting for breath.

Mendoza had hacked his way through the Portuguese right to where he could barely see in the thick gloom the standard of King Alfonso, rising and falling. Alfonso's ensign, Duarte de Almeida, was making an heroic struggle to keep it flying. Wounded in the right arm, he held the flag in his left. A Castilian arrow transfixed his left arm. He held the staff between his teeth until he fell, pierced through the body, while the Cardinal of Spain seized the Portuguese flag and bore it off. The fat Alfonso, puffing valiantly, gave ground. Their flag down, their king beaten back, a great hesitation like some slow fog began to drift over the mass of the tired Portuguese, who had eaten nothing since they left Zamora at daybreak. They gave way here, they drew in there. It was now quite dark.

Suddenly, with a mighty shout, the six battalions of mountain horse who had fled from Dom João's guns at the outset but had slowly reassembled in shame on the hillside, fell upon the disordered Portuguese. The whole line began to retreat. At the same time the Cardinal of Spain and the Duke of Alba drove them from the flank toward the river. In vain Alfonso and Dom João shouted their battle-cries. In vain the stouthearted Carrillo, blood from head to foot, the red cloak torn from his back, stormed and pleaded with them while he smote about him like some Homeric hero in the opaque night.

The flight became a panic. "Santiago!" cried the victors. "Castile! Castile for King Fernando and Queen Isabel!" The miserable Portuguese slew each other by mistake, they ran up the hills, they leaped into the swift river and were sucked under the cold waters by the weight of their armor. Bands of them rushed wildly about seeking their king and crying "Fernando! Fernando!" to avoid slaughter.

The carnage continued through half the night. Prince João and the remnants of his cavalry, after a skillful retreat, gained the heights above the river, where they wandered all night in the pouring rain and howling wind, shouting and lighting fires to guide their King in case he had escaped. Where was Alfonso? Nowhere among the rocks and wet defiles could the Portuguese find him. Nowhere on the battlefield could Fernando come upon a trace of him, though he remained there searching until morning. Nowhere among the twelve hundred corpses lying in the cold mud was the fat carcass of the gallant Alfonso.

Fernando ordered his troops to cease slaying the vanquished and make prisoners of them. Some two thousand were taken. Besides the royal standard, eight other illustrious banners were among the spoils. The dawn showed how utterly the invading host had been shattered. Characteristically laconic and roughly affectionate was the account of his triumph that Fernando sent to Isabel at Tordésillas. "Had it not been for the young chick," he added, "I would have caught the old cock."

That morning he had food and clothing given to the stragglers who came in to surrender. Most of the survivors, however, had fled to Toro, pursued to the very gates by Castilian cavaliers. Zamora was apprised of the disaster by the corpses that the swift Douro carried past the bridge next day.[5]

When the Archbishop of Toledo and other Castilian lords arrived at Toro, the Portuguese on the walls accused them of treachery to Alfonso, and refused to admit them until Prince João appeared and ordered the gates opened. It was a gloomy Carrillo who followed the Prince within the castle.

For some weeks to come there were thousands of survivors straggling about Castile, preying on the farms and towns, or slowly beating their way back to Portugal. It was suggested in Fernando's council that all of them be put to the sword. After the Portuguese defeated Fernando's grandfather at Aljubarrota, they had slain the vanquished to the last man. And now they had come bloated with pride into Castile, to loot the countryside and violate women, what could be more just than to give them a dose of their own medicine?

Fernando listened, pondering. The Cardinal of Spain gave his opinion:

"To kill one who surrenders is more like shameful vengeance than glorious victory. If you, cavaliers, should kill them in battle, it would be the deed of soldiers, but if they surrendered to you and then you slew them, it would be esteemed cruelty and would be offensive to the traditions of Castilian nobility. . . . Indeed, the idea is foreign to all virtue. . . . These Portuguese who are returning to Portugal are common people who came under the constraint or at the call of their king; and if they have committed acts of rapine in this kingdom, we should have committed the same in theirs if the King had taken us there. But Gonzalez de Mendoza, my grandfather, Lord of Alava, fought in that battle of Aljubarrota that you speak of, and having saved King Juan from death, returned to the conflict and was killed fighting, and so ended all my relatives there, and many others of the chief men of Castile. And it is no new thing, that with the pride of victory those cruelties you mention were done, for it is difficult to restrain the sword in the hour of wrath. But it would be an inhuman thing if ten days after the battle there persisted the rage to kill those who come asking pity. Never, please God, may such a thing be said, or such an example of us remain in the memory of living men. Let us strive to conquer and not think of vengeance, for to conquer is for strong men, and to avenge is for weak women."[6]

The chivalry in Fernando's nature assented to the Cardinal's wisdom. He released all prisoners and commanded that no one should prevent the return of the fugitives to their own nation.

Isabel, who had spent that Friday praying to Saint John the Evangelist for victory, was radiant with joy over her husband's success. It seems not to have occurred to her to claim a share in the credit. God had given the glory to Fernando. At a more fitting time she intended to arrange a public triumph for him and to build a fitting memorial to his valor. For the present she ordered all the clergy of Tordésillas to assemble and march through the streets, singing the *Te Deum*. The young Queen, thin and pale, but her eyes shining with happiness, came out of the palace barefoot, and thus she walked

over the rough stones of the streets to the monastery of Saint
Paul, where she went on silent white feet through the murmuring crowd to the high altar, and prostrated herself with
great devotion and humility, giving thanks to the God of
Battles.

IX

STANDING sadly in the midst of the wreckage of her
kingly inheritance, Isabel wondered how much of it
could be salvaged. Industries crippled, money almost
worthless, a hundred towns defying her authority under alcaides who ruled as petty kings, the people dying of famine
and pestilence, rogues everywhere preying on the miserable
peasants, a church in need of reform and a paralyzed government—such was the legacy of the Kings of Castile on that
spring morning in 1476. But the victory of Toro had saved
it from utter ruin, and the comparative peace that followed
gave the Queen an opportunity to plan the reconstruction of
her kingdoms. She found cause for hope, too, in the submission of various rebel barons.

Carrillo had ridden by circuitous ways to Alcalá. There
he barricaded himself, and there that other arch-rebel, the
Marqués of Villena, presently joined him. After a wait of
some months to see which way the tide was turning, the two
decided to sue for pardon. They persuaded Fernando's father,
with whom the Archbishop had continued to correspond
throughout the Portuguese war, to intercede for them. A letter
from the King of Aragon naturally carried much weight with
Fernando and Isabel.

About the same time there came a Franciscan monk with a
long message from the Archbishop, begging their Highnesses
remember his services in times gone by, and to forget his
later mistakes, "for so much the greater does the grandeur
and magnanimity of Kings show itself, the more grave the
error which they forgive those who come to beg their pardon."
After a great show of reluctance, but secretly pleased, Isabel

and Fernando forgave the two insurgents, upon Villena's delivering to them the keys of Madrid. The Archbishop had
some difficulty explaining to the Pope his various changes of
opinion. In one letter to Rome he admitted gravely that he had
made a serious error in judgment in thinking that Alfonso V
and Juana were the rightful heirs to the kingdom!

Isabel reaped other advantages from her husband's victory
at Toro. The Marshal Alfonso de Valencia, commanding the
fortress at Zamora, sued for peace through his relative Cardinal Mendoza. He delivered to the King, with the keys of the
fortress, the sumptuous bed and gorgeous furnishings that
King Alfonso V had abandoned in his flight. Fernando ordered
them sent to Alfonso at Castro Nuño, with his royal compliments. To a cavalier who suggested confiscation, the young
King replied, in high good humor, "We desire, if possible, to
rid the King of Portugal, my cousin, of the evil thoughts of
his mind, not of the good appendages of his person." Fernando
was usually magnanimous in victory.

Leaving Zamora in safe hands, the King and the Cardinal
went to Medina del Campo, where Isabel joined them, and
the three had a long conference. It was agreed that the Cardinal should write King Alfonso "informally" suggesting a
treaty of peace. This he did, only to receive a prompt refusal. For Alfonso had decided to go in person to France, to
solicit further aid from Louis XI. Meanwhile some of his
partisans in Castile continued the war, while others, like the
Count of Urena, made peace with the victors.

Going to Madrigal, the King and Queen assembled a Cortes
of the three estates. It was a stormy one, for the harassed
nation was clamoring for reforms. After the *procuradores*
had taken the oath of allegiance to the King and Queen, and
to the Infanta as heiress, there followed a long, passionate discussion of the notorious ills of the time. "No one paid his
debts if he didn't want to. The people were accustomed to all
disorders . . . and the citizens and laborers and peaceful
men were not masters of their own property, and had no recourse to anybody for the robberies and acts of violence they
endured. . . . Each man would willingly have given half
his goods, if he could purchase security for himself and his
family."[1]

Various remedies were suggested. The one that appealed

to Isabel and Fernando as most practical was that of Alonso de Quintanilla, to revive the *Santa Hermandad*, Holy Brotherhood. In the fourteenth century, this volunteer police force, little more than a local vigilance committee, had done much useful service. In general its function had been to defend local *fueros* or charters against the crown, but in the end it had become the instrument of the feudal nobility, rather than of the people. Isabel saw an opportunity to convert this old weapon of the privileged classes into an instrument of royal discipline. With her permission, the question was placed before the country. Two months later the delegates of all the eligible cities of Castile, Leon and Aragon met at Dueñas to vote on the proposal.

After much fiery Renaissance oratory, the Hermandad was re-established as a purely domestic police, with functions carefully limited to jurisdiction over murders, robberies, acts of violence generally, assaults upon women, defiance of laws and magistrates. The Cortes voted to authorize, for three years only, a force of 2,000 horsemen under a captain-general, the Duke of Villahermosa, bastard brother of the King, with eight captains under him. Every hundred householders maintained a horseman, well armed and equipped, ready at any moment to start in pursuit of a criminal. For every community of thirty families there were two *alcaldes*, magistrates, with plenary jurisdiction, though appeals from their decisions might be addressed to Don Lope de Ribas, bishop of Cartagena, and finally to the King and Queen in Council. But unless a criminal had good grounds for an appeal, the law gave him short shift. The mildest penalty he could expect was the loss of an ear, or a hand. A petty thief was relieved of one of his feet, to make sure that he would not repeat the offense. More often, the penalty was death. As soon as sentence was pronounced, a priest was fetched to hear the prisoner's confession and give him the last sacraments. Tied to the nearest tree, the convict was dispatched with arrows by the Hermandad. Evidently the authors of the ordinances of the Brotherhood were skeptical about the permanency of any moral reforms effected by force among criminals, for they commanded that the shooting follow the absolution "as speedily as possible, that his soul may pass from his body with the greater safety."

To Isabel and Fernando and most of their contemporaries, this stern and speedy justice seemed a matter of course. The sympathy that Enrique El Impotente had lavished on the criminal they reserved for the murdered man and his widow and children, the ravished woman, the family burned to death in the middle of the night by the lackeys of some degenerate baron. Blood flowed easily, life was incredibly cheap. Those who see death often, and may themselves be killed before they return to their homes, are not greatly concerned over the deaths of others. It was not that the Spanish were any more cruel than other western peoples. No country in Europe had ever got entirely free from the casual attitude of Imperial Rome toward human life; it would take the printing press, and the more refined tyranny of an industrial age to effect that. In England, a century later, it appears,[2] from 300 to 400 "rogues" including petty thieves, were hanged every year, and with no apparent disapproval is cited a report by the bishop of Lexovia to show that during the reign of Henry VIII alone, the gallows choked off 72,000 human lives for thefts alone—"great thieves, petty thieves and rogues," they are called—not to mention more serious offenders. Death was the penalty in England for rape, embezzlement of over forty shillings by a servant, "carrying horses or mares into Scotland," "sodomy and buggery," conjuring, forgery, "witchcraft, and digging up of crosses" slander, desertion, "letting out of ponds," "stealing of whatsoever cattle," counterfeiting, cutting of purses, and some hundreds of other offenses.

Only the determined eloquence of Quintanilla, pleading for the Hermandad, carried the reform against violent objections in the Cortes. Most of the nobles opposed the Brotherhood, some because it had failed under Enrique in 1465, some because it was expensive, some because they were astute enough to see in it the possibility of an alliance between the Crown and the common people against their own privileged order. The *Conversos* resented the reform for a similar reason.

The cost was to be defrayed out of taxation, each 100 households being assessed 18,000 maravedis—$3.60 a year for each household, if the maravedi be estimated at two cents. Towns refusing to pay the tax were excluded from the benefit of the Hermandad. Some of them refused for years to accept it, others were won over by the success of the experiment wherever it was tried. Perhaps the country as a whole would never have submitted if Count Haro, one of the great proprietors of the north, had not established it in all his dominions, as an example for others.

From the very beginning the institution was popular among the poor. They saw in it their only protection. It made little difference to them that in restoring justice the Queen would also acquire a small standing army, something almost unknown in the Middle Ages.

During the next three years one could hardly ride from one village to another without seeing on a tree by the roadside the strange fruit of a human corpse; or a body full of arrows tied to a stump, as a grim evidence that the Hermandad had been performing their duty. Isabel sentenced many of the criminals in person. Riding into a town with some troopers at her heels, she would announce that she had come to hold court, to show how justice could be administered without delay and without cost to the people. She would hear complaints, order reconciliations and restitutions, condemn the guilty to death, and go her way to another place. Corpses had been familiar sights to her from childhood. Many a time in her brother's reign she had seen the bodies of murdered men by the roadsides. Two years of bitter warfare had made death even more familiar to her.

Her soul, sickened by it all, cried out within her, night and day, for peace. But peace required order, and order, as Isabel saw, required political unity under a strong hand. There was more principle than vanity in her resolve to be a Queen in fact as well as in name. She could not forget that day when, walking with the Count of Benavente, she was accosted by a woman who came weeping to implore justice. Her husband had been slain in spite of his having a royal safe conduct, and the widow produced the Queen's letter, pierced by the sword that had ended the man's life, and stained with his blood.

"A cuirass would have served him better," said the Count, ironically.

Isabel was piqued.

"Count," she said, "do you wish then that there were no king in Castile?"

"Rather, *Señora*, I wish there were many."

"And why, pray?"

The Alcázar of Segovia, the Scene of Isabel's Heroic
Rescue of her Daughter, the Infanta Isabel

"Because then I should be one of them," said Benavente with a smile.

It was no smiling matter to the Queen. She tightened her lips and thought of a time to come when her safe-conduct would be more protection to a man than a coat of mail.

Her justice now filled the country with terror by its cold thoroughness. It was the more terrible because it was felt to be impartial and incorruptible. When the Queen held court at Medina del Campo, a poor woman knelt before her, sobbing and begging her protection. Her husband, a notary, had disappeared after a visit to the house of a wealthy noble, Alvar Yañez. Isabel commanded a search. The notary's body was found buried in the courtyard of Yañez's home. A brief trial disclosed that after inducing the notary to attest a forged deed to a neighbor's property, Yañez had murdered him to destroy the evidence of his plot. Confident that his enormous wealth and influence would save him, and calculating shrewdly on the Queen's piety and her well-known ambition to drive the Moors out of Spain, he confessed and offered her 40,000 ducats, a sum that would require six figures in our money, as a contribution toward the Holy War against the infidels of Granada. Isabel was advised by some of her Council to accept the large gift and pardon the criminal.

But Isabel "preferred justice to money"[3] and one of the evils she had resolved to abolish was the bribing of officials, the common expedient of Jews and *Conversos*.[4] The head of Yañez was struck off that same day. To avoid any imputation of mercenary motives, the Queen ordered the dead man's property distributed among his sons, although there were plenty of precedents to justify her in confiscating it, and she needed money.

Her rounds of justice led Isabel to Valladolid. Fernando had just met her there, when an urgent appeal came from his father, the King of Aragon. Taking advantage of the comparative quiet in the west, he hastened to Vittoria, assumed command of a huge popular army recruited in Old Castile and the mountains of the Asturias, and marching through Guipúzcoa, relieved Fuenterrabía, where Isabel's governor had been holding out against the French for three months. Louis XI, having no navy to support his army, gave up the siege. Fernando returned by way of the mountains with Count Haro, holding court, condemning criminals, restoring justice everywhere.

Isabel meanwhile had gone to Tordésillas, to be nearer Toro. As Alfonso's garrison there numbered only 300, she sent a force under Don Alonso Enriquez, Fernando's uncle, to take the citadel; but lacking artillery, they were compelled to retreat after a day of heavy fighting and serious losses. The Queen brought reinforcements and instituted a regular siege. Toro held out until July. Then a shepherd named Bartolomé, descrying an unguarded section of wall from a hill, informed a partisan of the Queen. The town was taken by storm. After Isabel had entered it in triumph, she sought out Bartolomé and gave him a pension, with perpetual immunity from taxes for himself and his descendants.

Two weeks later, while she was resting at Tordésillas, she had news from Segovia that made her blanch with fear. A serious revolt had begun, and her baby Isabel, guarded only by a handful of loyalists who were besieged in a tower of the Alcázar, was in danger of capture or death. As luck would have it, Beatriz de Bobadilla, the child's guardian, had come to Tordésillas to confer with the Queen.

Isabel suffered the anguish natural to a mother. Her imagination pictured the Infanta as a hostage in the hands of enemies, perhaps delivered to Alfonso V of Portugal; perhaps dead—all her trouble, all her life's work and Fernando's, all the hope and peace of Castile and Aragon, lost in a moment. Memories of the Segovia massacre of 1473 passed through her mind. She wasted no time in lamenting, however, but ordered horses saddled at once.

The messenger gave some details. During the absence of Andres de Cabrera, the governor, a disappointed office-seeker named Maldonado had smuggled several men, with weapons concealed under their laborers' garb, into the Alcázar. They killed the guard at the gate, they took his keys, they captured Mosen Pedro de Bobadilla, Cabrera's father-in-law. But they had not counted on the loyalty of the handful of troops detailed to guard the Infanta Isabel. These men, fighting furiously, retreated to the tower where the child and her nurse were, and resisted all attempts of Maldonado and his friends to dislodge them. Maldonado, taking possession of another tower, was compelled to institute a siege of the first. The tumult aroused the whole city. Men took arms and joined one side or the other. The majority, through prejudice against Cabrera, since he was a *Converso*, favored Maldonado. The rebels were in possession of all the Alcázar except the tower where the Princess was.

Don Juan Árias de Ávila, bishop of Segovia, himself the son of Jewish converts, threw his influence on the side of Maldonado, for he too had a grudge against Cabrera. The populace, encouraged by the bishop's eloquence, attacked the city gates, taking the gate of St. Martin and the gate of Santiago. A handful of Isabel's soldiers, barricading themselves at the gate of St. John, were holding out valiantly against furious odds. A messenger from the gate of St. John had ridden all night to notify the Queen of the disaster.

Isabel had with her at the moment only the Cardinal of Spain, her friend, Beatriz de Bobadilla, and the Count of Benavente. There was no time to assemble troops; besides, she could travel more rapidly without them. Four horses were saddled. She mounted one of them, and followed by her three friends, commenced a sixty-mile ride to Segovia. The sun glared on the white road, as hot as on the sands of Sahara. The dust, six inches deep, arose in clouds about her and her horse; it whitened them with powder, it blinded her eyes and rubbed the skin off her lips.

The Queen had not even thought of a change of clothing. Over the sandy plains she flew to Olmedo, tried to save time by cutting through the pine forest at Villaguilo, lost the trail, returned in exasperation to the roads, rested her horses a while at Coca, and during the night, when a cold wind came up with the August moon, pressed on to Segovia. At dawn they arrived within sight of the tower of the Alcázar, rising above that rocky spur that projects over the gray plain like the prow of a galley. All around them, barren and treeless, stretched the desolate waste—a cruel, inscrutable country. Was the princess still in that tower? Were they too late?

The Queen's approach having been noted from within the walls, the Bishop Don Juan Árias and several of the chief citizens came forth to receive her. The bishop addressed her with the greatest respect. Since the people, he said, were infuriated beyond measure, he had two earnest requests to make: first, for her own safety, that she would not attempt to enter by the gate of St. John, where there was sharp fighting; second, that she leave outside the walls Cabrera's wife, and his friend the Count of Benavente, since both were anathema to the mob. Several cavaliers added their respectful admonitions to the Bishop's.

The cold passion of Isabel's reply cut short their ceremonious speeches.

"Tell those cavaliers and citizens of Segovia that I am Queen of Castile, and this city is mine, for the King my father left it to me; and to enter what is mine I do not need any laws or conditions that they may lay down for me. I shall enter the city by the gate I choose, and the Count of Benavente shall enter with me, and all others that I think proper for my service. Say to them further, that they shall all come to me, and do what I shall command like loyal subjects, and cease making tumults and scandals in my city, lest they suffer hurt in their persons and their property."[5]

So saying she clapped spurs into her jaded horse, brushed past the bishop and the gaping cavaliers, and followed by her three friends, galloped through the gate of Saint John. She went directly to the Alcázar. Disregarding the Cardinal's advice, she pushed through the howling mob. Swords and spears flashed about her in the morning sun. She pressed on to the small courtyard near the tower. The Bishop followed, vainly trying to quiet the people. The mob surged around the little group.

"Kill them all!" they cried. "To the sword with the friends of the Mayordomo! Down with Cabrera! Storm the tower and kill them all!"

The Queen, silent, haggard and dusty on her white horse, faced them. The Cardinal leaned toward her. Urgently he begged her to have the gate of the Alcázar closed, that no more of the mob might enter the court. The Queen shook her head.

"Open the gates wider," she said, "and bid them all come in."

The gates creaked.

"Friends," shouted a cavalier, "the Queen commands that all come in, as many as can."

A murmur went over the crowd. The Queen! After a hesitation there was a forward seething of the human sea, and all overflowed into the court. The Queen waited for silence.

The Cardinal, indifferent to his own safety, watched her with a mixture of admiration and fear. Her words, clear and resonant, sped like arrows over the heads of the shoving and grumbling people:

"My vassals and servants, say now what you desire, for what suits you is agreeable to me, since it is for the common good of the city."

It was the complete confidence in her bearing and in her musical voice that silenced them. Fear would have been fatal, but Isabel in a crisis was no longer the tender mother and the womanly wife, but one of those *mugeres varoniles*, like Juana of Aragon and the Amazonian Countess of Medellin, in whom the cruel times and many hardships bred masculine qualities before which the most hardened ruffians quailed and hung their heads. "My city . . . my kingdom . . . my vassals and servants. . . ." Her attitude was always proprietary.

A leader of the mob, motioning for quiet, stood forth as spokesmen to relate their grievances at length.

"Señora," he began, "we have several supplications to make. The first is, that the Mayordomo Andres de Cabrera no longer have the keeping of this Alcázar!" The second . . ."

"What you wish, I wish. He is removed. I shall take possession of these towers and walls, and commit them to a loyal companion of mine, who will guard them with loyalty to me, and honor to you."

A howl broke from the crowd, a howl of triumph and approbation. "Viva la Reina!" It was the same motley swarthy multitude that had screamed those words to her that winter morning three years ago, when she rode out of this very court to be crowned. "*Viva la Reina!*" The people outside the gate took up the cry. In a trice the men who had been cursing Cabrera were clamoring for the blood of Maldonado and his partisans. The rebel leaders fled for their lives. By noon the towers and walls had been cleared of them, and the Queen was in complete possession of the Alcázar. Her first thought was to embrace the Princess, from whom she had so long been separated. Then she rode in weary triumph through the streets to the palace near the Church of St. Martin, followed by a mob that all but smothered her in their joy and admiration. From the steps of the palace she made a brief speech, promising them protection from the tyranny of Cabrera and all others, bidding them go peacefully to their homes, promising that if they would send a committee to her to explain all their grievances, she would have justice done. The multitude melted away. The Queen entered the palace, threw herself on a bed, and slept.

Subsequently, when she considered the complaints laid before her by the committee and sifted them to the bottom, she concluded that Cabrera himself was innocent of the charges against him, though some of his subordinates had committed minor tyrannies, and that most of the animus against him could be traced either to envy on the part of men who wanted his post, or to the strong "Old Christian" prejudice against him as an influential *Converso*. She reinstated him. That other *Converso*, Don Juan Árias, repented of his part in the day's work, bethinking him that the Queen might have a long memory and a long arm. The time was coming, though he little suspected it, when he would have a particular need of her friendship.

X

ISABEL had just met one emergency when she was summoned to cope with another. Having gone back to Valladolid late in September to meet the King on his return from
the north, she learned that the death of the Count of Paredes,
chief claimant to the title of Grand Master of Santiago, had
raised a new crisis in the affairs of the Order. The Count was
hardly cold in his grave when his principal rival, Don Alonso
de Cárdenás, marched at the head of his troops to Uclés,
where the *treces* and *comendadores* of the Order assembled at
his bidding to elect him Grand Master.

Isabel was vitally interested. She had no personal objection to
Cárdenas. On the contrary, she had valued him highly since
his exploit in taking a handful of cavalry to rout the four
thousand warriors and the nine choir singers of the Duke of
Medina Sidonia, and her judgment of him had been confirmed
by many reports of his fine generalship in Estremadura against
the Portuguese. It would be a serious blunder to offend a man
who could be of the greatest service in the coming war against
the Moors. On the other hand, the Queen had vivid and painful
memories of the woes brought upon Castile by the struggle
for the Mastership of Santiago between the elder Marqués
of Villena and Don Beltran de la Cueva. Such conflicts had
disturbed the public peace and impaired the authority of the
Crown. There was no room in her conception of the state for
powerful kingdoms within the kingdom. "*My* kingdom . . .
my people . . . *God's* service and *mine.*"

Infinite adroitness and tact were needed to carry out the
program she had conceived. Santiago was only one of three
military orders, all anachronisms with roots deep in the soil,

the race, they had kept Spanish, all sprung from the very necessities of the ancient death struggle with Islam.

The Order of Calatrava had got its name from a bloodily contested outpost commanding the passes between Castile and Andalusia. When the Knights Templar gave it up as untenable in 1157, King Sancho III offered it to any one strong enough to occupy it and hold it. Two Cistercian monks, one of whom had been a knight, accepted the perilous gift and led into the grim castle a band of Christians, whom they proceeded to organize, with the sanction of the Pope, into an order under the severe rule of Saint Benedict. They bound themselves to celibacy, silence in the refectory and the dormitory, abstinence four days a week besides the usual fasts; and the lay brothers, who bore the brunt of the defense, slept only in armor, with swords girt on in perpetual readiness. In a critical moment these monks and knights saved Christian Spain from being reconquered by the Moors. They grew and prospered until they could bring 1200 to 2000 belted knights into the field. As the Moors lost ground and were finally driven into the mountains of Granada, however, their *raison d'être* gradually was forgotten, and like many other human organizations they became at last a political machine, whose leaders tended to seek power rather than foster the ideal of their founders. Wars for the Grand Mastership had more than once divided the Order and the whole country, as when Don Pedro Giron, Isabel's most loathed suitor, prevailed over two other candidates. The Order of Calatrava ruled over fifty-six commanderies, sixteen priories, sixty-four villages and many forts. Its annual income was 50,000 ducats, an immense sum for the times.

Similar in form and purpose, but smaller, was the Order of Alcántara, organized to hold the outpost of Alcántara when it was taken from the Moors in 1214. Warfare in the Middle Ages being a sporadic and temporary affair, there were no standing armies and no garrisons. To supply the deficiency, a group of knights banded together under the Cistercian rule, wearing over their armor the white Cistercian mantle embroidered with a scarlet overcross. Like Calatrava, they had gone the way of all flesh as the need for their services disappeared. On Isabel's accession they had thirty-seven commanderies and fifty-three castles or villages.

But the most illustrious of the three orders was that Santiago, founded in the twelfth century to protect pilgrims going from all parts of Europe to the shrine of Sant' Iago (Saint James the Apostle) at Compostela, in Galicia.[1] Their great popularity and rapid growth may be attributed partly to the fact that they were laymen who adopted the mild rule of Saint Augustine rather than the rigorous one of Saint Benedict. With the king's permission the members might marry, provided they observed continence during Lent and Advent. As war with the Infidel languished under indolent kings, the knights turned to warring with one another, particularly over the great emoluments of their order. The election of a Grand Master often meant a civil war. That potentate enjoyed a greater income and more power than many of the kings. His sway extended over eighty-three commanderies, two cities, one hundred and seventy-eight boroughs and villages, two hundred parishes, five hospitals, five convents, and one college at Salamanca. In time of war he could lead into the field four hundred knights and a thousand lances—each lance meaning three to five men—all trained men "of the sword and of the shell," from the two symbols they wore, a red cross terminating in a sword, and a shell, probably a survival of their connection with Santiago de Compostela.

The body of Saint James, according to a tradition accepted as veracious by Mariana—whom Prescott, by the way, has grossly misrepresented—was taken to Spain by his disciples after his martyrdom in Jerusalem, and after a lapse of eight centuries was miraculously found. Shortly afterwards the Christians, fighting against overwhelming odds near Clavijo, saw an apparition of the Saint on a white horse, leading them against the Moors. They followed, and won the victory. From then on Santiago was the patron saint of Spain, invoked in every battle. His share in the building of the Spanish nation can hardly be overestimated. But in the fifteenth century the Order named for him was in danger of forgetting the heroic genesis of his cult.

Isabel saw plainly that Granada would never succumb to volunteer armies of crusaders loosely organized as in the days of chivalry. If chivalry was not dead, it was dying perceptibly, and gunpowder would soon give it the *coup de grâce*, for the simple reason that two or three plebeians with a lombard could blow up any number of men in armor, be their blood ever so blue or their hearts ever so stout. Gunpowder, in short, was destroying and creating a world. And in that new world of absolute monarchy, of which Isabel's genius had an intuition, there would be no room for military orders except as social survivals, decorations to flatter men's vanity. Powerless at present to destroy three such mighty states within the state, she planned instead to annex the powers of the masters to the Crown by asking the Pope to appoint Fernando to the vacancies, as each master died. The death of the Count of Paredes was her first opportunity. Isabel had dispatched a messenger to the Pope with her request, but before a reply could come, Cárdenas with his usual promptness in action had jeopardized her whole plan, perhaps her entire policy of royal supremacy.

Taking a small retinue the Queen started on her two-hundred-mile ride to Uclés. If her plan was to succeed she must arrive before the knights had time to elect a master. She hoped to reach Uclés by the end of the third day, but the roads over the mountains were so bad and it rained so steadily that she found herself, at dusk on the third day, in Ocaña, fifty miles from her destination. Her followers urged her to spend the night in the palace there, the palace she had fled from with Carrillo eight years before. But fearing that the election might be held next morning, she pressed on all night in the heavy downpour.

The chapter had concluded its business and was about to vote on the mastership when the door opened and the weary rain-drenched Queen walked silently into the midst of the astonished knights. She attacked the heart of the problem as usual, without any preliminary beating about the bush.

"Since the Master of Santiago is one of the great dignitaries of the realm," she said, "and has many revenues and dependencies, and many fortresses along the Moorish frontier, the Kings my ancestors have always kept it under their direct control, giving it to their second sons or some other royal person. And though the *comendador mayor* of Leon is most loyal to the King my lord and to me, I have decided that his Majesty ought to have the administration of the Mastership, and have so appealed to our Holy Father the Pope. For this reason I command you, as my loyal vassals and servants, to postpone your election, for it does not comport with the King's service, nor with mine, nor with the welfare of these realms."[2]

As usual, the Queen's self-possession carried the day. To Cárdenas, waiting at the Corral de Almaquer to hear of his election, her interference was most untimely. Before he had time to decide, however, what he would do, a message came from her bidding him "give up his solicitude for the dignity, since it did not comply with the King's service, nor with hers." If on inquiry he should be found to have a rightful claim to the office, she would see that it was bestowed upon him. Meanwhile he must wait upon her royal convenience.

Cárdenas submitted with good grace. After the first pang of disappointment he resumed his warfare on the Portuguese in Estremadura, serving her as loyally as if she had showered him with dignities. And as soon as Isabel had in her hands the Papal bull giving complete administration of the Order to Fernando, she made Cárdenas Grand Master. She could afford to be generous. She had conferred on him as a favor an office that he had claimed as a right, and as a condition of her gift, had exacted the promise of 3,000,000 maravedis a year from the income of the Order for the maintenance of forts along the Moorish frontier.

Thus again Isabel had increased the authority and dignity of the Crown. Further, she had deftly prepared for the complete concentration of the powers of all three orders in the hands of the King. On the death of Cárdenas in 1499, Fernando was appointed to the Mastership for life by Pope Alexander VI. Similarly he assumed the administration of Calatrava in 1487; that of Alcántara in 1492. Isabel was looking far ahead. Ultimately her foresight was to increase the royal revenues by the equivalent of over a million dollars a year.

Now, forgetting her great weariness and the wet and the cold in her satisfaction at having reached Uclés in the nick of time, Isabel returned to Ocaña, to wait for Fernando. He came from Fuenterrabía by way of Toro, stopping on the road to organize sieges at Castro Nuño, Cubellas and Siete Iglesias, and leaving in command of them his natural brother and Count Haro. Together the sovereigns proceeded to Toledo. There, at the Queen's orders, certain extraordinary preparations were being made.

Before the battle of Toro she had promised St. John the

Evangelist, to whom she was especially devoted, that if victory were hers she would give public thanks to God in his honor at Toledo, and would build a church there to commemorate his patronage and her husband's valor. A brief period of comparative quiet gave her the first opportunity to keep her word.

Cantering over the rolling brown *vega* in the afternoon, the King and Queen and their cavaliers saw the ancient city high on a hill, darkly outlined against the pale sky, like a rich mosaic of Moorish and Christian architecture. From the dome and spire of the Cathedral down to the hovels by the river bank and the long arches of the Roman bridge across the Tagus, a faint murmuring of music arose. Out of the northern Moorish gate, the Puerta de Visagra, came dancing boys in fantastic costumes, and musicians playing on divers instruments, and other children singing the song Isabel had heard that day at Ocaña when the populace rose up between her and the wrath of Enrique:

> Flores de Aragon, dentro Castilla son,
> Pendon de Aragon! Pendon de Aragon!

On a mule magnificently caparisoned with silks and cloth of gold, the bridle held by two pages of noble family, Queen Isabel entered the city, smiling happily, a slender figure with hair like molten copper in the sun. Fernando, in sparkling armor from head to foot, was mounted beside her on a great chestnut horse. Past the hermitage of San Eugenio, near the gate, they rode through the Moorish Zocober and the Calle Real to the Cathedral, where they met a procession of prelates, canons and priests who had walked from the Puerta del Perdon, at the other side of the city, with a crucifix raised before them, followed by an enormous crowd. On each side of the arch above the doorway of the great church stood an angel, and in the center another beautiful maiden crowned with gold, in a blue mantle, representing the Blessed Virgin. As the King and Queen dismounted, the angels began to sing:

"Tua est potentia, tuum est regnum, Domine; Tu es super omnes gentes: da pacem, Domine, in diebus nostris."

To the rhythm of the triumphal chant the procession entered the church. In the vast grove of marble and granite, the rich colors of sunlight filtered through stained glass mingled with the shadows about the young King and the beautiful Queen, kneeling in silence before the high altar. If success had made them somewhat lordlier to men, it had left them humbler before the Most High, and they never failed to give thanks for even the most insignificant successes. God, who might have given them the acid cup of defeat, had given them victory instead—to God, then, not to them, be the glory!

On the next day there was a second and more magnificent procession to the Cathedral. With a blaring of trumpets, and rolling of drums and the fluttering of many banners, they marched through the portal of their ancestor, Saint Fernando, who had freed Spain from the Moorish yoke by taking Córdoba, the Almohad capital, in 1235. Isabel, an expert in mob psychology, who never lost an opportunity to impress the Castilian imagination with the glitter of royalty on state occasions—she always remembered the slovenly boots of Enrique with something like a shudder—appeared that morning in a rich gown of white brocade, flowered with castles and lions of gold. On her brow sat the golden crown of Saint Fernando, afire with precious stones. From her shoulders fell a long mantle of ermine, the train of which was held by two pages with scutcheons of the arms of Castile on their breasts. Around her neck was the famous necklace of pearls and the collar of balas rubies, pale rose color in the sunlight, the largest of them, in the center, popularly believed to have belonged to King Solomon, when he sent to Spain, the ancient Tarshish of the Jews, for his gold and silver, his ivory and apes and peacocks.

After hearing High Mass, the King and the Queen walked to the tomb of their ancestor, Juan the first of Castile, who had been humbled by the Portuguese at Aljubarrota nearly a hundred years before. Over the place where he rested, Isabel draped the torn and bloody standard of Alfonso V, captured by the Cardinal of Spain in the battle of Toro. The wheel of time had reversed its poles: the vanquished was in the ascendant, Castilian honor had been redeemed.

Before leaving Toledo, Isabel bought several houses between the gate of St. Martin and the gate of Cambron, ordered them destroyed, and there had ground broken for the Franciscan monastery of Saint John of the Kings—for Kings (*reyes*) she often styled herself and Fernando, since the Spanish word is not restricted to the male sex. She engaged

Juan Guaz, the *maestro major*, a Fleming, as architect. Years would pass before the completion of the great single nave divided into four vaults, carved with the most delicate lacework in stone, no two arches alike anywhere. It was a work always dear to the Queen, the concrete expression of her love carved in imperishable stone. Everywhere in that church may be found the arms of Castile and Aragon with the cyphers of Isabel and Fernando interlaced with flowers, fruits, leaves and carvings of odd birds and weird beasts. The young Queen never tired of contributing gold chalices, jewels, trophies, tapestries, paintings to the memorial.

The sovereigns went from Toledo to Madrid. While they were there an ambassador with a blonde moustache came from King Edward IV of England, to negotiate a treaty allowing reciprocal privileges to merchants of both nations. Fernando had already begun to think of an alliance with England against the new French autocracy that had despoiled his father of Roussillon and Cerdagne; and he too, like his wife, was descended from the House of Lancaster. They received the Ambassador with all honor. As he desired to deliver a formal address before them, a platform was erected, that he might declaim with greater dignity and effect. He commenced a long harangue in Latin on the marvelous love his liege lord bore the most serene and puissant majesties of Spain, while Fernando and Isabel, who knew no Latin, must have wondered what he was talking about. Unhappily, when the diplomat was working himself up to a fine crescendo, the plank he was standing on gave way, and he was buried up to his arm-pits. The King and Queen, much mortified, looked as solemn as possible to keep from laughing. Before help could reach the Ambassador, he extricated himself and continued his discourse, true Briton that he was, without losing countenance.

After this comic interlude, there came a diplomatic communication of quite another tenor from the new king of Granada—Muley Abou'l Hassan his name was, and he was a Moorish potentate of the old fighting tradition. In 1476, Isabel had sent to ask him for the customary tribute. His answer was a refusal. It was believed in Castile that he was preparing to renew the ancient war that had languished under his voluptuous predecessors; that he looked back with regret to the glorious day in the previous century when 400,000

Moors had invaded the Christian kingdoms, and cherished some hope of emulation.

On the heels of Muley's refusal came the report that fresh Portuguese armies had entered Castile from Badajoz and Ciudad-Rodrigo; that Alfonso's Castilian allies were assuming the offensive from Castro Nuño, Cubellas and Cantalapiedra; that Alfonso V had arrived in Paris and was received with great honor by Louis XI. Fernando decided to crush the Castilian rebels in the west, once and for all, while Cárdenas went into Estremadura to repel the Portuguese. There remained a third, and in some respects more critical theater of war—the south, where the wildest anarchy reigned. There Isabel herself proposed to go.

The King and the Council objected that the risk was too great. There was no city or town in all southern Estremadura that she could use as a base of operations. Every fortress was in the hands of some petty tyrant whose crimes were so notorious that he dared not surrender for fear of being hanged. If Isabel asked for the delivery of a fort and was refused, she would be in the disadvantageous position of requesting what she could not command. While she assailed one place, others would rebel. The continuance of looting and burning while the Queen was in the neighborhood would injure her royal prestige incalculably. Better remain in a safe place such as Toledo, they said, where she could be in touch with all developments, until the King took the key positions of Castro Nuño, Cubellas and Siete Iglesias, and Cárdenas defeated the Portuguese.

The Queen listened to the advice, and as usual, calmly announced her own decision.

"I have always heard it said that the blood, like a good schoolmistress, always goes to repair the part of the body that receives some hurt. Now, to hear continually of the war that the Portuguese make as foes and the Castilians as tyrants, and to endure it with complacency, would not be the office of a good king; for kings who wish to reign have to labor. It seems to me that my Lord ought to go to those places beyond the mountain pass, and I to the other parts of Estremadura. . . . It is true that there are certain obstacles to my going, such as you have mentioned. But in all human affairs there are things both certain and doubtful, and both are equally in the hands of

God, who is accustomed to guide to a good end the causes that are just and are sought with diligence."

The King and the council acquiesced, knowing well that when the Queen spoke in that vein, further argument was useless. While Fernando took the field in the west, therefore, Isabel donned her armor again and rode south into the country of her foes the robber barons.

XI

DISMOUNTING at Guadalupe, Isabel sent one of her
secretaries ahead to demand the keys of Trujillo from
Pedro de Baeza, who held the fortress for the young
Marqués of Villena.

"I will deliver the keys to no one but the Marqués of Villena," said the Alcaide; and this was the reply the secretary
took back to her.

"Go back and tell him," said Isabel with an effort to remain
calm, "that if he will surrender Trujillo peacefully, I will
reward him with money and honors. If not, I will pull the
walls down about his ears."

The Alcaide sent back his defiance: "Tell your mistress
that the walls of Trujillo are not easy to pull down."

The greenish-blue eyes of the Queen grew dark with anger.
She cried, "Do I have to endure the dictation that my subject
presumes to lay down for me? Do I have to remain out of my
own city because of the hindrance that Alcaide thinks to put
in my way? Surely no good king would do it, and no more
will I."[1]

She ordered heavy artillery and troops sent immediately
from Sevilla and Córdoba, and called to her aid several nobles
of the vicinity. While waiting for the guns, she advanced on
two lesser places, Madrilego, a notorious robbers' den, and
Castilnovo. The Alcaides who held them agreed to surrender
if they and their men were pardoned for all crimes they had
committed. The Queen consented, on condition that all stolen
goods be restored. As soon as the keys were delivered and
the garrisons marched out, she commanded that Madrilego

be razed to the ground. Her lombards thundered at the walls and towers, until not one stone was left on another.

News of the fate of evil Madrilego spread terror among the tyrants of Andalusia. And as Isabel's artillery began to arrive before the walls of Trujillo, the Marqués of Villena suddenly made his appearance.

The Queen demanded the surrender of the town. The newly pardoned rebel coolly replied that first there was the question of the restitution of certain of his properties to be discussed.

"There can be no discussion," she said, "until I have the keys of Trujillo."

Villena ordered the Alcaide to surrender. The Queen entered the city in triumph, left the fortress in charge of a trusted captain, and rode on her way to Cáceres. There she settled a bloody feud over an election dispute. She garrisoned Badajoz and other frontier towns, and went to Seville.

That ancient city on the left bank of the Guadalquivir had been for uncounted centuries what Valdes called it—the symbol of light, the city of love and joy. It was Hispal to the Phoenicians, Hispalis to the Romans, Ishbilliah to the conquering Moslems, Sevilla to the Christians who recaptured it under Saint Fernando. As capital of Baetica it had been a pleasure resort for wealthy Romans; in its suburbs were born the emperors Hadrian, Trajan, Theodosius. Saint Gerontius preached there while Saints Peter and Paul were in Rome. Saints Justa and Rufina, the potters, were martyred there in 303 for refusing to adore the idol Salambo. The Moors, having conquered it, rebuilt it to their own liking, and as Isabel knew it, it was architecturally a Moorish city. The Cathedral, where the choir boys danced in gay costumes before the high altar on the feasts of Corpus Christi and the Immaculate Conception, had been a mosque turned into one of the finest Gothic structures in Europe. The delicate Giralda tower adjoining it, with the image of Faith above, had been the work of the Arab Al-Geber, inventor of algebra; and the Alcázar, which San Fernando adopted as his residence, had been the dwelling place of the Almarovid and Almohad kings—in fact, when Pedro the Cruel rebuilt it in the fourteenth century, he summoned from Granada workmen who had toiled on the Alhambra, to keep its Moorish character. The whole city, indeed, was Moorish, a bewildering labyrinth of narrow winding

streets and lanes, lined with one-story white houses inclosing
gay flowers and cool fountains in patios where the people
virtually lived most of the year. In Isabel's time, as now, it was
a sensuously charming city that seemed made for a perpetual
summer evening, drowsy with the scent of orange blossoms
in the light of the moon. The sound of guitars and castanets
came from the gypsy quarter at Triana, across the river, and
in patios and balconies everywhere were heard singing and
dancing, and the laughter of men and women.

Yet this city, in the year 1477, was reeking with corruption,
and trembling with hatred and fear. For, though the architecture was Moorish, the population was chiefly divided into the
two irreconcilable camps of Christianity and Judaism.

There was a large Jewish quarter, the *Juderia*, but the old
law compelling the Jews to reside in it was no longer enforced.
Far more numerous than the sad-eyed children of Israel were
those of their race who lived as *Conversos* among the Christians, intermarried with them, held the most influential and
lucrative offices, owned the most valuable property in the city,
and derived great incomes from merchandise, from money-
lending and from the busy slave market in which Moors and
blacks from Africa were bought and sold. To introduce one
more discord, the Duke of Medina Sidonia and young Don
Rodrigo Ponce De Leon, Marqués of Cádiz, had been fighting
pitched battles in and about the city for three years.

When Isabel approached Seville on a July morning in 1477,
a long procession of negroes from Triana in brilliant suits of
red, green and yellow came dancing from the gates along
the road to meet her. Light and joyous in their movements,
they seemed insensible even to the burning glow of the Andalusian sun, and flung arms and legs and lithe bodies in a frenzy
of rhythm until they were ordered to desist.[2] The Queen, on a
pale Andalusian mule, entered with her usual magnificence,
accompanied by a brilliant cortege of nobles, and of rich Jews
and *Conversos*, anxious to show their loyalty. The streets were
canopied with rich old tapestries stretched from one roof to
another, so that the royal cortege, glittering with gems and
purple and cloth of gold, might advance in a soft multicolored
shadow, over ground strewn with jasmine and roses from hundreds of gardens. Going first to the cathedral, Isabel knelt
before an ivory statue of Our Lady of the Kings that her

ancestor Saint Fernando had always carried in battle at his saddlebow, and gave thanks to God for all His mercies. Afterward she went to the Alcázar, the home of many kings. She walked through gardens where tufted palms swayed over pomegranates laden with blood-red fruits, and orange-trees with their spheres of gold. She sat, pensive and grave, in the judgment seat of San Fernando, in the Hall of the Ambassadors. And there she resolved to restore peace to laughing Seville. While the chief men of the city were hurrying about to arrange for her entertainment, she was calmly thinking of having some of them hanged.

Never, in the memory of its inhabitants, had any monarch had such a welcome in Seville. The "Twenty-Four" imposed a heavy tax to defray the expenses of the demonstration; ordered merchants to furnish fine Venetian velvet woven with gold for the hanging of the royal bed-chamber;[3] commandeered ornaments, laces, fine Oriental stuffs, for the Queen's uses; gave new uniforms to the militia; bade the heralds buy better horses.

The feasts and banquets that followed were brilliant. There were bull-fights in the great arena where the Romans had enjoyed the bloody sport fifteen centuries before. But the Queen looked with impatience at the procession of *alguaciles,* in archaic police uniforms, the *espadas* who waited with swords on foot to engage the huge black beast when he rushed out angered by the darts of the *banderilleros* and the waving red pennants of the *chulos;* the *picadores* on horseback, with spears or lances; a beautiful horse ripped open; the black snorting bull sinking at last to his death in the bloody sand, the *muleteros* with gaily caparisoned mules dragging the corpse from the ring —it only sickened her. Not that bloodshed troubled her particularly—when it was necessary. Wars were sometimes necessary, in her philosophy, and so were executions justly ordered by royal persons who had received authority from God. But this was different—it was unnecessary; and Isabel, on seeing a *torero* killed, forbade all bullfighting in future. Fernando and Mendoza, who knew how passionately the Andalusians loved the sport, said she was attempting the impossible. In the end she had to modify her rule, ordering that false horns, blunted, be fixed to the heads of the bulls. But if the Sevillanos imagined that the Queen was averse to bloodletting in a cause she considered necessary, they were soon to be disillusioned.

The festivities concluded, she demanded reports on the condition of the city from nobles and clergy. What she heard more than confirmed her apprehensions. Apart from the civil wars between great nobles, major crimes were daily commonplaces. Tales of murder, arson, rape, sodomy, blasphemy, every sort of theft and robbery, poured into the Queen's ears. The leading Christians of Seville, both lay and clerical, attributed the laxity in morals to the contact of the Christian population with *Conversos* who had given up Judaism without sincerely accepting Christianity. Fray Alonzo de Ojeda, a Dominican, advised her to establish an Inquisition. So did Philip de Barberis, Inquisitor in Fernando's kingdom of Sicily, who was then in Seville. Without such an instrument, they predicted, Christianity would soon disappear from the land, and Isabel and Fernando would be responsible.

"The Spanish Jews differed but little from the Christian population with regard to customs and education," says a Jewish authority. "They were fond of luxury, and the women wore costly garments with long trains, also valuable jewelry; this tended to increase the hatred of the populace toward them. They were quarrelsome and inclined to robbery, and often attacked and insulted one another even in their synagogues and prayer houses, frequently inflicting wounds with the rapier or sword they were accustomed to carry."[4] This was equally true of the Marranos; but they were even more disliked because as "Christians" they dominated activities from which the Jews were excluded.

The Queen had long known how acute the problem was in Seville, Córdoba, and Toledo. In her own time there had been several massacres of *Conversos*, besides the one at Córdoba in 1473. In Seville the "New Christians," numerous enough to consider retaliation in force, had secretly organized and armed a militia of more than 5,000 men, only to provoke a new massacre of which they were the victims. To put an end to this warfare once and for all was one of the chief objects of Isabel's policy.

She did not believe the antipathy between Christians and *Conversos* was racial. She would not have agreed with the gloomy view of the modern Jew who wrote that "Jew and

Gentile are two worlds—between you Gentiles and us Jews
there lies an unbridgeable gulf," though she might have agreed
with his "Wherever the Jew is found, he is a problem—a
source of unhappiness to himself and to those around him."[4a]
But the difference as Isabel saw it was chiefly religious, not
racial. She had no prejudice against those *Conversos* who sincerely attempted to practise the doctrines of Christianity. To
the end of her life she employed many of them in positions
of trust, and it was her opinion that the truly Christian Jews,
who gave up altogether the customs that marked the Jews as
a people apart, got on much better with their Christian neighbors. The final assimilation of millions of Jews by the Spanish
people seems to lend some confirmation to her theory. But
the impression prevailed in Spain that most of the *Conversos*
went to Mass on Sunday and to the synagogue on Saturday.
It was difficult to tell which of them were truly Christians
and which were Jews. The way of the mob was to murder
all indiscriminately. Isabel viewed such injustice with horror
and anger. But how to distinguish between the sincere and the
pseudo-Christian?

To ascertain whether the Inquisition was the best means to
accomplish her purpose, she asked Don Alonso de Solis, the
venerable Bishop of Cádiz, to investigate the situation in Seville
and report to her. But the crimes of Seville she intended to
deal with in her own direct way, under the existing laws. She
announced that every Friday she would hold, in accordance
with an old custom of the Kings of Castile, an *audiencia*, to
which all plaintiffs in criminal or civil causes might bring their
suits and obtain justice quickly and without cost.

All day Friday, during the next two months, the poor and
oppressed would go from the Plaza de la Monteria through
the Court of the Ladies with its fifty-two white marble columns into the Hall of the Ambassadors. There against a
background of blue glazed tiles, *azulejos*, and Arabian decorations, stood a high dais, draped with cloth of gold, on which,
gravely attentive, sat the young Queen. On one side, below
her, were several prelates and cavaliers; on the other, the
doctors of her Council; in front, three or four secretaries;
farther off, the alcaldes, alguacils and mace-bearers of the
court.

The number of plaintiffs fully justified the Queen's estimate of the need of hearings. As each petition was received by the secretaries, Isabel committed it to one of the councillors, with instructions that the evidence be examined diligently, and a decision returned in three days. She herself heard all doubtful cases and appeals. Soldiers began bringing in malefactors, great and small, rich and poor, from all parts of Seville and its environs. Murderers and other major offenders were taken out, given time to confess, and hanged without further ceremony. Goods were restored to owners in huge quantities.

As it became evident that the Queen was in earnest, supplications began to pour in from various influential people, some of whom offered her money if she would relent. But Isabel was impervious to bribery, to supplications, to threats and criticisms. She began to appear to the dismayed Sevillanos almost like a bloodless abstraction, the cold personification of mechanical justice. Even the wrongdoers who had not been denounced began to leave their homes by night. Four thousand persons fled from the city within a week.

So heavily did the Queen's mailed hand fall that at length the Bishop of Cádiz begged an audience with her, bringing with him a great throng of the wives, children, parents, brothers and sisters of the fugitives. Having great respect for the learned old man, she listened to his fervent rhetoric with the patience she had denied to others. The rigor of her magistrates, said the Bishop, had converted their joy into sorrow, fear and anguish. It was only natural that under a lax government like Enrique's, human nature should have followed the course of least resistance. So many in Seville were guilty that hardly a house was without a criminal, or an accessory in some way to crime. If the Queen continued to insist upon absolute justice, the city would be depopulated and ruined. Humbly, as she could see, and "with tears and groans," they all begged for mercy.

"True it is, most excellent Queen and Lady, that our Lord uses justice as well as mercy; but justice sometimes, and mercy all the time," said the old Bishop, "for if He used justice as He does mercy, all mortals would be condemned, and the world would perish. . . . Scripture enjoins mercy, and the Holy Catholic Church continually chants in praise of the mercy of God. The reign of justice is nigh to cruelty, and the prince is called cruel who, even though he has cause, does not use moderation in punishing."[5]

Frank words, these, to an autocrat of Isabel's temper; yet she listened thoughtfully, as she usually did to criticism, and concluded that there was something in what the prelate was saying—and after all, she had accomplished her end. She acceded to the request for mercy, by proclaiming a general amnesty covering all offenses save one—heresy. The exception was significant.

When Isabel first went to Seville, the Duke of Medina Sidonia had joined the *Conversos* in protesting against the Holy Brotherhood, but on being informed that she had no intention of bringing back the times of Enrique IV, he had eulogized the Queen's *audiencias* with all the assiduity he was master of. After the amnesty he had praises not only for the Queen's justice but for the Queen's surpassing mercy. He had, however, one suggestion to make: no matter how many judgments she pronounced, no matter how many *Hermanos* (members of the Brotherhood) ranged the roads from Portugal to Barcelona, there would be no peace in Seville and in Spain until she crushed and exterminated that notorious tyrant and criminal, that lawless, murderous, destructive, disloyal, treasonous viper, the Marqués of Cádiz. For years that graceless young reprobate had kept the city embroiled in civil war. Since Isabel's accession, he had been conspiring against her with the King of Portugal. Had he not married a sister of that other infamous rebel, the Marqués of Villena? The true reason why the Duke, always heart and soul devoted to Isabel, had been unable to aid her in the war against Portugal, had been the necessity of protecting her city of Seville against the Marqués.[6] She had no idea what trouble and expense he had been put to in her service. He accepted the burden in a cheerful spirit, for it was a pleasure to exhaust one's health and patrimony in the service of so great a Queen. Nevertheless all would be in vain if the Marqués roamed at liberty. The Duke begged the Queen to proceed against him as against a public enemy.

Opinion in Seville somewhat confirmed the Duke's account, for he was popular there. It was openly predicted that the Queen would never tame the Marqués without waging an expensive civil war against him. These prognostications having

reached the Queen's ear, she "conceived a great indignation
against Don Rodrigo."

Just how the feud between him and the Duke began, she
was unable to discover. Like the King Fernando, he was evidently nursed on battles—Bernaldez mentions his being
wounded as a boy in a pitched battle with the Moors in 1462.
Much younger than the Duke, he seems to have offended that
magnate's delicate sense of punctilio in some way difficult to
forgive or to apologize for. Both lived in Seville, and both
being meticulous on points of honor, their quarrel grew into a
civil war until all the city was full of armed men crying,
"Niebla!" and "Ponce de Leon!"

The account of Bernaldez shows graphically the sort of
anarchy that Isabel had to suppress everywhere before she
could begin the reconstruction of Spain. At one time the Marqués virtually sacked the city. Ruffians in his employ set fire
"unintentionally" to the doors of the Church of St. Mark to
drive out of it some of the Duke's partisans, and the whole
church burned down. The whole town, with a furious ringing
of all the church bells, joined with the Duke in driving Don
Rodrigo out of the city. He seized the strong fort of Jerez,
and made war in revenge on "all Andalusia." Subsequently,
on Monday, March 8, 1473, the two factions met at Carmona,
and fought a furious battle in which the two bastard brothers
of the Duke were killed, and Luis de Pernia, a brother-in-
arms of the Marqués, who had fought with him against the
Moors, was laid low with a ball from an *espingarda*. Both the
Duke and the Marqués vowed vengeance. They had been at
war continuously ever since—a period of four years.

The arrival of King Fernando and the consequent ceremonies in his honor temporarily diverted Isabel from her purpose to seize the Marqués and make an example of him. His
friends in the city, however, got wind of her displeasure, and
warned him of his danger. Instead of taking flight, he mounted
a horse one August evening, rode to Seville, with only one
servant, passed through the tortuous streets where his enemies
lived, till he came to the Alcázar, and asked for an audience
with the Queen.

Isabel had retired to her chamber, but on receiving the
startling intelligence that Don Rodrigo Ponce de Leon was
outside, she went forth and received him. She saw a man in

his early thirties, of middle height, though his powerful and
compact frame made him look shorter; a man with an open,
ruddy countenance, somewhat pock-marked; a face framed by
curly red hair and ending in a pointed beard of fiery red. Two
frank and fearless eyes calmly met the Queen's cool scrutiny.
Don Rodrigo made a bow in which there was respect but no
servility. She waited for him to speak.

"You see me here, most powerful Queen, in your hands,"
he began, "to show my innocence, and that being demonstrated, your royal highness may do with me what you please.
I do not come here with faith in any safe-conduct that your
royal majesty has given me, but I come with that which my
innocence gives me. Nor do I come to speak words, but to show
deeds; having no desire to weary your royal ears with denunciations of any one else, but only to save myself with the
truth, which always saves the innocent. Send, Señora, to
receive your fortresses of Jerez and Alcalá, which, as my
enemies have given you to understand, can be taken only with
difficulty, by many troops, with much waste of time; and if
those of my patrimony are needed for your service, I will
have them delivered from this your room, as I deliver my
person to you. And to avoid displeasing your Majesty, I refrain from saying how the Duke my adversary united the
greater part of the people of this city, and came to my house,
and drove me out of it, and despoiled me of my own land.
Nor do I even wish to cite the wrongs that he has done to
me and to mine, since your Highness will learn of these
through accurate sources. And above all, let your Royal Highness believe that I will console myself before enduring your
wrath and his pride. And if I correspond with the King of
Portugal, or do anything to your disservice, I call upon God,
who knows the secret of all hearts, as my witness, and you,
who have seen my public deeds."[7]

The Queen was immensely relieved. Her secretary wrote
that hearing his reasons, she was "*muy contenta*, since he
spoke briefly and with effect."

After a moment of thought she said: "Marqués, it is true
that I have no good reports of you; but the confidence that you
have shown in coming to me gives evidence of your blameless-
ness; and granting that you deserved punishment, your placing yourself in this manner in my hands would oblige me to

treat you with benignity. Deliver then those fortresses of mine, Jerez and Alcalá, and I will investigate the disputes between you and the Duke of Medina, and determine what may be just, protecting the honor of both of you."[8]

Isabel, with her knowledge of Andalusian character, had shrewdly put her finger on the sensitive point in the Marqués' nature—his aggrieved sense of honor. She was rewarded by seeing his proud reserve melt and his blue eyes shine with confidence and admiration, as he said:

"I hold you, Señora, in singular gratitude, that it pleases you to investigate those differences between me and the Duke, for your Royal Highness must certainly find that none exists, save the Duke's desire to rule this city alone, so that neither you, who are its mistress, can use your seignory, nor the cavalier native to it enjoy the place of his residence. And concerning the reports you have had of conversations I have entered into with the King of Portugal, against your service, on account of my brother-in-law, the Marqués of Villena, it is true that I am married with his sister, but marriage does not make it necessary that I should desire what he desires, nor follow the road that he follows—and if by chance, by any way public or secret, your Highness finds that I in those past times favored the cause of the King of Portugal, I will suffer with patience whatever penalty you may ordain for me. True it is, that in the past wars I have not served your Highness as I ought and as I desired, on account of the hindrances and great wars that were made for me on the part of the Duke, in which I certainly did not serve Portugal, as the Duke says, but resisted him, as all know."

Isabel smiled on the Marqués with that frank impersonal confidence that her greenish-blue eyes held for those whom she respected, and sent him away, her friend for life. With him went one of her captains to take possession of Jérez and Alcalá.

The submission of the Marqués was a great disappointment to the Duke and his friends, some of whom had hoped he would cause a new civil war which might bring both diversion and profit. Even more distressing to the Duke was the Queen's command that he deliver up seven fortresses illegally bestowed on him by Enrique IV. However, he yielded gracefully to the inevitable.

To another lawless noble, the Mariscal Saavedra, the Queen sent a demand for Tampa, which he occupied, and the powerful Utrera, which one of his henchmen held for him. He replied that King Enrique had given them to his father, and he saw no reason why he should be despoiled of them. Isabel brought up all her heavy lombards and turned them on the thick walls of Utrera. The siege lasted forty days, at the end of which time Alonso de Cárdenas, fresh from his triumphs in the west, took it by assault. The Alcaide and all but a score of his men were killed in the furious battle. Cárdenas took the twenty-two captives to Seville, where the King, learning that they were all notorious brigands, ordered them hanged.

Fernando had been engaged that summer in work similar to the Queen's. He had attempted to take Castro Nuño by storm and had failed, for it was on a high fortified hill and could not be commanded by artillery. There was nothing to do but leave a besieging army there to starve out the garrison.

The sovereigns, reunited at Seville in August, went to the Cathedral together to pray for a male heir. Fernando was beginning to see how useful children, even daughters, might be in the great European chess game that he hoped to enter after the restoration of peace. But, like all kings, he greatly desired a son. So did Isabel; "and with great supplications and sacrifices, and the pious works that she did," wrote Pulgar, "it pleased God that she conceived." Her child was expected in the summer of 1478.

Even during pregnancy the Queen seldom cancelled her engagements or relaxed in her energetic prosecution of public business. Her labors were prodigious. Yet there were always new reforms to be undertaken: there were more than one hundred private mints to be suppressed; money to be raised; castles to be taken; enormous estates, illegally given away by Enrique, to be resumed by the crown, naturally to the displeasure of the recipients. And meanwhile she found time to teach her daughter Isabel, and to be a patron of the arts.

In October the Duke of Medina Sidonia entertained the sovereigns at San Lúcar. Then, to show their impartiality, they went to Rota, where the Marqués of Cádiz gave them banquets more magnificent, if possible, than those of the Duke. All Isabel's powers of persuasion, however, failed to thaw Andalusian pride and punctilio to the point of reconciliation between the old foes. Hence she ordered both to stay on their estates, and not to enter Seville under pain of death.

About the first of December the Court returned to Seville for the winter. On Christmas Day that year, Isabel and Fernando issued the first known royal decree on printing. Thierry Martins or Dierck Maertens, the famous Alost and Louvain printer whose disappearance from 1476 to 1480 so long remained a mystery, appeared that winter in Seville, where he was called Theodoric the German, or Teodorico Aleman. Isabel's decree of December 25, 1477, makes him exempt from taxation, as "one of the chief persons in the discovery of the art of printing books, an art imported into Spain at great risk and expense, to enrich the libraries of the kingdoms, and providing more books for many learned men of our kingdoms, which redounds to the honor and utility of them and of our subjects." Any one who hinders Thierry or his workmen companions is threatened with civil and criminal prosecution and the confiscation of his property.[9] The first book printed in Spain was a collection of songs in honor of Our Lady, 1474, followed by an edition of Sallust, 1478, and a translation of the Bible into Castilian, 1478, by Father Boniface Ferrer. Even in vicissitudes of war, Isabel had found time to add to her father's collection of illuminated manuscripts, painfully done by hand. She immediately saw the possibilities of the new invention.

Seville, chastened by the Queen's justice and restored to tranquillity by her mercy, enjoyed a gay winter outwardly, whatever discontents may have rankled under the surface. Spring came, and with it some interesting news from Portugal. A wondrous mine of gold, discovered at St. George la Mina six years before, was making the Portuguese fabulously rich. It was said that the naked black barbarians would give a nugget as large as a man's fist for an old suit of clothes, or a few hawk's bells. From Seville, from Cádiz, from every port of Spain, caravels and galleys set sail, and one ship brought back 10,000 pesos ($100,000) in gold.

But the most common topic of conversation in the Court and all Spain was the Queen's approaching *accouchement*. Prayers were said for her in the churches of Castile and Leon, and there was great joy, and much ringing of bells and firing of cannon, when she gave birth to a son on the morning of

June 30th.[10] The King, according to ancient custom, commanded Garci Tellez, Alonso Melgarejo, Fernando de Abrego and Juan de Pineda to be present as witnesses with the midwife, a woman of Seville called *la Herradera*; and the tiny Prince, on his arrival, was committed to the care of a wet nurse of noble family, Dona María de Guzman. The people of Seville celebrated for three days and nights.

Prince Juan was taken to the Cathedral to be baptized on the ninth of July. Fortunately for curious posterity, there stood among the spectators a young priest with the eye of a society reporter, who set down all he saw in minute detail. The chapel where the baptismal font was, and the pillars of the whole forest of marble and granite, were draped with brocades and silks of all gay colors imaginable. Followed by the glad cries of the people, and held on a pillow of red brocade in the arms of a nurse, the royal child entered the Cathedral at the head of a splendid procession, including the court, the foreign ambassadors, the officials of Seville, and the great prelates and nobles of the South. First came Cardinal Mendoza, "the third King of Spain," followed by the distinguished godfathers, the Papal Legate, the Ambassador of Venice, the Constable of Castile, and the Count of Benavente.

In Spain no such ceremonial is complete without music. So there were *infinitos instrumentos de músicas*, including horns of all sorts from the highest piccolo to the throatiest basso-profundo. The magistrates of Seville carried the rods of justice in their hands, and all wore new robes of ornamental black velvet that the city purchased for the occasion. Don Pedro de Stuniga guarded a great silver dish containing the baptismal candle and the customary offerings. Before him, carrying the dish, walked a page so small that he held it atop of his head, steadying it with his hands, that the people might see that the offering was a great gold *excelente* made of 50 melted gold pieces. Walking beside this midget were two damsels of the Queen, and behind them two brothers of noble birth with a gilded pitcher and a golden cup for the ceremony. The high-born wet nurse was attended by four grandees of the court, and many other *caballeros* and notables. Last of all, in a burst of splendor, came the godmother, the Duchess of Medina Sidonia, carried, "for greater honor," on the haunches of the mule of the Count of Benavente, and followed by nine damsels clad in silk of different colors, with silken skirts and tabards. The Duchess herself, with a heavy chain at her neck, wore a rich skirt of brocade, embroidered with pearls, and a tabard of white satin lined with damask. At the feast that followed the baptism, the King and the Court were very festive and merry. King Fernando's pet dwarf, Alegre, was never more amusing. As he admired the tabard of the Duchess, she sent it to him after the banquet.[11]

Just a month later, on a Sunday in August, the Queen went to Mass to present the Prince at the temple, as the Infant Jesus had been presented in Jerusalem by His mother. The King went before her, very splendid on a small silver-gray nag. His Majesty wore a sumptuous brocade trimmed with gold and a sombrero bordered with thread of gold, and the trappings of his horse were of gold on black velvet. Queen Isabel sat on a small white horse with a gilded saddle and caparisons of gold and silver, and her silk skirt was woven with pearls. With her went the Duchess of Villahermosa, and no other lady. Following joyously were many musicians; and walking before their Majesties were the officials of the city, on foot, and the *grandes* of the court.

The nurse of the Prince followed on a mule, proudly bearing the Prince on a pillow in her arms. *Grandes* of the court surrounded her, and with her went the Admiral of Castile. "That day they said Mass at the bright altars of the Cathedral *muy festivamente*," wrote Bernaldez,[12] and all returned to the Alcázar.

Three weeks after this event the people of Seville and all Andalusia were terrified by a total eclipse of the sun. Scientists in the Dominican college at Salamanca had expected it, and observed it, but the populace were sorely troubled when the sun became black in the middle of the day, and the stars appeared as at night. With cries and prayers they rushed into all the churches to implore God not to destroy them. Bernaldez reports that the sun did not resume the natural clear color it had the day before the eclipse.[13] Astrologers looked solemn and gave various interpretations. Some said it was a good omen of the greatness of the King and Queen and of the mighty power that the Prince Don Juan would inherit. Others feared disasters for the Prince and Castile.

Over the heads of some unfortunate inhabits of Seville, at

any rate, a storm was indeed gathering. It was about this time that the Bishop of Cádiz reported the results of his investigation. He told the Queen what she had long suspected, that most of the *Conversos* were secret Jews, who had kept contact with the Jews of the synagogue. They were continually winning over Christians to Judaical practises. They were "on the point of preaching the law of Moses"[14] from Catholic pulpits. The Bishop saw no prospect of avoiding continual bickerings and crimes and massacres unless Their Highnesses removed the causes of these disorders. And this could be done only by enforcing the ancient laws compelling the Jews to live apart from the *Conversos* in *juderias*, where they could not proselytize; and by establishing a special court to punish those Marranos who were guilty of Judaizing and other offenses against the state religion. If these measures were not taken the Jews would sooner or later succeed in their design to destroy Christianity in Spain, to make it into a Jewish country, and to reduce the Christians to virtual bondage, political as well as economic.

How to distinguish between the Judaizing *Conversos* and the sincere Christian Jews by judicial process—that was still the question. And in the venerable Bishop's opinion it could not be done by the ordinary criminal courts of the state. Serious as the crimes against faith were in their effects on public morality, they were so secret that overt acts were difficult to prove. The test must be whether the accused Jew professing Christianity really believed and practised the teachings of the Christian Church or followed those of the synagogue and induced others to do likewise. An ordinary judge, though a lawyer, could not pass intelligently on matters purely religious. Therefore a religious court of inquiry was needed to pass on the orthodoxy of the accused before the state proceeded against him.

It is probable that the Bishop only voiced the growing conviction of both the King and Queen that there was no practical way to complete their ambitious program for the complete independence of Christian Spain except to borrow the spiritual powers of the Church. To them, as to all rulers of their time —Catholic and otherwise—unity of faith seemed the first essential of good government, and its enforcement the first duty of a King. If this appeared true in the days of peace, it was hardly likely to be questioned in wartime, when all governments everywhere insisted upon unity at any cost. And Castile was undoubtedly on the eve of a long and dangerous conflict.

To the Spanish Christian, descended from a long line of crusaders and taught from the cradle the glories of the perpetual war that could end only in the complete reconquest of Granada, any mention of the Moors was likely to conjure up recollections of the historic alignment of the Jews on the side of the enemy. What the children of Israel had done once, their descendants might do again. In any tribunal that could compel the *Conversos* to be loyal and besides make them pay a goodly share of the expenses of the imminent war, the "Old Christians" saw but a beautiful example of poetic justice. The Jews had invited the Moors into Spain; let the sons of the Jews pay for driving them out again. King Fernando is said to have made some such argument to the Queen.

Events were lending an edge to his logic. While the King and Queen were at Seville, their envoy came back from Granada with Muley Abou'l Hassan's reply to their final demand for the tribute. It was this:

"The Kings of Granada who paid tribute are dead, and so are the kings who received it."

He had no objection, however, to a three year truce, and Isabel and Fernando, having neither money nor men, were obliged to consent. The terms of the treaty permitted either side to make brief raids, and to capture any town that could be reduced within three days[15]—a concession to hotheaded frontiersmen whom neither government could restrain. But the treaty had hardly been signed when Muley invaded Christian Murcia with 4,000 cavalry and 30,000 infantry, destroyed the crops and drove off cattle. Taking the Christian town of Ciefa by storm within three days, he put all the inhabitants, men, women and children, to the sword, and withdrew at leisure to Granada.[16]

Isabel and Fernando were compelled to endure the humiliation of permitting him to escape unpunished after this atrocity. But they solemnly renewed the promise they had made in their marriage agreement nine years before never to rest while the Moslem held power in Spain. It took no prophet to foresee that the death grapple between Cross and Crescent would probably commence when the truce expired in 1481.

In 1478, about the time of Muley's raid, Fernando began ordering artillery from Italy,[17] and planning imaginary campaigns. It was obvious that the two chief bases of operations must be Seville and Córdoba. In both places the *Conversos* were numerous, rich and powerful. Seville, which had escaped the butcheries of 1473, was almost completely in their grasp. Their persecution would have been a foregone conclusion—granted the circumstances—under almost any military strategist who ever lived.

Isabel was an excellent strategist. Yet she strove to be just and merciful. Therefore when Cardinal Mendoza suggested that it was unfair to punish *Conversos* for heresy when so many of them had had no opportunity to be decently instructed in Christian doctrine, she was probably rather relieved to have an excuse for further delay. The Cardinal proposed to write a clear, simple and comprehensive catechism of the chief truths of the Christian religion, and have it expounded in all the churches of Seville and near-by places where the *Conversos* were numerous. The Queen gave him permission, and he began the labors that occupied him for the next two years.[18] But at the same time she secretly applied to Pope Sixtus, through her representatives at Rome, for permission to organize an inquisitorial court of the traditional type at Seville—the Inquisitors to be appointed by the Crown.

XII

INQUISITION—what a terrifying word! In its original Latin it signified "an inquiry," "a formal investigation." But to the modern ear it has become a discord full of sinister overtones, some vague perhaps, but undeniably sinister. It suggests torture chambers, flames, persecution, unjustifiable cruelty, fiendish injustice. How could those people, we ask, have done such things? And yet they were men like us. They were our own ancestors. Look at the effigies on some of those orange-tinted marble tombs in Spain.[1] They are not the faces of yellow Tartars or brown Bushmen or black voodoo doctors. They are the faces of our own western European stock, some of them fine, noble and sensitive; such faces as you might meet in Italy, in France, in Germany, in Poland, in Great Britain or Ireland; among professional men or business men in New York or Philadelphia clubs. It is difficult when musing on those profiles to retain much of the self-satisfied complacency with which one age looks down upon another. If faces tell anything, these bishops, these cavaliers, these stately ladies lying so silent on pillows of exquisite lace cut marvellously out of stone, were by no means our moral or intellectual inferiors. How then, did they govern by methods so incomprehensible to us? How could such a woman as we know Isabel to have been, give even serious consideration to the proposal that she have certain people condemned to the stake for offenses against the Church that she believed God had established for their salvation? And how did such a court as the Inquisition ever become associated with the Church founded by Jesus and propagated by a few Hebrew fishermen persecuted by their fellow Jews? The answers to these questions will be veiled to us, and Queen Isabel must remain the enigma of her many biographies, remote from the humanity we know, unless we stand in imagination at the curious cross-roads in history where she paused, and try to see through those blue-green eyes of hers, the actualities from which arose her problems.

The world to her was a vast battle-ground on which invisible powers and principalities had been locked for centuries in a titanic strife for the possession of men's souls. To her the central and significant fact of history was the Crucifixion. All that had happened in the fifteen centuries since then was explained in her philosophy of history by men's acceptance or rejection of the Crucified, and the key to many riddles lay in two of His utterances: "I came not to send peace, but the sword," and "He who is not with Me, is against Me." The peace promised to His children was in their souls, not in the world about them. The Church seemed to her like a beleaguered city, hated and misunderstood by "the world," even as He had predicted, but unconquerable. This view was an easy one to accept in a country where a Crusade had been in progress for eight centuries, nor was it difficult anywhere in Europe for those who knew the strange story of Europe as it appeared in the medieval songs and chronicles. For Christendom actually had been involved for nearly fifteen centuries in a mortal conflict against enemies within and without; chiefly Mohammedanism without, and heresy and Judaism within.

It seemed to her that whenever the Jews had been strong enough, they had persecuted Christians, from the Crucifixion on, and when they were too weak to do so they had fought the Gospel secretly by encouraging those Christian rebellions and secessions that were called heresies. They had stoned Saint Stephen and clamored for the blood of Saint Paul. They had cut out of the Old Testament the prophecies that seemed to Christians to refer so definitely to Jesus. Because of their turbulence against the first Christian converts, they had been expelled from Rome by the Emperor Claudius.[2] And whatever sympathy Isabel's human nature might have prompted her to feel for the cruel persecutions that Jews suffered later at the hands of Christians was tempered by her conviction that the children of Israel actually had called down upon themselves at the Crucifixion a very real and tangible curse, from which they must suffer until they acknowledged the Messiah who had been born to them. One can imagine her nodding with approval as she read Saint Luke's account of the labors of Saint Paul at Corinth: "Paul was earnest in preaching, testifying to the Jews, that Jesus is the Christ. But they gainsaying and blaspheming, he shook his garments, and said to them, 'Your blood be upon your own heads; I am clean; and henceforth I will go unto the Gentiles.' "[3] And Paul, the Jew, was in some ways the prototype of those Christian Jews who were so close to Isabel's throne throughout her reign. The dialogues of Pablo (Paul) de Santa Maria, a converted Jew who was Bishop of Burgos under Isabel's father, show vehemently the common attitude toward the historic Jew in her time. The Jews, he wrote, had climbed to wealth and high offices "by Satanic persuasion"; the massacres of 1391 had fallen upon them "because God stirred up the multitudes to avenge the blood of Christ"; and by these massacres He had "touched the hearts of certain Jews, who examined the Scriptures anew and abjured their errors."[4]

For the most part, however, the Jews had continued "gainsaying and blaspheming" through the fifteen weary centuries. When the collapse of Roman Imperial authority left to the Church the enormous task of assimilating and civilizing the barbarian millions, they had already spread through Europe, winning material wealth and influence among people whom they despised as less intelligent, and who hated them as aliens and creditors, and sometimes as extortioners. Their presence increased the difficulties of a Faith which was yet only a leaven in a mass of paganism. The Church, however, did succeed in her gigantic mission of imposing order and harmony upon the barbarians; in fact, by the time she had created the many-sided life of the thirteenth century, she had become virtually identified with society. This was inevitable, unless she was to remain a mere teacher, a clique, an élite group holding aloof from the masses—a conception obviously at variance with the wishes of her Founder. It was inevitable, but it carried with it the penalty of sharing in some measure in the fate of a society made up of human beings with all their follies and weaknesses. And one problem she had never solved was the one involving the children of Israel.

Meanwhile from without fell three great scourges: the

Vikings, the Magyars, and the Moslems. The menace of Islam was by all odds the most dangerous and enduring. Like the later Calvinism, it stood nearer to Judaism, in many respects, than to the Catholic Church; in fact, its doctrine, though under such obvious obligations to Christianity that it has been classified by some students as a heretical Christian sect, was partially an imitation of Judaism, having had its inception in the mind of a man influenced by the Jews of Mecca. It was to be expected that the Jews would be more friendly to this cult than to Christianity; and conversely, the Moslems, though they sometimes persecuted Jews, were generally more tolerant of them than Christians were.

Fierce, warlike, intolerant, the cult of Islam spread with incredible rapidity among the despairing peoples of the East. It was in some ways easier to accept than Christianity, for it flattered human nature where Christianity rebuked and disciplined it. It appealed to barbarian warriors because it made women their slaves and because it frankly preached conversion by the sword. Like a fire in a forest of dead trees, it swept over southern and western Asia, penetrated the interior and east of Africa, and ran along the northern coast until it commanded the Mediterranean, facing to the north a Christendom still wrestling with the task of civilizing the barbarians. The nearest, most vulnerable sector in the defense of Christendom was Spain, populous, rich, pacifistic, ruled by Christian Visigothic kings. Early in the eighth century, the Spanish Jews, through their brethren in Africa, invited the Moors to come and occupy the country.[5] Divided by civil disputes, the Goths were easily conquered by an invading army of Saracens.

Like a great dark tidal wave, the Moslem hosts now advanced northward over the whole peninsula. Some of the natives of the conquered territory remained there and became Mohammedans. The loyal Christians, however, driven into the mountains of the extreme north, united there in poverty to face the long and bitter prospect of winning back their lands by centuries of war. It was inevitable that they should link with the hated Moors the Jews who lived so prosperously under Abd er Rahman and other caliphs, serving them faithfully, and especially "trading in silk and slaves, in this way promoting the prosperity of the country."[6]

But the Moslems did not stop at the Pyrenees. While Muza,

their African governor, stood high on the mountain passes of
Navarre and imagined himself adding all Europe to the
empire that extended from the Oxus to the Atlantic, his men
were carrying fire and sword into Southern France. They
took Carcassonne, Béziers, Agde, Lodève. They held Arles and
Avignon for three years. Their raiding parties ascended the
Rhône, the Saône, and burned Autun. Though Toulouse re-
pelled them, they marched boldly on Tours. Charles Martel
saved Christendom.

In the train of the victorious Arabs, the Jews inevitably followed, and wherever they went, their uncompromising individuality began to influence their environment. An Archbishop
of Lyon in the eighth century complained of their "aggressive
prosperity" in southern Gaul. There, too, the Moslem culture
long persisted. Negro slaves from Africa were sold there long
after the Church had done away with slavery or elevated it
to serfdom in most parts of Europe. In fact, the society that
the troubadours sang for—rich, artistic, devoted to the good
things of this world—had many Asiatic characteristics, derived from both Moslem and Jew. So numerous and influential
were the Jews in Languedoc that some of the chroniclers called
it *"Judea Secunda."*[7]

In such a society, antagonistic as it was in so many ways
to orthodox Christianity, the so-called Albigensian heresy took
root. It is important to know who the Albigenses were and
what they believed and taught; for the Inquisition, as a permanent tribunal, was called into being to meet the questions
they raised. Had there been no Albigenses, there would probably have been no organized Inquisition for Isabel to introduce into Castile.

Up to that time, except for the scattered acts of intolerance
by individuals and mobs here and there, the Catholic Church
had been committed on the whole for twelve centuries to the
principle of toleration. Saint Paul had invoked only excommunication against heretics. Tertullian declared that no Christian could be an executioner, or serve as an officer in the army.
Saint Leo, Saint Martin, and others agreed that nothing could
justify the Church in shedding blood. There was some disagreement as to how far the Church might be justified in
accepting the aid of the State in coercing heretics, but Saint
John Chrysostom probably expressed the opinion of most of

the bishops of his time when he said, "To put a heretic to death is an unpardonable crime."

Up to the eleventh century, heretics, unless they belonged to the Manicheans or other sects believed to be anti-social, were seldom persecuted; and, if they were, it was the State, not the Church, which punished them. The use of force as an instrument of intolerance seems to have begun with the Emperor Constantine and his Christian successors, who, true to the Roman imperial tradition, treated heresy as a political crime, a form of high treason. Theodosius laid down the principle that "the just duty of the imperial majesty was to protect the true religion, whose worship was intimately connected with the prosperity of human undertakings."[8] Heretics were exiled and their property confiscated by the state; but the death penalty was enforced, generally, only against those who in some way were disturbers of the public peace, such as the Donatists, who organized riots and destroyed Catholic churches.

A change occurred about the year 1000. It was then that the Manicheans, under various names, spread from Bulgaria—hence their nicknames: Bulgars, Bougres and later Buggers—to all parts of Europe. Public resentment against them was strong, and in many places they were lynched by mobs. King Robert had thirteen of them burned at Orleans in 1022. Peter of Bruys, who burned some crosses on Good Friday and roasted meat in the flames, was burned at St. Giles in 1126. But at this time one frequently reads of bishops pleading for the lives of the heretics, and the civil authorities and the mob insisting upon "justice." In the middle of the eleventh century Pope Leo IX and the Council of Rheims affirmed the historic Catholic principle that the only punishment for heresy must be excommunication. They did, however, approve of imprisonment or banishment by the State, since in their opinion heretics were likely to corrupt the prevailing morality—as in fact many of them did.

It is interesting to note how men under stress of circumstances shift gradually from one point of view to another, believing all the while that they are consistent. In the twelfth century, with its development of canon law the revival of Roman law that the Renaissance had helped to bring about, there was a definite change of Catholic sentiment. From 1140 on we find the executions *"secundum canonicas et legitimas sanctiones"*; the canon law has added its authority to the civil; in short, the clergy become perceptibly involved in the persecutions. The Abbot of Vézelay and several bishops condemned nine heretics, of whom seven were burned at the stake. The archbishop of Rheims, Guillaume aux Blanche-Mains, sent two heretical women to the stake.

But it was the pontificate of the great and able Pope Innocent III, commencing in 1198, that marked the real beginning of a general rigor on the part of the Church toward heresy— the rigor that was to find its final and most extreme expression in Spain under Isabel. "Use against heretics the spiritual sword of excommunication, and if this does not prove effective, use the material sword," he wrote the French bishops. "The civil laws decree banishment and confiscation; see that they are carried out."

Why the new sternness? Why such words as these from the learned and benevolent statesman who was then the father of Christendom?

Innocent and the men of his time thought themselves justified by the nature and magnitude of the injury they were preventing the heretics of southern France from doing to society. In the year 1200 the various sects of Manichees, influenced originally by the orientals driven westward by the persecutions of the Empress Theodora, were prospering in a thousand cities and towns of Lombardy and Languedoc. They were especially numerous in Languedoc. Why were they so disliked by orthodox Christians?

Generally they called themselves *Cathari*, or the Pure, to indicate their abhorrence of all sexual relations. They were dualists, asserting that the evil spirit had marred the work of the Creator, so that all matter was an instrument of evil. Human life, therefore, was evil, and its propagation the work of the Devil. The Church of Rome was not the Church of Christ. The Popes were not the successors of St. Peter, for he never went to Rome, but of Constantine. The Church of Rome was the Scarlet Woman of Babylon, the Pope was Anti-Christ. They had only one sacrament, a combination of baptism, confirmation, penance and Holy Eucharist; this they called the *consolamentum*. Christ was not present in the Eucharist, and Transubstantiation was the worst of abominations, since matter, in any form, was the work of the Evil Spirit. The Mass was idolatry, and the Cross should be hated, not revered; love for Jesus should make his followers despise and spit upon the instrument of His torture. Such were the tenets of the Cathari.

They virtually repudiated the State as well as the Church. They refused to take oaths—a position which alone was sure to draw persecution in a feudal age when all loyalty rested upon the oath of allegiance. Some denied the authority of the State, some would not pay taxes, some justified stealing from "unbelievers," others denied the right of the State to inflict capital punishment. They opposed all war. The soldier who defended his country was a murderer.

To join the Cathari—the True Church, they called it—one promised to renounce the Catholic Faith and to receive the *consolamentum* before death. Thus one became a believer. The chief duty of a believer was to venerate the Perfected, or the Cathari, who were entitled to veneration by virtue of the presence of the Holy Spirit within them. A believer became one of the Cathari by receiving the *consolamentum*. After a year's probation he made this promise: "I promise to devote my life to God and to the Gospel, never to lie or swear, never to touch a woman, never to kill an animal, never to eat meat, eggs or milk food; never to eat anything but fish and vegetables, never to do anything without first saying the Lord's prayer, never to eat, travel or pass the night without a *socius*. If I fall into the hands of my enemies or happen to be separated from my *socius*, I promise to spend three days without food or drink. I will never take off my clothes on retiring, nor will I deny my faith even when threatened with death." The Perfected then gave their new brother the kiss of peace, kissing him twice on the mouth, after which he kissed the next man, who passed on the *pax* to all the others. If the candidate was a woman, the minister merely touched her shoulder with a book of the Gospels, since he was forbidden to touch women.[9]

The Cathari avoided meat partly because they believed in metempsychosis. But the tenet that chiefly drew on them the wrath and derision of the masses was their condemnation of all marital relations. Carnal intercourse, they held, was the real sin of Adam and Eve; and it was a sin, because it begot children. A woman with child was possessed of the devil, and if she died *enceinte* or in childbirth, she would surely go to Hell. "Pray God," said one of the Perfected to the wife of a Toulouse lumber merchant, "that He deliver you from the devil within you." Marriage was nothing but a perpetual state of sin; it was as great a sin, they declared, as incest with one's mother or daughter or sister; in fact, marriage was merely prostitution. They argued that cohabitation with one's wife was a worse crime than adultery, because it was not a temporary weakness to which a man surrendered in secret, but one that caused no shame, hence men did not realize how wicked it was. In times of persecution, however, men and women of the Perfected would live together to avoid detection, sleeping in the same bed while travelling, but never undressing, to avoid contact with each other.

Suicide was another dogma of the Cathari that did not increase their popularity with their Catholic neighbors. The *endura*, as they called it, had two forms: suffocation and fasting. The candidate for death was asked whether he wished to be a martyr or a confessor. If he chose to be a martyr, they placed a handkerchief or a pillow over his mouth, until he died of suffocation. If he desired to be a confessor, the Cathari left him without food, and sometimes without drink, until he perished of starvation. A sick man who asked for the *consolamentum* was urged to make his salvation sure by receiving the *endura*. In the middle of the thirteenth century, the *endura* was applied even to infants. A woman of Toulouse, named Guillemette, began the *endura* by bloodletting, then weakened herself by taking long baths, finally drank poison, and finding herself still alive, swallowed ground glass to perforate her intestines. The records of the Inquisition of Toulouse and Carcassonne show that the *endura* killed more victims than the public courts of the Inquisition.[10]

Such beliefs were a serious challenge to both Church and State, and Church and State met them with stern measures. The infidel Emperor Frederick II, influenced by Innocent's comparison of heretics to traitors, had them burned. But it was Pope Gregory IX who first established "an extraordinary and permanent tribunal for heresy trials"—the institution which became known as the Inquisition. The first attempts to ferret out the Cathari through inquiries by bishops and legates failed because of the secrecy of the sect. At that juncture, the establishment of the two great mendicant orders of Saint Dominic and Saint Francis of Assisi appeared to be "a providential interposition to supply the Church of Christ with what it most sorely needed."[11] To the Dominicans, in particular, since they were learned and skilled in theology, the work of inquiry was committed.[12] The organization they perfected was substantially the one that Isabel was urged to establish in Castile.

When the Inquisitors arrived in a city, they would summon every heretic to appear within a certain time, usually thirty days, known as "the term of grace," and confess. Those who abjured during this period were treated leniently and "reconciled." If the heresy was secret, a secret penance was imposed; if public, a short pilgrimage, or one of the usual canonical penances. Heretics who failed to come forward were to be denounced by good Catholics. The number of necessary witnesses was not specified at first. Later, two were required. At the start, only witnesses of good repute could testify, but later the Inquisitors, in their eagerness to uncover such a difficult quarry as heresy, took the depositions of criminals and heretics.

The defendant had no witnesses—naturally such persons would themselves be suspected as accomplices. "For the same reason the accused were practically denied the help of counsel. Innocent III had forbidden advocates and scriveners to lend aid or counsel to heretics and their abettors. This prohibition, which in the mind of the Pope was intended only for defiant and acknowledged heretics, was gradually extended to every suspect who was striving to prove his innocence. Heretics or suspects, therefore, denounced to the Inquisition, generally found themselves without counsel before their judge."[13]

To protect witnesses from being slain by the friends of the accused—and this frequently happened—their names were withheld from the prisoner. The only protection he had against this obvious injustice was that he was allowed to name all his mortal enemies, and if his accusers' names happened to be among them, their testimony was thrown out. Otherwise he must prove the falsity of the accusation against him—"practically an impossible undertaking. For if two witnesses, considered of good repute by the Inquisitor, agreed in accusing the prisoner, his fate was of course settled; whether he confessed or not, he was declared a heretic."

To be convicted of heresy meant death, in practice, in about one case out of ten. A prisoner found guilty could abjure his errors and accept a penance, or he could persist in his denial or in his opinion, and take the consequences. If he abjured, the Inquisitor dealt with him as he would with any other type of penitent, imposing a penance not as a punishment, but as "a salutary discipline to strengthen the weak soul and wash away its sin." He considered himself, in fact, the friend of the penitent—a point of view that the penitent must have found it difficult at times to share. The penance varied according to the decree of the offense: first, prayers, visiting churches, the "discipline," fasting, pilgrimages and fines; for more serious errors, the wearing of a yellow cross sewed on the garments—this was originally imposed on penitent heretics by Saint Dominic in all kindness to save them from being massacred by the mob—and finally, imprisonment for as long a time as was deemed necessary. One must remember that no stigma was attached to penance in the Middle Ages. Even kings who had sinned sometimes did penance in public, as Henry II did at the tomb of Saint Thomas of Canterbury, and were honored for it.

The Inquisitor never condemned any one to death. If a prisoner refused to abjure, the Inquisitor pronounced him a hardened and impenitent sinner, a heretic with no hope of conversion, and handed him over to the State, "the secular arm"; and the secular judge, to whom heresy was a major crime similar to treason, sentenced him to be burned. Thus by a legal fiction the Inquisitors persuaded themselves that they had nothing to do with taking the life of the heretic. A similar train of sophistical reasoning has enabled some Catholic writers to argue, as Joseph de Maistre did, that all the cruelty of the Inquisition was the State's and all the clemency the Church's. The truth is, however, that certain Popes threatened to excommunicate princes who refused to burn heretics handed over to them by the Inquisition. "It is, therefore, erroneous," says Father Vacandard, "to pretend that the Church had absolutely no part in the condemnation of heretics to death. It is true that this participation of hers was not direct and immediate; but, even though indirect, it was none the less real and efficacious."[14]

Evidently the Inquisitors felt uneasy about their own logic, and attempted to free themselves of the responsibility. In abandoning a heretic to the secular arm, they were careful to use the following formula: "We dismiss you from our ecclesiastical forum, and abandon you to the secular arm. But we strongly beseech the secular court to mitigate its sentence in such a way as to avoid bloodshed or danger of death."

Merciful words, these, and in accord with the best Catholic traditions of the ages. "We regret to state, however," observes Vacandard, "that the civil judges were not supposed to take these words literally. If they were at all inclined to do so, they would have been quickly called to a sense of duty by being excommunicated." In the beginning the formula was probably sincere.

If a heretic repented, but later returned to his errors, he was considered "relapsed" and forthwith handed over to the secular arm for burning. Even if he repented before he reached the stake the only mercy shown him was the privilege of being strangled before he was burned.

In general the Church, recognizing the frightful responsibility of the Inquisition, chose the Inquisitors with great care. As far as personnel went, the Inquisition was better than the State courts. Bernard Gui, a famous Inquisitor of the early fourteenth century, declared that an Inquisitor should be "diligent and fervent in his zeal for religious truth, for the salvation of souls, and for the destruction of heresy. He should always be calm in times of trial and difficulty, and never give way to outbursts of anger or temper. He should be a brave man, ready to face death if necessary, but while never cowardly, running from danger, he should never be foolhardy, rushing into it. He should be unmoved by the entreaties or the bribes of those who appear before his tribunal; still he must not harden his heart to the point of refusing to delay or mitigate punishment, as circumstances may require from time to time. In doubtful cases, he should be very careful not to believe too easily what may appear probable, and yet in reality is false; nor, on the other hand, should he stubbornly refuse to believe what may appear improbable, and yet is frequently true. He should zealously discuss and examine every case, to be sure to make a just decision. . . . Let the love of truth and mercy, the special qualities of every good judge, shine in his countenance, and let his sentences never be prompted by avarice or cruelty."

But in spite of the Church's insistence upon the impartiality of the judges, the monks made the criminal procedure of the Inquisition, as Vacandard says, "markedly inferior to the criminal procedure of the Middle Ages," though, "on the other side it must be remembered that the Inquisition dealt with many offenses which would have come before secular courts at an earlier or later date. The Inquisition dealt with murder, sodomy, rape, blasphemy and other crimes; and the offender fared better as a rule than he would if he had fallen into the clutches of the State alone."

In their attempts to make the procedure just, the Popes encouraged the Inquisitors to call in experts to consult with them, *periti* and *boni viri*. Sometimes as many as forty or fifty, including lawyers and other learned men, would hear evidence and give their verdict. This system, in which appear the beginnings of the modern jury, was unable to dispense true justice in that the jurymen did not have data enough to enable them to decide fairly, since only summaries of the evidence were read to them, and the name of the accused withheld, to avoid prejudice. Evidently it had not occurred to the Inquisitors that a crime must be judged with reference to the mentality and general character of the offender.

Even before trial the accused were sometimes treated with great cruelty. The cells in France were frequently narrow, dark, full of disease, unfit for human habitation; and though the papal orders were that life should not be endangered, in practice the accused sometimes died as a result of their incarceration in solitary confinement. On learning of this situation, the popes attempted to remedy it.

The use of torture was one of the most sickening abuses of the Inquisition. Perhaps the early Christians remembered Roman torture too painfully to use it against others; at any rate, it was not used until the revival of Roman law restored it during the Renaissance to courts that had known nothing of it during the so-called Dark Ages. "The earliest instances with which I have met," says Lea,[15] "occur in the Veronese code of 1228 and the Sicilian constitutions, and in both of these the references to it show how sparingly and hesitatingly it was employed." Innocent IV, in his bull "Ad Extirpanda," defends the use of torture by classifying heretics with thieves and murderers.

The commonest forms of torture were the rack and the strappado. The rack was a triangular frame on which the prisoner was stretched and bound so that he could not move. Cords, attached to his arms and legs, were connected with a windlass, which when turned dislocated the wrist and ankle joints of the victim. The strappado hoisted the prisoner by a rope tied to his wrists behind his back and attached to a pulley and windlass. After he was raised by the wrists to the top of a gallows, or near the ceiling of the torture chamber, he was suddenly left fall. The rope was pulled taut when he was within a few inches of the ground. Weights were sometimes tied to his feet to increase the shock of the fall.

As the canons of the Church forbade ecclesiastics to take any part in torture, lest they incur "irregularity" and be suspended until they had done penance and were pardoned, the torturing in the early days of the Inquisition was always performed by a civil officer. This scrupulous policy, however, caused so many delays that Alexander IV authorized the Inquisitors and their assistants to grant each other any necessary dispensations for "irregularities." From that time on—1260—the Inquisitor did not scruple to appear in the torture chamber.

The investigation ordered by Pope Clement V into the iniquities of the Inquisition at Carcassonne demonstrated that torture was used frequently. True, it was seldom mentioned in the records of the Inquisition, but only because a confession wrung from a victim by torture was invalid. This just provision the Inquisitors managed to evade by reasoning which men of our day find it difficult to follow. The prisoner was shown the instruments of torture and urged to confess. If he refused, mild tortures were used; if he persisted, more painful ones. When at last he confessed, he was unbound and carried into another room, where his confession, made under torture, was read to him, and he was asked to confirm it. If he didn't, he was taken back and tortured again. If he did, the confession passed as "a free and spontaneous confession, without the pressure of force or fear."

Another merciful regulation was that torture was not to be applied to any prisoner for more than half an hour, and never more than once. But in practice, "usually the procedure appears to be that the torture was continued until the accused signified his readiness to confess," says Vacandard, and as for torturing the victim only once, some Inquisitors evidently tortured him as many times as they thought necessary, explaining that the second torture was not a repetition but a continuance of the first, which had merely been suspended. "This quibbling," adds Vacandard, "of course gave full scope to the cruelty and the indiscreet zeal of the Inquisitors."

In the end, as the inquisitorial mind went from one quibble to another, torture was used even on the witnesses. After a prisoner had convicted himself, he could be tortured into betraying his friends.

Vacandard probably sums up the view of many modern Catholics when he says, after his frank statement of facts, that even if the Church today "were to denounce the Inquisition, she would not thereby compromise her divine authority. Her office on earth is to transmit to generation after generation the deposit of revealed truths necessary for man's salvation. That to safeguard this treasure she used means in one age which a later age denounces, merely proves that she follows the customs and ideas in vogue around her. But she takes good care not to have men consider her attitude the infallible and eternal rule of absolute justice."

Such, at any rate, was the cruel weapon that thirteenth century European society used to protect its integrity from a cruel and insidious propaganda. A crusade ended the Albigensian heresy in southern France. When some of the Cathari fled across the Pyrenees to Aragon, the Inquisition followed them there. But it had never been tried in Castile. Isabel did not believe that in its traditional form it could operate successfully there. For in the canonical Inquisition, so called, the bishops exercised a strong restraint over the Inquisitors, and she was inclined to believe that in Castile, where many bishops were *Conversos,* or related to *Conversos,* the tribunal would be allowed to die a natural death. She considered various means of preventing this as she rode along the river from Seville to Córdoba.

XIII

ISABEL REORGANIZES HER GOVERN-
MENT, MAKING THE CROWN SUPREME,
AND PREPARES TO ENTER THE GREAT
CRUSADE AGAINST THE MOHAM-
MEDANS

ISABEL found Córdoba, like Seville, in a state of anarchy. Horrible crimes went unpunished. Noblemen fought battles in the streets. The warfare between the *Conversos* under Don Alonzo and the Old Christians under the Count of Cabra blazed forth intermittently. Industry was paralyzed. The poor starved, or took to crime. To all these ills the Queen applied the same remedy that she had found so useful at Seville, though with a restraint born of experience.

Not long after she had established her Friday *audiencias*, the Queen found it necessary to look for a new confessor; and she summoned a certain Jeronymite whom Cardinal Mendoza had recommended: Fray Hernando de Talavera, Prior of the convent of Santa María, a pious and learned man whose grandparents had been converted Jews.

The monk sat in a chair and respectfully motioned to the Queen to kneel, as a penitent ought, by his side. Isabel was startled. Her confessors had always knelt beside her, by way of showing deference to her rank.

"Reverend Father," she said, "it is customary for both to kneel."

Fray Hernando replied, "The confessional, my daughter, is God's tribunal, in which there are no kings or queens, but only human sinners; and I, unworthy as I am, am His minister. It is right that I sit and you kneel."

The Queen knelt, and confessed her sins. Afterward she said,

"This is the confessor I have been looking for," and for several years she retained Talavera as her spiritual adviser.

From this generally accepted tradition some rather grotesque conclusions have been drawn by many solemn historians. It has furnished them with an easy way of explaining how a woman so kind, so conscientious and so enlightened, could have entertained the ugly thought of establishing the Inquisition. Now that it appears the Queen was like a humble child in the confessional, all is solved. She was "misled by monks," "priest-ridden," "dominated by prelates," "blinded by bigots of the cloister."[1] Such are the phrases that Prescott, Irving and a score of others have repeated one after another without proof, and in the face of much evidence on the other side. It would ·be interesting to know how these investigators would make their theory fit this undeniable fact:

The two priests who had most influence with the Queen at this period—1478 to 1480—were both opposed to the Inquisition. They were Cardinal Mendoza and Fray Hernando de Talavera.

It may be that the Queen never even mentioned the Inquisition in the confessional. A penitent confesses his sins, not his problems in general; and we must remember that Isabel, living in a society that took it for granted that heresy was a sin worse than murder, and that the ruler had not only the right but the duty to take life if the public welfare demanded it, considered the Inquisition anything but sinful. In her public capacity, as Queen, she occasionally withstood the highest dignitaries of the Church, when she believed them mistaken. As a woman, a private person, she was the humblest of penitents.

Months passed, and still she delayed her final decision. There were so many other problems besides the one in Seville. About this time, for example, she was incensed by reports she had concerning Carrillo. It appeared that the old conspirator was urging Alfonso V to make a second invasion of Castile. The Queen retaliated by placing an embargo on his revenues, and proclaiming in Toledo that she intended asking the Pope to remove him. At that his friends deserted him, and he was driven to seek a second reconciliation, through the archdeacon of Toledo, a learned and holy man whom the Queen esteemed. This time she pardoned Carrillo only on condition that he surrender to her seven towns belonging to the Crown that she had not felt strong enough to demand in 1476. Their delivery left the old archbishop helpless. The remaining four years of his life were wasted on alchemy and astrology.

There was no immediate prospect of peace with Portugal. Alfonso V had gone to France with every hope that he could persuade Louis XI to give him money and troops for the conquest of Castile. But Louis had other business in hand, including a war with the Duke of Burgundy. While he gave banquets to his "brother" of Portugal, and allowed him to take the keys of the cities and to free prisoners as if he were monarch of France, he was secretly poring over confidential letters from Cardinal Mendoza urging him to make an alliance with Fernando and Isabel. He was probably not long in seeing through Alfonso. De Comines wrote: "I am of the opinion that if our king had assisted him, as he was sometimes inclined to do, the King of Portugal might have succeeded in his designs; but by degrees the King's mind became changed, and so the King of Portugal was kept amused with fair words, and fed with hopes for a year or more."

Alfonso's growing disillusionment blackened into despair when he learned at the end of 1479 that Louis had concluded a treaty of peace with Isabel and Fernando. In February of that year Louis sent the Bishop of Lumbres to Isabel to tell her of the great pleasure it gave him to see her on the throne of her father, King Juan II, and to ask a renewal of their ancient friendship. A treaty was drawn up in which the high contracting parties agreed to be *"amigos de amigos, y enemigos de enemigos,"* against all persons in the world, except the Holy Father. The question of the return of Roussillon and Cerdagne to Fernando's father was to be arbitrated within five years.

The Treaty of St. Jean de Luz was such gall and wormwood to Alfonso that he wrote a letter to his son, Dom João, abdicating the throne and announcing that he would retire to a monastery. The Count of Faro argued him out of that determination, and he sailed with a heavy heart for Portugal, arriving just in time to see the fêtes in honor of the coronation of his son, who had taken him at his word. But Dom João dutifully permitted his father to remount his uncomfortable throne.

The fat king's ignominious home-coming gave impetus to a peace party led by his sister-in-law, the Infanta Doña Beatriz, aunt both to Dom João and to the Queen of Castile, and a most discreet woman. At this juncture she wrote Isabel secretly, asking for a meeting, in which perchance, "with the aid of God and of the glorious Virgin His mother, they would find a way to restore peace and concord" to the two kingdoms. Pope Sixtus assisted the peace faction by revoking the dispensation to Alfonso V to marry La Beltraneja, explaining that it had been obtained by misrepresentation of the facts. The marriage had never been consummated.

Isabel agreed to a meeting at Alcántara near the Portuguese border. But on the eve of her departure for that place, the war flamed up anew in Estremadura, where the Countess of Medellin, an illegitimate daughter of the elder Marqués of Villena, joined the enemies of the Queen.

Meanwhile Alfonso, having obtained funds from the confiscation of one of the Castilian fleets returning loaded with gold from St. George La Mina, equipped a new expedition under the Bishop of Évora, who crossed into Castile while Isabel was laying siege to Medellin. Alonso de Cárdenas met the invaders at Mérida, and after a bloody battle of three hours, defeated them. Isabel's situation was precarious. Supplies having given out, her army fought for days on bread and water.

To complicate matters further, the Queen found herself with child for the second time within a year. Prince Juan was hardly eight months old, and the third baby was expected in November. Fernando was obliged to go to Aragon, where his father's death in January had left him a crown and therefore new responsibilities. It was June before Isabel could go to Alcántara to meet Doña Beatriz, taking with her only a secretary and Doctor Maldonado of her Council.

After several days of conversation, the two women arrived at a complete understanding. Doña Beatriz had always considered her brother-in-law's invasion of Castile a chimerical piece of folly. She admired her niece. The treaty, therefore, was virtually Isabel's dictation. Alfonso would give up his title to Castile and remove the arms of Castile from his escutcheon. He would never marry La Beltraneja. That unfortunate Princess was to be free to do as she might please for six months, at the end of which time she must agree to marry Prince Juan when he became old enough (he was then a year old) or enter a convent. Prince Alfonso, younger son

of Alfonso V, would marry the Infanta Isabel, then nine
years old, both to remain during the interim in the custody of
Doña Beatriz at Mora. The Mina del Oro would remain
Portuguese. No subjects of Fernando and Isabel would go
there for gold. The Castilian rebels were to be freely pardoned,
with no loss of property. The treaty was to be binding for
five years.

It took Doña Beatriz nine months to persuade Alfonso to
ratify so humiliating a document. She did so only with the
help of Dom João, who bluntly told his father that the war
had been unjust, and his misfortunes a punishment from God.[2]
Alfonso consented at last, and the blare of trumpets in all
the cities of both kingdoms announced peace after a war of
four years and nine months. Juana La Beltraneja, rather than
wait for Prince Juan, chose to enter a convent. Fray Hernando
de Talavera was present when she took her vows. Her mother,
Queen Juana, had died four years before, at Madrid, forsaken and prematurely old, and had been buried in a tomb of
white marble near the high altar in the Church of St. Francis
at Madrid. Even in death, poor Juana had been embarrassing
to others. To make room for her, the bones of Ruy Gonzalez
de Clavijo, who had gone as ambassador to Tamerlane,[3] and
after his return had erected this great chapel of St. Francis
for his own burial place, were transferred elsewhere.

Isabel meanwhile had gone to Toledo. There in the old
Moorish city of seven hills, where the steep narrow streets are
cluttered with churches, convents and hospitals interspersed
with quiet shaded patios, she gave birth to her third child,
the ill-fated Juana the Mad, on the sixth of November. The
King, his business in Aragon concluded, hastened to his wife's
bedside; and some days later they went together, as was their
custom, to present the Infanta to God in the Cathedral.

As soon as her strength returned, Isabel began preparing
the program she intended to submit to the Cortes when it met
at Toledo in the spring of 1480. The moment had come, she
felt, to draw the last strands of authority into her own hands.
When the delegates assembled, she went before them, won
them with her beauty and the graciousness of her speech, and
proceeded with disarming frankness to take away from the
upper classes some of the privileges that they had guarded so
jealously against her ancestors.

The Hermandad, though still vigorously resisted by certain nobles, had proved on the whole so successful that the delegates voted to continue it and expand its functions.

The currency was stabilized by restricting all coining to the royal mint. More than a hundred aristocrats had been melting their own metal. When Isabel ascended her brother's throne, money was almost worthless in Castile.

Relentlessly, but with infinite tact and patience, the Queen forced her will upon the Cortes, playing off one estate against another, and especially using the good will of the commons and the clergy to lop off the privileges of the tyrannical nobles and increase the powers of the crown. It was an immense program that she laid before the *procuradores*; nothing less than a complete revision of the entire executive and judicial systems of the kingdom. In the reorganization of the royal council, *"nuestro consejo,"* she introduced a strong representation of the middle classes. As the government became more specialized and complex, it was important to take it out of the hands of great nobles who felt themselves rather above petty details and arduous labor, and give it to men accustomed to toil. The lawyers, mostly from the humbler orders, seemed to Isabel the most useful for her purpose. With all her exploitation of the popular reverence for royalty, the Queen was too intelligent to have much respect for "blood" alone. It was ability she looked for, and she used it and encouraged it wherever she found it. In consequence the new royal council consisted of one bishop, three cavaliers, and eight or nine lawyers. A tremendous revolution. Chiefly consultative, it had also administrative and judicial functions. The Cortes passed laws to prevent its encroaching upon the courts of justice.

Isabel divided her government into five departments: first, the Council of Justice, over which the King and Queen, and in their absence a President, officiated; second, a Council of State, dealing with foreign affairs, including the negotiations with the Court of Rome; third, the Supreme Court of the Holy Brotherhood; fourth, a Council of Finance; fifth, a Council for purely Aragonese matters. These departments maintained contacts with local governments through *pesquisidores* or inspectors, who made frequent visits to cities and towns, inquired into the execution of the laws, and reported abuses by governors and others. In this system, so useful at the time, Isabel was unconsciously sowing the seeds of the ponderous bureaucracy of later centuries.

From her own considerable experience as a judge, she realized the need of a new legal code to replace the cumbersome one based on the Visigothic *fueros*, those local privileges wrung from needy kings, and on the *Siete Partidas* of Alfonso X, which followed the Roman code of Justinian. The enormous task of compiling the new code was committed to Doctor Alfonso Diaz de Montalvo, who labored for four years compiling his eight thick tomes of *Ordenanzas Reales*. There were many mistakes, repetitions, and omissions, and Isabel ordered the jurist to do his work over. She was never completely satisfied with it—even in her will she left a request for still further revision of the laws.

By far the most unpopular task she imposed on the Cortes was the recovery of revenues illegally transferred from the Crown to various nobles by Enrique IV. In the days when the wealth of the Kings of Castile had been given to any who asked for it, there was hardly a noble house that had not been enriched by alienation of royal lands or revenues. Yet Isabel made the daring proposal that the Cortes command the return of at least a large percentage of this wealth to the Crown. She carried the measure with the powerful support of Cardinal Mendoza, whose disinterestedness was the more conspicuous, since his own family had been among the chief beneficiaries of Enrique's folly. At the Queen's request, the odious and intricate task of apportioning the wealth to be returned to the Crown was entrusted to her new confessor, Fray Hernando de Talavera, a man of courage and cool judgment. Fortified by the Queen's instructions to show no favoritism, he did what no man in Castile had dared hitherto attempt: he assessed the Admiral of Castile, Fernando's grandfather, 240,000 maravedis in yearly rents; the Duke of Alba, 575,000 maravedis; the Duke of Medina Sidonia, 18,000; Don Beltran, Duke of Albuquerque, 1,400,000. Altogether the royal treasury was enriched by some 30,000,000 maravedis. The heaviest exactions were levied on the family of Cardinal Mendoza, with his approval.

There was much grumbling, but the complacency of the great feudatories under such heavy demands showed how great a revolution had been accomplished. The same measure, in 1474,

On a Spanish Highway in the Fifteenth Century
(*From a Print in the Bibliothèque Nationale*)

would have been the signal for rebellion. But Isabel and Fernando had become absolute monarchs in the five melodramatic years since that December day when the herald in Segovia proclaimed the death of Enrique IV.

The Queen was as solicitous for Fernando's preëminence as she was for her own. She always referred to him with great respect as "my lord the King," and compelled even his relatives to show him a ceremonious deference. One evening when she had retired early, while the King in the next room was playing a long game of chess with his uncle, the Admiral Don Fadrique, she heard that nobleman exclaim with delight:

"Aha! I have beaten my nephew!"

Hastily throwing a wrap about her, Isabel thrust her head through the opening in the tapestry at the door, and said with frigid politeness: "Don Fadrique, my lord the King has no relatives or friends; he has only servants and vassals."

The times of King Enrique were past and Isabel had no intention that any remotely similar should return while she occupied the throne. She addressed even her old and intimate friend Beatriz Bobadilla by no more familiar term than *"hija marquesa"*—"daughter Marquesa." And the Admiral had another evidence of her impartiality about a year after the reform of Toledo, when the court was at Valladolid. His son, also named Don Fadrique, had a dispute in the Queen's palace with young Ramir Nuñez de Guzman over the beauty of women, and one word led to another, until Don Fadrique felt himself injured. The Queen, hearing of the quarrel, asked her *maestresala*, Garsilaso de la Vega, to take charge of Ramir while she herself commanded Don Fadrique to remain in his father's house and not leave without her permission. To Don Ramir, who was less robust than the King's cousin, she gave a safe-conduct, a more useful document, generally, than in the days when the Count of Benavente taunted her. But a few days later, as Ramir was riding on a mule through the Plaza of Valladolid, full of faith in the royal paper in his pocket, three men with masked faces suddenly appeared and gave him a beating with sticks. The Queen had no doubt who had instigated the assault. Although it was pouring rain, she mounted a horse and took the road for Simancas, where the Admiral's residence was, without waiting for even a servant or a squire.

When the Admiral came to the gate of his fortress, he was

greatly surprised to hear a familiar imperious voice in the rainy darkness: *"Almirante, dadme luego a Don Fadrique vuestro fijo, para facer justicia del, porque quebrantó mi seguro!"* [4]

"Señora," said the Admiral, "he isn't here, and I don't know where he is."

The Queen: "Since you cannot deliver your son, deliver to me this fortress of Simancas, and the fortress of Rioseco."

The Admiral gave the Queen the keys of both places, "since he didn't dare do anything else." The Queen, after a futile search of the castle, returned to Valladolid, a distance of twenty miles, in the driving rain.

Next day she was so ill that she could not get out of bed. Asked by her doctor what symptoms or pains she had, the Queen said, "This body of mine aches from the blows that Don Fadrique gave yesterday to my safe-conduct."

Her anger increased every day, until Don Fadrique's uncle, fearful lest the whole family suffer from her displeasure, urged the Admiral to give him up; in fact he took the young cavalier to the palace, and after representing that Don Fadrique was too young to understand the obedience due to kings and the sanctity of a royal safe conduct, begged her to receive him and to pardon him.

The Queen said shortly, "I do not wish to see Don Fadrique." She commanded an *alcalde* of her court to take charge of him, and to lead him publicly, like an ordinary criminal, through the plaza of Valladolid, and thence to the fortress of Arévalo, to be kept in solitary confinement with only the barest necessities. Even King Fernando, when he returned from Aragon, could obtain no concession from her but a commutation of Fadrique's sentence to exile in Sicily.

Don Ramir de Guzman seems to have been strangely unable to profit by the experience of others. The blows of the sticks still smarted in his soul until he conceived the insane idea of taking a second vengeance on Fadrique's father, the Admiral of Castile. The four horsemen he employed to beat that dignitary at Medina del Campo were repulsed by servants, and he himself fled to Portugal from the long arm of Isabel, who confiscated all his estates.

As Isabel sat sewing the buttons on her husband's shirts—for if we may believe Florez he never wore any but those her

skilful hands stitched for relaxation between dictating letters
and other cares of state—she had every reason to feel satisfied
with the first five years of her reign. For the first time she was
reasonably secure on her throne. Portugal was defeated; civil
peace had returned to Castile; the Cortes had granted her the
absolute powers she required; she had three children to guarantee the succession to her own blood. But she seemed aware
that all this was but a beginning. Greater events were impending.

The universal uneasiness, the expectancy of new shocks and
conflicts, was reflected in one of the historic ceremonies during
the Cortes of Toledo. Four hundred *comendadores* and *caballeros* of the Order of Santiago marched in their white mantles
surmounted by red crosses and cockleshells down the aisles
of the Cathedral, bearing their banners to be blessed for the
Moorish war. Cárdenas, the Master, knelt before the King and
Queen and delivered to them the flags and ensigns of Santiago.

"Master," they said, "God give you good fortune against
the Moors, enemies of our Holy Catholic Faith."

In taking back the flags and kissing the royal hands, Cárdenas was only following an old custom; but on this occasion
he did something more: he turned and impulsively asked permission to renew the war against the Infidel.

King Fernando replied, "We must first drive the Turks off
the shores of Italy."

He referred to what all men knew, the imminent danger that
overshadowed all Christendom as the conquering Mohammedans advanced through the Mediterranean. Something like
a chill spread through Europe when it became known in 1479
that the Grand Turk, Mohammed II, was besieging Rhodes.

Since Venice had abandoned the crusade in 1479, sacrificing
Christian Albania in the treaty of Stamboul to preserve her
own trade with the Levant, the only remaining Christian naval
power that offered any obstacle to the Turkish mastery of the
Mediterranean was that of the Hospitallers of St. John of
Jerusalem, who had withstood the Moslems on the Island
of Rhodes for a century, and had made themselves the terror of
the Infidel pirates. In 1480 Mohammed II brought all his
thunderbolts to bear on Rhodes with the intent of ridding
himself of so troublesome an enemy; but all his armament
could not prevail against the heroism of Pierre d'Aubusson and

his knights, who fought off the invaders for two months and at last repulsed them after a furious battle in the great breach opened by the Moslem artillery.

Having failed at Rhodes, the Great Turk dispatched his fleet to Italy. They sailed along the coast of Apulia, and on August 11, 1480, actually took by storm the city of Otranto in the Kingdom of Naples. Of the 22,000 inhabitants, the barbarians bound 12,000 with ropes and put them to death, thus helpless, with terrible tortures. They slew all the priests in the city. They sawed in two the aged Archbishop of Otranto, whom they found praying before the altar. On a hill outside the city, now known as Martyrs' Hill, they butchered many captives who refused to become Mohammedans, and threw their corpses to the dogs.

The consternation of Italy was indescribable. "In Rome the alarm was as great as if the enemy had been already encamped outside the walls," wrote Sigismondo de' Conti. . . . "Even the Pope meditated flight," and preparations were made at Avignon to receive him. He appealed to the Italian powers in these terms:

"If the faithful, especially the Italians wish to preserve their lands, their houses, their wives, their children, their liberty, and their lives; if they wish to maintain that Faith into which we have been baptised, and through which we are regenerated, let them at last trust in our word, let them take up their arms and fight." King Ferrante of Naples was at war with Florence, and his son Alfonso, Duke of Calabria, whose subjects the Turks were slaughtering, was 150 leagues away in Tuscany, fighting in the Tuscan War. Alfonso frantically marched to the defense of his dominions. Almost unaided, save by the Pope, who had even the sacred vessels melted to obtain money, he besieged the Turks in Otranto, and after six months recaptured the city.

The apathy of the Italian princes was incredible. Not until Ferrante threatened to join the Sultan in destroying them all did they bestir themselves with any vigor. The Pope, according to Sigismondo de' Conti, "would have witnessed with great indifference the misfortunes and losses of his faithless ally, had Ferrante's enemy been any one but the Sultan; but it was a very different matter when the common foe of Christendom had actually got a footing on Italian soil."

Of the foreign rulers, Isabel and Fernando were almost alone
in perceiving that the peril of Italy was the peril of all Christendom. They immediately dispatched the whole Castilian fleet
of twenty-two vessels to Italian waters to assist in the recapture of Otranto and to protect Fernando's kingdom of
Sicily. But it was characteristic of Isabel to stop at nothing
short of her utmost. At a moment when she had need of her
new revenues to complete her program of reform and to
prepare for the war with Granada that all men expected to be
resumed when the truce expired in 1481, she generously threw
all her energies and material resources into the major struggle
for the safety of Christendom. She formed the audacious design of raising a fleet powerful enough not only to defend
Italy and Spain, but if necessary to defeat the Turks on the
high seas and smash their whole offensive. Castile having done
its best for the present, she decided to equip the armada from
the northern provinces and launch it in one of the northern
ports. From merchants at Burgos she ordered huge supplies
of artillery, munitions, food, clothing, all manner of naval
stores.

The effort was tremendous, all the more so since public opinion among the mountains and along the protected northern
coast had to be whipped into enthusiasm. The men of Galicia
and Guipúzcoa had suffered less from the Moorish wars than
the Southern provinces had; yet they had contributed much to
the man-power of Castile in the War of the Succession, and
they were tired of wars and rumors of wars. Sicily to them
seemed very remote, Otranto only a word, the massacring
Turks like mythical goblins or werewolves. The Queen, therefore, commissioned Alonso de Quintanilla, who had been so
successful in organizing the Hermandad, to direct a vigorous
propaganda in the north, to let the mountaineers and sailors
know that if the Turks mastered Italy, their next logical stopping place would be Spain. But at first the royal officers were
badly received; there was rioting in several towns, and they
barely escaped from the mob with their lives.[5]

As the story of Otranto became generally known, the panic
that Castile and Aragon shared with Italy spread to every
corner of the peninsula. Men were asking, what would become
of the Christian kingdoms if the Turks came from the east, and
the Moors of Granada, their coreligionists, took the offensive

in the south against Andalusia? In such a case the situation of Castile would be perilous. But with secret enemies within her gates allied with the terrible foe without, her plight would be hopeless. In wartime every nation considers unity the indispensable condition of self-preservation. The doom of the *Conversos* in Castile, as a nation within the nation, was sealed with the landing of the Turks in Italy.

Otranto fell August 11. The news reached Spain some time in September. Isabel had long been keeping in reserve the Papal bull of November 1, 1478, authorizing her to establish the Inquisition in her kingdoms. On September 26, 1480, she issued the order that made it effective. The double signature—"Yo, el Rey, Yo, la Reyna"—marked the beginning of the last chapter in the slow resurrection of Christian Spain, and of a new and sad one in the weary annals of the children of Israel.

XIV

ISABEL AND FERNANDO DECIDE TO IN-
VOKE THE INQUISITION AS A WAR
MEASURE TO COMPLETE THE UNIFICA-
TION OF SPAIN

IN MEDIEVAL Spain the Jews came nearer to building a
New Jerusalem than at any time or place since their dis-
persion after the Crucifixion. Had they succeeded—and
several times they came perilously near success—they might
conceivably have managed, with Mohammedan aid, to destroy
the Christian civilization of Europe. Their ultimate failure
was caused chiefly by the life work of Isabel.

The date of their first migrations to the peninsula is disputed. But the evidence appears to indicate that they arrived
not long after Saint James the Greater first preached the gospel
of Christianity in Saragossa in 42 A. D. Some of those
expelled from Rome by Claudius may have settled in Spain.
Certain it is that they spread through the country very early
in the Christian era, and multiplied so rapidly that their presence constituted a serious problem for the Arian (unorthodox
Christian) Visigoths. They were not at first persecuted by the
Christians; but after the discovery that they were plotting to
bring the Arabs from Africa for the overthrow of the Gothic
kingdom, they were condemned to slavery by one of the councils of Toledo. Nevertheless by the beginning of the eighth
century they were numerous in all the chief cities, enjoyed
power and wealth, and even obtained through bribery certain
privileges denied to Christians.

That they played an important part in bringing the Saracens
from Africa in 709 is certain. In the invading army there were
many African Jews. Everywhere the Spanish Jews opened the
gates of cities to the conquerors, and the Moslems rewarded
them by turning over to them the government of Granada,
Seville and Cordoba. "Without any love for the soil where

they lived, without any of those affections that ennoble a people, and finally without sentiments of generosity," says Amador de los Rios,[1] "they aspired only to feed their avarice and to accomplish the ruin of the Goths; taking the opportunity to manifest their rancor, and boasting of the hatreds that they had hoarded up so many centuries." This is a severe indictment, and it would be most unfair to place all the blame for the Mussulman invasion at the door of the Jews. Neither their intrigues nor the Moorish arms could have prevailed, perhaps, if the Christian Visigoth monarchy had not fallen first into heresy and then into decadence. King Witiza led an unsavory life, published an edict permitting priests to marry, and so far flouted the Christian beliefs of his subjects that he denied the authority of the Pope. His successor, Roderigo, violated the daughter of Count Julian, who thereupon crossed into Africa and joined the Jews in prevailing upon the Moors to conquer Spain. The sons of Witiza, persecuted by Roderigo, also joined the enemy. And at the critical moment of the battle of Jeréz de la Frontera, Bishop Oppas, who had a grudge against Roderigo, went over to the Saracens and gave them the victory.

In the new Moslem state the Jews found themselves highly esteemed. It was under the caliphs that they attained the height of their prosperity. They studied and taught in the Arab universities, excelling particularly in astrology and medicine. Through their connections with Asiatic Jews, they were able to get the best drugs and spices; and through their wealth, acquired chiefly through usury, barter and the huge traffic in slaves, they obtained leisure for the pursuit and diffusion of culture. They expounded the philosophy of Aristotle, which flourished among the Arabs, before the Stagirite was known in Christian Europe.[2]

In Granada the Jews became so numerous that it was called "the city of the Jews." But the Saracens persecuted them at times. On December 30, 1066, the Moslems of Granada, infuriated by their exploitations, arose against them and slew 4,000. One of the caliphs expelled all Jews from Granada.

The gradual reconquest of the peninsula by the Christians did not at first trouble their marvelous prosperity. When Saint Fernando took Seville in 1224, he gave the Jews four Moorish mosques to convert into synagogues; he allowed them one of

the pleasantest sections for their homes, and imposed no conditions except to refrain from proselytising among Christians
and from insulting the Christian religion.[3] The Jews observed
neither of these conditions. Yet several of the later kings,
usually those of lukewarm faith or those especially in need of
money, showed them high favor. Alfonso VIII made one of
them his treasurer.

In spite of persecution now and then, they multiplied and
prospered until, toward the end of the thirteenth century, they
were a power, almost a state within the state, gradually re-
halting the reconquest. In Castile alone they paid a poll tax
of 2,561,855 maravedis in 1284.[4] As each adult male Jew was
taxed three gold maravedis, there must have been 853,951
men alone; hence the total Jewish population may well have
been from four to five millions—and this leaves out of account
large communities in Aragon and other sections. There are
no accurate figures for the total population of Spain, but most
of the estimates generally accepted are ridiculously low. More
probably there were at least 25,000,000 and perhaps as many
as 30,000,000 people in all the Spanish kingdoms at the beginning of the fourteenth century. Probably a fifth, or even a
fourth were Jews—a large minority, and they possessed an
influence out of proportion to their numbers. They became so
powerful that the laws against blasphemy could not be enforced
against them. It was so plain that they were above the law
that the Cathari of Leon used to circumcize themselves that
they might freely teach as Jews the heresy for which they
would be punished as Christians.[5]

The capital and commerce of the country were largely in
their hands, for they were almost the only bankers and money-
lenders in an age when usury was forbidden by the Church.
In Aragon they generally charged twenty per cent, in Castile
thirty-three and one-third per cent. During the famine of 1326
the Jewish *alhama* of Cuenca refused to lend money or wheat
for sowing, unless they received forty per cent interest, and
the town council was compelled by the distress of the people
to pay it. Carlos III of Navarre paid thirty-five per cent for
a loan of 2,000 florins in 1401, and in 1402 his wife, Queen
Leona, paid her Jewish physician four florins a month for a
loan of 70 florins, giving him her silver plate as security. As
the interest on the 70 florins amounted to 84 florins after

twenty-one months, she protested, and the Jew accepted 30 florins.[5] The citizen with taxes to pay, the farmer with no money to buy seed for his planting, the burgher held for ransom by a turbulent noble, turned in desperation to the Jewish money-lender and became his economic slave.

The government gradually passed into Jewish hands. Though the common people, the debtor class, hated them, the kings and great feudatories protected them, since it was convenient at times to borrow from them. Whenever the Jews made a loan, however, they asked for security, and frequently for some political concession. For example, a Jew would ask the King to "farm out" to him the taxes of a certain city or district; or the King, in desperate need of funds, would offer the privilege to the highest bidder, and a Jew usually got it. The profit of farming the taxes depended on the amount that the collectors could extort from the people. Isabel's brother Enrique carried the hated policy so far that he gave two of his Jewish tax collectors the power of life and death over the citizens whom they exploited. The Church in vain attempted to prevent the employment of Jews in public offices. The services they rendered to the monarchs as money-lenders, administrators, physicians and scientists made them indispensable. The people protested; the kings promised relief, but seldom gave it.

Confident and secure, the Jews lived with all the oriental ostentation of which their luxurious nature is capable. They took no particular pains to conceal their contempt for the lesser breeds without the law, who paid them tribute; they overdressed, they lived in grand houses, they entertained lavishly. Alfonso V of Portugal once said to Rabbi Ibn Yachia, "Why don't you stop your people from displaying a magnificence that Christians attribute to thefts committed at their expense? But you needn't answer me! I know that nothing but a massacre can cure them of that fatal pride of theirs."

With the reign of Pedro the Cruel in the middle of the fourteenth century, the history of the Jews in Castile enters on a new phase. Pedro, who was intensely hated, was popularly believed to have been a Jewish child, substituted in the cradle of the lawful heiress by Queen Maria, whose husband had threatened to kill her if she did not bear a boy. He was denounced by Pope Urban I as a rebel to the Church, "a fautor of Jews and Moors, a propagator of infidelity, and a slayer of Christians." He gave the Jews complete control of his government. They financed his war with his bastard brother Henry of Trastamara, Isabel's great-great-grandfather. The Moors also recognized a friend in Pedro, for 87,000 of them marched from Granada to help him in 1368. When Henry slew him— calling him *el fi de puta judio*—it was an unlucky day for both Jews and Moors.

As if their wealth and ostentation were not sure sooner or later to cause a repetition of their sad history, there fell on the Israelites a terrible misfortune such as no man could have predicted. All men suffered from it, but the Jews more cruelly than the rest.

The Black Death, killing 25,000,000 people in two years —at least half the population of Europe—was probably the worst catastrophe that had ever befallen Christendom. But the Jews suffered doubly. For they had hardly buried their dead when the populace, half crazed with fear and grief, revived the old cry, "Down with the Jews! The Jews did it! The Jews poisoned the wells!"

Straightway, all over Europe, the Israelites were put to the sword. In vain did Pope Clement VI attempt by pleadings and threats of excommunication to stay the fanatics, particularly in Germany. Following the example, as he said, of Calixtus II, Eugenius III, Alexander III, Clement III, Coelestin III, Innocent III, Gregory IX, Nicholas III, Honorius IV, and Nicholas IV, he denounced the tales attributing the calamity to the Jews as lies, and pointed out that the plague had been just as virulent in lands where no Jews lived. The massacres, however, continued.[6]

In Castile, the Jews escaped the major persecution until the Archdeacon of Ecija, Ferran Martinez, preached against them. In June, 1391, there was a general uprising in Seville; the mob rushed into the *juderia*, slew 4,000 and compelled the survivors to accept baptism. The furor spread to other cities. The total number of victims has been estimated as high as 50,000, probably, as Lea says, an exaggeration.[7]

These massacres created a new class of citizens: the *Conversos*, or *Marranos*, when referred to derisively. Thirty-five thousand were converted by the eloquence of Saint Vincent Ferrer, 4,000 being baptized in Toledo in one day. What his sermons and his miracles failed to accomplish, the fear of further atrocities effected. The Jewish population in Isabel's time had shrunk from some 5,000,000 or more to about 200,000.

What had become of the 4,800,000? If the Black Death slew, say 2,000,000, another two and a half million, at least, had become "New Christians." Some conversions were sincere; more of them were actuated by fear under persecution, or by motives of self-interest. "Their conversion was, however, only external, or feigned; at heart they adhered loyally to their ancestral religion. Though outwardly Christians, they secretly observed the tenets of the Jewish faith."[8] With the intelligence of their race, they saw that as acknowledged Jews they would be segregated, forced to wear a badge of inferiority and pay a poll tax, forbidden to have social or business relations with Christians, or to hold office in Church or State. But as professing Christians who heard Mass on Sunday, even though they privately attended the synagogue on Saturday, they could hold office, they could follow any career for which their abilities fitted them, they could even intermarry with the noble (but sometimes needy) families of Spain.

By the time of Isabel and Fernando, a great many of the ancient houses of the peninsula had Jewish relatives. *Limpia sangre*, "clean blood," was a distinction which many claimed, but not all had. The de Lunas, the Mendozas, the Guzmans, the Villahermosas, all had Hebrew strains. Certain Jewish traditions have gone so far as to include even the maternal grandmother of King Fernando; but the claim is based upon a misunderstanding, as Zurita and Mariana clearly prove.

What cannot be questioned, however, is that *Conversos* and their kin everywhere controlled business, government, taxation, all that was valuable, just as their ancestors had as Jews. Thus the massacres had only substituted for one problem another and much more intricate one. For as *Conversos*, the Jews were now capable of doing greater injury to Christianity through their influence upon the "Old Christians" with whom they mingled.

Even the Catholic Church in Spain was being directed and exploited to an astonishing extent by Jews when Isabel became Queen. As "Christians" they could now become priests, if otherwise eligible. A Jewish "convert" anxious to show his loyalty to his new religion, would dedicate one of his sons to the Church. And in the Church the Jews excelled just as they did in other fields; they mounted the hierarchy so rapidly that in Isabel's reign an impressive number of the bishops were of Jewish descent. Every church, every chapter, every monastery had influential Jewish connections; and in some dioceses Jews collected the ecclesiastical revenues.

To attribute all the corruption in the Church to them, as their enemies did, was of course unfair. Clerical discipline had broken down in other countries where the Jews were few; the Church had had to lower the standards of her priesthood after the Black Death; and the seventy-five years exile of the popes at Avignon as prisoners of the French Kings, had paralyzed the whole structure. But in Spain there was an additional cause of laxity and immorality, of cynicism and hypocrisy, in the presence of so many priests who did not believe the doctrines they taught.

It is not difficult to understand the indignation of Catholics against priests who made a mockery of the sacraments they pretended to administer. "No man could tell how many priests there were like Andres Gomalz, parish priest of San Martin de Talavera, who, on his trial at Toledo in 1486, confessed that for fourteen years he had been secretly a Jew, that he had no 'intention' when he celebrated Mass, nor had he granted absolution to the penitents who confessed to him."[9]

And there were others like Fray Garcia de Tapate, prior of the Jeronymite monastery of Toledo, who, when he elevated the Host at Mass, used to say, "Get up, little Peter, and let the people look at you," instead of the words of consecration; and who always turned his back on his penitents while he pretended to give them absolution.

The "New Christians," by another irony, became the bitterest persecutors of the poor despised Jews who had clung to the law of Moses at the risk of their lives. The Cortes of 1405, directed by ambitious *Conversos*, passed new and cruel laws against the people of the *juderias*. All bonds of Christians held by Jews were declared void; debts due them were reduced one-half; they must wear red circles on their clothing except when traveling. The ordinance of Queen Catalina in 1412 forbade them to shave or cut the hair round, to change abodes, to be farmers or collectors of taxes, physicians, surgeons, apothecaries, peddlers, blacksmiths, furriers, carpenters, tailors, barbers, or builders; to carry arms; to hire Christians; to eat with or bathe with Christians. "From the earliest times," says Lea, "the hardest blows endured by Judaism had always been dealt by its apostate children whose training had taught them the weakest points to assail, and whose necessity of self-justification led them to attack these mercilessly." Converted Jews had egged on the mobs in 1391. *Conversos* would be found high in the council of the Inquisition, directing its activities. Sometimes the Jews avenged themselves on the "New Christians" by falsely testifying against them before the Inquisition, and getting them burned as heretics. Isabel proceeded against such false witnesses with the utmost rigor. As an example she had eight of them executed, their flesh having been torn first with red hot pincers.

The *Conversos* were hated by the Old Christians even more than the Jews were. Bernaldez expresses his aversion to them in a famous passage that is, no doubt, a faithful reflection of the public opinion of his time:[10]

"Those who can avoid baptizing their children, do so, and those who have them baptized wash them off as soon as they return home . . . You must know that the customs of the common people before the Inquisition were neither more nor less those of the ill-smelling Jews, on account of the continual communication they have with them; thus they are gluttons and feeders, who never lose the judaical habit of eating delicacies of onions and garlic fried in oil, and they cook their meat in oil, using it in place of lard or fat, to avoid pork; and oil with meat is a thing that makes the breath smell very bad, and so their houses and doorways smell most offensively from those tit-bits; and hence they have the odor of the Jews, as a result of their food and their not being baptized. And notwithstanding that some have been baptized, yet the virtue of the baptism having been destroyed in them by their credulity and by judaizing, they smell like Jews. They do not eat pork unless they are compelled to; they eat meat in Lent and on the vigils of feasts and on ember days; they keep the Passover and the Sabbath as best they can. They send oil to the synagogues for the lamps. They have Jews who preach to them secretly in their houses, especially to the women very secretly; and they have Jewish rabbis whose occupation is to slaughter

their beasts and fowls for them. They eat unleavened bread
during the Jewish holidays, and meat chopped up. They follow
all the judaical ceremonies secretly so far as they can.

"The men as well as the women always avoid receiving the
sacraments of Holy Church voluntarily. When they confess,
they never tell the truth; and it happened that one confessor
asked a person of this tribe to cut off a piece of his garment
for him, saying, 'Since you have never sinned, I should like
to have a bit of your garment for a relic to heal the sick.'
There was a time in Seville when it was commanded that no
meat be weighed on Saturday, because all the *Conversos* ate it
Saturday night, and they ordered it weighed Sunday morning.

"Not without reason did Our Redeemer call them a wicked
and adulterous generation. They do not believe that God rewards virginity and chastity. All their endeavor is to increase
and multiply. And in the time when this heretical iniquity
flourished, many monasteries were violated by their wealthy
men and merchants, and many professed nuns were ravished
and mocked, some through gifts and some through the lures
of panderers, they not believing in or fearing excommuni-
cations; but they did it to injure Jesus Christ and the Church.
And usually, for the most part, they were usurious people, of
many wiles and deceits, for they all live by easy occupations
and offices, and in buying and selling they have no conscience
where Christians are concerned. Never would they undertake
the occupations of tilling the soil or digging or cattle-raising,
nor would they teach their children any except holding public
offices, and sitting down to earn enough to eat with little labor.
Many of them in these realms in a short time acquired very
great fortunes and estates, since they had no conscience in their
profits and usuries, saying that they only gained at the expense
of their enemies, according to the command of God in the departure of the people of Israel to rob the Egyptians. . . . Of
all this the King and Queen were assured while they were at
Seville."[11]

To some extent, at least, Isabel must have shared these
views, so that in yielding to an overwhelming pressure of public opinion in the early fall of 1480 she was doing no violence
to her own convictions. Mendoza's catechism had failed to
accomplish the miracle he had hoped for; it had only stirred
the *Conversos* to new laughter and blasphemies, and the

Cardinal was compelled to agree that no way remained but force.

Finally, on a cool day in September, the Queen unlocked one of the cunningly carved wooden chests in which her state papers were kept, and drew from it a document that had reposed there in profound secrecy since the last days of 1478. It was a piece of parchment, with a leaden seal hung on threads of colored silk. It was a bull issued at Rome on November 1, 1478, by Pope Sixtus IV. From its text it is possible to form an intelligent conjecture as to how the Spanish envoy at Rome had represented the situation to the Holy Father. After the usual preamble, the Pope wrote:

"The genuine devotion and sound faith manifested in your reverence for us and the Roman Church demand that, as far as we can in the sight of God, we grant your requests, particularly those which concern the exaltation of the Catholic Faith and the salvation of souls. We learn from your letter recently shown to us that in various cities, sections and regions of the Spanish kingdoms, many of those who of their own accord were born anew in Christ in the sacred waters of Baptism, while continuing to comport themselves externally as Christians, yet have secretly adopted or returned to the religious observances and customs of the Jews, and are living according to the principles and ordinances of Jewish superstition and falsehood, thus renouncing the truths of the orthodox faith, its worship, and belief in its doctrines, and incurring, without hesitation or fear, the censures and penalties pronounced against followers of heretical perversity, in accordance with the constitutions of Pope Boniface VIII, our predecessor of happy memory. Not only do they persist in their blindness but their children and their associates are infected with the same perfidy, and thus their numbers increase not a little. Due to the crimes of these men and, as is piously believed, to the forbearance of this Holy See and of those ecclesiastical prelates whose duty it is to examine into such matters, with God's permission, war and homicide and other misfortunes are oppressing those same regions to the offense of the Divine Majesty, the contempt of the aforesaid Faith, the danger of souls and the scandal of many. On this account you have humbly implored our apostolic kindness to extirpate

this dangerous sect root and branch from out your
kingdoms. . . .

"We rejoice in the Lord over your praiseworthy zeal for
the Faith and for the salvation of souls and express the hope
that you will exert every effort not only to drive this perfidy
from your realms, but also in our own times to subject to
your rule the kingdom of Granada and the territories that
border on it. We likewise trust that you will strive through
the workings of Divine Mercy to bring about the conversion
to the true faith of the infidels who are in these territories.
Thus, what your predecessors, owing to various obstacles,
found impossible of accomplishment you will bring to pass
unto the prosperity of the same true faith, the salvation of
souls, your own great glory, and the assurance of eternal happiness, for which you so earnestly pray. We wish to grant
your petitions and to apply suitable remedies to the evils you
mention. Yielding therefore to your entreaties, we willingly
permit the appointment of three, or at least two, bishops or
archbishops or other approved men, who are secular priests, or
religious of the mendicant or the non-mendicant orders, above
forty years of age, of good conscience and exemplary life,
masters or bachelors in theology, or doctors in canon law or
licentiates carefully examined, God-fearing men, whom you
shall consider worthy to be chosen, for the time being, in each
city and diocese of the aforesaid kingdoms according to the
needs of the places. . . . Furthermore to the men thus designated we grant, in regard to those accused of these crimes,
and in regard to all who aid and abet them, the same judicial
authority, peculiar rights and jurisdiction as law and custom
allow to Ordinaries and Inquisitors of heretical perversity."[12]

This text makes it clear that Isabel's agent in Rome had
represented the Inquisition to the Pope as a necessary war
measure during a Crusade; a temporary one—"for the time
being"; and one that would be conducted in cooperation with
the bishops, according to the practice that experience had taught
was needed to prevent abuses. As the royal petition reached
the Pope, the only new feature of it appeared to be the request
that he permit the sovereigns to name the Inquisitors. That
was unusual, but so were the conditions in Spain. Sixtus could
have had no idea that the Spanish tribunal would exist for
three centuries to come.

During the panic over the fall of Otranto—on September 26, 1480—the King and Queen published the bull as part of an edict establishing the Inquisition in Castile. The text of this document shows that their purpose was not merely to punish or to persecute for the sake of intolerance; it was in part at least to prevent a repetition of the ghastly massacres of the *Conversos*. The aim of the new court, the edict stated, was not only to punish the judaizers who sought to draw simple-minded Christians from the true faith, but also "to protect faithful Christians" among the *Conversos* "from unjust suspicion and persecution." Two Inquisitors were appointed: Fray Juan de San Martin, bachelor of theology, and Fray Miguel de Morillo, master of theology. They were given to understand in the plain language of the edict that their responsibility was no longer to the Pope but to the royal Crown. "We command you," said the edict, "to accept this office." Failure on their part to carry out the royal commands would be punished by the confiscation of their goods, and the loss of their citizenship; they could be removed at any time by the King and Queen.[13]

Isabel and Fernando may not have been aware at this stage that their ambassador at Rome had in reality tricked the Pope into granting them powers that would be used to the glory of the state and the discredit of the Church. Isabel, at least, despised all double-dealing; and it may be significant that her name appears less frequently than the King's on the correspondence with Sixtus. "Fernando had so contrived that the duty, which the Church was bound to perform, and which the Pope could neither refuse nor evade, of declaring where errors in faith existed, should be made subservient to the state purpose of detecting high treason, then identical with Judaism; while the Church itself could exercise no controlling influence whatsoever to stay the terrible retributions awarded by the criminal courts of the realm."[14] In short, the Inquisition, as Fernando arranged matters, was religious in form only; in spirit and purpose it was the instrument of the new Caesarism to which events had gradually led him. Its judges were to be Dominican monks; but the monks were servants of the State, not of the Church.

It is entirely possible that Fernando carried Isabel, as well as Sixtus, into deeper waters than she realized. Nevertheless, the Queen never shirked her share of the responsibility for the Holy Office. And there is no contemporary evidence to support the theory by which most of her biographers, anxious to reconcile her natural kindness and rectitude with her severity against the *Conversos*, have attributed her long delay to what would now be called "humanitarian" motives. All such well-intentioned efforts arise from a failure to understand the perilous conditions in which she labored—the war psychology of Spain, the challenge of the secret Jews allied to a nation within the new nation, the intensity of the popular distrust of them, and the extent to which the Queen probably shared it. She was, after all, the daughter of that uncompromising Queen who had pursued de Luna, the friend of Jews and *Conversos*, to his doom. She was the girl who had turned with disgust from the immoralities of Enrique's court where the *Conversos* held the palm, who had shuddered at the bare thought of being embraced by that lecherous *Converso* Don Pedro Giron, who had sickened on hearing men accuse that other *Converso* Juan Pacheco of poisoning her brother Alfonso. She had in her, after all, the blood of those Plantagenets who were so ruthless that men called them devils, of William the Conqueror, who, when his wife reminded him once too often of his bastardy, was said to have tied her long hair to the tail of his horse and to have dragged her about, to teach her the duty of a wife.

Isabel, the maid, had resolved to complete the reconquest and rehabilitation of Spain, and only the Moors and the *Conversos* stood in her way. And the mature woman who had calmly ordered the executions of so many thieves and murderers in the Jew-ridden city of Seville would hardly hesitate to exact conformity from those who were guilty of an offense which she considered even worse than theft or murder—heresy. To most people of the twentieth century the word "heresy" connotes merely an independence of thought, a difference of opinion. We are likely to forget that the mass of men in the Middle Ages nearly always associated it with some group whose tenets and activities appeared anti-social. In a dominantly Christian society, as Europe once was, heresy seemed something monstrous, diabolical. Men thought of heretics as respectable middle-class folk of our day think of militant anarchists. Even so gentle and charitable a woman as Saint Teresa of Ávila considered heresy worse than any other sin.

Comparing the human soul to a mirror, she wrote, "When a soul is in mortal sin, this mirror becomes clouded with a thick vapor, and utterly obscured, so that Our Lord is neither visible nor present, though He is always present in the conservation of its being. In heretics, the mirror is, as it were, broken in pieces, and that is worse than being dimmed."[15] Isabel would have agreed with this statement; it would have seemed to her only a logical conclusion from the premises contained in the teachings of Christ in her hand-illuminated New Testament.

In associating *Conversos* with the traditional foes, the sensual Mussulmans, Spanish Christians, even to this day, have imputed to them certain vices against which Christian communities have always reacted with severity. A modern Spanish scholar writes that "these unworthy practices, always existent, have epochs of recrudescence, as in the fifteenth century, through contact with the Moors, making necessary the *cedula* of the Catholic Queen, with the terrible chastisement of the bonfire."[16] A popular tract written by a converted Jew during the first years of the Inquisition went so far as to make the ridiculous assertion that "the Marranos invented sodomy." In the very nature of the case it was impossible for the Spanish Christian to be fair to the *Converso*; he saw in him only the ally of his ancient enemy. And it must be said that the deeds of the *Conversos* and of the Jews from time to time lent some color to the popular prejudices. After the massacres of 1473 the *Conversos* of Córdoba had attempted to purchase Gibraltar from King Enrique. It was generally believed that they intended using it as a base to bring hordes of Moors from Africa to reconquer all Spain.

Another reason for Isabel's delay was probably the simple fact that she did not feel herself quite strong enough to proceed until after the conclusion of peace with Portugal and the Cortes of Toledo. And it may be inferred that the *Conversos* who were so powerfully entrenched in her court did not see the royal hand raised above their heads without making strenuous efforts to avert the blow. Her closest friend, Beatriz, had married a *Converso*. Her confessor was of Jewish descent. Almost all her privy councillors and secretaries had Jewish ancestors on one side or the other—or both. Fernando's *escribano de racion*, a sort of treasurer, was the acute lawyer Luis de Santángel, one of a great family with ramifications all over Aragon and Castile. He was descended from the Jewish rabbi Azarias Zinello; an uncle, Pedro Martin, had been Bishop of Mallorca; other members of the family were farmers of taxes and of the royal salt works. King Fernando's government, in fact, was virtually in the hands of the *Conversos*. His *maestre racional* or Chief Treasurer, Sancho de Paternoy, his confidential friends and advisers, Jaime de la Caballeria and Juan de Cabrero; his cup-bearer Guilleo Sanchez, his steward Francisco Sanchez, his treasurer Gabriel Sanchez—all were of the seed of Abraham. It would have been strange if these shrewd and powerful politicians had not made every effort to dissuade the King and Queen from the step they were contemplating.

XV

CERTAIN MILLIONAIRES OF SEVILLE
PLAN TO SLAY THE QUEEN'S INQUISI-
TORS, AND ARE BURNED—BEGINNINGS
OF THE SPANISH INQUISITION

WHEN Morillo and San Martin arrived in Seville late in October, they presented their credentials to the chapter, and were escorted by the municipal council from the chapter house to the City Hall. The rich *Conversos* who controlled Seville looked on with sullen and skeptical indifference, and though they showed every outward courtesy to the emissaries of the King and Queen, managed to throw various difficulties in their way; for, as late as December 27, Fernando and Isabel found it necessary to issue a sharp *cedula* commanding all officials to render every possible aid. Meanwhile the court was being organized with Dr. Juan Ruiz de Medina as assessor, and Juan del Barco, one of the Queen's chaplains, as promotor fiscal or prosecuting officer. On the following May 13, were added Diego de Merlo, *Asistente* or chief magistrate of Seville, and the licentiate Ferrand Yanez de Lobon, as receivers of confiscations. It is evident that from the very outset the King and Queen counted upon the Inquisition to supply them with funds for the war against the Moors in Granada.

Meanwhile the Inquisitors had been taking much secret evidence and making some arrests. The *Conversos*, thoroughly alarmed at last, began to flee from Seville, as the *Sevillanos* had fled in 1477 from Queen Isabel's *audiencias*. Many went to the country estates of the great nobles, offering them money for protection, and the lords as usual accept it. Hearing this the two *friales* issued a proclamation, January 2, 1481, commanding the Marqués of Cádiz and other *grandes* to search their territories, seize all strangers and newcomers, and deliver them within fifteen days at the prison of the Inquisition; also to sequester their property, have it inventoried, and entrust it to reliable persons who should be accountable to the King and Queen. Failure to comply would result in the excommunication of the nobles, forfeiture of rank and property, prosecution by the Inquisition, and the release of their vassals from allegiance and taxes.[1]

The Marqués must have read this pronouncement with some amazement. Five years before he would have torn it in pieces and laughed to scorn the two simple monks who dared take such a tone with men accustomed to address kings on almost equal terms. Five years before two friars would probably not have dared send such a manifesto to Don Rodrigo Ponce de Leon. But times had changed.

The Marqués, though married to a daughter of the *Converso* Juan Pacheco, seized the "New Christians" and sent them to Seville. When the convent of San Pablo became overcrowded with the prisoners, the Inquisitors moved their headquarters across the river, to the great fortress of Triana. There in the gloomy, damp dungeons below the level of the river lay some of the richest and most influential men and women in Seville. The early Spanish Inquisition was one of the few persecutions in history in which the victims were chiefly millionaires and the common people applauded.

The trials commenced at once.

Since there was no longer any doubt that the Queen was serious, several of the most powerful *Conversos* met in the Church of San Salvador—a Catholic Church—to discuss means for protecting themselves. Catholic priests, priors, magistrates, government officials—all *Conversos* and secret enemies of the Church—were present. There were three of the "Twenty-Four" who ruled Seville, there were the major-domo of the Church, the Alcaide of Triana, and many other rich and powerful *Conversos*. Diego de Susan, a rabbi and a leading citizen of Seville, whose fortune was estimated at 10,000,000 maravedis, made a fiery speech demanding that they resist the Inquisition by force. He cried: "Are we not the principal men of this city in standing and the best esteemed of the people? Let us assemble troops; and if they come to take us, let us start an uprising with the troops and the people; and so we will kill them and avenge ourselves on our enemies!" All applauded this belligerent appeal, and they organized under leaders, one to collect troops, another to buy arms, another to raise money. Susan's proposal was generally commended, and plans were made for the uprising.[2]

Unhappily for him, Diego de Susan had a daughter so beautiful that she was known in Seville, a city of lovely women, as *la hermosa fembra*. She betrayed her father's secret to a Christian cavalier who was her paramour. Within twenty-four hours the Inquisitors knew the whole story.

The *Conversos* had played into their hands. Even if the plot had succeeded, there would probably have been the usual massacre in reprisal. As it was, their action seemed to confirm Queen Isabel's conviction that the *Conversos* considered themselves above the law and could not be reached by the ordinary processes of justice. Diego de Merlo proceeded to arrest the most notable men in Seville. One of the conspirators seized was Pedro Fernandez Venedera, major-domo of the Cathedral, in whose house were found hidden enough weapons to arm a hundred men. Susan and his accomplices were tried before a jury of lawyers—the traditional medieval *consulta de fe*. Several of the conspirators who confessed were given penances according to the degree of the offense, and six men and women of the ringleaders were condemned to be burned alive. If the sentence seems barbarous, it must be remembered that in other countries where there was no Inquisition, all who had any share in a plot to resist royal authority would have been cruelly executed for high treason—in England hanged, drawn and quartered, in France, boiled alive.

The first *auto de fe* in Castile was held February 6, 1481. The weather was damp, a sense of hopelessness had settled down upon the city, and only a few stragglers followed the procession, for the pestilence had returned and people were afraid of catching it. Two by two the civil officers and friars marched from the fort of Triana across the chill Guadalquivir to the marketplace of Seville, followed by the conspirators in the custody of men-at-arms. Mass was said in the Cathedral, followed by a sermon by Fray Alonso de Hojeda[3] who at last saw success rewarding his years of effort. The repentant judaizers confessed their errors, received their penances, and were reconciled to the Church. The assembly left the Cathedral and the *auto de fe* was over.

Outside the church the six condemned were delivered to civil officers of the city of Seville, who conducted them to the Campo de Tablada, beyond the walls. The six were tied to stakes, faggots were piled about them and the executioner approached, while the Dominicans made a last passionate appeal to the obdurate to repent and be reconciled. The torches were lighted, the flames flickered over the faggots and licked the feet of the condemned, the smoke curled round them. There were screams, the smell of burning flesh and hair, groans, a sickening silence.

A few days later three other prisoners were burned, including Diego de Susan, who, according to Bernaldez, who was in Seville at the time, "died a good Christian." If this be true, his execution must have been political, for high treason, rather than for heresy; for the Spanish Inquisition at this period did not execute the condemned, if they confessed even at the stake. Later such "relapsed" heretics were strangled before being burned.

La hermosa fembra found herself penniless, since her father's property was confiscated. She was hated by Jews as a parricide; but the Bishop of Tiberias took an interest in her and obtained admission for her to a convent. Her voluptuous nature eventually led her out of the cloister to a life of shame. Age withered her marvelous beauty, and she died in poverty, requesting that her skull be placed over the door of the house in the Calle de Ataud where she had plied her trade, as an example to others and a punishment for her sins.[4]

A new panic now scattered the *Conversos* in all directions. But the Inquisitors had guards placed at all the gates, and captured many. In one of the early *autos de fe* in Seville, 700 confessed, were reconciled to the Church and marched as penitents in a great procession.[5] Thousands, however, fled to the castles of nobles, to Portugal, and even to Italy.

The plague was now raging with violence, striking down Jew and Christian and *Converso* impartially. It was the same pestilence that periodically ravaged Europe during the fifteenth and early sixteenth centuries, perhaps a less virulent form of the Black Death, certainly very similar to what occasionally appears in our day as the bubonic plague. The first symptom was a bluish black boil under the arm-pit or on the palm of the hand. Then followed headache, vertigo, tottering gait, deafness, various pains and convulsions, swelling of glands and formation of buboes, coughing up of blood. The victim usually died in about ten days.

At the first appearance of the dreadful disease in any town, all fled who could. Those who had to remain built great bonfires on public squares and other open spaces, to purify the air, as they supposed, and prevent the spread of the infection. Processions were formed. Men and women did public penance for their sins. By the end of the century there were isolation hospitals in the principal cities, under plague doctors, volunteers; but in 1481 the sick were dependent upon the variable charity of their friends. The dead were buried by monks or by members of societies organized for the purpose by pious people.

"This year of 1481," wrote the curate of los Palacios, "was not propitious for the human race, but very contrary, and of very general pestilence." In Seville alone, 15,000 persons died of the plague during the summer. There were so many funerals that the Inquisition, by comparison, must have seemed a trivial affair, like the occasional shootings and decapitations of criminals. Beautiful Seville, that half-oriental pleasure-ground, was like a deserted charnel house. From the low white-washed houses, made for love songs and the strummings of lutes, came the wailings of the bereaved; no women laughed in the balconies, the gaudy flowers went to seed uncut, the oranges shriveled on the trees. Every day there were grim and silent processions of penitents in black hoods, horrible impersonations of death stalking through the crooked winding streets, bearing litters containing the corpses that no one else, not even kinfolk, would bury.

The *Conversos* begged Diego de Merlo to let them leave the city until the pest moderated. He mercifully granted the request, giving passes by which they might depart provided they took only personal effects needed for immediate use. More than 8,000 *Conversos*, mounted on horses, fled to Mairena, Marchena, Palacios; some continued to Portugal, others fled to Rome to appeal to the Pope. Many were hospitably received by the Marqués of Cádiz and the Duke of Medina Sidonia.

To escape the plague the Inquisitors moved their headquarters from Triana to Aracena.[6] There they delivered 23 judaizers, both men and women, to the secular arm, to be burned by the state. They burned the effigies of many *Conversos* who had fled the country, and the bones of condemned heretics exhumed from the churchyards. When the pestilence began to die out, they returned to Seville.

That summer they proclaimed a term of grace. It was customary in the earlier Inquisition to hold it at the beginning— perhaps the Susan conspiracy prevented. It was announced that during two months any heretic who voluntarily came forward and confessed would be pardoned, reconciled, given a penance and treated with mercy, provided he told all he knew of other judaizers or apostates. Hundreds of *Conversos* rushed in to confess. In their fear they betrayed friends and relatives, even mothers, fathers, sisters, brothers, sons and daughters. When they realized what they had done it was too late to draw back. Having confessed, they ran the risk of being "relapsed" and burned if they could not satisfy the Inquisitors of the complete sincerity of their conversions. In one *auto de fe* alone 1,500 of these penitents were reconciled, each wearing a yellow garment with a crimson cross on it, and walking barefoot to a church, where he showed his contrition and accepted his penance.

Even the Inquisitors were astonished to discover during the term of grace how extensive were the ramifications of the evil they were trying to suppress; they obtained names of suspects in Toledo, Córdoba, and even as far north as Burgos. They reported to the King and Queen that the *Conversos* were evidently almost all secret Jews engaged in undermining the Christian religion which they professed; and they demanded the extension of the Holy Office to other cities, wherever Jewish influence was strong. In Córdoba, the Inquisitors—four of them—began investigations in 1482. The first *auto de fe* was held there in 1483; and on February 28, 1484, Pedro Fernandez de Alcaudete, treasurer of the Cathedral there, was burned, his servants having killed an *alguazil* of the Inquisition when he was arrested for judaizing.[7]

There was no Inquisition in Toledo until 1485, perhaps because Archbishop Carrillo had already appointed a diocesan Inquisitor there. Instead, trials were held at Ciudad Real, commencing late in 1483 with an edict of grace. At the first *auto de fe*, November 16, 1483, the penitents who had taken advantage of the edict of grace were reconciled. Four persons were burned February 6, 1484, and thirty later in that month. When this tribunal was moved to Toledo in 1486, the *Con-*

versos organized a plot to cause a riot and slay the Inquisitors
and the chief Christian citizens and seize the city during a
procession on the Feast of Corpus Christi.[8] The conspiracy
was betrayed on and the six ringleaders were hanged.

When an assembly of the Inquisition was held in November,
1484, four years after Isabel had established the Holy Office
in Seville, only four cities were represented: Seville, Córdoba,
Jaen, and Ciudad Real. The tribunal at Segovia appears to
have been established later, and then over the vigorous protests
of the Bishop, Juan Árias de Ávila, the same who had met
Isabel at the gates one hot day in 1476. But one of the first
acts of the Inquisitors there was to condemn his Jewish mother
and father and grandmother as heretics and judaizers. He
drove them out of his diocese and sent a furious remonstrance
to Queen Isabel. When she refused to interfere with the processes of the court, the Bishop, realizing that the bones of his
ancestors would be publicly burned, went one night to the
church yard of la Merced, dug them up, hid them where they
could not be found, and fled to Rome to appeal to Pope Sixtus,
who protected him. Isabel wrote her ambassadors at Rome,
telling them what they were to say to the Pope to offset the
complaints of the bishop. He had dug up his ancestors' bones,
she declared, to conceal the fact that they were buried after the
Jewish manner, though they professed Christianity. She maintained that she acted only out of zeal for the Faith, and
denounced those who said her purpose was to gain money for
her own purse through confiscations. Any share of the confiscations appropriated by her had been used to educate and give
marriage portions to the children of the condemned.

The true history of the Spanish Inquisition has never been
written. Unfortunately most accounts until recently have been
based upon the work of Llorente, an employe of the Holy Office
in Spain, who was dismissed for alleged embezzlement, and
sought revenge by destroying records that did not support his
contentions, and using the others as the basis for an hysterical
and highly exaggerated account. Sectarian prejudice seized
upon his wild figures and built around them a monstrous legend
of fanaticism.[9] The actual records of the Holy Office, wherever
found, have compelled the most drastic revisions of his figures.
Altogether in Isabel's reign about 2,000 persons were burned
in all of Spain.[10] The contemporary accounts are few and

meagre. Public opinion undoubtedly approved of the Queen's measures, and the chroniclers appear to take the whole business as a matter of course, dismissing it briefly in a few pages. Bernaldez, chaplain to the second Inquisitor General, says that in Seville, from 1481 through 1488, 700 from all parts of Andalusia were burned and more than 5,000 cast into "perpetual" imprisonment, though these last were released five years later and compelled to wear *san benitos*. Among those burned were three priests, three or four friars, and a doctor of divinity who was a friar of the Trinity, called Savariego, "a great preacher and a great falsifier and heretical imposter, for he refused to come on Good Friday to preach the Passion, and stuffed himself with meat." The Cura of los Palacios had no reason to minimize the achievements of the Inquisition, for he heartily approved of it.

Pulgar, Isabel's *Converso* secretary, says that more than 15,000 accepted penance and were reconciled in his time; while others "who were guilty and would not confess" were executed. "And of these were burned at various times and in several cities and places nearly two thousand men and women" . . . . The sons of judaizers were barred from public office and from inheriting the goods of the guilty. Even the property of heretics long dead was confiscated. The sums thus realized, and fines collected from the reconciled, were considerable, and "the King and Queen commanded," wrote Pulgar, "that they should not be distributed for any purpose except in the war against the Moors, and in other things that were for the exaltation of the Catholic Faith." In the latter category she naturally included the share of the confiscations mentioned in her letter to her ambassador at Rome.

Four thousand families left the Andalusian country about Seville and Córdoba, to the injury of Queen Isabel's future revenues; "but estimating the diminution of her revenues very little, and holding very highly the cleansing of her lands, she said she put above any interest the ridding of the land of heresy, for she understood that this was for God's service and hers."

Isabel would have been greatly astonished if some prophetic angel had lifted a corner of the curtain of futurity and showed her the modern denunciations, sincere or pharisaical, of the court that she believed so necessary and so beneficent. She would have read that the Inquisition was responsible for almost all the imaginable ills of Spain except perhaps the cold winters and the hot summers; that it killed true religion, stifled literature and art, kept the people ignorant and brutal, crippled commerce and industry. The greenish blue eyes would undoubtedly have blazed with indignation, and with some reason. For the intellectual life of Spain was never more vigorous than in the century following the establishment of the Holy Office: The most brilliant epoch in her literature, the period that produced her three great poets, Cervantes, Lope de Vega and Calderon, coincides, curiously enough, with the time in which the Inquisition was most powerful. It was during that period that her greatest schools and universities were established, that foreign scholars flocked to Spain and were honored, that medicine and other sciences made their most notable gains. And in the material and political fields there was a parallel development. Never were the industries and commerce of Spain so prosperous, never was order so well maintained at home and prestige abroad than during the sixteenth century when Spain became the head of a new empire that overshadowed all Europe and the Americas. It would be grotesque to attribute all these results to the Inquisition. But the Inquisition certainly did not prevent their coming into being, and it did make possible the political unity that enabled the new nation to take advantage of the opportunities of the changing world.

Beyond a doubt the Inquisition completed the reform of the Church in Spain. In so doing, it also accomplished some less admirable ends. It imprisoned Saint Ignatius and impeded his work. It long threatened to suppress the autobiography of Saint Teresa. It annoyed other saints and writers in various ways. It perpetuated the absolutism and unwieldly bureaucracy of Spain long after the need for them had ceased. It was one of the instruments used by the enemies of the Society of Jesus to blacken it and bring about its suppression, especially in Portugal.

But of these matters the Queen foresaw nothing in the moment of her triumph. At no time, then or later, did she express the slightest regret over the instrument she had endowed with such powers. On the contrary, she frequently referred to it with pride, and a few years later we find her ambassador in England suggesting to Henry VII that "it is a pity, when Spain is purged of heresy, that Flanders and England should still be infected"; whereupon Henry, laying both hands on his breast, "swore that he would prosecute without mercy any cursed Jew or heretic that the Queen of Spain could point out in his dominions."[11] This promise he never kept, and the Inquisition made no headway in England or other parts of Europe. Save for the early tribunal against the Cathari, and the sporadic functioning of the Roman Inquisition, it was almost entirely a Spanish institution.

XVI

POPE SIXTUS CONDEMNS THE EX-
CESSES OF THE INQUISITORS AND
URGES THE QUEEN TO BE MERCIFUL—
WAR WITH GRANADA AT LAST

OF THE actual workings of the Inquisition during its
first year, Isabel and Fernando saw little or nothing,
for they were not in Andalusia. Having arranged matters there for the time being, they deemed it necessary to go to
Aragon, first to have Prince Juan formally acknowledged as
heir to that kingdom, and second, to expedite the sailing of the
great armada against the Turks. They left Córdoba about the
time when the plague returned to Andalusia. The King rode
east to visit his father's kingdoms. The Queen and the Prince
went north to Valladolid, perhaps because the delicate blond
boy was less likely to catch the pest on the dry hills of Old
Castile. They arrived in February, about the time when Susan
was being burned at Seville.

A month later Isabel and her son departed on horseback
for a three-hundred mile journey over arid wastes and bleak
mountains to the east coast. Arriving on April 16, they were
received with great ceremony by the people of Calatayud, where
King Fernando had already summoned the Cortes. The delegates met in the Church of San Pedro de los Francos on
Monday, April 30. There was much discussion about the
Turkish atrocities in Italy, for the gravity of the danger was
now realized everywhere in Spain; and the Catalans, always
independent with their sovereigns, aired some of their domestic
grievances. It was not until May 19 that they took the solemn
oath of allegiance to little Prince Juan, exacting in return the
oaths of the King and Queen to respect their privileges—an
obligation that the Prince himself was to renew at the age of
14. King Fernando then departed for Barcelona, to preside at
the Cortes there, while Queen Isabel remained as his lieutenant-

Missal of Isabel the Catholic
(*Royal Library at Madrid*)

general to dismiss the Cortes at Calatayud.[1] It was the first time in the history of Aragon that a woman had ruled, even pro tem. There was much murmuring and shaking of heads among the sticklers for precedent, but the Queen's composure and spirit of command as usual carried off the situation.

Meanwhile there were endless details to be arranged before the fleet could set sail against the barbarians. During May there was an assembly of fifty well armed vessels in the port of Laredo, under the command of Don Francisco Enriquez, son of the Admiral of Castile; and reinforcements from Galicia and Andalusia swelled the total to seventy. On June 22, a cool sunny day, a solemn high Mass was celebrated on the dock, the ensigns and standards were blessed, the great dark galleys with their high poops and bellied hulls weighed anchor, the canvas fluttered to the halyards, and under the cross of the Crusade and the colors of Saint James and the King and Queen, the armada stood majestically out to sea.

It was October 2 before the ships, having joined the fleet from Portugal, reached Otranto. The danger, when they arrived, had been averted, partly by the recapture of the city by the young Duke of Calabria, but chiefly in consequence of the unexpected death of Mohammed II.

Isabel heard of this event on her way from Calatayud to Saragossa to attend another Cortes. Saragossa was almost delirious with joy at the news. The popular satisfaction, in which Isabel and Fernando shared, was recorded with undisguised fervor by the faithful Bernaldez:[2]

"On the feast of the Holy Cross in the year 1481, there died and descended into Hell the Grand Turk, Emperor of Constantinople, called Mahomet Ottoman, who for more than thirty years had been waging war very cruelly against the Christians of Greece and its neighbors. . . . All Christendom in general took pleasure in this death, for no one can imagine the great terror that barbarous prince had instilled in the hearts of all Christians, because of the lands he had conquered, and those that he would desire and gain each day. . . . The King and Queen held great processions through the city, and sacrifices, and many other devotions and alms, because it pleased God to deliver Christendom from so mighty an enemy."

About the same time came intelligence of the death of King

Alfonso V of Portugal. Isabel and Fernando had a solemn high Mass of requiem sung for their former enemy, and prayed for the repose of his soul. Wars between Christian nations left no such bitterness as those with the Moslem.

Before the Court left Saragossa to continue its triumphal progress, ten of the leading Jews of the place waited upon the King and Queen and begged them to accept a gift. Bernaldez has left a detailed description of it: twelve heifers, twelve fine sheep sumptuously bedecked with ribbons and cloth of gold; and after these, an enormous silver vessel of singular design and skilful workmanship, whose argent legs were borne by twelve Jews, while a thirteenth held over it a rich cup full of gold coins, castellanos, and a fourteenth carried a beautiful jar full of silver. "And the King and Queen were delighted, and gave much thanks."

From Saragossa the royal party rode 160 miles to Barcelona, and then 200 miles to Valencia. At each place the chief nobles, prelates and commons tendered their homage both to the sovereigns and to the little Prince. The feasts at Valencia lasted fifteen days. At the end of the year the Court left Aragon to resume its long journey back to Castile. The Queen and the Prince arrived in Medina del Campo early in January.

In ten months she had ridden some 2,000 miles on horseback, had attended three parliaments, had assisted in launching an armada, had seen the Castilian and Aragonese kingdoms cemented in closer friendship by the oaths to Prince Juan. She had also conceived for the fourth time. The child was expected in the summer of 1482.

On reaching Medina, Isabel at once received an accounting from the Admiral and Count Haro, the regents she had left in charge, on the condition of her kingdoms. Civic peace had been restored everywhere . . . criminals were remarkably few . . . the plague had abated in Seville and Córdoba . . . there had been heavy rains in the south . . . the crops had been good and seed was abundant . . . the Moors of Granada were said to be preparing for war . . . the Inquisitors at Seville had reconciled some thousands of penitents . . . about a hundred *Conversos* from various parts of Andalusia had been burned.

Morillo and San Martin had taken the royal commands only too literally, proceeding with a zeal which seemed even to some Christians to be more vindictive than judicial, and assuredly going far beyond what either the Pope or the sovereigns had intended. Convinced that they were dealing with an insidious and intangible slayer of souls who worked by word of mouth instead of by steel or poison, they and their subordinates went to great pains to get evidence, and prosecuted the rich and powerful as rigorously as they did the lowly. Their psychology will seem familiar to any one who recalls the vagaries of mob psychology during the World War. In Boston the love letters of a German orchestra conductor were made public because he was suspected, and unjustly, of being a spy. An inflamed public imagination in Connecticut became almost hysterical when the senile governor announced in a speech that Germans were secretly drilling and collecting arms in that state. An inoffensive German musician near Hartford had a concrete foundation built for a new chicken-coop; ah! a gun base from which the Germans would shell the capitol! A wagon load of wire arrived for his chicken yard; any one could see that he was installing a wireless, to send military information to Berlin, and cause the death of American soldiers! It was a wonder the poor fellow was not hanged by the mob—there were many willing to assist, but fortunately they lacked leaders. The man's business, however, was ruined; he was arrested on a technicality, and kept in jail some months until his innocence was completely proved; meanwhile his wife and four children were left destitute.

The recollection of such incidents—they were common enough in 1917 and 1918—will help us to recreate the scene in Spain in 1481, and to realize that the Castilians and Andalusians of Isabel's time were not the monsters they have been painted, but poor human creatures, like ourselves. And so it happened that any Christian who dressed or acted like a Jew, or followed Jewish customs even of the most indifferent sort, was at once suspected. The out-and-out Jews, of course, were not troubled by the Inquisition. But if any Christian of Jewish descent bought his meat of a rabbi, or washed the blood from it in the Jewish manner, or gave his children Hebrew names, or wore his best clothes on Saturday, instead of Sunday, he was very likely to be denounced by his neighbors and dragged before the Inquisitors to be asked all sorts of questions in the hope that if he was a heretic he would betray himself. Many of the accused were released; others, who confessed to being secret Jews or to enticing others to adopt Jewish instead of Christian customs, were given penances; those who were convicted but refused to confess, or who lapsed after once being reconciled, were burned. On Saturdays the agents of the Holy Office climbed the roofs in certain sections of Seville where the *Conversos* dwelt, and noted which houses had smoking chimneys, and which not. The good Christians, of course, would be cooking as usual. But those who were secretly Jews would be observing the Sabbath.

Several hundreds of the suspected "New Christians" who had fled from Seville during the fall and winter without waiting to be arrested, went to Rome, always the safest refuge of the persecuted Jews, and presented themselves, with tears and lamentations, before Pope Sixtus.

It happened that about the same time, while Isabel and Fernando were still in Aragon, they decided that the activities of the *Conversos* in Saragossa and other eastern cities warranted an extension of the Holy Office to cover all the territories of the crown of Aragon; and they petitioned the Pope to permit them to appoint Inquisitors there. After questioning many of the *Conversos*, Sixtus came to the conclusion that the Inquisition in Seville—it has been called the abnormal or uncanonical Inquisition—was not at all the court of inquiry that he had intended it to be; that it was persecuting the innocent as well as the guilty, and ignoring the rules of canon law by which the earlier Inquisition had attempted to safeguard the legal rights of the accused. Morillo and San Martin had neglected to follow the papal command that they cooperate with the diocesan ordinaries. Furthermore, Sixtus believed that he had been tricked in 1478 by the Spanish ambassador at Rome.

On January 29, 1482, he despatched a brief to the sovereigns, flatly refusing to permit them to name Inquisitors for Aragon, and demanding an immediate reform of the tribunal in Seville to accord with the terms of his bull of 1478. He contemplated removing Morillo and San Martin from office, but out of consideration for Fernando and Isabel he would leave them their authority for the present, on condition that the abuses cease. The Pope's indignation blazed unmistakably under the polite formulas of the Roman curia:

"To our very dear children in Christ, health and apostolic benediction:

"We have never doubted that your original request for au-

thority from us to appoint Inquisitors of heretical perversity
in the kingdoms of Castile and Leon was motivated by zeal
for the Catholic Faith and by the sincere and worthy purpose
of leading to an acknowledgment of the way of truth, through
the diligent efforts of these Inquisitors, those who externally
professed themselves Christians, yet did not hesitate to follow
in practice the teachings of Judaical law and superstition. At
the time your request was made our own great zeal for the
faith led us to give the order that documents be drawn up
granting this deputation of authority. However, through the
instrumentality of that man who at the time in your name
petitioned the despatch of these documents, it came about that
since the explanation he gave us of their contents was vague
and confused and not as complete and definite as was proper,
the documents themselves contained much that contradicted the
decrees and customary procedure of our Holy Fathers and
Predecessors. This has led to numerous expressions of regret
and to complaints as much against us for issuing such documents as against your Majesties and against our beloved sons,
Michael de Morillo, Master of Theology, and John de San
Martin, Bachelor of Theology, whom, under the pretext of the
above-mentioned documents, you have named Inquisitors in
your city of Seville. The accusation is made that hasty action
and disregard of legal procedure on the part of these Inquisitors have brought about the unjust imprisonment and even
severe torturing of many innocent persons who have been unjustly condemned as heretics, despoiled of their possessions
and made to pay the extreme penalty. . . ."

Many of the fugitives, the Holy Father continued, "profess
themselves to be Christians and true Catholics." They have
fled to the Holy See, "the refuge of all the oppressed everywhere," and have appealed to him "with much shedding of
tears." He has discussed the situation with the Cardinals, many
of whom are of the opinion that Morillo and San Martin ought
to be removed. Nevertheless, rather than embarrass the sovereigns by seeming to condemn their appointments publicly,
the Pope is willing to let the two men retain office, on the
express condition that they adhere to the rules of the canon
law in future, "bearing in mind that if they conduct themselves otherwise than with zeal for the faith and the salvation
of souls, or less justly than they ought," they will be removed,

and others substituted for them. Sixtus concludes by earnestly
exhorting Fernando and Isabel to give him their assurance
that they will obey his stipulations, "as Catholic Kings ought"
so that henceforth "you will deserve to be commended before
God and men."³

Isabel investigated, and on finding that some of the complaints against Morillo and San Martin were only too well
founded, insisted upon their proceeding in accordance with
the canon law. But even before she received the Pope's reprimand, the Inquisition was pushed well into the background of
Castilian affairs by sudden and dramatic developments. The
long expected war with Granada had begun at last.

During the three years of the truce there had always been
intermittent raids and minor butcheries on the frontier. As
the time approached for the expiration of the agreement, Don
Rodrigo Ponce de Leon, Marqués of Cádiz, took it upon himself to organize an incursion of more than customary effect.
One fine October morning he led his cavaliers against Villa-
luenga, burned it to the ground, harried several villages of the
Sierra, slept under the very walls of Ronda, leveled the tower
of the Mercadillo, and after wasting some corn fields and
burning a few orchards, returned to his castle in high spirits,
feeling that he had at least partially requited Muley Abou'l
Hassan for his depradations in Andalusia.⁴ The event appeared
to be purely of local significance. Such raids had always been
permitted under the terms of the truce. But there was something more ominous in the air as the fateful year of 1481 drew
to its close.

That year the rains began early in Andalusia and Castile,
and continued without cease. Seville, already chastised by the
fires of the Inquisition, decimated by the plague that had increased in virulence since August, was set upon even by the
elements; for in December the swollen Guadalquivir engulfed
el Copero and other suburbs, and surrounded the low flats of
the city so menacingly that for three days and nights the terrified Christians, *Conversos* and Jews expected to perish in
the muddy waters.

On Christmas Day a heavy rain pelted all the orchards of
Andalusia; and in the mountains between Christian Spain and
Granada a howling tempest raged for three days and nights.
It was under cover of that storm, when men and beasts were

huddled under what shelter they could find, that Muley Abou'l Hassan began the war in earnest. He accomplished what all men believed impossible. He took Záhara.

Within fifty miles of Seville to the southeast, this fortress was the most powerful Christian outpost defending Christian Andalusia on the one side, and menacing the approach to Moorish Ronda a few miles to the east. The walled castle was perched on the top of a rocky mountain so high that no birds flew there, and the clouds drifted below it, hugging the broken cliffs on the side of the mountain. The very streets and many of the houses were hewn out of solid rock. There was only one gate, at the west, surrounded by massive bulwarks and turrets, and the only approach to it was by a winding steep road so jagged that in places it looked like a stairway cut out of granite. The place was considered impregnable, so much so that in all parts of Spain, a woman of irreproachable virtue was called a *Zaharena*. Hence the alcaide kept a careless watch, and a small garrison. A Christian renagade carried the news to Muley Abou'l Hassan.

On the night after Christmas, while Záhara sat securely in the clouds above the roaring of the tempest, Muley led a picked band of Moors from Ronda up the mountain side, planted scaling ladders on the wet walls, and entered the sleeping town. There were no sentinels on the walls and the Moors were in the streets, with naked scimitars, before the alarm was given. The cry, "El Moro! El Moro!" brought out the sleepy Spaniards, drawings their swords; but it was too late. Some were mowed down by the dark foe in the windy darkness, while others in panic leapt over the walls to death. At dawn, the women and children and old men, nearly 200 of them, were herded, half dressed, into the public square, and there in the cold rain, they were informed by Muley that they were to be taken to Granada as slaves. According to Washington Irving, the Moors drove them like cattle through the mountains and the broad *vega*. Those who fell were dispatched by a black fellow with a spear or a scimitar; the rest were goaded through the gates of Granada to be sold, while Muley rode to the Alhambra to receive congratulations on his feat of arms, and to send *alfaquis* to Africa, to inform the Barbary kings that the war had begun, and to ask their help. Lucio Marineo, a contemporary, says the Moors slew all the women and children.[5]

Being three hundred miles to the north of Záhara, Isabel and
Fernando heard nothing of the disaster until a messenger arrived at Medina del Campo a week later, while they were hearing Mass. They had expected something of the sort, but there
was nothing to be done in a military way until spring. Meanwhile they sent orders to the governors of castles on the frontier to strengthen their garrisons and maintain a strict watch.

Isabel had reached another great crisis in her life, and she
saw clearly that a long and difficult task lay before her. She
proposed to conquer a rich fertile kingdom of some 3,000,000
Moors, extending from Seville in the west to the Mediterranean; in the east to Murcia through mountains difficult of
access, interspersed with warm luxurious valleys. In the very
center of this kingdom, more than half a mile above sea level,
stood the high-walled city of Granada on the slope of the
Sierre Nevada, looking out to the west on the long *Vega de
Granada* by the River Jenil, and protected on the other side by
the Sierras, whose peaks of Veleta and Mulhacen, to the southeast, are well over 11,000 feet high, so that little was to be
feared in that quarter. All about, in a great circle, were a score
of powerfully fortified mountain cities, many of them considered impregnable. To lay siege to Granada alone would
require months, perhaps years, and no invader could afford to
remain long within sight of the red roofs of the Alhambra
with strong garrisons before him, ready to sally forth and cut
his communications, without first battering down, systemati-
cally, each of the subsidiary places. Mountains walled Granada
from the sea, and to the southwest were the Moorish ports of
Malaga and Vélez Malaga, and to the southeast Almería; to
the west Illora and Loja, Alhama, Ronda, Benameji and
Antequera; to the north, Moclin and Baza and Guadix; to the
east, more mountains; on all sides, mountains, with vines and
gardens at their feet and cowls of snow on their heads. The
Arab city sat secure like a king on a chessboard, well protected by bishops, knights and pawns; like some Castle Perilous, defended at many passes by champions.

What all good Castilian kings had dreamed of doing, what
her father had attempted and what the weaklings like her halfbrother had forgotten, Isabel proposed, with God's help, to
accomplish. Fernando would lead the Christian host, and she,
in her magnificent prime at thirty, would be recruiting agent,

commissary, purchaser of munitions, field nurse and hospitaler, and propaganda bureau, all in one. Her labors in the Portuguese War had been only a novitiate, to prepare her for the Crusade. Whatever the cost, however long it might take, she was resolved to conquer Granada. Like the men of Argos when they disembarked beside Ilion, she saw only the glimmer of victory. There was no soothsayer Kalchas to foretell that the years of blood between her and her desire would number ten.

XVII

ISABEL BEARS A FOURTH CHILD—SHE
HEARS OF THE HEROIC DEFENSE OF AL-
HAMA, AND THE DEFEAT OF THE
CHRISTIANS NEAR MALAGA

FERNANDO, handsome, bald and quietly self-confident in his thirtieth year, went into the Moorish war almost as light-heartedly as he had galloped into the lists during the feasts at Valencia, to split a few lances for the honor of his lady: it was a good game of chivalry, and God willing, he would win it. His spirit, though firm, lacked the diamond clarity and hardness of his Queen's. And differences of heredity and training gave them somewhat different viewpoints.

When the Queen looked at a map, she saw the Castile and Leon of her fathers, reconstructed; Granada wrested from the Moors, the Faith triumphant over all. Fernando saw Aragon, robbed of two provinces by Louis XI; Sicily to the east, vitally implicated in the fate of an Italy which was a discord of small bickering kingdoms; to the north, a united and expanding France. Beyond that there was a vague insignificant England which might, however, be coaxed on to annoy the King of France and keep him from troubling Spain, and in the Germanies, a possible friend or foe in Maximilian, the Hapsburg King of the Romans, parsimonious, thick-lipped, dull-witted. All these political realities struggled for one thing or another between an uncharted abyss of ocean to the west, and an unfathomed darkness of pagan Asia containing millions of Mussulman enemies to the east; between the chill Scandinavias that were only a name and the infinite expanse of sun and mystery that was Africa, whose known fringes swarmed with other Mohammedan enemies, glaring across the Mediterranean.

Here in Europe, as custodians of Roman culture, were a

few millions of more or less Christian souls, fighting with one another while cold and heat and darkness and the devil pressed in on them from all sides. The leaven that held this mass from being overwhelmed and obliterated was the Faith, the Church. Fernando began to visualize a united Italy, an England strengthened to make a balance of power against France, a Germany bound to Spain by matrimonial alliances—all joined under the spiritual fatherhood of the Pope to defend and per- petuate Christian civilization despite the barbarians of Asia and Africa. With singular farsightedness, Fernando in 1482 was beginning to envisage a Europe with geographical demar- cations very similar to those of 1914. If he had had his way he would have left the map almost as Napoleon did; but death repeatedly checkmated him.

In short, Fernando, as heir to the policies of Aragon and Sicily, was naturally drawn into the European scene; Isabel, as heiress to the miseries of Castile, unavoidably had her gaze drawn to Jews and *Conversos*, southern Moors, domestic problems, Portugal and the western ocean. Each saw, and to a great extent shared the viewpoint of the other. But Fernando's mind was the more flexible and accepted compromise more readily.

Left to his own courses, he would probably have followed the example of several of his ancestors; he would have waged a valiant medieval warfare against the Moors, defeated them, made the most favorable terms he could with them, then turned to gain an advantage over France; then perhaps, at a later, more favorable time, have struck the Moors again and taken what profit he could. He was always content to take small and sure gains; like a skilled and cautious gambler, he preferred to keep part of his resources in reserve. Even when he de- feated an enemy, he gave moderate terms rather than stake all in trying to gain more. He was always humble enough to learn from experience, and beyond any question, was the greatest and most able King of his time. Yet with all his prudence and skill, he fell just short of the one thing that could not be gained from experience: genius. That was Isabel's possession. Her contribution to his success was an intuitive sense that outran all calculation; the sixth sense that enables one to stake all when all seems lost, and win. It would be strange if such a wife and such a husband did not sooner or later find themselves at cross-purposes.

While they were making plans at Medina for a spring campaign of retaliation against Muley, their hand was forced in a measure by another exploit of the irrepressible Don Rodrigo, Marqués of Cádiz. In his late thirties, that high-spirited *magnifico* was the popular hero of Andalusia, and romantic ladies were comparing him to the Cid Ruy of immortal memory. Bernaldez, who knew him well, said that he was chaste, sober, a lover of justice, and "the enemy of all flatterers, liars, traitors and poltroons." He heard Mass each morning and knelt from beginning to end. Moorish women who fell into his hands were treated with knightly courtesy and scrupulous respect for their honor. In an age of lax morality, when even so devout a man as King Fernando had four illegitimate children, there was never a whisper of scandal about Ponce de Leon. Like Leonardo da Vinci, he had a passion for geometry applied to fortifications, and he liked music, though the conscientious Bernaldez adds that he preferred the notes of clarions and sackbuts, drums and trumpets.

To this cavalier, the loss of Záhara, a few miles east of his own fortress of Jerez and his city of Cádiz, seemed almost a personal insult, and since its recapture, at the present at least, was out of the question, he stroked his curly red beard and began to look about for a place where he might repay Muley with interest. Living as he did on the perilous frontier, he maintained a large number of spies, including some *Mudejares*—Christian Moors—to warn him of Moslem incursions and cattle raids. Shortly after Christmas one of them sought him out at his castle of Marchena with some interesting news. Alhama, a large and wealthy city, situated high on a fortified rock, with a steep, perilous ascent, was negligently guarded and might be taken by surprise. It was not on the frontier, like Záhara, but twenty miles inside the outposts of Granada, well within the circle of forts, and only twelve leagues from the capital itself. No one but a madman would attempt to take it, but for that very reason it might be surprised; and it commanded the road from Granada to Malaga and a wide sweep of the *vega*.

The Marqués sent a veteran soldier, Ortega de Prado, a veteran climber, to investigate. One moonless night Ortega scaled its walls, heard the sentinels pace to and fro, and concluded that the town was well guarded. But on climbing the battlements of the castle, he found them all unwatched. The lofty walls, rising out of the solid rock, might be mounted with scaling ladders, and from the castle an attacking party could get into the town. He descended, unobserved, and reported to the Marqués.

The Marqués did not proceed with the execution of his plan until he had sent a messenger to the King and Queen two hundred miles away, outlining the project and asking permission to attack. They thought it feasible. It would arouse the martial spirit in the south, and would stimulate recruiting for the spring campaign. They gave their consent.

The Marqués took into his confidence Diego de Merlo, chief magistrate of Seville; Sancho de Ávila, governor of Carmona, and the Adelantado of Andalusia. They assembled at Marchena 2,400 light cavalry and 3,000 foot, all unaware of their destination. They marched by night only, passed Antequera, and leaving their baggage by the river Yeguas, clambered through the narrow defiles of the sierra of Alzerifa. At midnight of the third day, they reached a deep walled valley, a mile and a half from Alhama. The Marqués now explained what they were about to do, and asked for volunteers to scale the walls of the castle, "men who would dare to die for honor, rather than endure shame." Only thirty of the hardiest and bravest climbers were chosen. Ortega showed them how to throw the scaling ladders over the wall. It was two hours before daybreak, on the last night in February.

The thirty mounted safely, stabbed a sentinal, and got to the guard-room before they were discovered. Cutting down the sleepy guards without quarter, they rushed into the streets, and before the town was aroused, were falling upon the sentries at one of the postern gates. Meanwhile, the Christian army, hearing the tumult in the dark, approached the walls with shouts and trumpet blasts, to confuse the garrison. Ortega de Prado at last leaped over a heap of Moorish corpses and managed to open the postern gate. The Christians poured into the citadel.

At daybreak, the townspeople, seeing how small a force of Christians held the castle, laid siege to it in the hope of receiving early aid from Granada. They barricaded the streets, and kept up a steady fire with cross bows, arrows and *espingardas*. Their artillery commanded the gate of the castle, on the side toward the city. Consequently, the Christians found themselves in a dangerous situation. If Moorish troops arrived from Granada before the city streets were swept clean of defenders, they were lost. The bulk of the army, still outside, assaulted the walls, planted scaling ladders, and swarmed up; the Moors fought them back with the courage of men defending their homes.

The Marqués, unable to sally forth from the castle by the gate, had a large breach made in the wall, and placing himself at the head of the troops, led them furiously into the street. From street to street, from house to house, from roof to roof, they pushed the Saracens back, fighting desperately all day, until at last the Moorish survivors took refuge in a mosque, whence they kept up a brisk fire with crossbows and arquebusses. The Marqués ordered his men to set fire to the mosque. The Moors rushed forth in panic and were killed or surrendered. Eight hundred were killed that day, and three thousand captives were taken, and distributed as slaves to the victors. In the dungeons under the castle, loaded with chains, were found many Christian captives, whose shackles were struck off.

The Andalusians now paused to inspect their booty. It was enormous. Alhama, in the middle of a prosperous agricultural district, was a rich mercantile and weaving town stocked with gold and silver, rare silks and taffetas, grain, oil and honey, horses and asses of the best breeds. Distributing and enjoying the spoils, and giving themselves the added pleasure of hanging on the highest turret a notorious renegade Christian who had betrayed many Christians to death at Moorish hands, the victors remained in Alhama from Thursday, the day of their conquest, until the following Tuesday. That morning Muley Abou'l Hassan appeared before the walls of Alhama with 3,000 cavalry and 50,000 infantry.[1] An old ballad represents him weeping when the news of the fall of Alhama, the apple of his eye and the key to Granada, was brought to him, and crying *"Ay de mi, Alhama!"* with inconsolable despair: "Woe is me, Alhama!" From the promptness with which he assembled his host and set out in pursuit, however, it may be inferred that he did not waste many hours in futile lamentations.

The situation of the Marqués and his troops seemed hopeless. Though he sent fleet messengers to the King and Queen in the north, to the city of Seville, and to neighboring lords, the only help within practical distance was a small force under his old friend, Don Alonso de Aguilar. Don Alonso would have hurried to throw himself into Alhama and die fighting with the Marqués, but it was too late. Pursued for some distance by Muley's cavalry, he reluctantly withdrew across the Sierras.

Muley returned in a savage mood to Alhama. As he came near the town, he saw the wild dogs feasting on the mangled bodies of the Moors slain in the night attack and thrown over the walls by orders of the Marqués. Muley, beside himself with rage, ordered an instant attack.

Wave after wave of Moors rushed with scaling ladders up the steep rocks, climbed up regardless of the stones, darts and liquid pitch poured from the battlements, were cut down with swords at the top, had their ladders overthrown, were brushed like flies from the great rock and lay in twisted silent heaps at the bottom. Muley had spent blood like water to no purpose. He cursed the fate that had permitted him to set out in his haste without artillery. Plainly, he could not take the fortress by assault.

He had a better plan. "Alhama the dry," having no wells or fountains, depended for its water supply upon a river that ran by its walls. If Muley could divert the channel of the stream, the Christians would die of thirst. He ordered his men to plant palisades in the river bed. The Marqués saw the danger immediately. At the head of his best cavaliers he descended, with drawn sword, through the narrow tunnel leading from the fort to the watering place, and wading knee deep into the cold water, fought hand to hand with the Moslems. In the end, when the river bed was choked with Moorish and Christian bodies, and the water literally ran red, the Christians had to retreat slowly, fighting, before overwhelming numbers of Saracens. The whole river was diverted except a tiny rill that trickled through the former bed.

Henceforth, to get even small quantities of water, Don Rodrigo and his men had to pass under the archery fire of the besiegers and fight their way step by step to the thin stream. Every drop of water was paid for with a drop of precious blood. It was in getting water that they incurred most of their heavy losses. And what they obtained was not sufficient for their needs. At the end of three weeks they were obliged to deny water altogether to the prisoners, some of whom died raving, and to ration it out almost drop by drop to the fighting men and their horses. Messengers slipped through the Moorish camps at night to carry frantic pleas for succor to Seville. No replies came back.

Isabel and Fernando were nearly 300 miles away when they learned of these happenings. The King sent swift commands to all the nobles in southern Andalusia to go to the relief of the heroic Marqués, and, taking leave of Queen Isabel the same day, he mounted his horse and galloped south, riding day and night.

Meanwhile the Marquesa of Cádiz, finding that there were no troops left in the neighborhood to send to her husband's relief, knew not where to turn in her anguish. The nearest lord with troops at his disposal was the Duke of Medina Sidonia, between Cádiz and Záhara. But the Duke and the Marqués were mortal enemies. Neither had gone to Seville since the Queen banished them.

It was no time, however, to stand upon *punctilios.* Proud as she was, the Marquesa valued her husband's life even above Andalusian honor, and she sent to the Duke imploring him to send men to the rescue.

The Duke replied immediately that to oblige so noble and so estimable a lady, and to rescue so valiant a cavalier and Christian warrior as the Marqués, would be an honor and a pleasure, and that he himself would go in person with all the troops at his command. He hastily ordered a mobilization of all the men who could be spared from the garrisons of the numerous cities in his domain, and offered high pay to all volunteers who would come at once with horses, armor and food. Don Alonso de Aguilar and his brother Gonsalvo de Córdoba were among the cavaliers who joined him. In an incredibly short time he was on his way east with five thousand horse and a large force of infantry.[2]

King Fernando meanwhile was riding pell-mell to the south with Don Beltran (de la Cueva), Duke of Albuquerque, and other great lords, to take command of the army that was being assembled. Fifteen miles from Córdoba, he turned east, planning to meet his troops on the road. Don Beltran remonstrated. There were plenty of bold leaders to lead the volunteers to Alhama, without risking the King's royal person in an enemy country, full of pitfalls. It was a tradition in Castile that the kings never rode into Moorish territory without powerful armies.

"Duke," said the King, "your advice might have been good if I had not left Medina for the avowed purpose of relieving these cavaliers in person. Now that I am so near the end of my journey, it would be unworthy of a king to swerve from my purpose before meeting with an impediment. I shall take the troops of this country who are assembled, and without waiting for those of Castile, with God's help I shall finish my journey."[3]

The King spurred on. Anxious to relieve the Marqués in person, he sent a swift courier to the Duke bidding him wait. But the Duke replied that if he did, it would be too late. The King was compelled to stop for news at Antequera.

Muley had to strike quickly at Alhama, or to give battle to the oncoming Christian host; and as the Moors generally preferred to wage a guerilla warfare, at which they were more skilful than the Christians, he chose the former alternative. Under cover of a feint at the opposite side of the town, his *escaladores* one morning at dawn managed to climb a precipice so steep that the walls on it were considered beyond the reach of ladders, and threw scaling ladders over the battlements before they were discovered. Seventy of them got into the town and sprinted for the gate, leaving behind them a trail of dead and wounded Christians. At the gate the Saracens stood back to back while some of their number made desperate efforts to admit the besieging army without. Hemmed in by Christian knights, they fell to the last man. Their turbaned heads were thrown over the walls, to roll down the mountain side to the feet of their friends.

That day Muley broke camp and marched over the sierra. The Marqués and his friends were wondering what this maneuver might mean, when they saw emerging from a cleft in the mountains to the west the banners of the Duke of Medina Sidonia. With a great flourish of those trumpets, flageolets, piccolos, sackbuts and kettledrums that he loved to hear when he went to the wars, the Duke marched through the gate of Alhama, with pennons fluttering their praise to the gallant defenders.

The Marqués, with tears in his eyes, advanced to meet the old enemy that he had sworn years ago to kill. Silently he held out his hand. The gray-haired duke embraced him, while the soldiers, who knew how matters stood between them, cheered like madmen. Stony veterans with their hands wet with Moorish blood felt another moisture in their eyes at the sight of this reconciliation. The age of chivalry was not quite dead.

The Marquesa of Cádiz had sent her major-domo in the Duke's army with a great supply of edibles. The Marqués ordered tables spread under tents in the plaza, and there gave a dinner to his rescuer and the cavaliers with him.

The event threw a strong light on the wisdom of Isabel's policy in handling recalcitrant nobles. The Marqués and the Duke, henceforth friends and brothers in arms, were among her most capable generals throughout the war. Other aristocrats whom she had humbled were offering her their swords and their lives, because they respected her. United under the same banner were several men who might have been executed under a regime less moderately firm than Isabel's: Don Beltran, whom she detested for the scandals he had caused; the Duke and the Marqués, who had shattered the peace of Seville for three years; Don Alonso de Aguilar and the Count of Cabra, who had done likewise in Córdoba; her foe the young Marqués of Villena—all were fighting loyally against the common enemy, instead of rending one another and preying upon the Crown and the people. Only one of the great brawlers of Enrique's reign was missing—the Archbishop of Toledo, who was keeping a rendezvous at Alcalá with a more peremptory sovereign. Weary of seeking his fortune through the illusions of astrology and alchemy, the broken old man died that year, consoled at last by the sacraments of the Faith that he had served so well and so badly.

The King, meanwhile, had returned to Córdoba, late in March, and there, a few days later, Isabel arrived at the head of the militia of Old Castile. A council of war was held to determine whether Alhama, isolated and surrounded by foes as it was, within striking distance of Granada, should be retained or destroyed and abandoned. Old border warriors shook their heads; the cost of keeping it would be prohibitive.

King Fernando, as usual, turned to the Queen with a look that said, "What is your opinion?"

"Keep it by all means," replied Isabel without hesitation. "Shall we give up the first place we have conquered? Such an idea should not be allowed even to enter our minds. It would encourage the enemy and discourage our people. What if it does cost labor and money and blood to retain it? Did any one here doubt when we began this war that it would cost infinite toil, money and bloodshed to carry it to victory? Let us hear no more of Alhama, except to maintain its walls sacred against all foes as a fortress granted us by God in the very heart of the enemy country; and let our only thought be how to extend our glorious conquest."

The Queen's counsel prevailed. It was decided that the King should attack Loja, the nearest large Moorish city to Alhama, as soon as preparations could be made. Sending a strong garrison with three months' provisions to Alhama, he appealed to all the cities and fortresses of Andalusia and Estremadura, to the holdings of the orders of Santiago, Calatrava and Alcántara, and even to Salamanca, Toro and Valladolid in Old Castile, to furnish allotments of bread, wine and cattle, half in June and half in July; and to send also cavalry and infantry, according to the quotas decided upon, and all the lombards and other artillery they could spare, with powder and ball. The armada which had returned from Italy after the Turkish retreat was sent to the straits of Gibraltar, to cut off reinforcements to Granada from the Barbary coast.

Isabel was no longer able to go from camp to camp on the mule which had lately supplanted her white horse. Yet she continued to despatch an enormous amount of official business every day, keeping her finger on the pulse of every province in Spain until the very day of her confinement. It was almost midsummer when the fourth of her children, another blond daughter, called Maria in commemoration of the Blessed Virgin, saw the light in the palace at Córdoba where the splendor of the Moorish Kings had once rivalled the glories of the caliphs of Bagdad. Prince Juan, hardly four, and the Princess Juana, not yet three, were taken to the Queen's bedside to see the new infanta. Their sister Isabel, a tall radiant girl of eleven, was still a hostage in Portugal.

It was still June when King Fernando, in Toledo armor inlaid with gold and silver, rode out of Córdoba with his new army. Leaving a considerable part of it, including the youngest recruits, at Ecija, he entered the enemy's land at the head of five thousand horse and eight thousand foot. Diego de Merlo, the Asistente of Seville, assured the King that even if Muley brought 80,000 Moors into the field, they would melt away before the swords of Christian cavaliers. Was not one Christian warrior worth a dozen of these turbaned jackanapes on their mountain ponies?

The Marqués of Cádiz, who had killed Moors in his fourteenth year, was not so confident. To his steady blue eye, the King's army looked too small to penetrate hostile country so far as Loja. But Fernando, impetuous in action as he was cautious in counsel, agreed with de Merlo. Sure of the justice of his cause and the élan of his army, he intended to make short work of the infidels and return to the larger game of European politics.

Arriving before Loja, he found the ground so broken up by hills, arroyos, and the deep channel of the river Jenil, that it was difficult to find a place for a united camp. The King was obliged to scatter his troops on different elevations separated by ravines; his own tents he pitched in an olive grove. The position was decidedly bad, for there was no room for cavalry to work, and the artillery did not command the walls of the town. The King's brother, the Duke of Villahermosa, whom Marineo calls the best captain of his time, pointed out that the Moors could dominate the camp with artillery and archery from a hill beyond called Santo Albohacen. Rather than retreat, the King decided to occupy the heights. The Marqués of Cádiz stormed the position, swept the Saracens away, and planted twenty guns there.

But Ali Atar, the governor of Loja, had learned something of strategy himself in the seventy years of his life. While he waited for reinforcements from Muley, he planted a large ambush one night near Albohacen, and at daybreak made a feint attack on the opposite side. When the Marqués and his cavaliers dashed forth, the assailants fled and were hotly pursued. Meanwhile, the Moors in the ambush occupied the heights. The Christians, perceiving that they had been duped, turned and fought their way back, this time against heavy odds. They recaptured the hill, but at a terrible cost of the lives of many of the bravest nobles in the host.

The King had begun the war with a blunder, as he had the War of the Succession. He admitted that the Marqués of Cádiz had been right, and with a heavy heart, for he was proud, consented to raise the siege and withdraw to Rio Frio, where troops from Córdoba could join him. The Marqués was to break camp first on Albohacen, the troops on lower ground covering his retreat. When the tents were struck on the heights, however, the Moors rushed out of Loja to attack. The Christians on lower ground fled in panic.

In vain Fernando rode among them, calling upon them to stand. With a handful of horsemen, he rushed into the face of the enemy with such fury that a whole squadron of them broke and scattered, and many leapt into the river. The King's mailed hand rose and fell above the *mêlée*; Moor after Moor went down before his spear. But enemy reinforcements surrounded him, and it was only a question of moments when he would be overpowered by sheer weight.

The Marqués of Cádiz, seeing the King's peril, gathered seventy horsemen and galloped to the rescue. He arrived just when Fernando had plunged his spear into the body of a Moor who was trying to wound his horse. The Moor fell forward in such a way that the King could not extricate the spear, nor could he draw his sword in that thick swarm of sweating bodies and blood and steel. A huge Moor raised his scimitar to despatch the King, when the spear of the Marqués caught him under the arm and crumpled him up. With the aid of the seventy, Fernando cut his way out and rejoined his retreating army. All day the King, the Marqués, and the flower of Andalusian chivalry threw themselves between the scurrying footmen and artillerymen, and the harrying Saracens, until at last the camp was evacuated. Leaving some of their guns behind, the Christians made their way slowly to Rio Frio, pursued by Ali Atar. Fernando, in silent gloom, rode back to Córdoba.

Sitting by the pale Queen's bedside, he explained what had happened. If Isabel had any criticism to make of "my lord the King" no chronicler has preserved it. But there is no doubt that she immediately saw the moral of the tale: the folly of attacking such places as Loja without bigger guns and heavier projectiles. They must raise money wherever they could and buy bigger guns. It seemed to them most fortunate that the Inquisition was beginning to provide funds from the sale of the properties of condemned *Conversos*.

Meanwhile, to keep up the spirit of his troops, the King led them into the *vega* of Granada to cut down the food supplies of the enemy by ravaging fields and villages. Muley Abou'l Hassan retaliated by making a great raid in southern Andalusia.

The first year of the war had been on the whole disastrous to the Castilians. Záhara and Loja had obscured the glory of Alhama.

While waiting for the funds essential to a continuance of the war on a larger scale, the King and Queen went to Logroño to checkmate the efforts of Louis XI to gain some forts in Navarre; and from there they sent to France, Germany and Italy for guns and munitions of war. During the winter Isabel began to study Latin, that she might understand foreign diplomats. Within a year she was able to speak it and write it correctly, if not elegantly.[4] After Christmas she went to Madrid to hunt wolves and boars in the neighboring forests. Spring found her fully restored to health, and ready for a second campaign against the Moors.

The year proved to be one of reorganization, of preparation, of continued propaganda among the sluggish people of the north. The Pope authorized the preaching of a crusade under the usual conditions, and Christian warriors began to arrive from France, Germany, Poland, England and Ireland. Sixtus also permitted the raising of 100,000 gold ducats— more than half a million dollars—on the ecclesiastical revenues of Aragon and Castile. The second year began with high hopes.

In March, just before the King and Queen returned to Córdoba to open the spring campaign, the great lords of the south collected at Antequera some 3,000 cavalry, the very pink of Andalusian chivalry, and 1,000 foot. All were eager to strike a blow at the Infidel—the only question was, where? The Marqués of Cádiz wished to attack Almojia, which one of his Moorish guides told him was weakly defended. But Cárdenas, Master of Santiago, also had Moorish renegades,

who had told him that a sudden raid in the Axarquia of
Malaga, a winding valley of herds and vineyards high among
the hills north of the city, would yield enormous booty with
slight danger. The nobles found the Master's plan more attractive than that of the Marqués. Why not ravage the Axarquia, they asked, and then take the rich city of Malaga by
assault?

News of the project evidently got abroad in Antiquera, even
beyond the confines of the camp, for when the four thousand
Christians set forth on Thursday morning, they were followed
by a long train of human vultures who seem to have sprung
up out of the ground overnight; "not the customary wretches
that hover about armies to plunder and strip the dead, but
goodly and substantial traders from Seville, Córdoba, and
other cities of traffic. They rode sleek mules, and were clad in
goodly raimant, with long leathern purses at their girdles, well
filled with pistols and other golden coin. They had heard of
the spoils wasted by the soldiery at the capture of Alhama, and
were provided with moneys to buy up the jewels and precious
stones, the vessels of gold and silver, and the rich silks and
cloths, that should form the plunder of Malaga. The proud
cavaliers eyed these sons of traffic with great disdain, but permitted them to follow for the convenience of the troops, who
might otherwise be overburdened with booty."⁵

All day they marched and all evening, sacking and burning
a few villages on the way, but curiously meeting no enemy
and taking no herds or other valuable booty. In the black of
night they found themselves spread out in a labyrinth of
ravines, with rocky crags ascending on every side. The silence
was unnatural; not a wolf howled, not a bird fluttered. Wearily
the crusaders paused, and lay down where they were to get
some sleep—all but the Marqués of Cádiz, who, commanding
the rear guard, could not shake off a premonition of disaster,
and decided to remain on watch all night. Suddenly, about midnight, a fearful yell sounded above them in the darkness. It
was answered by another across the valley and another and
another, until the echoes crossed and recrossed one another, and a shrieking and hooting as of all the fiends of
Hell brought the sleepy Christian warriors to their feet. Out
of the darkness came a shower of arrows. The invaders could
see no foe to strike. Ten thousand watchfires blazed forth

from cliffs and knolls.[6] With howls of triumph, the Saracens descended from the heights and fell upon the Christians, especially upon the vanguard under the Master of Santiago. In vain the Marqués of Cádiz led his cavaliers in the darkness to aid Cárdenas. Before daybreak the Christians were rushing in all directions among the rocky ravines, harried, panic-stricken, cut down by an invisible enemy.

Very few Moors accomplished this defeat, says Bernaldez, not more than 500 *peones* and perhaps 50 cavaliers, "and it appears that Our Lord permitted it, because undoubtedly the greater part of the people went with the intention to steal and barter, rather than serve God, as many of them testified and confessed." He admits that some good Christians were fighting solely for the triumph of the Faith, "but most of them were lusting for silks and fine horses."[7] The sleek gentlemen from Seville and Córdoba were captured and held for fat ransoms. But the Christian cavaliers died in the arid gullies, like flies in autumn.

The Marqués and his relatives fought back to back in the darkness until the first pallor of dawn revealed the ghastly scene of slaughter, and the Moors desisted out of weariness. As he rode among the corpses of his friends on the knoll that is still called la Cuesta de la Matanza, the Hill of the Massacre, he saw only a few living crusaders here and there. Two of his brothers, Don Diego and Don Lope, lay dead nearby, with a ring of fallen Moors about them. His nephews, Don Lorenzo and Don Manuel, lay face down in the sand. His third and favorite brother, Don Beltran, still sat on his horse; but even as he turned to rejoin the Marqués, a great chunk of rock, bounding down the mountain side, struck him full in the head, and he reeled over. The frightened horse went madly through the arroyo, riderless. The Marqués cried out in anguish. His Moorish guide brought him a fresh horse and bade him ride for his life. Arrows were beginning to whistle overhead. In the mountains the Moors were crying, "El Zagal! El Zagal!" Evidently the fierce brother of Muley Abou'l Hassan, the elder Boabdil known as "El Zagal," the Valiant, had arrived from Granada. The Marqués mounted the horse like a man in a trance and followed the faithful Luis.

Of all the Christian army, only a few found their way back to Antiquera. Some died of hunger and loss of blood. Some wandered for days, eating roots and herbs, until they were captured by Moorish peasants, or by the women of Malaga. Two hundred and fifty cavaliers, too weak to resist, were thus taken to the dungeons of Malaga, to be held for high ransoms. Five hundred of the infantry, commoners with no one to redeem them, were sold as slaves. The Moors spent several days gathering up the choice armor and weapons of the slain.

The Marqués of Cádiz shut himself up in his castle and remained in speechless sorrow for many days, until Queen Isabel bade him come to Córdoba to give her an account of the debacle. She listened in distress while he artlessly etched upon her imagination a stark picture of horror and desolation. There was not a noble house in Andalusia that did not have its lost hero. The Count of Cifuentes, Isabel's standard bearer, and his brother were led in triumph through the gates of Granada—so the Moorish spies of the Marqués had told him. "All this Andalusia," wrote Bernaldez, "was in a very great sorrow, and there was no drying of the eyes that wept in her and in a great part of Castile, wherever grief had touched."

After Don Rodrigo had gone, Queen Isabel went into her chapel and knelt a long time in the silence, praying.

XVIII

ISABEL HAS A SERIOUS DISAGREEMENT
WITH HER HUSBAND—END OF THE
FIRST PHASE OF THE CRUSADE

ISABEL has been called a mystic who managed to lead the life of a contemplative in the midst of an absorbing family relationship and an amazingly active public career, but there was nothing in her mysticism of that dreamy quietism from the east that denies the claims of reality and takes refuge in a subjective passivity. Like all the great western mystics—like Saint Teresa, like Saint Catherine of Siena, like Saint Ignatius Loyola—she was acutely conscious of the problems of this world and of her duties toward them, and like them she found in prayer the motive power for large and heroic actions. In every crisis she humbly laid her difficulties at the feet of God; but having appealed to Him with all confidence, she proceeded to do her part with an energy that would have commanded the admiration of those less articulate Yankee farmers whose motto was, "Trust God, and keep your powder dry."

If the concept of a crushing, irresistible Fate had occurred to her as she rode from town to town, from castle to castle, raising new levies and restoring the shattered morale of her people, she would have snapped her capable fingers at it. She would have despised it as she despised astrologers and fortune-tellers and all other manifestations of oriental distrust of the human will which are ultimately forms of despair. Deeply imbued as she was with the conclusions, if not all the processes, of the philosophy of Saint Thomas, she could not help seeing in the Fate that overshadowed Islam a roundabout form of unbelief; and surely if she had ever heard of Calvin's theology or Thomas Hardy's determinism, she would have considered them revivals of the hoary Manicheism. She believed in the will of God, yes, and that Will was all powerful; yet God was

246

a universal Father who so loved His children that He could and did limit his own omnipotence by the gift of their free will; and to those who besought Him with sincere faith He sometimes gave the power to do the impossible. Through the mazes of the problem of Will that has baffled so many metaphysicians, she moved with the decisiveness of Doctor Johnson refuting Berkeley by kicking a stone. Had any one demanded a proof that God answered human prayers, she would probably have replied, "He answers mine."

Her war was not only a conflict of kings and men, it was a death struggle of two philosophies, two different conceptions of the destiny of man; despair against hope, the stars against the saints, the centrifugal forces of Mohammedanism against the unifying and harmonizing tendencies of Catholic Christianity. Like all the Crusades, it propounds for those who are resolved to see only economic impulses at work in history a very pretty riddle: Why should a man with an ample estate in England or France leave wife and children to shed his blood at Ascalon or in Andalusia for some commercial advantage that he could not foresee, and probably knew nothing about, and most likely would have no share in? Greed, though naturally it played some part in those remarkable wars, will never explain them. Neither will differences of race. During the periods of tolerance there had been an incalculable fusion of the peoples of the peninsula by marriage. In 1311 the ambassadors of Jaime II of Aragon told Pope Clement that of the 200,000 inhabitants of the city of Granada, not more than 500 were of pure Moorish descent. There were Saracens fairer than the blue-eyed Castilians; there were Castilians darker than any Arab. Nor will climate account for the animosity between Granada and the rest of the peninsula. If the warm air of the south were the chief ingredient of a culture suggesting ripe fruit against a flowered wall in a flood of moonlight, an exotic eastern culture that pampered the senses and the passions as if their gratification were the chief end of life, then the Italians ought to resemble the Moors more than the Spanish. If the superstition of popular science that cold and forbidding landscapes make energetic and masterful peoples had more than a grain of truth in it, the Irish and the English, living on beautiful and fertile islands, ought to be too pacific to fight; the Italians of Julius Caesar's time should have been as easy to conquer as those in Attila's day, or during the Renaissance; the French Canadians should have overrun the western hemisphere, and the Eskimos should be lords of the earth.

The fact is that climate is insignificant in the life of a people, compared to the dynamic force of ideas. The Castilian was no more energetic than the Arab, but his energies were better disciplined. His religion, though in practise he was sometimes false to it, continually reminded him that even lawful pleasures and indulgences were but means to an end, and life itself a journey and a pilgrimage rather than a finality. Even at his worst he generally distinguished between passion and perversion; even in his crimes he despised softness and hypocrisy. His whole life was coordinated and made purposeful by a conviction of the supremacy, under God, of the human will. And if his intense preoccupation with this truth sometimes degenerated into fanaticism and cruelty, it produced on the other hand a long and radiant procession of saints and heroes.

With all their mathematics and horticulture and architecture, the Arabs had remained a barbarous people. If their love for excessive display and the brutality of their ethical principles were not evidence enough, an important index would be found in their attitude toward women. In truly civilized nations there is a balance between men and women, the spiritual equality of mates and comrades. A nation in which women dominate men is decadent. And a nation in which women are the slaves and chattels of men is barbarous. All the peoples who accepted the Mohammedan culture did in fact degrade women. The Koran hardly recognized them as human beings; it classified all mankind into twelve orders, of which the eleventh included robbers, sorcerers, pirates and drunkards, and the twelfth and lowest, women. One can hardly imagine women in Granada making such contributions to the common life as some of the notable women of Christendom made— Doña Lucia de Medrano, who taught Greek and Latin at the University of Salamanca; Doña Francisca de Lebrija, who took her father's chair of rhetoric at the University of Alcalá; Saint Catherine of Siena, who brought about the end of the Papal exile at Avignon; Queen Isabel herself.

Whether the degradation of women in Mussulman societies was only the usual concomitant of barbarism, or resulted more directly from the Prophet's dogma on polygamy need not be discussed here; but certain it is that polygamy in the concrete had brought great disorganization into the public and private affairs of Isabel's enemy, Muley Abou'l Hassan, King of Granada. It was his misfortune that two of his fairest wives were women of brains and ambition. For some years his favorite had been a Christian captive, Isabel de Solis, daughter of the governor of Martos, and a blonde of such passing beauty that the Moors called her Zoraya, Star of the Morning; and her son, Abu Abdallah Boabdil—also called Boabdil El Chico, the Little, to distinguish him from his uncle, Boabdil El Zagal—was recognized as heir to the throne of Granada, in spite of an astrologer's prophecy that he would cause its ruin. Unfortunately for this prince, his royal father, in his old age, conceived a grand passion for a new and younger wife, Ayesha. Zoraya was furiously jealous. Fearing her rival might bear a son capable of cheating Boabdil out of his inheritance, she incited the clan of the Zegries against Ayesha.[1] The Abencerrages took arms in defense of the younger woman. During the civil war that followed, Zoraya and Boabdil were imprisoned in the Alhambra, but managed to escape from the Tower of Comares by night and fled to Guadix. But after Muley's failure to retake Alhama the populace closed the gates against him and proclaimed Boabdil king. El Chico returned in triumph to the capital.

Muley Abou'l Hassan withdrew to Baza to meditate. One dark night he made his way back to Granada with 500 picked men, scaled the walls, expecting that the townspeople would join him as soon as they learned of his presence, and began to slaughter the guards. But the fortunes of Boabdil were still ascendant; the people took arms against Muley, and he was forced to flee to Malaga. All of his kingdom but Granada remained loyal to him. Nevertheless the rivalries of his wives had made a rift that was beginning to be useful to Fernando and Isabel.

Boabdil, a magnanimous and kindly man, but extremely indolent, had married Morayma, the daughter of old Ali Atar, who had humiliated King Fernando at Loja, and his enemies never wearied of saying that he preferred dalliance with her by the cool fountains of the Alhambra to manly exploits in the field against the enemies of Islam. These rumors having reached his father-in-law at Loja, the old warrior rode to

Granada to give Boabdil some seasonable advice. It was high time for him to distinguish himself in action. His father Muley had gained in popularity since his successful raid in Andalusia, and some fine day the volatile Arabs of Granada would welcome him back and cast Boabdil forth to the dogs, unless he bestirred himself. Why not lead an expedition against the Christian town of Lucena? The guard was careless and the spoils were rich.

Boabdil thought so well of the suggestion that he left Granada in April, 1484, with nine thousand infantry and seven hundred cavalry, harried the Christian villages on the way, and struck for Lucena.

At his approach, the Christian watch-fires blazed from mountain to mountain. The Count of Cabra started in pursuit with only 250 cavaliers and 1,200 foot. Throwing himself into Lucena, he helped to defend the place against the repeated attacks of Boabdil and Ali Atar; and when the Moors, knowing that there was no way to take the town except by surprise, began to withdraw to the border, he followed them.

Coming to where the Moors, in five battalions, were drawn up in a valley the Count said to his men: "Be not dismayed at their numbers, for God often gives the victory to the few over the many."[2] A fog drifted down from the hills, concealing the number of the Christians. The enemy retreated. Boabdil was captured fighting valiantly to cover the passage of his troops through a river bed.

The possession of Boabdil gave Fernando a singular opportunity to employ the consummate skill and subtlety in which he surpassed all other kings of his time. If his ignorance of Latin had kept from his ken the Roman maxim of statecraft, *Divide et impera,* he well understood the principle. He saw at once—and so did Isabel—that Boabdil as a prisoner was far less valuable than Boabdil in Granada, dividing the Saracens against Muley. Fernando purposed moreover to strengthen his claim to Granada by sending the captive back as his sworn vassal. Some of the royal councillors thought that Boabdil could not be trusted, but Cardinal Mendoza, "the third King of Spain" said that in Fernando's place he would not only send Boabdil back to Granada, but provide him generously with money.

The King, however, had no intention of spending on Boabdil the Unlucky the money he needed for guns. It was not necessary. Muley Abou'l Hassan offered to ransom the Prince, and intimated he cared little whether he was delivered alive or dead. But Zoraya, the mother of Boabdil, proposed more attractive terms:

If Fernando would recognize Boabdil as King of Granada, Boabdil would agree to hold his throne as vassal to Castile. He would pay a ransom immediately, an annual tribute thereafter. He would liberate four hundred Christian captives to be chosen by Fernando and Isabel, and seventy others every year for five years. He would render military service and attend the Cortes of Castile whenever summoned. His son, and the sons of twelve Saracen nobles, were to be delivered as hostages.

Before he agreed to these conditions, Fernando ravaged the *vega* of Granada to the very gates of the city, under the eyes of Muley and thousands of Moors whom civil war had made innocuous for the time being. He then signed the treaty. Afterwards the unfortunate Boabdil and fifty Moors his mother had sent for him were received at Córdoba with royal honors. All the great nobles of Castile and Andalusia were present. The King and Queen and Cardinal Mendoza gave the Saracens kingly gifts of blood horses and embossed armor and purses to defray their expenses while they remained guests at the court. Isabel graciously gave Boabdil her hand, but the King raised him up and saluted him as a brother monarch. The hungry sad eyes of the Moor glistened with gratitude.

Boabdil's son and the other hostages arrived in August. On the second of September the royal prisoner departed for Granada, cheered by the rabble of Córdoba, followed by an illustrious suite of Christian nobles, and accompanied by King Fernando, who rode at his side. Boabdil had a long, sensitive, almost ascetic face with hollow cheeks contradicted by sensual lips; his eyes were fairly bovine; his hair, falling to his shoulders, and his carefully trimmed beard with a cleft in the middle, had taken their color from the head of his mother Zoraya, the Morning Star. Altogether he looked so harmless, so unwarlike, so pathetically crushed that the emotional crowd felt sorrow for him, and many shed tears, particularly at the moment when he said farewell to the little Moorish boy he was leaving behind as an hostage.

Fernando escorted him until they met some Moorish cavaliers sent by Zoraya. The report they brought concerning the state of affairs at Granada was not reassuring to Boabdil. In fact, he waited until night, and entered privately by a postern gate of the Albaycin, the quarter where Zoraya maintained her own court in opposition to the one of Muley in the Alhambra. The next day, when the return of the captive king became known, scimitars were drawn on both sides, and the city was drenched in blood. Boabdil fled to Almería.

Muley, riding on the flood tide of popular esteem, felt that the time was auspicious for another great raid into Andalusia, and the man he picked to execute it was Bexir, the Alcaide of Malaga. This veteran assembled troops from several towns at Ronda, a town in the Serrania, high on a lofty rock surrounded by the chasm of the Rio Verde. It was the rallying point for many an incursion. No place on the frontier gave so much trouble to the farmers of the south. It was full of Christian spoils, and the dungeons under the bulky Alcázar were crowded with Christian captives. The inhabitants had the reputation of being especially warlike and aggressive; and there were so many Jews in it that it was known as "the Jew's town."[3] The alcaide was the Arab Hamet Ez Zegri, the scourge of the countryside.

The Saracen host, nineteen thousand strong, made for Utrera. But the Christian knights rallied to meet them, and on the banks of the Lopera, September 17, crushed them with great slaughter. Among the spoils were many horses and fine pieces of armor taken by the infidels in the mountains of Malaga. Seeing a great Moor on the back of a familiar looking horse, the Marqués of Cádiz slew him; and when the horse was brought to him he recognized the steed of his dead brother Don Beltran.

"*Ay de mi! mi hermano!*" he said.

Fernando and Isabel heard of this triumph at Vitoria, in Old Castile, where they had gone from Guadalupe in September. They ordered the *Te Deum* sung in the churches, and processions and feasts held in honor of the victory. Fernando sent the Marqués of Cádiz the royal robes he had worn the day the news reached him, and gave him and his heirs the privilege of wearing royal raiment on every anniversary.

Isabel sent her gown to the wife of Don Luis Fernandez Puertocarrero, who had distinguished himself in the battle.

On returning to Córdoba, the sovereigns gave a remarkable reception to the Count of Cabra, captor of Boabdil. Every punctilio of ancient Castilian etiquette was carefully observed, for Isabel had seen enough of the slovenly informality of Enrique's court. She knew how the Castilians, from long contact with the Moors, loved barbaric splendor and ceremony; and although she issued an edict against the extravagant funerals that were popular curses in her day, she never hesitated to exploit the national weakness for the sake of restoring the royal prestige. It was her policy to bestow great honors sparingly, that they might appear an especial mark of distinction. She had noticed that men who could not be bought for money would die for a piece of ribbon or a smile from a queen. Of money and lands she gave with extreme caution which her enemies, forgetting how little she had and how urgent were her needs, attributed to parsimony; but when she did make gifts, they were the rich and generous ones of a woman who despised half measures.

When the Count of Cabra arrived at the gates of Córdoba, he found waiting to meet him the Cardinal of Spain in scarlet robes, the King's brother, the Duke of Villahermosa, and a long train of notables in velvet and silks and gold. To the sound of warlike music, they passed through the mellow old city that Pompey had loved and Caesar had destroyed, until they arrived at the palace, where the King and Queen awaited them, seated on a lofty dais covered with cloth of gold. The monarchs arose. Fernando advanced five steps to meet the victor, who knelt and kissed his hand. The King raised him and embraced him. Isabel took two steps forward and gave her hand to the Count to kiss.

Cushions being brought, the Count was asked to seat himself, a rare privilege in the Castilian royal presence, while their Majesties resumed their places on the throne. Beside him, near the King, sat the Duke of Nájera, the Bishop of Palencia, Don Alonso de Aguilar, and Don Gutierre de Cárdenas. On the Queen's left were Cardinal Mendoza, the Duke of Villahermosa, the Count of Monte Rey, and the Bishops of Jaen and Cuenca.

Music from unseen instruments now sounded through the

hall of audience as twenty of the Queen's ladies, in magnificent gowns of many brilliant colors, entered, and having curtseyed to twenty cavaliers who came forward to bow, hands on hearts, began with them a square measure of stately gravity. The dance ended, the King and Queen retired to dine, while the Count, graciously dismissed, went to the palace of Cardinal Mendoza to be guest of honor at a great banquet. A week later the King and Queen invited him to supper; and on that occasion the Queen danced with the King, and the slender Infanta Isabel with the Count of Cabra. Afterward, the Count supped at the same table with the King, the Queen and the Princess. The supper and the merrymaking continued until one o'clock in the morning.

Isabel measured out her smiles at Court functions as conscientiously as she did her money and her offices. When she received several Portuguese cavaliers, one of their countrymen stood beside her to tell her the precise degree of condescension the rank of each entitled him to.

Feasts and triumphs were ending a year that had begun badly. And the finale was as glorious as it was unexpected. On the twenty-ninth of October, the Marqués of Cádiz recaptured Záhara by a surprise attack in broad daylight, without the loss of a man. At the risk of his life, he scaled the wall in a lonely part at high noon, when no one would have expected an attack. The Moors were startled from their siestas to behold within their gates an enemy whose name and exploits were becoming legendary. Seeing his army outside, they surrendered and were allowed to leave peaceably.

Thus ended the third year of the war. It had been so far the traditional war of forays and ravages. But Isabel was storing up powder at various arsenals along the frontier, she was having stone bullets made at Constantina, she was planning a different sort of conflict, a modern war of sieges, for 1485.

All was going merrily, when the death of Louis XI of France disturbed the equilibrium of Europe.

Louis for some time had been meddling in the affairs of Navarre, where his sister was regent for young François Phœbus. It was bruited about the chanceries of Europe that he was arranging to marry Phœbus to none other than Juana La Beltraneja, then residing at the Portuguese Court. This was the worst possible news to Queen Isabel. Juana had long been the skeleton at the feast of her triumph, and Louis's move seemed to veil a threat of reviving her pretensions and setting up a claim to the throne of Castile for the French house reigning in Navarre.

The Spanish sovereigns attempted to parry the thrust by offering Prince Phœbus their own daughter Juana, then three years old. But Phœbus died, and was succeeded as heir to Navarre by his sister Catherine, 13 years old. Isabel and Fernando then proposed a marriage between this princess and their four-year-old son, Prince Juan. The Regent Madeleine refused, giving the disparity of ages as an excuse. As difference in age was generally of secondary importance in these royal arrangements, Isabel suspected Louis of further and more dangerous intrigues. At this point the Spider King died. Saint Francis de Paula, who gave him the last sacraments, made him promise to return Roussillon and Cerdagne to King Fernando.

One of the first acts of Louis's successor, his son Charles VIII, was to repudiate the deathbed promise. He was an amiable but fatuous youth with a touch of megalomania, and for the time being, at least, completely under the thumb of his aunt, the Regent Anne de Beaujeu. In the boy king's weakness Fernando thought he saw his opportunity to recapture his lost provinces by force. It would be necessary to suspend operations against Granada for a year; but what of it? The opportunity might never come again, and the troops and artillery assembled for use against the Moors in 1485 were providentially available for a sudden and triumphant campaign in the north.

Isabel refused even to discuss such a possibility. What, turn back now and lose the fruits of three years' labor and blood? Encourage the Moors, and discourage the Castilians, and earn the contempt of all Christendom and the derision of all infidels? Never, while she had breath.

Fernando argued that the war against France would be an eminently just one.

"Señor, it is very true that your war is a just one," said Isabel, with that adamant sweetness and calm that she found so impenetrable a buckler on such occasions, "but my war is not only a just one, but a holy one."

The King warmly defended his policy. The Moorish war, when all was said, was a foreign war, whereas the one with France would be a war to recover what was his own. There was no dishonor involved in suspending the war with the Moors, but he would incur a great dishonor if he were to permit himself to be despoiled of his father's lands by force, and do nothing to recover them. There was an opportune moment for everything, and in this business there would never again be such an opportunity as now, when the King of France was a boy, with a weak government. The longer Fernando postponed action, the firmer would Charles's hold be on Roussillon and Cardagne, and the more secure his title, and the inhabitants, seeing so long a time pass without an effort to bring them back to their former allegiance, would lose hope, and reconcile themselves to the government of France. The cavaliers and citizens of those places were continually imploring Fernando to come to their rescue. How could he refuse when the opportunity seemed so providential?[4]

All this reasoning failed to swerve Isabel from her determination to prosecute the Moorish war. She had a logic of her own, and it was not Fernando's logic.

When the royal pair left Vitoria, January 12, for Tarragona, Fernando had decided to ask the Cortes of Aragon for troops, and to make war on France without Isabel's help. They reached Tarragona on the 19th. The Cortes had already met on the fifteenth, but in the absence of the King, had been prorogued. The sessions were not resumed until February 12, and lasted a long while, for the Catalans, to whom insurgency was a tradition and a pleasure, refused to send delegates on the ground that the holding of the Cortes in their territory violated their constitution. When at last the Catalans attended, Barcelona and Valencia remained recalcitrant. Time passed, and nothing was done. Fernando, who wanted money and troops for his war against France, fought parliamentary battles with the Catalans and the Valencians while his hopes melted day after day. A final appeal to Isabel was futile. She replied that he had promised to carry the Moorish war to a successful termination, and ought to keep his word. Fernando again refused.

The Queen, therefore, left Tarragona with the Cardinal of Spain and other Castilian *grandes*, and took the road to

Córdoba, 400 miles away. She went to Toledo for Easter, remained there three days, and then began a rapid recruiting tour of Andalusia, stopping at Ubeda, Baeza, Andújar and Jaén, and returning to Córdoba in April.

The Andalusians responded in great numbers to her fiery sincerity. She assembled at Antiquera a formidable army of 6,000 horse and 12,000 foot in which there was more artillery than any Spanish army had ever had before, master gunners and engineers having arrived that spring from Germany and France. "The Queen ordered brought a great number of carts and timbers and iron and stones necessary for lombards and other artillery."

There were many surgeons in the army, who were to care for the sick and wounded without charge; and there were six great tents, equipped by Isabel with beds and medicines and bandages, which aroused great wonder among the troops, and were called "the Queen's Hospital." It was the first military hospital in history. Isabel's field nurses anticipated the Red Cross by more than three hundred years.

Don Alonso de Aguilar led the vanguard of the Queen's army; the Marqués of Cádiz commanded the second battalion, with the Master of Santiago and Gonsalvo de Córdova, who had his first important command; a third battalion followed under the Duke of Medina Sidonia and the Count of Cabra; and the rearguard was made up of the knights of Alcántara and the Andalusian cavaliers from Jerez and Carmona.

Isabel, mounted on a war horse, watched this host, her own army, file through the gate of Antequera into the plains. For forty days they marched through rich valleys and over fertile plateaux, burning villages, and destroying crops. They proceeded to the seacoast near Malaga, and repulsed the Moors who sallied out to attack them, but did not attempt to storm the city. Perhaps the Queen was unwilling that any one but Fernando should have the glory. Having made a circuit of Coin, Cazarabronela, Almería, Castaina, Gatero and Alhaurin, the army returned laden with spoils to Antequera.

Fernando remained at Tarragona pleading with the stubborn Catalans for funds to raise an army. Had they consented, no doubt he would have waged war without Isabel's aid; but the Aragonese, long overtaxed to pay for the wars of his father, and jealous of their democratic constitutions, checkmated him. He ordered the proroguing of the Cortes of Valencia May 1, and that of Aragon May 13. On their final refusal to give him additional troops, he left his sixteen-year-old natural son, Don Alonso de Aragon, Archbishop of Saragossa, to preside at the Cortes. He had suddenly come to a humiliating but necessary decision. He notified Isabel that he would go south and lead the Castilian army as usual.

Leaving Tarragona May 30, he reached Córdoba in June, took charge of Isabel's army, and appeared before Illora June 11th. He battered his way into it in nine days, ravaged the countryside to the gates of Granada, and returned to Córdoba. Making a second campaign that summer, he smashed his way into the powerful fortress of Setenil in September. The Queen's new artillery was doing its work. The Marqués of Cádiz exultantly exclaimed that the Moorish forts were built to withstand the old guns, and the ballistas and battering rams with which Fernando had had to fight in 1484, but never could resist the new lombards. Isabel was overjoyed at the success of her policy, both as to the war and as to her husband. She greeted Fernando affectionately on his return to Córdoba, and they went to Seville to spend the winter.

Whether Fernando admitted that he had been wrong, or whether Isabel said, "I told you so," no historian has left any record; but an undated letter in the King's handwriting, the original of which is in the collection of autographs at Madrid, may perhaps have been written during the stormy spring when Isabel rode to Toledo while Fernando was vainly attempting to win over the Aragonese delegates:

"*Mi Señora*,—Now at last it is clear which of us two loves best. Judging by what you have ordered should be written to me, I see that you can be happy while I lose my sleep, because messenger comes after messenger and brings me no letters from you. The reason why you do not write is not because there is no paper to be had, or that you do not know how to write, but because you do not love me, and because you are proud. You are living at Toledo, I am living in small villages. Well! one day you will return to your old affection. If you do not, I shall die, and the guilt will be yours.

"Write to me and let me know how you are. There is nothing to be said about the affairs which keep me here, except what Silva will communicate to you, and what Fernando

Pulgar has told you. I beg you to believe Silva. Do write to me.

"The affairs of the Princess must not be forgotten. For God's sake remember her, as well as her father, who kisses your hands, and is your servant.

THE KING."[5]

XIX

POPE SIXTUS IV, like Saint Peter, was a fisherman and the son of a fisherman who arose from obscurity to eminence through merit. On account of his nepotism and his connection with the Spanish Inquisition, he has been represented by historians following the seventeenth century English tradition as cruel, unprincipled, tyrannical, avaricious —a composite of all unchristian traits. To find out how much truth there may be in this picture, we must discard all the partial, distorted and falsified summaries of his correspondence with Queen Isabel, and go back to the original texts.[1] They are exceedingly difficult to read, for a single sentence, though perfectly constructed, will run on sometimes for two whole pages of supple and beautifully cadenced Renaissance Latin. But out of these first hand records, if one takes the trouble to translate them, emerges a very definite personality.

The first important disagreement between this Pope and Queen Isabel—and for this our principal authority must be the chronicle of her secretary Pulgar—occurred early in 1482, when Sixtus decided to bestow the vacant see of Cuenca upon his nephew, Raffaello Sansoni, Cardinal of San Giorgio. Queen Isabel had already planned to ask for the appointment of her own chaplain, Alonso de Burgos. She wrote the Holy Father, reminding him that in the past Rome had allowed the kings of Castile to make ecclesiastical appointments as a special privilege, "considering that with great cost of their blood as Christian princes they had won back the land from the Moors;"[2] furthermore, as some of the benefices included fortified places of strategic importance on the Moorish frontier, it was necessary to commit them to trustworthy men familiar with the situation.[3]

Sixtus replied, according to Pulgar, that in making appointments to spiritual offices he was not bound to consider the wishes of any prince on earth, except as he might deem it advisable for the service of God and the welfare of the Church.[4]

Isabel's ambassador hastened to assure the Pope that she did not wish to set any limit to his authority; "but it would be a reasonable thing to consider the arguments previously alleged."[5]

Sixtus declined to change his decision. Fernando and Isabel then commanded all their subjects at Rome to leave the city, under pain of having their property in Spain confiscated by the State, and threatened to call a general council of all the princes of Christendom "on this and other matters." The Spaniards at Rome obeyed the injunction.[6]

Sixtus was not anxious to have a general council, for there was always the possibility that it might end in another schism. Therefore he commissioned a layman, Domingo Centurion, to visit the court at Medina del Campo and attempt to reach an understanding. The King and Queen replied to this envoy, however, "that the Pope had dealt with them more unjustly than with any Catholic prince, and they would seek what remedies they could and ought,"[7] and ordered him to leave the country, though they were careful to add that any messenger of the Sovereign Pontiff naturally would receive safe conduct and immunity. But Domingo Centurion, instead of retiring from the field, wrote a conciliatory reply that "somewhat tempered the indignation of their majesties."[8]

Meanwhile he found a powerful intercessor in Cardinal Mendoza, who begged Fernando and Isabel, for the sake of the unity of Christendom, to make peace with the Pope. The Cardinal also wrote the Holy Father, explaining the peculiar situation in Spain with such good effect that Sixtus consented to revoke the appointment of Sansoni to the see of Cuenca, and to recognize Isabel's candidate.[9]

The Queen henceforth nominated all bishops appointed in her realms, and it is generally agreed that she named "learned men of good lives, and preachers of good doctrines, whose lives were an example to others,"[10] and often forced bishoprics

on men so humble and unselfish that they preferred to remain
in monasteries. But from the Catholic standpoint, whatever
the political exigencies of Spain may have been, the Pope was
right and Isabel was wrong in this controversy. The privilege
she demanded had often been abused by other rulers, to the
great detriment of the Church; and Sixtus was contending for
the principle for which Saint Gregory VII had toiled and Saint
Thomas of Canterbury had died, the principle now universally
accepted in the Catholic Church. It was unfortunate that
nepotism was involved in his invocation of it.

A controversy of far greater moment commenced in the
same year, 1482, with the Pope's bull of January 29 threatening to remove the Inquisitors unless the King and Queen
insisted upon their following the canon law. The King and
Queen, through their ambassador at Rome, probably explained
the abuses of Morillo and San Martin to the Pope by representing that the cases of heresy were so numerous that no two men
could possibly give adequate attention to all; for on February
11, 1482, Sixtus appointed eight Inquisitors for Castile and
Leon, saying that they had been recommended to him by the
sovereigns "for their purity of life, love and zeal for religion,
gentleness of manners, extensive learning and other virtues."[11]
The seventh man he named was *Thomas de Turrecremata,
baccalaurius*—Tomás of Torquemada, prior of the Dominican
convent of Santa Cruz at Segovia.

It would seem that some at least of the new appointees—including Torquemada, for we know that he refused a bishopric
—were by no means eager to assume the arduous and perilous
labors of an Inquisitor, for the Pope deemed it necessary to
command them, "in remission of their sins and in the love of
God," to lay aside all fear and accept the office "in a spirit of
fortitude" because of the expediency of the affair "and in hope
of eternal reward . . . that the inner root of this perversity
may be torn up through your care and solicitude, and the
vineyards of the Lord, after the little foxes have been driven
off, may bear abundant fruit"[12]—referring to a verse in the
Canticle of Canticles, "Catch us the little foxes that destroy
the vines; for our vineyard hath flourished."[13]

Sixtus again mentioned the complaints he had had of Morillo and San Martin, and repeated with emphasis that the
letters authorizing their appointment contained much that was

contrary to the opinions of the Church fathers and the common observance of the Church, because the situation had been "confusedly" explained to him by the Spanish ambassador. The Inquisitors had proceeded indiscreetly and unjustly in Seville, he said, and in disregard of proper legal procedure. He commanded the eight new Inquisitors to proceed "prudently and carefully," within the rules prescribed by the canons.

A sharp change of policy is observable in this document. Previously Sixtus had allowed Fernando and Isabel to appoint the Inquisitors. Now, although he accepted their nominations, he made the appointments himself, and reserved to himself or his successors the right to revoke them. His distrust of Caesar becomes increasingly apparent.

Two months later, April 17, 1482, he permitted Fernando to extend the Inquisition to Aragon; but in October he suspended the permission, no doubt on receipt of new and more forceful complaints from the *Conversos* flocking to Rome, and perhaps as a rebuke to the impatience of the King. For on May 13, while the Court was at Córdoba, Fernando had written His Holiness a vigorous letter, protesting against the letters of pardon that Sixtus continued to give the fugitives in Rome. Some of the New Christians returned to Spain with their letters, only to find their estates confiscated and their lives in danger. Fernando asked the Pope to revoke the concessions made, saying they had been obtained by "the importunate and astute persuasions" of the *Conversos*, and that he did not intend to honor them; but he signed himself, "Your Holiness's very humble and devoted son, who kisses your holy feet and hands, the King of Castile and Aragon."[14]

In September of the same year Queen Isabel wrote the Pope independently of Fernando, and later, probably in December, sent an autograph letter, assuring Sixtus of her filial obedience and devotion, protesting that the *Conversos* in Rome, with their usual duplicity, had deceived him about their "conversions" and the situation in Spain generally, and suggesting that a remedy for existing abuses be sought in the creating of a Court of Appeals, not at Rome but in Spain, where the judges would be familiar with the peculiar local conditions. The text of her communications has not been found, but its tenor is clear from the reply of Pope Sixtus, dated February 23, 1483, to "your letter written by your own hand." Cardinal Borgia, the Vice-Chancellor, had read the Queen's letter to him some while before, he said, but ill health had prevented his making an earlier reply. After approving of her nomination of Cardinal Mendoza to the see of Toledo to succeed Carrillo, he continued:

"Your letter is full of your piety and singular devotion to God. We rejoice exceedingly, daughter very dear to our heart, that so much care and diligence are employed by Your Highness in those matters so eagerly desired by us"—evidently, from the context, justice and mercy. Yet the Pope assured the Queen that he was not wholly lacking in sympathy for her attitude toward the judaizers in Spain, and had not been deceived by them. "We have always striven to apply suitable remedies for the wretched folly of those people, as for a pernicious disease," he wrote, and a little later he referred to them as a "treacherous and wicked kind of men." He approved of the Inquisition as such, and even in its extension, provided the Inquisitors did not act cruelly and against the provisions of canon law.

Evidently Isabel had written that she had made every effort to follow the Pope's wishes, for he replied, "It is most gratifying to us that you should conform to our desire, in punishing the offenses against the divine Majesty with such care and devotion. Indeed, very dear daughter, we know that your person is distinguished by many royal virtues, through the divine munificence, but we have commended none more than your devotion to God and your enduring love for the orthodox faith."

Though she seemed to fear he might believe that in punishing "those faithless men who, pretending to the name of Christians, blaspheme and crucify Christ with judaical treachery," she was actuated "more by ambition and by greed for temporal goods than by zeal for the faith and for Catholic truth, or by the fear of God," the Pope added, "be assured that we have had no such suspicion.[15] For if there are not lacking those who, to cover up their own crimes, indulge in much whispering, yet nothing from that source can persuade us of any evil on your part, or that of our very dear son, above-mentioned, your illustrious consort. Your sincerity and devotion to God are known to us. We do not believe every spirit. If we lend our ears to the complaints of others, we do not necessarily lend our mind."[16]

The Pope promised to discuss with the Cardinals the Queen's petition for a Court of Appeal in Spain; "and according to their advice, so far as we may be able before God, we shall endeavor to grant your will. Meanwhile, very dear daughter, be of good spirit, and cease not to pursue this pious work, so pleasing to God and to us, with your usual devotion and diligence; and be assured that nothing will be denied to Your Highness that can honorably be granted by us."

The Pope made it clear, however, that while he did not blame the King and Queen personally for the abuses at Seville, he was far from being convinced that all the complaints of the New Christians were groundless or hypocritical. "Since we behold, not without wonder, that which proceeds, not from your intention or that of our previously mentioned beloved son, but from your officials, who, having put aside the fear of God, do not shrink from laying the scythe to an unseemly harvest, from breaking our provisions and the apostolic mandates . . . without being hindered or retarded, as is obvious, by any regard for censures—this, since it is offensive to us, and foreign to your custom and station, and the respect due to us and to the apostolic chair and your own equity, we have caused to be written to Your Serenity. Therefore we urge and require that you carefully avoid censures of this kind, to be feared by any of the faithful whomsoever, nor suffer so evident an injury to be inflicted upon us and upon this Holy See; and in this manner let it be carefully provided lest the liberty and apostolic right which your illustrious progenitors, to their great glory, were zealous to defend and increase, may not appeared to be wronged or diminished in the time of Your Highness. For thus the Lord, in whose power are Kings themselves, will direct your desire, the favor of the apostolic see aiding you; He will cause your posterity and your affairs to flourish; and all things will happen to Your Highness, walking in the right way, according to your wish."

With these solemn words the Pope concluded. He discussed the matter with the Cardinals, and in consequence decided to try the expedient suggested by the Queen. On May 25, 1483, he issued a bull saying that "although it is the sole and peculiar right of the Roman See, over which we preside, not by our

own merits but by the Lord's disposing, to receive the complaints and appeals of all that are heavily oppressed, and take
them to the bosom of our mercy," yet in the present instance
he was willing to appoint as judge for Castile and Leon, the
learned Inigo Manrique, Archbishop of Seville, with authority
to receive all appeals, including those pending in the Roman
Curia, and to extend protection to those deserving it.

Sixtus did not allow Fernando and Isabel to appoint Manrique, but named him directly, and notified him personally of
the appointment in a brief despatched the same day, bidding the
Archbishop accept the burden of the office. It would be
grievous and laborious, said Sixtus, but his merit would be
all the greater in the eyes of God and of the Holy See.

On the same day the Pope removed from office Christopher
de Galves, Inquisitor in Valencia, who, he said, had acted
impiously and imprudently. The Pope notified both the sovereigns and Manrique of his decision, and asked the Archbishop
to cooperate with the Crown in seeing to it that the harsh
activities of Galves ceased immediately.

The new Court of Appeals was not successful, possibly on
account of the age of the Archbishop and the magnitude of
his task, possibly on account of the interference of King Fernando. Fugitive *Conversos* from Seville continued to arrive in
Rome, asking the protection of the Pope and asserting that
the Court of Appeals was so severe that they dared not appeal
to it.

Although Sixtus received them with great kindness, his
health was now failing and he was beset with many vexing
problems. In 1482 his nephew Girolamo Riario had joined the
Venetians in their war against Ferrara and Naples, and Papal
troops under Roberto Malatesta had defeated the Neapolitans
near Nettuna. The Pope made peace, to prevent Venice from
growing too powerful for the future security of Italy. In retaliation the angry Venetians threatened in 1483 to bring the
Turks back into Italy. Their ambassador left Rome in February, 1483. Sixtus proclaimed an interdict against Venice, and
Louis XI expelled the Venetian ambassadors from Paris.
The Venetians then threatened to call a general council to depose Sixtus. He replied that he was willing to have a general
council, provided it was held in the Lateran at Rome.

All this while the Pope had kept an anxious eye on the progress of the new Court of Appeals at Seville. Morillo was probably removed from office, for when an assembly of the Inquisition was held in 1484, that domineering official had disappeared. And on August 2, 1483, the Pope issued a pronouncement of historic importance, which definitely put an end to the uncanonical or abnormal inquisition. In a bull ten pages long, addressed not to the sovereigns but *"ad futuram rei memoriam"* he reviewed the Spanish Inquisition at some length, summarized his previous bulls, as a matter of record, and recalled the reasons why he had appointed Manrique. He professed himself entirely displeased with the experiment. Cases before the Archbishop or his deputies had been subject to long and unfair delays, on the pretext that the Archbishop himself would give attention to them, but the royal officers had shown contempt for his authority. In future, said the Pope, "we wish that the said Archbishop shall proceed not by himself only, but through the official jurisdiction of his ordinaries, with the said Inquisitors," in expediting appeals. Complaints from Seville indicated that the rigor of the Inquisitors "exceeded the moderation of law." The accused were denied safe access to the Court of Appeals, and many *Conversos* of both sexes who had Papal letters of pardon were afraid to present them, since they heard that their effigies had been burned by the secular officials.

After conferring with the most learned of the Cardinals, the Pope decided to have all such cases reopened, heard, and determined with justice and expedition. "And meanwhile, because the shame of public correction has led the erring ones into such a wretched state of despair that they choose rather to die with their sin than to live in disgrace, we have resolved that such persons must be relieved, and the sheep who are lost must be led through the clemency of the Apostolic See to the fold of the true Shepherd, Our Lord Jesus Christ." Therefore he commanded that complete freedom of appeal be guaranteed all persons, and that all penitents, whether heretics or judaizers, be received, absolved and admitted to penance secretly and circumspectly. Even those pronounced heretics or burned in effigy or otherwise punished must be allowed the full liberty of appeal, and when absolved and penanced must be completely reinstated and unmolested in any way. *Conversos* whose appeals were pending in the Roman Curia must not be prosecuted under any pretext. "They must be treated and considered as true Catholics."

Anticipating the lines that Shakespeare[17] put into the mouth of Portia a century later, Sixtus concluded:

"Although human nature is surpassed in all things by the divine nature, *it is mercy alone that makes us like to God*, in so far as human nature itself is capable . . . and therefore we ask and exhort the said King and Queen in the heart of our Lord Jesus Christ, that imitating Him, whose way is always to pity and to spare, they should wish to spare their citizens of Sevilla and the natives of that diocese who recognize their error and implore mercy, so that if henceforth they (the penitents) wish to live, as they promise, according to the true and orthodox faith, they may obtain indulgence from their majesties just as they receive it from God . . . and that they may remain, abide, live and pass safely and securely, night and day, with their goods and their families, as freely as they could before they were summoned on account of the crimes of heresy and apostasy." Any who oppose the Pope's desires are threatened with the indignation of God and the most severe censures and penalties of the Church.[18]

Eleven days later, August 13, 1483, Sixtus dispatched a brief suspending the operation of the bull of August 2, explaining that some to whom he had shown it had raised new objections which he wished to consider more fully. Historians have dealt most unjustly with Sixtus on this score, without giving any English versions by which the reader might form his own opinion of what the Pope actually said. Lea ridicules the claim that "the papacy sought to mitigate the severity of the Spanish Inquisition," but passes over in silence all the fervent and obviously sincere utterances of Sixtus and other Popes that prove his statement false. Llorente makes the error of saying that Sixtus "revoked" the bull of August 2—as if a suspension with the intent to reconsider and perhaps amend were equivalent to revocation. Bergenroth states that Sixtus suspended his bull *the following day*, as if he had whimsically changed his mind over night! The more popular Sabatini informs his wide public that "the brief" (sic) of August 2 "does not appear to have been even dispatched." Yet it was dispatched, for we know that it was received by the bishop of Évora in Portugal and published by him on January 7, 1484—

five months after its temporary suspension August 13—a strong indication that after due consideration Sixtus permitted his first text to stand;[19] and the Bishop later cited this bull of August 2 in censuring the Inquisitors of his diocese for their severity. Since Lea and Sabatini, at least, had access to the documents published by the Royal Academy of History of Madrid in 1889—they mention them—their misrepresentation of Sixtus cannot be attributed to ignorance alone. After all the efforts that have been made to paint this Pope as black as possible, the fact remains on record that Sixtus, after his merciful plea of August 2, continued receiving appeals and granting letters of indulgence, in the spirit of his bull of that date. It is of record, too, that the succeeding Popes Innocent VIII and Alexander VI both insisted upon the observance of the merciful principles laid down by Sixtus in that document. But the argument is clinched in a still more emphatic way, as will appear later, by no less a personage than Torquemada himself.

The controversy between the Holy See and the Spanish crown had now reached what appeared to be an acute stage. Sixtus felt that he had taken the only position possible for the head of the Church with the information before him. But Isabel and Fernando still believed that the Pope did not fully understand the gravity of the Jewish problem in Spain, and that his policy, if carried out, would throw the Inquisition ultimately into the hands of the Spanish Bishops, so many of whom were of Jewish descent that, granting their faith to be sound, their natural sympathies would be fatal in the end to the Holy Office. This, in fact, was exactly what had happened in the past, and Sixtus himself had recognized the difficulty to the extent of requesting, early in 1483, that bishops and ordinaries of Jewish descent refrain from any participation in the Inquisition.

The upshot of all this was a compromise. Queen Isabel probably pleaded that the abuses could be eliminated by a complete reorganization of the Holy Office under a responsible head, and at the suggestion of the invaluable Cardinal Mendoza she recommended to the Pope Fray Tomás de Torquemada, Prior of the Dominican convent of Santa Cruz at Segovia, whose qualifications had been amply demonstrated during the year and a half since his appointment as one of

the eight. In October, 1483, Sixtus appointed this man Inquisitor General for Castile and Leon, and a few days later
added Aragon, Catalonia and Valencia to his jurisdiction. By
virtue of his office, the Prior became a member of "Our Council" and confessor to their Majesties.

Few men in history have been more cruelly caricatured by
ignorance and malice than this self-effacing man of prayer
who had vast and terrifying powers thrust upon him against
his wish. A search of contemporary sources discloses no facts
to support the monstrous legend that sectarian and rationalistic
prejudice has built up about his memory. The genesis of the
legend is not difficult to trace. Propagandists eager to discredit Spain and the Church began by judging the Inquisition
on partial or false evidence, by the standards of another age,
and pronounced it wholly evil. From that point they reasoned
that any man involved in it must have been wicked. The Inquisitor General must therefore have been a Nero of iniquity.
A similar reasoning in the year 2300—assuming for the sake
of argument that say, capital punishment should be abolished
before that date—could brand as bloodthirsty scoundrels and
hypocrites all the judges who have pronounced sentence of
death during our age. Thus our historians have dealt with
Torquemada. But when one follows the legend back to the
fifteenth century, it gradually dissolves, leaving a picture of
a pleasant, kindly, industrious, able and modest man whose
chief ambition in life was to imitate Jesus Christ.

The modern man who gasps incredulously at this essential
and incontrovertible conception has probably fallen into the
common but very unhistorical fallacy that sees only one side,
the merciful side, of the complex character of the Redeemer.
But to Torquemada the Christ was not some remote character
in history, but an ever-present and living God. He held that
mystical concept of the Crucifixion which is at least as old as
Saint Augustine and as modern as a certain striking sonnet by
E. A. Robinson: that the Passion of Christ was perpetuated
as long as there were ambitious Caesars, fickle rabbles, Caia-
phases and Annases, denying Peters and betraying Judases in
the world.

During the long years in his bare cell at Segovia the Dominican monk had meditated on this idea; and though the Christ
to whom he prayed daily was merciful above all things, He

was not only the pardoner of the woman taken in adultery, not only the preacher of the Sermon on the Mount, not only the healer and the divine consoler, but also He who foretold in burning words the destruction of Jerusalem and the punishment of the Jews for rejecting Him; who said that it would be better not to be born than to give scandal to a child; who spoke of an actual Hell and a day of Judgment; who scourged the money-changers out of the Temple on that first memorable Palm Sunday when He solemnly reminded the Jews of the prophecy that *the stone rejected by the builders would become the head of the corner,* and concluded with this startling prediction: "Therefore I say to you, that the kingdom of God shall be taken from you, and shall be given to a nation yielding the fruits thereof. *And whosoever shall fall on this stone shall be broken; but on whomsoever it shall fall, it shall grind him to powder."*

Fray Tomás, like Queen Isabel, like all devout Catholics, had often pondered on such words as these, set down by one of the first Jewish Christians; and he had read in the same chronicle that five days afterward the Jewish multitude, deceived by their leaders, had cried, "His blood be upon us and upon our children." And looking beyond his monastery walls, the friar had beheld for many years the rocky city of Segovia, where Don Juan Árias de Ávila had had the seventeen Jews executed in 1468 for the murder of a Christian boy on Good Friday, where the unscrupulous Pacheco had incited the massacre of 1474, and where every day the powerful Jews and *Conversos* continued to reject the Crucified, openly mocked and blasphemed Him, and by their exploitation of Church and State strove to bring His work to nought. That some strong hand should intervene to prevent the total wreckage of the Christian culture by its most determined enemies seemed to him only reasonable and just. This was perhaps the dominant idea in the man's mind; and it is particularly important to notice it, since it was also the key to the psychology of Queen Isabel, who is chiefly responsible for making him an historical character.

Whether Torquemada himself had Jewish blood in his veins has been disputed. Pulgar, himself a "New Christian," said that he had. Zurita denies this, saying that he was "a person of holy life, and of clean and noble lineage."[20] He was a nephew of the illustrious Cardinal Torquemada, and was born in Valladolid in 1420. At the time of his appointment as Inquisitor General, therefore, he was sixty-three years of age.

For twenty years he had been quietly presiding over an exemplary monastery and giving his monks the example of a selfless and studious life. Strict as he was with others, he was even more so with himself, for he never ate meat, he slept upon a bare plank, he wore no linen next to his skin. He was industrious and persistent. He was incorruptible by either bribes or flattery, and thus immune from one of the most telling weapons of the Jews and the crypto-Jews. Nor could the violence to which they resorted when other means failed deter him from doing his duty as he saw it, for he was fearless. The spiteful paragraph that Lea devotes to his character mentions that he went about with a retinue of 250 armed familiars of the Holy Office and 50 horsemen, and that he was so fearful of assassination that he always kept on his desk the horn of the unicorn, supposed to have mysterious powers of discovering and neutralizing poisons. Thus is added the touch of superstition needed to complete the conventional lampoon of a medieval friar. But it is clear that Lea follows the vindictive Llorente in taking these details from Paramo. Contemporary evidence is lacking—although it is probable enough, to be sure, that Queen Isabel insisted on the Prior's having an adequate guard to prevent his assassination.

The chroniclers of his time—and they are frank enough in laying bare the weaknesses of great men—unanimously pay tribute to his lofty character, his administrative efficiency, and the confidence he inspired in the King and Queen. Two Popes, Sixtus IV and Alexander VI, praised his zeal and his wisdom. Severe he was with those whom he believed guilty, that is undeniable. But it is not true that he enjoyed inflicting pain for the mere sake of persecuting; nor was he a fanatic, as Savonarola was. A fanatic is a man from whom some idea, true or false, has shut out part of reality. But Torquemada saw the world about him very clearly, and knew just what he was doing. And money meant so little to him that he spent all of the great sums given him by the grateful King and Queen out of the confiscations, on various charitable and religious works—built the beautiful monastery of Saint Thomas Aquinas at Ávila, enlarged the one of Santa Cruz at Segovia, and erected some fine buildings in his native town of Torquemada.

The selection of Torquemada, as Lea admits, "justified the wisdom of the sovereigns."[22] He commenced with calm energy to reform and reorganize the Holy Office. He discharged Inquisitors who were unjust or temperamentally unfit, and named others in whom he had confidence. In general he made the procedure of the tribunal more lenient, and he seems to have striven in every way possible to avoid the mistakes and abuses of the earlier French Inquisitors. He forbade the Inquisitors and other persons attached to the Holy Office to receive presents, under pain of excommunication, dismissal, restitution and a fine of double the gift—and he was a man to enforce his regulations. He insisted upon clean and well ventilated prisons which were far better than those maintained by the civil authorities all over Europe. Every effort was made to safeguard the legal rights of the accused person; he was allowed counsel, and he could name his enemies, whose testimony, if they were among the witnesses, was then discarded. Torture was used, but sparingly, and only when other means failed to elicit a confession from one against whom there was strong evidence. Secret absolution was allowed where the crime had been secret.

To provide funds for the Moorish war, the Inquisition adopted some expedients that are offensive to all our notions of equity. If an accused person did not appear when summoned, he could be condemned as a heretic, his effigy could be burned, his goods could be confiscated and his children thus not only disgraced but deprived of their heritage. A dead man, known to have died a heretic, could be exhumed and burned, and all his property confiscated, even if his children were orthodox, though they generally were not. Torquemada ruled, however, that if a man executed as a heretic had children under age, part of their father's property must be granted to them, and their education entrusted to proper persons. Queen Isabel was particularly interested in this aspect of the matter, and in numerous cases provided for the children of the deceased.

If we remember that heresy was considered very much like high treason, and that high treason was punished everywhere in Europe not only by the most cruel kind of death but by

confiscation of the estates of the guilty, the attitude of the
Spanish sovereigns and of the Holy Office seems moderate by
contrast. Compare the notarial records of a trial in the Spanish
Inquisition under Torquemada, for instance, with those of
some of the treason trials in England under Henry VII, Henry
VIII, or Queen Elizabeth—consider, for instance, how Sir
Edward Coke discredited the testimony of Sir Walter Raleigh,
on trial for his life, on the ground that he was already guilty
of the crime for which he was being tried!—and the advantage
is all on the side of the Inquisition.[23]

The royal correspondence concerning the affairs of the Holy
Office appears to have been conducted chiefly by King Fernando. That he used the Inquisition as a source of revenue
to finance the Moorish Crusade can hardly be doubted. According to a memorial address to Charles V by the Licenciado Tristan de Leon in 1524, the enormous sum of 10,000,000 ducats
was realized from the confiscations of condemned heretics during the period of the war. Yet Fernando seems to have been
sincere in his efforts to repress harshness and delay on the
part of Inquisitors, even when he lost money by interfering.
His letters to them, urging leniency and justice, could not
have been hypocritical, for they were meant to be confidential,
and remained hidden for centuries. His scrupulous attention to
the smallest appeals, even from obscure condemned persons in
remote places, and his many orders revoking confiscations or
granting alms to the children of the accused, show a desire
to be merciful and just that even Lea, no friend of the Holy
Office, repeatedly acknowledges with praise.

Many of the 2,000 victims of Torquemada would undoubtedly have been put to death by the criminal courts of the
State, even if there had been no Inquisition. For he enlarged
the scope of the tribunal to include numerous offenses that
were only "implicit" heresy. Thus the Inquisition punished
bigamists, blasphemers, church robbers, priests who married
women and deceived them as to their status, priests who se-
duced women and induced them not to confess the sin, usurers,
employes of the Inquisition who violated female prisoners,
mixers of love potions, pretended saints and mystics, and "all
who speculated on the credulity of the public."[24]

If an institution is to be judged, as de Maistre insisted, not
only by the evils it caused but by those it prevented, the verdict

of history must be that in the long run the Spanish Inquisition proved to be a life-saving organism, in the sense that it
averted more deaths than it caused. Not only was Spain free
from the terrible religious wars that cost hundreds of thousands of lives in the countries where Protestantism obtained a
foothold, but she escaped almost completely the terrors of
witchburning, which claimed 100,000 victims in Germany and
30,000 in Great Britain.[25] When the witch-hunting craze swept
over Protestant Europe, Spain was not immune from that
curious impulse to persecute; but the Inquisitors claimed jurisdiction over witchcraft and necromancy, and after an investigation they announced that the whole business was a delusion. A dabbler in the black art was whipped or penanced here
and there, but few if any lives were lost.[26]

If Vacandard is right in estimating that about one-tenth of
the persons accused were executed in the early Inquisition
against the Cathari, it would appear that Torquemada's courts
were far more merciful. For during his whole regime more
than 100,000 persons were placed on trial, but only two per
cent—about 2,000—were put to death. In other words, Torquemada's Inquisition was only a fifth as deadly as the thirteenth century tribunal.

On taking office, the Prior of Santa Cruz proclaimed an
edict of grace, during the term of which thousands of judaizers
confessed and were reconciled. After he formed a Suprema, or
High Court, he organized four inferior tribunals at Seville,
Córdoba, Jaén and Ciudad Real, and in 1484 he held a general synod of all Inquisitors at Seville, in the presence of the
King and Queen, to impress upon all of them the need of
fairness and uniformity. Several of the instructions issued by
the assembly—numbers 3, 8, 10, 23, and 24—plainly are
intended to carry out the merciful requests made by Pope
Sixtus in his bull of August 2, 1483. And in December of
the same year the Inquisitor General issued fourteen instructions that have somehow escaped the attention of most historians of the Inquisition, perhaps because Llorente omitted
them. One paragraph in particular sheds illumination on two
or three controversies of first importance. It proves beyond a
doubt the falsity of Lea's contention that the Popes did not
"attempt to mitigate the severity of the Spanish Inquisition."
It indicates clearly that while Torquemada submitted to the

supreme authority of the Holy See, he found as a Spanish judge that the merciful rulings of Pope Sixtus were something of a hindrance to him in his difficult task. It demonstrates that Sixtus not only allowed his bull of August 2, 1483, to stand, but in so doing created a precedent that Innocent VIII followed. It shows too, that while Isabel and Fernando went so far as to prepare an order forbidding the use of papal letters of indulgence in Castile, they forebore to publish them pending an appeal to Innocent.

"Since in the time of Pope Sixtus IV of good memory," wrote Fray Tomás, "there emanated from the Roman court certain orders and bulls and excessive rules for penitence against equity *to the detriment of the Inquisition and its ministers*, Their Highnesses command that letters and provisions be read which together are general for all the realm, by which are prevented and can justly be prevented the execution of the said orders and bulls if any persons ask for them and desire to use them *until the Pope may be consulted* and informed of the truth by command of Their Highnesses; for it is not to be presumed that the intention of the Holy Father would be to cause any hindrance to the affairs of the holy Catholic faith; *but the said provisions of Their Highnesses shall not be published until it is seen whether Pope Innocent VIII, newly elected, will concede certain bulls and mandates in place of those which have been sent from his court to the detriment of the Holy Inquisition.*"[27]

There could hardly be a more convincing testimony of the delicacy of Torquemada's position, his temptation and that of the sovereigns to sacrifice the interests of the Church to the royal supremacy, and the restraint the Popes exercised over the Holy Office and over the impatience and the pride of kings than this complaint of an Inquisitor General that the Roman Curia had issued excessively merciful rules "to the detriment of the Inquisition." The decision of Innocent was adverse, and both Torquemada and the sovereigns were compelled to accept it.

A month later Torquemada issued fourteen additional instructions, chiefly concerned, like the first, with carefully safeguarding the imposition of fines and confiscations, and preventing the negligence, corruption or excessive rigor of the Inquisitors. He commands them to send full information

Torquemada, Inquisitor-General of Castile

of all the affairs of the Holy Office either to "our lord the King, or to me." The confiscations, he says, are "to pay the costs of the war and of other pious works, and to pay the salaries of the Inquisitors and other ministers engaged in the Holy Inquisition." Accused persons who are sick or have some other good excuse when summoned before the Inquisition must be treated mercifully even if they appear after the expiration of the Edict of Grace. . . .

When the King and the Queen went to Tarazona early in 1484 to preside at the Aragonian Cortes, they took Torquemada with them to make arrangements for the revival of the Inquisition there; and because the opposition was even greater than it had been at Seville, they first took the precaution of demanding from all the delegates a promise to accept the jurisdiction of the Holy Office. On the fourth of May, Torquemada appointed as Inquisitors for Aragon Fray Gaspar Juglar and Maestre Pedro Arbues of Épila, canon of the Cathedral at Saragossa, both Dominicans.[28] The Inquisitor General himself apparently arranged the first *auto de fe*, held in the Cathedral at Saragossa, and four persons were penanced and reconciled. There were no executions.[29]

The penitents were fined, however, and the "New Christians," who had been so secure in their wealth and power that they had openly attended the synagogues and mocked the Christian religion, saw clearly that the King and Queen counted on them for a large pecuniary harvest. They began to organize to prevent the threatened confiscations. Most of the political power of Saragossa and of all Aragon was theirs. The governor of Aragon was a *Converso;* so were most of the members of the Cortes, most of the judges, most of the lawyers. Aragon, in fact, was being ruled by a Jewish plutocracy operating through the crypto-Jews who professed Christianity.

With such influence it was not difficult for them to organize a formidable protest against the Inquisition on the ground that it was contrary to the *fueros*, or charters of liberties, to confiscate property for heresy, or to prosecute without giving the names of witnesses. This was calculated to appeal to the strong national pride and independence of the Aragonese. A great meeting of the four estates of the realm was held in protest, and two monks were sent to Córdoba, whither the sovereigns had returned, to ask them to quash the Holy Office.[30]

When these protests failed to move Fernando and Isabel, the Jews had recourse to a weapon they had often found useful in Spain. They collected huge sums of money to bribe officials of the Court to influence the King and Queen. It appears that they even attempted to bribe the sovereigns themselves. "They offered large sums of money," says Zurita, "and (promised) on that account to perform a certain designated service, if the confiscation were removed; *and especially they endeavored to induce the Queen, saying that she was the one who gave the more favor to the General Inquisition.*"[31] But the Queen had made up her mind, and could neither be persuaded nor bribed.

It is strange that when bribery failed the Jews were not deterred by the unfortunate ending of the Susan conspiracy in Seville from a similar resort to violence. Perhaps their greater political authority persuaded them that they could defy the double Crown. A large group of Jewish millionaires who outwardly professed Christianity held a meeting in the Mercado in the residence of Luis de Santángel, head of the numerous family of bankers, money-lenders, lawyers and farmers of taxes, who were descended from the converted Rabbi Azarías Ginello. Among them, besides Santángel himself, were Sancho de Paternoy, Chief Treasurer (Maestre Racional) of Aragon, who had a seat in the synagogue of Saragossa, though he pretended to be a Catholic; Juan Pedro Sanchez, brother of King Fernando's treasurer; Alfonso de la Caballeria, Vice-Chancellor of Aragon; Pedro de Almazan, Mateo Ram, Juan de la Badia, and others—all men of high influence. They decided to have the Inquisitors murdered, as a warning to the sovereigns. Don Blasco d'Alagon undertook to collect a fund of 10,000 reals to reward the assassins. Juan de la Badia assumed the direction of the affair, and hired several desperadoes.

The conspirators sent a letter to Gabrial Sanchez, King Fernando's treasurer for Aragon, who was then with the Court at Córdoba, telling him the whole plan. He replied, giving his approval, and predicting that the murder would end the Inquisition in Aragon.

The original plan was to kill Pedro Arbues de Épila, the Assessor Martin de la Raga, and the new Inquisitor Micer Pedro Frances—for Juglar died soon after his appointment, poisoned, it was said, by some *rosquillas* (sweet-cakes) given him by some crypto-Jews.[32] Gradually, however, the plans appear to have centered more and more about the person of Pedro Arbues.

All accounts agree that he was a holy and learned man of retiring disposition, who had accepted the office of Inquisitor at the royal command with the greatest reluctance, having no taste for authority and knowing how perilous the task would be. His activities so far had consisted largely in obtaining evidence of judaizing. He was an eloquent preacher and had preached at the second *auto*, June 3, 1484. He is said also to have had the gift of prophecy.

Plans for his assassination were carefully developed for several months, during which, considering the large number of accomplices of both sexes, secrecy was preserved with remarkable success. Three times the cutthroats assembled at various churches to waylay the Inquisitors, but each time the victims escaped. On one occasion they planned to throw the Assessor Martin de la Raga into the river, but he happened to have two cavaliers with him.

On the night of September 14, 1485, the assassins sought Pedro Arbues at his lodgings, and later at the Church, where he was accustomed to pray; but he eluded them. The following night they hid themselves in the Church and waited for him in the darkness among the pillars.

At midnight a dim white figure came through the door of the cloister. It was the Inquisitor Arbues, and in one hand he held a short lance—for he evidently knew of the design upon his lodgings—and in the other a lantern. Walking to a spot below the pulpit on the epistle or right side of the altar, he laid his lantern and the lance beside a pillar, and kneeling down before the Blessed Sacrament was soon lost in prayer, saying the office of Matins. The assassins crept slowly along the dark aisles until they came to the flickering edge of the circle of light in the center of which knelt the Dominican in his white robe.

"There he is, give it to him!" whispered de la Badia to the French Jew, Vidau Durango.

Stealing up behind the priest from the choir, Durango leaped forward and stabbed him in the back of the neck. The other ruffians closed in, and Esperandeo ran the kneeling man twice through the body with a sword. Peter Arbues cried out, "Praised be Jesus Christ, that I die for His holy faith!"[33] and fell, while the assassins fled.

When the clergy of the Church came running in with lanterns, the wounded man repeated the same words, says Zurita, "and others in praise of Our Lady, whose hours he had been reciting."

Before dawn, the streets were crowded with angry men, crying, "To the fire with the *Conversos!*" and undoubtedly one of the periodic massacres would have ensued, if Don Alonso de Aragon, the Archbishop and King Fernando's natural son, had not mounted a horse and ridden among the mob, assuring the people that justice would be done.

Peter Arbues died in the middle of the following night. During the twenty hours since the assault he had spoken no word against his murderers, "but always glorified Our Lord till his soul left him." He was buried the following Saturday[34] in the Cathedral close to the spot where he had fallen. As he was laid in the sepulchre in the presence of a great throng, some of his blood which had fallen profusely on the flag-stones and had dried there, suddenly liquefied and bubbled up; and to this fact, says Zurita, "Juan de Anchias and Antic de Bages and other notaries who were present testified with public acts." Lea suppresses the highly important fact that records were made by eye-witnesses of considerable intelligence, and dismisses the miracle with a characteristic sneer.

From the day of his death Peter Arbues was venerated in Saragossa as a martyr. It was said that the holy bell of Villela had tolled for the fourth time, untouched by human hands, on the night of his murder. In 1490 the city government of Saragossa commanded that lamps be kept burning day and night at his tomb; and King Fernando and Queen Isabel caused to be built on the spot a fine statue bearing the inscription, "Happy Saragossa! Rejoice that here is buried he who is the glory of the martyrs." He was canonized June 29, 1867, by Pope Pius IX. Thousands of persons still pray at his sepulchre, which, by an interesting coincidence, is near the spot where Saint James the Apostle first preached the gospel of Christ in Spain.

Far from having the effect that the Jews had hoped for, the assassination of Saint Peter Arbues gave the Inquisition a free hand in Aragon. As soon as the King and Queen learned of the event, they sent orders through Torquemada from Córdoba that every one concerned in the crime must be tracked down and punished. Scores of fugitives, including whole families of prominent Jews, fled to France and other countries. The chief offenders, however, were caught before they crossed the borders and executed at various times during the following three years. On June 30, 1486, the hands of Vidau Durango were cut off and nailed to the door of the House of Deputies, after which he was beheaded and quartered. Juan de Esperandeo suffered a similar fate. Juan de la Badia, another of the chief assassins committed suicide in prison by breaking a glass lamp into pieces and swallowing the fragments, on the day before he was to have been executed in January, 1487. His corpse was dragged through the streets and beheaded. Mateo Ram, who supervised the murder, had his hands cut off and was then burned.[35]

With public opinion now strongly on its side, the Holy Office proceeded with vigor to prosecute the powerful New Christians who had been openly insulting and ridiculing the Christian religion. In a series of inexorable trials, during which every effort at bribery and corruption failed, Torquemada little by little shattered the power of the great Jewish plutocracy of Aragon, and turned the proceeds of the numerous confiscations into the war chest of the Moorish Crusade. In this he had the whole-hearted support of King Fernando and Queen Isabel.

XX

ISABEL TASTES THE BITTERNESS OF
DEFEAT, SHAKES OFF DESPAIR, AND
MOVES A MOUNTAIN

CÓRDOBA was a beautiful city in the spring of 1485, but it was not what it had been when the caliphs made it their capital. Gone were the mosques with minarets of burnished gold, the marble palaces with cool halls inlaid with mosaics, the fountains, the arabesques, the cornices of beaten gold, the chests inlaid with malachite and silver, the furnishings of mother-of-pearl and ivory. Gone was the date palm that the first Ommiad had brought from Syria and planted in his garden, to call to mind his old home in Damascus. Gone were the times when a man could walk ten miles in a straight line by the lamps of the city after sundown. The caliph with the income of 20,000,000 gold pieces per year, and his 10,000 skilled workmen, his 13,000 silk looms, his wives, his concubines, his eunuchs and his slaves from many nations—all were crumbled up in the dust of history. Time had swept away the summer afternoon of Islam and restored the western vigor of Rome. Trumpet calls again shivered against the walls as in the days when Julius Caesar humbled the city, and the fields across the river were pied with tents of many colors, and the pennants of a hundred cities. And on the very site of the ancient Temple of Janus, a Byzantine mosque that Abd er Rahman had built was being used as a Christian Church.

There, one April morning, in a forest of porphyry and jasper and lapis lazuli, Queen Isabel knelt at Mass and prayed for victory. All about were exquisite traceries and mosaics. The sanctuary was paved with silver, the pulpit was of ivory inlaid with gold and gems, and everywhere hung lanterns—thousands of them—made of filigree work like priceless lace. There was something barbaric in the overwhelm-

ing accumulation of riches and spoils that cluttered those bewildering vistas; one sighed for the more spiritual grace of
the Cathedral at Seville.

Queen Isabel preferred the comparative simplicity of her
own chapel, and usually heard Mass there. Her altar was covered with brocade and satin studded with precious stones and
pearls of great value, and before it, on silk rugs of many rich
colors spread over the floor, stood massive silver candlesticks
of subtle workmanship. The ornaments were all of gold and
silver, and the vestments were of choice silk or satin, for the
Queen, like the woman with the alabaster box in the gospel,
felt that nothing was too good to lay at the feet of her Lord.
Yet there was nothing gaudy or ostentatious; all was simple,
harmonious, regally severe. Even the seats reflected an orderly
mind, for they were carefully arranged according to rank.
First, on the right, sat cardinals, then archbishops, then ambassadors, then bishops. On the left were constables, admirals,
dukes, marqueses, counts and other cavaliers in the order
named.[1]

She listened so attentively that if any of the priests or
choristers who chanted the psalms or the beautiful liturgy of
the Mass happened to mispronounce a Latin word, or slur
over a single syllable, she made a note of it; and afterwards
she corrected and instructed the delinquent, as a master might
take to task a pupil.[2]

She was then thirty-four, serene and thoughtful of countenance, somewhat settled, but still comely as on the day of
her coronation. In dress she followed the prevailing fashion.
A lady of rank usually wore long full garments with graceful
lines. The gown, with a tight bodice and a girdle tied in a
looped knot at the front, fell over the ankles to the ground,
revealing only the tips of the square-toed shoes. Over this a
cloak was drawn across the figure from the left and caught
under the right arm, falling at the sides in long folds. Ladies
often wore veils, and over them a hood-like covering that
met under the chin and was draped over the breast in small
horizontal folds.[3] The Queen wore few jewels, except on state
occasions.

After Mass, while breakfasting with the King, she opened
her voluminous mail. Afterward they mounted horses and
rode through the city to inspect the camp. A blind man could

have found it easily by the noise. For the heavy lombards from Italy were discharging their great stone bullets at targets by the river bank, and the booming was like a victorious music in the ears of the Queen.

The reorganization of the army was almost complete. During the winter Isabel had engaged Don Francisco Ramirez, a famous Madrid engineer known as *El Artillero*, and it was largely due to his ability that when the campaign of 1485 began, the Castilian army had expert smiths, powder-makers and gunners from France, Germany and Flanders, and could boast of the best artillery in Europe.

Cannons were not exactly new—they had been used in the East from the earliest times. Isabel's ancestor Edward I had had projectiles of 300 pounds hurled at the siege of Stirling, a century before, and Mohammed II had used cannon-balls twice as heavy at Constantinople in 1453. "Bumbardos, canones, culverynes, fowelers, serpentynes et alios canones quoscumque" had been familiar in the wars of the fifteenth century; yet the most useful of them, the lombards, were still clumsy contraptions mounted on ox-carts and incapable of being pointed right or left, up or down. They were Italian guns, made of thick iron bars 12 feet long and two inches wide, clamped together with iron hoops. The weight of the ammunition—they threw marble bullets of about 165 pounds in Isabel's army—prevented rapid ignition of the powder, so that the gunners were congratulated when two lombards together fired 140 shots in a day. Each lombard, dragged by oxen or mules, was followed by a wagon loaded with marble bullets about 14 inches in diameter. Isabel had projectiles of iron made for pieces of small calibre—*robadoquines, cerbatanes, pasavolantes* and *buzanas*. To provide supplies for the artillery, arsenals were scattered in many small places along the frontier between Córdoba and Seville.

Foreseeing the difficulty of using guns in mountainous country, she sent 2,000 sappers with the army to make roads, keep the artillery in motion and construct works of circumvallation. During the remaining campaigns they opened roads through mountains. Under her orders they filled in valleys, threw bridges of cork-oak over streams, dammed up rivers, and turned aside mountain torrents that would have swept away bridges and roads.

Isabel and Fernando with their Children at Prayer
(*From a Painting in the Prado*)

It was in 1485 that Fernando and Isabel began to import troops from Switzerland. "These are warlike men who fight on foot, and are resolved never to turn their backs to the enemy. And for that reason they wear defensive arms only in front, and not on the other parts of the body. These people serve for pay abroad, and take part in wars that they believe just. They are good Christians and pious."[4] In employing these mountaineers the Spanish sovereigns were taking a leaf from the notebook of Louis XI. The immortal *tercios* of Spain were formed on the model of the Swiss, and even excelled them, as Machiavelli remarks, for besides being warlike, they were nervous, frugal and sober.

In medieval warfare it was the privileged classes, the men who brought about wars and chiefly benefited by them, who occupied the dangerous places in the front ranks and shed their blood most freely. The farmers and artisans for the most part remained in their fields and at their benches; when they did serve, it was for so many days a year, or for a limited period. The infantry was considered an auxiliary arm, to do menial tasks such as digging trenches and holding horses, and to support the cavalry. Standing armies were unknown, except for such mercenaries as the *condottieri* in Italy, and garrisons were usually temporary. But all that was changing rapidly. A mixture of sulphur, charcoal and saltpetre was making possible a warfare in which the common people would have the privilege of risking their lives for years at small pay, for the benefit of other men who sat safe at home collecting the spoils.

The host that Isabel saw marching out of Córdoba on April 5, 1485, was a highly efficient organization of 29,000 men, including 9,000 cavalry, in whose ranks fluttered the pennants of all the noble houses of Castile and Andalusia. Don Beltran de la Cueva, no longer the young and handsome cavalier who had defended the passage of arms for the beauty of Queen Juana, was among the lords who took the field that day.

The King captured by storm Benamaquex, Coin and Cartama in quick succession. When Benamaquex, which had returned to its Moorish allegiance, was retaken, 108 of the inhabitants were put to the sword or hanged on the battlements, as an example. Coin was razed to the ground, for it was too large to be garrisoned. Altogether 70 Moorish towns were destroyed.

Fernando now intended marching on Malaga, but on being informed by the Marqués of Cádiz that Ronda, "the Jews' town," had few defenders—having sent its troops to aid Malaga—he abruptly changed his plan, marched swiftly against it, and gave the Moors the first demonstration of the powers of his new artillery. Balls of tow, steeped in pitch, oil and gunpowder, fell on their roofs and set fire to them; by night the city was like a great furnace. Next day the people surrendered, and were allowed to leave with their effects for Barbary or elsewhere. Those who chose to remain in Spain had lands assigned them by the King, and whether Moors or Jews, were allowed freedom of worship.

When the dungeons of Ronda were opened, hundreds of Christian prisoners came tottering forth. Some were almost naked, except for a few filthy rags; chains clanked at their ankles; their beards and hair were matted, or fell to their waists. They were fed and clothed and sent to Córdoba.

Isabel was waiting for them there on the steps of the Cathedral. Some fell on their knees before her, and the Queen wept with them. She commanded food, clothing and money to be given them. Emaciated hands were held up in blessing, and feeble voices cried, *"Viva la Reina!"*

Although she was ill and nervous and pregnant for the fifth time, the Queen went to Vaena with Cardinal Mendoza and Prince Juan, to be nearer the scene of the important events that seemed imminent.

The Count of Cabra had asked permission to storm Moclin, a stronghold commanding the northern approach to Granada, and the King, after a council of war, had allowed him a large force of cavalry for the purpose. The Master of Calatrava was to follow with 10,000 men, and the King, making a feint in another direction, was to turn and surround the town.

Queen Isabel sat in the tower of the castle of Vaena, waiting for tidings of victory. With her were Prince Juan, the three princesses, and Cardinal Mendoza. Suddenly, on the side of the opposite mountain, they saw mounted men were coming from the direction of Moclin. News at last! But as the couriers rode into the town there was a disappointing silence. Then arose from the streets the wailing of women, stricken women who had lost husbands or lovers. The Queen in the tower knew what had happened before the dusty horsemen were brought into her presence. The Count, on his way through the mountains, had been ambushed by El Zagal, and defeated with terrible slaughter.

After the messengers had gone, the Queen sat in a gloomy silence that reminded those about her of her mother, eking out the days of a living death at Arévalo. It was perhaps the only time when her will to victory faltered during the long war. But the great Cardinal of Spain consoled and encouraged her until she shook off the temptation to despair and assembled her inner resources for a new effort.

Presently came letters from the King. Three leagues from Moclin he had heard of the Count's defeat. Question: should he retreat, as caution urged, or advance quickly and stake all on one desperate assault?

Isabel held a council of war. The Cardinal was present, and among others, the Bishop of Jaén, Don Garcia Osorio. During the discussion, the Bishop made a valuable suggestion:

Between Moclin and Jaén, on either side of a deep rock valley, stood twin castles, Cambil and Albahar, connected by a high bridge across the Rio Frio. Even if the King took Moclin, he would have these two giants at his back commanding the Christian country to the north. By taking them first, and they would be easier to storm than Moclin, he could advance more easily the next season to Moclin, and thence to Loja and Granada.

The Queen and the Cardinal thought the plan excellent. A courier carried their decision to the camp, and Fernando adopted it. He sent the Marqués of Cádiz with two thousand cavalry to cut off the two castles from the surrounding country. He himself followed with the rest of the army and the artillery. Queen Isabel and the Cardinal went to Jaén, to be near the scene of operations.

All went well until the King pitched his camps on the heights about Cambil and Albahar. Then he made an alarming discovery. It was impossible to bring his heavy guns through the only narrow rugged path that led over the mountains, along perpendicular crags and precipices.

The new peril called forth the amazing energies of the Queen in a way that reminded her lieutenants of the invincible

Lady Isabel of the Portuguese War. Although she expected a fifth child in three months, she insisted upon riding over the rocky crags near Jaén to inspect the terrain. She looked at the mountain that stood in the way of her new guns. And she decided that the mountain must be removed.

Six thousand sappers and pioneers, "by order and solicitude of the Queen,"[5] started digging and blasting a new road on the mountainside, so high up on the steep slope that "a bird could hold on there with difficulty." They worked day and night, filling up valleys, breaking rocks, cutting down trees, in one place leveling a whole hill. The Bishop of Jaén, superintended the work, for he knew the country well, and at times wielded a pick and shovel to encourage the men, while the Queen looked on, silent and determined. When funds gave out, the Cardinal paid the workmen. In just twelve days they made nine miles of traversible road, and the Moors, who had been laughing at the chagrin of the Christians, looked out one morning to see the black noses of heavy lombards, drawn by great oxen, come slowly through a gap in the mountain side.

As soon as the artillery was in position high on the neighboring mountainsides, Ramirez began to batter the towers and walls about the ears of the Moors. It was not long before they submitted, and were allowed to depart for Granada.

This was in September. The Court returned to Córdoba, planning to spend the winter there. The Queen's confinement was expected in December.

From November 11 until Christmas day it rained almost continuously. The Guadalquivir flooded the arsenals of Seville, covered a great part of Triana and swept over the monastery of las Cuevas, so that the monks had to escape in boats. All Seville was surrounded, and could get no food for three days. As Córdoba was in similar danger, the tired and heavy Queen, at the urging of the King and her physician, prepared to travel north.

At this moment, hastily going over her voluminous daily correspondence, she opened a letter from Rota that bore the crest of Don Luis de la Cerda, Duke of Medina Celi. He was the son of that lisping Don Gaston de la Cerda who had died at forty, *vencido del amore de las mugeres,* "vanquished by the love of women,"[6] and next perhaps to the Duke of

Medina Sidonia, and the Marqués of Cádiz, he was the richest man in Andalusia, with an income greater than the Crown's.

The Duke wrote—we have not his letter, but we have his summary of it in a later epistle—that for the past two years he had had living in his palace at San Lucar, on the southern coast, one Cristóbal Colomo, "who came here from Portugal and wished to go to the King of France, to undertake to find the Indies under that king's protection and by his aid. I myself offered to send him from El Puerto with three or four caravels, for he didn't ask for any more."[7] But on seeing that the enterprise was one which fell within the jurisdiction of the Queen, Don Luis felt that he ought to write her for instructions. The design of Cristóbal Colomo to reach certain eastern islands by sailing west seemed to him very reasonable; and in case the man succeeded, he would like the credit to go to her rather than to the King of France.

Isabel, related by blood as she was to the royal house of Portugal, whose enterprise had already broken the silence and dissipated the horrors of the western ocean, might have been keenly interested but for the Moorish war, then in a critical phase. Even under the circumstances she could have allowed the Duke to send Colomo with a few well-equipped galleys or caravels, and he could well afford the expense. But she had not spent years of effort in reducing the arrogance of the great nobles only to give them royal privileges and additional wealth at this late day.[8] The royal edicts forbidding Spanish subjects to sail on voyages of discovery without royal permission gave her control of the situation. She could investigate the claims of Colomo, and if they seemed feasible, find a way to use him later. She wrote Don Luis a reply substantially as follows:

"Send Cristóbal Colomo to Córdoba and we shall hear what he has to say when we return."

The Cardinal invited the royal family to spend the winter at his palace at Alcalá de Henares. They went there from Córdoba; and there in Carrillo's former residence, on the fifteenth of December, the Queen brought into the world her fifth and last child. It was a girl named Catalina, destined to be known in history as Catherine of Aragon, first wife of Henry the Eighth.

XXI

AN ITALIAN SAILOR WITH AN IDEA AP-
PEARS AT COURT——FERNANDO SHOWS
HIMSELF A GREAT LEADER OF MEN——
SOME VICTORIES OVER THE MOORS

A MAN in his late thirties, with prematurely gray hair that added a touch of nobility to a solemn and rather morose countenance, rode on a mule through the western gate of Córdoba on a warmish day in January, 1486. The sun was bright after the long rains, the air perfumed with the scents of new flowers. The white-washed houses and gilded turrets sparkled like a city of alabaster and gold. The narrow zigzagging streets——let us imagine the scene ——were full of people——silver-smiths and leather-workers with Moorish faces, silk-weavers, farmers from the country driving mules and ox-carts, a *torrero* with a red sash, a lady on a little mouse-colored mule, a Franciscan in a brown cowl, a squad of men-at-arms in leathern jerkins, with arquebuses over their shoulders; a knight on a black horse with gleaming cuirass and helmet, and a scarlet cloak woven with gold threads over his shoulder; a beggar, a thief, a white-clad Dominican on a mule followed by two servants of the Inquisition, armed to the teeth; a Jew with a long beard. But the man with grayish hair rode on without looking to the right or the left until, in the next street, he came to the great Cathedral with nineteen doors of polished brass. Hardly glancing at it, he turned the head of his mule to the left and continued a little way until he came to the Alcázar. There he dismounted, tied his mule to a post, and walking into the palace with the same abrupt directness, asked for their Majesties, the King and Queen of Castile.

The attendants, suspiciously eying the somewhat frayed cloak of the stranger, and listening disdainfully to the bad Spanish that he spoke rapidly in a loud nervous voice, were on the point of ejecting him when he presented a letter addressed to their Serene Highnesses by the Duke of Medina Celi. That put a different face on the matter. He was led into the presence of Don Alonso de Quintanilla, the Royal Treasurer. To that nobleman he explained that he had a plan to communicate to their Majesties, which would be greatly to their advantage, and that of all Christendom, and that he would discuss it with no one else.

In that case, said Don Alonso, faintly amused, the visitor must wait until their Highnesses returned to Córdoba for the spring campaign. Meanwhile, knowing from their letter to the Duke of Medina Celi that they desired to speak with him, the Treasurer would gladly provide lodgings for him as a guest.

Cristoforo Colombo, or as he generally called himself in Spain, Cristóbal Colón—though he was also known as Colom and Colomo—had three months to wait about the court, supported at public expense, but growing more impatient each day under his gloomy self-restraint.

It was late that spring when the Court returned, for their Majesties were delayed in the north by much business. After the Queen's churching, they had gone to Madrid, to thank the chapter there for money contributed to the war fund, and to beg the Dean and the chapter to preach the Crusade with all fervor. Returning to Alcalá de Henares, they had then ridden to Segovia and Medina del Campo, swinging around in a hundred-mile semicircle to Béjar to console the Duke of Alba, who had been widowed. Thence they had gone through Guadalupe to Córdoba, arriving April 28th.[1]

Meanwhile Christopher Columbus, to give him his English name, had been having a liaison with a girl named Beatriz Enríquez de Arana, the daughter of poor parents, and making some powerful friends. A man with the presence of a Roman senator, with courtly manners picked up from noble patrons, and with the adaptability of a good actor, he seems to have taken by storm most of the principal advisers of Isabel and Fernando. Alonso de Quintanilla introduced him to Cardinal Mendoza, to Prince Juan's tutor, the Dominican Fray Diego de Deza, who later became Archbishop of Seville and, although of Jewish ancestry, second Inquisitor General of Spain; to Fray Hernando de Talavera, Prior of Prado; to the Aragonese *Converso*, Juan Cabrero, *camarero* of the King; to

Queen Isabel's girlhood friend Beatriz de Bobadilla and her husband; to Doña Juana de la Torre, nurse of Prince Juan, and other notables. Every one of these exalted persons received Columbus with kindness, agreed with him that his plans were reasonable, and promised to help him gain the royal consent necessary to start on his voyage of discovery. Others who encouraged him from the beginning were Gabriel Sanchez, Royal Treasurer for Aragon, Gaspar Gricio, the Castilian Secretary, the King's Aragonese secretary Juan de Coloma, and somewhat later, the rich bank-lawyer, Luis de Santángel, in whose house, only the year before, the conspirators had planned the assassination of Pedro Arbués. Santángel was now the King's *escribano de racion*, clerk of supplies, a man more powerful for the time being, than even the Inquisition; for while his relatives and friends were being burned in Aragon, he remained in the royal service—protected by Fernando, it would seem, from the zeal of Torquemada's officials.[2] He was a statesman and financier of ability; besides, the King had probably borrowed money from him. On the whole, Columbus was helped from the beginning by the leading men in Spain.

Who was Columbus and what did he want? His own accounts of himself at various times are conflicting, and do not wholly explain the mysteries of his origin and early life. He was a Ligurian, born in one of the little villages outside Genoa—the latest to claim the honor is Cogoleto, a small fishing town—probably about the year of Queen Isabel's birth, 1451;[3] the son of a wool-comber, Domenico Colombo, and his wife Susanna Fontanarosa. Christopher seems to have been a weaver at Savona, his father's birthplace, until late in 1472.[4] That year he made a voyage to Chios, and in 1476 he sailed in a merchantman from Genoa to England; but, his ship having been attacked at Saint Vincent and disabled, he took refuge at Lisbon. There he married Felipa Moniz Perestrello, and there, in 1480, his son Diego was born. After a voyage to Guinea, he received from his mother-in-law the papers of her husband, Perestrello, was moved thereby to become a maritime discoverer, and asked the aid of Dom João, King of Portugal. A committee of two bishops and two doctors—one "that Jew Joseph" whom Columbus bitterly blamed afterwards for the unfavorable report—advised against the project, and described Colombo as a visionary. Dom João, however,

retained an interest in him as late as 1488, when he invited him
to return to Portugal, in a letter which has only increased the
mystery of Columbus's early life by its hint of his having run
afoul of the law, either for debt or for some crime or mis-
demeanor. "And as you may have some fear of our justice,
because of certain things that render you obligor," wrote the
King, "by these presents we guarantee that neither upon your
arrival, nor during your sojourn, nor at the time of your departure, shall you be arrested, held, accused, cited or prosecuted
for any cause, be it civil or criminal of any nature whatsoever." This throws but little light on why Columbus left
Portugal, taking his little son Diego. The commonly accepted
belief that his wife was then dead seems to be contradicted by
what he wrote years later: "When I came from such a great
distance to serve these Princes, I abandoned a wife and children, whom, for this cause, I never saw again."[5]

Whatever his reasons for leaving his family, he sailed for
Spain; or he may have taken a ship for Huelva, where his
brother-in-law lived, intending to go from there to France. A
storm drove the caravel ashore at Palos. The Ligurian and his
son asked for food and shelter at the Franciscan monastery of
La Rabida. Fray Antonio Marchena, a monk skilled in astronomy and cosmography, heard him explain his project,
and immediately kindled with enthusiasm. So did Fray Juan
Perez, prior of the monastery, who had at one time been
Queen Isabel's confessor. The friars persuaded Columbus not
to go to France, but to give Spain the opportunity to reap the
glory of his discoveries. They suggested his appealing to the
Duke of Medina Sidonia or the Duke of Medina Celi, either
one of whom could equip three vessels and never miss the
money. The former rejected him; the latter sent him to the
Court.

When the King and Queen returned to Córdoba, April 28,
they heard nothing but favorable reports of the stranger who
wanted to sail west to arrive at the east. It was probably early
in May when they received him in the great hall of the
Alcázar. They bade him explain his project, and while he was
speaking in his rich strong voice, whose cadences became almost metrical as he warmed to his subject, they studied him.
He was fairly tall and robust, with sandy hair turning gray,
and a long freckled face that flushed as he spoke. His light

gray eyes shone like those of a man with a vision. His nose, hooked like the beak of an eagle, suggested an acquisitive and domineering nature. Father Bernaldez, whose guest he was a few years later, called him "a man of very high talent, but without much learning,[6] very skilled in the art of cosmography and of the proportioning of the world, who thought, from what he had read in Ptolemy, and from other books, and from his own ingenuity, that the world in which we are born and move about is fixed in the sphere of the skies, but doesn't touch any part of the skies, nor does it join anything else of solidity, save land and water, embraced in sphericity within the dizzy vacuity of the heavens. And he thought that by going he would find much gold. And he thought that this world and firmament of earth and water was all traversable round about by earth and water, according to the reckoning of Sir John Mandeville; and whoever wished, if he had ships, could sail west, from the right of San Vicente, and return by Jerusalem and Rome and Seville."[7] It was gold that Columbus emphasized for the benefit of the King, who was always in need, but he probably looked at the Queen when he mentioned the uses that might be made of the gold—the crusade against the Moors, and perhaps even a crusade for the recovery of the Holy Sepulchre; and then, there were the souls of the heathen of the Indies, who might be converted to Christianity.

The Queen liked Columbus from the start. There was enough poetry in her to perceive what could not have escaped Cardinal Mendoza: that the Italian was essentially a poet, a man of stupendous imagination; perhaps even a bit of a liar. His Eminence, who in his youth had translated the Odyssey and the Æneid into Spanish, because his poet-father regretted being unable to read them, knew as well as anybody that there is more truth in the fancies of poets than in the catchpenny wisdom of the world. And of all persons the Queen was hardly the one to think little of any man for attempting the impossible.

Could Columbus, by any chance, be of Jewish ancestry? He was sometimes called Colom; and in an *auto de fe* at Tarragona some people named Colom were made to wear *sanbenitos* on confessing that they secretly practised Jewish rites. If he were, he would say nothing about it, naturally. What difference did it make whether he was or not? The Queen constantly had

about her trusted Jews whose conversion to Christianity she
felt to be sincere—in fact, she often found them the best
Christians. Time would show whether this man's frequent
expressions of faith in Christ were from the heart, or the lip
service of a clever actor. Isabel was no fool, as those who
tried to pass off counterfeit piety on her sometimes discovered.
It might be significant that among those who recommended
Columbus were several of the great *Conversos*—Santángel,
Sanchez, Cabrero, de Deza. On the other hand, he had even
more champions among the Old Christians of the Court. In
fact, no one has ever unearthed any evidence that Columbus
had Jewish blood. The theory has been deduced from characteristics supposed to be exclusively Jewish—as though they
were not to be found in every race. Lacking proof, posterity
must accept the man's own word—confirmed by evidence—
that he was an Italian with Christian ancestors.[8]

As for his project, Isabel did not need to be convinced that
the world was round, any more than Father Juan Perez did,
or Luis de Santángel, or Cardinal Mendoza. It was a fact
accepted by most persons of any education at all. Aristotle
had argued from the shadow cast by the earth in lunar eclipses
that it must be a sphere, and Aristotle had long since entered
the Spanish universities by way of Islam. Columbus had read
Aristotle's opinion in the *Imago Mundi* of Cardinal Pierre
d'Ailly. Heraclitus, a pupil of Plato, discovered the rotation of
the earth on its axis. Aristarchus, two and a half centuries before Christ, propounded the heliocentric theory, and was called
a blasphemer for his pains by the Stoic Cleanthes, who wrote
a tract demanding that he be silenced. Eratosthenes measured
the angle of obliquity of the ecliptic within half a minute of
one degree, and made a fairly correct estimate of the earth's
circumference. Within Isabel's lifetime the learned Aeneas
Sylvius Piccolomini, who became Pope Pius II, had written
"Almost all agree that the shape of the earth is round."[9]

It was generally believed, however, that the earth was larger
than it is. How wide the ocean was between Spain and the
Cipango and Cathay described by Messer Marco Polo, whether
that ocean could be safely crossed in a reasonable time, what
storms, winds, whirlpools or other dangers there might be—
those were the moot questions. But there were even more practical considerations. When ships were needed to blockade the

Moors on the Mediterranean, and money was desperately required to pay troops and buy guns and munitions, it seemed unwise to spend perhaps 2,000,000 maravedis—$30,000 to $40,000—on a project that was, after all, hypothetical. At any other time, Queen Isabel, following the sure intuition that had discerned the worth of the Marqués of Cádiz and Gonsalvo de Córdoba, would have risked that much on Columbus. But she was a woman of single purpose.

The more calculating King could not have failed to see also the wisdom of deferring action until Columbus was well separated from his patron the Duke. Besides, he admitted frankly that he knew nothing of cosmography, and would like to hear the opinions of some experts. Columbus said the earth was only one-seventh water; how could he prove that? Fernando suggested referring the proposal to a learned commission. With the Queen's consent, he appointed her confessor, Fray Hernando de Talavera, President of the Junta; and Columbus was turned over to the good graces of that gentle theologian.

The memory of the Ligurian's words was muffled in the royal minds almost at once by the blare of trumpets and the neighing of steeds. It was in that year that the Christian kingdoms put forth their greatest effort to bring the war to an end. An army of 52,000, well armed and equipped, assembled in the valley of the Guadalquivir; and the camp was a city of silken pavilions under pennants and heraldic devices from all parts of Christendom. Soldiers from every nation in the West had come to serve under the silver standard of the Holy Cross, presented to the King and Queen by Pope Sixtus IV. Gaston du Leon and other chevaliers had arrived from France. Lord Scales (Earl Rivers), whose battle-axe at Bosworth Field the year before had helped to place his brother-in-law, Henry VII, on the throne of England, brought with him a hundred English archers, with long bows and cloth-yard arrows, and two hundred yeomen, armed cap-a-pie, with pikes and battle-axes. There were Irishmen, too, in this campaign. In March of the following year King Fernando gave a "passport and recommendation"—the document is in the archives of Simancas—to "Ubertus Stantum (Staunton), an Irishman, who had distinguished himself by his valor against the Moors in the town of Loja, and on a former occasion in Tangiers."[10]

King Fernando was extremely tenacious when his pride

was touched. Just as he had gone back to Toro to wipe out the stigma of his first defeat, so he now returned to the scene of his humiliation at Loja, "the right eye of Granada." He found the Moors of all factions uniting against him. Muley had died, and his corpse had been taken to Granada, slung over a mule, like a laborer's. His brother El Zagal and his son Boabdil, alarmed by the preparations at Córdoba, made peace and divided the kingdom between them. Boabdil led an army to take charge of Loja, evidently in the hope of averting the threatened siege, for he sent Fernando word that he held the city as the loyal vassal of the Kings of Castile. Fernando replied that Boabdil had forfeited that privilege by making an alliance with El Zagal.

The Christian host marched on Loja. The Marqués of Cádiz led the vanguard of 17,000 men to storm the heights of Albohacen. A long and bloody battle ensued. As the Christians planted their flags on the height, Boabdil sallied forth with Ez Zegri and the best cavalry of Granada, to attack them on three sides. The Marqués was in grave danger when King Fernando arrived with the main body, while Lord Scales gave the Spanish an exhibition of northern tactics. Dismounting from his horse, says Bernaldez, "with a battle-axe in his hand, and with a band of his men in a wedge behind him, all armed like him with axes, he rushed forward among the Moors, with stout and valiant heart giving blows right and left, killing and knocking them flat, and neither courage nor might failed them; and when the Castilian mountaineers who came with the Duke of Infantado saw this, they followed the English without waiting a moment, and did such execution among the Moors that they turned their backs in flight." Scales fought his way into one of the suburbs of Loja, but as he climbed a scaling ladder, a Moor on the wall above hurled a great stone that smashed the Englishman's front teeth and killed three of his men. He was stunned, but on coming to, refused to leave the field.

From the heights of Albohacen the King's artillery filled the town with fire and destruction to such good effect that the Moors surrendered at the end of a week. Fernando entered Loja May 28. When the silver cross appeared on the highest turret, with the banner of Santiago and the flags of Fernando and Isabel, the whole army cried "Castile! Castile!" and knelt, singing the *Te Deum.* The bishops then consecrated the mosques as Christian churches. Gonsalvo was left in command of the garrison; the host marched on.

On hearing the good news, Queen Isabel at Córdoba walked barefoot to the Cathedral to hear Mass and offer thanks to Almighty God. And when another letter came from the King, begging her to visit the camp, for he wished to consult her and her presence would be good for the morale of the army, she hastened to comply. By that time the King had moved to Llora. He smashed its heavy walls with his great lombards in four days, and occupied it on Thursday, June 8. On Friday the host moved on to Moclin, and it was there that the Queen overtook them.

The Marqués of Cádiz, the Duke of Infantado and many other glittering cavaliers met her and the Princess Isabel at the Rock of the Lovers, to escort them to the camp. As they approached, they saw the whole army drawn up in battle array in the wide plain at the left of the road, four miles from the camp. Fifty thousand Christian warriors passed in review before the great Queen, each battalion lowering its colors before her in salute. The flags of a hundred cities, commencing with Seville, flashed before her in the sun, and the rhythmical undulations of sparkling helmets and gray armor and silk and gold made a sea of glory, passing like an endless pageantry in a dream.

At last came the King and the great lords of Castile. Queen Isabel, riding a chestnut mule, on a magnificent silver saddle-chair, made three reverences to His Majesty, and the King made three reverences to her. She took off her hat, leaving on her auburn hair a silk net or cowl which showed her cheeks uncovered. The King embraced her and kissed her on the cheek. Then he rode to the Infanta Isabel, embraced her, kissed her on the mouth, and gave her his blessing.[11] Last of all the nobles who came to pay their respects was Lord Scales. His magnificence smote all hearts with wonder. He made a low obeisance to the Queen, and then one to the King, while his great horse curveted and pranced.

Afterward the Queen, who had heard of the Englishman's valor at Loja, thanked him with the smile that made men glad to die for her, and expressed sorrow for the loss of his front teeth.

"It is a small thing," said Scales, "to lose a few teeth in the service of Him who gave them all to me. Our Blessed Lord, who built all this house, has merely opened a window in it, that he may more easily see what passeth within."[12]

The Queen was delighted with him. Next day she sent him twelve magnificent Andalusian steeds, two beds with coverings of gold brocade, and some fine linen and stately tents for his men. This was the last appearance of Lord Scales in the chronicles of the Moorish War. A year later he was killed in France.

The ceremonies concluded, the crusaders began the siege of Moclin. They had 2,000 cannon of various sizes, and plenty of munitions, besides the reserves stored in great depots at Medina del Campo, Madrid and Fuenterrabía, and in arsenals along the frontier. All day they poured a fire of red hot stone and iron balls into the city. The Moors were terrified; and when one of their towers, used as a powder magazine, blew up and scattered the mangled bodies of its defenders through the town, they surrendered.

The Queen's presence lent a new solemnity to the entrance of the Christians to Moclin. A great procession was formed: first, the standard of the Cross, then the multicolored banners of the army, then the King and Queen, with the choir of the royal chapel chanting the *Te Deum laudamus*, followed by a long train of cavaliers. As the choir paused in their chant, the King and Queen heard faintly, as if from underground, a chorus of voices singing ecstatically, *"Benedictus qui venit in nomine domini."* All stopped and listened, marveling. The explanation suddenly dawned upon them. Under the street were the dungeons where the Christian captives were kept.

The wretched prisoners were led forth, blinking in the unaccustomed light, but still singing hysterically and weeping. The Queen was much moved by the sight of their emaciated, half-naked bodies and matted hair and beards. As they knelt at her feet she spoke words of consolation, and commanded that food and clothing, and money be given them.

Caring for the captives and the wounded, and directing the enormous line of communications, the Queen followed her victorious army through the *vega* to a point six miles from the walls of Granada. They took the bridge of Pinos after sharp fighting, and returned to Córdoba. Nothing was needed to complete a triumphant year but the news of a new civil war in Granada between Boabdil and his uncle, El Zagal, whom he publicly accused of having poisoned Muley Abou'l Hassan.

But unfortunately Granada was only a small segment of the long battlefield of an Islam whose unbroken empire extended from Gibraltar eastward to Cathay; and out of the east, in retaliation for the success of Fernando and Isabel, was arising a new menace to all Christendom. The armies of Bajazet II had already overrun Moldavia in 1484 and conquered the important strongholds of Kilia and Akjerman, while a Turkish navy, greatly magnified, crossed the Mediterranean. And in 1486 all the Mussulman powers, alarmed by the progress of the Christians in Spain, hastily patched up their quarrels and planned a new offensive on all sectors. Even the Sultan of Egypt laid aside his feud with Bajazet to make a league against the new Spanish nation. They agreed that while Bajazet launched a great fleet against Fernando's kingdom of Sicily, the Sultan would send a huge army from Africa to Spain to reinforce the Moors of Granada. It was the gravest crisis since Otranto fell in 1480.

Pope Innocent VIII, a kind, charitable man of fifty-four, with weak eyes and feeble health, who was completely dominated by the strong-minded Giuliano della Rovere,[13] nephew of Sixtus IV, had no money in his treasury. He had become involved in the Barons' War against Ferrante of Naples and Lorenzo de Medici; and Ferrante's son, Alfonso of Calabria, had invaded the Papal territory to the gates of Rome. Innocent appealed to the Emperor, but it was Fernando and Isabel who saved him by negotiating for peace with their cousin Ferrante, for which the Pope thanked them, February 10, 1486.

Freed from this embarrassment, Innocent turned his attention to the Turkish War, notified Fernando of the project against Sicily, and exhorted him to protect his possessions. In May, 1486, the Pope issued a bull calling upon all Christendom to join the Crusade against Islam. But in general, the appeal fell on ears made deaf by selfishness.

XXII

WHEN Queen Isabel learned of the New Mohammedan offensive, the King was planning to open the campaign of 1487 by storming Baza, but the news from Africa made a change of plan necessary. She suggested that Fernando cut off Granada from Africa by descending to the Mediterranean seaboard and attacking the three fortified ports, Vélez Malaga, Malaga and Almería, that were the southern outposts of the Moorish kingdom. The greatest was Malaga, called "the hand and mouth of Granada," because supplies of men, troops and ammunition from Africa constantly passed though its harbor, in spite of the Christian blockade. But as it would be costly to take and hold Malaga while Vélez Malaga remained in Moorish hands, the King decided to attack the latter place first.

A crusading army of 70,000—20,000 cavaliers and 50,-000 infantry, left Córdoba on the eve of Palm Sunday, 1487. An earthquake had shaken the city the night before, but as it chiefly damaged the old Moorish Alcázar, it was considered a good omen. Isabel remained at Córdoba, waiting for news. Letters, blunt and affectionate, came daily from the King.

The army crossed the plain like a great glittering snake, and disappeared in the southern hills. The Queen had sent ahead 4,000 pioneers to smooth out the roads, which in many places were little more than mule-paths, rising from yawning chasms and ravines to the tops of dizzy precipices. They passed slowly, paying for every mile with blood as well as toil, for the Moorish mountaineers harried them continually. But at last they filed down from the snows into the warm valley of

Vélez, and shouted with joy to see the blue mirror of the Mediterranean.

The King established his camp on a mountain slope above the town, near the powerful fort of Bentomiz. It was a dangerous position, and the artillery was miles away in the mountain passes, but the King was confident that the town could not get help from Almería or Granada before he blew down its walls with his new guns.

Suddenly, while he was dining, he heard shouts on the hillside and looked out to behold his troops flying before a large force of Moors. Disarmed except for a cuirass, Fernando seized a lance, rushed from the tent crying, "Here I am, Fernando! Turn, Castilians, and stand with me!" and hurled himself into the swarm of Saracens. A groom who followed him was struck down. The King impaled the Moor who had struck the blow. But the enemy surrounded him, yelling, and undoubtedly would have despatched him, if the Marqués of Cádiz had not arrived with Garcilaso de la Vega and dragged him to safety.

Several days passed before Isabel learned of her husband's narrow escape. She trembled as she read the letters from the camp, and went to the Cathedral to offer thanks. Later she gave Vélez Malaga a coat of arms showing the King striking with his lance, the groom dead beside him, and the Moors flying.

Meanwhile a still graver peril hung over Fernando and his whole army. For El Zagal, on the approach of the Crusaders, had collected reinforcements from Baza, Guadix and Almería, and leaving a sufficient garrison at Granada, led to the relief of Vélez a well-disciplined army of 30,000 lightly armed, swift warriors. He made his way by night, like a silent wolf, along the mountain range from Granada to Bentomiz. Before dawn the Crusaders saw his signal fires on the mountain top behind and above them, and the answering flames on the towers of Vélez. They were in a precarious situation.

The King commanded a strict watch to be kept day and night. He never undressed, he slept little, he was everywhere in the camp, tireless and observant of the minutest details. Meanwhile he sent a fast courier to the Queen, begging her to send whatever reinforcements she could.

He had more need of help than he knew, for El Zagal was

formulating a bold plan to exterminate the Christian army in the middle of a certain night. He wrote a note to the Alcaide of Vélez, ordering him to light an answering fire when he saw one on Bentomiz, and then to lead forth his men and fall upon the enemy, while the Moors from Granada attacked from above. This note the Arab King gave to a fleet runner, to carry through the Christian camp that night.

Isabel had no troops to send her husband. She was now thirty-six, and was beginning to show the effects of overwork and privation. But as in the days after the disaster at Toro, twenty years before, when she whetted the wrath of the Castilians against the Portuguese, the challenge of the impossible drew forth her astonishing reserves of energy and resourcefulness. She was in the saddle day and night, making a swift round of cities and castles, ordering supplies, thinking even of medicines and nurses, and as a last resort calling to arms all men in Andalusia under seventy years of age. Old veterans of the border warfare forgot their rheumatism under the fascination of the Queen's voice and face, took their swords and lances from the walls, and reported at the camp at Córdoba, where she marshalled them. Her faithful Cardinal Mendoza, too, came at her call. He was growing old and infirm, so that he was no longer able to keep pace with her. Yet he offered high pay to all who would take arms and follow him, and he once more buckled on his armor and mounted a horse, to take command of the Queen's army of rescue.

They were too late. Before they could reach the scene, the attack was launched from the heights of Bentomiz. Fortunately, however, the messenger of El Zagal had been captured going through the Christian camp, and Fernando had his army silently drawn up at night, waiting. When the fire shot up on the tip of Bentomiz, there was no answer from Vélez. Yet El Zagal was so confident of success that he attacked at the appointed time. He was repulsed with great slaughter, and the Moors, seized with panic, broke and fled through the darkness.

Next day Isabel's artillery arrived through a pass in the mountains. Little else was needed to complete the discouragement of the people of Vélez except the news that Granada had refused to re-admit the defeated El Zagal, thus ending the hope of another relief expedition. When Fernando offered them easy terms, for he was eager to press on to Malaga, they accepted. They were allowed to depart with all their effects save arms, and to live anywhere in Spain except near the sea. One hundred twenty Christian captives were liberated and sent to the Queen at Córdoba.

The surrender of Vélez was followed promptly by that of Bentomiz, Comares and the strong forts of the Axarquia. The crusaders marched over the mountains, high above the Mediterranean, to the west, until one morning, May 7, they saw the rich and beautiful city of Malaga far below them, between two powerful forts, by the curve of the tranquil sea. The vast walls rose out of the water into great castles and mighty towers, among which were hanging gardens like those of Babylon, stately cedars and palms shading fountains and patios, groves of oranges and pomegranates, and outside the walls to the lee, many vineyards and variegated farmlands.

The garrison was composed chiefly of *Gomeres*, fierce and expert warriors from Barbary, commanded by that Hamet Ez Zegri who had been Alcaide of Ronda, a daring and resourceful leader. "The heart of Ez Zegri was hardened like that of Pharaoh," wrote Bernaldez, "and he made the hearts of his people hard with vain hopes."

The Marqués of Cádiz asked for the post of danger, as usual, and pitched his camp on a hillside opposite the castle of Gibralfaro, where the battlements of the town were most accessible.

For several days the siege continued without success. The walls of Malaga were old but powerful, and the Moors, grown accustomed to the heavy lombards, were learning how to repair breaches. One day the Marqués attempted to storm the walls near Gibralfaro. Another day the Moors sallied out and attacked his camp, to be repulsed only after a most desperate hand to hand struggle.

A pestilence that had been raging in the neighboring villages spread to the Christian camp, slaying more soldiers than the Moors did. Added to this, supplies were running low, and there was danger of famine. A great Castilian fleet of caravels and galleys appeared off the coast, however, with food, munitions, and seven enormous lombards, which were set up in the camp of the Marqués, and christened by the gunners "the Seven Sisters of Ximenes." Still the Christian morale re-

mained at low ebb, while the defenders took hope from tales
brought them by renegades and camp-followers. It was said
that the besiegers were running short of powder and that
Queen Isabel had written the King, advising him to give up
the siege.

As soon as Fernando got wind of these rumors, he wrote
the Queen, begging her to visit the camp. She set out at once
with the Infanta Isabel, the Cardinal, and Fray Hernando de
Talavera. At her request, the batteries were silenced on the
day she arrived, and a new demand for surrender was made.

The Moors took the cessation of firing as a confirmation of
what they had heard of the shortage of powder in the Christian camp. They were jubilant, and they found further encouragement in the predictions of two dervishes. One of these,
a hermit from Tunis call Ibrahim Algerbi, who had long
brooded on the wrongs of Granada, announced that Allah had
sent an angel to reveal to him how to save Malaga from the
Christian dogs. He asked for volunteers; and four hundred
warriors, fired by his eloquence, agreed to follow him wherever
he might go. Marching at night by a roundabout way to a
height above the Christian camp on the further side, they
rushed suddenly into the invading army, at his instructions,
and attempted to fight their way through to the city. While
the Castilians sprang to arms and cut them to pieces, the
santon, Ibrahim, knelt among the rocks and prayed, and thus
the Christians found him at dawn. Taken before the Marqués
of Cádiz as a prisoner, he said that he was a prophet to whom
Allah had revealed how and when Malaga should be taken;
but he would reveal the secret to no one but the King and
Queen. The Marqués, with a shrug, commanded the man to
be taken to their Majesties. He might or might not have
information of importance; there could be no harm in questioning him.

The King was taking his siesta, and the Queen desired to
wait and interview the prisoner with him; hence Ibrahim was
led to a nearby tent, where Doña Beatriz de Bobadilla, Marquesa of Moya, was playing chess with Don Álvaro of Portugal. The dervish supposed them to be the King and Queen.
He asked for a drink of water. While the guards were fetch-
ing it, he drew a scimitar from under his burnoose and threw
himself upon them. Don Álvaro fell senseless, with a deep

gash in his head, the Marquesa was saved by the guards, and the dervish was cut to pieces. His hacked remains were thrown by a catapult over the walls of Malaga. The defenders retaliated by butchering a noble Christian prisoner and sending his body to the Castilian camp, lashed to the back of a mule.

The Queen's presence, however, did change the whole aspect of the siege. It was almost an article of faith in the Spanish camp that wherever she went, victory was sure to follow. There was something about her trim armored figure on a war-horse and the confident tilt of her chin that inspired courage and hope. When the troops passed in review before her, they uttered a thunderous shout of welcome, audible on the city walls. The Queen visited the camp of the Marqués, heard the roar of the Seven Sisters of Ximenes which were fired at the walls in her honor, and saw great chunks of stone topple from the towers and mosques of Malaga. She inspected the enormous hospital of several tents, she visited the sick and bound up wounds with her own hands. Her influence radiated through the whole army. There was no cursing or brawling while she was there. Many friars and priests said Mass every morning as in a great city, and preached throughout the camp, says Bernaldez, "to those who were healthy as well as to the sick." The singers of the chapels of the King and Queen sang daily for Mass and Vespers, and marched, chanting, in solemn processions. Over the wide city of silk and linen shone the silver cross given by Pope Sixtus, and in the sight of it the priests gave the crusader's absolution to all who might die in the holy struggle for the Faith. It was like a great mushroom city. There were even bells to chime the hours of the watches—forty great silver ones with musical tones of varying pitch, that rang joyously day and night. The continual sound of the bells—forbidden by the Koran—and the sight of the cross, adds Bernaldez, "gave very bad solace to the Moors." They said mockingly, "What, you have no cows, and yet you bring cowbells?"[1]

In a very few days the Queen transformed the camp; and fortune, as usual, followed in her train. A great fleet arrived with additional supplies. From over the mountains came the Duke of Medina Sidonia with a large reinforcing army, raised at his own expense, to swell the numbers of the Christians to well over 80,000. "The people were growing somewhat weary of the assessments of taxes to cover the great costs of the siege," said Bernaldez; but once more the clergy and the churches of the land saved the day with subsidies, and the Duke of Medina contributed 20,000 gold doblas.

Fernando was determined now more than ever to batter his way into the city. But since the Queen begged him to avoid all unnecessary bloodshed, he ordered firing to cease, and promised the inhabitants their lives, liberty and property if they surrendered, but stern vengeance if they compelled him to use force. Hamet Ez Zegri, confiding in the promises of an astrologer who had a miraculous white banner under which he said Allah had promised to give victory to the Saracens, contemptuously refused.

The Seven Sisters of Ximenes thundered away again, while Ramirez mined one of the towers of Malaga and blew it up with gunpowder. The frightened inhabitants, reduced to eating dogs and cats after their last horses were consumed, pleaded with Ez Zegri to make peace, but he retired with his *Gomeres* to the fortress of Gibralfaro, swearing that he would die fighting. On the advice of his astrologer, he sallied out under the white banner against the camps of the orders of Santiago and Alcántara. His Moors fought with fanatical abandon. Not until their prophet fell and his banner disappeared in the dust did they fly for the city, to be cursed by the relatives of their slain comrades.

Ali Dordux, a rich merchant of Malaga, now asked for terms. The King would not receive the messengers, for he was still angry over the rejection of his terms. "Let them go to the devil," said he, and ordered all his heaviest guns to fire a broadside against the walls.[2]

Nothing could be more humble than the next letter from the starving people. It began:

"Almighty God be praised: May God exalt our lords the monarchs, the King and the Queen, greater than all the kings and all the princes!

"Felicitating you on the grandeur of your state, and kissing the ground under your feet, your servants and slaves the people of Malaga, great and little . . . recognize well their error, and place themselves in your hands."

Fernando replied that if they had surrendered at first, he would have granted easy terms; but since they had put him to such expense of treasure and blood, they must submit to his mercy. He would make no promises.

Malaga surrendered rather than starve, and Fernando and Isabel entered the city as conquerors August 18, after a siege of three months and eleven days. Six hundred Christian captives, released from the dungeons, prostrated themselves before their deliverers, and, "as many as saw them gave thanks to God, and wept with them for joy." They "came forth so thin and yellow with the great hunger that they all desired to die."[3] Many were of noble Castilian families. Some had been buried in the dungeons for ten, fifteen or twenty years.

Ali Dordux, who negotiated for the city, received a pardon for his family and forty families of his friends; but the rest of Malaga found the King's mercy a bitter draught. The *Gomeres* in the castle were all condemned to slavery, except the chivalrous Ibrahim Zenete who had spared some Christian striplings in the attack on the camp of Santiago, "because he saw no beards." Twelve Christian renegades were executed by a method borrowed from the Moors; they were tied to stakes, and pierced with pointed reeds thrown by horsemen riding past on the gallop, until many wounds brought death. Some Moorish converts to Christianity who had returned to their own faith were burned as relapsed heretics. The Moors who had surrendered, confiding, as they did, in the well-known mercy of Isabel, were disillusioned, for her appeals to the King met with adamant refusals. He had promised to teach these people a lesson, and he would do so. It would help later with Granada.

He acceded to her request only to this extent: Instead of selling all the people into slavery, he agreed to ransom them, each individual at the rate of thirty gold doblas. All their gold, silver and jewels would be accepted immediately as part payment, the rest to be paid within eight months. If the residue remained unpaid in eight months, all should be considered as slaves. The Moors were compelled to accept the terms. Each one was given to a Christian family to feed and maintain as a servant. After the eight months, having been unsuccessful in raising the balance of the ransom money, eleven thousand of them were sold as slaves.

Four hundred and fifty Moorish Jews, the majority of them women, were ransomed by Abraham Senior, a Jewish millionaire, chief rabbi of Castile, who had aided Isabel and Fernando with loans so large that they had felt obliged to farm out to him some of the taxes; and in return he devised an efficient system of taxation that helped to make possible the financing of the long war.

After the end of the campaign, the King and Queen went to Saragossa to attend the meeting of the Aragonese Cortes. The victories of the year had revived warlike enthusiasm throughout Spain; and when they addressed the delegates in the Casa de Deputacion by the banks of the Ebro, the Aragonese appropriated a large sum to continue the war, acclaimed the nine-year-old Prince Juan as their future sovereign, and knelt to take the oath of allegiance to the rather pale boy with beautiful yellow hair who looked out with such grave benignity upon the cheering crowd. He must have reminded Isabel of her brother Alfonso, the boy king of Ávila, who had been lying for twenty years beside their father in the Cartuja de Miraflores.

From Saragossa the Court went to Valencia, where the King made certain reforms in the administration of justice. Thence they went south along the east coast to Murcia; and it was there the army assembled for the campaign of 1488.

It was an unfortunate one, and the fault was partly Fernando's. Taking advantage perhaps, of the Queen's admiration, and her joy over his escape from death, he sent troops that he could ill spare to aid the Duke of Brittany in his rebellion against Anne de Beaujeu, regent for young Charles VIII. A rebellion against the French Crown was too good an opportunity to let slip without an attempt to recover Roussillon and Cerdagne. Queen Isabel consented most reluctantly, and the result justified her misgivings. In the defeat of the French rebels at St. Aubin du Cormier, July 27, 1488, more than 1,000 Spanish soldiers were killed or captured.

Fernando could hardly have chosen a more unfitting time to commit a blunder. For it was in the spring of that year, 1488, that the new Turkish offensive, so long threatened, and so carefully prepared, terrified all Christendom. A Turkish fleet of 55 galleys, all triremes, left the Hellespont May 16, with huge convoys of transports laden with horses, heavy artillery and supplies, and an army of 100,000 men.[4] Their objective was Fernando's kingdom of Sicily. Fernando's spies

in Constantinople informed him the Moslems counted on using
Sicily as a base to bring men, food and munitions from the
Barbary coast, conquer Italy and overrun Europe.[5] But first
they must take the island of Malta, 58 miles from Sicily and
180 miles from Africa. The safety of Europe depended on
the defense of Sicily, and the safety of Sicily depended on the
defense of Malta. Fernando sent 50 caravels to reinforce his
Sicilian fleet and assist Pierre d'Aubusson, the heroic old
Grand Master of the Knights of St. John, who had commanded the defense of Rhodes in 1480. Meanwhile the defenses of Sicily, Malta and Gozo were greatly strengthened;
and Fernando divided the enemy by sending a fleet to sack
the rich cities on the coast of Tripoli. The Turkish attack failed
because Christendom, chiefly through the efforts of Pope Innocent and King Fernando, had been prepared. On the fourteenth
of July, the Pope congratulated Fernando on his victories in
Spain, for which he said the Christian people of the whole
world were indebted to him; and the Holy Father hoped that
he would continue to be vigilant in the defense of Sicily, on
which so much depended.[6]

Fernando's French gamble, however, and the great effort
for the defense of Sicily, crippled his resources in the 1488
campaign against the Moors. He left Murcia June 5, with
only 19,000 men, including 5,000 cavalry. Vera, Vélez el
Rubio and Vélez el Blanco, small places, surrendered without
resistance, and the King marched toward Almería on the sea.
The place resisted valiantly. Fernando, lacking the strength
to storm it, withdrew, and led his host to Baza. But El
Zagal was there, with a large garrison, and the walls were
powerful.

The chastened King, leaving a frontier guard under the
command of Luis Fernandez Puertocarrero, disbanded the rest
of his army, and went to the Cross of Caravaca, in the
hills of Murcia, to do penance for his sins, and to pray for
victory. There he knelt in the dirt before the famous shrine
where so many miracles had been performed, and bowed his
head and beat his breast, like David of old.

El Zagal could see nothing in Fernando's retirement but a
confession that his money and his man-power were exhausted,
and the great Christian effort virtually at an end. He assumed
the offensive all along the frontier. His cavalry pounced on

Christian towns, drove off herds of cattle, led men, women and children into slavery. From Almería, Tavernas and Purchena the Saracens carried fire and sword into Murcia, on the east; and on the west front, many who had submitted to Castile returned to their old allegiance, and began slaying Christians.

As if God and nature had turned against King Fernando and his people, the year ended in floods, storms, and pestilence. Wrecks of ships were scattered along every coast in Spain; roofs were torn off houses by the winds; stone towers were laid prone; the Guadalquivir encircled Seville in an angry embrace and lashed the low buildings with its muddy yellow waters until the inhabitants feared total destruction. In Córdoba that year more people died of the plague than in the lethal year of 1481.[7]

Queen Isabel spent the winter praying and fasting, begging for money, raising troops in remote districts where there had been no intensive recruiting, purchasing food, supplies, and munitions, and discussing with the King the strategy of the next campaign. By spring, they had managed to assemble 13,000 horse and 40,000 infantry. Isabel went to Jaén with the Cardinal and Prince Juan, to be near the scene of action, while Fernando advanced against Baza, the most powerful of the remaining outposts of Granada, and the key of Guadix and Almería. When Baza fell, the way would be clear for the final thrust against the capital.

Baza was tremendously strong, built in the plain, protected in the rear by fortifications rising to the precipice of a mountain, and in front by massive walls and turrets, flanked by fortified suburbs checkered with gardens and orchards. The commander was Cidi Yahye, a skilful strategist. His garrison was swollen by contributions from all the cities of the plain to more than twenty thousand men, each one, he estimated, worth five besiegers. He had food and munitions for a siege of fifteen months. When he saw Fernando establishing his camp in the gardens outside the suburbs, he sent his nimble and lightly armed cavalry forth to attack. The Christians, bewildered in the labyrinth of trees and irrigations, fought at a great disadvantage for twelve hours, with heavy carnage on both sides, until the Moors, contesting every yard of ground, withdrew in the darkness.

After a council of war, the King decided to relinquish his perilous position. It was a difficult operation, but he accomplished it by a stratagem. While the rear of the camp withdrew, the tents in the gardens nearest the walls were left standing, as a camouflage; and when they were lowered after sundown, the main body of Christians was on the march.

The new camp was safer, but it was too far from the city. The King called a second council of war. The Marqués of Cádiz advised giving up the siege and ravaging the countryside until the next year, when Baza, having consumed its supplies, could be taken with small loss of life. Communications were difficult; the army was already on short rations; there was not enough artillery, and the soldiers were suffering from disease, in addition to many wounds from the battle of the gardens.

The King decided to retire, and had his generals announce that he did so to save the men from further suffering. A remarkable demonstration followed. A sound like the soughing of a wind through a field of cornstalks passed over the host. It was a broken cheer, not of joy over the King's decision, but of gratitude for his consideration; and the crusaders cried, "Let us fight here until we take the city!"

Fernando's heart was touched, but as his doubts and scruples remained, he sent a letter to Isabel at Jaén, asking her advice.

The Queen's reply was characteristic. Baza must be taken at any cost. Another retreat would be fatal to the spirit of the people and ultimate success. If the King and the army would continue the siege, she guaranteed on her part, with the help of God, to send them money, food, munitions and men, all that might be needed, until the fall of the city. How Isabel was going to accomplish all this, she had no idea, but she knew it must somehow be done. Money was the first need. She pawned her gold and plate, priceless heirlooms from her ancestors; and she sent all her jewels by speedy messengers to Valencia and Barcelona, where they were pledged to Jewish money lenders—her pearl necklace, her balas rubies, even the jeweled crown of Saint Fernando.

The money thus obtained saved the Crusade. The valley before Baza grew that summer into a great military market, teeming not only with troops but with caravans of merchants, blacksmiths setting up forges, skilled artisans and cunning armorers from Toledo beating out steel, saddlers and harness makers from Córdoba, tent-makers, doctors and nurses receiving the sick and wounded in hospital tents, couriers bringing despatches from all parts of Europe.

Under the Queen's direction, six thousand pioneers broke a new road through a mountain side, to make way for the heaviest new lombards from Venice. Supplies of wheat came from England,[8] for there had been a shortage in Andalusia.[9] A great line of convoys was established over the Sierras. When the rains washed out a path by which mules carried supplies to the camp, the Queen had another broken, parallel, and as soon as the first was repaired, established a one-way traffic, the mules approaching Baza by one route, and leaving it by the other. It was estimated that 14,000 beasts of burden were going back and forth.

Among the strangers who approached Baza on mules that summer were three men in brown Franciscan robes. Two of them came from the East, having journeyed all the way from Jerusalem with a threat for the King and Queen from the Grand Turk Bajazet II.

The third came from the west, alone and mysterious, looking neither to right nor left, lost in his meditations. The Queen, on her way to the camp with her attendants, might have passed him in a great cloud of dust, and he might have looked up with his irritable frown as he drew to one side of the road. And if Isabel had seen him, she might even have noticed that the long sombre face framed in brown sackcloth was the face of the adventurer Cristóbal Colón, the poet with the gray eyes, who had spoken about that business of the islands in the West, and the palaces of Kubla Khan.

XXIII

FERNANDO AND ISABEL WIN THE
MOORISH WAR AND ENTER GRANADA
IN TRIUMPH

THE pawning of Isabel's jewels was the turning point
in the Crusade, and the fall of Baza marked the beginning of its third and last phase. The first had been
the old feudal war of excursions and alarms. The second had
been the systematic war of sieges, in the modern fashion,
against the circle of fortresses protecting Granada. The last
was to be a war of attrition, choking off the resources of the
Arab capital before the final stroke at its walls.

Isabel arrived in camp in her usual magnificent state one day
in November, after a storm had washed out a large section of
the Christian camp and left the troops tired and discouraged.
As she came within sight of the city, even the Moors thronged
the battlements to catch sight of the mighty Queen to whose
beauty and goodness they paid a romantic tribute in their
songs, even while they feared her as a foe. Turbaned heads
appeared silently on the mosques and turrets while the King
welcomed the Queen and the Cardinal, and the shouts of the
crusaders rose above the drums and clarions and re-echoed
against the walls of Baza.

Next day Cidi Yahye, reasoning that the Queen's arrival
meant a continuation of the siege with new vigor and intelligence—such was her reputation among her enemies—asked
for terms of peace, and on St. Barbara's day, December 4,
surrendered.

Meanwhile the King and Queen received in audience the
three men in brown cowls who had come from the East and
the West. The two from Jerusalem were Franciscan friars sent
by the Sultan of Egypt to warn them that if they did not
cease the war against Mohammedans in Spain, he would put
to the sword all the Christians in Palestine and destroy their

churches and the Church of the Holy Sepulchre at Jerusalem. Isabel received the friars with great kindness, gave them a grant of a thousand ducats a year for their convent, and sent back in their charge a rich embroidery, the work of her own hands, to be hung in the Church of the Holy Sepulchre. They took word to the Sultan that she would commission an embassador to him at a later date, to go more fully into the questions he raised. Thus she gained time; and eventually she dispatched Peter Martyr to make a treaty with him.

The third man in a cowl had come to make another request for two or three ships in which to sail west to the Indies. From this time on he often appeared in the Franciscan habit, for like Dante and other great men of the Middle Ages, he was a member of the Third Order of St. Francis. Disappointment and ridicule had developed the strong religious side of his nature, and he may have been doing penance for the liaison which resulted in the birth of his natural son Fernando at Córdoba in 1488. The suggestion that he was merely seeking to impress the pious queen is a reflection on his great histrionic abilities, for if he was acting, he certainly overplayed the part during the rest of his life. There is not much doubt that he believed himself to be divinely chosen by God to unite the western with the eastern world. Of the American continent, of course, he had no suspicion, believing that one body of water, dotted by islands, extended from Gibraltar to the marvelous city of Kinsai in China.

The Junta assembled by the Prior of Prado, Fray Hernando de Talavera, to consider his proposals in 1486, had reported against him after many interviews and delays. For this a great deal of undeserved abuse has been heaped upon Talavera. Yet Columbus himself acknowledged later that the Prior had been one of his earliest and most helpful champions. The other members of the Junta were *sabios e letrados e marineros,* wise and learned men and mariners. According to Dr. Maldonado, the only one of them whose name we know, they were unanimous in pronouncing the Admiral's theories impracticable, and in advising the King not to accept them, at least during the Moorish war. But Columbus himself seems to have been chiefly to blame for this report. We have the word of Hernando Colón, his son and biographer, that he did not explain his plan completely to them, fearing that they might steal his material and attempt to make secret use of it, as he believed the Portuguese had. The commissioners, therefore, did not have all the facts before them, and his lack of frankness must have made an unfavorable impression.

Even so, the King and Queen were unwilling to lose sight of the fluent navigator with the striking personality, and they intimated that as soon as the Moorish War was ended they would reconsider their decision. Meanwhile they gave him a pension of about 3,000 maravedis a month. This was not a large sum by any means,[1] but it sufficed to keep him alive without labor. And Isabel's generosity to a somewhat eccentric stranger of whose utility she was not entirely convinced may perhaps be gauged by the fact that Antonio de Lebrija, a noted grammarian who taught at the University of Alcalá in Columbus's lifetime, received only 3,333 maravedis a month in salary. When the Queen's funds no longer permitted her to continue Columbus's allowance in 1489, she commanded all owners of inns to feed and clothe him and his two sons. But Columbus was impatient. Like every man with a single dominant idea, he considered all else in the world of secondary or slight importance. The truth of his later complaint that during seven years —1485 to 1492—he "received aid from no one, except from Friar Antonio de Marchena" (in another place he speaks of "two friars who always were constant") and was repulsed and laughed at by all must be appraised in the light of the facts: for two years he was maintained in the luxurious palace of the Duke of Medina Celi, at the Duke's expense; during the next three years he received a pension almost equal to the salary of one of the most famous university professors; thereafter, he was lodged without expense at inns. During all this time he received from the King and Queen, the Cardinal, and many of the greatest personages in Spain, the kindness and encouragement that might have been expected from the aristocracy of a civilized country. Indeed, considering that Castile was in the middle of a life-and-death conflict of ten years, and had hardly recuperated from the anarchy of the reign of Enrique IV, his reception was remarkable.

Columbus, with all his mighty powers of will and of endurance, had the defects of his virtues; he could not understand or tolerate opposition. His sensitiveness to criticism amounted almost to a delusion of persecution. During his whole life there was always some one whose rascality or ingratitude he blamed, instead of himself, for his misfortunes. In a marginal note to his copy of Pierre d'Ailly's *De Imagine Mundi*, he attributes the refusal of Dom João of Portugal to "the Jew Joseph"— *el judio Josepho*—the physician and astrologer Dr. Vecinho, whom the canny King had sent to Guinea to measure the altitude of the sun, as a means of checking up on Columbus's theories, and who reported adversely. And in Castile, where everyone honored him, he found that "all" were against him. Yet immediately after the Junta of Córdoba had advised the monarchs against the voyage, he received a warm invitation from the Dominicans of Salamanca University to visit them as their guest and discuss his plans. For this kindness he was indebted chiefly to Fray Diego de Deza, formerly confessor to the Queen and tutor to Prince Juan. The Queen esteemed his piety, learning and loyalty so highly that she had made him Bishop of Salamanca, and he was now teaching theology in the university there.

Students from all parts of Europe went to study under men like Deza and Lebrija. The nobles of Spain sent their sons, and poor boys, if worthy, were taught without charge. The University had a larger enrollment than Yale or Princeton has today; in 1488 there were more than 6,000 students, and it was there, as guest of the Dominican college of St. Stephen, that Columbus spent several months, holding informal discussions with the monks who were professors of cosmography and other sciences. The famous "council of Salamanca," in which several generations of sentimental historians have imagined Columbus as the man of science contemptuously refuting the errors of ignorant and bigoted monks and being repulsed by their folly, is simply a myth. There was no "council of Salamanca."[2] There were several conferences in which Columbus, and not the monks, appears to have lugged quotations from the Church Fathers into a scientific discussion in his answer to the hard practical questions of the Dominicans. His quotations from the prophecies of Isaias and his assurances that God had directly commissioned him to "open the gates of the western seas" were probably received with that polite but skeptical raising of the eyebrows that Catholic priests usually bestow on tales of miraculous visions and divine revelations from uncertified mystics; it is likely they hurt Columbus more than they helped him in that milieu. But on the whole, the impression he made was favorable. The Dominicans were henceforth among his champions, and Bishop Diego de Deza never ceased to intercede for him with the King and Queen.

It was in consequence of the reports of Deza, after certain conferences of the Dominican astronomers and mathematicians in the farmhouse of Valcuebo, owned by St. Stephen's College, that the King and Queen ordered the reopening of the case, and the payment of a regular stipend to the inspired adventurer.

Isabel could hardly have failed to sympathize with a man who, like her, refused to be swerved from the road he had taken, and paid no tribute to the impossible. The poet and the artist in her—or was it the woman?—instinctively felt the destiny of this dreamer so facile in images. Where Fernando, the cool man of business, detected inconsistencies and small discrepancies, Isabel's more intuitive mind leaped to the central fact of a man of genius willing to risk his life to bring a vast mystery within the limits of actual knowledge. Yet at this moment, with the blockade of Granada still to be effected, she had no intention of allowing any one's dream, however gorgeous, to prevent the realization of her own vision of a united and orderly Spain. She was obliged to dismiss him once more, therefore, with kindly words and a smile of hope. Columbus wrapped his brown monastic habit about his powerful form and silently departed from Baza. What happened to him during the next two years, no one has yet discovered.

The army left Baza, December 7, to strike for Almería on the south coast. The King led the main body. Isabel was to follow with the rear guard.

The winter had settled down over the gusty mountains when the Queen set out on the perilous journey over the most desolate and savage part of the long Sierra. Surrounded by shivering cavaliers muffled in cloaks, she rode over icy peaks above the clouds, and down through valleys where the sun never penetrated. It had cost her twenty thousand lives—17,000 by disease—to take Baza. Hundreds more perished on the way to the Mediterranean, frozen to death during the bitter nights.

Almería surrendered without a siege. El Zagal, who was growing old, came out to meet the Christian monarchs. When he knelt before them, Fernando raised him up and embraced him. "His appearance touched my soul with compassion" wrote Peter Martyr, "for though a lawless barbarian, he was a King, and had given proofs of his heroism." In return for his allegiance Fernando allowed him a large sum of money, the nominal title of king, the valley of Alhaurin, and half the salt pits of Maleha.

The King and Queen spent Christmas very joyously by the salt-scented beaches of Almería, and in the afternoons they went hunting mountain boars along the wooded coast nearby.

For the first time in the war, Isabel knew that ultimate victory was a certainty. At the beginning of 1489 the morale of the Spanish people had almost broken under the long strain, and "there was much murmuring against the King." But the fall of Baza and Almería had turned the grumbling into rejoicing. What remained now but to march up to the walls of Granada and batter them down?

This Fernando and Isabel were urged to do; but on discussing the possibilities with the Cardinal and the Marqués and others, they came to the conclusion that the cost in lives would be less if they cut off the supplies of Granada in 1490, and forced a comparatively bloodless victory in 1491. It was futile to ask Boabdil to surrender while he had a great fortified city full of men and supplies; and even if he were inclined to keep his oath of allegiance to the Castilian sovereigns, his subordinates would not allow him to, so long as they had hope of reinforcements from Africa. The King, however, went through the form of demanding the delivery of Granada, reminding Boabdil that he had promised, after his capture at Lucena, to give up the capital if the Christians should take Baza, Almería and Guadix. The refusal of Boabdil gave Fernando the opportunity he sought of denouncing him as a pusillanimous traitor, false to his feudal lord, and therefore, entitled to no mercy or consideration.

Isabel was not sorry to turn from camps and sieges to the peaceful business of planning the marriages of her children. Having been betrothed by her own parents at the age of six, she took it as a matter of course that the personal happiness of those born on the steps of a throne must be subordinated to the public good. It probably never occurred to Fernando and Isabel to question the propriety of using their children as instruments to limit the power of France and strengthen Spain.

They sought an alliance on the east with Maximilian, the King of the Romans, by negotiations for the double marriage of Prince Juan and the Princess Juana, respectively, to the Emperor's daughter Marguerite and his son Philip the Fair. To bind a treaty with England against France in March 1489, they agreed to give their youngest daughter, Catalina, to Prince Arthur of Wales, as soon as both were old enough.

When the treaty with Henry VII was signed, great jousts and bull fights were held at Medina del Campo. Roger Machado, the Richmond king-at-arms who accompanied the English ambassadors, wrote afterwards, "They speak of the honor that is paid to ambassadors in England, but surely it does not compare with the honor they show ambassadors in the realm of Castile." Doctor Saloage, the English envoy, made a long address in Latin, to which the Bishop of Ciudad Rodrigo replied; but "the good bishop was so old, and had lost all his teeth, that one could understand him with great difficulty."[3] Machado describes the King and Queen of Spain with some minuteness. Fernando had "a rich robe of cloth of gold, woven entirely of gold, and furred with a costly trimming of fine sable." Isabel appeared in "a rich robe of the same woven cloth of gold . . . and over the said robe a riding hood of black velvet, all slashed in large holes to show under the said velvet the cloth of gold in which she is dressed." Furthermore, "crosswise over her left side" she wore "a short cloak of fine crimson satin furred with ermine, very handsome in appearance and very brilliant." Her jewels—this was before she pawned them to pay for the siege of Baza—were magnificent. Her necklace was of gold and jeweled roses. The ribbon at her breast was adorned with diamonds, rubies and pearls. And the pouch of her white leather girdle, wrote the observing Machado, was set "with a large balas ruby the size of a tennis-ball, between five rich diamonds and other stones the size of a bean." Her costume was not worth a penny less than 200,000 gold crowns in his estimation. In 1490 the diamonds and the balas rubies were in the keeping of money lenders of Valencia and Barcelona. But they had previously served their purpose in dazzling the English ambassadors so that the miserly Henry VII would give as large a dowry as possible to Catalina, who was already spoken of in Spain as "the princess of Wales."

Machado describes her in Isabel's arms, looking at a tourney, a singularly beautiful child.

To arrange Catalina's marriage and a favorable alliance, Isabel and Fernando had sent to England a doctor of civil and canon law, Roderigo Gondesalvi de Puebla, who had served them well as a magistrate of Ecija in Andalusia; described as lame, parsimonious, shrewd, enormously vain and indifferently honest; probably of Jewish ancestry, for his daughter was later arrested by the Inquisition. Henry VII received him in state, flattered him, made him his own. After he was received at the royal table, he reported that he saw thirty-two ladies of angelic beauty attending Queen Elizabeth of York. Invited to look upon little Prince Arthur asleep, he reported him "fat and fair, but small for his age" of twenty months. During the same year the good Doctor attempted to arrange a marriage between the chivalrous James of Scotland and King Fernando's illegitimate daughter Juana. Knowing that James would not ally himself with a bar sinister, Puebla told him that Juana was Fernando's daughter by a clandestine morganatic marriage contracted before his union with Isabel. James was attracted by the proposal, and the Doctor, proud of his subtlety, wrote Fernando what he had done, only to receive a contemptuous reprimand. It was a foolish lie, said the King, and could not fail to be detected.

In 1486 the sovereigns had offered the Princess Isabel, a slender girl of nineteen with blonde hair and coloring like her mother's, to the young Charles VIII; but the Regent, Anne de Beaujeu, who was planning his marriage with Anne of Brittany as a means of completing the union of France, made no reply. The Spanish monarchs in the following year renewed the negotiations, offering Anne a prolongation of power and 400,000 crowns for her consent. When Anne refused, Isabel and Fernando turned toward Portugal. The King had seen in a French marriage an opportunity to make a dicker for the return of Roussillon and Cerdagne, but the Queen from the beginning, true to Castilian tradition, had desired an understanding with the Portuguese. With the aid of her aunt Doña Beatriz and the Castilian party at Lisbon, she at length succeeded. In April, 1490, before the beginning of the spring campaign, the Infanta was married by proxy to Dom Alfonso, heir to the throne of Portugal. Thus for the first time in more

than a quarter of a century, Queen Isabel was relieved of ap-
prehension over a possible revival of the claims of her niece,
La Beltraneja, who had left her convent and was living in state
at the court of Lisbon. The Portuguese have always maintained her legitimacy.

All the chivalry of Spain assembled at Seville for the wedding and the magnificent fêtes that followed. Cardinal Mendoza performed the ceremony on Easter Sunday, April 18,
and Don Fernando de Silveira was proxy for Prince Alfonso.
The Princess had 70 maids of honor and 100 pages. The
festivals and tourneys were held in an inclosed field on the
banks of the Guadalquivir, shaded from the sun by enormous
canopies of silk embroidered with heraldic devices, and surrounded by galleries hung with silk brocade and cloth of gold,
where the Queen and the princesses and the great ladies of all
Spain looked down on the festivities. The King broke several
lances, and was much admired for his horsemanship and his
fine figure. The Marqués of Cádiz and the Duke of Medina
Sidonia appeared in the lists; there were jousts every day. In
the evenings the ladies, mounted on mules, were lighted from
the banquet halls to their lodgings by cavaliers. "There were
eight or nine torches," says Bernaldez, "for each lady."[4] Seville
was once more the city of love and of youth. The rose-strewn
patios and streets were full of voices and the strumming of
many instruments, and the tapers going to and fro on the
river were like myriad fireflies. The festivities lasted until the
Feast of the Holy Cross, May 3.[5]

Later in the year, November 11, the Princess went to Portugal with Cardinal Mendoza and a magnificent escort.[6] She
was married to Alfonso November 22 with a pomp greater, if
possible, than at Seville. The Portuguese court had brought
artists from France, Flanders and England six months before
the event to make preparations for the jousts and balls. The
Princess was greatly admired, and the magnificence of her
gowns and jewels, said by the court gossips to be worth 12,000
florins, impressed all beholders, as Queen Isabel had intended,
with the munificence of the royal crown of Castile. And best
of all, the Princess, like Queen Isabel and all her children,
found love in marriage.

The Queen of Castile was happy. But much as she loved
her daughters, she reserved for Prince Juan an especial devo-

tion. He had very fine blond hair falling to his shoulders; a handsome face with thoughtful blue eyes; and rather spindly legs, for he was delicate from birth. The Queen called him "my angel." It seemed to her that for him, next to God, she had chiefly toiled and sacrificed; for him she had won the Portuguese war, hanged thieves and murderers, burned heretics, carried fire and sword into the cities of Granada; and for him in particular she desired the sort of education that a good king should have.

The Prince was fond of music, and though he had a rather thin and mediocre tenor, enjoyed singing. The chapel master used to take five children with good voices to the palace to sing with him. He played with taste and some skill on the organ, the clavichord, and the flute. To prevent his being isolated like the ill-taught Charles VIII of France, Queen Isabel carefully chose ten boys as his companions, five of his age and five older ones, who were treated as his peers in the palace and competed with him on equal terms in all his sports. When she observed that Juan was too much inclined toward economy, she urged him to be generous and magnanimous: to keep the hand closed to courtiers, climbers and flatterers, but open to faithful servants and all unfortunates. The state of his health made it difficult sometimes to carry on the rigorous training in martial exercises that a King ought to have, and he was frequently under the care of physicians. Nevertheless, he learned to ride well, to joust and to hunt. When his sister Isabel was married, he was twelve years old. He could handle a sword as well as any of the boys of his age in the palace and like a true knight, kept it by his pillow when he slept.

That year his father invited him into the field for the first time, and when the King rode out of Seville at the head of his chivalry and his men-at-arms, the Prince was beside him, proudly erect in his small suit of chain mail.

The crusaders—5,000 horse, 20,000 foot—marched through the fertile fields and blooming orchards of the Moors, burning and leveling anything that might give them food or supplies, until they came within sight of the red towers of Granada, and there, by the great Moorish canal, within earshot of their walls, the King conferred knighthood upon Prince Juan of the Asturias. The Duke of Medina Sidonia and the Marqués of Cádiz were sponsors; and the Prince in turn laid his gemmed Toledo sword on the shoulders of several other boys of noble families.

The army resumed its destructive march over the *vega.* While they were returning with their spoils to Córdoba, Boabdil marched swiftly with a large force against the Christian port of Sobrena. Fernando at once left Córdoba in pursuit, and Boabdil retreated.

The Christians made a second expedition through the *vega,* destroying whatever they had overlooked in the previous raid. El Zagal, finding himself as unpopular in his shrunken kingdom as he had been at Granada, sold his remaining castles to the conquerors and crossed the sea. He was seized and made blind by order of the King of Fez.

With a sole enemy remaining in Granada, Fernando and Isabel resolved to end the war in 1490. Nothing now, it appeared, could prevent their success except the lack of money. They solved the problem partially by levying a general war-tax on all Jews in their kingdoms.

As the crucial year approached, all Europe became interested in the struggle, and volunteers were coming from all countries to be in at the death. On April 11, 1491, a high-spirited army of 50,000 men left Córdoba for the final campaign.

The Queen and the Infantas remained at Alcalá la Real, while the King and the Prince led the host into the *vega,* sent through the Alpujarras several raiding parties that destroyed nine villages and collected great stores of foodstuffs, and stopping at los Ojos de Huecar, some four miles from Granada, on the twenty-sixth, laid out a great quadrangular camp. As soon as the position was properly fortified, the Queen and the Princesses arrived to inspect it, and were met with great ceremony by the Marqués, now the Marqués-Duke, of Cádiz. His cheeks were hollow from a long illness during the winter, and his beard, which had been fiery red when the Queen spared him twelve years before, was turning gray. But he bowed with the same grave courtesy, and begged her to accept his own tent for her lodgings. He had had it made especially for the Holy War; it was the stoutest and most exquisite in the whole camp, "and the queen was well lodged in it."[7] Other tents, for the Duke had many, were provided for the Princesses.

One night in July—it was on Thursday, the fourteenth, says the meticulous Bernaldez—the Queen, unable to sleep because of the flickering of a taper in her sumptuous quarters, asked one of her damsels to remove it to the adjoining tent. This was done, and Isabel fell asleep. All the camp was silent except for the pacing of sentries and of officers going their rounds. Suddenly the wind shifted and the flame of the candle was blown against the silken stuff of a tent flap. It leaped up the wall, it spread to another tent, and to another; in a little while it was a great conflagration whipped by the rising wind through the city of silk and brocade, consuming the pavilions and tents. There were screams of women and shouts of soldiers; cries of "Fire!" "Treason!" "The Moors! The Moors!" "Save the Queen!" An answering murmur arose in Granada as the Moors mounted the walls and gazed in wonder at the pillar of fire and smoke in the midst of the black *vega*.

Queen Isabel, aroused by the shouting and the smell of smoke, rushed into the next tent, where the King was sleeping soundly, and woke him. They rescued the Prince and the Infantas, who were sleeping nearby. Then they both mounted and rode through the blazing camp to allay the panic of the troops. By that time the wooden barracks between the royal tents and the city of Granada had caught fire, and were blazing away in the dry July air. The whole camp was quickly reduced to cinders.[8]

The first fear of all was that the Moors had set fire to the camp and were preparing to attack in force. But to forestall this possibility the Marqués of Cádiz had already taken 3,000 of his men into the plain, and there they waited till dawn. If the Moors understood their opportunity, they failed to profit by it.

As soon as it became known next day that Queen Isabel's wardrobe had been destroyed, Gonsalvo de Córdoba sent her his wife's. The Prince of Youth had become the handsome veteran of forty, chaste, fearless, magnanimous to the weak and the poor, terrible to his foes; and Isabel's favor would yet make him the Great Captain of history.

"Your household," she said in thanking him, "has lost more by the disaster than mine has."

"Señora," replied Gonsalvo, "it is no disaster that gives my wife and me the privilege of serving your Majesty."

King Fernando ordered an attack on the walls of Granada to keep up the morale of his troops and to prevent the Moors from exulting too much over the charred remains of the camp. Isabel's reaction was characteristic. "God has permitted this to happen to test our faith," she said. "If we stand firm He will yet give us the victory;" and she commanded the army to rebuild the camp at once, not in linen and silk, but in stone. Foundations were dug, rocks were drawn from the neighboring hills, and day after day the buildings arose in the sight of the puzzled Arabs. The whole army, swelled by new recruits to 80,000, engaged in the work, and within three months, as if by a miracle, a complete new city, with towers, battlements and walls, stood in the midst of the plain. Two principal streets in the form of a great cross, ran north and south and east and west to four gates, through a public square large enough to contain the whole army. From the topmost tower was raised the silver cross of the Crusade, with the banners of Santiago and of Castile and Aragon. "Call the city Isabel, after the Queen!" cried the cavaliers and the soldiers. But she insisted upon its being named *Santa Fé*, Holy Faith.

The King had forbidden those costly skirmishes in which the light-armed Moors usually had the advantage. But when the bands of Saracen cavalry failed to draw fire from their enemies, individuals among them began riding close to the Christian camp, with challenges to personal combat. At first the Christians responded; but after Fernando had lost some of his best men, he forbade all duels of any sort. "Hunger alone will win the city for us," said Isabel to the French ambassador.

Among the Moors, however, there was a cavalier named Yarfe, a giant in stature and a madman for courage and strength. One day he rode to the very edge of the Christian camp and rising in his stirrups, hurled a javeline toward the royal quarters. The missile stood quivering in the ground, only a few feet from the Queen's tent, and on it was found an insulting note marked "for the Queen of Castile."

Hernando Perez del Pulgar—not the Queen's secretary, but another known as *El de las Hazañas*, He of the Exploits— vowed vengeance. That night, with fifteen chosen companions, he rose to a certain little postern gate of Granada where there were only a few unmounted guards. While his companions cut them down, Hernando dashed through the streets of the sleeping city. At the principal mosque he dismounted, knelt to say a prayer and to dedicate the church to the Blessed Virgin, and nailed to the door with his dagger a placard bearing the words,

"Ave Maria!"

He fled for the postern gate. By that time the street was full of Moorish soldiers attacking his companions. He bowled over some, struck down others, cut his way to the gate, and rejoined his friends. All galloped back to Santa Fé without the loss of a man.

One Saturday in August, the Queen expressed a desire to see Granada and the camp from a high place. The Marqués of Cádiz provided a great escort, to make sure of her safety; and a splendid train of cavaliers rode out of the camp, with their Majesties and Prince Juan and the three Princesses, to the village of Zubia, on the mountain side to the left of Granada, where there was a fine view. The Marqués of Villena and Don Alonso de Aguilar stationed their forces on the slope above the village, while the Marqués of Cádiz drew up his army in battle formation in the plain below. Thus the Queen and her children were almost surrounded by a ring of steel. They entered a house in the hamlet, and going to the terraced roof, looked down with delight on the red towers and tiled roofs of the Alhambra, and the massive wall too great in circuit for any army to encircle.

The Moors, however, supposed that the Christians were offering them battle; and as they always counted on their superior fleetness in cavalry actions, they came out in great numbers under the gallant Muza. Queen Isabel, unwilling to have her curiosity cost the lives of Christian soldiers, sent orders to the Marqués of Cádiz not to attack, and to accept no challenges. The Moors rode near. They discharged arrows into the Christian ranks. Some of them came near enough to throw spears. Still the Spanish host stood silent and immovable. The Moors laughed and hooted.

One of them, a gigantic man on a fiery black horse, came forward alone, his visor down, a scimitar of Damascus steel at his side, and over his great buckler a lance from which floated the device that showed who he was. It was Yarfe, the colossus, who had thrown the insulting spear at the Queen's quarters. A murmur of anger passed over the Christian host, but it swelled into a cry of rage when they saw dragging in the dust and tied to the tail of Yarfe's horse, the placard inscribed, "*Ave Maria*" that Pulgar had pinned to the door of the Mosque.

That was more than Christians could endure. Garcilaso de la Vega, a young Castilian, galloped to Zubia, threw himself on his knees before King Fernando, and begged permission to avenge the insult to Our Lady. The King nodded. Garcilaso remounted, closed his visor, spurred his steed, and sped down to the plain, his four black plumes rising and falling as he went. Yarfe saw him coming, and was ready for him. The two came together with a shock that could be heard on the mountain side. The Queen held her breath in fear, and prayed for her champion.

The great weight of the Moor had thrown Garcilaso well back in his saddle, and he nearly lost his seat, but he recovered his balance and drew his sword, while the scimitar of Yarfe made a flashing arc in the sun. Time after time they closed, the swords rose and fell, both were wounded in several places. Garcilaso, worn down by the might of the Moor and by his own heavy armor, was growing tired. Perceiving this, Yarfe suddenly reached over and with his gorilla-like arms dragged him from his saddle. Both fell entangled to the ground, while their horses galloped away. Queen Isabel saw the huge Saracen place his knee on the breast of her champion, saw him raise his dagger to plunge it into the throat of the vanquished. A wail of despair ascended from the Christian army. While they watched, horrified, fascinated, they saw the Moor fall backward into the thick dust. Garcilaso painfully arose and stood looking down at his dead foe. He had shortened his sword, and when Yarfe raised his arm, plunged the point into his heart.

Remounting, he galloped back with the "*Ave Maria*" hoisted triumphantly on the point of his sword.[9] The army roared its applause.

Muza now ordered his army to attack the Christians below the village. The Marqués of Cádiz, considering himself free under the circumstances to disregard the Queen's commands, gave the word. With cries of "Santiago! Castile!" the Christian cavalry spurred into action. The Queen and the Princesses threw themselves on their knees and prayed aloud. After bitter fighting, the Moors broke and fled for Granada, pursued al-

Christopher Columbus
"The Adventurer, the Poet with the Gray Eyes"

most to the gates. Two thousand of them were killed or captured. There was no Christian cavalier, says Bernaldez, whose lance was not dyed in Moorish blood that day. Only a few of the Spanish were killed, "and the King and Queen were well pleased with this victory, especially because the Queen had been the cause of it."[10]

When the royal party rode to where the Marqués-Duke was reassembling his troops, to congratulate him, he said,

"Señora, this victory has come from God and from the good fortune of Your Highness."

"Duke," replied the Queen, "we have been indebted to your good fortune before this, and it is you who have brought it about."[11]

The victory went into history, however, as "the Queen's skirmish." To commemorate it, Isabel erected at Zubia a monastery dedicated to Saint Francis, to whom she had prayed during the battle, and in the garden of the cloister planted a laurel tree.

The Moors made no more sorties. When the autumn came and food began to run short, Boabdil yielded to the clamors of the growing peace party and asked for terms.

The treaty was drawn up at Churriana, a small village near Granada, on the twenty-eighth of November, by Gonsalvo de Córdoba, who spoke Arabic well. The Moors were allowed freedom of worship and the possession of their mosques. Their laws were respected, but their magistrates must submit to the royal authority of Castile. They were free to preserve their language and costume. Possession of their property was guaranteed them, and the right to dispose of it as they might see fit. They would be exempt from all taxes for three years, after which time they must pay taxes at the rate they had paid them to their former sovereigns. They might remain where they were, undisturbed in their occupations, or emigrate. If they chose to migrate to Africa, vessels would be provided and they would be transported free of charge. Hostages were required. Boabdil was granted a small territory in the Alpujarras, and was to be acknowledged as an independent sovereign there. The garrison of Granada was to have the honors of war. All fortresses and artillery must be delivered within sixty days.

Such were the magnanimous conditions that Isabel and Fernando offered their vanquished enemies, and the Moors accepted without much hesitation. The date for the formal surrender was fixed for January 2, 1492.

Boabdil came forth with melancholy dignity at daybreak on the second, attended by only fifty cavaliers. Isabel and Fernando met him at the village of Armilla, a mile or more from the city. El Zogoybi, the Unlucky, looked more noble in defeat than he had ever looked on his throne in the Alhambra, and all hearts were filled with pity for him. As he bent to kiss Fernando's hand, the King prevented him; whereat Boabdil kissed his conqueror's arm. Then, as he delivered the keys, he said in a steady voice:

"We are your slaves, invincible King; we deliver up this city and kingdom to you, not doubting you will treat us with clemency and moderation."[12]

The King handed the keys to Isabel, and she in turn to Prince Juan, who gave them to the Count of Tendilla, newly appointed governor of Granada.

Meanwhile Cardinal Mendoza was leading the Christian vanguard into Granada, and with him went Fray Hernando de Talavera, now Bishop of Ávila, whose privilege it was to hoist the standards. Presently on the highest tip of the Torre de la Vala flamed forth the silver cross of the Crusade, and beside it the pennon of Saint James, the patron of the Christian warriors of Spain for centuries.[13] "Santiago! Santiago!" shouted the soldiers in Granada and the army without, kneeling in the dust. And the King and Queen, with Prince Juan and the Infantas, fell on their knees and gave thanks to God for their victory. Then appeared the pennants of Isabel and Fernando, while the army, with a great voice, cried, "Castile! Castile! for the invincible monarchs, Don Fernando and Doña Isabel!"[14]

Isabel's eyes, very blue that day, were shining with triumph and joy. All her own struggles and sufferings, all the pains and labors and bloodshed of her kingly ancestors, all the wounds and deaths of the thousands of Christian knights who had fought so doggedly for the recovery of this sacred soil, all the shame and agony of Christian women and children who had perished befouled in Moorish dungeons—all the mighty epic of Christian Spain was consummated and justified in that glorious moment. The faith of a woman had prevailed.

The sovereigns did not enter the city until four days later,

January 6, the feast of the Epiphany, when they rode grandly through the gate to the principal mosque, already consecrated as a Christian church by Fray Hernando. After giving thanks at High Mass, they continued to the Alhambra, passed through the Gate of Justice, entered the presence chamber, and sat on the seats of the Emirs of Granada. It was the first time that Christians had had authority there for 777 years.

All the great dignitaries of the country joined in the acclamations when the herald-at-arms cried, "Granada, Granada, for the illustrious Kings of Castile!" Fray Hernando was there, his good Jewish face happy over the triumph of his royal penitent. She had already offered to make him Archbishop of Granada, and he had refused, because he said he was unworthy; but the Queen insisted, and as usual must have her way. There were the Marqués of Cádiz and the Duke of Medina Sidonia; and there were the Master of Santiago and Gonsalvo de Córdoba and many others whose swords, once devoted to civil anarchy, had been consecrated to the holy cause of the Crusade by the Queen's genius. There was Cardinal Mendoza, the oldest and most faithful of all her friends; who could say how much she owed to his wisdom? Even Fray Tomás de Torquemada, the Inquisitor General, was there, having ridden south to be present at the triumph to which he had contributed his share.

Luis de Santángel, the King's trusted *escribano de racion,* was there too, but he probably took no great pleasure in meeting Fray Tomás de Torquemada, for in April of the previous year, the indefatigable hunter of heretics had at last tracked down the millionaire conspirator and had put him on trial in spite of the King's friendship. Fernando has been commended even by Lea for his impartiality; for several of his *Converso* associates were punished by the Inquisition. But it is difficult to avoid the conclusion that he shielded Santángel. We find that the wealthy lawyer, after renouncing his errors, did penance by walking in a public procession in a yellow sanbenito, whereas some of his less fortunate relatives had been burned for the murder of Peter Arbues. There is of course a possibility that he was not as guilty in that affair as history has represented him to be. His cousin, also named Luis de Santángel, fled to Bordeaux to escape the Inquisition, and the two have sometimes been confused.

In the great happy throng there stood morosely aloof at some distance a tall powerful man in the brown cowl of a Franciscan, from which the lean and melancholy face of Cristóbal Colón looked over the heads of the cheering cavaliers toward the King and the Queen, as if to say, "I wish all these trivialities were over, so that you would pay attention to *my* affair."[15]

Boabdil the Unlucky was not present. He had already set out for Purchena with his mother Zoraya and his wives and servants. When he reached the edge of the Alpujarras, he turned to take his last look at the golden city of his ancestors, and two great tears fell from his dark eyes. His mother, Zoraya, who had said nothing until then, remarked,

"You may well weep like a woman for what you have failed to defend as a man."[16]

Boabdil crossed the hill and vanished in the shadows.

XXIV

THE CONQUERORS OF BOABDIL WALK
IN THE GARDENS OF THE ALHAMBRA,
AND DECIDE TO SEND CHRISTOPHER
COLUMBUS OVER THE WESTERN OCEAN

ALL Europe joyfully celebrated the reconquest of Granada:
for who could fail to see an epic grandeur in the final
triumph of a people who had contended with an alien
foe for eight centuries? Men felt that the regaining of Granada
in the west was a compensation for the loss of Constantinople
in the east. Some years later the Moslem would advance to
the gates of Vienna at a moment when the unity of Europe
was being shattered by a new heresy, and the freedom of the
seas was yet to be snatched from him at Lepanto; but never
again would he threaten Christendom seriously from the west.
Bonfires blazed and churchbells rang deliriously from the
Mediterranean to the North Sea.

King Fernando's letter announcing the victory to Pope Innocent VIII reached Rome on the night of February 1, a
month after the event. The Pope and all the Cardinals went
in solemn procession next morning from the Vatican to the
Spanish Church of Saint James, to offer a Mass of thanksgiving, after which the Holy Father gave his benediction. The
rejoicings lasted several days. Cardinal Raffaele Riario entertained the Spanish envoys with a dramatic representation of
the conquest of Granada and the triumphal entry of the King
and Queen. Cardinal Borgia delighted the Roman people by
an exhibition of the Spanish popular sport, the first bullfight
they had ever seen.[1]

When the news reached England, King Henry VII commanded all the nobles and prelates who were in the Court to
march with the Lord Mayor and Aldermen of London in great
solemnity to the Church of Saint Paul. There the Lord Chancellor addressed them, saying, "These many years the Chris-

tians have not gained new ground or territory upon the infidels, nor enlarged and set farther the bounds of the Christian world. But this is now done by the prowess and devotion of Fernando and Isabel, sovereigns of Spain, who to their immortal honor have recovered the great and rich kingdom of Granada, and the populous and mighty city of the same name from the Moors . . . for which this assembly and all Christians are to render laud and thanks to God, and to celebrate this noble act of the King of Spain, who in this is not only victorious but apostolical, in the gaining of new provinces to the Christian faith." The whole assembly then marched through London, singing, *Te Deum Laudamus*.[2]

Queen Isabel meanwhile was enjoying the first leisure she had known since childhood, and in beautiful surroundings. She walked with her children through the pillared halls and pleasure rooms of dead caliphs, and she wandered among fig trees and pistachios, cypresses, oranges, laurels and roses in those incomparable gardens of the Alhambra that extended from the palace down through the shady ravine of Los Molinos. Everywhere were pools and fountains under arcades and arches of green; everywhere brilliant colors, delicate fragrance, the songs of birds. The Moors, skilled beyond all men in irrigation, had made an earthly paradise of a dry vega; all about her the Queen saw aqueducts, canals, pumps and chain-wells, waterwheels, every device for making a desert habitable. On every side she found acacia, myrtle, ilex, tamarisk, guelder roses, crimson oleanders, white Arabian jasmine in endless profusion, the blood-red flowers of the pomegranate; every imaginable fruit, every conceivable vegetable; fields of golden sugar cane, meadows of pale saffron like those she remembered near Arévalo. On every hillside as far as she could see were white-walled houses, orange groves, luxuriant gardens hedged in by cypresses, and in the distance, melting into the blue sky, the snowy peaks of the Sierra Nevadas.

In these peaceful surroundings the Queen rested, and contemplated her kingdoms with some satisfaction. She had reigned eighteen years, and the country that she had found bankrupt, drenched with blood, sick with despair, had become a peaceful and prosperous whole. The population, in spite of the military casualties, had increased rapidly during the decade of the Moorish war. Hundreds of families who had migrated

to France and Portugal in the time of anarchy had returned
to enjoy the security and peace established by the Holy Brotherhood. Castile alone had from 10 to 12 millions of people.
Granada added another 2,000,000. Aragon also had become
populous as foreign merchants and farmers settled there after
the reforms of King Fernando. By the end of the fifteenth
century, the total population of Castile and Aragon and their
nearby dependencies was probably not far from 20,000,000.
If there were many racial strains and many conflicting tem-
peraments, from the proud insurgent Catalan to the comfort-
loving Moor, they were now united by common commercial
interests and a common rule, and except for the Jews and
Moors, a common religion.

When Isabel became Queen in 1474, the Crown revenues
had shrunk to 885,000 reals. In 1482, after the rents alienated
by Enrique had been resumed, they amounted to 13,000,000.
At the end of the Moorish war the Queen owed a tremendous
war debt, and was hard pressed for money. But in another ten
years she would have an income of 26,000,000 reals. The
revenues of cities and towns had increased in proportion.

Add to all this that Spain had emerged from the Crusade
as one of the leading powers of Europe—a fact that interested
the King even more than it did the Queen—and it is evident
that Isabel had good reason to be pleased. But even in the
gardens of the Alhambra there was no place so sheltered
that the cares of mortal life could not penetrate it. The burden
of administration followed her. And then there was the great
sorrow of the Princess Isabel, who had gone to Portugal the
previous autumn to marry the heir to the throne.

In July, after six months of happiness, Prince Alfonso was
killed by a fall from his horse while hunting, and his young
widow returned, grieving, to her parents in Spain. Moving
among the lovely mosaics of the Alhambra like a slender
shadow in black robes, she was inconsolable. She prayed and
fasted so rigorously that even her pious mother begged her
to be moderate. She spoke much of entering a convent. She was
tired of courts and thrones and vanities, and wanted peace.
The King and Queen remonstrated patiently.

Then there was the business of Cristóbal Colón. After a disappearance of many months, that solemn-eyed vendor of
dreams with the head and bearing of a Roman senator had

suddenly reappeared at Santa Fé before the surrender of
Granada, and since then had been like a shadow at the heels
of any who might have access to the royal ear. Through Luis
de Santángel, Bishop Diego de Deza, the Marqués of Moya
and other friends he renewed his supplications to their Majesties until they received him in audience. The Queen was as
favorably impressed as before, and if she had not been ab-
sorbed in the final events of the Crusade, would probably have
consented. The King was less willing to believe that Columbus
was a man chosen by God for a particular mission, and suggested referring the matter once more to a committee. This was
a convenient way of postponing a decision until a more suitable time, and avoiding a break with Columbus.

No record has been found of this committee's findings, but
they are supposed to have been unfavorable. Columbus's impatience, and the high and mighty tone he took, even with
monarchs, may have irritated some of his questioners. Some
of them, at least, knew more about science in general than he
did, and finding certain of his propositions rather wild—for
he depended much on Sir John Mandeville[3] who described a
Terrestrial Paradise on a mountain so high that it almost
touched the moon—may have doubted others more worthy of
credence. It was probably Columbus's poetry, rather than his
science, that offended. A Dominican astronomer, asking a
stranger why he was so sure of finding land to the west within
a thousand leagues, and receiving some such answer as, "I
am sure, because Our Divine Lord has told me that I should
find land there, for the propagation of the news of His passion and death," or "St. Augustine said—" would probably
have shrugged a little skeptically—not that he disbelieved in
divine revelation, but that he questioned the authenticity of
this particular one. We may conjecture the tone of Columbus
from what he writes in a subsequent letter to the sovereigns.
There was, for instance, a miraculous voice that whispered to
him in the night,

"God will cause thy name to be wonderfully resounded
through the earth, and will give thee the keys of the gates of
the ocean, which are closed with strong chains."

The Queen, who saw the hand of God in all the mazes of
her own life, could readily believe this; but the less intuitive
mind of Fernando looked for objective evidence.

A Patio of the Alhambra, Whence Isabel Sent Columbus
on his Voyage of Discovery

Whatever the details may have been, Columbus left the Court in anger and sorrow, decided to go to France, and started on his way to the seacoast. Fortunately he stopped once more at the Franciscan monastery of La Rábida, overlooking Palos. The good Prior, Father Juan Perez, was delighted to see him again, to talk cosmography with him, to hear the latest tidings of the Crusade that was thrilling all Europe. It has been conjectured that Columbus in his bitterness may have described his plans more frankly to the priest than he had at the Court. At any rate, Friar Juan declared that his going away was preposterous; nor could he believe that the Queen would permit Castile to lose so much glory. He called in a learned physician of Palos, Garcia Fernandez, and Father Antonio Marchena, the astronomer, who heartily agreed. They sent a sailor to the Queen with a letter.

Fray Juan wrote that Columbus was undoubtedly right in his hypothesis, that whoever sent him would gain glory and riches, and the eternal reward of those who propagate the Faith; for he was convinced that Columbus was as sincere in his piety as he was daring and sound in his speculations. Such an opinion from her old confessor, confirming her own impressions, influenced the Queen so profoundly that she sent back 20,000 maravedis in gold florins by the messenger, that Columbus might buy new clothes and a mule; and she bade him return to Court.

"Our Lord has listened to the prayers of His servant," wrote Fray Juan Perez with joy. "The wise and virtuous Doña Isabel, touched by the grace of Heaven, gave a favorable hearing to the words of this poor monk. All has turned out well."

Columbus returned to Santa Fé supremely confident that nothing remained but to sign the contract and assemble his crews. Looking back on that time in his old age, he wrote, "In all men there was disbelief"—by no means an accurate statement—"but to the Queen, my lady, God gave the spirit of understanding and great courage, and made her heiress of all as a dear and much-loved daughter." But Isabel was hardly prepared for the terms that he was about to lay down for her.

Standing before the King and the Queen in the Hall of the Ambassadors, in the Alhambra, the Ligurian weaver evidently informed them, with a lordly air, that it was not merely a

question of three ships and 2,000,000 maravedis. For himself
he wanted nothing, but he had two sons, he was obliged to
think of his posterity. If he failed, he would pay the penalty
with his life. But if he succeeded, his achievement would be
so glorious that all the world would ring with the praises of
the monarchs who sent him; and surely it would not look well
if the man who brought them so much glory did not have
titles and emoluments commensurate with his deeds. Columbus,
as usual, spoke as though his projects were already achieved,
and had little patience with anyone who insisted on regarding
them as unproved hypotheses. And on this occasion he addressed the Kings of Castile in the tone of one monarch treat-
ing with another.

He demanded to be made Admiral of all the seas and countries he was about to discover, the title to remain his during
his life and to descend to his heirs. He was to be Viceroy and
Governor of all continents and islands he might find. He
must have a tenth part of all merchandize—pearls, gold or any
other wealth—to be found, gained, bought or exported from
the countries he was to discover. If any disputes arose over
mercantile matters between those countries and Spain, he was
to be the sole judge. He reserved the right to contribute the
eighth part of the expenses of all ships which might traffic
with those lands, and in return to receive an eighth part of the
profits—this last because he had already tried to overcome
the reluctance of the sovereigns by offering a contribution
of 250,000 maravedis, part of which had been promised him
by the Italian banker Gerardi, of Seville.

The Queen looked at the King, and the King kept staring,
speechless, at Columbus. Fernando had never heard such a
preposterous thing in his life. What, give a man titles and
rewards for something he had not yet done? Viceroy! Admiral! What, make a foreign nobody the social equal of the
King's uncle, the Admiral of Castile? It was well that Don
Fadrique, his grandfather, was not alive to hear that suggestion; his comments would have been vigorous and profane.
Discoverers in Portugal and Spain were commonly rewarded
by captaincies and pensions. The title of Admiral was reserved
for those of the blood royal, or related to it. It was all so
fantastic that the King did not even get angry.

Isabel, too, foresaw the difficulty of bestowing so high a

title upon a foreigner in jealous Castile. The Castilians and Andalusians had never entirely forgiven King Fernando for being an Aragonese. What would they think of making an Italian woolcomber an Admiral? And yet the Queen liked Columbus none the less for his pretensions. There was something attractive in the very magnitude and majesty of the man's effrontery. Only a great man or a lunatic would dare talk in that vein, and this fellow seemed sane enough. Most women are rather drawn to braggarts if their intuition tells them there is ability behind the boasting. And Isabel, of all women, was capable of understanding a man of heroic imagination, who snapped his fingers, as she always had done, in the face of what others believed to be impossible. His piety, of course, did him no harm in her estimation. And perhaps she found it a little amusing that a composite of Odysseus, Amadis de Gaul, poet and mystic monk should also contain a strong dash of Italian peasant acquisitiveness. The chosen instrument of Providence wanted his share of the proceeds, and he wanted it in black and white, for he trusted in no verbal contracts. But King Fernando himself was expert at driving a bargain; and Isabel with all the largeness and generosity of her soul, was capable of haggling if she thought some one was trying to cheat her. But when all was said and done, she was compelled to admit that the King was right. Columbus's demands were preposterous.

The Italian bade a dignified farewell to the monarchs, this time, as he thought, forever. He left the Alhambra, mounted his mule, rode sadly out of the gate and took the road to the west. This was late in January, 1492.

He must have said good-by, however, to some of his friends at court, for he had hardly left the Alhambra when three of them hastened to the Queen to beg her to reconsider—Beatriz de Bobadilla, Marquesa of Moya, Alonsa de Quintanilla, and Luis de Santángel.

Why should the rich *Converso* have put himself to so much trouble over an irascible visionary? "Santángel, an experienced man of affairs and an astute politician, could not be suspected of lending any support to vain chimeras," writes a modern Jew. "It is hard to avoid the impression that he was interested in the project in a way that we cannot now establish."[4] In an attempt to answer this riddle, the theory has been advanced that Columbus promised Santángel large profits from the enslavement of the people of the Indies.[5] The Jews and *Conversos* had always been active in the slave traffic in Spain. And a subsequent letter from Columbus to Santángel will be found to contain some circumstantial evidence tending to support the theory. But conclusive proof that Santángel helped Columbus in the expectation of future profits is lacking. All that we know is that the millionaire lawyer did hasten to the Queen on this occasion, and according to Bishop Las Casas, Columbus's biographer, addressed her in these words:

"Señora, the desire I have always had to serve the King my lord, and Your Highness, and if it be necessary to die for your royal service, has compelled me to appear before Your Highness and to speak of a matter which does not touch me personally, nor am I unaware that it lies beyond the rules and limits of my office, but in the confidence that I have always had in the clemency of Your Highness and in your royal generosity, and that you will consider the affection in which I speak. . . . I say, Señora, that considering many times how generous and constant a spirit God has given to Your Highnesses, to assume grand and praiseworthy undertakings, I have marvelled much that you have not accepted such an enterprise as Cristóbal Colón has offered you, in which so little will be lost in case of failure, so much good be accomplished (in case of success) for the service of God and the benefit of the Church, with so great an exaltation of the royal state of Your Highnesses and the prosperity of all these your realms."

If the Spanish sovereigns lost their opportunity, he went on to say, and some other king took it up, the Queen would reproach herself all the rest of her life. Her enemies would deride her, her fame and the prestige and honor of her kingdoms would suffer exceedingly, her descendants and all posterity would blame her for excessive caution. Columbus appeared to be "a wise and prudent man and one of sound reason."

Isabel evidently felt the force of Santángel's vigorous argument, even though she may have wondered what his motive might be. The grandeur of soul with which Columbus had thrown to the winds all hope of help from Spain rather than compromise his demands had made her regret that she had not managed in some way to detain him; he was, undoubtedly, a great man. As for his titles, she agreed with Santángel that if he failed and was lost, no harm would have been done; on the other hand, if he added new realms to Spain, he would deserve to be an Admiral. The Queen, after all, had given high offices to men of lowly birth, when their merits warranted. But there remained the question of money. The Castilian treasury was bare.

Isabel did not offer to pawn her jewels; they were already pledged as security for war debts. But Santángel pointed a way out of the difficulty. He happened to know that the Holy Brotherhood, of which he and Francisco Pinelo were treasurers, was well supplied with funds received from taxes for its maintenance, and at the command of the Queen he advanced 1,140,000 maravedis out of the society's public funds to Archbishop Talavera[6] to equip Columbus's expedition. At the same time, and from the same funds, he repaid a loan of 1,500,000 to Isaac Abravanel. Both these sums were returned to the Hermandad during the next two years with interest.[7]

All of Columbus's demands were granted in the "capitulations of Santa Fé" drawn up by the secretary Juan de Coloma and signed by the sovereigns April 17, 1492. It is impossible to say whether Fernando in signing them remembered that the bestowal of privileges on an alien was forbidden by the *Ordenamiento de Alcalá*, and expected that the courts might later declare the contract void.

The town of Palos, for some offense against the Crown, was sentenced to provide two caravels, fully manned and equipped, for a two months' voyage. Later, their Majesties agreed to defray the cost of a third ship. The Admiral, now Don Cristóbal Colón, a grandee of Castile, proceeded to Palos, to organize his expedition.

Isabel remained at Granada until Pentecost that year. She spent a great deal of time in reflection over certain reports the Inquisitor General had submitted on the activities of the Jews. In particular she pored over the dossier of a unique murder trial in which the accused were five Jews and six *Conversos*; and late in March, she came to a momentous decision.

XXV

ISABEL and Fernando signed their names on March 31, 1492, to a document commencing thus:

"You know, or ought to know, that since we were informed that there were certain evil Christians in these our realms who judaized and apostatized from our Holy Catholic Faith, on account of the considerable communication of Jews with Christians, we commanded the said (Jews) in the Cortes which we held in the city of Toledo in the past year 1480, to go apart in all the cities, towns and places of our realms . . . and gave them Jeweries and separate places where they might live, hoping that with their segregation the matter might be remedied. And moreover we have endeavored and given orders to have inquisition made in our said realms and seignories; which, as you know, has been done for more than twelve years, and is done; and many guilty persons have been sentenced by it, as is well known. . . . (Yet) there remains and is apparent the great injury to the Christians which has resulted and does result from the participation, conversation and communication which they have held and hold with the Jews, who have demonstrated that they would always endeavor, by all possible ways and manners, to subvert and draw away faithful Christians from our Holy Catholic Faith, and separate them from it, and attract and pervert them to their wicked belief and opinion, instructing them in the ceremonies and observances of their law, holding fasts during which they read and teach them what they have to believe and observe according to their law, causing them and their sons to be circumcized . . . notifying them of the Passover feasts before they come . . . giving them and taking to them from their houses unleavened bread and meat slaughtered with ceremonies . . . persuading them as far as possible to hold and observe the law of Moses, giving them to understand that there was no other true law but that; the which is clear from many utterances and confessions, not only by the Jews themselves, but by those who were perverted and injured by them, which has resulted in great harm, detriment and opprobrium to our Holy Catholic Faith."

Although they had long known of this situation, the sovereigns had hoped that the expulsion of the Jews from Andalusia, where they were doing the greatest harm, would suffice. But it had been plainly demonstrated that the crimes and offenses of the Jews against the Faith were increasing daily, and that nothing would remove the root of the trouble but to drive them from the kingdom. "For when *some serious and detestable crime* is committed by certain ones of a certain college or university, it is right that the college or university be dissolved and annulled, and that the lesser be punished for the greater and the ones for the others; and that those who pervert the good and honest life of cities and towns by the contamination that can injure others be expelled from among the people, even for more trifling causes which are injurious to the Republic. How much more so for the greatest, most perilous and most contagious of crimes, as this is?

"On this account, we with the counsel and advice of many prelates and noblemen and cavaliers of our realms, and of other persons of knowledge and conscience in our council, having given much deliberation to the subject, have decided to command all of the said Jews, men and women, to leave our kingdoms, and never to return to them." All but those who chose to be baptized must depart by July 1 and not come back under pain of death and confiscation. Any who received or sheltered the Jews after the date assigned would have all their goods confiscated. But until the time appointed for the exodus, all Jews would remain under the royal protection, and no one must hurt them or their property under pain of death. The Jews must take out of Spain no gold, silver, minted money, "nor other things forbidden by the laws of our kingdoms, save in merchandize not prohibited or concealed."

For more than four centuries historians have been condemning this law and its authors without deigning to examine the reasons why the King and Queen took so radical a step, and under what circumstances. Public opinion in Spain at that time was undoubtedly with them. It was widely believed that the edict was the direct result of a request by the young Prince Don Juan. According to a story in the Libro Verde de Aragon, King Fernando's Jewish physician, Maestre Ribas Altas, used to wear about his neck a golden ball hung on a gold chain. One day when he was calling at the palace, the Prince opened the ball and found inside a tiny parchment on which was painted a figure of the crucified Christ with one of the physician in an unspeakably obscene and insulting posture. Don Juan was so shocked and disgusted that he became ill, and did not recover until his father promised to expel all the Jews. This tale has been pretty generally rejected. Yet the fact remains that Fernando and Isabel did permit their personal physician to be burned at the stake. We know this from the account of the penancing of a woman named Aldonza at Saragossa in 1488, for judaizing; the record says she was the mother of Doctor Ribas Altas, the King's physician, who was burned previously on account of the picture that Prince Juan found in the gold ball, and that this was the cause of the expulsion of the Jews.[1] Lea concludes that the doctor's execution could have had nothing whatever to do with the exodus, since it happened some years before the edict of 1492.[2] But Lea forgets—though he himself mentioned it on the previous page[3] —that Fernando and Isabel had been contemplating the expulsion of the Jews for several years. They had issued an edict expelling the Jews from Andalusia in 1482, the second year of the Inquisition, though they had later suspended the order; and Fernando, in 1486, had caused all Jews to be expelled from the archbishopric of Saragossa, where Ribas Altas was burned. No final conclusion can be formed on this matter until further evidence is obtained.

However this may be, and granting that innumerable lies were circulated about the Jews, it is a great mistake to assume their complete innocence of all the crimes attributed to them. In June, 1485, at the critical time when Queen Isabel almost broke down in the tower of Vaena on hearing of the defeat of the Count of Cabra near Moclin, the Jews and crypto-Jews of Toledo planned to seize that city during a procession on the feast of Corpus Christi and murder many Christians;

but the plot was detected and punished by the Inquisition.[4]
On Good Friday, 1488, a rabbi and several Jews mocked a
large wooden crucifix at Casar de Palomero and toppled it
over in the dust. Three of them were stoned to death in the
ensuing riot, and the rabbi was burned by the Duke of Alba.[5]

Very deeply rooted was the belief of the Spanish Christians
that Jews sometimes showed their hatred for Christ and his
teachings by crucifying Christian boys on Good Friday, or by
vituperating wax images of the Redeemer. In fact, a Cortes
under one of Isabel's ancestors had passed a law saying,

"And because we have heard it said that in some places
the Jews have made and do make remembrance of the Passion
of Our Lord Jesus Christ in a scandalous fashion, stealing
boys and placing them on the cross, or making wax images
and crucifying them when they could not obtain boys, we
command that if such a thing be done henceforth in any place
in our seignory, if it can be ascertained, all those who are
implicated in the deed shall be arrested and brought before
the King; and when he shall know the truth, he ought to command that they be put to death very ignominiously, as many
of them as there may be."[6]

The charge here given legal sanction cannot be dismissed
as a mere evidence of fanaticism or propaganda, for the fact
is that from time to time Jews actually were convicted of
such crimes. It was the Bishop Juan Árias de Avila, son of
Jewish converts, who passed sentence of death on seventeen
Jews of Segovia in 1468 for the crucifixion of a Christian
boy; and the fact that this incident was long suppressed even
in certain editions of Colmenares' *History of Segovia*, though
it may be read in his autograph manuscript, shows how successful and how insidious has been the great conspiracy to
distort the history of fifteenth century Spain.

Another crime of the same sort during the most anxious
years of the Moorish War—1487 or 1488—gave Torquemada
a powerful argument for the expulsion of the Jews, and was
one of the chief factors, if not the decisive one, in the decision
of Fernando and Isabel. It was the "serious and detestable
crime" referred to indirectly in their edict of March 31.[7] Only
four months previously, in November of 1491, the whole nation had been stirred to wrath by the publication of the sentence. The burning of the two Jews and six *Conversos* who

were convicted did not appease public opinion, and the grave danger of another general massacre as horrible as that of 1391 must be reckoned among the weighty considerations that urged the King and Queen to their decision.[8]

The complete record of testimony in the trial of one of the accused has been available since Fidel Fita published it in 1887 in the Bulletin of the Royal Academy at Madrid from the original manuscript in his possession.[9] Since then it has been no longer possible to pretend successfully that it was a popular myth or a bit of anti-Jewish propaganda released by the Inquisitor General to justify the edict of March 31. Yet almost no notice has been taken of this invaluable source-material outside of Spain. Mr. Sabatini gives a lengthy account of it in his "Torquemada and the Spanish Inquisition," but makes two omissions of the gravest character. And in Lea's four fat volumes on the Spanish Inquisition, the whole case is dismissed with a sneer in one paragraph. Lea records that "in June, 1490, a *Converso* named Benito Garcia . . . was arrested at Astorga on the charge of having a consecrated wafer in his knapsack. The episcopal vicar, Dr. Pedro de Villada, *tortured him repeatedly* till he obtained a confession implicating five other *Conversos* and six Jews in a plot to effect a conjuration with a human heart and a consecrated host, whereby to cause the madness and death of all Christians, the destruction of Christianity and the triumph of Judaism. Three of the implicated Jews were dead, but the rest of those named were promptly arrested and their trial was carried on by the Inquisition. After *another year spent in torturing the accused, there emerged a story of the crucifixion at La Guardia of a Christian child*, whose heart was cut out for the purpose of the conjuration. The whole tissue was so evidently the creation of the torture chamber that it was *impossible to reconcile the discrepancies* in the confessions of the accused. . . . The Inquisitors finally abandoned the attempt to frame a consistent narrative, and November 16, 1491, the accused were executed at Ávila."[10]

If this be true—let us keep in mind the italicized words and see whether or not the record confirms them—there is a ruthlessly logical conclusion which appears to have escaped the notice of Lea and some of the others. If the Inquisitors sent eight men to a shameful death without being convinced beyond a reasonable doubt of their guilt, the honest verdict of history cannot shrink from finding not only Torquemada and his judges but King Fernando and Queen Isabel, Cardinal Mendoza and several of the most illustrious professors of Salamanca University guilty of complicity in one of the most brutal judicial murders on record. But let us see, if possible, what really happened before venturing an opinion:

In June, 1490, a woolcomber named Benito Garcia, a *Converso* of about sixty years, stopped at an inn at Astorga. Some drunkards rifled his knapsack and found in it what appeared to be a Host from the altar of a Catholic Church. They dragged him to the vicar, Dr. Villada, who had him tortured twice—once with the "water cure" and once by two twists of a rope. The record we have of his confession on Trinity Sunday, June 6, says nothing of the Host or of any murder, but gives at some length what Benito revealed about the judaizing of certain friends. In his youth he had voluntarily become a Christian, but about five years ago a secret Jew named Juan de Ocaña had urged him to give up Christianity, "saying that he should not believe in Jesus Christ, nor Holy Mary, and that the Law of Moses was the true one . . . and he believed it, and . . . performed many judaical actions," such as staying away from Mass, eating meat on Fridays, and so on. He observed certain Jewish rites in the house of Ça Franco and his son Yucé, two Jews of Tenbleque.[11] And ever since then he had been really a Jew at heart. During the past five years he had made false confessions to the curate at La Guardia, and had never received Holy Communion, believing that "it was all humbug, the *corpus Christi*," and that "when he saw the *corpus Christi*, or they took it to any sick person, he despised it and spat."[12]

On the first day of July, 1490, Ça and his son Yucé, a lad of twenty, were arrested in consequence of Benito's revelations, and taken to the prison of the Inquisition at Segovia. This prison had formerly been the house of the Marqués and Marquesa of Moya, who had donated it to the Holy Office.[13] The use of a former residence of the Queen's personal friend Beatriz de Bobadilla and her husband Cabrera suggests how scrupulously Torquemada had sought to avoid one of the abuses that had crept into the thirteenth century Inquisition. The prisoners were kept on the two lower floors, and the

Inquisitors had their offices above. From now on Yucé becomes the chief character in the mystery, for the dossier of his trial is the only one so far discovered, out of eight. Parts or fragments of others, such as the above confession of Benito, are included only as they have a bearing on the case of Yucé.

During July the young Jew became ill, and thought he was going to die. The Inquisitors sent a physician, Antonio de Ávila, a resident of Segovia, to prescribe for him. This Antonio was probably a converted Jew, for he understood Hebrew, and Yucé begged him to ask the Inquisitors to send him "a Jew who would say to him the things that the Jews say when they wish to die." Here was an opportunity which the Inquisitors were not slow to grasp. On July 19, 1490, they sent one "Rabbi Abrahan" to console the young prisoner. In reality the rabbi was a learned master of theology, Fray Alonso Enriquez, also a converted Jew whose name originally was Abraham Shesheth.[14] During the conversation the "rabbi" asked why Yucé had been arrested. Yucé answered evasively, and as a matter of fact he had no definite knowledge on the point, for no charge had been made against him. The rabbi then said that if Don Abraham Senior knew of the case, he might get Yucé off, and he himself would ask him. Now, Don Abraham Senior was none other than the chief rabbi of Castile, a member of the synagogue of Segovia, and a man so rich, powerful and capable that the King and Queen had made him their factor general. The mention of his name encouraged Yucé to confide to the "rabbi" that he had been arrested for the *mita* (death) of a *nahar* (boy) after the manner of *otohays* (that man), and he was willing to have Don Abraham Senior know it, but no one else, "for the love of the Creator." The "rabbi" departed, promising to return.

On the same day the physician Antonio de Ávila made a sworn deposition before a notary that he had overheard Yucé tell the "rabbi" that he had been arrested for the murder of a *nahar* after the manner of *otohays*, which he took to refer to Jesus Christ, "for so the Jews call Him in vituperation." According to Antonio, Yucé said this happened about eleven years before. Here is a discrepancy, for all other references to the crime place it about 1488. But as Fita reasonably suggests, Antonio's hearing may have been bad, or he may have confused the Hebrew words for "eleven" and "two," which have similar sounds. Fray Alonso confirmed this conversation under oath October 26, 1490, and added that he visited the prisoner a second time eight days later, but could get nothing out of him. On that occasion Yucé appeared to be in great fear of Antonio, the physician, he said.

What had happened in the meantime? Had some intimation of Yucé's startling admission reached the synagogue of Segovia, and had some influential person found a way to warn the young Jew to say nothing? This is Fita's conjecture. But when Yucé made a sworn deposition more than a year afterward—September 16, 1491—describing his conversation with the "rabbi" and confirming the statements of Fray Alonso and Antonio, he apparently had no idea that he had been imposed upon.

Whether or not Benito had spoken of a murdered boy in his confession at Astorga we may not know until his dossier has been found. But the striking admission of Yucé to the "rabbi" must have shown the Inquisitors at Segovia that they were on the track of big game. Undoubtedly they went directly with their evidence to the Inquisitor General, who was then in Segovia at the convent of Santa Cruz, of which he was still prior. He considered the case so important that when the King and Queen summoned him to Court, on their leaving Córdoba for Granada August 20, he deferred his journey for several days to organize the investigation.

On August 27, 1490, Torquemada commanded three of his most trustworthy judges to take charge of the case—Doctor Pedro de Villada, abbot of San Millan and San Marciel; Juan Lopes de Cigales, canon of Cuenca, and Fray Ferrando de Santo Domingo. He directed them to take possession of the persons and property of Yucé and Ça Franco, of Rabbi Mosé Abenamías of Zamora, of the four Franco brothers of La Guardia ("New Christians," not related to Yucé and Ça); and of Juan de Ocaña and Benito Garcia, both *Conversos* of La Guardia. "And since at present we are occupied in many and arduous affairs," wrote the Inquisitor General, "we cannot act in person, but confide in your fidelity, knowledge, experience and good conscience" to investigate thoroughly, "sentence and relax to the secular arm those whom you find guilty, and absolve and set free those who are without blame."

The arduous business mentioned by Torquemada was probably the summons to Granada. We know, too, that about this time he had a conversation with Don Abraham Senior, in which he pleaded for certain tax concessions for the citizens of his native town of Torquemada. The great rabbi refused, saying he had already assigned the revenues of Torquemada for that year to Diego de la Nuela, but would do otherwise in future. It is a pity that we have no complete record of the conversation of the two powerful opponents, the rabbi and the inquisitor, disguising their hostility under polite phrases.

The dossier of Yucé now shows a lapse of two months, which may perhaps have been caused by efforts of influential Jews to have the proceedings quashed. The next examination of the prisoner by the Inquisitors was on October 27, 1490. He told them that about three years before, "more or less," he had gone to La Guardia in the archbishopric of Toledo to buy wheat to make unleavened bread for the Passover of Alonso Franco, a shepherd, one of the four brothers. Alonso asked why it was necessary to have unleavened bread, and Yucé explained. They talked of one thing and another, until at last Alonso made the extraordinary confidence that he and his brothers one Good Friday had crucified a boy "in the form in which the Jews had crucified Jesus Christ."

All this time there is no indication of any attempt to torture Yucé. When at last he was *threatened* with torture a whole year later, the fact was set down very casually, as a matter of course; and from time to time the torture of other prisoners was faithfully recorded by the notaries. The Spanish Inquisitors seem to have had none of the squeamishness of their thirteenth century forerunners about mentioning the *"tormentos"* by which evidence was obtained. When nothing is said of torture in connection with a confession, therefore, it is safe to assume that no torture was applied.

After another unexplained delay, during which the Inquisitors were probably examining the Francos of La Guardia, they transferred Yucé and the others to Ávila. The reason for this does not appear. Perhaps the prison at Segovia was too near the wealthy synagogue to which Don Abraham Senior belonged. Hernando de Talavera, former confessor to the Queen, must have given his consent to the transfer, for he was then Bishop of Ávila and his approval was necessary.

Six months and a half after Benito's arrest—Friday, December 17, 1490—Yucé was placed on trial and formally accused of judaizing and murder by the Promotor Fiscal (or prosecutor) Guevara, who declared that the young Jew had attracted Christians to his belief, told them "that the law of Jesus Christ was a false and pretended law and that no such law was ever imposed or established by God. *And with faithless and depraved mind he was associated with others in crucifying a Christian boy on a Good Friday, somewhat in the same way and with such enmity and cruelty as his ancestors had crucified Our Redeemer Jesus Christ,* mocking him and spitting upon him and giving him many blows and other wounds to scorn and ridicule our holy Catholic Faith and the Passion of our Savior Jesus Christ." Finally, the Promotor Fiscal said that Yucé had been engaged, as a principal actor, in an outrage upon a consecrated Host, with the intent of causing the Christians to go insane and die, and the Christian religion to perish, and the Jews to gain possession of the goods of all the Catholic Christians. He demanded sentence of death, saying, "And I swear before God and before this cross, on which I place my right hand, that I do not make this demand and accusation against the said Yucé Franco maliciously, but believe him to have committed all that I have said."·

"It is the greatest falsehood in the world," replied Yucé, according to the notary Martin Peres; and he denied every charge the Promotor had made.

The Inquisitors then asked him whether he desired counsel, and he said yes. They appointed the Bachelor Sanç and Juan de Pantigoso—for under Torquemada's rulings each prisoner was allowed two lawyers—to represent him. Five days later, December 22, Yucé asked for Martin Vasquez of Ávila as additional counsel, and the request was granted at once. On the same day Vasquez read to the Court the reply that the Bachelor Sanç had drawn up in rebuttal of the Promotor's charges. It was a vigorous and able defense, obviously the work of a good lawyer. First, he denied the jurisdiction of the court of Ávila, since Yucé lived in the diocese of Toledo. Further, he said the charge was "very general, vague and obscure; for in his accusation the said Fiscal does not express, nor clearly, the places, years, months, days, times, nor persons in which and with whom he says my client committed the crimes he accuses him of." And Yucé, being a Jew, could not properly be accused of heresy or apostasy. If the Inquisitors admitted the accusation, it would be prejudicial to their consciences, and if they did, Sanç would appeal from their decision. Finally, he entered a complete denial of all the charges. His client was but a boy so ignorant that he did not even know the Law of Moses, and so engrossed in his trade of shoemaker that he had no desire to judaize among Christians. If he had offended, he had done so unwittingly. Certainly he had nothing to do with crucifying a boy or making a charm with a Host. The attorney demanded that Yucé be set free, and his good name and all his property restored to him. Otherwise he asked that the Promotor Fiscal be instructed to give a bill of particulars, with names and places.

On January 22, the Fiscal replied that he was not obliged to be more specific than he had been, in such a case as this, and asked that testimony be admitted and the case put to the proof. The Inquisitors ordered both sides to present evidence in thirty days.

Sanç had scored a point for the defense when he denied the jurisdiction of the Court, and Torquemada, who was always a stickler for regularity, had to send to Cardinal Mendoza, then at Guadalajara, for permission to try Yucé at Ávila instead of at Toledo. The Cardinal wrote a letter, February 12, 1491, delegating his faculties as Ordinary to the Inquisitors at Ávila.

On the ninth of April following, Benito Garcia was placed in a room directly under Yucé's, and the two conversed, as the Inquisitors had intended they should, through a hole in the floor.

"Jew," said Benito, "have you a needle to give me?"

"Only a shoemaker's needle," replied Yucé. "Where are you?"

"In this prison, below. And know that your father, Don Ça Franco, is here."

"He couldn't be!"

Benito said he had seen him, for the *padres* had confronted them to see whether they knew each other. Benito, who seems to have been a garrulous fellow, said among other things that "he had become a woolcomber in an evil hour, and that the devil had led him there; and the dog of a doctor (Villada), had given him two hundred lashes in Astorga, and a torment of water; and another night two *garrotes.*" The lashes, as will appear presently, were not a torture, but a punishment. A *garrote* was the twisting of a cord about the arms or legs of a prisoner. It would appear from this statement that Benito was tortured twice at Astorga. He told Yucé that he had told them enough to burn him.

Presently Yucé began playing on a guitar.

"Don't play!" cried Benito from below. "Have sorrow for your father, for the Inquisitors have told him that little by little they are getting enough to burn him."

Benito heard Yucé say his morning prayer commencing, *"Helohay nesamá,"* and on one occasion he asked the young Jew to pray to the Creator to take them out of this prison, but he had little hope of it; for under torture he had said "more than he knew"—*mas de lo que sabia,* a phrase that might mean "more than was true" or "more than he meant to tell."

On the following Sunday Benito remarked that these In-quisitors were gods, and Yucé answered—according to what he told the Inquisitors afterwards—"Don't say so!"

"I say that they are worse than Antichrists," insisted Benito. And he added that Antichrist was he who was a Jew and turned Christian; and that his father had cursed him when he turned Christian forty years before. Presently he asked Yucé to lend him a knife that he might mutilate himself in such a way as to remove the evidence of his having been circumcized.

"Don't do that, you'll die," said Yucé.

"Die, Hell!"[15] retorted Benito. "I'd rather die that way than be burned."

He then scoffed at the Christian religion at some length, saying it was all idolatry, and asked several questions about the Jewish religion, which Yucé answered. "The Prior of Santa Cruz is the greatest Antichrist," declared Benito. He advised Yucé, if he ever got free, to tell the Alcaide Pena of La Guardia, who had influence with the Queen and would get them all out of prison. The two hundred lashes given him at Astorga, he said, were for beating his children because they had gone to a Catholic church. And all the reward he had ever got for contributing to a new holy water fount for a church was the water cure at Astorga. He declared that "for the eyes that he had in his face he would not confess or know anything; that he, for what he had known, had lost body and soul; that they held him prisoner for his property, and for no other reason; and that if he got free, he would go to Judea."

This, at least, was what Yucé related to the Inquisitors when they made him a visit later on the same day. So far he had been careful not to incriminate his father or himself, or any living Jews. He sealed the fate of the *Converso* Benito, however, by telling the Inquisitors, on the same day, that Maestre Yuçá Tazarte, a Jewish physician, then deceased, had told him that he had asked Benito to get a consecrated Host, and Benito had got it by stealing the keys of the Church of La Guardia and hiding them in the river. On that occasion Benito was arrested, but managed to get himself cleared after two days in jail. Tazarte, who it appears was a wizard as well as a doctor, told Yucé that he had planned to make the Host into a cord with certain knots, and to send it to Rabbi Peres, a Jewish physician of Toledo.

On the next day, April 10, 1491, the young cobbler told the Inquisitors that about four years before, more or less, his brother Mosé, now dead, told him that he and Tazarte, the four Christian Francos of La Guardia and Benito had made an agreement to use a consecrated Host in a charm to bring it about that "the justice of the Christians" could not harm them. Mosé asked Yucé to join them, saying he had the Host in his possession. Yucé replied that he was on his way to Murcia, and did not care to. The conjuration failed. Two years later Mosé said that he and Tazarte had been to La Guardia to arrange for a second one.

Yucé voluntarily sent for the Inquisitors on May 7, 1491, saying he wished to declare more. He now remembered that he had asked his brother Mosé where the conspirators could hold the conjuration without knowledge of their wives, who were all Catholics. Mosé replied, in some caves between Dosbarrios and La Guardia, on the road going to Ocaña.

A month later, June 9, Yucé told the Inquisitors that about four years before he had gone "one evil day" to Tenbleque to be bled by Maestre Yuçá Tazarte. And he heard Mosé say that Tazarte and the Francos of La Guardia had made a

charm *with the heart of a Christian boy* and a consecrated
Host, that the Inquisitors might die if they attempted to take
any action against the conspirators.

After a few more weeks in prison, Yucé made some highly
interesting revelations on July 19, 1491, asking immunity for
himself, and being promised it on condition that he tell the
whole truth. He explained his failure to confess previously by
saying that all the conspirators had sworn an oath that if
they were arrested, they would tell nothing for a year, the
period within which Tazarte promised that the Inquisitors
would die, should they attempt anything. As Yucé had been
arrested July 1, 1490, the year was up, and he had waited
a few more days, evidently, for good measure.

Put under oath according to the Jewish form, he said that
about three years before all the prisoners were present in a
cave between La Guardia and Dosbarrios, a little apart from
the road on the right hand side going from La Guardia to
Dosbarrios. Alonso Franco, one of the "Christians" of La
Guardia, showed them the heart of a boy, which seemed not
many days out of the body, and a Host, which he said was
consecrated, both in a wooden box. Tazarte took them in his
hand and went to a corner, where he said he had to make a
certain conjuration to cause the Inquisitors to go mad and die
within a year after they attempted anything.

The Inquisitors asked where the heart came from. Yucé
replied that he did not know. But Alonso Franco said that
he and some of his brothers had crucified a Christian boy and
taken the heart from him. On a later occasion they had given a
second consecrated Host, wrapped in parchment and tied
with purple silk, to Benito, to take to a Jew named Mosé
Abenamías, a rabbi, in Zamora, with a letter saying they were
sending him a yard of cloth. Yucé thought Benito had gone
first to Santiago, and then to Astorga, where he was arrested.

That afternoon Yucé remembered having seen the *Conversos*—the Francos, Benito and Juan de Ocaña—take a
Christian boy, three or four years old, into the cave, and
after they had stripped him, they crucified him on some crossed
poles, and gagged him, buffeted him, pulled his hair, whipped
him, spat on him, and crowned him with some thorns from
a gorse bush. Alonso Franco opened the veins of both his
arms and let him bleed for half an hour, and caught the blood

from one arm in a copper cauldron, and that from the other in a "yellow cup such as they call *toscas* in Ocaña." Lopé Franco whipped the boy, and Juan de Ocaña crowned him with thorns. Juan Franco opened the little victim's side with a knife. Garcia Franco, the fourth brother, took out the heart from under the breast and put a little salt on it. Benito gave the boy buffets and pulled his hair. Maestre Tazarte spat on him, struck him, and pulled his hair. So did Mosé, the dead brother of Yucé. But Yucé and his father Ça did nothing; they were only innocent onlookers.

Garcia and Juan Franco took the small corpse from the cave, Juan holding the hands and Garcia the feet. Yucé didn't know where they buried him, but later heard Tazarte say they had buried him in the valley of La Guardia. Yucé told Tazarte that it was *mal siglo de Dios* when he and his father got mixed up in such business.

Alonso kept the heart until they all gathered in the cave a second time, when Tazarte made his *conjuro*. Was it day or night? asked the Inquisitors. Night, said Yucé, and they had candles of white wax in the cave, and hung a cloak over the entrance to keep the light from being seen.

Asked whether any boy had been missing thereabouts at that time, he said he heard one was lost in Lillo, and one in La Guardia had gone with his uncle to the vineyards, and had never after been seen. The Francos in their business came and went to Murcia. They could easily have got a boy on the road, and no one would know. They had sardine barrels on their wagon, and some were empty. A boy could have been hidden in one of them.

All this was told by Yucé little by little in answer to numerous questions. Afterwards his deposition was read to him, and he confirmed it under oath.

Armed with the information they had, the Inquisitors turned their attention to Yucé's father, Ça, whom Yucé had definitely placed in the cave; and on the next day the old man —he was eighty—was sworn after the Jewish manner. He admitted that he and Yucé were in the cave between La Guardia and Dosbarrios, and that they saw the others bring a Christian boy and crucify him. It was the *Conversos*, however, who did this. He and his son Yucé were only spectators. The notary, summarizing his deposition, added, "And he saw his son Yucé Franco give a little push to the boy, as is more fully set forth in the confession of the said Don Ça Franco, Jew." The dossier of Ça, containing his full confession, has not yet been found. But it is clear that he implicated Yucé. Probably the Inquisitors told him enough of Yucé's confession to make him believe that all was known, and further denial useless. Nothing is said of Ça's being tortured on this occasion.

During July, Benito was again placed under Yucé's room, and their conversations were carefully noted by an *alguacil*, who was listening. Yucé asked "Why did you accuse me?" and Benito replied, "Keep quiet, for I have not said anything about you."

On September 16 Yucé was asked whom he had talked with in the prison at Segovia. He related his conversation with "Rabbi Abrahan." What had he meant by the *mita* of a *nahar* after the manner of *otohays*? The crucifixion of the boy in the cave by the Francos of La Guardia, said Yucé.

During the last week in September, the torture was applied to Benito, to Juan Franco, and to Juan de Ocaña, separately. All confessed, and their confessions agreed with Yucé's in all essentials. The discrepancies are slight, and such as commonly occur between two eye-witnesses of one event. Garcia Franco, placed under Yucé's room, told him that Benito had been tortured. If any of the others were tortured, he said, they must deny everything.

All this time the Inquisitors were trying to learn more about the identity of the murdered boy, and to incriminate Rabbi Abenamías at Zamora. He was examined later by another tribunal, but exculpated himself.

Three of the prisoners—Yucé, Benito and Juan de Ocaña —were asked separately on October 12 whether each would repeat his confession in the presence of the others. On consenting, they were confronted, and all repeated what they had said before. The stories agreed in all the main points, as to the boy, the crucifixion in the cave, the time. Yucé and his father and Juan Franco were confronted on the seventeenth, with similar results. "They said it was true enough," wrote the Notary Juan de Leon. Juan Franco admitted having cut out the child's heart.

All that had directly implicated Yucé so far had been his

father's statement about the "little push" he gave the boy; but Benito now proceeded to draw him further into the vortex. He told the Inquisitors on October 20 that Yucé had pulled the child's hair and whipped him with the rest, saying they should crucify him, that "it was all humbug, the law of the Christians," that the enchantment would cause all Christians to die and end their law, that they were all idolaters, and so were their saints. Benito confirmed this next day under oath.

On the same day Juan de Ocaña confessed that when the little victim was being scourged, his executioners all addressed him as though he were Jesus Christ, saying, "Traitor, deceiver, who when he preached preached lies against the law of Moses, now you shall pay here for the things you said in that time!" And the five Jews—Ça and his two sons and Tazarte and David all said, "Now you shall pay here what you did in another time. For you thought to undo us and exalt yourself. All the worse for you! You have thought to destroy us, but we will destroy you as a false deceiver!" And when they crucified him, said Juan de Ocaña, *Yucé drew blood* from his arm with a little knife. Asked where the boy was from, the witness said Mosé, deceased brother of Yucé, had brought him from Quintanar to Tenbleque on the back of an ass; and that he was the son of Alonso Martin of Quintanar, so Mosé said; and that Mosé and Yucé and their father Ça and Tazarte had brought him to the cave on the ass. In fact, it was Yucé who summoned the Franco brothers of La Guardia and Benito to the cave.

Here is the most serious discrepancy, for Yucé had said that Alonso Franco had obtained the boy. But as Sabatini has suggested, it is possible that Juan de Ocaña suspected or was told by the Inquisitors that Yucé had incriminated him, and in his fury sought revenge by placing both Yucé and Ça in major roles, to ensure their being burned with him. This view is supported by the fact that one of the Franco brothers of La Guardia afterwards confessed to having obtained the boy.

On October 21, 1491, the Promotor Fiscal Guevara added to his indictment of Yucé the charge of having vituperated Christ in the person of the boy, accused him of being a principal in the crime, and demanded judgment.

Now comes a most important part of the trial, of which

absolutely no mention is made in Sabatini's long account or in Lea's summary paragraph. It is highly important not only in its bearing upon the probable guilt or innocence of the accused, but in the new light it throws upon Torquemada's methods. The Inquisitor Fray Ferrando took all the evidence in the case to Salamanca, to the monastery of Saint Stephen where Columbus had been received with such kindness after his rejection by the Junta of Córdoba, and there, on Tuesday, October 25, he submitted the whole dossier to a jury, including several noted Renaissance scholars who occupied the principal chairs at the University of Salamanca. There were seven members of this jury—Maestre Fray Juan de Santispiritus, professor of Hebrew; Maestre Fray Diego de Bretonia, professor of Sacred Scripture; Fray Antonio de la Pena, Prior of the monastery and candidate for a master's degree in theology; Señor Doctor Anton Rodriguez Cornejo, professor of canon law; Doctor Diego de Burgos, professor of civil law; Doctor Juan de Covillas, professor of canon law in the college of the city of Salamanca, and Fray Sebastian de Hueta, religious of Saint Stephen's monastery.[16] Probably some of these men had discussed Columbus's plan with him, and had helped to have his case reopened.

Each member of the jury was placed under oath, laying his hand on the cross and the holy gospels, and swearing to keep the proceedings secret until sentence was determined, and to "determine and speak the truth and vote on this process according to God and their consciences." After three days they returned a unanimous verdict of guilty against Yucé and declared that he ought to be relaxed to the secular arm and all his goods confiscated.[17] All that we have is their verdict in Yucé's case; but it is a fair assumption that all eight dossiers were submitted to them.

On October 26, the day after the meeting of the jury, the Promotor Fiscal and Yucé both appeared before the Inquisitor Villada, and demanded access to the depositions of all witnesses. The Inquisitor ordered copies and transcriptions of all the depositions to be given to each of the parties, with all facts and circumstances by which the names of witnesses could be learned omitted—this was customary to prevent the murder of witnesses by the relatives of the accused—and gave the parties three days to file objections.

Yucé asked—probably under instructions from his counsel —for the names as well as the depositions of the witnesses against him, with a declaration of the day, month, year and place "of each thing"; for he admitted nothing except what he had already confessed, and still denied active participation in the crime. If the names and details were withheld, he would appeal "to whom the law provided" and he called upon the said notary to witness it. Guevara, the Promotor, objected, threatening to appeal on his side if the Inquisitor granted Yucé's request. But the Inquisitor overruled the objections of the Promotor, "for he was ready to do justice," he said, and he ordered the depositions given to Yucé, with the new details. The names apparently were withheld, however, for three days later he complained on this score when he presented a long and skilful defense drawn up by the Bachelor Sanç. He proceeded on the assumption that the chief witnesses against him were Juan Franco, Benito, and Juan de Ocaña, and he demanded that their testimony be excluded because of its discrepancies, because they had already confirmed his confession in his presence, and because they were all criminals and accomplices in the crime and hence untrustworthy. Under the rules of the Inquisition, wrote Sanç, the evidence of criminals could be admitted only when it concurred so indubitably as to force upon the judges the conviction of its truth; but such was not the case here.

Sanç made the further point that since the witnesses against Yucé had previously sworn to the contrary of what they now confessed, they were perjurers; "and being such, no faith ought to be given them or can be attributed to them." Their testimony was given with malice and hate on account of the truth that he spoke against them before the Inquisitors. "Since they know that their condemnation is certain, they wish that I likewise should be condemned with them." He pleaded that he was a Jew and only a boy when the crime was committed, and repeated that though he was present he was only an innocent onlooker.

Taking up the testimony of his enemies individually, Yucé said that Juan Franco's was vague and general, and did not state anything specific that Yucé had done to make him a principal. Benito had deposed that Yucé struck the boy and drew blood from his arm with a little knife, but he was the

only one who said so. As for Juan de Ocaña, he had testified
that Yucé struck the boy and spat in his face, whereas it was
Juan de Ocaña himself who had done these things.

Yucé's defense was that of a man fighting desperately for
his life, and under the circumstances it was a good one. The
Inquisitors allowed the Promotor Fiscal three days in which
to reply to it. He entered a general denial, and demanded that
since it was obvious that Yucé was not speaking the truth,
the Inquisitors formally put him to the *quistión de tormento*,
since "in a case of law of. this kind it is demanded and
permitted."

The Inquisitor Villada said that he had heard all the Promotor had said, and that he felt obliged to deny his request
for the torture of Yucé. A second request of the Promotor
must have been granted, however, for four days later we
find Yucé being taken to the torture chamber for the first
time. The Inquisitors urged him "affectionately, with all humanity" to tell the truth. If he did so they would treat him
mercifully, so far as conscience and justice would allow. As
Yucé's reply was not convincing, they ordered Diego Martin
to take him to "the house where the torments were given,"
and there he was stripped and tied to a ladder by hands and
feet. This form of torture, known as the "water cure," had
been substituted by Torquemada for the more violent methods
used in the thirteenth century; and barbarous as it appears to
us, it was undoubtedly far less dangerous to life and limb than
the strappado and the rack had been, nor did it inflict the
excruciating mental torment of certain "third degree" methods used by the police in some of our American cities. The
prisoner's nostrils were gagged, his jaws held apart by an
iron prong, and a piece of linen placed over his mouth. Water
was slowly poured into the cloth, carrying it into the throat.
The prisoner must swallow what water he could to make
room for air to pass into his lungs. He experienced all the
fear and some of the sensations of suffocation without actually
suffocating; and if he squirmed, the cords hurt his limbs.
Furthermore, if he proved too stubborn, the attendant gave
the cords a twist or a *garrote*.

Yucé was now informed that if he would not confess all
he knew he alone would be responsible for whatever happened
to him; and the young Jew, rather than take the "water cure,"

said he would tell all he knew. Fifteen questions, formally drawn up in advance, were propounded to him. Where had Juan Franco obtained the boy? In Toledo; Juan had told him so before the others; and had kept the child in the inn called La Hos at La Guardia a whole day until the night of the crucifixion. Juan had said that when he went to Toledo to sell a cartload of wheat, he saw the boy in a doorway, and enticed him away with a nougat.

The Inquisitors were still curious as to why they had crucified the boy, insteading of killing him in some other way to obtain the heart. Yucé replied that it was to insult Jesus Christ; and at this point, under fear of torture, he attributed to Benito and to the four Franco brothers some very lewd and blasphemous gibes, spoken to the child but intended for the person of Jesus. The murderers jeered also at the Blessed Virgin, and repeated a scurrilous account of the Incarnation that had been current among Jews for centuries.

In each case it was Tazarte the wizard who spoke first, and the others—all but Yucé and Ça—imitated him. Pressed further by the Inquisitors, Yucé now admitted that he and his father had joined in the chorus of foul insults. Tazarte had spoken first, then the Jews followed, and finally the Christians took up the vituperations, crying, "Villain, traitor, trickster," and more scurrilous epithets.[18]

Asked further about the Host sent to Zamora, Yucé said that Rabbi Abenamías himself was not to perform the second enchantment, but was to have it done by a certain "wise man" of that town. Where had the Host been obtained? Alonso Franco had got it in the Church of Romeral, from the sexton or sacristan. This was the Host given to Tazarte with the boy's heart. But where did the other Host come from, that they had given to Benito? Alonso Franco said he had got it from the Church in La Guardia. Yucé didn't know who had given the Host to Alonso. It was Alonso who first set the plot in motion by appealing to Tazarte for supernatural aid after he had been made to march in a procession as a penitent by the Inquisitors of Toledo.[19]

Two days later, when Yucé was asked to confirm this confession he asked to have it read to him, and when it was read, said it was all correct, except that Garcia Franco and Juan Franco together had brought the boy to the cave, one remaining with him at La Hos, the other going to La Guardia and saying that he had broken the cart and had left the axle (no doubt the one used as part of the cross) to be repaired. And Yucé added further that he had been one of the six signers of the letter that had been given Benito to take to Zamora with the Host. Also, Tazarte had told them a filthy anecdote about the person of Jesus Christ.

The day after Yucé's confession, his old father was summoned. After the usual formula, he said that it was Tazarte who had invited him and his sons to join the plot, saying that it was necessary to have five Jews in it as well as five Christians, to ensure its complete efficacy. The old Jew was now placed on the *escalera* and given a jar of water. Then, his tongue having been loosened, he was asked what words were spoken to the crucified boy. He confirmed Yucé's testimony, saying that all had cried, "This villainous preacher!" and "You, why do you call yourself God, why do you do it? Are you not a man like us and the son of a man? . . . Go for a rogue! Why do you deceive the people? What a traitor you are, swindler, seducer of the world, liar—preaching such things!" First Tazarte said these things, then the Jews, then the Christians.

Why were such things said? To vituperate Jesus Christ, said Ça. Why had they crucified the boy instead of killing him some other way? This was necessary to cause all Christians to go insane and die, so that the Jews would remain lords of the land.

That same day Juan Franco was placed on the *escalera*. Asked what the vituperations were, he said they had all cried, "Death to this little traitor, our enemy who goes deceiving the world with his words and calls himself Savior of the world and King of the Jews!"

In all these torture scenes—which are frankly described in contrast to the evasive methods used earlier in France—it is significant that the tenor of the answer is never suggested by the form of the Inquisitor's question. There are no queries such as "Did any one call Jesus Christ a traitor? Did any one deny that he was the Savior of the world? Did any one do this or say that?" On the contrary, what our lawyers call leading questions appear to have been very carefully excluded by the scrupulous Torquemada. The questions are of this sort:

"Who was present? What did they do? Why was this done?
Who did it first?" It is impossible to believe after reading
the testimony in Yucé's dossier that the evidence came from
any source except from the prisoners themselves. The claim of
Jewish writers that it was concocted by the Inquisitors for
propaganda purposes might be more plausible if the testimony
had been made public; but the fact that it remained hidden for
four centuries strongly supports the internal evidence of its
authenticity.

Benito was questioned again—without torture—on November 4; and he now remembered that all had said, "Crucify
this enchanter who called himself our King and said our temple had to be destroyed! Crucify him, this dog, crucify him!"
And they called him "deceiver and enchanter," and said "that
he was the son of a corrupt woman, and the son of Joseph,
and that he wished to destroy the Jews and their law, but they
would destroy him." Otherwise he confirmed what Yucé and
Ça had said.

It will be noted that all the confessions agree as to the
tenor of the vituperations, but differ somewhat in phraseology.
This is all the more convincing. If the recollections of various
witnesses corresponded word for word, the fact would be
highly suspicious. But human testimony does vary in just this
way.

On November 11, 1491, the Inquisitors submitted their
evidence to a second jury of learned men in Ávila. There were
five of them: the Licenciate Álvaro de Santa Estevan, Queen
Isabel's corregidor for the town of Ávila; Ruy Garcia Manso,
Bishop Talavera's provisor; Fray Rodrigo Vela, guardian or
head of the Franciscan monastery at Ávila; Doctor Tristan,
canon of Ávila; and the Bachelor Juan de Sant Estevan, son
of the corregidor. The notary Martin Peres was instructed
to ask each of them separately two questions: first, whether
the Inquisitors had jurisdiction over Yucé and Ça and could
lawfully pass judgment on them; and second, whether the
accused were guilty and ought to be relaxed to the justice of
the secular arm. Each of the learned men, "according to God
and his conscience," gave an affirmative answer to both
questions.

Twelve educated men, all under oath, passed upon the evidence in this case in addition to the three Inquisitors, and all voted for conviction.

On November 14 four of the prisoners—Yucé and Ça, Benito, and Juan de Ocaña—were confronted. Their confessions were repeated, and all agreed and were ratified. Juan Franco was then brought in, and in the presence of the others he admitted that he had brought the boy from Toledo. It was he, too, who had taken out the boy's heart, and his brother Alonso had opened the veins in the arm. And he and Alonso had taken the boy from the cave, Juan holding the feet and Alonso the arms, and had buried him near Santa Maria de Pera—"as he had said in his confessions," wrote the notary —and that they buried him with a large hoe which their brother Lopé brought along. Juan also said (and Benito admitted this) that Benito had helped him look for a boy in Toledo, but it was Juan who found one at the Door of the Pardon in the Cathedral at Toledo. Afterward—and this we learn from a letter of the notary Gonzalez to the officials of La Guardia November 17—Juan Franco took the Inquisitors to the place where the child was buried, and they found a hole there; but nothing is said of the finding of any remains. However, if Fita's conjecture is correct that the Jews of the synagogue of Segovia knew of Yucé's first confession, it is not unlikely that some one of the prisoners may have got word to friends outside, who removed the evidence. In a book written later by the parish priest of La Guardia, the belief is expressed that since the Holy Child, as he became known immediately, had shared in the passion of Jesus Christ, he had also been permitted to share in the glory of His resurrection.

The case was now complete, and justice followed swiftly. The *auto de fe* was held on Wednesday, November 16, in the presence of all the citizens of Ávila and a great number of people from villages for many miles around, for the whole country was now ablaze with horror and wrath. The sentence of the Court, reviewing the evidence at some length, was read, and the prisoners relaxed to the secular arm. After they were given into the custody of Queen Isabel's corregidor, Álvaro de Sant Estevan, they were tied by his men to the stakes. All of them then made final confessions of guilt, which were taken down by the notary Anton Gonzalez and which confirmed all their previous admissions. Benito, in spite of his previous boast that he would die a Jew, now declared that he was sorry for his sins and wished to die a Christian. He was reconciled to the Church by one of the friars; and so were two other *Conversos*, Juan Franco and Juan de Ocaña. These three, therefore, were strangled before they were burned.

Yucé and his father Ça, however, died as Jews, roasted over a slow fire.

The notary Gonzalez, writing to the officials of La Guardia the following day, urged them to set up a suitable monument on the spot where Juan Franco had pointed out the grave of the boy, and not to allow any one to plow there or otherwise disturb the spot, "since Their Highnesses (the King and Queen) and Cardinal Mendoza had yet to visit it." An inscription on a tablet erected in La Guardia in 1569 gives the name of the *Santo Niño* as "Juan, son of Alonso Pasamontes and Juana La Guindera." Monuments were erected to his memory, and he was venerated by many people as a saint.

Two days after the *auto de fe*, the Inquisitors examined one Juan, who was sacristan of the Church of Santa Maria at La Guardia, where according to Yucé's confession, Alonso Franco had obtained the second Host. Why Villada put off interviewing this witness until after the executions remains one of the puzzles of the case, but the notarial record clearly gives the date as November 18.

The sacristan, evidently a New Christian, confessed that he himself had promised the Host to Alonso, who was his uncle, and who had asked for it on two occasions. But Alonso sent Benito for the Host, and Benito assured him they were going to do no harm with it, but much good would come of it. This was about two years ago, he thought. Asked whether he believed that the consecrated Host was the true body of Jesus Christ, Juan said he always believed it; but Benito told him that while it would be a sin to give him the Host, it would not be heresy, so that the Inquisition could not punish him. He took the keys from an earthenware vessel where the priests kept them, and opened the pyx containing the Host. There were two consecrated Hosts in it, and he gave one to Benito. Benito offered him an unconsecrated Host to put in the place of the one taken, but the sacristan refused to do that. Here the record breaks off, and we do not know what happened to the sacristan. We do know, however, that he corroborated the strange story of Yucé Franco.[20]

The testimony was not published, but Yucé's sentence was read the following Sunday from the pulpit of the Church at La Guardia, and the news spread rapidly from village to village. There were riots everywhere against the Jews, and at Ávila a Jew was cruelly stoned to death by the angry mob.

Torquemada must inevitably have presented the sentence of the Court, and probably the whole record of the case, to the King and Queen as the most powerful kind of evidence to justify the course he advocated—the expulsion of all the Jews. We know for a certainty that their Majesties had the case brought to their attention in various ways. The Jews of Ávila appealed to them for protection against the infuriated populace, and Isabel and Fernando sent them a letter of safe conduct from Córdoba, December 16, 1491, forbidding any one to harm the Jews or their property, under extreme penalties, ranging from a fine of 10,000 maravedis to possible death.[21] .

This merciful step was taken by the King and Queen during the ferment of the last month of the siege of Granada. Two weeks later they entered the Moorish capital in triumph; but just before they did so they took time to commend and reward the Inquisitor General and the three Inquisitors of the Court at Ávila for the excellent work they had done in bringing Yucé Franco and his accomplices to justice. The La Guardia crime is not specifically mentioned in the royal edict of January 4, 1492, but there can be no doubt that it is the one referred to. It commends "the devout father Fray Tomás de Torquemada, prior of the monastery of Santa Cruz of Segovia, our confessor and of our council" and states that he has delegated certain judicial powers "in the Bishopric of Ávila and its diocese." He is given authority to transfer and sell all the property confiscated for the use of Their Highnesses—presumably in the La Guardia case—and to use the money "for the expenses and salaries of the Señores Inquisitors and their officers" and for other extraordinary expenses.[22]

During the next few weeks, while Columbus was unsuccessfully negotiating with the sovereigns for his titles and profits, Fray Tomás of Torquemada was also at the Alhambra, urging them to do what they had long contemplated doing—to go to

the very heart of the Jewish problem by expelling all Jews
from Spain. This they decided to do, and on March 31 they
issued the famous edict.

Naturally the Jews, through their powerful friends at Court,
made every effort to avert the catastrophe. The millionaire
Abraham Senior, chief rabbi of Castile, and Isaac Abravanel
may have offered the sovereigns 30,000 ducats, as the story
goes, to revoke the edict; but the assertion that Torquemada
prevented their accepting by throwing a crucifix on the table
and shouting that they were betraying Christ for 30,000 pieces
of silver as Judas did for 30 is extremely improbable and must
be dismissed as a legend of later fabrication. There is no
contemporary evidence for it, and it is not consistent with
what we know of the sovereigns and Torquemada in this
connection.[23]

The Jews, however, would naturally mobilize their great
wealth to prevent the final destruction of their dominion in
Spain. "They lived mostly in the larger cities," wrote Bernaldez . . . "and in the most wealthy and prosperous and fertile
lands . . . and all of them were merchants and venders, and
lessors and farmers of taxing privileges and stewards of
manors, cloth shearers, tailors, cobblers, leather dealers, cur-
riers, weavers, spicers, peddlers, silk merchants, jewelers, and
had other similar occupations. Never did they till the soil, nor
were they laborers, nor carpenters, nor masons; but all sought
easy occupations and ways of making money with little work.
They were a very cunning people, and people who commonly
lived on gains and usuries at the expense of Christians, and
many of the poor among them became rich in a short time.
They were very charitable among themselves, one to another.
If in need, their councils, which they called *alhamas*, provided
for them. They were good masters to their own people. . . .
They had among them very rich men, who had great wealth
and estates, worth a million or two million, as for example
Abraham Senior, who leased most of Castile."[24]

When it became evident that the King and Queen, who were
all-powerful now that the war was over, would undoubtedly
enforce the edict, Abraham Senior and his son became Christians rather than relinquish their great wealth and power. The
Chief Rabbi of Castile was baptized June 15, 1492, at Santa
Maria de Guadelupe. His sponsors were the King and Queen

and Cardinal Mendoza, and he took the name of Ferrand Perez Coronel. The distinguished Spanish Catholic family of that name are his descendants.

Most of the Jews, however, began selling their goods and preparing to leave. "When the gospel was preached to them," wrote Bernaldez, "their rabbis preached the opposite to them, and encouraged them with vain hopes, telling them they considered it certain that all this trial came from God, who wished to lead them from captivity and bring them to the promised land; and that in this exodus they would see how God would perform many miracles for them, and lead them from Spain with wealth and honor. And if they had any mishap or misfortune on land, they would see that when they went upon the sea, God would guide them, as he had guided their ancestors out of Egypt. The rich Jews paid the expenses for the exodus of the poor Jews, and showed much charity for one another, so that only a very few, and those of the most needy, were converted. It was a common belief among the Jews, the simple as well as the learned, that wherever they wished to go the strong hand and extended arm of God would follow with much honor and riches, as God through Moses had miraculously led the people of Israel from Egypt."

Obliged to dispose of all their property that was not portable within three months, the Jews were virtually at the mercy of their purchasers, who, it may be inferred, included large numbers of the rich *Conversos*. The prohibition against carrying gold and silver out of the country increased the difficulty. Hence, says Bernaldez, a Jew would give a house for an ass, and a vineyard for a tapestry or a piece of linen. Nevertheless "it is true that they took an infinite amount of gold and silver secretly, especially cruzados and ducats ground between the teeth, which they swallowed and took in their bellies. . . . The women in particular swallowed more, and one person is said to have swallowed 30 ducats at one time."

When the appointed day approached—the time had been extended by the King and Queen to August 2—the Israelites caused all the boys and girls over twelve years of age to marry, so that each girl might go under the protection of a husband. And so, "putting all their glory behind them, and confiding in the vain hope of their blindness," wrote the curate of Los Palacios, "they gave themselves over to the travail of the road, and went forth from the lands of their birth, little and great, old and young, on foot and on horses and asses and other beasts, and in carts, each one pursuing his way to the port to which he had to go. They stopped on the roads and in the fields, with many labors and misfortunes, some falling down, others getting up, some dying, some being born, and others sick; and there was no Christian who did not grieve for them. Everywhere the people invited them to be baptized . . . but the rabbis encouraged them and caused the women and boys to sing and play tambourines and timbrels to make the people merry.

"When those who were to embark from Puerto de Santa Maria and Cádiz saw the sea, both men and women shrieked and cried out, praying for God's mercy and thinking they would see some miracles; but they stayed there several days and had so much misfortune they wished they had never been born." At last they set sail in 25 ships, but had to bribe the pirate Fragosa with 10,000 ducats—evidently they had found some way to defeat the royal order concerning money—to let them sail for Cartagena. Some, however, returned to Castile and were baptized. But most went to Arcilla, and thence to Fez.[25]

Others proceeded to Portugal and were allowed, on payment of a large tax, to enter. Some went to Navarre, others straggled as far as the Balkans, where their descendants to this day speak a dialect containing many fifteenth century Spanish words. A large group finally settled at Saloniki, and formed there a colony which persisted until 1914, when the members were compelled to migrate, and went to New York, where they still keep many of the characteristics of the Spanish Jews. But most of the exiles, as Bernaldez said, "had sinister luck, being robbed and murdered wherever they went."

The most terrible sufferings of the wanderers were inflicted by the lust and cruelty of the Moors on those who sailed from Gibraltar to the Kingdom of Fez. The Jews had once been very powerful in that kingdom, and one of them, a man named Aaron "so enjoyed the protection of the King of Fez," said Bernaldez, "that he conducted himself and gave orders in the kingdom as he pleased, and the Moors were angry, and made a riot against the King and the Jews, and killed the King and Aaron, and then went into the *Jeweries*, in which there were over 2,000 households in the city, and put them (the Jews) to the sword, and killed and plundered, and left only those who said they would be Moors" . . . but "many of the Jews remained secret Jews, as in Spain before the Inquisition, and the new King said he would find out whether they were Moors or no, and he commanded that those who wished to be Moors" might remain and be free, but the Jews must be subject to certain severe conditions, always going on foot, wearing distinctive garb, and so on. And "the Jews, fearing to be killed, became Moors, but remained secretly Jews."[26] Thus in Mohammedan Fez the story of the Jews parallels that of their brothers in Christian Spain. On this occasion the King of Fez offered to protect the Jews, and allowed them to hire bands of Moorish soldiers for the purpose; but he secretly gave orders to the men to rob them on the road.

Having seized all the property of the exiles, the Mussulmans violated the women and girls under the very eyes of their husbands, fathers and brothers, and slew any of the men who dared to protest. Evidently these barbarians, too, had heard the tale, widely circulated, that the Jewish women had swallowed gold, for after dishonoring them they ripped their bellies with scimitars to search for the ducats.

Some of the survivors staggered on till they reached Fez, naked, starving and swarming with vermin. Others returned to Arcilla, and begged the Count of Borva, the Spanish governor, "to have them baptized, for the love of Jesus Christ, in whom they believed, and to let them return to Spain." He received them with much kindness, fed and clothed them, and had them baptized. So many were baptized that the priests had to sprinkle them with a hyssop in groups. During the next three years bands of them continued to straggle back to Spain, convinced that their sufferings were a punishment for their rejection of Christ.

Bernaldez obtained estimates from the rabbis who returned to Spain of the total number of exiles; and today, after the wild computations of Llorente have been rejected, the figures of the curate are generally accepted as authentic, by both Jewish and Gentile scholars. A "very acute" rabbi named Zentollo, one of the ten or twelve rabbis that Bernaldez baptized, told him that in Castile there were more than 30,000 Jewish households, and in Aragon 6,000—making a total of more than 160,000 persons.[27] These figures, of course, dispose of the legend that the expulsion of the Jews directly caused the economic ruin of Spain.

"A hundred of them came here to this place of Los Palacios," wrote Bernaldez, "and I baptized them, including some rabbis," whose eyes, he added, were at last open to the truth of the prophecies of Isaias "and many other prophecies of the advent, incarnation, birth, passion and resurrection of Our Lord Jesus Christ which they confessed in Hebrew to be true and to have been accomplished in the coming of Our Lord Jesus Christ, whom they admitted they truly believe to be the true Messias, of whom they said they had been ignorant through the hindrance of their ancestors, who had forbidden them, under pain of excommunication, to read or hear the Scriptures of the Christians."

XXVI

COLUMBUS THE POET SAILS FROM
PALOS — ISABEL CONTEMPLATES A
PEACEFUL AND PROSPEROUS COUNTRY
—HER NEW CONFESSOR

ON THE Thursday when the Jews were hurrying out of Spain, Don Christopher Columbus stood on a hillside near the harbor of Palos and watched the setting of the sun in a tranquil sky. Above him were vineyards heavy with grapes, and still higher, on a promontory, the low buildings of the monastery of Santa María La Rábida, looking out into the western ocean. Below him, in the harbor, were three small vessels, newly calked, ready for sea. The wind, which had been contrary, had shifted to the east, and blew steadily toward the Elysian fields, the land of Avilion, the isles of Saint Brendan, the palaces of Kubla, the earthly paradise of Sir John Mandeville, the land of heart's desire that Columbus had dreamed of these many years. The great moment was at hand, God had sent a good wind, and the next day was Friday, always a lucky one for Columbus and for Spain. Tomorrow!

The Admiral, armed with royal authority, had gone to Palos in the middle of May. He had had no end of trouble with his ships and his crews. Neither the ship owners nor the sailors of the town shared the fluent Italian's confidence in himself as a navigator, and all put so many obstacles in his way that the King and Queen were obliged to send a sharp reminder that he was their officer. The calkers did their work so badly that it had to be done over. Some of the ill will may be explained, perhaps, by the fact that the town resented having been sentenced, for some offense against the Crown, to furnish two of the vessels. But the Admiral had a most influential friend in the person of Fray Juan Perez. And it was probably through the kindly Franciscan that he won the support of Martin Alonzo Pinzon, the most expert and popular sea captain in Palos.

It was not difficult to convert Martin Alonzo to the project, for he had been cherishing the same dream ever since he visited the Vatican library at Rome and conversed with the cosmographer of Pope Innocent VIII; in fact, he had even made copies of the Vatican maps of the western seas, with islands marked on them. According to the testimony of Pinzon's son in a later lawsuit, Columbus promised the captain half the profits if he would make up the balance of the money needed for the expedition, and persuade the sailors of Palos to enlist. It appears that the Crown of Castile contributed 1,000,000 maravedis, and that Columbus paid 167,542 maravedis, making the total cost of the expedition 1,167,542 maravedis, or, if we estimate the maravedi at two American cents of 1929, the sum of $23,350.84.[1] Just how much of Columbus's share was paid by Pinzon, we do not know.

When the men of Palos learned that Martin Alonzo had agreed to go in command of the *Pinta*, with his brother Francisco as pilot, and that Vicente Yañez Pinzon would captain the *Niña*, ninety of them enlisted for the voyage. There were seamen from Palos, Huelva, Seville, Moguer and other nearby places; and there was one Tallarte Lajes (Arthur Lawes?) of England and one Guillermo Ires (William Harris?) of Galway, Ireland. There were also some converted Jews, including the ship's physician, Maestre Bernal, who had lately been penanced by the Inquisition.

The ships, contrary to the accepted legend, were good solid sailing vessels, well adapted for the voyage, as Columbus later admitted, but as small as safety would allow, by his own request, to permit them to enter shallow harbors and coast along strange shores. His flagship, the *Maria Galante*, which he renamed the *Santa Maria* in honor of the Blessed Virgin, was probably of 100 tons register, with a displacement of a little over 230 tons fully loaded. She was about 128 feet long, according to the computations of the experts who built her replica in Seville in 1928,[2] and was 26 feet in the beam at the main-deck. She carried a crew of 52.[3] The *Pinta* and *Niña* were smaller, perhaps of 50 tons each, with a crew of 18 apiece. All the ships had decks, with three masts and a square lateen sail, and mounted guns. They were provisioned for a year's voyage.

The Admiral carried with him a letter from King Fernando and Queen Isabel to the Great Khan or Prester John or whatever other oriental potentate he might encounter when he landed on the shores of Asia. It was written in Latin, and read thus:

"Don Fernando and Doña Isabel, by the grace of God King and Queen of Castile, of Leon, of Toledo, of Galicia, of Aragon, of Valencia, etc., etc. . . .
To King ——:
We have heard that Your Highness and your subjects entertain great love for us and for Spain. We are informed, moreover, that you and your subjects very much wish to hear news from Spain. We therefore send our Admiral, Christopher Columbus, who will tell you that we are in good health and perfect prosperity.
                              Yo, El Rey   Yo, la Reyna
Granada, April 30, 1492."⁴

Columbus's purpose as he prepared to set sail is clearly reflected in the introduction to the Journal of his first voyage. After speaking casually and without emotion of the expulsion of the Jews, he says:

"Your Highnesses, as Catholic Christians and Princes, loving the Holy Christian Faith and the spreading of it, and enemies of the sect of Mohammed and of all idolatries and heresies, decided to send me, Christopher Columbus, to the said regions of India, to see the said Princes and the peoples and lands, and learn of their disposition, and of everything, and the measures which could be taken for their conversion to our Holy Faith."

Columbus went not to find a new trade route, but as a missionary explorer; and his last acts before sailing were consistent with his lofty view of the enterprise. On that Thursday evening, August 2, he and his men confessed their sins to Fray Juan Perez in the little Church of La Rábida. Next morning early they received Holy Communion before they broke their fast, and placed themselves under the protection of God. Fray Juan blessed the ships, the ensigns of the Holy Cross and of the King and Queen were hoisted to the mastheads, and at eight o'clock, after the women of Palos had cried their last farewells to their men, Columbus weighed anchor at the bar of Saltes "in the name of the Most Holy

Trinity"—it was with these words that he began all his undertakings—and put out to sea. A fair wind still blew from the
east. The people on shore watched the square rigged *Santa
María* and her two little consorts until they vanished where
the sea melted into the sky.

A courier naturally carried the last messages of Columbus,
and the news of his sailing, to Queen Isabel. He found her
still at Córdoba, but living in seclusion and wearing the
deepest mourning for Don Rodrigo Ponce de Leon, Marqués-
Duke of Cádiz, who had recently died at Seville. He had been
the outstanding hero of the Moorish war, and in the eyes of
the ladies of the court, he was greater even than the Cid Ruy
of immortal memory. Not only Fernando and Isabel, but the
whole court went into mourning for him. By an odd coincidence, his reconciled enemy, the Duke of Medina Sidonia,
followed him to the tomb within a week.

The chronicles of 1492 mention the sorrow of the sovereigns and the courtiers for Don Rodrigo, but say nothing of
how Isabel received the news of the departure of the Jews
on the second of August and the sailing of Columbus on the
third. In fact nothing at all is said of the epoch-making event
at Palos. Modern Jewish writers have endeavored to link the
two happenings together, and to find a compensation for the
exodus in the discovery of a New World where perhaps might
be found at last the New Jerusalem, the Promised Land. Dr.
Meyer Kayserling devotes considerable space to the theory that
the American Indians might have been the lost tribes of Israel.
Isabel, too, undoubtedly linked together the exodus and the
discovery—for they were repeatedly mentioned as among the
achievements of her reign—but from quite another point of
view.

To Isabel it seemed most significant that in the single year
of 1492, three events contributed to the glory of Spain and
of the Christian religion; first, the conquest that ended all
fear of Mohammedan dominion; second, the final delivery of
the new nation from all danger of exploitation by internal
enemies of the Christian Faith; and finally, the opportunity to
carry the gospel of Christ to millions of benighted souls across
the seas. In all this the Queen saw a manifestation of the divine
will.

The Court went to Saragossa before the end of August,

and thence to spend the winter at Barcelona. That flourishing seaport, now a rival of Venice and Genoa since the Turks had destroyed much of the Italian commerce in the East, had always been a favorite residence of both the sovereigns. The people were intelligent, industrious, joyous and pleasure-loving; the streets had an air of briskness and success that appealed to a woman who could not understand failure. It was an intelligent city. There was a University established by Pope Nicholas V; besides an academy of natural sciences, and a college of medicine and surgery, while the Board of Trade provided free instruction for thousands of pupils. It was a thriving city. One of the first banks in Europe had been established there in the twelfth century; and the mutual benefit societies, including the famous one of Our Lady of Hope, made loans without interest to persons in need. It was a city of docks and arsenals and warehouses; of clean streets, fine homes, beautiful gardens; of men from all nations landing from all manner of ships that brought into the cluttered harbor the world's riches, from spices and perfumes of the East to the choice wool of England. Trade there was not considered a degradation, as in Castile; in fact, the merchants were conspicuous in the senate and in the executive council, for Barcelona was ruled by a commission form of government.

A benevolent despot like Isabel may have viewed with distrust some of the free institutions which the Catalans were always so ready to defend with their blood. But she could understand and admire their passion for the fine arts. Since the days of the troubadours they had given a great poetry prize every year. The poems were inscribed on parchment of different colors, enamelled in gold and silver and richly illuminated. They were publicly recited by the poets and a wreath of gold was laid on the winning poem, while the victorious poet was escorted to the royal palace by minstrels, cavaliers and merchants, "thus manifesting to the world the superiority which God and nature have assigned to genius over dulness."

Barcelona was one of the few large Spanish cities where the Inquisition found hardly any work to do. The Catalans had destroyed the Jewish *alhama* in 1395, and from 1400 on had allowed no Jew to live in Barcelona. Many "New Christians," however, had settled there. The first tribunal was established

in 1488. It is one of the few of which we have accurate
statistics covering the early years of the Inquisition. In Barcelona and seven neighboring towns there were thirty-one
autos in ten years. Ten persons were strangled and burned, 13
burned alive, 15 burned dead, 430 burned in effigy, 116 penanced with prison and 304 reconciled after voluntary confessions. In short, out of 433 prisoners, 23 were executed in
a decade.[5]

Isabel was approaching the apogee of her glory. All the
way from Córdoba to the east coast she had ridden through
a country that showed traces of a new prosperity. Andalusia
was a blooming garden, Castile was producing abundant crops
of corn and wheat. Thousands of men whom despair had
driven previously to crime were now earning their livings in
various industries. The great glass works of Barcelona rivaled
those of Venice. Fine woolens from the looms of Castile were
exported to all parts of Europe. The silk industries of Seville
were employing as many as 130,000 workmen. The leather
trade of Córdoba was flourishing; Granada made velvets too
fine to be imitated; Toledo and Valencia wove carpets. Every
city was like a great singing workshop; farms that had long
been fallow were green with vegetables and grain. Isabel even
took measures to stop the deforestation that had produced bleak
areas of treeless deserts; she passed special as well as general
ordinances for the conservation of the forests about Madrid
and Medina del Camp, and planned a broader program which,
if followed by her successors, would have eliminated one of
the causes of the later economic decline.

Freed from the anxieties of war, she turned eagerly to the
pursuits that had been dear to her father. She was a generous
and consistent patron of all the arts and sciences. The study
and practice of medicine flourished during her reign. She
encouraged the beginnings of botany and zoölogy—one of the
earliest treaties was written during her reign by Francisco de
Oviedo. It was to her that Alonso de Córdoba dedicated his
astronomical tables; and under the patronage of her protegé,
Diego de Deza, Bishop of Salamanca, the Jewish astrologer
Abraham Zacuto prepared his *Almanach Perpetuum*, with
tables of the sun, moon and stars which Columbus used. Andres
Laguna made anatomy an indispensable part of medical studies.
Hospitals were established by the King and Queen at Granada,

Salamanca and Santiago. The vast field of archaeology was opened; Alexander Geraldini, one of the tutors of the Prince Juan and the infantas, gathered a collection of Latin inscriptions into a "corpus"; Professor Lebrija studied the Roman circuses and naumachies at Mérida and deduced their antique measurements; Juan Guas de Sepulveda excavated milestones on the old Roman road between Mérida and Salamanca; Luis de Lucena made a collection of ancient coins. Florian de Ocampo was the first to publish these findings in archaeology.

When Isabel became queen there was only one important university in Spain, that at Salamanca. Before her death there were several, all endowed by her or by men she had raised to power. There were 6,000 students at Salamanca and 2,000 at Alcalá de Henares, and the lecturers included some of the most noted humanists of the later Renaissance. The sort of life a college student was expected to live may be inferred from the routine prescribed for Don Gaspar, son of the Count of Olivares, a student at Salamanca in the sixteenth century. He is counseled to live in a well-kept house, with sufficient servants; to maintain suitable relations with teachers, professors, and servants, not omitting his washerwoman; and to be scrupulous in all matters of etiquette. "Each evening, after having prayed to God and retired, Don Gaspar shall make his examination of conscience. He shall go frequently to the sacraments, and communicate on great feast days, or at the least, fulfil this duty once a year. He shall keep a memorandum of his communions in a special notebook. His servants shall communicate more or less frequently according to their station. Don Gaspar shall be charitable without ostentation, but with the generosity suitable to his birth and position. He shall give each year in alms a sum equal to one tenth the expenses of his household. One fraction shall be given to the poor in the street, another to ordinary beggars at the door. . . . Don Gaspar ought to live in good company, and in the choice of his associates to have a greater care for virtue than for other qualities. Let him take warning that flatterers and those who show a desire to please their superiors profit by their faults if they believe them naïve."[6]

It was only a generation after this that Erasmus wrote, "The Spaniards have attained such eminence in literature that they not only excite the admiration of the most polished nations of Europe, but likewise serve as their models."[7] Salamanca was known through Christendom as "the Spanish Athens." One of its noted professors was Lucio Marineo, a Sicilian scholar, who was invited to court in 1500, and labored there with such success that it was said "no Spaniard was considered noble who showed any indifference to learning." But perhaps the most respected of the teachers at Salamanca was Aelio Antonio de Lebrija the philologist. After five years of study at Salamanca and ten in Italy he had returned to Spain to teach at his Alma Mater at the beginning of Isabel's reign. Scholars came from all parts of Europe to hear his lectures and to read his works. He resigned in 1488 to compile his Latin lexicon under the patronage of Cardinal Zuniga. After the Cardinal's death, Lebrija became one of the tutors of Prince Juan, and was appointed official historiographer to succeed Pulgar. This post he held until the death of Queen Isabel, when he returned to Salamanca.

At Salamanca the studies included grammar, rhetoric, dialectics, arithmetic, geometry, astronomy and music; at Alcalá, logic, philosophy, medicine, Hebrew, Greek and Latin, rhetoric, grammar and music. The medieval Spanish, like the Greeks, considered music an essential part of every education, "the support of true wisdom," and no person was thought educated who was not well trained in singing and in playing of various instruments. Ruy Sanchez de Arévalo, in the beginning of the *Vergel de Principes*, addressed to Enrique IV the following eulogy on music: "The fifth excellence of this noble art and of this worthy exercise consists in disposing and directing men not only toward the moral virtues, but also toward political virtues that prepare them well to reign and to govern. And it is for this end that the virtuous exercise ought to be recommended to kings and princes." The Jesuit historian Mariana expressed a similar thought: "By song, Princes can understand how strong is the influence of laws, how useful order is in life, how suave and sweet is moderation in our desires. The King ought to cultivate music to distract his soul, to temper the violence of his character, and to harmonise his affections. In studying music, he will understand that the happiness of a republic consists in the exact proportion and the just accord of the parties."

Isabel showed her approval of this principle not only in the

Replica of the "Santa María," the Flagship of Columbus
(*"Art and Archaeology"*)

education of Prince Juan, but in her consistent patronage of the art. She liked to have about her cavaliers who were good musicians. Garcilaso de la Vega, the knight who killed the giant Yarfe before the walls of Granada and who was sent later as Ambassador to Rome, was an excellent harpist. Francisco Penalosa, another Spaniard, was one of the most brilliant musicians in the papal choir where Palestrina, half a century later, was to lay the foundations of modern music. Isabel hardly ever traveled anywhere without musicians about her. In her chapel she had more than 40 trained singers,[8] besides organists and players on the clavecin, the lute, the viol, the flute and other instruments. She took them to camp when she went to war, and during her lifetime music was played even at the *autos de fe*—by no means an astonishing circumstance if we remember that the word *auto* to a Spaniard suggested a joyful reconciliation of a penitent to the Church of God, rather than an execution. A great collection of *cancioneros* and other music was assembled at the Queen's orders in the Alcázar at Segovia.

From now on Isabel the just and able administrator took precedence over Isabel the Crusader. She issued a *pragmática* against costly and ostentatious funerals, in which she argued that it was inconsistent for Christians, believing in the immortality of the soul, to waste so much money on "vain and transitory things." She illuminated manuscripts. Very likely she continued to make Fernando's shirts. She took her spinning wheel to a convent where she heard discipline had grown lax, and spent a day toiling there as an example to the nuns. Thus in a limited degree she prepared for the reforms of the glorious Saint Teresa of Ávila a generation later. She nominated for the hierarchy holy and erudite priests. Rarely was she mistaken in her judgment of men.

It was at this period, just after the close of the Crusade, that she discovered the Franciscan friar Ximenes de Cisneros and set him on the high road to greatness. Having compelled her favorite confessor, Fray Hernando de Talavera, to accept first the bishopric of Ávila and, after the surrender of Boabdil, the new archbishopric of Granada, she found herself in need of a spiritual adviser who could accompany the court wherever it went; and she asked Cardinal Mendoza to recommend some one. The Cardinal named Ximenes, a monk whom he had been employing in certain business at Toledo.

The son of poor parents, Ximenes, like many others, had received a free education at Salamanca, and after graduating with high honors, had been sent to Rome to continue his studies. He was extremely ambitious. On returning to Spain, he took with him a letter from the Pope granting him the first vacant benefice in the diocese of Toledo. The vacancy happened to fall at Uzeda. But Archbishop Carrillo, who had promised it to a friend of his own, clapped Ximenes into jail and kept him there for six years.[9] The young man emerged from his long solitude a humble and steady-eyed ascetic, and joined the Observantine or more rigorous wing of the Franciscan order. Carrillo had died. Mendoza recognized the talents of Ximenes, and made use of them.

When Isabel appointed this friar her confessor, he accepted with great reluctance, for he had no love for the glitter of the Court. He proved, however, so worthy a successor to Talavera that Isabel began planning to raise him to the hierarchy. It was only too evident that Cardinal Mendoza could not live much longer. During his last illness, which dragged through the year 1494, Isabel visited him to console him and to receive his final advice as to the future government of the kingdom. After a long conversation, Mendoza suggested that she appoint Ximenes to succeed him. He reminded her that in the hands of great nobles like Carrillo the See of Toledo, with its immense revenues, had been almost a rival to the crown and the source of many ills to Church and State. He advised the Queen to limit her appointments to worthy men of the middle class.

When the Cardinal died at the beginning of 1495, Isabel startled the Court by letting it be known that she intended to ask the Pope to appoint the humble Ximenes. It now transpired that the King had views of his own concerning the appointment of Mendoza's successor; indeed, he had already promised the position to his natural son, Don Alonso of Aragon, the talented young Archbishop of Saragossa. But Isabel, whose marriage treaty gave her the right to make all ecclesiastical nominations in Castile, indignantly rejected the candidacy; and unless human nature is far more variable than it appears to be, it is likely that His Majesty on that occasion was reminded of several matters that he would prefer to have forgotten. Besides Don Alonso he had three other illegitimate children. Doña Juana, his daughter by a lady from Tarega, in Catalonia, afterwards married the Constable of Castile. His two others daughters became nuns, and both died prioresses of the convent of Santa Clara de Madrigal. Queen Isabel had received Doña Juana at Court, with marked kindness. But she flatly refused even to consider Don Alonso for the See of Toledo, and sent her own nomination to the Pope.

Pope Alexander VI appointed Ximenes in a bull that reached the Queen at Madrid during the Lent of 1495. On Good Friday, after she had made her confession, as usual, to the lean visaged Franciscan, she summoned him to an audience, and after a brief conversation handed him a parchment sealed with lead, saying:

"Reverend Father, you will see by these letters what are the commands of His Holiness."

Ximenes kissed the parchment reverently, according to the custom; but when he opened it and saw the words "To our venerable brother Francisco Ximenes de Cisneros, Archbishop-elect of Toledo," he turned pale, and handing the bull to Queen Isabel, said abruptly, "These letters are not for me," and departed without ceremony.

"Come brother," he said to his companion Ruyz, as they took the road to Ocaña, "we must leave here as soon as possible."[10]

It required six months of pleading on the part of the Queen and certain friends of Ximenes, as well as a second bull from Pope Alexander, commanding acceptance, to shake the resolve of the monk. He was finally consecrated in the presence of the King and Queen October 11, 1495, at Tarazona.

After his elevation he continued to wear coarse cotton, to sleep on bare boards, and to eat simple convent fare. Only at the Queen's and the Pope's insistence did he put on the gorgeous robes of his office when he said Mass in the cathedral. His enemies—and he had some in his own order—saw in this an evidence that he had yielded to the seductions of power; and one Sunday a zealous young Franciscan preached a fiery sermon in his presence on the vain pride of ecclesiastics tempted by high office to betray the ascetic principles of the Little Poor Man of Assisi. After Mass Ximenes sent for the priest, and receiving him alone in the sacristy, began in silence to take off his vestments. Under the silk and the cloth of gold his critic beheld a rough garment of sackcloth bound with the cord of Saint Francis, and under that a hair shirt, next to the skin. Ximenes smiled and walked away, leaving his critic in tears.

This was the man who guided Isabel's conscience from 1492 until the end of her life. With her aid he united the Spanish Franciscans, who were divided into Conventuals and Observatines by a dispute over their rule, and imposed a severe discipline on the clergy of his diocese—the beginning of a reform that spread through all Spain, without the bloody civil wars which were soon to rend northern Europe. Ximenes was also an ardent patron of learning. He spent eight years establishing his University at Alcalá, taking professors from Salamanca for the purpose and introducing one remarkable innovation: he had the rector chosen by the students instead of by the faculty. One of his greatest achievements was the assembling of the Complutensian[11] Polyglot Bible, comprising all the known texts of Holy Scripture in various languages. For this arduous and complicated undertaking, he engaged the greatest scholars in Europe, and through the aid of Pope Leo X obtained translations of all the manuscripts existing in the Vatican, and in the libraries of various convents and churches in Italy. As the art of founding type was elementary, there was great difficulty with the dead languages, particularly Hebrew, and Ximenes went to much trouble to have his type properly cast at the foundry attached to the University. The work took him many years; a complete copy of the Bible was given him only in the last months of his life.[12] After Isabel's death he averted a civil war by making peace between Fernando and Philip the Fair; he was Inquisitor General; he became Regent after Fernando's death, ruled with great wisdom, saved the dearly won unity of Spain, led an army to Africa to take several Moorish towns at his own expense, and was repaid by the ingratitude of the young Charles V, who on his accession summarily discharged the greatest prime minister in Spanish history. Peter Martyr of Anghera wrote of Ximenes, "Behold an Augustine in his piercing intellect, a Jerome in his self-inflicted penances, an Ambrose in his zeal for the Faith."

Peter Martyr was another of Isabel's protegés. He had

come from Italy to Spain in 1487 at the invitation of the Count of Tendilla, and had taken service in the Crusading army, saying, "I have deserted the Muses for Mars." Isabel, finding him learned and pious, engaged him to tutor Prince Juan, and after the fall of Granada, he organized a complete school, like the Schola Palatina of Charlemagne, for the Prince and his ten young companions. Peter was discouraged at first. "Like their ancestors, my pupils hold letters in slight esteem," he wrote. "They consider them an obstacle to the career of arms, which alone they judge worthy of honor." But the Queen was as unyielding in the discipline of her children as she was in extirpating heresy or in conquering Moors. She insisted on their learning Latin, and she succeeded so well that Princess Juana could make extemporaneous speeches in Latin, and Catalina—Catherine of Aragon—was said by Erasmus to be "a literary miracle for her sex." But it was Prince Juan, "my angel," who first gave hope to his instructor.

Peter found ways of sugar-coating his instructions to suit the chivalrous ideals of the sons of crusaders. When the Court was at Saragossa in September, 1492, he wrote, "My house is filled all day with young nobles who, reclaimed from vulgar amusements to devote themselves to study, are now convinced that letters, far from being an obstacle, are rather an aid in the career of arms. . . . It has pleased our royal mistress, the model of every exalted virtue, that her cousin-german, the Duke of Guimarães, as well as the young Duke of Villahermosa, nephew of the King, should stay at my house the whole day—an example which has been followed by the principal cavaliers of the court."[13] When Peter gave a lecture on Juvenal at the University of Salamanca in 1488, so many of his pupils tried to help him to his chair that he could hardly reach it. As the discourse lasted two hours and a half, some of the lazy students showed their impatience by stamping, to the great annoyance of the lecturer. But at the end the audience hoisted him to their shoulders and bore him to his lodgings "like a victor in the Olympic games."

He was eloquent. But what appealed to Queen Isabel even more than his eloquence was his frank distrust of eloquence. He saw danger in an uncritical admiration for Greek and Roman culture. "Eloquence," he wrote, "is at the service of the soul, but if the soul is perverted, it uses eloquence as a poison to corrupt manners. Nobody ought to devote himself to the study of eloquence unless first he has turned to virtue, and learned to live well as well as to speak well."

Under the tutelage of such a philosopher, the fifteen-year-old Prince made rapid progress in the virtues and accomplishments of a king. To prepare him better for the glorious destiny that seemed to wait upon him, the Queen gave him a house of his own, for whose accounts he was responsible, and there he lived with his ten companions, like a young monarch surrounded by his court. On certain days the Queen sent lawyers and statesmen to sit in his council, as if it were the Great Council of Castile, while the Prince asked questions and gave judgment on real and imaginary problems.

Isabel was proud of him, yet her ambitions were somewhat more modest than Fernando's. She was content to have him rule a free, united Spain, prosperous and Christian. But Fernando was beginning to imagine his descendants uniting with the House of Austria to be heirs of the Holy Roman Empire. He had betrothed Juan and Juana to the heirs of the Emperor Maximilian. He strove constantly to prevent France from overrunning Europe. He conceived of a united Italy under some prince of his own house.

"No reproach attached to him," wrote Giucciardini,[14] "save his lack of generosity and his faithlessness to his word." This judgment, though not without some foundation, is much too severe. Fernando was parsimonious not so much from inclination as from the necessities that his lofty schemes forced upon him. He certainly did not hoard money, as Henry VII did. "Contrary to the belief of all men," wrote Peter Martyr, "he died poor." He was lacking, no doubt, in Isabel's liberality. "When between the King and Queen there was discussion as to the fitting reward of any particular service, she on her part always gave more than the sum on which the two had determined," wrote Lucio Marineo.[15]

If the King was sometimes faithless, the charge came generally from those who had tried to cheat him, and failed. He was dealing with master liars like Louis XI, Henry VII, Ludovico Sforza and Philip the Fair, and he met them with their own weapons. When he outwitted them, they denounced him with all the fervor of the unscrupulous.

Fernando and Isabel kept several secretaries constantly engaged, and they usually sent three copies of any important message by three different couriers traveling by different routes. Most of the messages were in code. Bergenroth is mistaken[16] in attributing the introduction of cipher into Spain to their secretary Almazan; for Fernando had used it in correspondence with his father in 1478.[17]

The following note sent by Isabel in 1491 to Dr. Puebla in London, is typical:

"Considering the question whether the town of 102 (Granada) be 90 (conquered) or 39 (not) 90 (conquered), we are constructing a 188 (fortress) there (Santa Fé) in which we intend to have good 97 (troops) and all that is necessary to 94 (besiege) 102 (Granada) or at least to watch her so closely that it shall 39 (not) be necessary to 94 (besiege) her now."[18]

Almazan, a brilliant converted Jew who was one of the later secretaries of Fernando and Isabel, perfected a system so involved that it was never completely deciphered until the latter half of the nineteenth century. In one of his codes each letter had fifty symbols. In another, the signs were so numerous that the key is like a dictionary. Each vowel had five equivalents, each consonant four. Words of no significance were sometimes intermingled. The word *enviando* (sending), for example, was elaborately represented by the symbols "DCCCCLXVIIII, *le*, N. o, γ, malus, ϛ." "Malus" has no significance. The other symbols in order stand for en, vi, a, n, d, and o.

It was under cover of such necessary precautions that Fernando succeeded Louis XI as the most subtle and farsighted diplomat in Europe, spinning a web from which few of his contemporaries completely escaped and from whose consequences the modern world is not yet wholly free. It was Fernando, for instance, who paved the way for the union of England and Scotland by suggesting to Henry VII that he give his daughter Mary to James V in marriage—this to soothe James's irritation at being denied a Spanish princess. Henry, a parvenu king sitting on his throne insecurely, needed the support of both Fernando and James. To buy off James, then a champion of the English pretender Perkin Warbeck, he reluctantly consented. The issue of the marriage of James and Mary was the unfortunate Mary Stuart, whose son ruled all Great Britain as James I. All of this sequence King Fernando,

assisted by Queen Isabel, set in motion because he had promised James V one of his own daughters, and found it convenient to break the promise. It was also imperative at the
time that he pose as the friend of Henry VII. For great
events were impending, and Fernando had a rôle planned for
Henry.

XXVII

EUROPE in 1492 was a chessboard that must have been inviting to a man of Fernando's talents. Out of the ferment of the Renaissance and the decay of feudalism was emerging a new political concept, a nationalism assuming the form of absolute monarchy and commonly employing the cynical maxims of Machiavelli. This royal absolutism used two Renaissance discoveries—gunpowder and the printing press—to achieve and perpetuate its power; not knowing that in the end gunpowder and the printing press would destroy it. It was a despotism full of menace to the Church, even when it protected her; indeed, without its powerful support the Lutheran revolt would have been a passing phenomenon with no important historical consequences, and England would have remained part of a comparatively homogeneous society. But of the dangers lurking in the Caesarism that he had employed so successfully in Spain, Fernando probably had no accurate prevision. What he did see was that England, under the miserly but sagacious Henry VII, was becoming a power to be reckoned with. And he noted, with positive alarm, that the new political despotism in France was threatening to disturb the peace and balance of all Christendom. For the sceptre of Louis XI had fallen into dangerous hands.

Charles VIII was then twenty-two years old, with a rickety body, a weak puny face on which were superimposed a hawk-like nose, a heavy underlip overshadowing a scanty beard, and fine eyes that usually stared murkily from under heavy lids. Though flabby of will, he was extremely obstinate; and he was ignorant, for his father had let him grow up with no instruction in Latin except *"Qui nescit dissimulare, nescit regnare,"* and little else besides. He found a compensation for his inadequacies in conceiving of great designs far beyond his power to execute. He liked to think of himself as a Caesar or a Charlemagne. Best of all, he fancied himself regaining the Holy Sepulchre at Jerusalem. But in Charles's crusading zeal there was an admixture of shrewd self-interest quite foreign to the spirit that animated Richard of the Lion Heart and Saint Louis. In his dreams of restoring and protecting the glories of Christendom there was interwoven a baser pattern of imperialism. In the great epic of his journey to Jerusalem he seemed to see himself taking the Kingdom of Naples *en passant*. He had inherited a rather shadowy claim to it through the house of Anjou.

The personal weakness of Charles found a fertile field for its vegetation in the political weakness of Renaissance Italy. After Ferrante of Naples had besieged Rome during the Barons' War, and had spurned the efforts of Fernando and Isabel to make peace, Pope Innocent VIII had been so eager to end the disgraceful situation that he had followed the advice of Cardinal Giuliano and had appealed to Charles for protection. In May, 1486, Charles had sent new ambassadors to Rome to seek the investiture of Naples. The envoys of Isabel and Fernando strove to frustrate their efforts. Cardinal Borgia and the French Cardinal Balue had a violent dispute in a consistory. At length, largely through Spanish efforts, Ferrante was induced to make peace.

A few months later, however, he murdered the Pope's envoy and expelled the Papal troops from Aquila. Encouraged by the King of Hungary, he again openly defied the Pope. Innocent now invited Charles VIII and the Emperor Maximilian, who had just signed a treaty of peace (July, 1489), to restore order in Italy, and then to lead all Christendom in a Crusade against the Turks, who were making new conquests in the east. When the two kings declined, Innocent threatened to leave Italy to its bickerings. A second papal exile at Avignon seemed inevitable, when the Pope suddenly became seriously ill.

On his partial recovery he continued throughout the autumn of 1489 to plan for a crusade, and to this end he assembled a great congress of all Christendom at Rome in 1490. Mean-

while, the previous year, the Grand Master of the Knights of
Saint John had sent him a most useful prisoner in the person
of Prince Dschem, rebellious brother of the Sultan of Turkey,
whose value as a hostage lay in the fact the Sultan lived in
mortal fear of his release. At the Congress of 1490 Dschem
promised that if he gained the sultanate with the aid of the
Christians he would withdraw the Turkish forces from Europe
and give up Constantinople. Innocent's plan was a bold one
to gain by diplomacy what Christendom had failed to accomplish by arms. But his efforts were defeated by the selfishness
of the Christian princes. Charles and Maximilian began their
quarrel anew. There were many disputes in the Congress. All
through its sessions, Venice, placing its commercial advantage
before the good of Christendom, kept the Sultan informed of
the proceedings.

Pope Innocent, a sick and disappointed man, died July 25,
1492.

The election that followed was the most deplorable in the
annals of the Christian Church. Charles VIII sent 200,000
ducats to an Italian bank to finance the election of Cardinal
Giuliano. Naples and Milan were at drawn daggers over their
candidates. Ferrante of Naples, at the request of King Fernando and Queen Isabel, proposed the name of Pedro Gonzalez de Mendoza, Cardinal of Spain. But the wealth of
Cardinal Borgia turned the scales in his favor. He won by a
single vote, that of the almost feeble-minded Cardinal Gher-
ardo, 95 years old.

Queen Isabel was bitterly disappointed. "The days of distress and confusion began for the Roman Church," says Von
Pastor; "the prophetic words of Savonarola were fulfilled"—
Savonarola, that small, sallow-faced Dominican friar with
the aquiline nose and the piercing fiery eyes, who had snubbed
Lorenzo the Magnificent and had burned the pagan art treasures of Florence; whose voice, predicting the humiliation and
reform of the Church and the scourging of Italy for her sins,
had already reverberated through the land.

The new Pope, who took the name of Alexander VI, promised to be a father to Christendom, to keep peace, and to unite
Europe against the Moslems. He evidently intended to do so,
and there were many who expected that he would reform his
own life and apply his undeniable ability to the great problems

of his office. But it soon became apparent that Alexander had forgotten his resolutions, and it was not long before he was openly devoting himself to the task of making his children rich and powerful. Men began recalling the dream that Savonarola had had in the previous advent, in which he saw in the midst of the sky a hand bearing a sword on which was written, *"Gladius Domini super terram cito et velociter."*

In the spring of 1493 Fernando and Isabel sent Count Haro to Rome to offer their obedience to the new Pope. According to the unreliable Infessura, the Count protested in the name of the Spanish sovereigns against the protection Alexander was giving to the Spanish "New Christians" fleeing from the Inquisition. It is a fact that Alexander, throughout his pontificate, was so kind to the fugitives of Jewish descent that in Spain he was derisively spoken of as "The Jew" and "The Marrano." Like Innocent VIII he definitely followed the spirit of the bull of Sixtus IV dated August 2, 1483, insisting that all penitent *Conversos* be admitted to penance, and that the right of appeal to Rome be given them at all times—a proof that the bull of Sixtus was by no means considered to have become null and void. It is a noteworthy fact, too, that all the official acts and documents of Pope Alexander relating to matters of faith and morals were orthodox and correct.

Alexander was not under the domination of the strong will of Cardinal Giuliano. Nor was he sympathetic with the ambitions of Charles VIII. Giuliano, however, hastened to Paris and urged the young King to invade Italy. Ludovico Sforza, regent for the duke of Milan, also sent him an urgent invitation, for he needed Charles's help against Ferrante of Naples and was shortsighted enough to disregard the warning of a diplomat who said, "After the King of France has dined with the King of Naples, he will sup with you." But perhaps the most influential of Charles's friends in Italy was Savonarola, who hailed him as the Champion of God.

In all this, King Fernando of Spain saw a delightful opportunity. He had never forgotten that Roussillon and Cerdagne were still in French hands, and before he went to Barcelona for the winter of 1492-3 he renewed his demand for their return. It was a particularly favorable moment, since Charles, having jilted Maximilian's daughter Margot and having married Maximilian's betrothed, Anne of Brittany, found himself

in need of help—the Spanish sovereigns might be able to pour
a little balm of some kind on the double wound of the Emperor. Besides, Charles had almost made up his mind to cross
the Alps, and he was loth to leave his frontiers exposed to
an invasion by Fernando, whose well-trained veterans of the
Moorish War had nothing to do at the moment. The young
monarch therefore decided to buy off Fernando and Isabel
before he embarked on his Italian venture. While they were
at Barcelona he sent envoys to win their friendship. Nothing
could have suited them better.

The result was the Treaty of Barcelona, signed January 8,
1493. Charles agreed to return Roussillon and Cerdagne without the payment of the 200,000 crowns his father had lent
Juan II of Aragon. Fernando promised not to oppose, but to
help in any way possible, the laudable plan of Charles to lead
a new crusade for the recovery of Jerusalem, and pretended
not to see that the real objective was not the Holy Sepulchre,
but the conquest of Naples. The Spanish sovereigns bound
themselves "to assist the King of France against all his enemies,
without exception, and in particular against the English, who
are old foes of the French." In fact they would aid him against
any persons in the world except the Holy Father.

In the same treaty Fernando and Isabel engaged their royal
word and faith as Christians not to conclude, or permit to be
concluded, any marriage of their children with any members
of the royal family of England or Austria, without first obtaining the permission of Charles.[1]

The treaty signed, Charles with a light heart completed his
preparations for emulating the example of Hannibal.

Meanwhile Fernando and Isabel in a quiet way began taking certain precautions of their own. Isabel passed a law forbidding any man in her realms to ride on a mule, under pain
of death.[2] This custom, borrowed from the Moors, had nearly
cost her the Moorish war, for in a country where more than
100,000 able-bodied men were riding on mules, she had found
it difficult to assemble 10,000 mounted on horses, for cavalry.
"At first there were many executions under the law by the
magistrates of the King, and they enforced it in such a way
that even Dukes, Counts and Marqueses and other great lords
feared it and observed it all the time that the Queen Doña

Isabel lived."³ In future wars she intended having cavalry available.

But while Fernando was recovering his patrimony and drawing Charles into the Italian net, an incident occurred that nearly put an end to all his schemings. Like the Kings of Castile, he was in the habit of holding every Friday a criminal and civil court, where the poor might have justice without cost, without delay, and without being victimized by the cupidity and hypocrisy of quibbling lawyers. Naturally these *audiencias* were popular, and the King found himself besieged by petitioners from morning until night. One Friday, on the vigil of the Immaculate Conception, he arose from the judgment seat at twelve o'clock, having heard evidence and given judgment since eight, and walked down a flight of steps toward an open space called the Plaza of the King. Many cavaliers and citizens attended him, and with him walked his treasurer, Gabriel Sanchez. As Fernando reached the bottom step, and turned his head to part with Sanchez, a man who had been hiding in a corner leaped out and struck the King from behind with a cutlass, inflicting a deep wound from the top of the head to the ear, and down the neck to the shoulders. If the King had not turned his head at that precise moment, the blade would have cloven through his skull to the shoulders; as it was, the gash was dangerous. Putting his hands to his head, he cried, *"Santa María, val!* Holy Mary, defend me!"⁴ while the people looked on, too astonished to move.

A cry of "Treason! Oh, what treason!" filled the plaza, and a dozen men leaped on the assassin, while a page drew a poniard to dispatch him. Fernando, having recovered his self-possession, said, "Don't kill that man!" and the guards bore the struggling assailant to prison.⁵ A great hubbub arose in the city.

Isabel's first intimation of the event was hearing the crowd outside the palace shouting, "The King is dead! They have killed the King!"

The courtiers, the merchants and the sailors had armed themselves and were running through the streets, some weeping, some praying, some cursing and denouncing the authors of the deed. "France is the traitor!" cried some. "Navarre is the traitor!" cried others. "It was a Castilian!" said the Catalans. And the Castilians of the Court retorted with, "It

is none but a Catalan!" A bloody battle in the streets might
have ended this dispute if some one with presence of mind
had not sent forth a herald who shouted, "The King is alive!
The King is alive!"

Next the rumor spread that the plot aimed also at the lives
of Queen Isabel and the prince and princesses. Galleys were
made ready in the harbor, and the Queen arranged to send her
children on board. But an examination of the prisoner, Juan
de Canamas, disclosed that he was, as Bernaldez says, a *loco
imaginativo y malicioso*, acting on his own initiative; an ugly
peasant with a warped body, one of a class that Fernando had
released from serfdom. He declared that the Devil had whispered in his ear that he was the rightful ruler of Aragon, that
the King was usurping what belonged to him, and that he had
only to strike to recover his title.

The King was willing to have the lunatic released, but the
nobles of Barcelona, in their mortification and their anxiety
to show their disapproval of the attempt on the King's life,
insisted upon the full penalty for treason, a most cruel death.
"First he was put in a cart and taken all over the city, and
then they cut off the hand with which he struck the king, and
then they plucked off one nipple with tongs of red-hot
iron; then they plucked out one eye, then they cut off the
other hand; then they plucked out the other eye, and then the
other breast, and then the nostrils, and then they caught up
the whole body with burning tongs, and cut off his feet. And
after all his members were cut off, they stoned him and burned
him and cast the ashes to the wind."[6] Such was the decree; but
Isabel sent a monk to absolve the condemned, and commanded
that he be strangled before the execution of the barbarous
sentence.

The King's condition remained critical for several days;
his temperature was high, and there was danger of a hemorrhage. The Queen, almost distraught, remained at his bedside
day and night. There was always a great crowd outside the
palace, and when the King had a relapse after he appeared to
be recovering, the rumor was revived that he was dead, and
he finally had to show himself at a window to allay their fears.
After it became certain that he would not die, people who had
promised pilgrimages and mortifications for his recovery began to perform them. Some were seen going barefoot through

the streets, some went on their knees to various churches and shrines.

The miraculous great bell of Villela, a few miles from Saragossa, whose inexplicable tolling always announced some disaster to the royal house of Aragon, had been heard to strike on the day of the assault on Fernando—its fifth tolling since the Moorish conquest eight centuries before. But Fernando at last recovered, "and he said that this punishment had been given him for his sins."[7]

During the King's illness Isabel found some consolation in corresponding with her former confessor, Talavera, now Archbishop of Granada. She wrote:

"Very pious and very reverend Father: Since we see that kings, like other men, are exposed to mortal accidents, it is a reason why they should be prepared for death. And I say this, although I have never doubted it, and have reflected on it for a long time; for grandeur and prosperity made me think of it all the more, and fear to reach the end of life without sufficient preparation. But the distance is great from the firm belief to the realization from concrete experience. And since the King my Lord has seen death near at hand, the experience was more real and more lasting than if I myself had been at the point of death—not even at the moment of leaving the body would my soul endure anything similar. I cannot say or explain what I suffer. Indeed, then, before I touch death again— please God it may not be in such a way—I should like to be in other dispositions than those in which I find myself at this moment, and particularly as to my debts. Inform yourself of all the cases where it seems to you there can be restitution and satisfaction of the interested persons, and how this may be effected; send me a memorandum of it,—it will be the greatest peace in the world for me to have it. And having it, and knowing my debts, I shall labor to pay them."

In a later letter she corrects certain details of her first account of the attack on the king.

"The wound was so great, as Doctor Guadalupe said—for I could not find the courage to look at it—that it penetrated four inches, and was twelve inches long. My heart trembles to speak of it. . . . But God, in His mercy, decreed that it should be in a place where the wound would not be mortal, for, the nerves and the spine having been left untouched, it soon became evident that there was no danger of death. Afterward, the fever and the danger of a hemorrhage alarmed us; the seventh day, he was so well that I wrote you and dispatched a courier to you—much relieved, although I was nearly mad from lack of sleep. And then after the seventh day he had an access of fever so great that he suffered the greatest anguish he had yet endured. And that lasted a day and a night of which I will not say what Saint Gregory says in the office for Holy Saturday, but it was a night of Hell; so that you may believe, Father, that never was the like seen among the people at any time, for officials ceased their work, and none paused to speak with another. All was pilgrimages, processions and almsgiving, and more hearing of confessions than ever in Holy Week, and that without being asked by any one. And in the churches, in the monasteries, night and day, without cease, ten or twelve friars were praying—one can't tell all that happened.

"God, in His goodness, wished to have pity on us, for when Herrera left, taking you another letter from me, His Lordship was very well, as I told you. He has continued so, thanks be to God, so that he has got up and goes here and there. To-morrow, if it pleases God, he will be able to mount his horse, and go about the town and visit the house where we are going to live. And great has been our pleasure at seeing him about, as great as our sadness was before; indeed, he has brought us all back to life! Every one wept for joy.

"I don't know how we shall thank God for so great a grace —many virtues would not suffice to do it. And what shall I do, who have none? Please God, henceforth I shall serve Him as I ought. Your prayers and your counsels will aid me in this, as they always have helped me."

Isabel's keen sense of her own sinfulness and unworthiness must be laid to her humility. The evidence appears to be that her "sins," like those of Saint Teresa, were peccadilloes seen in the mirror of a sensitive conscience—errors of omission in the stress of great affairs, lies told in haste and in conflict with unscrupulous rivals, unpaid war debts which she could hardly have been expected to pay sooner. So far as personal morality is concerned, even her bitter enemies have found her blameless. There was in fact something almost virginal in her character to the day of her death; even her later utterances have a quality that calls to mind the little yellow-haired girl of Arévalo. Errors she certainly committed, for she was human, but if a sin is a deliberate violation of one's conscience, as the Church has always taught, then it must be said that Isabel was what Washington Irving called her, "one of the purest and most beautiful characters in the pages of history."

Archbishop Talavera still exercised his prerogative of scolding his royal "daughter" by mail, whenever he heard a report that seemed to indicate a falling away on her part. How closely he scrutinized her personal conduct, and how humbly the autocratic queen comported herself before a spiritual adviser may be inferred from one of her letters to him:

"As for the French people supping at table with the ladies, that is a thing they are accustomed to do. They do not get the custom from us, but when their great guests dine with sovereigns, the others in their train dine at tables in the hall with the ladies and gentlemen, and there are no separate tables for ladies. The Burgundians, the English, and the Portuguese also follow this custom, and we on similar occasions do likewise. . . . I say this that you may see there was no innovation in what we did, nor did we think we were doing anything wrong in it. . . . But if it be found wrong after the inquiry I will make, it will be better to discontinue it in future. . . . As for the bullfights, I feel with you, though perhaps not quite so strongly. But after I had consented to them, I had the fullest determination never to attend them again in my life nor to be where they were held."

Yet when the good Archbishop wrote her that he had disturbing reports of the richness of her gown on a certain occasion when she entertained the French ambassadors, Isabel defended herself with a vigor that reveals the elemental woman beneath the royal penitent. Her dress was not new, she wrote, nor were those of her ladies—in fact her own was only "made of silk, and with three bands of gold as plainly as possible," and she had worn it before in the presence of these identical Frenchmen—a humiliating experience, surely, for any woman. Some of the *men's* costumes may have been extravagant, she admitted, but it had not been by her orders, nor by her example.

It was about this time—March, 1493, while the Court was still at Barcelona—that the first news came from Christopher Columbus, who had been missing for nearly eight months.

His letters to the King and Queen—and it is inconceivable that he should not have notified them first—have not been found. But the general tenor of his report may be conjectured from letters he wrote to two of the most powerful *Conversos* of the Court, Gabriel Sanchez and Luis de Santángel who undoubtedly showed them to the sovereigns.

The letter to the astute Sanchez, treasurer of Aragon, was signed "Christoferens, Admiral of the Armada of the Ocean," and began thus:

"As I know you will take pleasure in hearing of the success of my undertaking, I have determined to send you an account of the occurrences of my voyage and discoveries. Thirty-three days after my departure from Cádiz I arrived in the sea of India, where I discovered many islands, inhabited by innumerable people. Of these I took possession in the name of our fortunate monarch, with public proclamation and colors flying, no one offering any resistance. I named the first of these islands San Salvador, thus bestowing upon it the name of our Holy Savior, under whose protection I made the discovery. The Indians call it Guanahanyn. I gave also a new name to the others, calling the second Santa María de la Concepcion, the third Fernandina, the fourth Isabela, the fifth Juana. In the same manner I named the rest. Arriving at the one last mentioned, I sailed along its coast, toward the West, discovering so great an extent of land that I could not imagine it to be an island but the continent of Cathay . . .

"These islands are of a beautiful appearance and present a great diversity of views. They may be traversed in any part, and are adorned with a great variety of exceedingly lofty trees, which to appearance never lose their foliage, for I saw them as verdant and flourishing as they exist in Spain in the month of May, some covered with flowers, others loaded with fruit, according to their different species and their season of bearing. . . . The nightingale and countless other birds were singing, although it was the month of November when I visited this delightful region."

He speaks in a rather general way of towns, fields, drugs, gold and metals.

"The inhabitants of both sexes . . . go naked as they were born, all except a few females who wear at the waist a green

leaf, a portion of cotton, or a bit of silk which they manu-
facture for the purpose."

They are timid, peaceable people, ingenuous and honest,
and so generous that "they would trade away their cotton and
gold like idiots, for broken hoofs, platters and glass. I prohibited their traffic on account of its injustice, and made them
many presents of useful things which I had carried with me,
for the purpose of gaining their affection in order that they
may receive the faith of Jesus Christ, be well disposed towards
us, and inclined to submit to the King and Queen our Princes,
and all the Spaniards, and furthermore that they may furnish
us with the commodities which abound among them and we
are in want of."

The Indians thought Columbus and his companions were
men from Heaven, and brought them food and drink. On the
Island of Hispaniola, Columbus had "fixed upon a spot for a
large city," which he called *Navidad,* "Nativity." There he
built a fort, and left in charge a garrison with arms and provisions for a year, and a caravel, "after having assured them
the friendship of the king of this part of the country. These
people are a friendly and amiable race, and the king took a
pride in calling himself my brother. Even if their sentiments
should change, and they should become hostile towards us, they
will not be able to effect any injury to those who remain at
the fortress, as they are destitute of weapons, go naked and
are very cowardly; so that those whom I have left there will
be able to retain the whole island in subjection without any
danger, if they adhere to the regulations with which I charged
them."

There were other Indians in an island beyond Hispaniola,
who were regarded by their neighbors as exceedingly fe-
rocious; "they feed upon human flesh"; but of these Columbus
saw nothing. He had also heard of an island where the people
had no hair, and possessed larger quantities of gold. Finally,
to sum up, "I am obliged to promise the acquisition, by a
trifling assistance from their Majesties, of any quantity of gold,
drugs, cotton and mastick . . . also any quantity of aloe, and
as many slaves for the service of the marine[8] as their Majesties may stand in need of.

"And now ought the King, Queen, Princes and all their
dominions, as well as the whole of Christendom, to give thanks

to our Savior Jesus Christ who has granted us such a victory
and great success. Let processions be ordered, let solemn festivals be celebrated, let the temples be filled with boughs and
flowers. Let Christ rejoice upon earth as He does in Heaven,
to witness the coming salvation of so many people, heretofore
given over to perdition. Let us rejoice for the exaltation of
our faith, as well as for the augmentation of our temporal
prosperity, in which not only Spain but all Christendom shall
participate."

About the same time another of the great *Conversos*, Luis
de Santángel, *escribano de racion,* received from Columbus a
letter substantially the same as that of Sanchez and dated
"on board the Caravel, off the Azores, February 15, 1493."

Presently came letters to the Court from Portugal, stating
that a terrific storm had driven him into the port of Lisbon,
and though an envious Portuguese chronicler said that the
Admiral went there to crow over King João and show him
his parrots and naked Indians, he was entertained with all
the honors commonly paid to royalty. He was on his way to
Barcelona to report in person to their Majesties.

XXVIII

COLUMBUS arrived at the bar of Saltes at daybreak on March 14, 1493, and entered the harbor of Palos that noon. It was disappointing to learn that the Court was at Barcelona, nearly six hundred miles away. However, there would be all the more cities and towns to pass through in triumph, and Columbus can hardly be blamed if after all his years of waiting and of obscurity, he took full advantage at last of what might prove his only opportunity to dramatize himself on a wide stage. Courts are cruel and the favor of kings is variable. And as if his poetic soul already whispered to him that after six months of applause he would be almost a forgotten man, the weaver who thought that he had been to the waters of Cipango and the shores of Cathay received the acclamations of the people of Palos with a natural swelling of the heart, and immediately set off like a conqueror on an imperial progress through Seville, Córdoba and a dozen other great cities that lay on the route to Barcelona, far in the northeast.

He entered Barcelona with a burst of splendor in the middle of April. Many young cavaliers and noble merchants, followed by the populace, came forth from the gates to receive him, as if he had been a Roman victor returning from the wars. The first to enter the city were the six Indians he had brought from the lands of Kubla Khan, painted and befeathered, and shivering with cold. After them walked the sailors of Columbus's crew, carrying live parrots, stuffed birds and animals from the Indies, weapons and implements of the Indians. At last came Columbus on horseback, in silken doublet and hose, with a new velvet bonnet and a gorgeous cloak flung over his shoulders—the Admiral of the Ocean Seas attended by the chivalry of Spain.

To show signal honor to the discoverer of new lands, the King and Queen had ordered their throne placed in public, before the Cathedral, under a canopy of gold brocade, and there, with Prince Juan on one side of them, and the venerable Cardinal of Spain on the other, they received him. As Columbus knelt to kiss their hands, they raised him. Indeed, they stood up, as if he were a person of the highest rank, and begged him to be seated in their presence—a courtesy commonly extended only to princes of the blood. The wool-comber's son who had been jeered at because his cloak was patched would hardly have been human if he had not felt the elation of that moment, but he carried off the situation with a grave and gracious dignity.

He gave a brief summary of the events described in the log of his voyage, which he presented to their Majesties, and as he spoke, his imagination conjured up not only what he had seen, but the shapes of things unknown that he intended to discover—gold and pearls, great cities, mighty empires; for the actualities he related, amazing as they were, proved a little pale beside the promises he had made, based upon the accounts of Marco Polo and Sir John Mandeville. When he concluded, Isabel and Fernando and the Prince knelt and raised their hands and voices in gratitude to Heaven. All the Court followed their example, and Columbus and his sailors too, while the choir of the royal chapel, accompanied by many instruments, sang the *Te Deum Laudamus*, and all arose to form a joyous procession through the city. Isabel must have felt the pleasure of one whose judgment of a man has been confirmed by the event. She invited the Admiral to dine with the royal family and promised him a new fleet for a second expedition. While the Admiral described the wonders of Asia, Prince Juan hung upon every word uttered, and at the end asked for one of the Indians for a servant. The request was granted, but the Indian soon died, for the Spanish climate was too much for him. The King and Queen sponsored the six aborigines when they were baptized.

For a whole month Columbus was the hero of the court. He was seen riding horseback in the park with King Fer-

nando and Prince Juan. He was entertained at supper by
Cardinal Mendoza. His praises were sung in London, Paris,
Vienna, at the court of Pope Alexander VI, and especially at
Genoa. Sebastian Cabot, his fellow countryman who was to
emulate his example, pronounced the discovery "a thing more
divine than human."

Few had any doubts that the islands he had found were
near the mainland of Asia; it seemed that this daring man
had actually arrived at the east by sailing west—he had annihilated the great mystery, he was what he had claimed to be,
the man God had chosen to bring to pass the prophecy of
Seneca in the chorus of *Medea*. Not everyone, however, was
certain that the Admiral had actually reached the waters of
Asia. A note of caution is discovered in the earliest reference
in print to the discovery, an *oratio* by Cardinal Bernardino
Carvajal at Rome in 1493:

"And Christ placed under their rule the Fortunate Islands,
the fertility of which has been ascertained to be wonderful.
And he has lately disclosed some other unknown ones *towards
the Indies* which may be considered among the most precious
things on earth, and it is believed that they will be won over
to Christ by the emissaries of the King."

Columbus's journal, abbreviated by his biographer and
friend Las Casas, so that we sometimes have the words of the
Admiral in the first person and sometimes only summaries in
the third person,[1] may still be read as Isabel read it that April
in Catalonia. He tells how he made for the Canaries, and then,
September 6, after certain repairs, boldly sailed west. On the
eleventh they saw part of the mast of a ship of about 120 tons
floating in the water. On the night of the fifteenth they beheld
"a remarkable bolt of fire fall into the sea at a distance of four
or five leagues." It drizzled next day, but from then on there
was nothing but very pleasant weather. "The mornings were
most delightful," wrote the Admiral. "Nothing was wanting
but the melody of the nightingales to make it like Andalusia
in April." He encouraged the sailors by pointing to some
patches of green weeds, and said, "The continent we shall find
further ahead." But on the seventeenth the sailors were terrified when the Admiral noted, for the first time in history,
the magnetic variation of the needle, a whole point from the

north. The Admiral invented a very ingenious explanation to quiet the men; the compass was correct, but the north star, instead of being stationary, as all had supposed, evidently revolved about the pole like a lantern—what could be more simple? After that "they were all very cheerful, and strove which vessel should outsail the others." They saw tunnies, and a live crab. The Admiral said he saw a white bird called a waterwagtail, which does not sleep at sea. On the eighteenth a pelican came aboard. The Admiral said they never went more than twenty leagues from land; there must be islands near. He was then in the middle of the Atlantic Ocean.

The wind blew so steadily from the east that the sailors began to say that it never blew in any other direction in that ocean, hence they could never return home, but must sail west forever. Fortunately on the twenty-second the wind changed. The Admiral, seeing the hand of God in everything, said, "this head wind was very necessary to me, for my crew had grown much alarmed." The next day the sea was so smooth and tranquil that the sailors murmured, saying they had got into an ocean where no winds blew. But they were presently astonished to see the waves rise without a wind. The Admiral recorded, "The rising of the sea was very favorable to me, as it happened formerly to Moses when he led the Jews from Egypt."

He had differences of opinion with Martin Alonzo Pinzon. At sunset September 25, Pinzon cried that he saw land, and the crew of the *Pinta* sang the *Gloria in excelsis Deo*, the other crews joining in. Sailors of that period commonly sang at their work, and the Admiral had them all sing every evening the beautiful hymn called the *Salve, Regina*:

> Hail, holy Queen, Mother of Mercy, hail,
> Our life, our sweetness and our hope!
> To thee do we cry, poor banished children of Eve,
> To thee do we send up our sighs,
> Mourning and weeping in this valley of tears.
> Turn then, most gracious Advocate,
> Thine eyes of mercy towards us,
> And after this our exile
> Show unto us the blessed fruit of thy womb, Jesus.
> O clement, o loving, o sweet Virgin Mary,
> Pray for us, o Holy Mother of God,
> That we may be made worthy of the promises of Christ!

But on this occasion the chanting of the ninety voices withered into a disappointed silence when the "land" turned out to be a cloud.

The Admiral now began to conceal from the crew the true distance they had gone. October first he told them they had sailed only 584 leagues, whereas his own reckoning showed 707. He would lop a few leagues off the reckoning each day. The weather continued fine. "Many thanks to God," wrote the Admiral in his log.

On the sixth of October Pinzon urged Columbus to alter the course from west to southwest, where he thought there would be islands. Columbus, who appears to have found Pinzon very irritating, refused. But on the next day he shifted his course from W. to W. S. W., giving as his reason that the birds were flying toward the southwest, and that "the Portuguese had discovered most of the islands they possessed by attending to the flight of birds." If Columbus had continued to follow the inner voice of his own genius instead of Martin Alonzo and the birds, he would have landed on the North American continent in a few days. As it was, he discovered land on the fourth day.

In his journal he says nothing of any "mutiny" or threats to mutiny by his crew. The story of the mutiny, like that of the dying sailor whose secret Columbus was supposed by certain historians to have appropriated, must be dismissed as a later fabrication. Years after Columbus's death, a sailor, Francisco Vallejo, a relative of Pinzon, declared that Pinzon had to quiet a disturbance in Columbus's crew, and to persuade the Admiral to continue. But as Harrisse observes,[2] the "inane" story was told "a half century after the alleged event, by an individual in the employ of the Pinzons and their blood relation, repeating, on his own authority, what these last had taught him to say in the course of a lawsuit that they lost before the Council of the Indies."

On the evening of the eleventh the Admiral saw a moving light ahead. The three crews chanted the *Salve, Regina* with unusual fervor; and the next morning they landed on an island which Columbus called San Salvador, "Holy Savior." It was on a Friday, always a lucky day in the Admiral's life and in Spanish history.

It is not certain which of the islands of the Lucaya Archi-

pelago is the San Salvador of Columbus. It may have been
Watling Island. It may have been Grand Turk, or Turk's
Island, which corresponds to Columbus's description of San
Salvador as "flat, without any lofty eminence, surrounded by
a reef of rocks, and with a lake in the center."

Naked savages gazed with wonder and delight as the "celes-
tial men" landed. Columbus bore the royal standard, and each
of the Pinzons carried a banner of the Green Cross, containing the initials of the names of the King and Queen each side
of the cross, and over each letter a crown. The Indians swam
out to the ships.

"As I saw that they were very friendly to us," wrote the
Admiral in his journal, "and perceived that they could be
much more easily converted to our holy Faith by gentle means
than by force, I presented them with some red caps and strings
of beads to wear upon the neck, and many other trifles of
small value, wherewith they were much delighted. . . . But
they seemed on the whole to me to be a very poor people. They
all go completely naked, even the women, though I saw but
one girl. All whom I saw were young, not above thirty years
of age, well made, with fine shapes and faces; their hair short,
and coarse like that of a horse's tail, combed toward the fore-
head, except a small portion which they suffer to hang down
behind, and never cut. Some paint themselves with black . . .
some white, others with red."

The first person that Isabel and Fernando notified of the
momentous discovery was Pope Alexander VI. Their chief
aim, they explained, had been the discovery of new lands
and the extension of Christianity. A year later they called
upon him to avert a possible war between Spain and Portugal
by arbitration. The Portuguese had been the leaders in previous discoveries; Diaz in 1487 had rounded the Cape of Good
Hope. When Columbus visited Dom João in Lisbon on his
return, the King expressed the fear that San Salvador might
be in Portuguese territory.

Pope Alexander drew an imaginary line through the Atlantic to protect each nation in the right to its discoveries. All
discovered to the west of that line should belong to Spain,
since Columbus had sailed west; all to the east should be
Portuguese, since their activity had been along the coast of
Africa. As Dom João was not quite satisfied, the Spanish Pope,

with remarkable impartiality, shifted the arbitrary line 370 leagues west of the Cape Verde Islands. A great deal of buncombe has been written about this papal bull. Alexander has been accused of dividing the whole world between Spain and Portugal, to the exclusion of France and other nations, and of attempting to dispose of the liberties of later Americans by grant. The folly of this criticism is apparent when one remembers that when Alexander issued his bull in 1493 he had no idea that the American continent existed. Like every one else, including Columbus, he supposed that certain islands had been discovered near the shores of Asia, and he acted to prevent a war over these islands.[3] On June 7, 1494, the two nations agreed to abide by the Pope's ruling in the Treaty of Tordésillas, which gave Portugal her later title to Brazil.

Isabel decided to send the Admiral back to the Indies, not only to make further discoveries and to spread the gospel, but to colonize; and by September, 1493, she had assembled seventeen ships and about 1500 men, including soldiers, farmers, artisans, young cavaliers in search of gold and adventure, and missionary priests and monks. Since the New World had no domestic animals or agricultural products useful to civilized man in the "Indies," she had the armada well stocked with all kinds of seeds, wheat, barley, oranges, lemons, bergamots, melons and other fruits and vegetables, the first to be planted in America; and all manner of beasts, cows, bulls, goats, horses, pigs, hens, rabbits. Her genius provided for the fecundation of the whole virgin continent, so rich in soil but poor in products. The armies of *conquistadores* who carried civilization later from the Atlantic to the Pacific, lived on the great droves of swine descended from the eight pigs that Columbus took on his second voyage.

In return for these benefits the New World gave to the Old "a root that looked like a carrot and tasted like chestnuts"—the potato, a truly American product, Irish only by adoption. And when Columbus sent men to explore the interior of an island in November, 1492, they came back saying they had found natives who carried a lighted brand to kindle fire, and perfumed themselves with certain herbs they burned. This burning was accomplished in a Y-shaped pipe made of a hollow tube, the two points of which were inserted in the nostrils of the Indian when he "perfumed" himself, and thus

The Arms of Boabdil
Tableware Used by Columbus and his Crew

the fumes of the herbs were inhaled through the nose. The Y-shaped pipe was called a *tabago*. The first European who had the temerity to imitate the savages in this curious custom was Luis de Torres, a Jew who had become a Christian just before he sailed with Columbus as interpreter.

Of more useful commodities the explorers found very little. "There were no beans, chick-peas or vetches or lentils or lupines or any quadrupeds or other animals, excepting some small dogs," wrote Bernaldez, quoting what Columbus related during a visit to the good curate at Seville. There were, however, certain very peculiar animals "which look like large rats, or something between a large rat and a rabbit, and are very good and savory for eating, and have feet and paws like rats, and climb trees. The beast thus described by Christopher Columbus to his breathless listeners in Spain was undoubtedly the "island" possum. He told of many kinds of lizards he had seen. On a certain island he had seen one "as large around as a yearling calf, and as smooth as a lance; and several times they undertook to kill it, but could not, on account of the thickness of the hide, and it fled into the sea." As for the Indians, added Bernaldez, "besides eating lizards and snakes, these Indians devour all the spiders and worms that they can find, so that their beastliness appears to exceed that of any beast in the world."[4]

In October, 1493, after six months of glory, Columbus set sail a second time in quest of the shores of Cathay.

Meanwhile Fortune, thus far having favored Isabel in all her undertakings in the west, was beginning to reward Fernando's long and patient efforts north and east. For Charles VIII had taken the bait laid out for him; he was preparing to invade Italy.

In spite of the warnings of his wisest counsellors, he imagined that when he had given Fernando two provinces and obtained his promise to assist him against all foes except the Holy Father, he had nothing further to fear from that quarter. By the treaty of Étaples he had bought the friendship of Henry VII for 750,000 gold crowns. By the treaty of Senlis he had restored to the Emperor Maximilian Artois, Charolais and Franche-Comté. He felt that he had disposed of all obstacles between him and the conquest of Naples.

He had 20,000 infantry, 3,600 men at arms, and 8,000 well-trained Swiss, with a plentiful supply of heavy artillery; but, needing money and cavalry, he sent secretly to Fernando, reminding him of the Treaty of Barcelona and asking for men, for financial aid, and for the use of the harbors of Sicily as bases for his fleets. He informed the Spanish monarch that he was commencing an expedition against the Turks, a project that all Christendom would naturally approve. He spoke incidentally, as though it were a fact of no importance, of taking Naples.

Fernando and Isabel sent Alonso de Silva to speak with him at Vienne. In the name of his master and mistress, de Silva congratulated Charles on his zeal and promised him all possible aid against the Mussulmans, although he felt it to be his duty to point out that the right of conquests of the Moors in Africa had been reserved by papal brief to Castile. As for Naples, the Kings of Spain must reluctantly refrain from co-operating, since that kingdom was a fief of the Holy See, and the high contracting parties at Barcelona had expressly agreed to do nothing inimical to the Pope.

Charles stormed out of the room without making a reply. Having gone so far with his plans, he resolved to continue without the aid of Fernando. In August, 1494, he left Grenoble, and crossed the Alps with the largest army that had invaded Italy since the barbarians.

It was a grotesque campaign. The mercenary armies of the Italian states, led by the *condottieri*, melted away like shadows. Towns opened their gates to the conqueror. Having stopped at Asti for a month of riotous pleasures with Ludovico El Moro, he advanced in leisurely fashion southward, and appeared before Rome on the last day of December. "The sword has arrived," cried Savonarola at San Marco in Florence. "The prophecies are on the eve of fulfilment, retribution is beginning, God is the leader of this host!"

The Eternal City was in a panic. While Pope Alexander and the Cardinals took refuge in the castle of San Angelo, the French King, like a modern Caesar, rode into the city at the head of his chivalry. It took from three in the afternoon till nine in the evening for the long files of mercenaries to make their entrance—Swiss and German men-at-arms, Gascon crossbowmen, mounted French noblemen in heavy armor, wearing silk mantles and gilt helmets; Scottish archers in kilts, marching to the squeak of bagpipes; and finally, in the midst of a bodyguard of dismounted noblemen bearing iron maces, the youthful King of France with Cardinals Giuliano and Ascanio beside him, like giants glistening in the wavering light of thousands of torches; and trailing after the column, thirty-six bronze cannon, eight feet long, rumbling over the ancient *Via Lata*, now the Corso.

The scatterbrained youth with the gilt circlet on his brow had laid bare, with hardly the loss of a man, the fatal weakness of Renaissance Italy. The Italian states had become over-civilized; they had become so enamored of ease and luxury, of books and art, that they had forgotten how to fight. Each state had left its defense to mercenaries who cared for nothing but collecting their pay. Superficially their history reads as if they were constantly embroiled in bloody wars. The battles were frequent, but they were virtually sham battles. In one of them, that "raged" all day long, only one man was killed, and he was smothered by the weight of his armor. After a "battle," the prisoners were usually released, without ransom. The opposing armies would sometimes declare a holiday and play games. The *condottieri* refused to attack any towns by night, or to fight winter campaigns. It was inevitable that such troops should flee without resistance before the invincible Swiss and other well-drilled warriors that marched under the banner of Charles. All that the French needed, observed Pope Alexander ironically, were children's wooden spurs to egg on their tired horses, and some chalk to mark their lodgings for the night.[5]

XXIX

FERNANDO AND ISABEL OUTWIT
CHARLES, AND MAKE SPAIN A GREAT
EUROPEAN POWER—THEY PLAN SOME
ROYAL MARRIAGES FOR THEIR CHIL-
DREN

THE success of Charles was a valuable lesson to several statesmen, but to none more than to King Fernando of Aragon and Castile. That deep contriver was maturing his plans very secretly. He had already sent to Sicily a strong fleet with 3,000 picked men on board under Gonsalvo de Córdoba, the Great Captain, who was recommended for this command by Queen Isabel. At the same time Fernando sent Garcilaso de la Vega to Rome to assure the Holy Father of the loyalty and obedience of Spain, and to organize the Italian States against the invader.

Garcilaso might have been too late if Pope Alexander had not displayed an unexpected courage and determination in the face of the conqueror. Charles had entered Rome with every intention of causing the Pope to be deposed. Both Cardinal Giuliano and Savonarola had urged him to enter Italy for that purpose—Giuliano because he expected to become Pope in Alexander's place, and Savonarola from loftier motives. And it is likely that all three imagined that Alexander would surrender the tiara rather than face a Council investigating, under French auspices, his simony, his nepotism, and his immoral life. But Alexander refused to play the part assigned to him. Although the Roman barons who had promised to defend him deserted him at once, he drew up his majestic figure on the crumbling ramparts of San Angelo, and calmly defied the young King with the bronze cannon, the Italian traitors, and the cardinals who had joined the cabal of Giuliano. After two weeks it was Charles who submitted, acknowledging Alexander as the true Pope, "with all imaginable humility," says Commines; to the intense disgust of Giuliano. Many a pope more saintly than Alexander might have made a less brilliant demonstration of the moral power of the Papacy to tame what appeared to ‚be irresistible brute force. As soon as Charles had offered his obedience, he strove to wheedle the Pope into granting him the investiture of Naples, but Alexander remained firm. There was nothing for Charles to do—at least so he decided—but to leave Rome.

Meanwhile Garcilaso and the other Spanish envoys, acting on instructions from the farseeing Fernando were quietly beginning their work. They went from one Italian Prince to another, rebuking them for their weakness, and appealing to their faith, patriotism and hatred of the foreigner. Reproaching Ludovico Sforza for his treachery to the rest of Italy, they dangled before him the bait of a marriage with one of the Infantas of Spain. Thus they laid the foundation for an alliance of the Pope, Venice, Milan, the Empire and Spain to protect the Holy See and Italy from the megalomania of Charles.

All that Fernando now required was a good occasion for war, and Charles furnished it by marching against Naples, taking Cesare Borgia along as an hostage. The Spanish envoys, who had been waiting for precisely what happened, followed him, and overtaking him on the road, publicly complained of the French ill-treatment of the Spanish ambassador Alonso de Silva at Vienne and of his actions towards the Pope, which, as Isabel and Fernando later wrote Henry VII, were such that "the Turks would not have treated him worse," nor had such an outrage "ever before been committed by Christians against the Viceroy of God." The French had committed many atrocities in Rome, especially against the Spaniards, "who were dead as soon as they were seen." The envoys concluded by demanding that Charles release Cesare, restore Ostia and other lands of the Church that he had seized, give up his attempt on Naples, and submit the whole question to arbitration. When Charles refused, as he was expected to do, the ambassador Fonseca tore up the treaty of Barcelona, crying, "The die is cast. It is in God's hands. Arms shall decide it."

Charles, in a fury, heightened by the sudden disappearance of Cesare, continued to march on Naples. King Alfonso II abdicated, and his son Ferrante II was obliged to flee, as the

Neapolitans, tired of the tyranny of the bastard Aragonese line, threw open the gates February 22, 1495, and sang hymns in honor of their "deliverer." A month later, after the French had looted their town and dishonored their women, they switched their allegiance to the Spanish.

On the last day of March the organization of the League of Venice, carefully promoted by Garcilaso in many night conferences, was completed. A force of 24,000 horse and 20,000 foot was to be raised in Italy to defend the Holy See and the Italian states against Charles. King Fernando of Spain agreed to use his fleet and his army to restore his cousin to the throne of Naples. Forty Venetian galleys would attack the French forts on the Neapolitan coast. Ludovico, Duke of Milan since the opportune death of his nephew, promised to desert Charles, for the League, to expel the French from Asti and to block the passes of the Alps, shutting off reinforcements from the north. Both Fernando and Maximilian agreed to invade France. All the powers were to contribute to the joint expenses. So secretly did Garcilaso do his work that even Commines, the French minister at Venice, knew nothing of the formation of the League until the Doge made a public announcement of it.

Early in May, 1495, Charles made his formal entry into Naples, clad in robes of scarlet and ermine, the imperial crown on his head, the sceptre in one hand and a globe, the symbol of sovereignty, in the other, while the Neapolitans hailed him as their august Emperor.

Four days later Gonsalvo de Córdoba with his 3,000 picked men landed in Sicily and prepared to cross into Calabria to relieve Naples. Charles found himself facing a different sort of campaign from the one he had just completed. But it was the threat of an invasion of France that threw him into a panic, just as Fernando had foreseen. Leaving a garrison of 9,000 troops in Naples, he set out, May 20, for the Alps.

The League was too slow in mobilizing to cut him off effectually, but some of the allied troops met him at Fornovo di Taro. After a sharp battle, in which he proved himself no coward in the field, he withdrew, having lost heavily, and retreated across the Alps.

Gonsalvo de Córdoba, after futile efforts to get reinforcements or supplies from a Spain still paying for the Moorish war—"let them live off the country," wrote King Fernando, when the Great Captain complained—proceeded to conquer Calabria in a brilliant campaign by the sheer force of his genius. His siege of Atella was one of the most skilful in history. At the Pope's appeal he marched against Ostia, where a French garrison under a notorious freebooter had cut off the supplies and destroyed the commerce of Rome, and took it by storm. He entered Rome in triumph and was hailed as its deliverer. Pope Alexander publicly bestowed upon him the Golden Rose.

King Fernando was never reimbursed by his allies of the League for his expenses in driving Charles out of Italy, nor had the Emperor Maximilian kept his promise to invade France; but on the whole, the Spanish sovereigns had reason to congratulate themselves on what Fernando's diplomacy and Gonsalvo's strategy had accomplished. The reorganization that Isabel had begun in the Moorish war had been completed in Italy under the Great Captain. Meanwhile, Isabel and Fernando were beginning to form a national militia. They passed laws regulating the equipment of each citizen according to his property, and forbidding the seizure of a man's arms for debt. Somewhat later, they had a census taken of all persons capable of bearing arms. By an ordinance signed at Valladolid in February, 1496, they commanded that one of every twelve inhabitants between twenty and forty-five years of age must be engaged in military service, either in the field, or in suppressing disorders at home. The conscripts were paid during service and excused from taxes. A general review and inspection of troops and arms was to be held every year, and prizes given to the best accoutred. For the first time since the Roman eagles were withdrawn, Spain now had a standing army. The civil liberties of the Middle Ages had been destroyed, and the absolutism which had been the natural reaction to anarchy was made permanent.

All this was but a beginning. For just as Isabel had opened a New World to the west, so Fernando, with her aid, brought the Spanish genius out of the isolation of the peninsula into the full light of the European stage, to advance in triumph along the dangerous road of empire. Almost over night Spain had become the greatest power in Europe. Up to the conquest of Granada and the discovery of the New World, it was Isabel who played the dominant part, as a rule, in the royal team. But from then on Fernando gradually assumed the mastery. His character was one of those that mature slowly; it was not fully formed until the latter part of the Crusade. From then on it became more and more evident that he was the wisest and most prudent king of his time. "If you consider his actions," said Machiavelli, "you will find them always great and extraordinary." He began to look even beyond Europe. With the decay of the empires of Genoa and Venice, what was to prevent Aragon from extending her sway from Sicily along the north coast of Africa to Syria, reviving the ancient empire of the east and ruling from the pillars of Hercules to the Golden Horn? For himself and for Isabel, such a consummation seemed remote. But for Prince Juan it was a possibility. As human beings the King and Queen could hardly have failed to find the prospect exhilarating; and from now on they were constantly employed in attempting to realize it by arranging marriage alliances calculated to place every one of their four daughters on a throne and to ally Prince Juan with the Hapsburgs who ruled the Holy Roman Empire.

In January, 1493, Fernando and Isabel had promised Charles in the Treaty of Barcelona not to make any matrimonial arrangement with England. Yet in March, two months later, they made a treaty with Henry VII, agreeing to send Catalina to London as a bride when she was twelve, and Prince Arthur fourteen. There is no doubt that they played false with Charles, probably justifying their course by the knowledge that Charles all the while was deceiving them as to the true purpose of his "crusade."

Henry was anxious to ally himself with the Spanish house, as a counterpoise to France and a guaranty of his own unstable throne. Indeed, it was he who had made the first overtures at a time when he feared Scotland as well as France, and most of all Perkin Warbeck, "Duke of York" an imposter who was received even by the Emperor Maximilian as the son of Edward IV, and therefore as the legitimate king of England. When France became a menace to Spain, and Isabel and Fernando sent ambassadors to England in 1488, Henry, shrewdly calculating that the demand for his goods had risen, asked a marriage portion five times greater than his envoys had demanded in Spain. Why should not the King and Queen of Spain be liberal? he asked of Dr. Puebla; the money would

come not out of their coffers, but out of the pockets of their
subjects. Puebla replied, with a courteous smile, that the English ought to be content with whatever marriage portion the
Spanish monarchs chose to give, for it was not usual for them
to condescend to allow their daughter to marry into a family
that might any day be driven out of England. In one of the
interviews with the lame Doctor, Henry uncovered his head,
said the most flattering things of Fernando and Isabel, and
every time he pronounced their names made a reverential gesture with his bonnet. After some very plebeian haggling on
both sides, the marriage was arranged. Henry agreed to make
war on France whenever Fernando did, and not to make peace
unless France restored Roussillon and Cerdagne.

After the Italian War Fernando and Isabel maneuvered
Henry into a position where they virtually dictated all his foreign policy except with France, by alternately promising to aid
him against Perkin Warbeck, and threatening to abandon him
at a time when all Europe wavered between Perkin and Henry.
But at last Henry caught Perkin and had him hanged. Up to
that time Fernando had always addressed him as "Cousin."
From then on he called him "Brother." During all this bar-
gaining Catalina had been engaged to Arthur by treaty several
times. She was a sturdy, rather phlegmatic girl, kind, studious
and pious. It was finally agreed that her marriage portion was
to be 200,000 scudos, each scudo worth 4s 2d; half to be paid
at the time of marriage, and the rest within two years. The
dower of the Princess was to consist of a third part of the
revenues of Wales, Cornwall and Exeter.

About that time Henry heard something of the treaty of
Barcelona, in which Fernando and Isabel, only two months
before, had bound themselves to assist Charles against all his
enemies "and particularly against the English," and it was
only natural that he should be curious as to its contents. Evidently he inquired through Puebla, and Fernando and Isabel,
in November, 1495, wrote him an explanation. The King of
France, their much beloved and very dear brother and ally,
had restored to them their counties of Roussillon and Cerdagne.
In the treaty between Spain and England, they reminded
Henry, there was a clause by which they were at full liberty
to receive from their beloved brother, the King of France,
their counties of Roussillon and Cerdagne. These having been

restored, they had concluded their alliances, fraternity, brotherhood and confederation with France; which they were the more
entitled to do since Henry had not signed nor sworn to nor
delivered the treaties he made with them before the Treaty
of Barcelona.

When Charles VIII entered Rome, Isabel and Fernando
wrote Henry begging him, with other Catholic princes, to
come to the assistance of the Holy Father. Henry replied that
there was no more zealous Christian in the world, and no one
more disposed to aid the Holy See, than he. But he could
not believe the Pope was really in danger, for he had not told
him so, and communication between Rome and England was
not obstructed. Isabel and Fernando replied that the Pope had
not written to Henry because he was afraid his messenger
would be intercepted—presumably in France—and he had
therefore written to them, asking them to write to other Christian princes. But even that was not necessary, for every good
Christian would hasten to assist the Pope, without being asked
to do so, as soon as he knew that the Pope was in danger.
Soon afterward, Dr. Puebla wrote them that it was true no
appeal from the Pope had reached England, and this astonished
him, "because the authority of the Pope is very great in England, and his letter would have produced much effect."

At this period the Spanish monarchs were very cool on the
subject of the marriage of Catalina and Arthur, for they were
trying to draw Henry into the League of Venice. They declared they would not give a marriage portion of more than
100,000 crowns—32,800,000 maravedis, or nearly three-quar-
ters of a million dollars; but they empowered Puebla to draw
up a new agreement. This was the status of the Princess Catalina in 1496.

Isabel, the beautiful young widow of the Portuguese Prince
Alfonso, had lived virtually the life of a nun since the tragic
death of her husband six months after marriage. Her mother
and her sisters had attempted in vain to console her and to
draw her attention to the worldly duties of those born on the
steps of the throne. When her husband's brother, Dom Manoel,
became king of Portugal in 1495, he immediately asked for
her hand. The proposal pleased the King and Queen, for an
alliance with Portugal might perhaps lead to a union of the
whole peninsula. But the Princess would not even discuss it,

nor did her parents insist. In one of Queen Isabel's letters she said that since the Princess would not consider a new marriage, they would probably have to send her sister María to Portugal.

This was embarrassing, because King James of Scotland had made a request for one of the daughters, and Fernando and Isabel were anxious to please him, for they were using him as a club to force Henry VII, who feared him, into a war with France. Queen Isabel solved the difficulty by writing Dr. Puebla in London that if there were a fifth daughter, they would gladly give her to the King of Scotland; but since there was no other, she was about to send an ambassador to James "to keep him in suspense as much as she is able." James was duly kept in suspense until a satisfactory understanding was reached with Henry.

The second daughter, Juana, had already been promised to the young Archduke Philip the Fair, son of the Emperor Maximilian. Isabel and Fernando had taken advantage of Maximilian's pique against Charles to clinch this alliance, and that of Prince Juan to the Archduchess Margot. Juana was now sixteen years old, slim, dark, and so closely resembling her grandmother Queen Juana of Aragon that Isabel used to address her teasingly as *suegra*, mother-in-law. In temperament, however, Juana was more like her maternal grandmother at Arévalo. She was moody, melancholy, given to fits of sullenness and inexplicable depression. Of all the four daughters she alone lacked physical charm. She was jealous of her sisters. She resented her mother's discipline, and at times showed a great impatience with religious instruction and observance. Such was the young girl who was to be sent to Flanders as the bride of a careless, sensual and pleasure-loving boy.

Fernando and Isabel were using all their ingenuity to isolate Charles VIII in such a way that he would not make a second invasion of Italy; and in every letter to Dr. Puebla they urged him to draw Henry into the league against the French King. The Doctor replied in June, 1496, "Would to God the Archduchess (Juana) would soon go to Flanders. She will be able to do much good in England and in Flanders, especially if she is wise as the daughter of such parents is expected to be."

To this Isabel replied, evidently under great stress, that she was informed that Charles was assembling a great army to make a new descent upon Italy. The Pope was much afraid, and had appealed to Spain for protection. Fernando had gone to Catalonia to raise a large army, and Isabel remained near the frontiers of Navarre to superintend in person the preparations for war. She intended sending her daughter, the Archduchess, to Flanders. But now was the right time, she added, for Henry to show his devotion to the Pope.

Most of the diplomatic letters found in the archives of Simancas and elsewhere are signed "Ferdinandus et Isabella," making it possible for Isabel's biographers to place most of the onus of any sharp dealing upon the broad shoulders of the King. But at this period, when the sovereigns were separated, the Queen's signature alone appears on the letters to England, so that one may judge how far she yielded to the inferior ethics of the international game. The frankness and fearlessness of the old Isabel are still apparent, and there is a pulsating vigor, characteristically hers, that is missing from the joint correspondence; there is a freshness of epithet, an aptness of metaphor and simile—much of the charm, the power and the individuality of the woman of genius.

There are also some new and less agreeable qualities. The Queen is nervous and tense, and occasionally writes something that illustrates the observation of Pulgar that "she was naturally truthful, and desired to keep her word, though it happened in those times and in certain vicissitudes brought about by certain persons, and by the great events of the times, that she was made to swerve from it sometimes." But the Queen generally has a good excuse when she departs from the strict path of truth, and being very feminine, has probably convinced herself of its complete validity. And it must be said that at the period when this trait becomes most noticeable, she is exactly forty-five years old, a difficult age for most women.

Through Isabel's letters of 1496 runs one dominant idea: to prevent another war between France and Spain in Italy by bringing about a war between France and her "brother" Henry. There is a letter, dated July 10, whose bearer appears to have fallen into the water on his way to England, for the paper has been wet and in many places has decayed so that the words in cipher are illegible. It is apparent, however, that the Queen is trying to impress upon her ambassador that she and Fernando are acting chiefly out of devotion to the Church. She writes indignantly that Charles wishes to treat the Pope as his sacristan; "and considering the weakness of Italy, there is no doubt but that he will very soon conquer it if the King of England and the King and Queen of Spain do not henceforth assist it effectually. We have the intention to do so, with the help of God. The King of England will see how much reason he has to do so. . . . Send us a very long and very clear account of the whole business, and write us such a despatch as we expect from the Doctor de Puebla. We do not expect that you will send us a worse despatch than our other ambassadors, who all send us very good despatches on all things we wish to know. We expect more from you because we know that you have more capacity than they."

The Queen has begun to suspect that Puebla is more devoted to the interests of Henry VII, who has flattered him, than to those of his own employers. She plans to send another envoy to England to investigate Puebla's activities. At present she flatters him. In one letter she addresses him as "My counsellor and ambassador," and in another, "Virtuous and intimate friend."

In the waterlogged letter she writes that Henry must prevent Charles from "destroying and setting on fire the whole of Christendom, as he has hitherto done." But farther on she says, "Though this business is the business of God and of the Church, to defend which all we Christian Princes are obliged, there might be mixed in it something of . . . our own interest. . . ."

Isabel has offered part of Catalina's marriage portion in jewels and ornaments. Henry has refused, but at length has agreed to take a fourth in that form, provided the rest is in ducats. He cannot understand how Isabel and Fernando can spend such great sums in Flanders, and yet make so many conditions concerning the English marriage. Puebla writes her that "there were never kings so much praised as they are by Henry, and by the whole English nation; and never was an ambassador so much esteemed and flattered" as he. Evidently, too, Henry has become a little curious about an embassy that Fernando and Isabel have sent to France at the time when they are urging him to fight Charles. In her reply Isabel explains the whole affair:

"He sent his ambassadors to us twice, as above said; and although they came about things of little importance and less effect, and in fact to put us off with ridiculous impostures and trivialities, yet that he might have no grounds for saying that it was he who had obtained peace, attributing to himself that which we have desired and procured, and in order that neither by word nor in deed should he take advantage of it, we have sent him these messengers. . . . Moreover, in order, if it were possible, to avoid all the many evils and calamities which follow upon war, not only would we send one and more embassies, but, if necessary, we would even go in our own person, sparing ourselves no trouble whatever."

During the fall of 1495, Isabel was with the King at Tarazona; in January, 1496, at Tortosa, recruiting; and from April to July at Almazan, repairing defenses against a possible French invasion of Spain. Late in July she went to Laredo, on the northern coast, with the sulky Juana. In August she wrote Henry that the Archduchess had already gone aboard her ship, and begged him, if the vessel were obliged to put into an English port, to give her a cordial reception.

On the following day she made a more determined attempt to persuade Henry to declare war on France. "If you should see that he shows any signs of making war upon France," she wrote Puebla—if we may believe the unreliable Bergenroth, who decoded and translated all this correspondence, "then it appears to me that, in order to gain him over more entirely to come to an open rupture, you should speak to him in the following manner. Tell him that matters might be so arranged with the Pope that he should give him a crusade in this kingdom, he presenting to His Holiness either the half of what it would produce, or perchance he might prevail on the Pope to be content with a third, in which case the larger proportion would be his. Say to him, moreover, that we ourselves would obtain this for him, taking it in hand as though it were our own affair."

It was a monstrous proposal that Isabel, in her almost hysterical fear of France, was committing to paper. She could hardly have believed that Alexander VI would even consider granting a bull of crusade for an invasion of France by England, even though he had reproved Charles in 1495 for "committing horrible cruelties, murdering women and children in the churches, and behaving more furiously than even the Turks," in the Italian campaign. Her letter is very clearly that of a highly strung woman whose nerves are stretched taut by anxiety and overwork, and who clutches at a ridiculous expedient because it is the only one that happens to occur to her in a crisis. She goes to the length of assuring Henry that he will be doing Charles a service if he makes war on him. "If the King of France will continue to carry things with a high hand, putting reason entirely out of sight, then it would of a certainty be doing him a good office to prevent him from further following the road to ruin which he is taking. . . . In order to do this, there does not appear to us a better course to take than for the King of England to make war upon him." Isabel goes on to argue that in this event, Charles would give up his plan, make terms, and thus "restore peace to Christendom without prejudice to any one, in addition to which it would greatly benefit the said King of England our cousin." By making war, she adds, Henry will "put the finishing stroke to a thing of immense and universal good."

A few weeks later Isabel heard with much satisfaction that Henry had entered the league against Charles, and desired the early conclusion of the marriage of Catalina and Arthur. She wrote Dr. Puebla, evidently for Henry's ear, that she had a high opinion of him as a "prince of great virtue, firmness and constancy." She loved him very much, and hoped that after the marriage of their children a much more intimate friendship would exist between them than between any other princes. The marriage treaty of Medina must be renewed, but with certain additional clauses, one of which was that "the conclusion of the marriage must be kept most secret, in order that the King of Scotland may not hear of it."

Isabel bade farewell to her daughter Juana on August 22, and with many misgivings watched the sails of her caravel disappear to the north in a swelling sea and a cloudy sky. The eccentric girl showed no emotion or regret at leaving her mother. She seemed more interested in the weather and the ship, both of which she detested. She was hardly to be blamed, for the weather was foul, and the voyage, even under the fairest skies, was bound to be dangerous and uncomfortable in a four-masted vessel with a double tower at the stern, and wide bow and narrow poop, all rolling like a cork in the heavy wind. Juana would have preferred to remain at home, but there was no help for it, Charles VIII would probably have made her a prisoner had she attempted the journey by land, and as for staying at home, it was not likely that a Spartan like Isabel would allow one of her daughters to break off any enterprise on account of mere physical inconvenience.

There is a very pretty story[1] about Isabel's return to land after saying adieu to Juana. A storm having risen, the little bark in which the Queen was being rowed to shore could not make the land. The sailors spoke of taking the Queen in their arms to the land. But Gonsalvo de Córdoba, who could not endure the thought of his sovereign's being touched by plebeian hands, "leaped into the water, clad in cloth of gold studded with jewels, received the precious burden, which he hardly touched, and carried it like a holy relic to the dry gravel."

A charming tale, but alas, this was in August, 1496, and Gonsalvo was hundreds of miles away, in Italy, laying siege to the town of Atella. He was absent from Spain from 1495 to 1498.

Isabel had no news of her daughter for several months, during which reports of wrecks washed up on the Biscayan coasts kept her in a continual state of fear and remorse. At last she heard that her armada, after scattering in a storm and stopping at Portland for repairs, had reached Flanders.

This intelligence came indirectly, but not from Juana. The Archduchess made no reply to her mother's letters, and left three gracious messages from Henry VII unanswered. The Flemings had received her with enthusiasm, but Philip, who was hunting in Luxembourg, did not take the trouble to meet her until a month after she landed, when he saw her at Lille. Poor Juana's wedded life was beginning under indifferent auspices; and to make matters worse, she at once fell desperately in love with Philip, who cared nothing for her.

The armada which took Juana to her fate was to bring back on the return voyage the sister of Philip to be married to Prince Juan. In Margot of Austria the Queen believed that she had found the best possible mate for him. This charming, intelligent and attractive princess had been sent to Paris at the age of four to be affianced to Charles VIII, and had been brought up carefully by Charles's older sister, Anne de Beaujeu, in a coterie of young noble damsels to whom the stately and learned Regent read Greek philosophers, Church fathers, Renaissance humanists, poets and romancers, giving them an education that any Italian princess might have envied. Under her tutelage, Margot became a skilled huntress—by no means a fault in the eyes of Queen Isabel—and was very proud of her collection of wolves' heads. After she had borne the title of Dauphine for seven years, Charles had jilted her at the command of the Regent, to marry Anne of Brittany and thereby unite that province to France. For two years more, Margot remained at the French court, as a sort of hostage, until in May, 1493, after the peace of Senlis, she was sent home to her angry father. She was extremely popular in France, and the people cheered her when she left to live in retirement at Namur. Late in the winter of 1496, when the channel was covered with white caps, this young princess, accompanied by the seasick and homesick damsels who had attended Juana, set sail for Spain to become the bride of the delicate and sensitive boy with blond hair whom Queen Isabel called "my angel."

XXX

COMPLAINTS ABOUT COLUMBUS DUR-
ING HIS SECOND VOYAGE—HIS CHAR-
ACTER—MARRIAGE AND DEATH OF THE
PRINCE DON JUAN

WHILE Queen Isabel was at Almazan waiting for Juana to sail, she was notified of the return of Columbus from his second voyage, and she sent him a summons to Court, for she had been wondering what had become of him. Besides, she had been getting certain disquieting reports and complaints for which she desired an explanation from his own lips. A few weeks later he appeared before her at Laredo, shockingly changed. During his thirty months of absence his beard had grown, his face had become aged and lined by sickness and care, and instead of the gay attire in which he had last appeared, he had returned to the brown habit of Saint Francis, so that on the whole he would have looked more like a hermit than an admiral of Castile, but for that touch of gloomy majesty that never forsook him. He came to a Court where he had many enemies and backbiters, and few staunch friends save the Queen, the young Prince Don Juan, and the royal nurse. But he was received with honor, and found every one eager to hear of his new adventures.

After a voyage of some five weeks he had found himself among six little islands of the Antilles. It was Sunday, November 3, 1493. The crews, according to the custom of Columbus and of the Spanish and Portuguese explorers generally, knelt on the decks and gave thanks to God for their safe voyage, and sang the *Salve, Regina*; then, as there was no harbor on the island nearest them, they proceeded to the next. This the Admiral called Guadalupe, for he had promised the monks of Our Lady of Guadalupe in Estremadura that he would name some place after their monastery. The crews went ashore and discovered several interesting facts.

They found that curious fruit known as the pineapple, for example, and some wild geese, and a village with square huts, very filthy. And what was most disconcerting, they found the idyllic picture they had drawn of man in a state of nature revised by the ruthless hand of fact. Peter Martyr, ecstatically echoing Columbus, had already written of these communists, "It is certain that the land among these people is as common as the sun and water; and that 'mine and thine,' the seeds of all mischief, have no place with them. They are content with so little, that in so large a country they have rather superfluity than scarceness, so that they seem to live in the golden world without toil, in open gardens, not intrenched with dykes, divided with hedges or defended with walls. They deal truly with one another, without laws, without books and with judges. They take him for an evil and mischievous man who takes pleasure in doing hurt to another, and although they delight not in superfluities, yet they make provision for the increase of such roots whereof they make their bread, contented with such simple diet, whereby health is preserved and disease avoided."[1] Whether or not such rhapsodies as Peter Martyr's were the seeds, as Marius André alleges, of Rousseau's philosophy and other modern illusions about uncivilized man, the fact remains that the communists of Guadalupe were not contented with so simple a diet as the potato and the turnip. In several hamlets the Spaniards found human limbs hung from the rafters of the huts, as if curing for meat. They found the head of a young man recently killed, still bleeding, and some parts of his body roasting before the fire, while others were being boiled with the flesh of geese and parrots.[2]

Somewhat depressed, the explorers continued on their way to Española (Hayti), arriving off the coast near the fortress of La Navidad November 22. Naturally, their first wish was to speak with the thirty-nine comrades whom they had left in the stockade. Some Indians who came aboard told them the garrison were well, though "some had died of sickness and others had quarreled among themselves." Going ashore, however, the Admiral found no trace of his men. The fort had been burned to the ground. Every man, Englishman and Irishman and all, had been killed.

As soon as he found a suitable site, Columbus landed, and commenced building the first Christian town in the New

World, which he named Isabela, after the Queen. There, on
the feast of the Epiphany, 1494, the first High Mass in
America was solemnly offered up, either by Fray Bernard
Buyl, the apostolic delegate of Pope Alexander, or, as Fita is
inclined to believe, by Pedro Arenas. The news was received
in Europe with rejoicing. "Columbus has begun to build a city,
as he has lately written to me," recorded Peter Martyr, "and to
sow our seeds and propagate our animals. Who of us shall
now speak with wonder of Saturn, Ceres and Triptolemus,
traveling about the earth to spread new inventions among
mankind?"

But the Admiral was not content to settle down as a coloniz-
ing governor; his unfulfilled promises of gold, the children of
his imagination, scourged him on to new quests. He ransacked
Hayti in vain. Then he resumed his exploration of Cuba, which
he called Juana, and which he was positive was the continent of
Asia. After sailing 335 leagues along the coast, he compelled
all the crews of the fleet to make depositions before a notary
that it was a continent, and threatened to fine any one who
affirmed the contrary. The Indians were less willing than the
sailors to humor him. "He asked the Indians if it was an island
or terra firma," wrote Bernaldez, evidently echoing the Admiral, "and as they are a bestial people and think that all the
world is island and do not know that anything can be firm
land, nor do they have letters or ancient memorials, nor do
they take pleasure in anything but eating and women, they
said that it was an island."[3] After an exploration of the coast
of Jamaica, Columbus returned to Cuba with the hope of
finding a channel through the "continent" so that he might
circumnavigate the globe, returning to Spain by way of the
Ganges, Jerusalem and the Mediterranean.[4]

All this news was sent by returning caravels to the Queen.
But she had other intelligence from unofficial sources, and it
troubled her not a little. Complaints that reached her in growing volume and bitterness indicated that the Admiral, with all
his vision and greatness of soul, was far from being an ideal
executive. Some accused him of being too severe, others of
being too lenient. He was impatient and overbearing. The very
qualities that had swept aside all opposition and carried ninety
anxious men with him across the Atlantic were such as usually
make it difficult for their owner to get on harmoniously with

other men except in the stress of great actions that subdue all other spirits to his. And Columbus appears to have quarreled sooner or later with most of the people who had close relations with him.

During his absence on one of his exploring expeditions, Fray Bernard Buyl (or Boyle) boarded a ship with Captain Pedro Margarite, commander of Columbus's troops, and sailed for Spain to appeal to the King and Queen from what they described as the tyranny of Columbus and his brother. For this the anti-clerical historians have censured the priest harshly, giving all the benefit of the doubt to Columbus, though no evidence has been found of the exact cause of their differences. From what is known of the characters of the two men, it would be more reasonable to blame the Admiral and exonerate the friar. The latter was a Benedictine of the famous abbey of Monserrat. He was skilled and experienced as a peacemaker, for Fernando and Isabel had previously sent him to Paris to negotiate with Charles VIII for the return of Roussillon and Cerdagne. There he came under the powerful influence of Fray Francisco de Paula, who was known all over Europe for his sanctity and who persuaded Louis XI on his deathbed to agree to return Fernando's provinces, for the sake of the peace of Christendom. Fray Buyl, too, had labored in this cause, and so successfully that when he went to Seville to sail with the Admiral, the King and Queen wrote him, September 5, 1493,

"Devout Fray Buyl: Since we know the pleasure it will give you to know the good state in which, thanks be to God, the matter of the restitution of Roussillon stands, for which you have so labored, we have decided to let you know of it, as you see by the letter which we are writing to the Admiral Don Cristóbal Colón."[5]

Though a member of the rigorous order of Saint Benedict, Buyl was so inspired by his friend Fray Francisco de Paula that when the Saint organized a still more austere Order of Hermits, known as the Hermits and later as the Minims of Fray Francisco de Paula, he joined it, and was sent to Spain as Vicar-General in 1492 to organize some monastic communities. Pope Alexander commissioned him as first delegate to the New World at the request of the King and Queen, and after his denunciation of Columbus, Fernando and Isabel sent him on important embassies to Rome, where his conciliatory spirit was of value both to the Church and to Spain. As late as December 7, 1504, we find King Fernando writing his Captain General in Roussillon an order to have the detractors of Fray Buyl severely punished, and suggesting that they deserve to be hanged.[6]

Yet the just Queen realized that Columbus was working under no ordinary difficulties. He had taken with him on the second voyage a large number of gentlemen adventurers, who, taking his promises literally, expected to pick up gold nuggets on the ground without labor or discomfort and to return to Spain in glory. Where was the gold? Where was the glory? And who was this upstart Italian, that he should force hidalgos of Castile to build fences and dig ditches in his accursed town? Unfortunately, too, the King had released many convicts from jails to serve with the Admiral, and they proved unmanageable, once they were clear of civilization. Worst of all, the site picked for the town of Isabela was found to be unhealthy, and at length, after disease had taken a heavy toll, had to be abandoned. Columbus was prostrated for several months. A more patient executive than he might have failed under the circumstances.

Nothing in his career has been more embarrassing for his eulogists than his venture into the slave traffic, and nothing has furnished more useful ammunition for the proponents of the theory that he was of Jewish ancestry. For with all his genuine piety he was singularly lacking in the traditional Catholic instinct that held in abhorrence the enslavement of human beings; a scruple which the Jews did not share, since they regarded other races as inferior to their own and hence justly to be exploited, whereas the Church from the beginning preached the universal brotherhood of man. It is significant that slavery in Europe persisted longest where Jewish influence was strong, as in Languedoc, Andalusia, and later in England and Holland, long after its definite abolition in all Catholic countries. In Isabel's time theologians disagreed as to whether it was just to enslave male prisoners of war taken from infidel nations, and some of them justified it in Spain as a retaliation for the Mohammedan custom of enslaving Christian men, women and children.

Columbus had written the King and Queen early in 1494

suggesting that some of the cannibals of the Caribbean be sent to Spain as slaves. He argued that it would be doing them a service to wean them from their taste for human flesh, and to teach them the tenets of the true Faith. Isabel put him off by writing that she would answer his proposal later.

In April, 1495, four ships arrived in Seville, loaded with Indian captives sent by the Admiral. The King and Queen authorized their sale, evidently in the belief that they were male prisoners of war; for Columbus had sent them news of a battle in which his three hundred men-at-arms, aided by bloodhounds, had vanquished 100,000 Indians. Five days later, however, the Queen issued the following order:

"The sale of slaves must be absolutely suspended, and payment for them not made until we have had time to consult with informed persons, with theologians and canonists, as to whether in good conscience it is permitted to continue with this affair. Especially must Antonio de Torres send us at once the letters which he has from the Admiral, that we may learn with what motive he has sent these men as slaves to Seville."

The Queen was still under the impression that only male captives had been sent. But Bernaldez, who saw them at Seville, recorded that they were "five hundred souls, Indian men and Indian women, all of good age, from twelve years up to thirty-five or thereabouts . . . and they came just as they used to go in their own country, as they were born, and they had no more shame for it than wild animals, and all were sold. They proved very unprofitable, for they died all the more, since the climate was trying to them."[7]

Evidently the slave traders of Seville had done their work before the arrival of the Queen's order. But her conferences with theologians and canonists had so convinced her of the injustice of the sale that she commanded all the Indians to be freed and sent back to their homes in the New World. Unhappily all the five hundred died before the merciful command could be carried out.

How Columbus justified his action to the Queen, history has not recorded. Bernaldez says that the Admiral seized the Indians in retaliation for the burning of Navidad and the murder of his garrison. However this may be, it is a fact that in the epic of his life, which moves like a Greek tragedy to its appointed close, the sale of the slaves must be considered the turning point, as even his most enthusiastic biographer, the Bishop Las Casas, has noticed. Indeed, if Columbus had died after his first voyage, his unique service to the Faith, to Spain, to humanity in general would have remained essentially the same. He returned to Hayti with almost incredible glory and prestige, which nothing can take from him. From then on misfortunes closed in about him like dogs on the trail of a wounded lion. But in all vicissitudes he remains the man of will, the heroic man, made of the same stuff as Oedipus Rex, the mad Lear confronting the thunderbolt, Odysseus the man of many wanderings.

This poet has two ruling passions that keep him from the spiritual destiny to which his lofty imagination invites him. He is vain, he is avaricious. His vanity begets self-deception and a passion for self-justification. He craves gold and power and admiration. For a time these weaknesses defeat the man of faith, and the poet becomes a publicity agent for the man of gold and power. But suffering will bring him to himself. The latter part of his life will be a spectacle of increasing patience, of ascetic self-control practiced among licentious men in a strange world, of humility painfully acquired after many failures and rebuffs, of avarice transmuted by faith into an ambition to spend his gold for the recovery of the Holy Sepulchre, of vanity submerged in reverence and hope.

Returning to Spain in the spring of 1496 with two hundred passengers and thirty Indians, including the hostile chief Caonabo, he got lost among the Caribbee Islands, and when he finally put to sea after a month of wandering, his supplies were so reduced that he was obliged to restrict every one to a daily allowance of six ounces of bread and a pint of water. None of his pilots knew their way across the Atlantic; each contradicted the others and disputed the Admiral. Some of the sailors wanted to throw the Indians overboard to save their food for the Spanish. Others, half insane from hunger and thirst, proposed eating them. Caonabo and some of the rest died and were buried at sea. The hideous voyage lasted three months. It was a crew of emaciated, half-starved, fever-stricken wretches that crawled from the caravels at Cadiz on June 11. Last of all, in a monk's robe, sadly came the Admiral. His procession across Spain was vastly different from the one in 1493. His popularity was gone. Every one was saying, "Great cost and little gain;"[8] every one was calling him a humbug.

Isabel probably saw his weaknesses as clearly as any one. But invariably his virtues appeared to overshadow them and leave him greater than any of his critics. It was no light matter, either, even if she had been so disposed, to dismiss an official who had rendered such distinguished services. In the end she told him that she would continue the experiment for the glory of God and of His Church, even if the islands yielded nothing but rocks and stones. She had spent more money, she said, on enterprises of less importance, and would consider all she had disbursed well employed, for it would result in the spread of the Catholic religion and the good of Spain. Those who spoke ill of the project were not her friends nor those of the King. At Columbus's request she revoked an edict of the previous year, allowing individuals to explore and settle in the Indies, and she publicly proclaimed her gratitude to the Discoverer and her intention to protect him in all his privileges. To complete his triumph, she granted his suit for a third expedition, the clearest proof, perhaps, that she still trusted him in spite of all the complaints against him.

At the same time she made it plain that there must be no more slaves. Columbus obeyed. But five years later he interpreted his instructions liberally enough to give an Indian to each of his men as a body servant. When Isabel heard of this at Granada, her greenish-blue eyes flashed with anger, and she exclaimed, "Who authorized my Admiral to dispose of my subjects in this manner?" and had the natives sent back to America.

The Admiral remained in favor, but he had to wait some months for his six ships. One reason was that the King and Queen were at Burgos, preparing for the reception of the Princess Margot, then on the high seas, and her wedding to the Prince. Columbus partly refuted those who said he was no navigator by predicting what course Margot would follow and approximately when and where she would arrive.

The King and the Prince, taking Columbus's advice, rode to Santander to receive the Princess. As the Admiral had predicted, she arrived there a few days later, and came ashore to the sound of music and the shouts of cavaliers and populace. She was a girl with a piquant French charm, witty and joyous, intelligent and versatile. Her hair was blond, and if undone, would have fallen to her feet. Riding to Burgos between the King and the Prince, she related all that had happened on the long voyage, especially during a storm that had driven her into Southampton. In the worst of the tempest, when the sailors expected the ship to founder, Margot had written her own epitaph in verse and sewed it on her wrist band as a mark of identification in case her body was washed ashore:

> "Ci-git Margot, la gentil damoiselle,
> Qu'eut deux maris, et si, mourut pucelle."

> ("The gentle damsel Margot here lies dead,
> Who had two husbands, and so died unwed.")

Before the cavalcade reached Burgos, Don Juan and the Hapsburg princess were in love, to the delight of the King and Queen and all Spain. The marriage was celebrated almost immediately, on Palm Sunday, before a great assembly of nobles, prelates and ambassadors, by the Archbishop of Toledo, Ximenes de Cisneros, and the blond prince of nineteen and his blonde princess of eighteen walked out of the great Cathedral like the happy characters of a fairy tale, amid the flash of gold and jewels, and the blessings of the people.

Fernando and Isabel overwhelmed Margot with their generosity. A list of their gifts found in the archives of Simancas includes pearl necklaces, bracelets, girdles, chains, rings, earrings, diamonds, emeralds, rubies, gold and silver—even the celebrated Aragonese necklace that Fernando had given Isabel as a wedding present. But Isabel was not content with that. Her crown jewels and others had been in pawn at Valencia and Barcelona since she had raised 2,000,000 florins on them to finance the siege of Baza in 1488. She still owed a quarter of the sum received. She paid it, recovered her balas ruby necklace, and gave it to Margot. "All the jewels offered to the Princess," said the Queen's treasurer, "are of such perfection and of such value, that those who have seen them have never seen better." And there were furnishings without end—plates, braziers, candlesticks of gold, silver basins, bed furniture, hangings of brocade and damask, Flanders tapestries, enameled caskets filled with chemises and tabards of silk, headdresses of fine linen embroidered with threads of gold and silver, the saddles and caparisons for four mules.

After the usual tourneys, feasts and processions, Juan and Margot rode in triumph through the kingdoms of Castile and Aragon, fêted everywhere, symbols of eternal youth and love.

Queen Isabel watched them go with mingled emotions. The problem of choosing a mate for Juan had been weighty, for his delicate constitution had been a constant worry since his birth in Seville during the hectic summer of 1478; but the choice of Margot, the most eligible Princess of Europe, had seemed ideal.

Of all Queen Isabel's ambitions only one remained unsatisfied—the one concerning the Princess Isabel. Although she had never attempted to force the will of her eldest child, she had clung to the hope that grief would yield to time, and permit a second marriage. Dom Manoel of Portugal still loved her, but the Princess long remained indifferent. After her brother's marriage, she consented, but with an extraordinary proviso: the King of Portugal must agree to drive all the Jews out of his realm. Manoel hesitated, for the Portuguese Jews were rich and influential, and had rendered distinguished services to the Crown. Nevertheless he was not sorry, perhaps, to have an excuse to rid himself of subjects who were rapidly taking into their own skilful hands the management of all the new foreign trade and phenomenal prosperity that Portugal had gained through her discoveries. The Jews were expelled, and with them many who had been driven from Spain in 1492. The Princess Isabel prepared to go to Portugal a second time as a bride.

At that moment, when the Queen's cup of worldly success seemed not only full but overflowing, a courier overtook her with disturbing information. Prince Juan was not well. His physicians had already intimated that his infatuation for his bride might have dangerous consequences, considering his youth and frailness. They now went further, and advised his complete separation for a time from the lovely Princess. The King was inclined to follow the suggestion of the doctors, but the Queen would not hear of such a thing.[9] Perhaps her mother's heart divined that the humiliation and grief of such a forced separation would be a more bitter potion to Don Juan than death itself.

Margot remained with her husband. He recovered, and they continued on their happy way to Salamanca, while the Queen went with the King to Alcántara in September, for the wedding of the Princess to King Manoel. There were brilliant fêtes and jousts for several days, and the whole affair was more magnificent, if possible, than the previous ceremony at Seville.

After her daughter departed for Portugal, Queen Isabel was compelled to take to her bed, for the strain of the festivities had been too much for her, and her tremendous energies, long overtaxed, were beginning to wear down at last. Next day came a courier from Salamanca with bad news. Prince Juan had developed a high fever after the feasts in his honor at Salamanca, and the physicians sent word that his condition was alarming.

The King mounted a horse and posted to Salamanca, more than 100 miles away, while Isabel remained in an agony of suspense.

When Fernando reached his son's bedside, the physicians had given up hope, and the Prince was reconciled to the prospect of death. He bade his father and mother to be of good cheer, and submit to the will of God. He himself had known nothing but happiness and blessings in his short life, he said, and he would die without regret. He told his father that Margot had conceived, and he commended her and the unborn infant to the kindness of his parents, and his own soul to God. Fray Torquemada, the Inquisitor General, who had hastened to Salamanca at the King's summons, heard the dying boy's confession and gave him Holy Communion and Extreme Unction.[10]

The King, according to Bernaldez, comforted the Prince much when the last hour approached, saying, *"Fijo mucho amado*, have patience, since God calls you, who is a greater King than any other, and has other kingdoms and seignories greater and better than any we might hold or might hope to give you, and they will last you forever. Therefore be of good heart to receive death, which comes once inevitably to all, with hope to be immortal henceforth and to live in glory."[11] Thus he spoke, and when the Prince had sighed his last, closed the boy's eyes, and wondered, perhaps, why death, that had spared him in so many perilous battles, should strike down a happy youth on the threshold of life. The Prince died October 3, 1497, and "thus was laid low the hope of all Spain," sadly wrote Peter Martyr, his tutor.

The King had sent courier after courier to Alcántara, reporting every slight symptom that might be interpreted favorably, and keeping up the Queen's hopes until the last, perhaps in the belief that a miracle might yet happen. Now, as soon as the body of Juan was laid in state in the Cathedral of Salamanca, amid the lamentations of the university students and townspeople, he chose to be the first to break the tidings to the Queen.

Isabel gave a cry of relief, for she imagined his coming signified that the Prince was out of danger. The King's face, however, disillusioned her before he spoke.

"Tell me the truth, Señor!" she demanded.

"He is with God," replied Fernando.

The great Queen stood pale and shaken. "This was the first knife of sorrow," said Bernaldez, "that pierced her heart." Then she bowed her head, and said,

"God gave him, and God has taken him away. Blessed be His holy name!"

The King and Queen shut themselves up with their grief for several days while the church bells all over Spain tolled for the Prince, and people everywhere put on mourning, draped the walls and gates of every city in black and suspended all public and private business for several days.

When at last the sovereigns emerged from their retirement, they faced the world with such fortitude that all marveled at their self-control. Peter Martyr wrote, "The sovereigns force themselves to hide their grief, and they succeed. As we watch them, crushed by the weakness of our souls, they look calmly, eye to eye, at those about them. Where do they get such a power to hide their feelings? It seems as if, clothed as men, they were not beings of human flesh, and that their nature, harder than diamond, did not feel their loss."

But under the serene exterior of Queen Isabel there was a fatal wound. The world would never be to her as it had been, for she had learned at last the meaning of the word "impossible."

XXXI

ISABEL REBUKES POPE ALEXANDER
AND IS REBUKED IN TURN—SAVONA-
ROLA—COLUMBUS COMES BACK FROM
HIS THIRD VOYAGE IN CHAINS

QUEEN ISABEL lived seven years after Don Juan was laid in his beautiful tomb at Ávila; seven years of illness, anxiety, penance, self-mortification, and preparation for leaving a world that she no longer regretted. Although people at first saw little outward difference in her, and although her firm will continued to the end to fill her kingdoms with the impulses of her clear mind and lofty spirit, she knew well enough that life was passing her by. In that very year there entered Salamanca University a boy of fourteen named Hernando Cortes, who was to carry the standards of Castile and Aragon to the blood-drenched altars of Mexico where priests plucked out the hearts of maidens to appease an idol. And in the army of the Great Captain there was a soldier named Pizarro, whose son Francisco would win for Spain the incredible gold of Peru. And a boy in Germany who was being beaten vigorously by his father every day was growing into the Martin Luther who was soon to shatter the unity of Christendom for which Isabel had toiled so earnestly all her life. And in a castle in Guipúzcoa there was a boy of eight who was soon to be a page in King Fernando's court and finally to be a *conquistador* of souls—Saint Ignatius Loyola, whose life work would be to restrict the work of Luther to northern Europe. But the new order rising about her was like some receding pageant to the tired Queen.

The world was slipping away from her little by little as death removed her associates. Cardinal Mendoza, whose contribution to her greatness can hardly be overestimated, had left her only the consolation of praying before his tomb, the earliest Renaissance monument in Spain. Fray Tomás of

Torquemada, who had ensured the permanence of her life-work, died in 1498 at the age of seventy-five, and those who opened his tomb to remove his remains reported that a singularly sweet and agreeable odor emanated from it; causing many to go there and venerate him as a saint, though the Church has never given her sanction; and his place was filled by Bishop Diego de Deza, Prince Juan's tutor and Columbus's patron. Charles VIII of France had died an early death, the victim of his excesses. And in Italy there had been another political death that was having its repercussions in Spain—that of Alexander's favorite son, the Duke of Gandia, who had married Doña Maria Enriquez, a cousin of King Fernando.

Returning from a banquet late one night in 1497 with his brother Cesare and others, the Duke left them to take a lonely road along the Tiber with a mysterious domino who, it was believed, was conducting him to a rendezvous with a lady. He was never again seen alive. His body, the throat cut, was found several days later in the river.

The Pope, whose affection for his family was deep and sincere, was heartbroken, and retired to grieve and fast alone, while all Rome went wild with fears and rumors. Some accused Ascanio Sforza, some the Orsini; still others the unscrupulous Cesare Borgia, brother of the murdered man. The mystery was never solved, and the opinion gained currency that some jealous husband had quietly taken his midnight revenge on the Duke. Oddly enough, the name of the lady of mystery never found its way into history, save in the richly laden pages of Bernaldez, then the chaplain of the second Inquisitor General, Deza. He tells us categorically that the Duke was on his way to visit Madam Damiata, and gives a detailed account of the murder, though he errs in the date.[1] Far from accusing Cesare, he blames the Sforzi. He must have had excellent sources of information, for many persons in the court were on intimate terms with Garcilaso de la Vega, Gonsalvo de Córdoba, the Duke's widow, and perhaps the exiled Bishop Don Juan Árias de Ávila, who was Pope Alexander's guest.

The effect of the tragedy on Alexander was such that it seemed likely to change the course of his life. At the consistory of June 19, he declared that he would give seven tiaras to recall the Duke to life. "God has done this in punishment for our sins," he said frankly before all the cardinals—for what-

ever else was said of him, he was never accused of hypocrisy—
and proceeded with a remarkable statement in which he said,
"May God forgive the murderer. We, on our part, are resolved
to amend our own life and to reform the Church. We renounce
all nepotism, and we will begin the reform with ourselves."
The sorrowful old man appointed six cardinals to organize the
reform of the Papal court. He even wrote King Fernando of
Spain that he contemplated resigning the tiara. Fernando did
not take the resolution very seriously, for he wrote the Pope
advising him to do nothing hastily, and spoke of "the healing
hand of time."

Alexander's intention to reform was undoubtedly sincere.
The cardinals, especially Caraffa and Costa, set about in great
earnest to draw up a program for the Catholic Reformation, a
program that would have anticipated the great work of the
Council of Trent, if it had been vigorously enforced. But
Alexander had gone too many years in his old ways to give
them up suddenly without some such drastic action as leaving
Rome and his associations and perhaps going into a monastery;
and that he lacked courage to do. Consequently the reformation
was first postponed and then forgotten, until, as Pastor remarks, his last state became worse than his first. Henceforth
he fell completely under the domination of Cesare's strong will,
and so incurred the hatred of Cesare's numerous enemies. The
wildest and most scandalous tales were now circulated about
the Borgias. Their faults were exaggerated into enormities,
after the Renaissance fashion, and nothing was too wicked to
attribute to them. Strange phenomena, believed to be of dire
portent, were related. The powder magazine in the castle of
San Angelo was struck by lightning. The city became hysterical
over the tale of a monster said to have been found on the banks
of the Tiber. The Venetian ambassadors reported that it had
"the body of a woman and a head with two faces. The front
face was that of an ass with long ears; at the back was an old
man with a beard. The left arm was human; the right resem-
bled the trunk of an elephant. In place of a tail it had a long
neck with a gaping snake's head at the end. The legs, from the
feet upwards, and the whole body were covered with scales
like a fish."[2]

From San Marco the mighty voice of Savonarola thundered
prophecies of woe. This man, one of the most appealing fanat-

ics in history, had made himself virtually dictator of Florence, and in spite of the efforts of the Medici and other powerful enemies to silence him, had preached with increasing violence against their sins and those of Pope Alexander.

The Pope, who was indifferent to attacks of a personal nature, made no effort to curtail the monk's liberty of speech so long as he attacked none of the sacred doctrines of the Church; and Savonarola might have gone on prophesying indefinitely if he had not invaded a most delicate political field by calling upon Charles VIII of France, time after time, to return to Italy and reform the Church, since God had chosen him for that mighty work. To the end of his life the friar remained under the illusion that Charles was an instrument of the Most High. But neither the Pope nor the Italians outside of Florence could see in the frivolous young rake on the French throne the man qualified for so austere a work. They were all in mortal fear of the French. And a second French invasion was the very last thing that the King and Queen of Spain desired.

Even after Savonarola invited Charles to return, however, Alexander dealt with him moderately and without vindictiveness. At length he forbade him to preach. But the Prior of San Marco defied the command, and during the lent of 1497 preached more violently than ever. In May the Pope excommunicated him. Savonarola then declared from the pulpit that all who persecuted him were enemies of Christ. He wrote the Emperor and the Kings of France, Spain, England and Hungary early in 1498 that "The hour of vengeance has arrived. God desires me to reveal His secret counsels and to announce to all the world the dangers to which the bark of Peter is exposed in consequence of your slackness . . . I assure you, *in verbo Domini*, that this Alexander is no Pope at all and should not be accounted such; for besides having attained to the Chair of Saint Peter by the shameful sin of simony, and daily selling Church benefices to the highest bidder, besides his other vices which are known to all the world, I affirm that he is not a Christian and does not believe in the existence of God, which is the deepest depth of unbelief."

Suddenly the Florentines, who had attributed supernatural powers to Savonarola, turned against him on finding that many of his prophecies were false. He was left naked to his powerful enemies, and neither the Medici nor Alexander were likely to neglect their opportunity. He was seized by the Florentines, tried, tortured and hanged with two other friars, in April, 1498.

Charles VIII had died a few days before. His cousin, Louis XII, who succeeded him, at once assumed the title of King of Jerusalem and the Two Sicilies and, as a descendant of one of the Visconti, that of Duke of Milan. Obviously he intended a second descent upon Italy. It was an unmistakable challenge to King Fernando of Spain and Sicily.

To make the situation more alarming, Pope Alexander, who had been the soul of the Italian resistance to the French "barbarians," as they were called south of the Alps, was now led by various circumstances to lend an ear to certain overtures from Louis XII. Venice had made an alliance with the new French monarch. The Colonna and Orsini combined to make war on the Pope. Cesare wanted to resign the cardinalate—he had taken only minor orders and his distinguished talents were military, not spiritual—to marry some Princess and to become a great secular lord. And events conspired to make the offer of Louis to lead a new crusade rather tempting, for Alexander shared with the more admirable Popes who preceded and followed him a desire to unite Europe somehow against the constant menace from Islam.

In 1496 the Turks had taken some Hungarian fortresses and had made serious inroads into Moldavia. In 1498 the Turks and Tartars ravaged Poland far and wide. "The land was strewn with corpses," and the Moslems plundered and burned all the towns on the hills and plains around Lemberg and Przemysl as far as Kanczug. But what alarmed Italy most was the offensive that resulted, August 26, 1497, in their taking Lepanto, the last important Venetian post on the Gulf of Corinth. At the same time 10,000 Turkish horsemen from Bosnia raided the mainland of Venice. They devastated the whole country as far as Tagliamento and even near Vicenza, slaying or enslaving all the inhabitants. In 1499 they harried the seaboard of southern Italy. In the autumn of that year Alexander called a council of all Christian powers, but the response was discouraging.

Louis, on his part, desired an annulment of the marriage, never consummated, that he had been forced by Louis XI to contract with the lame Princess Jeanne, who was later canonized as Saint Jeanne de Valois. There is no doubt that under the laws of the Church he was entitled to an annulment, and one was granted after a commission appointed by the Pope had examined the evidence. Louis, as a token of gratitude, made Cesare Duke of Valentinois.

The Catholic Sovereigns, for such was the title bestowed upon Fernando and Isabel by the Holy See in 1497, in recognition of their many services to the Faith, were indignant on learning of these evidences of the Pope's leaning toward France, and in concert with Portugal they attempted to frighten Alexander by threats of a general council to depose him. The Portuguese envoys, on November 27, 1498, criticized the Pope to his face, without mincing words, for his nepotism, his simony and his French policy. "The demeanor of the Portuguese envoys," wrote Ascanio Sforza, "is all the more unpleasant to the Pope since he believes their Spanish Majesties to be at the bottom of it, and that the Spanish envoys, who are daily expected, will say the same things, or worse."

The ambassadors of Fernando and Isabel arrived December 19, and three days later "they appeared before the Pope," says von Pastor, "with that display of anxious concern for the welfare of the Church which Fernando's successors were so apt at employing, while, in fact, their aims were entirely political." The chief spokesman of the delegation, Don Felipe Ponce, began by informing Alexander that he was no Pope at all, and that his election had been uncanonical. The Pope interrupted him, according to Zurita, who narrates the whole conversation, to say that he did not hold the Pontificate illegally, as the King and Queen of Spain held their kingdoms, since "they had occupied them without just title and against conscience . . . and they were usurpers." He added that he was not Pope by virtue of the obedience that they gave him, but was Pope without it, since he had been canonically elected, for all had concurred in his election without a dissenting voice.

When Felipe reproached him for alienating the property of the Church, Alexander said that he had not, though he had intended giving Benevento to the Duke of Gandia.³ But Fernando held Sicily and Cerdagne unjustly, he declared, for these were of the patrimony of Saint Peter and belonged to the Church. He accused Garcilaso de la Vega, who was present, of having concocted false reports about him.

One of the envoys asserted that the death of the Duke of Gandia was a divine chastisement for the sins of Alexander. The old man drew himself up to his majestic height and retorted that in that case Fernando and Isabel were more severely punished than he was, for they were now (since the death of Prince Juan) without direct successors, and that this was doubtless God's judgment on them for their encroachments upon the rights of the Church.[4]

There was another animated conference at which both Spain and Portugal were represented. Lopez, one of the envoys, told Alexander that he was not the lawful head of the Church. Von Pastor is not quite right in saying that the Pope "in his anger threatened to have him thrown into the Tiber."[5] What Alexander said, according to Zurita's chronicle, was that "if Cesare were in Rome he would answer them as they deserved, and that in the time of Pope Sixtus the Count Geronimo had told the ambassadors of the sovereigns of Spain that he would throw them into the Tiber."[6]

Alexander was in a critical situation. The probability that Spain and Germany would renounce their obedience to him was freely discussed. The general fear of a new schism probably explains why Christopher Columbus, in settling his estate on his son Diego on February 26, 1498, commanded him to employ his wealth in the crusade against the Turks, "or in assisting the Pope if a schism in the Church should threaten to deprive him of his seat or of his temporal possessions." Perhaps it was just as well for the Admiral that this declaration did not come to the notice of his royal patrons. As for the Pope, he extricated himself from his difficulty by promising to restore Benevento to the Church, to send his children away from Rome and to carry out certain other reforms; and he made large concessions to Fernando and Isabel for the control of ecclesiastical affairs in Spain.

While all these happenings touched the interests of Queen Isabel, the records show her leaving active participation to an increasing extent to the King, and withdrawing into a more personal life, in which the affairs of her children engaged her attention more than anything else. It was a sad road that she elected to follow, for every one of her offspring either died young or lived unhappily. A curious fatality seemed to pursue them. Standing by the white marble tomb of Don Juan she may have thought more than once of the solemn words of Pope Sixtus in his letter of February 23, 1483, "urging and requiring" that she avoid any severity that would discredit the Church; "for thus the Lord, in whose power are Kings themselves . . . will cause your posterity and your affairs to flourish." Another Pope had now assured her envoy that the death of Don Juan was a divine punishment for those encroachments on the rights of the Church in which Fernando had been the leading actor and she in a greater or less degree, an accomplice. A similar explanation of the misfortunes of the royal children has been advanced by Jewish writers.

After the death of Prince Juan, Isabel had treated his young widow with the greatest tenderness, and had awaited her confinement in the hope that there would be another heir to the throne. But the posthumous child was born dead, early in 1498, and as Margot had no other ties to bind her to Spain, and had always found the stiffness of Castilian court etiquette a nuisance, she decided to return home; and Isabel and Fernando sent her away, laden with honors and gifts, in 1499. She subsequently married the Duke of Savoy, but was again widowed three years later, and rejected several royal suitors, including Henry VII in the days of his decrepitude. For eight years she ruled the Netherlands with marked ability as governor-general for her nephew, Charles V. On her tomb at Bourg-en-Bresse—she died in 1530—are the words *"Fortune, Infortune."*

The succession to the throne of Castile now devolved upon the young Queen of Portugal, and as she expected a child in the summer of 1498, there were high hopes that she might have a son who would unite all Spain and Portugal. Isabel and Fernando invited her to Castile to be recognized by the Cortes, a necessary procedure, for Philip the Fair had already claimed the succession for himself and his wife Juana, regardless of the seniority of the Queen of Portugal. After the Castilians had taken an oath of allegiance, Fernando and Isabel went to Saragossa with the Portuguese monarchs to solicit a similar action from Fernando's subjects. But the Aragonese, as usual, had a long and vigorous debate; at the end of which they decided that their laws and precedents did not permit them to recognize the title of a woman to the throne, though they agreed to take the oath of allegiance to the child of the Portuguese Queen, if she bore a boy; unless, however, King Fernando should have male issue. This last proviso was occasioned by the fact that Queen Isabel was ill for several days during the sessions of the Cortes, and it was said openly that she would not live long. It was expected that after her death Fernando might be urged by political exigencies or by the need of an heir to marry again.

At last, one Thursday noon in September the Queen of Portugal was delivered of a boy in the palace of the Archbishop of Saragossa. An hour later she died in the arms of King Manoel and her parents.[7]

The Cortes, true to its word, immediately acknowledged the Infante Miguel, who was now the lawful heir to all Spain and Portugal.

All Queen Isabel's remaining hopes and affections became centered in his tiny person. She kept him always with her, hovered over his cradle day and night, transferred to him all the dreams she had had for Don Juan. But alas for the hopes of Queens! Within two years little Miguel followed his mother to her tomb in the monastery of Saint Isabel at Toledo.

Bernaldez, philosophizing on the fortune that strikes down kings and peasants, wrote, "The first knife of grief that passed through the soul of the Queen Doña Isabel was the death of the Prince, the second was the death of Doña Isabel her eldest daughter, the third was the death of Don Miguel her grandson, with whom she had consoled herself. And from that time on, the Queen, Doña Isabel, so illustrious and very virtuous and very necessary to Castile, lived without pleasure, and cut short her health and her life."[8]

Maria, most fortunate of all Queen Isabel's daughters, lived to be thirty-five. In 1500, after a decent interval, the King of Portugal asked for the hand of this beautiful Princess, and she married him, bore him six sons and two daughters.

Of the Archduchess Juana in Flanders only the sorriest reports had reached Spain. It was said that she was wildly jealous of Philip, with good reason, and was unhappy and morose. Queen Isabel was so disturbed by the reports that she sent to Flanders the assistant prior of the Dominican monastery of Santa Cruz in Segovia, to try what his influence might accomplish. Juana received him with kindness. He wrote the Queen that she was very handsome and stout, and quite advanced in her pregnancy. He endeavored to persuade her to be reconciled to her mother, to whom she had not written, and for whom she made no inquiries. She was suspicious and moody in her attitude toward the sub-prior. She did not confess her sins for the Feast of the Ascension, he wrote, although her two confessors were in attendance.

Queen Isabel then attempted to reach Juana's affections through Fray Andreas, who had gone to Flanders as the Archduchess's confessor. He appealed in every way conceivable to Juana, but she would have none of him or his ministrations.

After a trip to England to investigate the activities of Dr. de Puebla—whom he described in a letter to the sovereigns as "a liar, a flatterer, and calumniator, a beggar, and not even a good Christian" on account of his Jewish opinions—the assistant-prior of Santa Cruz continued his efforts to win over the Archduchess. He wrote the Queen that her household was under a religious rule like that of a convent and that the Archduchess had some of the qualities of a good Christian. She was in a most difficult situation. She was not permitted to have anything to do with the management of her own household. Madame de Aloyn and the counsellors of the Archduke had so intimidated her that she did not dare hold up her head. She had not a maravedi for alms, even though she wished to give some. During her pregnancy she had asked the Estates for the usual allowance. They awarded her sixty thousand florins, payable within three years, but she got nothing of it, for it was paid into the exchequer of the Archduke. All the Spaniards who had gone to Flanders with the Archduchess were living in misery, and Philip did nothing for them.

Juana's allowance was distributed in favors to the Flemish courtiers, and she knew nothing of it until they sent her the paper to sign. She observed that as they had not consulted her, they might at least have spared her the trouble of signing the paper.[9]

At last, on the feast of Saint Matthias in 1500, she was delivered of a boy, Charles. As Juana, since the death of Miguel, was now the legitimate heiress of the throne of Castile, little Don Carlos, as he was known in Spain, would one day inherit a vast empire, including Spain, Naples, Sicily and all the lands of the Hapsburgs—the Germanies, Flanders and the rest—as the Emperor Charles V. Queen Isabel predicted this on hearing of the day of his birth, saying, "The lot falls on Matthias."[10]

Of all the children there remained with Isabel only the youngest, Catalina; but the beginning of her long martyrdom was at hand. A treaty satisfactory to both nations was finally drawn up and ratified in August, 1498. The friendship between them and their successors was to last forever. Henry professed himself delighted. De Puebla had previously asked that Catalina be taught French, "for the English Queens do not know Latin, and understand Spanish even less; and added that the Princess "should accustom herself to drinking wine; in England the water is not good, or when it is, the climate does not permit one to drink it."

After the treaty was concluded, Henry urged that the Princess be sent to England as soon as possible. On Whit-Sunday, 1499, in the chapel of Bewdley Manor, she was married by proxy to Prince Arthur by the Bishop of Coventry and Lichfield, Dr. Puebla representing the Princess.

Queen Isabel deferred sending Catalina to England as long as she could think of any excuses, not only on account of her youth, but because she distrusted Henry. Her ambassador Don Pedro de Ayala wrote her that the English were a superstitious people who believed in prophecies and fortune tellers. King Henry, he added, had lately asked a certain priest who had foretold the death of Edward IV and of Richard III, "to tell him in what manner his latter end would come. The priest, according to common report, told the king that his life would be in great danger during the whole year, and informed him, in addition to many other unpleasant things, that there are two parties of very different political creeds in his kingdom. . . ." Henry had aged so much during the last two weeks that he seemed to be twenty years older. He was growing very devout. "He has heard a sermon every day during Lent, and has continued his devotions during the rest of the day. His riches augment every day. I think he has no equal in this respect. If gold coin once enters his strong boxes, it never comes out again. He always pays in depreciated coin. . . . All his servants are like him; they have quite a wonderful dexterity in getting other people's money."

De Puebla, who had been recalled to Spain in 1499, but had been sent back to his post, wrote about the same time, probably at Henry's dictation, that "now that Perkin and the son of the Duke of Clarence have been executed, there does not remain a drop of doubtful Royal blood," the only Royal blood being the true blood of the King, the Queen, and above all, of the Prince of Wales—though why his blood should have been more royal than that of his parents, the ambassador did not state.

In March, 1500, de Ayala wrote that Henry was "very sorry" that the Princess had not yet been sent. He had made "very great" preparations to receive her. "If she should not come this year, he and his whole kingdom will suffer very great losses." Isabel and Fernando promised to send her at the first opportunity. Nevertheless a whole year later, in March, 1501, the Queen was making her excuses to Dr. Puebla. The revolt of the Moors in the Alpujarras was one pretext. The plague in London was another.

All this time, Dr. Puebla was between the Devil and the deep sea. He wrote plaintively to the Queen's secretary that he was in want, and could not get his salary. King Henry had written to Spain for permission to have him made a bishop, or to marry him well in England, he said, but Fernando and Isabel had ignored the requests. Dr. Puebla at that period, according to the report of the sub-prior of Santa Cruz, was living at a very disreputable lodging house in London. He ate at the English court as often as possible, to save money, and when he appeared, King Henry would say, "Here comes the old Doctor a-begging."

While the last hagglings concerning the Princess's going, her money and jewels, her reception and her status in England were being dragged out, the affairs of Columbus were giving renewed uneasiness to the King and Queen. The Admiral had begun his third voyage rather unauspiciously in May, 1498, by knocking down one Ximenes de Breviasca, a *Converso* employed by the Indian office, who had irritated him beyond further endurance, and kicking him about the dock at Cádiz.

It was during this voyage, however, that the Admiral discovered Trinidad. And on the following day, August 1, 1498, he saw the American continent from his deck, and, according to Las Casas, named it Isla Santa, thinking it, naturally, to be another island. Thus to Columbus belongs the glory of having been the first European to look upon the mainland of the western world, even if he died in ignorance of the fact. His crew went ashore, but he himself was prevented by illness from doing so. On Friday, August 3, Columbus discovered the point of Paria (Venezuela) which he called Gracia, believing it to be another island. Vespucci's letter to King René of Sicily claiming to have discovered the continent in 1497 was a fabrication which he never dared to publish in Spain. It was the opinion of Las Casas that the New World ought to be called Columbus, Columbo, or by the names he gave the continent— Santa (Holy) or Gracia (Grace).

When at last he arrived in Hispaniola at the end of August, the Admiral found himself much hated because of the stern rule of his brother and adelantado, Bartholemew, whom he had left in command during his absence. A revolutionary party was formed among the colonists under the leadership of Francisco Roldan, a bold and able but turbulent man, with the intent of ousting the whole Columbus family. The island was soon divided into two armed camps. Both Columbus and Roldan wrote the King and Queen, each blaming the other and exculpating himself. Fernando and Isabel decided to send an impartial investigator to settle the dispute. They commissioned Francisco de Bobadilla, a cavalier who had won their confidence, as commander of a wing of the army at the siege of Malaga,[11] to proceed to Hispaniola, and place under arrest any disturbers of the peace. It is likely that they had in mind the rebels against the authority of Columbus.

When Bobadilla arrived, the Admiral, after a long period of lenient parleying with the rebels, had finally had a young Spanish nobleman hanged. Bobadilla concluded that the Admiral's incapacity as an administrator was the cause of the trouble; he arrested him, had him taken aboard ship in chains, and sent him to Spain. When the ship's captain offered to take off the chains, Columbus insisted on wearing them, and thus, in November, 1500, he landed in Cádiz, crippled by gout, white-haired, painfully aged by exposure and suffering. But under all circumstances, right or wrong, sick or well, rich or poor, he preserved a certain sublimity of bearing and a grandeur of phrase that leave him always, despite all that has been and can be said against him, the great figure, the heroic man. If Columbus had been a thief, he would have taken purses with a lordly air; if he had been a beggar, he would have held out his hand with the gesture of an emperor.

On shipboard he wrote to Doña Juana de la Torre, who had been Prince Juan's nurse, a letter evidently intended to be passed on to Her Majesty:

"Most virtuous lady: Although it is a novelty for me to complain of the ill usage of the world, it is, nevertheless, no novelty for the world to practise ill usage. Innumerable are the contests which I have had with it, and I have resisted all its attacks until now, when I find that neither strength nor prudence is of any avail to me; it has cruelly reduced me to the lowest ebb. Hope in Him who created us all is my support: His assistance I have always found near at hand. On one occasion, not long since, when I was extremely depressed, He raised me with His divine arm, saying: 'O man of little faith, arise, it is I, be not afraid' I offered myself with such earnest devotion to the service of these princes, and I have served them with a fidelity hitherto unequalled and unheard of. God made me the messenger of the new heaven and the new earth, of which He spoke in the Apocalypse by Saint John, after having spoken of it by the mouth of Isaias; and He showed me the spot where to find it."

The reference to "the new heaven and the new earth" was a felicitous accident, considering that Columbus still thought he had been to Asia. In the same letter he repeated his promises of fabulous wealth. "Already the road is opened to the gold and pearls, and it may surely be hoped that precious stones, spices and a thousand other things, will also be found. Would to God that it were as certain that I should suffer no greater wrongs than I have already experienced, as it is that I would, in the name of Our Lord, again undertake my first voyage."

He never doubts that his name will be cleared of the charges against him and, as he defends himself, sorrow wrings eloquence worthy of Cicero or of Edmund Burke from the pen of the self-educated wool-comber:

"God is just, and He will in due time make known by whom and why it has all been done. Let them not judge me as a governor who had been sent to some province or city under regular government, and where the laws could be executed without fear of danger to the public weal or subjection to any enormous wrong. I ought to be judged as a captain sent from Spain to the Indies to conquer a nation numerous and warlike with customs and religion altogether different to ours; a people

who dwell in the mountains, without regular habitations for
themselves or for us; and where, by the divine will, I have
subdued another world to the dominion of the King and
Queen, our sovereigns; in consequence of which Spain, that
used to be called poor, is now the most wealthy of kingdoms.
I ought to be judged as a captain who for so many years has
borne arms, never quitting them for an instant. I ought to be
judged by cavaliers who have themselves won the meed of
victory; by knights of the sword and not of title-deeds."

What queen, what woman, could read such words and remain indignant?

When the Admiral walked through the streets of Cádiz in
chains, a murmur of pity and indignation swept through the
town. The tide of public sentiment was turned in his favor; he
was a martyr to the officiousness of bureaucrats. Consequently
when he appeared in the presence of the King and Queen at
Granada, the battle was more than half won. It was at this
period that he used to go about, according to Las Casas,
dressed somewhat like a Capuchin. Of the legend that Isabel
wept when she saw him, and that the Admiral was so touched
by her sympathy that he fell on his knees and burst into sobbing, there is no contemporary evidence, nor does Columbus's
son Hernando mention it in his biography. The earliest reference to it appears to be that of Herrera.

Once more Columbus had triumphed over his enemies. Not
only did he escape punishment, but he was publicly vindicated
and retained all his titles and privileges. Nevertheless, the King
and Queen appear to have decided that it was no longer wise
to entrust him with administrative duties. In his place they
sent Nicholas de Ovando to Hispaniola with the title—no doubt
to spare Columbus's feelings—of temporary governor.

It is to be noted that Fernando and Isabel inflicted no recorded censure upon Bobadilla to justify all the vilifications
that historians have heaped upon him. He remained in favor
of at Court, and was much honored. Peter Martyr, a friend of
Columbus, did not blame him, and Las Casas, the sympathetic
biographer of the Admiral, says that "even after his death no
one dared attack his probity and his disinterestedness."

Columbus now published a book of prophecies, in which he
predicted that "there is no doubt that the world must end in
155 years"—hence the need of completing his discoveries to

make possible the salvation of all men. God had chosen him through Isaias, he wrote Prince Juan's nurse, to disclose the new regions before the consummation. He must have been a little crazed from his sufferings at this period, yet he never ceased to be magnificent. Notice the tone of the letter he writes to the bank of Saint George in Genoa in 1502, making them his trustees for certain benevolences:

"High and noble Lords: Although the body walks about here (Spain), the heart is constantly over there (Genoa). Our Lord has conferred on me the greatest favor ever granted to any one since David. The results of my undertaking already appear, and would shine greatly, were they not concealed by the blindness of the government. I am going again to the Indies under the auspices of the Holy Trinity, soon to return, and since I am mortal, I leave it with my son Diego that you receive every year, for ever, one tenth of the entire revenue, such as it may be, for the purpose of reducing the tax upon corn, wine and other provisions. If that tenth amounts to something, collect it. If not, take at least the will for the deed. I beg of you to entertain regard for the son I have recommended to you. Messer Nicolo de Oderigo knows more about my own affairs than I do myself, and I have sent him the transcripts of my privileges and letters for safe keeping. . . . My lords the King and Queen endeavor to honor me more than ever. May the Holy Trinity preserve your noble persons and increase the most magnificent House."

Though Isabel had no great faith in Columbus's prophecies, she must have retained her confidence in him as a navigator; and even Fernando felt that the Admiral's plan to find a water route through the supposed continent—Cuba!—was sound. No better proof could be asked than their consent to send him on a fourth voyage, stipulating that he keep away from Hispaniola, where Ovando was. It was not the custom of the sovereigns to spend large sums on sentimentalities or without the hope of some return.

Columbus went, and once more failed gloriously. Shipwrecked for eight months among hostile Indians on the island of Jamaica, sick, betrayed, denied entrance to the port that he had discovered—he still kept his unconquerable spirit, and one cannot read his letters, as the Queen did, without feeling that the world lost an epic poet of the first rank when he elected to live in action what he might have written on parchment. Here is his description of a storm;

"I had already made four leagues when the storm commenced, and wearied me to such a degree that I absolutely knew not what to do; my wound reopened, and for nine days my life was despaired of. Never was the sea seen so high, so terrific, and so covered with foam; not only did the wind oppose our proceeding onward, but it also rendered it highly dangerous to run in for any headland, and kept me in that sea which seemed to me as a sea of blood, seething like a caldron one day, and one night burning like a furnace, and emitting flashes in such fashion that each time I looked to see if my masts and my sails were not destroyed these flashes came with such alarming fury that we all thought the ship must have been consumed. All this time the waters from heaven never ceased; not to say that it rained, for it was like a repetition of the deluge. The men were at this time so crushed in spirit that they longed for death as a deliverance from so many martyrdoms. Twice already had the ships suffered loss in boats, anchors, and rigging, and they were now lying bare without sails."

And this is his description of a vision that he had in his sickness, when he was on the point of despairing:

"I toiled up to the highest part of the ship, and, with a quivering voice and fast-falling tears, I called upon Your Highnesses' war-captains from each point of the compass to come to my succor, but there was no reply. At length, groaning with exhaustion, I fell asleep, and heard a compassionate voice address me thus: 'O fool, and slow to believe and to serve thy God, the God of all! What did He do more for Moses, or for David His servant, than He has done for thee? From thine infancy He has kept thee under His constant and watchful care. When he saw thee arrived at an age which suited His designs respecting thee, He brought wonderful renown to thy name throughout all the earth, and thou wert obeyed in many lands, and didst acquire honorable fame among Christians. Of the gates of the Ocean Sea, shut up with such mighty chains, He delivered to thee the keys; the Indies, whose wealthy regions of the world, he gave thee for thine own, and empowered thee to dispose of them to others, according to thy pleasure. What more did He do for the people of Israel, when He brought them out of Egypt? Or for David, whom from a shepherd He made to be king in Judea? Turn to him, and acknowledge thine error—His mercy is infinite. Thine old age shall not prevent thee from achieving any great undertaking. Abraham was above a hundred years when he begat Isaac; and was Sarah youthful? Thou criest out for uncertain help. Answer! Who has afflicted thee so much and so often, God, or the world? The privileges and promises God hath made to thee He hath never broken; neither hath he said, after receiving thy services, that His meaning was different, and to be understood in a different light; nor does He inflict suffering, in order to make a show of His power. His acts answer to His words; and He performs all that He promises, and with interest. Such is His custom. Thus have I told thee what thy Creator hath done for thee, and what He doth for all men. Even now He partially shows thee the reward of so many toils and dangers incurred by thee in the service of others.' I heard all this, as one almost dead, and had no words to reply, and could only weep for my errors. He that spoke to me, whoever he was, concluded by saying, 'Fear not, but trust; all these tribulations are written in marble, and not without cause.'"

This untutored man had genius of the highest order. His most commonplace utterances had a quality that is found only among a few writers of surpassing power, and especially among writers belonging to the most richly endowed of all races, the Jews. To better the mighty cadences and the emotional sincerity of his prose, one must go back to Isaias, the Book of Job, the Apocalypse of Saint John, the letters of Saint Paul.

XXXII

WHILE Queen Isabel was reading the letters of Columbus among the gardens of the Alhambra, King
Fernando was watching Italy like a cat before a
mouse-hole. The mouse who had gone into the hole was Louis
XII of France, a much more intelligent mouse than Charles had
been, and the cheese that drew him there was Naples. After
buying off all his foes, and spending much money improving
his army, especially the artillery, he had sent the French over
the Alps again in 1499, under Trivulzio, and by August 10
they had reached Asti. They took Annone, Valenza, Tortona,
Alessandria; Ludovico Sforza fled from Milan, and Louis was
virtually master of Italy. Nothing remained but to march into
Naples.

All the efforts of King Fernando to keep Louis out of Italy
had proved futile. A diplomat of less astuteness might have
left the field to the powerful enemy, or begun a conflict whose
issue was doubtful. But Fernando's bag of tricks was not yet
empty. He reasoned cannily that Louis, remembering the unfortunate experience of Charles would hesitate to go into
Naples leaving behind a troublesome foe who might invade
France. This was exactly what Louis dreaded, and his fear
betrayed him into making a fool's bargain with Fernando. By
a secret treaty signed November 11, 1500, they agreed to divide
the kingdom of Naples between them. Louis was to be king of
Naples and to have Terra di Lavoro and the Abruzzi, Fernando
to be grand duke, holding Apulia and Calabria. They deposed
Fernando's cousin, Federigo of Naples, on the ground that he
had betrayed Christendom by appealing for aid against Louis
to the Turkish Sultan Bajazet II; nor could Federigo com-

plain, since the Spanish sovereigns had long before warned him that they would not tolerate his appealing to the Moslems. Federigo first learned of the partition treaty of Granda and his own ruin when he received a bull from Pope Alexander, assenting to his deposition.

Five months before he made his arrangement with Louis, Fernando had taken the precaution to send Gonsalvo de Córdoba very quietly to Sicily with 70 ships, 600 cavalry and 5000 of the crack Spanish infantry. While the Great Captain was on his way, the Turkish question became acute. The Mussulmans had taken from the Venetians the island of Cephalonia (Homer called it Samos) near the coast of Greece, and in consequence commanded the Venetian seas from the citadel of Saint George, a position hitherto believed impregnable. They then captured Modon, and impaled all its inhabitants, and followed up this atrocity by the conquest of Navarino and Koron. The Venetians experienced the worst panic they had known since the fall of Negroponte.

The Pope addressed an urgent bull of crusade to all Christendom, telling the princes of the fury and cruelty of the Moslems and their hatred of the Christian name, and urging all to unite for the common preservation. The purpose of the Turks, he said, was first to conquer Rome, and then to subjugate all Christian populations. Consequently the Roman Church had now formally declared war against the hereditary foe. To meet the expenses of the Crusade, he levied a tithe on all Church benefices without exception, and on all officials in the Papal States. A tax of half as much was imposed upon the Jews. All who resisted were threatened with excommunication.

In a consistory of September 11, 1500, the Pope and cardinals decided to send the Spanish fleet, then at Sicily, against the advancing Turks, and so notified Gonsalvo. Legates were sent all over Europe to arouse the princes. Henry VII of England contributed four thousand pounds to the Crusade, though he declined to send ships. The forty-one cardinals in Rome gave a total of 45,376 ducats to the cause, and the Pope promised 40,000 ducats on his own account as long as the war should last. It is certain that Alexander was making a sincere effort to be the true father of Christendom in this crisis, though he could have done more if he had not committed himself to the advancement of Cesare, who had conquered the Romagna and seemed likely to make himself King of all central Italy. At this time Paolo Capello wrote, "The Pope is now seventy years of age; he grows younger every day."

Late in the autumn of 1500 Gonsalvo joined the Venetian fleet with sixty-five of his Spanish vessels, and they proceeded against Cephalonia. Though the Turks fought furiously with poisoned arrows, liquid fire, boiling oil and rocks, the walls were mined and the Christians recaptured the stronghold after a siege of fifty days.

For this, the first defeat inflicted upon the Turks in their victorious advance westward, King Fernando received from the Pope the title of Defender of the Faith—the same that Henry VIII of England was to receive for his defense of the Catholic Church against Luther—and Gonsalvo, entering Venice in state, was showered with princely gifts, which he distributed among his troops with his usual magnificence. His victory at Cephalonia had saved Venice and perhaps Europe. The Turks grew tired of the war and made peace with Venice, and for the next twenty years western civilization was comparatively free from the fear of the Mohammedan invasions, while the Sultans wrestled with the new power of Persia. Queen Isabel learned of the triumph of her Great Captain with joy, and ordered processions and masses of thanksgiving. Gonsalvo proceeded to Naples to take possession of his master's half of it.

Up to this point Fernando could claim with some plausibility that he had been actuated chiefly by zeal for the Church. But from now on his devotion to his own interest became more apparent. He had probably instructed Gonsalvo to quarrel with his French allies when the moment seemed opportune. Friction had inevitably arisen between the two armies over the boundary line and other matters. Gonsalvo acted quickly, and in less than a month had seized all of Calabria, both French and Spanish, except the important and almost inaccessible city of Taranto, where the adherents of King Federigo of Naples were making a last rally about his young son, the Duke of Calabria. This stronghold, on the site of the fort that had defied Hannibal, had the sea on one side, and the Mare Piccolo, an island sea 12 miles in circumference, on the other. Its only connection with the mainland was by two bridges, well fortified. In one of the most skilful of his sieges, the Great Captain cut off its communications to the landward and starved it into surrender.

He put the young Duke of Calabria on a galley, in violation of his oath, and sent him to Spain. It was an act entirely foreign to the magnanimous character of Gonsalvo, and one that always troubled his conscience, even though he had acted upon orders from King Fernando. On his deathbed he said that in all his life he had done only three things that he regretted, and one of them was the breach of his oath at Taranto.

The French received Swiss reinforcements, but Gonsalvo was left, as usual, to fend for himself, without money, supplies or reinforcements. King Fernando appears to have calculated that the Great Captain's genius could find a way of making one man do the work of four; and they could always live off the countryside. Gonsalvo with his little force was therefore obliged to fall back to Barletta, which he defended with memorable patience and skill. It was there, in one of many duels between French and Spanish cavaliers, that Bayard, the "knight without fear and without reproach," slew the enormous Spaniard Alonso de Sotomayer in the presence of the two armies.

Gonsalvo then made a rapid march over a hot sandy terrain to Cerignola, reaching its heights with a fagged army at the close of the day. The French overtook him at dusk, giving him barely time to dig a few trenches and to utilize a sunken road somewhat as the English did three centuries later at Waterloo; and there, in the gathering darkness, the two armies joined battle. Gonsalvo crushed the enemy in a short and bloody action, with a loss of fewer than 100 Spaniards to 4000 Frenchmen. Next morning he shed tears over the corpse of the French commander, young de Nemours, his former friend and companion in arms.

In May, 1503, after one of the most brilliant campaigns in the annals of warfare, the Great Captain entered Naples in triumph, and the Neapolitans, who had had seven kings in eight years, complacently took the oath of allegiance to King Fernando and Queen Isabel. Spain had become the dominant power in Italy.

During all this while Fernando and Isabel had been holding their court principally at Granada. After the death of the Infante Miguel, July 20, 1500, the Queen had remained in retirement for some days, and was inconsolable; but at length she recovered her usual composure, and began interesting herself in the attempts that were being made to convert the Moors of the state of Granada to Christianity, for she feared that so long as they remained Mohammedan there would be danger of their conspiring with the Moslems of Africa to disrupt the dearly bought unity of Spain.

Since 1492 the work of conversion had been under the direction of Hernando de Talavera. He had learned Arabic, and had insisted that his priests do likewise, and he had caused parts of the New Testament and the catechism to be translated. At the same time he scrupulously observed the provision of the treaty of 1492 that no Saracen was to be compelled to change his religion. Many voluntary conversions resulted, however, from the kindness and wisdom of this grandson of Jewish converts. Little by little he made friends among the Moors, both rich and poor; he spent the revenues of his diocese in charities, and the purity and nobility of his life preached to the Mohammedans with such silent eloquence that they called him "the great *alfaqui* of the Christians."

Apparently the King or the Queen, or both, considered the rate of conversion too slow, for in the autumn of 1499 they summoned the more energetic Ximenes de Cisneros, Archbishop of Toledo, to assist Talavera at Granada. Since Fernando had long resented the appointment of Ximenes to the see he had desired for his son, Don Alonso de Aragon, it is a fair assumption that Isabel was chiefly responsible for the presence of the man who had succeeded Talavera as her confessor. When the King and Queen went to Seville in November, 1499, both prelates remained at Granada.

The dynamic nature of Ximenes was not content with the slow gains of Talavera. Making liberal gifts to the chief *alfaquis* of the Moors, he began inviting them daily to his palace to discuss religion with him, and with such effect that many of them became Christians. The baptism of the Moorish scholars influenced the people as Ximenes had expected. On one day, December 18, 1499, he baptized 4,000 of them by aspersion. Bells, so odious to Mohammedans, were heard ringing in Granada; and Ximenes on that account was called "*alfaqui campanero.*"

The irreconcilables countered by stirring up a rebellion that spread through the kingdom of Granada. Bernaldez says that the Queen sent Ximenes to Granada in the first instance "in

Ximenes, Primate of Castile
Isabel's Greatest Spiritual Adviser

order to get rid of many nuisances that arose from the situation—murders and acts of rapine that the Moors along the sea coast committed and consented to, for they came by night and seized whole towns and fought all the Christians who were in them." These disorders, instead of diminishing, began to take on the aspect of a revolution after the successful preaching of Ximenes. He retaliated with characteristic vigor by having the ringleaders arrested.

Up to this point he had observed the treaty, but in his exasperation over the revolt he commanded the prisoners to receive instructions in the Christian religion from his chaplains, and when some of them refused, punished them severely. Into the harsh custody of his henchman, Pedro Leon, he delivered among others the noble Ez Zegri, who had fought so valiantly in the defense of Granada. Leon chained him with heavy irons and deprived him of food for several days, until at last Ez Zegri asked to be taken before Ximenes. He told the Archbishop that in a vision the night before, Allah had commanded him to become a Christian. He was fed, baptized, and given the Christian name of Fernando Gonsalvo, in honor of the Great Captain, with whom he had crossed swords in the Granadine war. During the rest of his life he remained a zealous Christian and a devoted follower of Ximenes.[1]

"None ought to be forced to become Christians," wrote the Jesuit historian Mariana in criticising a similar intolerance on the part of the King of Portugal; the Church had always forbidden the forcible conversion of non-Catholics, and even the Inquisition claimed jurisdiction only over the baptized. But the success Ximenes had had with Ez Zegri and certain others inspired him to a further disregard of the time-honored principle. After causing several thousand copies of the Koran and other Mohammedan books, with the exception of works on medicine, to be burned on the public plaza, he compelled the descendants of renegades from Christianity to be baptized, even against the wishes of their parents. The grandson of a man who had turned from Christianity to Mohammedanism for example, might be forcibly "converted," though he himself had never been a Christian. This peculiar attempt to stretch the jurisdiction of the Church was bitterly resented by the Moors; and the end was what might have been expected.

One day when Salzedo, the major-domo of Ximenes, went

to the Albaycin to arrest the daughter of an apostate, the girl screamed frantically, the Moors ran to her rescue, killed the *alcalde* who accompanied the major-domo and would have slain Salzedo himself, if a woman had not hidden him under her bed. The whole Albaycin, taking arms, flocked to the palace of Ximenes with the intent of doing away with him.

The Archbishop's servants defended him in a siege that lasted all night until the Count of Tendilla arrived in the morning with troops from the Alhambra. Greatly outnumbered, the Christians remained on the defensive for nine days and nights. A herald sent by the Count of Tendilla was murdered by the angry Moors, and various attempts by Ximenes to make peace with them were laughed to scorn. All the Christians might at last have been butchered, but for the intervention of a man who understood the ultimate weakness and folly of mere physical force.

It was the Archbishop Talavera who saved the situation. Attended by a single chaplain carrying the archiepiscopal cross before him, he left the palace on foot, crossed the square, as calm and benevolent as if he were setting out to preach a sermon, and slowly walked toward the place where the howling mob was thickest. The hoots and the jeers subsided into a murmur, and the murmur into a hush, as the white-haired old man faced the mob and raised his hand for silence. There was no one in the Albaycin who did not know the great *alfaqui* of the Christians.

The Archbishop spoke a few words in Arabic. A smile of understanding passed over the fine face worn thin by many vigils and fastings. The Moors nearest him fell upon their knees. Some of them went nearer and kissed the hem of his robe. Since the time of Saint Leo there had seldom been a clearer manifestation of the power of moral excellence over brute force.[2]

Tendilla took advantage of the diversion to make overtures to the Moors, offering his wife and children as hostages, and a truce was made.

Ximenes, who had resolutely refused to flee from his enemies, wrote letters to the King and Queen, explaining all that had happened and assuring them that the worst was over. When a noble of Granada offered him the services of an Ethiopian slave who could run fifty leagues in two days, he gladly accepted, and entrusted his letters to the black. But on the way to Seville, where Isabel and Fernando were, the slave got drunk, and arrived five days late. Meanwhile the sovereigns received highly colored and emotional accounts of the uprising from unofficial sources.

The King was mightily enraged, especially against Ximenes. "Ah!" he cried. "Does it not appear to you, Señora, that your Archbishop in a single hour has placed in jeopardy all that the Kings our ancestors and we ourselves have won in so long a time and with so great cost in toil and bloodshed?"

Robles, who reports Fernando's words, adds that "la reyna le disculpava todo quanto le era posible." Nevertheless, Isabel ordered Almazan to write Ximenes a demand for an immediate accounting, and to censure him for his negligence in failing to report.

Ximenes went to Seville and explained. He probably represented that peace in Granada would never be permanent until the cause of friction—the Mohammedanism of the Moors—was removed, and that the proximity of Granada to Africa might in the end result in a second conquest by the Moslems. He was so successful in his apologia that the sovereigns adopted the policy he suggested of giving the Moors their choice between prosecution for high treason and baptism.

Politically, at least—though the conversions were insincere, as Peter Martyr observed—the results appeared to justify the counsel Ximenes had given, for nearly all the Moors in the city of Granada were baptized. But in the following year, when Ximenes was busy erecting his great University at Alcalá de Henares, a new and fierce revolt broke out among the Alpujarras, the mountains running southeast from Granada. Many of the friars who had been sent to preach to the people were murdered. In Daydin and Benahabis the Moorish women and boys stoned to death two priests who had been tied to trees with matted grass. The Sultan of Egypt sent threatening letters to Spain, and in answer to appeals from their coreligionists in Granada, Mohammedans came by night from Africa in their swift lateen-rigged boats with sails like a shark's fin, to burn and slay in the Christian hamlets near the sea.[3]

Eight hundred Christian cavaliers assembled in Andalusia to carry the sword of reprisal into the villages of the Alpujarras. The Count of Tendilla captured Huecar. Fernando himself took command of an army that marched on Lanjaron and seized it in the early spring of 1500. The uprising was sternly repressed. But a more spirited one flamed forth in the Sierra Bermeja, west of Granada. The Moors murdered Christian priests and sold Christian women as slaves in Africa. In one great memorable night raid, Don Alonso de Aquilar, brother of the Great Captain, was slain.

Fernando marched swiftly to avenge his general's death. Rather than endure his wrath, the Moors asked for terms of peace. The King, after conferring with Queen Isabel and Ximenes, informed them that they might have their choice between exile to Africa, and baptism. Most of them chose baptism.

Thus came into existence that class of unwilling Christians known as the Moriscos, of whom a half million were finally expelled under Philip III in 1609. Their going was a serious economic loss to Spain, for they were excellent farmers, who understood the importance of irrigation. But considering how few of the Moors left the country in 1501, it is difficult to understand by what glib reasoning historians have arrived at the conclusion that their expulsion contributed to any significant extent to the decline of Spanish commerce a whole century after Fernando and Isabel had bequeathed to their posterity a peaceful, united, happy and prosperous nation.

That Spain did ultimately suffer a decline, economically and politically, is notorious. The causes of that decline were various, but they were not those that have been most widely accepted. The Church cannot be held responsible, for Spain reached her greatest material prosperity precisely at the period when the Church exercised the most complete influence over the lives of the people. Nor was it the Inquisition, for Spain was at the height of her glory when the Inquisition was most active. It was not, as certain enemies of Spain have alleged, the plague of syphilis. It has been rather generally believed that the disease first appeared in Europe during the First Italian War; that some of Columbus's sailors had carried it from the New World to the camps of Italy. The earliest acceptation of this theory seems to be in Mariana: "During this war of Naples was first discovered a new kind of sickness communicated chiefly by illicit intercourse. The Italians called it the French disease, and the French the Neapolitan disease; the Africans the Spanish disease. The truth is that it came from the New World, where this disease is very common, and was carried to Naples by the Spaniards;[4] as the best informed people believe, the Spanish soldiers at that time took it to Italy and Naples."

Mariana may be correct in saying that the Indians had the disease, but his belief that it was unknown in Europe before 1492 is contradicted by the fact that the Italian physician Guglielmo Salicetti, who kept careful case histories in the thirteenth century, recognized the symptoms and referred them to their true cause;[5] and there are evidences that the plague existed in ancient Persia and Egypt. There are no historical records pointing to anything like an epidemic in either Italy or Spain during the closing years of the fifteenth century.

One factor often overlooked was the failure of Spain to perfect her means of transportation, a neglect arising largely from the habitual dependence of the people upon mules. After the death of Isabel there was a gradual return of this Moorish custom; hence wagons were little used, and there was but slight need of good roads. Spain suffered also from deforestation, which Isabel sought to prevent, but her successors permitted. The country paid, too, for the extravagance, the weakness and the reckless ambition of later kings. But on the whole it appears that Christopher Columbus, by one of the ironies of history, unintentionally dealt one of the deadliest blows to the nation that gave him his greatness.

Within a century the population of Spain was reduced by half through emigration to the New World, where the most ardent and adventurous of her chivalry scattered to fall under Indian arrows or disease or to settle and perpetuate the civilization of Greece and Rome in the American wilderness. The fever of migration was so intense that in a single generation after Columbus had penned his rhapsodies on gold and glory, some of the cities of the peninsula were actually depopulated and the Venetian ambassador, Andrea Navagiero, who traveled through the country in 1525, recorded that in Seville scarcely any inhabitants were left but the women.[6] The gold that ultimately came by shiploads from the mines of Mexico and Peru hardly compensated for so great a loss in man power. In many ways, indeed, it proved a curse to the nation that Isabel had just instructed in peaceful toil and frugality. Prices rose with the circulation of money, and the new demand for foreign products crippled some Spanish industries and eventually ruined others. A new class of wealthy parvenus, to whom titles were given with foolish prodigality, perpetuated a mischievous tradition that toil was dishonorable.

There appears to be one more cause, which for some mysterious reason has been passed over in complete silence by all our historians.

"There can be no doubt," says the Jewish Encyclopedia, "that the decline of Spanish commerce in the seventeenth century was due in large measure to the activities of the *Marranos* of Holland, Italy and England, who diverted trade from Spain to those countries. . . . When Spain was at war with any of these countries, Jewish intermediation was utilized to obtain knowledge of Spanish naval activity."[7] Furthermore, it appears from the same source that the Spanish *Conversos* who settled in London acquired within a century an almost complete monopoly of English trade with the Levant, the Indies, Brazil, and especially with the Netherlands, Spain and Portugal. "They formed an important link in the network of trade spread especially throughout the Spanish and Portuguese world by the *Marranos* or secret Jews. Their position enabled them to give Cromwell and his secretary, Thurloe, important information as to the plans of Charles Stuart in Holland and of the Spaniards in the New World. Outwardly they passed as Spaniards and Catholics; but they held prayer meetings at Cree Church Lane, and became known to the government as Jews by faith."[8]

There is a suggestion here of a fascinating and unexplored chapter of history, in which the tragic figure of the wandering Jew, defeated in his attempt to destroy the Catholic Church and build a New Jerusalem on its ruins in medieval Spain, is seen playing a large part in bringing low the greatest Catholic nation of Europe at the moment of its final triumph, and transferring the dominion of the seas and of world politics to the anti-Catholic power of modern England. It would be interesting to know to what extent they instigated or encouraged the revolt in the Netherlands which Philip II attempted to suppress by the Inquisition. That they had something to do with these matters is highly probable, for they supported Calvinism and other anti-Catholic movements just as they had the primitive heresies and the Mohammedanism of the Middle Ages. It is one of the curiosities of history that they paid off the score of the Spanish Inquisition at the strategic moment when Spain, in spite of all her phenomenal powers of recuperation, had exhausted herself at last like a good mother in the stupendous effort to colonize and civilize vast portions of the western hemisphere.

XXXIII

THE PRINCESS CATALINA MARRIES THE
PRINCE OF WALES—QUEEN ISABEL'S
LAST CAMPAIGN—HER ILLNESS AND
DEATH

THROUGH sunshine heavy with the scent of white jasmine and red oleander, there came again into the gardens of the Alhambra, without trumpets or drums, the peace of old times. The leaves fell noiselessly into the fountains, and at dusk the cool wind from the Sierras on the face of the *vega* was like the voice of an old monk bringing peace to a young sinner; but there was to be little more peace in this life for the Princess Catalina. The two ultimate pretexts—the stormy weather and her mother's ill-health—had been exhausted, and Puebla, who suspected Henry of lending a friendly ear to counter proposals from France and the Empire, had written frantically, "For the love of God, don't put it off and don't give him an excuse for a change of policy!" And at last the sick and world-weary Queen had brought herself to the point of saying farewell to her only remaining child.

The English, a little skeptical after so many postponements and excuses, were delighted, and made great preparations for her reception. King Henry sent letters to all the lords in England, Ireland and Wales, enjoining them to be ready to receive the Princess on the twenty-fifth of May. The jousts were to last forty days. All made ready to welcome Catalina—known to England as Catherine. Thirteen knights were to be created, twelve by Prince Arthur and one by the King. Two hundred and thirty Knights of the Round Table were to assemble. One of King Henry's secretaries wrote his nephew, a clergyman in Spain, that the Spaniards would have no reason to complain of England as they had complained of Flanders. "In Flanders many a Spaniard has died from starvation. But I tell you that as many as like may come with the Princess of Wales, and none of them will die of hunger. If they die it will be from too much eating."

But the departure of Catalina was delayed once more by the uprising of the Moors in the mountains about Ronda. Queen Isabel wrote De Puebla that the Princess would leave as soon as the King returned from the mountains. She would try to reach Coruna, the port of embarkation, at the time agreed upon. But the journey would be very long, and the Princess had suffered from a low fever. Although she was better now, it would be imprudent of her to expose herself to the fatigue of quick traveling. She must proceed by easy stages.

This was in April, 1501. On May 7, Isabel wrote that the King had been detained longer than he had expected by the rebellion of the Moors of Ronda. . . . Wishing to see his daughter before her departure, His Majesty had accepted the capitulation offered to him by the Moors, and pardoned the rebels. It would have cost him much more time to subdue them by force. He was therefore at liberty to leave Ronda, and had written that he would start that very day for Granada. Queen Isabel herself was suffering from fever at that time.

King Fernando reached Granada May 15, but as the Princess was ill with the ague, there was another delay. On the twenty-first she left the Alhambra to begin the painful journey of five hundred miles to the port of Coruna, in the extreme northwest. She took with her 150 attendants, including Doña Elvira Manuel, first lady of the bedchamber; several ladies of honor, carefully chosen, for Henry had asked to have only beautiful ones; a major-domo, a master of ceremonies, a chief cup-bearer and trenchant; a confessor, two chaplains and an almoner, pages and equerries, gentlemen in waiting, a cook, a purser, a baker, a sweeper and others of high and low degree. Henry had asked to have the number restricted, since he "did not propose to starve them as the Archduke Philip had starved the Spaniards in Flanders." King Fernando and Queen Isabel did not accompany the Princess, that she might travel faster; besides, the Queen was too ill to ride.

Catalina found the heat so intense that she had to stop frequently, and took two months for the journey. She reached Guadalupe July 5, and arrived at Coruna, July 20. Illness and bad weather caused further delays, so that she did not set sail until August. A furious storm nearly confounded the armada,

causing it to return to the Spanish coast and seek refuge in
the port of Laredo. Embarking a second time, September 27,
the ships had got as far as Ushant when they were overtaken
by a *vendabal*, (south wind) with thunderstorms. During all
the rest of the voyage they had thunderstorms every four or
five hours. It was October 2 when the tired and miserable little
Princess landed in the harbor of Portsmouth.

"She could not have been received with greater rejoicings,"
wrote the Licentiate Alcares to Queen Isabel, "if she had been
the Savior of the world." As soon as she left the boat, Catalina, like a true daughter of her mother, went to a church in
procession to give thanks to God for her deliverance from the
perils of the sea.

A month after Catalina landed, Henry VII left Richmond
to meet her on the way to London, and with him rode the
Prince of Wales. The Prothonotary of Spain informed him
that according to the orders of King Fernando and Queen
Isabel, the Princess was not to converse with him or with
Prince Arthur until the day of her marriage—for Isabel had
at last after much correspondence wrung from Henry a reluc-
tant promise of a second marriage ceremony. The English
King, whose coarser nature could not understand the delicate
amenities of the Spanish Court, disregarded the injunction,
and insisted upon speaking with the Princess at Dogmerfield.
The Prince, arriving shortly after, also met her. Catalina proceeded to Chertsey, while His Majesty returned to Richmond.

The Prince and the Princess were married November 14,
1501, at the altar of Saint Paul's Cathedral in London, before
an immense concourse. Catalina was fifteen years old; her husband sixteen.

The news was a relief to Queen Isabel, for until the very
last moment she had not been certain that Henry would not
make some new arrangement with another power, and send
Catalina home, as Margot had been sent home from Paris.
But Henry wrote that he much admired the beauty of Catalina,
and her agreeable and dignified manners. "The union between
the two royal families and the two kingdoms is now so complete," he wrote, "that it is impossible to make any distinction
between the interests of England and Spain."

Prince Arthur informed his wife's parents that he had

"never felt so much joy in his life as when he beheld the sweet face of his bride."

Within six months the Prince was dead, and Fernando and Isabel, alarmed by reports of Henry's indifference to the comfort of their daughter, were sending frantic requests to the English court for her immediate return to Spain. They demanded from Henry the 100,000 scudos which had been paid as a first installment of the marriage portion of the Princess; they demanded that the towns and lands assigned to her as her dowry be delivered, and they begged their "brother" to send her to Spain "in the best manner, and in the shortest time possible." At the same time they authorized the Duke of Estrada, their ambassador, to conclude a second marriage between Catalina and Henry, Prince of Wales, since the young widow declared that her marriage with Arthur had never been consummated. She was only at the beginning of the years of suffering which were to end with her divorce by Henry VIII and the final shattering of that Christian European unity to which Fernando and Isabel had devoted their lives and the lives of their children. Isabel wrote Puebla that the death of Prince Arthur had revived the affliction caused by her former losses; "but the will of God must be obeyed."

Two weeks later, in May, 1502, the Spanish sovereigns wrote a most urgent letter to Puebla. They said they expected confidently that Henry would at once fulfil his obligations toward their daughter. They had been told that Catalina had been advised to borrow money, because the King of England would not provide for her. If she were really to do that, it would reflect great dishonor upon Henry. Puebla must tell the Princess and her advisers not to borrow money. "Such a thing is unheard of." When the Queen of Portugal, their daughter, became a widow, she received all she wanted from the new king of Portugal, and they had never had to send her a farthing. When the Princess Margot was widowed in Spain, they provided for all her wants, as though she had been their own daughter. Neither her father nor her brother Philip had sent her the smallest sum of money; if they had done so, Fernando and Isabel would have considered it an insult, and would not have accepted it.

In June they wrote that some persons had advised the Princess of Wales not to accept what the King of England had offered her (presumably because it was so small). "The advice is bad. She must accept all she can get."

Queen Elizabeth of England had been kind to Catalina, and after Arthur's death had sent a black litter borne between two horses to fetch her to Croydon Palace. But Elizabeth died in childbirth the following winter. The very letter of Doctor de Puebla that notified the Spanish Court of her death intimated that King Henry "was not disinclined to marry the Princess of Wales." Queen Isabel wrote the Duke of Estrada her opinion of this, April 11, 1503:

"The Doctor has written us concerning the marriage of the King of England with the Princess of Wales, our daughter, saying that it is spoken of in England. But as this would be an evil thing, one never before seen, and the mere mention of which offends the ears, we would not for anything in the world that it should take place. Therefore, if anything be said to you about it, speak of it as a thing not to be endured."[1]

For the next seven years Catalina was doomed to a most wretched life while her father and Henry bargained about her dowry, her plate, her household, and the long and tiresome details of the agreement under which she was at last married to Prince Henry. Fernando sent her very little money, evidently in the belief that if he did not do so, Henry would be compelled by shame, if not by generosity, to provide for her. But Henry, whose position on the throne was now secure, was never troubled by either shame or generosity. Several years later the princess wrote her father that her servants and maidens had no money to buy clothes. She herself sometimes had to borrow money for food. All this time Fernando was using her as a special ambassador. She was skilful and trustworthy, and kept him well informed.

Queen Isabel, too, has been accused of employing her daughter for political purposes, and abandoning her to the cold charity of Henry. The facts hardly justify so severe a judgment. Isabel lived only two years after the death of Prince Arthur—two years of sickness, anxiety and discouragement. Her letters to England show the most earnest desire to have Catalina sent home, unless her position could be made secure by a marriage to Prince Henry. The betrothal of Catalina to the Prince of Wales, just before Isabel's death, naturally ended all talk of the return of the Princess. If the great Queen could have foreseen the consequences of this match, her last moments would have been greatly embittered.

Her letters to Estrada are full of solicitude. "Should the King of England not be willing immediately to settle the betrothal of the Princess of Wales with the Prince of Wales . . . in that case, the Princess of Wales shall depart at once for Spain. She shall do so, moreover, without waiting to recover the 100,000 scudos of the portion of which the King of England has to make restitution, should he not immediately give them." . . . However, "such a thing was never known as that the daughters of Castile, after being portioned by their parents, should have to give up the portion they had brought with them, in case of the dissolution of the marriage and their becoming widows. But, that it should be given to the father of the husband is certainly a thing unheard of, nor has such a thing ever been spoken of or agreed to. On the contrary, it has sometimes happened that they have been taken without any portion, and dowered by their husbands. Because, in addition to being the daughters of such monarchs as we are, respect is likewise had to the fact that in Spain daughters inherit, which is not the case in France. . . . It would not be consonant either with reason, or with right, human or divine, but would, on the contrary, be a most barbarous and dishonest proceeding, if the King of England, provided he could, were to keep by force that which the Princess of Wales took with her, and which belongs to her."[2]

Henry had urged the Spanish sovereigns to send Catalina to England, promising to be a father to her. But his conduct was cold, stingy and heartless almost consistently except when he saw some advantage in a temporary gift. Even after her betrothal to Prince Henry in 1503, her condition was in no way improved. To make matters worse, she was almost constantly ill from the effects of the English climate, and in 1504 was almost given up by the physicians who had bled her and repeatedly purged her in an attempt to cure her of a cough and a fever.

As Catalina could not marry her husband's brother without a dispensation, King Fernando wrote to Rome requesting one of Alexander VI. But Alexander was prevented from granting it by an unforeseen circumstance. "The forbearance of God," says Von Pastor, "had reached its appointed term."

At the age of seventy-three, the Pope was vigorous and in high spirits, and looked forward to a long pontificate. Nothing appeared to trouble him, and he laughed at the vicious lampoons published by his political enemies. When Cesare wanted them punished, he said, "Rome is a free city, and here every one has a right to say and write what he likes."[3]

On August 6, 1503, the Pope and Cesare and several others dined with Cardinal Adriano de Corneto at his villa. All who were present became ill of the Roman fever, which was raging with unusual virulence. Alexander took to his bed August 12. On the eighteenth his life was despaired of. He confessed, received Holy Communion, and died that evening. His enemies circulated the report that he had been poisoned, and a later version of the tale represented him as having drunk by mistake the poisoned cup he had ordered given to his host! But all the evidence is against this fabrication.

Queen Isabel was frankly pleased to hear of Alexander's death, and ordered Masses said in thanksgiving to God for delivering His Church from the author of so many scandals. But even if he had been the monster that his foes depicted, it would never have occurred to her to leave the Catholic Church, or to reject its teachings or the authority of the Holy See; she would no more have thought of that than the modern American would think of destroying the Constitution or abolishing the Presidency because of the scandals of Harding's administration. She saw that the truth of the Church's doctrines did not depend upon the perfection of the human nature through which it must work. Christ Himself had said, "It must needs be that scandals come, but nevertheless woe to that man by whom the scandal cometh."[4] Even at the Last Supper there was a Judas Iscariot.

"Priests are forgiven nothing," said De Maistre, "because everything is expected of them; and the vices lightly passed over in a Louis XIV become most offensive and scandalous in an Alexander VI."[5] But Isabel's dislike of Alexander was not wholly prompted by zeal for the Faith. Irritation at his leniency to Jews and pseudo-*Conversos* played some part in it. This personal prejudice somewhat blinded her to his virtues, of which there were not a few. He was a patron of art, literature and science. He surrounded himself with learned men, and had an especial predilection for jurists. He loved the theatre, and did much to encourage the drama. In pontifical ceremonies his majestic height made him an impressive figure. And it must be said that he scrupulously fulfilled the foremost duty of his office to transmit to posterity the teachings of Christ in their original integrity and purity, with the accumulated decisions of what might be called the Supreme Court of Christendom, interpreting the principles and applying them to specific cases.

Fernando and Isabel now threw all their influence on the side of the reform party that sought the free election of a good Pope. The King wrote Estrada, commanding him to ask Henry's aid in this work.

"Say likewise from us," he wrote, "that he has already witnessed the injuries inflicted of late upon the Church and upon Christendom, on account of there not being a good Pope. He must see how much it imports the Church and Christendom, that the Pope be righteously elected, and how necessary it is for the service of our Lord, and the wise government of the Church, and for the purpose of making resistance to the infidels, and securing the peace and welfare of Christendom. We therefore entreat him very affectionately that he will be pleased to write to his ambassador who is at Rome, saying that if the Pope should not be already elected, he should, conjointly with our ambassador, endeavor to have a good Pope elected . . . and that the College of Cardinals should not be deprived of the liberty of making the election canonically."[6]

In spite of the attempt of King Louis XII to have one of his minions elected, the reform party prevailed, and the Cardinals chose the irreproachable and highly respected Pope Pius III. Queen Isabel celebrated the event with pomp, and welcomed his brief reign as the beginning of the great and needed reform by which the Church was to purge itself of the stains that a dying civilization had left upon it. There was reason to rejoice, for the most regrettable, if not the most anxious, days of the Church were past.

By this time—1503—it was pretty generally known throughout Europe that the great Queen had almost run her course, and there was much wagging of heads over what would happen after her death.

Juana, the heiress to Castile since the death of Miguel, was plainly becoming insane, and her conduct kept the Queen in continual anxiety.

Late in 1501, Fernando and Isabel had invited her and her husband Philip to Spain to be formally acknowledged by the Cortes. They came by way of France, and were highly honored and flattered by Louis XII, who desired to separate Philip from Fernando. When at last they reached Madrid in January, 1502, Philip caught the measles, and had to receive his father-in-law in bed. On recovering, he went with his wife and the King to Toledo, where Queen Isabel and Cardinal Ximenes awaited them. The Queen showed much pleasure at the meeting, and Juana manifested an unusual affection for her mother. Having a male heir, Carlos, the Archduke and Juana were acknowledged in Aragon as well as in Castile. Philip, however, soon professed himself bored by the banquets, games and tournaments given in his honor, and announced that important business necessitated his return to Flanders immediately. As he planned to go through France, he offered to act as representative of the King and Queen in negotiating a peace with Louis XII.

This was at the stage in the Second Italian War when Gonsalvo, having conquered most of Calabria, was defending Barletta. Philip arranged the peace and sealed it by the treaty of Blois, whereby he agreed to marry his son Charles to the infant daughter of Louis. But he betrayed his father-in-law by agreeing, on Spain's behalf, to the division of Naples, as in the treaty of Granada, and at the request of Louis, he notified the Great Captain in Italy that peace had been concluded. But Gonsalvo, on the point of marching to Cerignola, had probably had secret instructions of another tenor from Fernando; at any rate, he ignored Philip's communication, and proceeded to crush the French, while Fernando denounced the treaty of Blois. Philip continued on his pleasurable way to Flanders.

Juana, who was then expecting a second child, remained at the Spanish Court, a prey to despondency caused by his absence and by jealousy of his mistress in Flanders. As soon as her son Fernando was born, in March, 1503, she demanded to be sent home; but by that time the war with France had begun afresh on the northern borders, and traveling was dangerous. She was therefore compelled to remain with her mother. "She raged like a lioness at being kept in Spain," said Peter

Statue of Queen Isabel in the Memorial Chapel
at Granada

Martyr, and accused every one of being in a monstrous plot to keep her away from Philip. People began calling her Juana la Loca—"crazy Jane."

Enraged at being outwitted by Fernando, Louis, in 1503, launched a great triple offensive against Spain. One army was to invade Italy, another to cross the border near Fuenterrabía, a third, of 20,000 men, to penetrate Roussillon.

Fernando hastily raised an army in Aragon to defend his territory. In the midst of his recruiting, he heard that Isabel was dying at Segovia, three hundred miles away. He dropped everything and rode day and night until he reached her side.

The Queen was ill, but not as seriously as rumor had represented. When the King returned to Aragon to lead his army against the invaders, she arose, and with something of her old spirit raised troops and supplies, while her household spent several days in fasting and prayer and visiting all the churches in the city. Fernando was again victorious; but when the Queen heard that the danger was past, and the French in disorderly flight to the north, she sent the King a letter begging him to remember that the French were a Christian nation, and not to drive them to despair by cutting off their retreat to their own country; by no means to permit any unnecessary bloodshed. The King, to please her, did not even make prisoners of the French fugitives, but contented himself with their evacuation of the country. Oviedo believed that if Fernando had chosen to continue the pursuit, he could easily have penetrated to the heart of France and conquered it. He adds that the King desisted not only on the Queen's account, but at the solicitation of the second Inquisitor General, Bishop Diego de Deza, who reminded him that it was immoral to invade another Christian nation.

King Fernando's action furnishes an excellent illustration of the medieval ethics of war. Not only was warfare less bloody and less protracted as a rule than in modern times, but there was nothing like the intense hatred of one nation for another. Christians hated Mohammedans, and with some reason, but there was generally a feeling of the solidarity and common interest of Christendom which has not existed since the time of Luther. When one nation invaded another—and that sometimes happened—it was likely to find the weight of Catholic opinion, the European League of Nations, unsympathetic, as Charles VIII and Louis XII did when they despoiled Italy.

Isabel's last effort left her weak and almost exhausted. But there was no time yet for rest, no time yet for peace, for Juana was behaving deplorably in the palace at Medina del Campo, where she had been placed under the supervision of the Bishop of Burgos. No one could quiet her, and she was threatening to travel alone through France to rejoin her husband in spite of all the dangers of the frontier roads.

One cold and stormy November evening, she fled half-clad to the city gate, which was already closed. The Bishop of Burgos came in haste to plead with her, but Juana turned her back and would not listen to him. She imperiously commanded the guards to open the gate, while the Bishop forbade them to do so. The Archduchess threatened, implored, wept, shrieked, clung to the iron bars in despair. Thus she spent the long night in the howling wind and the dark.

Next day came messages from the Queen begging her to return to the palace, and with them came the Admiral Enriquez and the Archbishop Ximenes, with instructions from the Queen to detain the Archduchess, "as gently and as graciously as possible;" for Isabel was too ill to ride forty miles in the middle of the night. The Queen left Segovia during the day, however, and on the second night arrived in Medina del Campo. Juana addressed her with anger and bitterness. "She spoke so disrespectfully and so little as a child should address her mother," wrote Isabel afterward, "that if I had not seen the state of mind she was in, I would not have suffered it for a moment." It was a severe ordeal for the ceremonious Queen, especially before a crowd of gaping citizens and yokels. However, in the end her will prevailed, and Juana sullenly returned to the palace.

The Archduchess left for Flanders in the spring of 1504, greatly improved in body and mind at the prospect of seeing the husband whom she idolized. Philip at first received her with kindness, and on the surface they appeared reconciled, until Juana struck his mistress and cut off her beautiful hair one evening in the presence of the whole court and the foreign ambassadors. The Archduke cursed her and swore that he would have nothing more to do with her.

The story was buzzed immediately through all the capitals

of Europe. Queen Isabel was sick with grief and shame. Her health had suffered much from the incident at Medina, but after the hair-cutting episode she failed rapidly. "Cursed fruit of the tree that bore her," wrote Peter Martyr of Juana; "ill-fated seed of the land that gave her birth was this daughter for her mother." It was well for the Queen that she could not foresee the time when Juana would keep the corpse of her husband with her for months, expecting it to come to life, and the long decades that she would spend as a captive, by orders of the Emperor Charles V, her first-born son.

As soon as the weather permitted, Queen Isabel was taken to Medina del Campo, in the midst of wheat and saffron fields to which the memories of her brief happy girlhood were drawing her as time closed in upon her. To Medina she had gone with Beatriz de Bobadilla to see the fair, to Medina she had ridden on that last birthday of her brother Alfonso, and to Medina she had taken Prince Juan in 1481 to escape the pestilence. The Castillo de la Mota was a favorite residence, full of friendly ghosts and fragrant recollections.

On Holy Thursday, twelve beggars from the streets were brought into the palace, and King Fernando, following the example of his Lord, knelt humbly before the tattered odds and ends of humanity and washed their feet—a custom still observed by the Kings of Spain. On the following day, Good Friday, the King and Queen fasted and prayed with their usual rigor; and on that day occurred an event that struck all hearts with terror. A violent earthquake, accompanied by a loud and peculiar noise in the air overhead, rumbled through Andalusia and parts of Castile. It was particularly destructive in Seville, Carmona and other places in Andalusia. As Father Bernaldez, that indispensable chronicler, was hearing confessions in the Church of Los Palacios, he looked up and saw the belfry tower swaying back and forth; then the roof creaked as if many persons were running across it, and finally the whole church began to lurch from one side to another. The good curate ran to the statue of Christ on the altar, crying out to Jesus and the Blessed Virgin to save the people with whom the church was filled. Some screamed and ran out; others followed the priest's example and knelt praying before the statue. Fortunately for historians as well as for the curate, the walls held, and no one was hurt. Other churches were not so fortunate. Many were razed, houses tumbled down, people were killed and injured. Learned men were saying that the same sort of thing happened before the death of Charlemagne, as all readers of the French chronicles knew. Some evil was about to befall Spain.

That summer both the King and the Queen were ill with the prevalent fever. Fernando recovered, but Isabel, more anxious about him than about herself, developed symptoms of dropsy, and from that time on had no illusions that her life would be prolonged, nor had she any wish to remain longer in a world that seemed to her so futile. Hearing that people were going on pilgrimages and marching in processions all over Spain for her recovery, she asked them not to pray for the health of her body but for the salvation of her soul. And on October 12, the twelfth anniversary of the landing of her Admiral in San Salvador, she signed her last will and testament.

She desired her body to be taken to Granada and placed without unnecessary expense or ostentation in a simple tomb of humble design. The money that would otherwise have been wasted upon an extravagant funeral was to be distributed in the form of dowries for twelve poor girls—always a favorite charity with Isabel—and the ransom of Christian captives in the hands of the African Moors. She would not even permit the vanity of embalming for her body, that it might more quickly return to dust.

As the funds in the Castilian treasury were small, as usual, compared to the great expenses of the government, the Queen asked that the number of officials in the royal household be reduced, and gifts and revenues alienated without sufficient cause by the Crown, revoked.

Her love for King Fernando, which appears to have grown and deepened, in spite of occasional jealousies, since that day when she first saw him, a young prince, in Valladolid, shines through her testament with characteristic frankness and warmth. "Should the King, my lord, prefer a sepulchre in some other place, then my will is that my body be transported there and laid by his side, that the union we have enjoyed in this world, and through the mercy of God may hope again for our souls in heaven, may be represented by our bodies in the earth."

She provided for the personal maintenance of the King a sum "less than I could wish, and far less than he deserves, considering the eminent services he has rendered the state": half of all the net profits of the discoveries in the Indies, and 10,000,000 maravedis a year assigned on the *alcabalas* (a ten per cent tax) of the military orders. In case her daughter Juana was unable for any reason to rule, the Queen desired Fernando to act as regent until the majority of their grandson Charles; and in this she was actuated, she said, "by the consideration of the magnanimity and illustrious qualities of the King, my lord, as well as his large experience, and the great profit which will redound to the state from his wise and benevolent rule." She was compelled by Castilian law to require to him the usual oath on undertaking his duties as Regent.

Finally, "I beseech the King my lord that he will accept all my jewels, or such as he shall select, so that, seeing them, he may be reminded of the singular love I always bore him while living, and that I am now waiting for him in a better world; by which remembrance he may be encouraged to live the more justly and holily in this."

Even in her last moments Isabel saw clearly the evils that were likely to come upon Castile following her death, and sought to avert them. Six weeks after signing her will and only three days before her death, she wrote a codicil. She appointed a commission to make a new codification of the laws, a reform that she had twice accomplished, but never to her complete satisfaction. She recommended an inquiry into the legality of the *alcabalas*, a ten per cent tax on commerce, which she implies was not intended to be perpetual, and ought not to be made so without the consent of the people—showing that after she had accomplished her purposes by a necessary concentration of authority, her democratic instinct led her to look backward to the free institutions of her ancestors. Further, she most earnestly enjoined her successors to treat the Indians in the new possessions beyond the seas with the greatest kindness and gentleness, to redress any wrongs they might justly complain of, and to carry on the sacred work of civilizing them and converting them to Christianity. And with characteristic foresight she insisted that Gibraltar was necessary to the safety of Spain, and must never be given up.

Her duty accomplished, the Queen returned to her prayers. Clad in a Franciscan robe, she confessed, received Holy Communion, and consoled the friends who came in tears to pay their last reverence. Archbishop Ximenes, who was engrossed in building his university and preparing his polyglot Bible, hurried from Alcalá to give her his last consolation. Prospero Colonna, one of her visitors from Italy, told the King that he had come to Spain "to see a woman who from her bed of sickness rules the world." A Franciscan brought from Jerusalem a stone slab from the Holy Sepulchre, part of which he gave to the Queen, who received it with the greatest reverence. "We sit sorrowful in the palace all the day long," wrote Peter Martyr, "tremulously waiting the hour when religion and virtue shall quit the earth with her."

It stormed almost continually that November. On the twenty-sixth the skies were dull gray, the rain beat against the castle walls, the rivers were in flood, and wind whistled over the melancholy *vegas*. The Queen felt that her moment was near. She received the sacraments again, and was anointed, signifying by a gesture that she did not wish her feet uncovered during the ceremony. She then became unconscious. Toward noon she recognized the King at her bedside, smiled weakly, folded her hands, turned her eyes upward in hope and supplication, and gently breathed out her pure and luminous soul. There was a silence in the great chamber; then a sobbing, and a wailing of women.

"My hand falls powerless by my side for very sorrow," wrote Peter Martyr to Archbishop Talavera. "The world has lost its noblest ornament; a loss to be deplored not only by Spain, which she has so long carried forward in the career of glory, but by every nation in Christendom, for she was the mirror of every virtue, the shield of the innocent, and an avenging sword to the wicked. I know none of her sex, in ancient or modern times, who in my judgment is at all worthy to be named with this incomparable woman."[7]

The next day, after King Fernando had announced the Queen's death and taken the oath as regent, in accordance with her wishes, a cortege of cavaliers and prelates wrapped in black cloaks of mourning and mounted on horses and mules with black caparisons, left Medina with the unpretentious black litter containing the body of the Queen, still wrapped, according to her wishes, in a coarse Franciscan robe. They had hardly left the city when a terrific tempest of rain and wind burst over them. The cavalcade went slowly on; through Arévalo, where the Queen had spent her girlhood; through Toledo, where she had joyously celebrated Fernando's victory at Toro in the flush of her young womanhood; through Jaén, where she had saved the Christian cause and completed the building of the Spanish nation by pawning her jewels to finance the siege of Baza.

During the three weeks of the journey they saw neither sun nor stars. Roads were almost impassable, bridges had been swept away, the fields and plains were lakes and the small rivers roaring torrents in which now and then a horse would tumble, to be drowned with his rider. "I never encountered such perils," said Peter Martyr, who followed his lady's remains to their last resting place, "in the whole of my hazardous pilgrimage to Egypt." It was still storming, December 18, when the drenched pilgrims carried their silent burden through the gates of the city that the great Queen had conquered, through the gates of the Alhambra where she had sent forth Christopher Columbus to discover a world, and laid it in the Franciscan monastery.

The clouds lifted that day, and the sun shone, but it looked down upon a Spain from which something vital had passed forever. For some persons it was a Spain most tragically changed. King Fernando had lost his good genius; and twelve years of vexations with Philip and Juana remained to him. A few months after Isabel's death he married the beautiful young Germaine de Foix, in the hope of having a male heir, but their child died, leaving the succession to Charles V. Archbishop Talavera was accused by the Inquisition under the cruel third Inquisitor General, Lucero, and had difficulty clearing himself. Gonsalvo de Córdoba returned to Spain to be dismissed by King Fernando, who distrusted so powerful a general. But of all the persons who discovered that their most loyal friend had left the earth, the most desolate, perhaps, was the little Princess Catalina at Westminster. On the very day of her mother's death, November 26, 1504, she felt unusually depressed. On that day she wrote two letters home, one to King Fernando, saying she had no letters from him all that year, and the following to her mother:

"I have written three letters to you, and have given them to Doctor de Puebla to forward with all care. I wish to know above all things else how your health is. Although the Archduchess has written that your daily attacks of ague and the consequent fever have disappeared, I cannot be satisfied or cheerful until I see a letter from you. I have no other hope or comfort in this world than that which comes from knowing that my mother and father are well."

Columbus had arrived at San Lucar from his fourth voyage two weeks before the Queen died. After twenty-eight months of cruel adversity his spirit was yet unbroken, and he was on his way north to Medina del Campo to ask her for one more expedition, when the news of her death reached him, early in December. As if he had almost an intimation that he was to spend his remaining seventeen months of life in futile attempts to induce Fernando, Philip and Juana to send him on a fifth journey, the rugged old man wrote the news with a heavy heart to his son Diego, and added, "The principal thing is to commend affectionately and with great devotion, the soul of the Queen our lady to God. Her life was always Catholic and holy, and prompt in all things in His holy service; for this reason we may rest assured that she is received into His glory, and beyond the care of this rough and weary world."

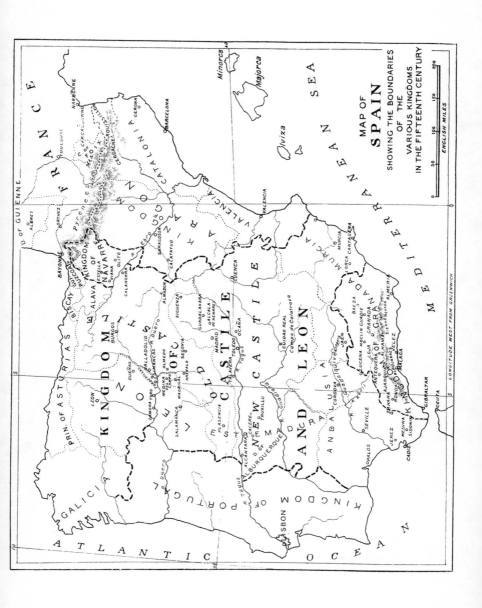

MAP OF
SPAIN
SHOWING THE BOUNDARIES
OF THE
VARIOUS KINGDOMS
IN THE FIFTEENTH CENTURY

ENGLISH MILES

0   50   100   150   200

SELECTED BIBLIOGRAPHY

(Asterisks indicate authors contemporary with Queen Isabel, and books either contemporaneous or containing original documents or other valuable source material.)

AMADOR DE LOS RIOS, DON JOSE. *Estudios historicos, políticos y literarios sobre los Judíos de España.* Madrid, 1848.
Historia Social, política y religiosa de los Judíos de España y Portugal. 3 vols. Madrid, 1876.
ANDRÉ, MARIUS. *La Véridique Aventure de Christophe Colomb.* Paris, 1929.
Art and Archaeology. August, 1929.
BELLOC, HILAIRE. History of England.
Europe and the Faith.
The Jews.
The Catholic Church and History, in the Calvert Series.
*BERGENROTH. Calendar of State Papers. Volume I.
*BERNALDEZ, ANDRÉS. *Historia de los reyes católicos Don Fernando y Doña Isabel.* Sevilla, 1869.
BETHENCOURT, DON FRANCISCO FERNANDEZ DE. *Historia general de la monarquía española, casa real y grandes de España.* 9 vols. Madrid, 1897.
BOISSONADE. *La Réunion de la Navarre à la Castille.* Paris, 1893.
Bullarium Romanum. Turin edition.
*CASTILLO, DIEGO ENRIQUEZ del. *Crónica del rey Don Enrique el Quarto.* Second edition. Madrid, 1787.
Catholic Encyclopedia, The.
CHESTERTON, G. K. The Everlasting Man.
CLEMENCIN. *Elogio de la Reina Católica.*
COLMENARES, DIEGO DE. *La historia de la insigne ciudad de Segovia.* 1640.
*COLUMBUS, CHRISTOPHER. Journal of the First Voyage, transcribed by Las Casas; edited by Van Wyck Brooks.
*COLUMBUS, CHRISTOPHER. Select Letters, edited by R. H. Major. London, 1870.
*COLUMBUS, FERNANDO. History of the Life and Actions of Admiral Christopher Columbus and of His Discovery of the West Indies. English translation in Churchill's Collection of Voyages.
*COMMINES, PHILIPPE DE. *Mémoires.*
Cortes de Leon y de Castilla.
CRUMP, G. C. AND JACOBS, E. F. The Legacy of the Middle Ages. Oxford, 1926.
DE WULF, MAURICE. Philosophy and Civilization in the Middle Ages. Princeton, 1922.

Dictionnaire de Théologie Catholique. Paris.

DIEULAFOY, JANE. *Isabelle La Grande*. Paris, 1920.

Dublin Review. Vol. 9, pp. 163-199. The Holy See and the Inquisition. 1867.

*FITA, FIDEL. *Boletin de la real academia de la historia*. Volumes 9, 11, 15, 20, 23.

FLOREZ, ENRIQUE. *Reinas Católicas*.

GUGGENBERGER, A. General History of the Christian Era, 3 vols. St. Louis, 1918.

HARE, CHRISTOPHER (MRS. ANDREWS). A Queen of Queens. London, 1906.

*HARRISSE, HENRI. *Christophe Colomb, son origine, sa vie, ses voyages, sa famille et ses descendants, d'après des documents, inédits, tirés des archives de Gênes, de Savone, de Séville et de Madrid. Etudes d'histoire critique*. 2 vols. Paris, 1884.

Christophe Colomb devant l'histoire.

Christophe Colomb et ses historiens espagnols.

Christopher Columbus and the Bank of St. George. Privately printed. New York, 1888.

HEFELE, DR. VON. *Der Cardinal Ximenez*. Canon Dalton's translation. London, 1860.

HOLLAND, DR. WILHELM LUDWIG. *Zur Geschichte Castiliens: Bruchstucke aus der Chronik des Alonso de Palencia*. Tubingen, 1850.

IBARRA Y RODRIGUEZ. *Don Fernando El Católico y el descubrimiento de America*. Madrid, 1892.

IRVING, WASHINGTON. The Life and Voyages of Christopher Columbus. 2 vols.

The Conquest of Granada. 2 vols.

Jewish Encyclopedia, The. New York.

KAYSERLING, DR. M. Christopher Columbus and the Participation of the Jews in the Spanish and Portuguese Discoveries. New York, 1894.

LEA, DR. HENRY C. The Inquisition in the Middle Ages. 3 vols.

*The Inquisition of Spain. 4 vols.

*LLORENTE, J. A. *Histoire critique de l'inquisition d'Espagne.*

LOEB, ISIDORE. *Revue des Etudes Juives*. Vols. 15, 18, 19, 20.

LOPEZ DE AYALA, DON JERONIMO, CONDE DE CIDILLO. *El Cardenal Cisneros, Gobernador del Reino*. Madrid, 1921.

*MARIANA, JUAN DE, S. J. *Historia general de España*. 2 vols. Madrid, 1780.

*MARINEO, LUCIO (SICULO). *Sumario de la clarissima vida y heroycos hechos de los Católicos Reyes don Fernando y doña Ysabel de inmortal memoria*. Madrid, 1587.

*MARTYR, PETER. *De Orbe Novo*. The Eight Decades, translated by MacNutt.

Opus Epistolarum.

McCARTHY, DR. CHARLES H. Columbus and His Predecessors. Philadelphia, 1912.

Columbus and the Santa Hermandad in 1492: The Catholic Historical Review. Volume I, p. 38.

McNabb, Vincent, O. P. The Catholic Church and Philosophy, in the Calvert Series. New York, 1927.
*Mingo Revulgo. Coplas.
Moreno, Martin Martinez. Historia del Martirio del Santo Nino de La Guardia.
*Navarrete. Colección de los viages.
Nervo, M. le Baron Gonzalve de. Isabella the Catholic, Queen of Spain. Translated by Temple-West. London, 1897.
Nickerson, Hoffman. The Inquisition. Boston, 1923.
*Palencia, Alonso de. Tres decadas de las cosas de mi tiempo.
Paramo. De Origine et Progressu Sanctae Inquisitionis. Madrid, 1598.
Pastor, Ludwig Von. History of the Popes. Vols. 4, 5, and 6.
Paz y Melia, A. El Cronista Alonso de Palencia. Madrid, 1914.
Plunket, Ierne. Isabel of Castile and the Making of the Spanish Nation.
Polo, Marco. Travels. Translated by John Masefield. New York, 1926.
Prescott, W. H. History of the Reign of Ferdinand and Isabella. 3 vols. Mexico.
*Pulgar, Hernando de. Crónica de los Reyes Católicos.
Claros Varones de Castilla.
Letras.
Quintana, Don Manuel Jose. Memoirs of Gonsalvo Hernandez de Córdoba. English translation by Joseph Russell. London, 1851.
*Real Academia de la Historia. Boletin. Vols. 5, 6, 9, 11, 13, 16, 20, 23.
Reinach, Salomon. Apollo.
Roselly de Lorgues, Count. Christophe Colomb.
Sabatini, Rafael. Torquemada and the Spanish Inquisition.
Samuels, Maurice. You Gentiles.
Stone, Eliza Atkins. A Brief for the Spanish Inquisition.
Teresa of Jesus, Saint. Autobiography. Translated by David Lewis. New York, 1916.
Thacher, John Boyd. Christopher Columbus, His Life, His Works, etc. 2 vols. New York, 1903.
Vacandard, E. The Inquisition. Translated by Father B. L. Conway, C. S. P. New York, 1915.
L'Inquisition: Dictionnaire de Théologie Catholique.
Wassermann, Jacob. Columbus, Don Quixote of the Seas. 1930.
Zuñiga, Diego Ortiz de. Anales de Sevilla.
*Zurita, Jerónimo (1512-1580). Anales de la corona de Aragon. Vols. 4 and 5. Saragossa, 1610.

NOTES

FOREWORD

1. Dr. Lea is so violently prejudiced that his conclusions are untrustworthy and his methods sometimes reprehensible, but he is an indefatigable hunter of facts and documents. His *Inquisition of the Middle Ages* and *History of the Inquisition of Spain* are useful, provided the student takes the trouble to verify his references.
2. Vol. XI, p. 485
3. Mariana, *Historia general de España.*

CHAPTER I

1. Amador de los Rios, *Historia de los Judíos de España y Portugal,* Vol. III, p. 62.
2. He was a diplomat, a scholar, and one of the chief contemporary chroniclers of the reign of Enrique IV and the first part of Isabel's.
3. Castillo, *Crónica del Rey Don Enrique el Quarto, cap.* I, 1787 edition.
4. The Stuttgart portrait seems to bear out this impression of Alonso de Palencia.
5. Amador de los Rios, *Historia de los Judíos,* Vol. III, p. 34, note 1.
6. A. Paz y Melia, *El Cronista Alonso de Palencia.*

CHAPTER II

1. Hernando de Pulgar, *Crónica de los reyes católicos.*
2. Enrique's two principal chroniclers were Castillo, his chaplain, who recorded chiefly his virtues, and Palencia, who despised him and evidently took pleasure in exposing his vices. Many Spanish historians, including Zurita, commend the veracity of Palencia. One of his latest champions is Señor A. Paz y Melia, who makes out a plausible case in *El Cronista Alonso de Palencia,* Madrid, 1914.
3. Pulgar, *Claros varones de Castilla.*

CHAPTER III

1. This is Palencia's description of Queen Juana's damsels.
2. Pulgar, *Crónica.*

CHAPTER IV

1. Pulgar, in his *Crónica,* attributes the death of Don Pedro to an *esquinencia.* Prescott and others have translated this as "quinsy,"

488

but Colmenares, in his *Historia de la insigne ciudad de Segovia* (*Lib.* II, *cap.* 33) explains that the Old Spanish word *esquinencia* is "a sickness which today they call *garrotilla*", or croup. He adds that Don Pedro's brother, the Marques of Villena, died of the same ailment.

2. Mariana, *Historia general, Lib.* XXIII, *cap.* iv.
3. Lea, *The Inquisition of Spain*.
4. Amador de los Rios, *Historia de los Judíos*, Vol. III, p. 147.
5. Paz y Melia, *El Cronista Alonso de Palencia*.
6. *Historia general, Lib.* XXIII, *cap.* iv.
7. Isabel's secretary Pulgar, himself a *Converso*, is the authority for this.
8. Amador de los Rios rejects the story in his *Estudios sobre los Judíos de España*, p. 161: "*Ni Isabel la católica podia hacer semejantes promesas á un fraile oscuro,*" etc.
9. Pulgar, *Crónica*.
10. Pulgar, *Crónica*.
11. Pulgar, *Crónica*.
12. Pulgar, *Crónica*.
13. Pulgar, *Crónica*.

CHAPTER V

1. The claim of Dr. Meyer Kayserling and other Jewish writers that Fernando was the grandson of the beautiful Jewess Paloma of Toledo appears to be based upon a midunderstanding of some sort. Mariana dismisses the whole story as groundless gossip (*Historia general*, Vol. II, *Lib.* 16, *cap.* xviii) and shows that Paloma was not the mother but the wet-nurse of one of the ancestors of Fernando's grandfather, the Admiral Don Fadrique, a whole century before, in the reign of Pedro the Cruel. Zurita (*Anales de la corona de Aragon*) says that Fernando's maternal grandmother was Doña Marina de Córdoba. The Semitic characteristics that appear in one of the portraits of Fernando, representing him as a youth, are lacking in others.
2. Castillo gives the full text, *Crónica, cap.* 136.
3. Lucio Marineo, *Sumario de la clarissima vida y heroycos hechos de los católicos reyes don Fernando y doña Ysabel de inmortal memoria*, pp. 142-3.
4. Isabel's breviary is in the British Museum.
5. Castillo, *cap.* 144. This undated letter is given also by Pulgar.

CHAPTER VI

1. Guggenberger, *General History of the Christian Era*, Vol. I.
2. F. M. Powicke, *The Legacy of the Middle Ages*. Oxford, 1926.
3. It is difficult to understand why Lavisse and other historians have gone on repeating the calumny that the Riarios were sons of Sixtus long after Von Pastor disproved it. See *History of the Popes*, Vol. IV, p. 234, note.

4. Von Pastor, *History of the Popes*, Vol. IV, p. 239.
5. Von Pastor, *History of the Popes*, Vol. IV.
6. *"Apenas quedó gallo que no se mirase con espanto á la mañana solitario en los desiertos peldanos del gallinero."*—Palencia.
7. Pulgar, *Crónica*.
8. Lea dismisses this occurrence somewhat vaguely as "an accident" without giving his grounds for believing that it was not intentional.
9. *Fortalitium Fidei*, by Fr. Alonso de Espina; Latin text in *Boletin de la real academia de historia*, Vol. IX, p. 354.
10. "Executando en el cuantos afrentas y crueldades sus mayores en el Redentor del mundo."
11. This bishop was a son of the converted Jew Diego Árias de Ávila, treasurer of Enrique IV.
12. Segovia.
13. This occurred thirteen years before the Inquisition was established in Castile.
14. This important passage has been omitted from several editions of Colmenares. It appears, however, in his original autograph manuscript, in the archives of the Cathedral at Segovia. It is given also in the edition of Diego Diez, Madrid, 1640, and in the edition printed at Segovia in 1921, *cap.* XXXIII, no. 2.
15. Amador de los Rios, *Historia de los Judíos*, Vol. III, pp. 162-3.
16. Amador de los Rios, *Historia de los Judíos*, Vol. III, pp. 161 *et seq.*
17. Mariana, *Historia*.
18. Mariana, *Historia, Lib.* XXIV.

CHAPTER VII

1. Amador de los Rios, *Historia de los Judíos*, Vol. III, p. 226; Zurita, *Anales*, Vol. IV, *Lib.* XIX.
2. Pulgar, *Crónica*.
3. Pulgar, *Crónica*.
4. Pulgar, *Crónica*.
5. Pulgar, *Crónica*. The sixteenth century historian Mariana adopted the Portuguese view that Isabel was an usurper.
6. Bernaldez, *Historia de los reyes católicos*.
7. Pulgar, *Crónica*.
8. Pulgar, *Crónica*.
9. Pulgar, *Crónica*.
10. Pulgar, *Crónica*.
11. Pedro de Mendano, son of a currier of Paradinas. Bernaldez, *Historia, cap.* xxi.

CHAPTER VIII

1. Pulgar, *Crónica*.
2. The canonization of Isabel as a saint has been urged strongly in Spain during the past year.

3. Pulgar, *Crónica.*
4. Pulgar, *Crónica.*
5. This battle has been reconstructed by information pieced together chiefly from the chronicles of Pulgar and Bernaldez.
6. Pulgar, *Crónica.*

CHAPTER IX

1. Pulgar, *Crónica.*
2. In *Holinshed's Chronicle,* as recorded by William Harrison (1577).
3. Marineo, *Sumario.*
4. The author does not know whether Yañez was a *Converso* or an "Old Christian."
5. Pulgar, *Crónica.*

CHAPTER X

1. According to a very early and persistent tradition, Saint James the Greater was the first to preach Christianity in Spain. Returning to Jerusalem, he was martyred there in 42 A. D. His followers took the body to Spain and buried it in Galicia, where Compostela now is. During the bloody persecutions ordered by Roman emperors and the disorders following the Gothic invasions, the Christians who survived were scattered, and the sepulchre of the Apostle became first neglected and then forgotten. About 800 A. D. the site was revealed by supernatural lights gleaming over a thicket in the darkness of a wood. A bishop ordered the wood cleared away, and found under the thicket a mound of earth, which was excavated. Inside was a marble inclosure containing a body which investigation convinced him was that of Saint James. Numerous miracles were reported at the shrine there established; and Pope Leo III, at the request of King Alonso and the Emperor Charlemagne, set the seal of his approval upon the new popular devotion to Santiago by transferring the See of Iria to Compostela. A fine example of how Spanish historians have been misrepresented in our language may be found in Prescott's statement (*History of the Reign of Ferdinand and Isabella,* Vol. I, p. 307, note) that "Mariana . . . doubts the genuineness of the body, as well as the visit of the Apostle, but like a good Jesuit, concludes, 'It is not expedient to disturb with such disputes the devotion of the people, so firmly settled as it is.'" Apart from the fact that Prescott has violently wrenched a sentence from its context and weakened the force of *"en especial tan asentadas y firmes como esta es,"* by translating it "so firmly settled as it is," it is worth noting that Mariana emphatically declares his belief in the whole Santiago tradition! In our times," he says, "certain learned and grave persons have raised a difficulty over the coming of the Apostle Santiago to Spain; others . . . over the finding of his sacred body. . . . It would take great

space to treat of this question fully; and I do not judge it to be expedient to change the devotions of the people with such disputes and contentions, *especially* when they are so solid and well-established as this one is. *Nor do the reasons they bring forward seem to us so conclusive that the more numerous and more weighty testimonies of Popes, Kings and ancient authors and saints, stainless and unexceptionable men, do not militate more powerfully on the side of the truth. Finally, after weighing the arguments on both sides, I assert that few sanctuaries in Europe are better attested and confirmed than ours of Compostela."* *Historia general, Lib.* VII, *cap.* x; see also *Lib.* IV, *cap.* ii.

2. Pulgar, *Crónica*.

CHAPTER XI

1. Pulgar, *Crónica*.
2. Jane Dieulafoy, *Isabelle la Grande*.
3. Jane Dieulafoy, *Isabelle la Grande*.
4. *Jewish Encyclopedia*, Vol. XI, p. 499.
4ᴬ. Maurice Samuels, *You Gentiles*, p. 10.
5. Pulgar, *Crónica*.
6. Pulgar, *Crónica*.
7. Pulgar, *Crónica*.
8. Pulgar, *Crónica*.
9. There are two facsimiles of this decree in the Yale Library.
10. Bernaldez, *Historia, cap.* xxxii. Prescott's date is an error.
11. Bernaldez, *Historia, cap.* xxxii.
12. Bernaldez, *Historia, cap.* xxxiii.
13. Bernaldez, *Historia, cap.* xxxiv.
14. Bernaldez, *Historia, cap.* xliii.
15. Zurita, *Anales de Aragon*.
16. Mariana, *Historia general, Lib.* XXIV, *cap.* vii.
17. Pulgar, *Crónica*.
18. Other historians do not agree with Mariana in his view that "the principal promotor and founder of this court was the Cardinal of Spain, moved to it by the great corruption caused by the intermingling of Christians, Jews and Moors." *Historia general, Lib.* XXIV.

CHAPTER XII

1. There is a fine effigy of the brother of Don Beltran de la Cueva, in the Museum of the Hispanic Society in New York City.
2. Acts of the Apostles, XVIII, 2; Suetonius, *Claudius*, XXV.
3. Acts of the Apostles, XVIII, 6. Pablo de Santa Maria, mentioned just below, was formerly Selemoth Ha-Levi, tutor of Isabel's father. He was converted upon seeing an apparition of the Blessed Virgin.
4. Amador de los Rios, *Historia de los Judíos*, Vol. III, p. 66.
5. *Jewish Encyclopedia*, Vol. XI, p. 485.
6. *Jewish Encyclopedia*, Vol. XI, p. 485. Rabbi Lewis Browne, in his *Stranger Than Fiction*, p. 196, says that "under the tolerant

rule of the Mohammedans, the Jews began to prosper. They who had been poor and bedraggled pedlars for centuries, now became wealthy and powerful traders. They traveled everywhere, from England to India, from Bohemia to Egypt. Their commonest merchandise in those days was slaves. On every highroad and on every great river and sea, these Jewish traders were to be found with their gangs of shackled prisoners in convoy." Albert M. Hyamson (*A History of the Jews in England*, p. 5) makes the interesting observation that the Jewish slave traders were probably indirectly responsible for the conversion of Britain to Christianity. "The British slaves who, in the Roman market-place, attracted the attention of Gregory, and directed it towards Britain, were most probably introduced into Italy by Jewish merchants."

7. "If the truth were fully known," says Rabbi Lewis Browne in *Stranger Than Fiction* (p. 222), "probably it would be found that the learned Jews in Provence were in large part responsible for the existence of this free-thinking sect (the Albigenses). The doctrines which the Jews had been spreading throughout the land for years could not but have helped to undermine the Church's power." For a vivid account of Southern France in the thirteenth century, see Hoffman Nickerson, *The Inquisition*. New York, 1923.

8. Lea attributes to Saint Leo an intolerant speech of the Emperor. The fact is that most of the churchmen of the time protested against the death penalty that the Empire decreed for heresy.

9. Vacandard, *The Inquisition*, p. 63, English translation.

10. Vacandard, *The Inquisition*, p. 72.

11. Lea, *The Inquisition in the Middle Ages*.

12. Saint Dominic himself was never an inquisitor, although he preached to the Cathari.

13. Vacandard, *The Inquisition*.

14. Vacandard, *The Inquisition*.

15. Lea, *The Inquisition in the Middle Ages*.

CHAPTER XIII

1. A recent echo of this legend appears in Jacob Wassermann's *Christopher Columbus, Don Quixote of the Seas*, English translation, p. 41: "She was dependent on the dignitaries of the Church for her opinions."

2. Lucio Marineo, *Sumario*, p. 70.

3. There is an interesting account of Clavijo's embassy in *Tamerlane*, by Harold Lamb.

4. Pulgar, *Crónica*.

5. Pulgar, *Crónica*.

CHAPTER XIV

1. Amador de los Rios, *Estudios sobre los Judíos de España*, p. 21.

2. Although the Catholic Church owes a debt to both Arabs and

Jews for the Hellenic thought they transmitted to her, it must be said that Aristotelianism in Islam and Judah remained sterile, whereas the Catholic philosophers of the Middle Ages made it the point of departure for a new synthesis which was brilliant, original and profound. In view of the familiar charge that the Church stifled independent thinking, it is interesting to notice that the greatest Jewish and Mohammedan philosophers were usually laymen, often opposed and persecuted by the rabbis and priests. In Catholic Europe, on the other hand, the most daring philosophers were commonly priests and monks, often of high station in the hierarchy, and much honored by the official Church —Thomas Aquinas, for example, was canonized. The vitality of Saint Thomas's thought is indicated by the fact that in our day it has been reconciled to modern science by the late Cardinal Mercier and other neo-Thomists. See McNabb, *The Catholic Church and Philosophy*, in the Calvert Series, pp. 33 *et seq*; also Olgiati-Zybura, *The Key to the Study of St. Thomas*. St. Louis, 1925.

3. *Jewish Encyclopedia*, Vol. XI.
4. Lea, *The Inquisition of Spain*.
5. Lea, *The Inquisition of Spain*.
6. Lea, *The Inquisition of Spain*.
7. Lea, *The Inquisition of Spain*.
8. Dr. Meyer Kayserling, *Christopher Columbus and the Participation of the Jews in the Spanish and Portuguese Discoveries*.
9. Lea, *The Inquisition of Spain*.
10. Sabatini gives a somewhat garbled translation of this passage in his *Torquemada and the Spanish Inquisition*. For example, he translates the word *manjarejos,* which means "delicacies", as "garbage"; and *oler*, which has a neutral connotation like our word "smell," as "stink".
11. Bernaldez, *Historia, cap.* xliii.
12. The complete Latin text is given in the *Boletin*, Vol. IX, p. 172.
13. The Spanish text of this edict is published in the *Boletin*, Vol. XV, p. 448 *et seq.*
14. Dublin Review, Vol. IX, p. 172.
15. Autobiography, chap. xl. par. 9.
16. Paz y Melia, *El Cronista Alonso de Palencia.*

CHAPTER XV

1. Complete text, including Pope Sixtus's bull of November 1, 1478 and the royal order of September 26, 1480, is printed in the *Boletin*, Vol. XV, p. 453 *et seq.*
2. Amador de los Rios, *Historia de los Judíos*, Vol. III, p. 248.
3. Bernaldez, *Historia*.
4. Amador de los Rios, *Historia de los Judíos*. Vol. III, p. 249, note.
5. Bernaldez, *Historia*.
6. Bernaldez, *Historia*.
7. Lea, *The Inquisition of Spain*.

8. Lea, *The Inquisition of Spain*. See also *Boletin*, Vol. XI, p. 293.
9. Prescott followed Llorente's errors with blind confidence, but undoubtedly in good faith. It remained for later investigators to expose the dishonest methods of the dismissed secretary of the Inquisition who wrote in a spirit of spite, first carefully destroying the documents that did not support his thesis.
10. The later Inquisition, of course, does not fall within the scope of this work.
11. Bergenroth, *State Papers*, Vol. I.

CHAPTER XVI

1. Zurita, *Anales de la Corona de Aragon, Libro* XX, *cap.* xli.
2. *Historia, cap.* xlv.
3. The Latin text followed is that published in the *Boletin de la real academia de la historia*, Vol. XV, p. 459. A long sentence in the part of the text quoted has been broken up for the convenience of modern readers unaccustomed to Latin style.
4. Bernaldez, *Historia*.
5. *Sumario*, p. 88.

CHAPTER XVII

1. Bernaldez says 80,000.
2. Bernaldez, *Historia, cap.* liii; Irving, *The Conquest of Granada*, Vol. I.
3. Pulgar, *Crónica*.
4. Marineo, *Sumario*.
5. Irving, *The Conquest of Granada*.
6. We are indebted to Bernaldez for the statistics.
7. Bernaldez, *Historia, cap.* lx.

CHAPTER XVIII

1. As Martin Hume has shown, Washington Irving, in his *Conquest of Granada*, is in error when he makes Ayesha the mother of Boabdil and Zoraya her younger rival. The same mistake is followed by Jane Dieulafoy, in *Isabelle la Grande*, and by others.
2. Irving, *The Conquest of Granada*.
3. Dr. Meyer Kayserling, *Christopher Columbus and the Participation of the Jews in the Spanish and Portuguese Discoveries*.
4. Pulgar gives the King's argument at length.
5. Bergenroth, *State Papers*, Vol. I.

CHAPTER XIX

1. Fita has published authenticated texts of the bulls of Sixtus pertaining to the Inquisition in the *Boletin*, Vol. XV, pp. 442-490, and has pointed out numerous errors and omissions in the versions given by Llorente.

2. Pulgar, *Crónica.*
3. Pulgar, *Crónica.*
4. Pulgar, *Crónica.*
5. Pulgar, *Crónica.*
6. Dr. Hefele, in *Der Cardinal Ximenes,* says that the Spanish left Rome as a protest against the Pope's leniency toward the *Converso* fugitives, but the evidence does not appear to support this view.
7. Pulgar, *Crónica.*
8. Pulgar, *Crónica.*
9. Pulgar, *Crónica.*
10. Pulgar, *Crónica.*
11. *Boletin,* Vol. XV, p. 462.
12. *Boletin,* Vol. XV, p. 462.
13. *Canticle of Canticles,* II, 15.
14. Bergenroth, in the introduction to the first volume of his *Calendar of State Papers,* quotes Fernando directly as saying, *"Haec concessiones sunt importunae et eis nunquam locum dare intendo. Caveat igitur Sanctitas Vestra impedimenta sancto officio concedere."* What the King actually wrote was, *"Et si per dictorum neophitorum importunas et astutas persuasiones la concessa forsitan fuerint eis nunquam locum dare intendo. Caveat igitur S. V. contra dicti negotii prosequtionem* (sic) *quicquid impedimenta concedere et si quid concessum fuerit revocare et de nobis ipsius negotii cura confidere non dubitare."* Bergenroth's misquotation has made the King call the Pope's concessions importunate, whereas it is obvious that Fernando was referring to the "importunate and astute persuasions" of the *Conversos.* It is to be hoped that Bergenroth was more accurate in decoding and translating the diplomatic correspondence of Fernando and Isabel, for his work is still the only available source on certain aspects of their relations with Henry VII and others. The complete text of Fernando's letter is published by Lea in the appendix of his *History of the Inquisition of Spain,* Vol. I. Bergenroth gives the same reference, *Arch. Gen. de la corona de Aragon* in *Barcelona, Registros,* Vol. 3684.
15. This document has been very generally misrepresented. The *Jewish Encyclopedia* informs us that Sixtus hinted that Queen Isabel was urged to rigor "by ambition and greed for earthly possessions, rather than by zeal for the faith and true fear of God." The Pope said just the opposite. And Prescott makes the equally absurd statement (Vol. I, p. 313) that Sixtus was "quieting the scruples of Isabella respecting the appropriation of the confiscated property."
16. *Boletin,* Vol. V, p. 468.
17. See *Shakespeare, Actor-Poet,* by Clara Longworth de Chambrun, for an interesting study of the sources of Shakespeare's philosophy. His tutor was the Jesuit martyr, Father Edward Hall.
18. *Boletin,* Vol. XV, pp. 477-487. Llorente's text is defective.
19. The text published by Fita in the *Boletin,* and followed in this

work, is the one received by the Bishop of Evora. See *Boletin,* Vol. XV, pp. 477-87, *et seq.*

20. *Anales de la corona de Aragon,* Vol. XX, *cap.* 49: "Era varon de santa vida, y de limpia y noble linage." The word "limpia" (clean) was used of blood in which there was no Jewish admixture.

22. *The Inquisition of Spain,* Vol. I, p. 174.

23. The evidence of an actual trial under the Inquisition of Torquemada will be summarized in its proper place in Chapter xxv.

24. Hefele, *Der Cardinal Ximenes,* p. 356, Dalton's translation.

25. Lea, *The Inquisition of Spain.*

26. Lea, *The Inquisition of Spain,* Vol. IV, pp. 217-24.

27. Lea published the Spanish text of these instructions in the appendix of the first of his four volumes on the Inquisition of Spain. He was the first to publish them, but his English text does not show that he took advantage of his valuable find to correct the obvious errors he makes at the expense of the Papacy and of the truth.

28. Zurita, Anales, *Lib.* XX, *cap.* 65.

29. At a second *auto,* June 3 two men were executed. According to a *Memoria de diversos autos* that Lea publishes, Pedro Arbues preached the sermon. There is no evidence in the document that he imposed the sentences. This is the only *auto* that he could have had any connection with, for no others were held for eighteen months, and his death occurred in September, 1485. Lea considers the *Memoria* authentic, though he admits that the handwriting is of the seventeenth or eighteenth century, and that there are discrepancies with other records.

30. Zurita, *Anales, Lib.* XX, *cap.* 65.

31. Zurita, *Anales, Lib.* XX, *cap.* 65.

32. Lea, *The Inquisition of Spain,* Vol. I, p. 244.

33. Lea omits these words, though he makes liberal use of other parts of Zurita's narrative. See *The Inquisition of Spain,* Vol. I, p. 250, for a very prejudiced account of the whole affair.

34. Zurita, *Anales, Lib.* XX, *cap.* 65. Lea says, on his own authority, that the funeral was two weeks later, but gives no reason for controverting Zurita's statement that it occurred "on the following Saturday."

35. *Memoria de diversos autos,* Lea, *The Inquisition of Spain,* Vol. I, Appendix.

CHAPTER XX

1. Marineo, *Sumario,* p. 142 *et seq.*

2. Marineo, *Sumario.*

3. A recumbent figure of the lady of a certain knight of Santiago, now in the Museum of the Hispanic Society in New York, gives a fairly complete idea of the fashion in Isabel's time. The author is indebted to this anonymous lady, and to a pamphlet of the Society, for the details mentioned.

4. Pulgar, *Crónica.*
5. Pulgar, *Crónica.*
6. Pulgar, *Claros Varones de Castilla.*
7. The text of the Duke's letter has not been found, but a later one to Cardinal Mendoza, in which he refers to it, is printed in Bergenroth's *Calendar of State Papers,* Vol. I.
8. Ibarra y Rodriguez, *Don Fernando El Católico y el descubrimiento de America.*

CHAPTER XXI

1. Ibarra y Rodriguez, *Don Fernando El Católico y el descubrimiento de America.*
2. Santángel did public penance as an abjuring heretic in 1491.
3. Some guesses have put this date as early as 1436, and in the present year (1930) a Peruvian engineer has produced a new Columbian theory based upon that premise; but Henri Harrisse has shown conclusively that Columbus could not have been born before 1446. See *Christopher Columbus and the Bank of Saint George,* privately printed, New York, 1888.
4. Corsica, then Genoese territory, is one of the numerous "birthplaces" of Columbus.
5. Navarrete, Vol. II, p. 255.
6. *"Hombre de muy alto injenio, sin saber muchas letras."*
7. Bernaldez, *Historia, cap.* cxviii.
8. Two of Columbus's latest biographers, the Catholic Marius André and the Jew Jacob Wassermann, argue for the Jewish theory, but without advancing any real evidence.
9. *"Mundi formam omnes fere consentiunt rotundam esse,"*
10. Bergenroth, *State Papers,* Vol. I.
11. Bernaldez, *Historia, cap.* lxxx.
12. Bernaldez, *Historia, cap.* lxxx.
13. He later became Pope Julius II.

CHAPTER XXII

1. Bernaldez, *Historia, cap.* lxxxvii.
2. Bernaldez, *Historia, cap.* lxxxiv.
3. Bernaldez, *Historia, cap.* lxxxv.
4. Zurita, *Anales, Lib.* XI, *cap.* lxxix.
5. Zurita, *Anales, Lib.* XI, *cap.* lxxix.
6. There is a copy of this brief in the *Boletin,* Vol. XV, p. 585.
7. Bernaldez, *Historia.*
8. Bergenroth, *State Papers,* Vol. I.
9. Bernaldez, *Historia, cap.* xci.

CHAPTER XXIII

1. About $60 a month.
2. Jacob Wassermann is the latest biographer of the Admiral to repeat this legend of Washington Irving.

3. Gairdner's *Memorials of Henry VII*; Bergenroth, *State Papers*, Vol. I.
4. Bernaldez, *Historia, cap.* xcv.
5. Bernaldez, *Historia, cap.* xcv.
6. Bernaldez, *Historia, cap.* xcix.
7. Bernaldez, *Historia, cap.* ci.
8. Mariana (*Historia general, Lib.* XXV, *cap.* ix.) says the King seized buckler and lance and rushed out naked, thinking the Moors were surprising the camp; Zurita (*Anales, Lib.* XX, *cap.* lxxxix) says he had on a shirt; see also Bernaldez, *cap.* ci.
9. Irving, *The Conquest of Granada.*
10. Bernaldez, *Historia, cap.* ci.
11. Bernaldez, *Historia, cap.* ci.
12. Mariana, *Historia general, Lib.* XX, *cap.* ix.
13. Zurita, *Anales, Lib.* XX, *cap.* xcii.
14. Zurita, *Anales, Lib.* XX, *cap.* xcii.
15. Columbus mentions in his Journal that he was present at the triumph in Granada.
16. Zurita, *Anales*; Irving, *Conquest of Granada.*

CHAPTER XXIV

1. Von Pastor, *History of the Popes*, Vol. V.
2. Lord Bacon, *Henry VII*, quoted by Prescott.
3. "Sir John" was probably Jehan la Barbe, a physician, of Liége, who used the actual journey of the Franciscan monk Odoric to China about 1300 A. D. as the basis for his own imaginary wanderings.
4. Jacob Wassermann, *Columbus*, English translation.
5. Marius André, *La Veridique Aventure de Christophe Colomb.* Paris, 1929.
6. Isabel had made him Archbishop of Granada after the reconquest.
7. Dr. McCarthy, in *Columbus and His Predecessors*, has unraveled the mystery about the source of the funds for the first voyage. Previously it had been asserted by various historians, including Lea (*The Inquisition of Spain*, Vol. I, p. 259) that Santángel advanced the money for Columbus's first voyage out of his own pocket; and André contended that he did so at huge interest.

CHAPTER XXV

1. Lea, *The Inquisition of Spain*, Vol. I, p. 133.
2. Lea, *The Inquisition of Spain*, Vol. I, p. 133.
3. Lea, *The Inquisition of Spain*, Vol. I, p. 132.
4. *Boletin de la real academia*, Vol. XI, pp. 292-3; also Lea, *The Inquisition of Spain*, Vol. I, p. 168.
5. Lea, *The Inquisition of Spain*, Vol. I.
6. *Partidas*, VII, *tit.* xxiv, *ley* 2. This law was passed under King Alfonso the Wise.

7. *Boletin,* Vol. IX, pp. 353-40.
8. *Boletin,* Vol. IX, pp. 353-40.
9. *Boletin,* Vol. XI, pp. 7-160.
10. *The Inquisition of Spain,* Vol. I, pp. 133-4. In a footnote Lea refers the reader to his more extended discussion of the La Guardia case in *Chapters from the Religious History of Spain.* A perusal of the twenty pages he devotes to the trial of Yucé Franco will convince the careful student of Dr. Lea's intellectual dishonesty. Not only does he omit all mention of the two juries to which Torquemada, in his desire to be just, caused the evidence to be submitted, but he clearly falsifies the record. He says (p. 452) that *on December 17, 1490,* the Prosecutor Guevara simply charged Yucé with "a conspiracy to procure a consecrated host with which, and the heart of a child, a magic conjuration was to be wrought. . . . Curiously enough," adds Dr. Lea sagely, "up to this time the crucifixion of the victim and the insults offered to Christ, which ultimately formed so prominent a part of the story, seem not to have been thought of. . . . It was not until the close of the trial . . . that on October 21, 1491, the promoter fiscal asked permission to make to his denunciation an addition which charged the crucifixion of the child, with the blasphemies addressed to Christ." If this contention of Lea were true, the case against Yucé would stand on flimsy foundations indeed. But the record plainly gives the lie to Dr. Lea. It was *on December 17, 1490,* that Guevara swore a solemn oath in court that he believed that Yucé "was associated with others in crucifying a Christian boy one Good Friday . . . mocking him and spitting upon him, and giving him many blows and other injuries to scorn and ridicule our holy Catholic Faith and the Passion of our Savior Jesus Christ." The crime was committed, said Guevara, "somewhat in the way, and with the same enmity and cruelty with which the Jews his ancestors crucified our Redeemer Jesus Christ—quasi de la forma é con aquella enemiga é crueldad que los judíos sus antepasados crucificaron á nuestro Redentor ihesu christo, escarnesciendole é escupiendole é dandole muchas bofetadas é otras feridas por vituperar é burlar de nuestra santa fe católica é de la pasion de nuestro Salvador ihesu christo." See *Boletin,* Vol. XI, p. 14.
11. Benito said Mose and Yucé Franco, but later corrected his error. Mose was the brother of Yucé.
12. *Boletin,* Vol. XI.
13. *Boletin,* Vol. XXIII, p. 411.
14. *Boletin,* Vol. XXIII, p. 420.
15. "E el dicho benito le respondió que moriese con el diablo; que más quería morir así que ser quemado."—*Boletin,* Vol. XI, p. 36.
16. *Boletin,* Vol. XI, p. 69.
17. *Boletin,* Vol. XI, p. 69.
18. *Boletin,* Vol. XI, pp. 81-87.
19. Fita believes that this was probably early in 1487.
20. *Boletin,* Vol. XI, p. 109.

21. *Boletin*, Vol. XI, p. 420.
22. *Boletin*, Vol. XXIII, p. 427.
23. The earliest authority for this legend seems to be Paramo, p. 144.
24. Bernaldez, *Historia, cap.* cx.
25. Bernaldez, *Historia, cap.* cx.
26. Bernaldez, *Historia, cap.* cx.
27. Lea says that "the estimate of Bernaldez is probably as nearly correct an estimate as we can find."—*The Inquisition of Spain*, Vol. I, p. 142. M. Isidore Loeb estimated that 165,000 emigrated, 50,000 accepted baptism, and 20,000 died. Lea considers these figures too high.

CHAPTER XXVI

1. John Boyd Thacher, in *Christopher Columbus, His Life, His Works*, etc., Vol. I, p. 490, estimates 1,167,542 maravedis at only $7,203.73 in our money; and this conclusion is accepted by Dr. McCarthy in *Columbus and His Predecessors*, p. 136. Dr. McCarthy adds, however, "It has been calculated that about $80,000 would now be required similarly to equip and maintain a fleet for the same time. In other words, $7,203.73 had in the fifteenth century the purchasing power possessed by about $80,000 in the twentieth century." The author of this work has translated maravedis into dollars of 1929 by reference to statistics on purchasing power in wheat, corn and other staples. Hence his opinion that the maravedi was worth about two American cents of 1929.
2. A photograph of the replica was published in *Art and Archaeology*, August, 1929.
3. Marius André says some friars from La Rabida accompanied the expedition, but mentions no authority for this unusual opinion.
4. Bergenroth, *State Papers*, Vol. I.
5. Lea, *The Inquisition of Spain*.
6. Jane Dieúlafoy, *Isabelle la Grande*.
7. *Epistle* 977.
8. Marineo, *Sumario*.
9. Von Hefele, *Der Cardinal Ximenes*, p. 6.
10. Von Hefele, *Der Cardinal Ximenes*, p. 36; Gomez, pp. 10-11; Robles, *cap.* xiii, p. 76.
11. From Complutum, the ancient Latin name of Alcalá de Henares.
12. For an excellent discussion of the Polyglot Bible and of Ximenes generally, see Dr. Von Hefele's *Der Cardinal Ximenes*, Dalton's translation.
13. *Epistle* 115.
14. *Storia d'Italia*.
15. Marineo *Sumario*.
16. *Calendar of State Papers*, Vol. I, Introduction.
17. Paz y Melia gives some of the texts in *El Cronista Alonso de Palencia*.
18. Bergenroth, *State Papers*, Vol. I.

CHAPTER XXVII

1. There is a summary of the treaty in Bergenroth's *State Papers*, Vol. I, p. 43; see also Du Mont, *Corps Universel*, III, 297.
2. There was a similar law in England, decreeing death for the taking of horses into Scotland.
3. Bernaldez, *Historia, cap.* cxvi.
4. Bernaldez, *Historia, cap.* cxvi.
5. Bernaldez, *Historia, cap.* cxvi.
6. Bernaldez, *Historia, cap.* cxvi.
7. Bernaldez, *Historia.*
8. Marius André has advanced the theory that Columbus intended from the beginning to promote a slave traffic, and had won the support of the rich crypto-Jews by promising them large profits on transactions in human flesh. He advances no convincing proof, however; and the phrase "for the service of the marine" certainly suggests that Columbus may have intended to take only male slaves, captured in war. There is considerable probability, as the context here shows, that he had in mind the bloodthirsty cannibals, the Caribs, who harassed the natives of Hispaniola.

CHAPTER XXVIII

1. Jacob Wassermann solemnly explains in his *Christopher Columbus,* pp. 80-1, that the "I" and "The Admiral" alternately used in the narrative known as the Journal of Columbus "are strongly opposed manifestations of himself. They were two persons of different rank, different responsibility and different importance, one of these a suspicious, feverishly excitable, dream-tormented, weary, obstinate man, and the other, a being not wholly of this world—the instrument of divine power, an infallible spirit." Evidently Herr Wassermann has not heard that the original text of the Journal was lost, and that the text we have was transcribed by Las Casas, who sometimes gives the Admiral's direct words in the first person, and sometimes summarizes them in the third. Psychoanalyzing a man who has been in his grave more than 400 years seems to be a task of some difficulty, even for a popular novelist.
2. *Christophe Colomb et ses historiens espagnols,* Paris, 1892. Yet Marius André revives the hoary legend in 1928, without suggesting any new evidence in its favor!
3. For a fuller treatment of this subject, see Von Pastor, *History of the Popes,* Vol. VI, p. 159 *et seq.*
4. Bernaldez, *Historia, cap.* cxx.
5. Commines, *Mémoires.*

CHAPTER XXIX

1. This episode is related by Christopher Hare (Mrs. Andrews) in *A Queen of Queens,* and by Madame Dieulafoy in *Isabelle la Grande.*

CHAPTER XXX

1. Palencia, *Tres decadas de las cosas de mi tiempo*, I, *Lib.* III.
2. Peter Martyr, letter to Pomponius Laetus.
3. Bernaldez, *Historia, cap.* cxxiii.
4. Bernaldez, *Historia, cap.* cxxiii.
5. Fidel Fita, in *Boletin*, Vol. XX, pp. 160-178.
6. Fidel Fita, in *Boletin*, Vol. XX, pp. 176-7.
7. *Historia, cap.* cxx.
8. Bernaldez, *Historia.*
9. Peter Martyr, *Epistle* 176.
10. Madame Dieulafoy's statement that Peter Martyr gave the last sacraments to Don Juan appears to be contradicted also by the fact that Peter did not become a priest until 1505.
11. Bernaldez, *Historia, cap.* cliii.

CHAPTER XXXI

1. Bernaldez, *Historia, cap.* cli; Von Pastor, Vol. VI.
2. Von Pastor, *History of the Popes.*
3. Zurita, *Anales*, Vol. V, pp. 159, 160.
4. Von Pastor, *History of the Popes*, Vol. V, p. 64.
5. Von Pastor, *History of the Popes*, Vol. V, p. 64.
6. Zurita, *Anales*, Vol. V. *cap.* xvi.
7. Zurita, *Anales*, Vol. V, p. 155.
8. Bernaldez, *Historia, cap.* cliv.
9. Bergenroth, *State Papers*, Vol. I.
10. A reference to *Acts*, I, 26.
11. Marineo, *Sumario*, p. 107.

CHAPTER XXXII

1. Von Hefele, *Der Cardinal Ximenes.*
2. Von Hefele, *Der Cardinal Ximenes.*
3. Bernaldez, *Historia, cap.* clxv.
4. Mariana, *Historia general, Lib.* XXVI, *cap.* x.
5. Dr. J. J. Walsh, *Thirteenth, Greatest of Centuries*, p. 83.
6. *Viagge fatto in Espagna.*
7. *Jewish Encyclopedia*, Vol. XI, p. 501.
8. *Jewish Encyclopedia*, Vol. V, p. 168. "Cromwell was by no means unacquainted with the resources and wide activities of the rich Sephardi Jews of the Continent," says Albert M. Hyamson in his *History of the Jews in England*, p. 176. "The Spanish and Portuguese trade was in their hands; the Levant trade also to a considerable extent. Jews had helped to found the Hamburg Bank, and were closely connected with the Dutch East and West Indian Companies. As bullion merchants, also, Jews were prominent, and, in addition, many of them owned fleets of merchantmen. The second reason for Cromwell's favor was the great assistance

these crypto-Jews of London and their agents on the Continent were to the government of the Commonwealth. And, when employing them on secret service, he was well aware of their true faith." Carvajal, a secret Jew who went to England as Portuguese ambassador, was enormously wealthy, and placed a whole army of continental agents and spies at the disposal of Cromwell. The share of the Jews in promoting the Protestant Reformation is pointed out by Rabbi Lewis Browne in *Stranger than Fiction*, p. 248 *et seq*. Luther, he observes, studied Hebrew with Reuchlin, a pupil of Jewish scholars in Italy, and the Jews, "by their very presence in Europe . . . had helped to bring the heresy into being. But once it was born, they let it severely alone." Browne is right, too, in discerning that Liberalism is of Jewish origin. "It was little wonder that the enemies of social progress, the monarchists and the Churchmen, came to speak of the whole liberal movement as nothing but a Jewish plot," he says on p. 305. Liberalism, he adds, "was the Protestant Reformation in the world of politics . . . Incidentally, however, it brought complete release at last to the Jew." The *Jewish Encyclopedia* recalls that Luther was said to be "a Jew at heart," and that he remarked on one occasion, "If I were a Jew I would rather be a hog than a Christian."

CHAPTER XXXIII

1. Bergenroth, *State Papers*, Vol. I, p. 295.
2. Bergenroth, *State Papers*, Vol. I.
3. Von Pastor, *History of the Popes*, Vol. VI, p. 112.
4. Saint Matthew, XVIII, 7.
5. *Du Pâpe*, II, chap. xiv.
6. Bergenroth, *State Papers*, Vol. I, p. 314.
7. *Epistle* 279.

INDEX

A

Abravanel, Isaac, 341, 368
Aguilar, Alonso de, 84, 235, 464
Alba, Duke of, 345
Albigenses, 171
Alcalá, University of, 316, 384
Alcalá la Real, 324
Alcántara, peace of, 185
Alcázar, 381
Alexander VI, Pope, 78, 263, 269,
    272, 333, 383, 391, 404, 422, 440
  arbitrary division of world, 407
  death, 474
  diplomacy in Spain, 79
  dispensations to Inquisition, 180
Alfonso II, King, 413
Alfonso V, King of Portugal, 51,
    129
  at French court, 185
  a threat to Spain, 102
  battle in defense of his court, 44
  character, 44
  death, 222
  education, 26
  Grand Master of Santiago, 28, 33
  heir to throne, 33
  illness, 47
  importance at court, 35
  imprisonment, 31
  meeting with Isabel, 30
  proclaimed king, 36
  sent to the court of Enrique, 24
  war against Isabel, 108
Alfonso of Portugal, Prince, death,
    335
  marriage, 321
Algerbi, Ibrahim, 305
Alhama, 232
  wealth of, 234
Alhambra, 327
  description, 334
Almanach Perpetuum, 378
Almazan, secretary, 387
Almeria, 301, 319
  surrender, 318
Alonso of Aragon, 382, 460
Altas, Ribas, 344

America, commodities discovered in,
    409
  first descriptions of, 399
  vegetables, 427
Anne of Beaujeu, 255
Anne of Brittany, 392
Antilles, the, 426
Antiquera, army assembled at, 257
Aragon, Inquisition refused by Pope,
    224
  rebellions in, 56, 95
  refusal to help Fernando, 257
Arbues, Peter, 331
  death, 280
Arenas, Pedro, 428
Army, Spanish, campaign of 1488,
    309
  camp rebuilt, 326
  conflagration in camp, 324
  devastation by, 323
  foreign volunteers, 324
  imported troops, 285
  munitions, 284
  reorganization, 284
  size of, 285
  winter marches, 318
Arthur, Prince, death, 471
  marriage, 468
  marriage plans, 418
Ascanio, Cardinal, 411
Autos-da-fé, 365, 378
Avignon, 390
Ávila, 367
  royal pageant at, 36
Ávila, Antonio de, 348
Ávila, Juan Arias de, 216, 271, 345,
    439
Ayala, Pedro de, 448

B

Bajazet II, Sultan, 456
Balue, Cardinal, 390
Barcelona, University of, 377
Barons' War, 390

505

If you have enjoyed this book, consider making your next selection from among the following . . .

The Facts About Luther. Msgr. Patrick O'Hare....................13.50
Little Catechism of the Curé of Ars. St. John Vianney.............. 5.50
The Curé of Ars—Patron Saint of Parish Priests. Fr. B. O'Brien...... 4.50
Saint Teresa of Ávila. William Thomas Walsh.....................18.00
Isabella of Spain: The Last Crusader. William Thomas Walsh........16.50
Characters of the Inquisition. William Thomas Walsh...............12.00
Blood-Drenched Altars—Cath. Comment. on Hist. Mexico. Kelley....16.50
The Four Last Things—Death, Judgment, Hell, Heaven. Fr. von Cochem 5.00
Confession of a Roman Catholic. Paul Whitcomb................... 1.25
The Catholic Church Has the Answer. Paul Whitcomb.............. 1.25
The Sinner's Guide. Ven. Louis of Granada......................11.00
True Devotion to Mary. St. Louis De Montfort.................... 6.00
Life of St. Anthony Mary Claret. Fanchón Royer.................12.00
Autobiography of St. Anthony Mary Claret......................10.00
I Wait for You. Sr. Josefa Menendez............................ .75
Words of Love. Menendez, Betrone, Mary of the Trinity............ 4.50
Little Lives of the Great Saints. John O'Kane Murray..............16.00
Prayer—The Key to Salvation. Fr. Michael Müller................. 7.00
Sermons on Prayer. St. Francis de Sales........................ 3.50
Sermons on Our Lady. St. Francis de Sales...................... 9.00
Sermons for Lent. St. Francis de Sales.........................10.00
Passion of Jesus and Its Hidden Meaning. Fr. Groenings, S.J.........12.00
The Victories of the Martyrs. St. Alphonsus Liguori.............. 7.50
Canons and Decrees of the Council of Trent. Transl. Schroeder......12.00
Sermons of St. Alphonsus Liguori for Every Sunday...............13.50
A Catechism of Modernism. Fr. J. B. Lemius.................... 4.00
Alexandrina—The Agony and the Glory. Johnston................. 3.50
Blessed Margaret of Castello. Fr. William Bonniwell.............. 5.00
The Ways of Mental Prayer. Dom Vitalis Lehodey................11.00
Fr. Paul of Moll. van Speybrouck.............................. 9.00
St. Francis of Paola. Simi and Segreti.......................... 6.00
Communion Under Both Kinds. Michael Davies................... 1.50
Abortion: Yes or No? Dr. John L. Grady, M.D................... 1.50
The Story of the Church. Johnson, Hannan, Dominica.............16.50
Religious Liberty. Michael Davies............................. 1.50
Hell Quizzes. Radio Replies Press............................. 1.00
Indulgence Quizzes. Radio Replies Press....................... 1.00
Purgatory Quizzes. Radio Replies Press........................ 1.00
Virgin and Statue Worship Quizzes. Radio Replies Press.......... 1.00
The Holy Eucharist. St. Alphonsus............................ 7.50
Meditation Prayer on Mary Immaculate. Padre Pio............... 1.00
Little Book of the Work of Infinite Love. de la Touche............ 1.50
Textual Concordance of The Holy Scriptures. Williams............35.00
Douay-Rheims Bible. Leatherbound...........................35.00
The Way of Divine Love. Sister Josefa Menendez................16.50
The Way of Divine Love. (pocket, unabr.). Menendez............. 7.50
Mystical City of God—Abridged. Ven. Mary of Agreda............18.50

Prices guaranteed through June 30, 1993.

Prices guaranteed through June 30, 1993.

Raised from the Dead. Fr. Hebert...........................13.50
Love and Service of God, Infinite Love. Mother Louise Margaret. 10.00
Life and Work of Mother Louise Margaret. Fr. O'Connell.......10.00
Autobiography of St. Margaret Mary......................... 4.00
Thoughts and Sayings of St. Margaret Mary................... 3.00
The Voice of the Saints. Comp. by Francis Johnston........... 5.00
The 12 Steps to Holiness and Salvation. St. Alphonsus......... 6.00
The Rosary and the Crisis of Faith. Cirrincione & Nelson....... 1.25
Sin and Its Consequences. Cardinal Manning.................. 5.00
Fourfold Sovereignty of God. Cardinal Manning............... 5.00
Catholic Apologetics Today. Fr. Most....................... 8.00
Dialogue of St. Catherine of Siena. Transl. Algar Thorold....... 9.00
Catholic Answer to Jehovah's Witnesses. D'Angelo............. 8.00
Twelve Promises of the Sacred Heart. (100 cards)............. 5.00
St. Aloysius Gonzaga. Fr. Meschler.........................10.00
The Love of Mary. D. Roberto............................. 7.00
Begone Satan. Fr. Vogl.................................... 2.00
The Prophets and Our Times. Fr. R. G. Culleton..............10.00
St. Therese, The Little Flower. John Beevers.................. 4.50
St. Joseph of Copertino. Fr. Angelo Pastrovicchi.............. 4.50
Mary, The Second Eve. Cardinal Newman.................... 2.50
Devotion to Infant Jesus of Prague. Booklet.................. .75
The Faith of Our Fathers. Cardinal Gibbons..................13.00
The Wonder of Guadalupe. Francis Johnston................. 6.00
Apologetics. Msgr. Paul Glenn............................. 9.00
Baltimore Catechism No. 1................................. 3.00
Baltimore Catechism No. 2................................. 4.00
Baltimore Catechism No. 3................................. 7.00
An Explanation of the Baltimore Catechism. Fr. Kinkead.......13.00
Bethlehem. Fr. Faber......................................13.50
Bible History. Schuster....................................10.00
Blessed Eucharist. Fr. Mueller.............................13.00
Catholic Catechism. Fr. Faerber........................... 5.00
The Devil. Fr. Delaporte................................... 5.00
Dogmatic Theology for the Laity. Fr. Premm.................15.00
Evidence of Satan in the Modern World. Cristiani.............. 8.50
Fifteen Promises of Mary. (100 cards)...................... 5.00
Life of Anne Catherine Emmerich. 2 vols. Schmoger...........37.50
Life of the Blessed Virgin Mary. Emmerich..................13.50
Manual of Practical Devotion to St. Joseph. Patrignani..........12.50
Prayer to St. Michael. (100 leaflets)........................ 5.00
Prayerbook of Favorite Litanies. Fr. Hebert.................. 8.50
Preparation for Death. (Abridged). St. Alphonsus.............. 7.00
Purgatory Explained. Schouppe.............................12.50
Purgatory Explained. (pocket, unabr.). Schouppe.............. 7.50
Fundamentals of Catholic Dogma. Ludwig Ott................16.50
Spiritual Conferences. Tauler..............................10.00
Trustful Surrender to Divine Providence. Bl. Claude........... 4.00
Wife, Mother and Mystic. Bessieres......................... 7.00
The Agony of Jesus. Padre Pio............................. 1.00

Prices guaranteed through June 30, 1993.

At your bookdealer or direct from the publisher.

Prices guaranteed through June 30, 1993.

Born in 1891 in Waterbury, Connecticut, William Thomas Walsh, prominent historian, educator and author, gained international attention for his Spanish historical biographies, *Isabella of Spain* and *Philip II*, both of which have been translated into Spanish, as have *Saint Teresa of Avila* and *Characters of the Inquisition*. These works represent a contribution to historical literature unsurpassed in the twentieth century. *Isabella of Spain* was a great success in Spain just before and during the Spanish Civil War, and it was also translated into French and German; *Philip II* received favorable attention from both the *New York Times* and the *London Times*. Mr. Walsh also wrote a perennially popular little book entitled *Our Lady of Fátima*, as well as several other works, and for two decades he contributed short stories, articles and poetry to national magazines. William Thomas Walsh's educational background included a B.A. from Yale (1913) and an honorary Litt.D. from Fordham University. In 1914 he married Helen Gerard Sherwood, and the couple had six children. For 14 years Mr. Walsh directed the English department of Roxbury School in Cheshire, Connecticut; he did newspaper reporting during World War I; and he held the position of Professor of English at Manhattanville College of the Sacred Heart, New York City, for many years. In 1941 he received the Laetare Medal, which is awarded by the University of Notre Dame in recognition of distinguished accomplishment for Church or nation by an American Catholic, and in 1944 he was awarded two honors: Spain's highest cultural honor, the Cross of Comendador of the Civil Order of Alfonso the Wise, and the 1944 Catholic Literary Award of the Gallery of Living Catholic Authors. William Thomas Walsh died in 1949.